# MATTHEW'S
# MAJESTIC
# GOSPEL

**Titles by Ivor Powell**

*Bible Cameos*
*Bible Gems*
*Bible Highways*
*Bible Names of Christ*
*Bible Nuggets*
*Bible Pinnacles*
*Bible Promises*
*Bible Treasures*
*Bible Windows*
*Mathew's Majestic Gospel*
*Mark's Superb Gospel*
*Luke's Thrilling Gospel*
*John's Wonderful Gospel*
*The Amazing Acts*
*Exciting Epistle to the Ephesians*
*David: His Life and Times*
*What in the World Will Happen Next?*

# MATTHEW'S MAJESTIC GOSPEL

## IVOR POWELL

kregel
PUBLICATIONS

Grand Rapids, MI 49501

Cover design: Alan G. Hartman

**Library of Congress Cataloging-in-Publication Data**
Powell, Ivor 1910-
    Matthew's Majestic Gospel

    Includes index and bibliography.
        p.     cm.
    1. Bible. N.T. Matthew—Commentaries. I. Title.
BS2575.3.P68     1986          226'.207          86-10401
                                                           CIP
ISBN 0-8254-3544-7 (pbk.)

        2 3 4 5 6 printing / year 97 96 95 94 93

# CONTENTS

*Preface* . . . . . . . . . . . . . . . . . . . . . . . . . . . . . . . . . . . . . . . . . . . . . . . . 11
*Introduction* . . . . . . . . . . . . . . . . . . . . . . . . . . . . . . . . . . . . . . . . . . . . 13
THE FIRST CHAPTER OF MATTHEW . . . . . . . . . . . . . . . . . . . 19
    Introduction to Chapter One 19
    The Ancestry of Jesus (1-17) 20
    The Announcement About Jesus (18-25) 24
THE SECOND CHAPTER OF MATTHEW . . . . . . . . . . . . . . . . . 31
    Introduction to Chapter Two 31
    The Experiences of the Wise Men (1-12) 33
    The Enquiry of the Wicked Monarch (3-8, 16) 36
    The Efficiency of the Warning Messages (12-13, 19-23) 43
    The Exasperation of the Weeping Mothers (16-18) 46
THE THIRD CHAPTER OF MATTHEW . . . . . . . . . . . . . . . . . . 51
    Introduction to Chapter Three 51
    The Strange Servant (1-4) 54
    The Successful Service (5-6) 58
    The Striking Sermon (7-12) 62
    The Submissive Son (13-17) 67
THE FOURTH CHAPTER OF MATTHEW . . . . . . . . . . . . . . . . 72
    An Increasing Danger (1-11) 72
    An Important Decision (12-17) 80
    An Invitation to Discipleship (18-22) 83
    An Inspiring Development (23-25) 86
THE FIFTH CHAPTER OF MATTHEW . . . . . . . . . . . . . . . . . . 89
    Introduction to the Sermon on the Mount 89
    The Delights of the King's Citizens (1-12) 91
    The Description on the King's Citizens (13-16) 102
    The Distinction Among the King's Citizens (17-20) 104
    The Demands of the King's Citizens (21-26) 105
    The Determination Within the King's Citizens (27-37) 107
    The Devotion of the King's Citizens (38-48) 110
THE SIXTH CHAPTER OF MATTHEW . . . . . . . . . . . . . . . . . 113
    Give Graciously (1-4) 113
    Pray Privately (5-13) 116

Forgive Freely (14-15) 120
Fast Faithfully (16-18) 120
Trust Triumphantly (19-34) 123
A Supplement to the Study of the Lord's Prayer 129

THE SEVENTH CHAPTER OF MATTHEW . . . . . . . . . . . . . 134
The Need to be Considerate... *"Judge Not"* (1-6) 134
The Need to Communicate... *"Ask, Seek, Knock"* (7-12) 136
The Need to be Converted... *"Enter Ye In"* (13-14) 138
The Need to be Careful...
*"Beware of False Prophets"* (15-23) 140
The Need to be Concerned... *"The House Fell"* (24-29) 142

THE EIGHTH CHAPTER OF MATTHEW . . . . . . . . . . . . . . . 146
Saving the Suppliant (1-4) 146
Surprising the Soldier (5-13) 150
Serving the Savior (14-17) 155
Sifting the Superficial (18-22) 158
Stilling the Storm (23-27) 161
Subduing the Spirits (28-34) 163

THE NINTH CHAPTER OF MATTHEW . . . . . . . . . . . . . . . . 167
Removing a Distressing Guilt (1-8) 167
Reclining With Dubious Guests (9-13) 170
Replying to Doubtful Grievances (14-17) 173
Raising a Dead Girl (18, 23-26) 176
Reaching a Definite Goal (19-22) 179
Restoring a Departed Gift (27-31) 181
Responding to a Discerning Group (32-34) 184
Revealing a Delightful Grace (35-38) 186

THE TENTH CHAPTER OF MATTHEW . . . . . . . . . . . . . . . 188
The Privilege of the Preachers... *"He called them"* (1-4) 188
The Power of the Preachers...
*"He gave them power"* (5-8) 191
The Preparation of the Preachers...
*"Provide nothing"* (9-15) 193
The Persecution of the Preachers...
*"They shall deliver you up"* (16-23) 196
The Persistence of the Preachers... *"Fear not"* (24-31) 197
The Promise to the Preachers...
*"I will confess you"* (32-33) 200
The Problems of the Preachers...
*"They of his own household"* (34-38) 202

The Payment to the Preachers...
*"A Prophet's Reward"* (39-42) 203
THE ELEVENTH CHAPTER OF MATTHEW ............208
  A Great Concern (1-6) 208
  A Gracious Compliment (7-19) 211
  A Grievous Condemnation (20-24) 216
  A Glorious Communion (25-27) 218
  A Godlike Compassion (28) 221
  A Gentle Companion (29-30) 222
THE TWELFTH CHAPTER OF MATTHEW ..............224
  The True Witness (1-8) 224
  The Triumphant Work (9-14) 227
  The Timely Withdrawal (15-21) 229
  The Terrifying Warning (22-37) 231
  The Three Wonders (38-42) 235
  The Thrilling Word-Picture (43-45) 237
  The Troubled Woman (46-50) 239
THE THIRTEENTH CHAPTER OF MATTHEW ..........242
  Introduction to Chapter Thirteen 242
  The Sower...*Sowing* (1-23) 244
  The Wheat and Tares...*Spoiling* (24-30, 36-43) 251
  The Mustard Seed...*Succeeding* (31-32) 253
  The Leaven...*Seasoning* (33) 253
  The Savior...*Speaking* (34-43) 256
  The Treasure...*Searching* (44) 260
  The Pearls...*Sacrificing* (45-46) 260
  The Dragnet...*Separating* (47-53) 264
  The Citizens...*Sinning* (54-58) 266
THE FOURTEENTH CHAPTER OF MATTHEW ..........269
  Jesus Remembers a Worker (1-12) 269
  Jesus Removes a Worry (13-21) 273
  Jesus Rescues a Walker (22-33) 277
  Jesus Receives a Welcome (34-36) 280
THE FIFTEENTH CHAPTER OF MATTHEW ............284
  Christ's Memorable Preaching (1-20) 284
  Christ's Marvelous Patience (21-28) 289
  Christ's Miraculous Provision (29-39) 293
THE SIXTEENTH CHAPTER OF MATTHEW ............300
  The Denial of Foolish Desires (1-4) 300

**8**      CONTENTS

The Danger of False Doctrines (5-12) 302
The Declaration of a Fervent Disciple (13-20) 304
The Demands of a Faithful Devotion (21-28) 309

THE SEVENTEENTH CHAPTER OF MATTHEW ........313
The Shining Face (1-8) 313
The Sincere Followers (9-13) 317
The Sad Father (14-21) 319
The Strange Fish (22-29) 321

THE EIGHTEENTH CHAPTER OF MATTHEW ..........327
The Importance of a Child (1-14) 327
The Inspiration of the Church (15-20) 332
The Illustration of Compassion (21-35) 334

THE NINETEENTH CHAPTER OF MATTHEW ..........340
Jesus Explains the Law (1-12) 340
Jesus Exhibits Love (13-15) 346
Jesus Expounds About Life (16-26) 348
Jesus Examines Losses (27-30) 352

THE TWENTIETH CHAPTER OF MATTHEW ...........356
The Men and Their Money (1-16) 356
The Master and His Message (17-19) 362
The Mother and Her Mission (20-28) 363
The Multitude and the Miracle (29-34) 369

THE TWENTY-FIRST CHAPTER OF MATTHEW ........374
The Arrival of the King (1-11) 374
The Anger of the King (12-17) 377
The Action of the King (18-22) 381
The Answer of the King (23-27) 384
The Announcements of the King (28-46) 386

THE TWENTY-SECOND CHAPTER OF MATTHEW ......395
The People at the Lovely Wedding (1 14) 395
The Presence of the Listening Witnesses (15-22) 402
The Problem of the Lonely Widow (23-32) 405
The Power of the Lord's Words (33-46) 408

THE TWENTY-THIRD CHAPTER OF MATTHEW ........413
The Importance of Being Nothing (1-12) 413
The Danger of Knowing Everything (13-32) 416
The Awfulness of Being Condemned (33-36) 421
The Tragedy of Being Lost (37-39) 423

THE TWENTY-FOURTH CHAPTER OF MATTHEW......426
    Be Warned..."*Not Yet.*" (1-13) 426
    Be Wise..."*Listen.*" (14-28) 431
    Be Watchful..."*Look.*" (29-35) 435
    Be Waiting..."*Any Moment.*" (36-44) 438
    Be Workers..."*Constantly.*" (45-51) 441

THE TWENTY-FIFTH CHAPTER OF MATTHEW........444
    The Ten Virgins...*A Great Slumber* (1-13) 444
    The Ten Talents...*A Great Stupidity* (14-30) 451
    The Sheep and the Goats...*A Great Surprise* (31-46) 456

THE TWENTY-SIXTH CHAPTER OF MATTHEW........460
    The Dastardly Goal (1-5) 460
    The Devotional Gift (6-13) 463
    The Disgusting Greed (14-16) 466
    The Displayed Graciousness (17-30) 468
    The Denying Guests (31-35) 474
    The Dozing Group (36-56) 476
    The Detestable Gathering (57-68) 483
    The Disturbing Guilt (69-75) 485

THE TWENTY-SEVENTH CHAPTER OF MATTHEW.....488
    The Betrayer of Jesus...*His Turmoil* (1-10) 488
    The Judge of Jesus...*His Troubles* (11-26) 492
    The Death of Jesus...*His Triumph* (27-56) 498
    The Burial of Jesus...*His Tomb* (57-66) 510

THE TWENTY-EIGHTH CHAPTER OF MATTHEW......514
    The Radiant Messenger (1-8) 514
    The Risen Master (9-10) 517
    The Reporting Men (11-15) 519
    The Royal Message (16-20) 521

# INDEX OF HOMILIES

1. Naomi and Ruth...*Who came home to Bethlehem*     29
2. The Wise Men...*Who looked through a starry window*     48
3. "I Am Not Worthy"     69
4. The Divine Lawyer... *And the dramas
   in the court house*     143
5. The Savior's Strangest Utterance     205
6. The Jordan Management Consultants     206
7. The Gold Digger...*And the way he staked his claim*     260
8. Peter...*Whose ardor was somewhat dampened!*     281
9. The Syrophenician...*Who tried to deceive Christ*     292
10. The Crowd...*That knelt down and reached heaven*     294
11. Peter...*And his greatest fishing story*     324
12. Christ In the Midst of His People     338
13. The Husbandman...*Who paid strange wages*     360
14. The Guest...*Who refused a wedding garment*     400
15. The Disciples...*Who had sleeping sickness*     447
16. The Great Wedding...*And the people who came late*     449
17. The World's Greatest Battle     478
18. A Gracious Wife...*Who believed in dreams*     495
19. Simon the Cyrenian... *The most privileged man
    in the world*     500

# PREFACE

This commentary on Matthew's Gospel, in common with the companion volume on Mark's Gospel, is the product of my serious illness in November of 1983. At that time, and even before I began to regain my health, I was aware of the fact that God had spared my life that I might write these books. Constantly since that time, I have endeavored to fulfill my obligation to the Lord and His people.

Readers of the earlier volumes will quickly discover this commentary is different from its predecessors. It was my custom to place homilies at the end of chapters, but that has now been changed. It became obvious that pastors across the country appreciated my alliterative style, and it was their influence which suggested the same method be used throughout the expository sections of this volume. Some homilies may still be found at the end of sections and chapters, but I have tried to supply expositions in homiletical style so that maximum help may be brought to all who preach and teach the Word of God.

Almost all the content of this volume came from my many years of *living with the Book*! Nevertheless I pay tribute to a few authors whose writings have influenced me, some of whom I have quoted. I have made reference to the *Pulpit Commentary* which has been my constant companion throughout the years. Josephus, the Jewish historian, has always seemed an old friend of mine, and throughout this volume frequent reference is made to his outstanding descriptions of ancient events. To the best of my ability, I have tried to indicate the authors and other sources from whom, and from which, I have made quotations. Nevertheless, as I have said, nearly all the content of this commentary is the product of many years of study.

I am extremely grateful to my publisher and to my wife, Betty, who carefully edited every chapter. Her service has always been of incalculable worth. I am aware that if Christ tarries, this book will be used by a great number of pastors and evangelists long after I have gone to be with the Lord. It is to those servants of Christ, I gladly dedicate this commentary. May they have as much pleasure preaching the message as I have had writing it.

IVOR POWELL

Santa Barbara, California

# INTRODUCTION

It is probably true to say that more has been written about the Gospel of Matthew than about any other Gospel. Nevertheless, this only becomes noticeable when a detailed study is made of the book. Throughout the centuries its authorship has been challenged, its content criticized, and frequently a new educationalist has appeared to discredit the entire volume. It is not my purpose to condemn what any other commentator has written, but it is necessary to mention briefly the more vital aspects of the findings of scholarship.

The word *synoptic* is derived from two Greek words, and means "giving or constituting a general view", or, "presenting the same or similar point of view." It is the name given to the first three Gospels. All students know that the Gospels of Matthew, Mark, and Luke basically describe identical events, and often the expressions of the three authors have a remarkable resemblance. It is true that each writer had a point to prove, and an individualistic way of achieving his purpose. Matthew-Levi, a Jew, firmly believed Jesus to be the Messiah, and endeavored to prove this to his Hebrew readers. Mark set out to portray the Savior of Simon Peter, and, consequently his Gospel is one of continuing action. Luke, who obtained much of his material from Paul and other early Christians, set out to prove that Jesus was indeed the God-man, perfect in every detail of His humanity. To repeat, each author had his own method of reaching his literary goal. Nevertheless, it must be remembered that only Matthew had been a traveling companion of the Lord. He alone of the three writers could claim to have been an eyewitness of the things described in his book. To appreciate intelligently the Gospel of Matthew, it is necessary to consider seven facts.

## MATTHEW HAD BEEN AN EYEWITNESS

He had never been a member of the inner circle of three disciples, and therefore had not been on the Mount of Transfiguration, nor in the home of Jairus when the little girl was raised from the dead. Matthew had not been present to see the Lord's agony in the Garden of Gethsemane, and it is understandable why he had to seek detailed information of these events. Nevertheless, he had been with the Lord from the beginning, and for most of the deeds and words of Jesus, had no need to seek information. He was present when miracles were performed; he listened when Jesus delivered His tremendous messages. If any person had challenged the authenticity of Matthew's record, the writer could have said, "I was there when it happened."

## MATTHEW WAS A MAN ACCUSTOMED TO KEEPING BOOKS

This disciple had been trained to do the work of a tax gatherer, and this entailed being an accountant. Each day, he sat at his table by the side of the main highway running through Galilee, where each caravan had to halt and pay dues. The work of collecting the taxes had been sublet to minor officials, but the authorities insisted they be given an appropriate amount. Publicans were detested because, in addition to the legitimate taxes, anything collected above went into the pockets of the tax gatherer. When the governor, or man in charge of customs, came to examine the records, Matthew of necessity had to be able to open his records and satisfy the investigating officer. It has been claimed by certain theologians that this was the real reason why Jesus called Matthew to be a disciple. There is no record of any itemized service; he was not a preacher; apparently he did very little to command admiration. Matthew was a book man accustomed to writing records, gathering facts, accumulating evidence. It is extremely interesting to read the writings of Papias who was a Bishop of Hierapolis, a few miles north of Laodicea. This man was one of the earliest theologians of the church, and he exercised his ministry toward the close of the first century and at the beginning of the second. Writing of Matthew, Papias said, "He collected the sayings (of Jesus) in the Hebrew tongue, and each interpreted as he was able" ( *Eusebius,* History III. 35:15-16). If this is correct it would fit into the pattern already described, namely, that Matthew, the eye-witness, wrote what he knew, but he collected what he did not know from other sources. If those other sources were the disciples, then it is easy to understand how Matthew knew the details of things which he had not witnessed.

## MATTHEW'S GOSPEL WAS PLACED FIRST IN THE CANON OF NEW TESTAMENT WRITINGS

At first, there were no written records of the ministry of Jesus. The message was probably memorized and orally passed on from one

Christian to another. Eventually, the need for written records became obvious, but the growth of the New Testament as we now have it, covered a period of years. The Gospels were written and afterward came the Epistles of various authors. Writers of anything connected with Jesus became men greatly esteemed, and consequently, many books came into being. Some were of more value than others, and therefore a choice was forced upon the church — which to accept as authentic and which to reject. "The canon of the New Testament, as commonly received at present, was ratified by the third Council of Carthage (A.D. 397) and from that time was accepted throughout the Latin Church" (*Unger's Bible Dictionary*, p. 178). The Church Fathers of those days had to decide which book should be first in the 27 to be included in the authorized list, and they chose the Gospel according to Matthew. That fact in itself suggests the very high esteem in which they regarded the book and reveals the wide acceptance the Gospel had received throughout the universal church.

## MATTHEW WAS RECOGNIZED TO BE THE AUTHOR BY EARLY CHURCH LEADERS

A. Lukyn Williams, writing in the *Pulpit Commentary*, Introduction to Matthew, pp. xiv-xv, says, "That Matthew wrote in Hebrew (Aramaic), the early church seems to have held as certain." The testimony is so important, that it must be quoted at length. *Papias* about circa A.D. 130, wrote, "So then Matthew composed the oracles in the Hebrew language, and each one interpreted them as he was able." *Irenaeus*, circa A.D. 180, wrote, "Now Matthew among the Hebrews published a writing of the Gospel in their own language, while Peter and Paul were preaching in Rome and founding the church." *Origen*, circa A.D. 230, wrote, "Having learned by tradition concerning the four Gospels, which are alone indisputable in the Church of God under heaven, that there was written first that which is according to Matthew, who was once a publican, but was afterward an apostle of Jesus Christ, and it was issued to those who once were Jews but had believed, and was composed in Hebrew." *Eusebius*, circa A.D. 330, wrote that when Pantaenus, circa A.D. 190, the first teacher of the Alexandrian school, went to India to preach the gospel, "he found that the Gospel according to Matthew had preceded his appearance, and was in the hands of some who already knew Christ, to whom, Bartholomew, one of the apostles, had preached, and had left behind him the writing of Matthew in the very character of the Hebrews, and that this was even preserved until the time referred to.'' Eusebius went on to say, ''Of all the disciples of the Lord, only Matthew and John have left us written memorials, and they, tradition says, were led to write only under the pressure of necessity. For Matthew, who had at first preached to Hebrews, when he was about to go to others also, committed his Gospel to writing in his native tongue, and thus compensated those from whom he was withdrawing himself for the loss of his presence.''

## MATTHEW THE TAX COLLECTOR FREQUENTLY MENTIONS MONEY IN HIS GOSPEL

Matthew surely smiled when he wrote about the question of giving taxes to Caesar (see Matt. 22:17-22). He had experience of giving money to the representatives of the emperor. The account mentioned in chapter eighteen seemed to be the kind of thing the former tax gatherer could expound for hours. It concerned a man who owed his master ten thousand talents ($262,800,000) and yet, although he was forgiven that tremendous debt, refused to forgive a fellow laborer who only owed one hundred pence ($7.50). Then in chapter twenty, Matthew writes of the dispute over wages in the vineyard. He was fascinated by money; it reminded him of what he did before he met the Lord. Sometimes it is possible to see a lot of light through small holes. The references to money in this Gospel are tiny chinks through which we see the life and thoughts of the author.

## MATTHEW WAS A JEW SPECIALLY ENABLED TO WRITE TO FELLOW JEWS

Matthew's book is the Gospel to the Jews. No writer could have been more fitted to write it. Even before Jesus called him to be a disciple, he looked for the appearance of the Messiah. Matthew was a student of the Old Testament, and was aware of what had been predicted by the prophets. When he became convinced that Jesus of Nazareth was the Messiah, he remembered what had been predicted, and every promise seemed to be fulfilled in his Master. Thus, when Matthew wrote his Gospel for Jews, frequently he referred to the law and the prophets. One of the key statements used throughout the book is, ''Then was it fulfilled which was written by the prophets.'' Matthew believed in the establishment of the Messianic Kingdom and, as his Gospel indicates, firmly believed Jesus would be the One to make his dream come true.

Everything about his Gospel was written to influence the members of his race, and these facts are to be found throughout the entire volume.

## MATTHEW'S GOSPEL EMPHASIZES WORDS NOT DEEDS

Matthew's Gospel is different from the other Gospels in that it contains sections exclusively devoted to instruction. The Sermon on the Mount is expressed in 111 verses. Possibly the Lord, from time to time, repeated some of His sayings, but Matthew asserts the entire message was delivered at one time, or at least, during one session on the hillside. It would have been impossible for a listener to memorize all those precepts spontaneously, and since recorders were unknown in those days, obviously someone made notes of all the Lord uttered. Matthew was the only man capable of performing that task. If Peter and the others were men of the pulpit, Matthew was the man with a pen! His Gospel is outstanding in that it emphasizes words not deeds! He devotes 53 verses in chapter thirteen to describing the parables of the kingdom, and again it becomes obvious that notes were made during the original discourse. It would appear that when Jesus called Matthew-Levi, He did so that He might have within His small company, a talented librarian! With these thoughts in mind, we can now proceed with our study of this great Gospel.

# The First Chapter of Matthew

THEME: *The Ancestry and Birth of Jesus*

OUTLINE:
   I. The Ancestry of Jesus (Verses 1-17)
   II. The Announcement About Jesus (Verses 18-25)

## INTRODUCTION TO CHAPTER ONE

Let it be candidly admitted that few, if any, books had such an inauspicious beginning as did the Gospel of Matthew. No modern author would even think of presenting a manuscript to a publisher, if his book began with a list of over forty uninteresting names reaching back into antiquity. Let it be further admitted that although this chapter is the introduction to the New Testament, few Christians read the Old Testament names, and of those who do, very few discover anything of interest. If the New Testament were any other book being lifted from a shelf in a book shop, the casual reader would take one look at the introduction, and then hurriedly return the volume to its place. To an ordinary person there is nothing but boredom forthcoming from such uninteresting material. It is necessary therefore to ask why Matthew chose this strange way of beginning his Gospel.

All British citizens find interest in Americans who, every year, visit Britain to trace their lineage. Apparently, the travelers desire details of their origin, and visit places where information may be found. There is, of course, a great building known as Somerset House where records are preserved, and in the course of every year, thousands of visitors are courteously received by the officials. Questions are asked and answered; records are studied, but when the documents fail to supply what is needed, the anxious Americans often proceed to old churches throughout Britain in the hope that sextons or librarians may be able to trace the ancestry even further back in time. British people laugh when some of these Americans become shocked when they discover their ancestors were pirates, cut-throats and horse thieves! Nevertheless, this indicates many people are anxious to trace their beginnings.

This fact was very obvious in ancient Israel. If we may be permitted to quote another example, it is only necessary to draw attention to Hitler's Nazi Germany, and remember how constant emphasis was placed on the necessity of having a pure bloodline. When the authorities discovered a person's ancestor had been a Jew, he was considered unclean, and alas, millions of these people were exterminated in the infamous gas ovens of the country. There is reason to believe that ancient Israel was even more insistent on a pure line. From various ancient writers we learn the reason for this interest in pedigrees. The Jews set the greatest possible value on purity of lineage. If in any man there was the slightest admixture of foreign blood, he lost his right to be called a Jew and a member of the people of God. A priest, for instance, was bound to produce an unbroken record of his pedigree stretching back to Aaron; and, if he married, his wife-to-be had to produce her pedigree for at least five generations. Herod the Great was always despised by the pure-blooded Jews because he was half an Edomite. We learn that even Herod attached such importance to these genealogies that he had the official registers destroyed, so that no one could prove a purer pedigree than his own.

When Matthew, in an effort to introduce his Messiah to Jewish readers, began his Gospel, he recognized the importance of proving the purity of the lineage of his Master. If there were the slightest doubt about this detail, orthodox Jews would never exhibit any interest in what was being said or written. It was therefore necessary for the author, at the beginning of his book, to stress the ancestry of Jesus. That would be the first thing for which Jews would look. Whereas modern readers of the Gospel might be repelled by an apparently boring introduction, all Hebrew readers would be fascinated by the details supplied from sacred records. Matthew was a very shrewd man; he knew exactly what he was doing!

## SECTION ONE

*Expository Notes on Matthew's Roller-coaster of Names*

The book of the generation of Jesus Christ, the son of David, the son of Abraham. Abraham begat Isaac; and Isaac begat Jacob; and Jacob begat Judas and his brethren; And Judas begat Phares and Zara of Thamar; and Pharez begat Esrom; and Esrom begat Aram; and Aram begat Aminadab; and Aminadab begat Naason; and Naason begat

**Salmon; And Salmon begat Booz of Rachab; and Booz begat Obed of Ruth; and Obed begat Jesse; And Jesse begat David the King (vv. 1-6).**

## MATTHEW'S STRANGE START

"The book of the generation of Jesus Christ, the son of David, the son of Abraham." That first introductory statement of Matthew represented genius; indisputably, he was led of the Holy Spirit even in his choice of words. There were many outstanding names in Jewish history, but the two greatest were Abraham and David. Abraham was the father of the nation, and David its king. The patriarch represented the earliest beginnings, when Israel was but an idea in the mind of God. On the other hand, David the king provided the evidence needed to prove the reliability of Jehovah's promise to make Israel a great nation. All Jews looked back to Abraham with profound reverence; when they remembered David, they were filled with pride.

Matthew knew the prophet Nathan had spoken to David, saying, "I will set up thy seed after thee, which shall proceed out of [thine own body], and I will establish his kingdom. He shall build an house for my name, and *I will establish the throne of his kingdom forever....And thine house and thy kingdom shall be established forever before thee: thy throne shall be established forever* " (2 Sam. 7:12-16). Matthew was aware that Jews considered this to be a Messianic prediction. Solomon, David's son, had built a temple, but his kingdom had been divided and ultimately destroyed by Babylonian armies. Jews firmly believed that from David's descendants would arise a new king, and even the Pharisees and scribes taught this truth. When Herod the king asked for information about the coming Messiah, they said that He would be born "in Bethlehem of Judaea: for thus it is written by the prophet, And thou Bethlehem, in the land of Judah, art not the least among the princes of Judah: for out of thee shall come a Governor, that shall rule my people Israel" (Matt. 2:4-6).

Matthew was absolutely sure that the anticipated Messiah had arrived. His Master, Jesus of Nazareth, fulfilled all the requirements, but before his readers would accept his views, they had to be persuaded of their accuracy. Therefore, the apostle went to great lengths to discover from ancient records, important evidence; and when his tables of genealogy were completed, he wrote the details to support his claims for Jesus.

**And David the king begat Solomon of her that had been the wife of Urias; And Solomon begat Roboam; and Roboam begat Abia...and Manasses begat Amon; and Amon begat Josias; and Josias begat**

Jechonias and his brethren, about the time they were carried away to Babylon. And after they were brought to Babylon, Jechonias begat Shealtiel...Matthan begat Jacob; And Jacob begat Joseph the husband of Mary, of whom was born Jesus, who is called Christ (vv. 6-16).

## MATTHEW'S SUGGESTIVE SUMMATION

"So all the generations from Abraham to David are fourteen generations; and from David until the carrying away into Babylon are fourteen generations; and from the carrying away into Babylon unto Christ are fourteen generations" (v. 17). Momentarily, we are jumping ahead of ourselves! Matthew mentions many other names, but we shall appreciate their importance when we have considered his summary of them all. Matthew divides the generations into three categories, each with fourteen. Some names represent greatness; others are dismal. This resembles a rollercoaster when the nation was lifted to unprecedented heights of glory, only to be plunged back into the horrifying depths of defeat and shame. Let us consider these three periods of fourteen generations. Beginning with Abraham, when the nation was nothing, Matthew traces Israel's history to unprecedented greatness when David reigned triumphantly. Alas, our rollercoaster now begins to plunge into the depths of ignomy and shame. The path of history descends to the time when the Babylonian armies ravaged the nation, destroyed the temple, and carried many thousands of people to a living death in a foreign land. Then Matthew, with the skill of a Spirit-filled genius, proceeds to show that all was not lost. Israel had failed, but God had not forgotten His covenant. He traces the lineage down to Christ, the fulfillment of every Messianic promise, the hope of Israel, the One whose kingdom would never end.

It might be to our advantage if we now analyze Matthew's summation. (1) *Resplendent Glory.* From a tribe of wandering nomads, God had built a tremendous nation. Tents had been replaced by palaces, poverty by unsurpassed wealth, insignificance by undying fame. (2) *Recurring Guilt.* The chosen people had rebelled; they who had received much blessing from Jehovah had been unfaithful. They had made idols, and violated every covenant made with God. The prophets had been stoned; the entreaties of God had been spurned, and their inexcusable conduct led to disaster. (3) *Redeeming Grace.* Matthew was thrilled to be able to announce that God had found a remedy for the ills of the nation. He who had sent Moses, Samuel, David and many others, had now sent His Son. After the darkness of the night of gloom, Matthew was thrilled to announce "The Sun of Righteousness is arising with healing in His wings."

*MATTHEW'S SUBLIME SAVIOR...* "*Jesus who is called Christ.*"

The time has now come to examine carefully the names mentioned in this long list of ancestors. The lineage as supplied in this chapter, resembles a line of trees in the autumn. Some are very drab and colorless, but here and there along the row a few trees are resplendent with beauty. They command attention. "*And Salmon begat Booz of Rachab*" (v. 5). I think again of the Americans who dislike discovering their ancestors to have been cut-throats, pirates and horse thieves! Who would expect to find a harlot among the forebears of Jesus? "And Joshua the son of Nun sent out of Shittim two men to spy secretly, saying, Go view the land, even Jericho. And they went, and came into an harlot's house, named Rahab, and lodged there." The rest of the story, as told in Joshua, chapter six, tells of the courage and obedience of this woman. When Jericho fell, Rahab was delivered, and ultimately became one of the most distinguished ladies in Israel. When she married Salmon, who was in all probability one of the spies she had sheltered, Rahab forsook her questionable practices and began a new life. Soon she gave birth to a son, and with her husband decided to name him Booz or Boaz (Ruth 2:1). (See the special homily at the end of this chapter.)

"*And Booz begat Obed of Ruth*" (v. 5). Matthew's list of names might resemble a main highway through a country, a highway leading to a desired destination. Yet, here and there, our guide momentarily stops to indicate a beautiful scene close to the road. Rahab was one; Ruth was another. These women were both Gentiles! Naomi had gone with her husband to the land of Moab, where increasing sorrow devastated her soul. There had been two weddings and three funerals, and Naomi was heartbroken. When she indicated a desire to return to her homeland, Ruth, the daughter-in-law, refused to be left behind, and so into the city of Bethlehem came this young woman from a far country. The account of her marriage to Rahab's son, Boaz, is one of the loveliest stories in history, but who would have thought that such a woman would be found among the ancestors of the Lord? Surely God, through Matthew, was trying to teach the world that Jesus would be the Savior of Gentiles as well as Jews; He would welcome sinners as well as saints!

It is worthy of note that Matthew was very careful in his choice of words concerning the birth of Jesus. Constantly throughout the writing of the genealogy he had written the word "begat." "...Matthan *begat*

Jacob; And Jacob *begat* Joseph the husband of Mary, *of whom was born Jesus,* who is called Christ'' (vv. 15b,16). One mistake from Matthew's pen could have caused endless controversy. It could *not* be truthfully said, "Joseph begat Jesus." The Lord was brought into the world with the aid of a Jewish mother, but He was begotten of God through the Holy Spirit.

## SECTION TWO

*Expository Notes Concerning the Birth of Jesus*

**Now the birth of Jesus Christ was on this wise: When as his mother Mary was espoused to Joseph, before they came together, she was found with child of the Holy Ghost. Then Joseph her husband, being a just man, and not willing to make her a public example, was minded to put her away privily (vv. 18-19).**

Throughout the history of the Christian church, the doctrine of the Virgin Birth of Christ has been consistently challenged. Today, there are many clergymen who reject its implications and some denominations which condone the actions of their representatives. For example, one representative clergyman in the denomination wrote, "The virgin birth is a doctrine which presents us with many difficulties, and it is one of the doctrines on which the church says that we have full liberty to come to our own belief and our own conclusion." Furthermore, writing in the *Pulpit Commentary,* the Rev. A. Lukyn Williams, states: "It may, however, be justly said that the words are in themselves rather a record of the feelings of Joseph and Mary about the Incarnation." The explanation infers that, as people attribute to God credit for any personal pleasure, so the parents of Jesus described the birth of Jesus as a direct answer to their prayers; that His coming was through the kindness of God who had graciously answered their prayers. Hence, "...she was found with child of the Holy Ghost." There exists many ministers who ridicule the account of the miraculous conception, and there are theological seminaries where the entire story is rejected. In all honesty, it must be said, the time has arrived when every preacher should know what he believes, and every church should be aware of its pastor's theological views.

It is extremely difficult to harmonize the above interpretation with Matthew's statement "Joseph, [Mary's] husband, being a just man, and not willing to make her a public example, was minded to put her away privily [privately].'' If, as has been suggested, these parents were celebrating a magnificent answer to their prayers, they should have been proclaiming their joy from the housetop! Some churches do not compel their representatives to accept and preach this disputed doctrine; ministers are free to interpret the Scriptures as they desire. It is necessary to ask a very direct question. Are the Scriptures reliable or not? The Bible teaches that Joseph was NOT the father of Jesus. We are therefore entitled to ask who was the father? However distasteful it might appear to be, the fact remains that unless Mary's child was conceived of the Holy Spirit, Jesus was an illegitimate child, born out of wedlock. Furthermore, His mother had enjoyed illicit associations with an unknown man, even when she was betrothed to Joseph.

''Nevertheless, to bring this debatable issue to a very decisive head, the question must be asked, What is the alternative to this old story? If Christ were not born as Luke describes, *then how was He born?* Mary was engaged to Joseph, and in Jewish law an engagement was as binding as a wedding ceremony. Either party guilty of breaking that contract was liable to severe punishment (death by stoning). The *New English Bible* translates Matthew 1:18-21 as follows, 'This is the story of the birth of the Messiah. Mary, his mother, was betrothed to Joseph; before the marriage, she found that she was with child by the Holy Spirit. Being a man of principle, and at the same time wanting to save her from exposure, Joseph desired to have the marriage contract set aside quietly. He had resolved on this when an angel appeared unto him...' It is very evident that Joseph was not the father of Mary's child. If the miraculous element be denied, then who was the father? These are not pleasant thoughts, but the time has come when students must decide what they intend to believe and preach. There are no illegitimate children on earth; there are only illegitimate parents, and if modern interpretations are to be accepted, then we must go the whole way and admit once for all, that Mary was an unfortunate young woman whose moral lapse initiated her into the ranks of unmarried mothers. Somewhere along the line, unknown to her sweetheart, she had associations with another man, but her unwanted child ultimately overcame this social handicap to become the most famous figure in Jewish history. Maybe some of the critics who reject the story of the virgin birth would like to explain to a waiting world how the second miracle was even greater than the one they rejected as impossible'' (Condensed from ''A Necessary Introduction to the Study of the Virgin Birth of Jesus,'' in the author's commentary on *Luke's Thrilling Gospel,* pp. 39-41).

But while he thought on these things, behold, the angel of the Lord appeared unto him in a dream, saying, Joseph, thou son of David, fear not to take unto thee Mary thy wife: for that which is conceived in her is of the Holy Ghost. And she shall bring forth a son, and thou shalt call his name JESUS: for he shall save his people from their sins. Now all this was done, that it might be fulfilled which was spoken by the Lord through the prophet, saying, Behold, a virgin shall be with child, and shall bring forth a son, and they shall call his name Emmanuel, which being interpreted is, God with us (vv. 20-23).

It should never be forgotten that this story has an Eastern setting. Even today, wedding arrangements are vastly different from those found in Western nations. During my years in Africa, I was often amazed to find among the native people, weddings were an economic adventure; wives were bought! The price varied according to the status of the bride's family, but generally the bridegroom, in order to obtain the consent of his in-laws to-be, had to give ten cows for his bride and one extra fat cow to the mother-in-law! A baby boy was unwanted by parents, for they knew they would have to help provide cows when the time came for him to be married. Baby girls were welcomed with open arms; if they lived, they would someday, through their marriage, enrich the family. Girls were often promised at birth, and claimed later when they were old enough to wed. I knew of one very serious problem which arose on a mission station when the promised bride sought sanctuary; she did not wish to marry the man to whom she had been promised. The custom still exists in India. To understand this situation is to appreciate the events connected with the marriage of Mary to Joseph.

A Jewish wedding was generally arranged in three stages. *First* came the engagement. This was an agreed arrangement when the girl, often very young, was promised to a man chosen by her parents. This seems strange to Western people, for often the bride and bridegroom had never met. Parents, and parents alone, were responsible for the continuance of the family name, and it was their task to find a husband for their daughter. *Second,* there was the betrothal. It was the equivalent of an engagement party. What had been arranged earlier, was then ratified. At this point in the proceedings, the entire affair could be cancelled if either bride or bridegroom objected. However, once the matter had been agreed, there was no way of escape. The engagement lasted for one year. During that time, the couple was considered to be man and wife, although the marriage was never consummated. If the man wished to end the contract, he could do so by divorce proceedings, but the woman could do nothing. *Finally,* after one year of preparation, the marriage service was held, and festivities continued for several days. It is against this background we must consider the relationship existing between Joseph and Mary.

At some earlier date, Mary had been promised to Joseph. Then, she had been officially engaged or "espoused" to him, and it was during the following twelve months that she became pregnant. Ordinarily, this would have been a devastating catastrophe, and if Joseph denied having had intercourse with his promised wife, she would have been tried and sentenced to death by stoning. This was in accordance with Jewish law. Writing of such a situation, Moses said: "But if this thing be true, and the tokens of virginity be not found for the damsel: Then shall they bring out the damsel to the door of her father's house, and the men of her city shall *stone her with stones that she die:* because she hath wrought folly in Israel, to play the whore in her father's house: so shalt thou put evil away from among you" (Deut. 22:20-21).

Joseph was terribly shocked when he discovered Mary's condition. This had happened during the twelve months when they should have been eagerly preparing for the consummation of their own marriage. Lesser men might have accused her before the elders of the city, but "Joseph her husband, being a just man, and not willing to make her a public example, was minded to put her away [privately]." He loved the girl too much to permit her being stoned, and yet could hardly condone her crime! The only solution seemed to be in secrecy, during which they could be quietly divorced, and somewhere, somehow, both could begin living separate lives. Joseph was contemplating these things when the angel appeared to remove his doubt.

*GOD'S PROVISION*

"And she shall bring forth a son, and thou shalt call his name JESUS: for he shall save his people from their sins" (v. 21). During the lifetime of Ezekiel, God had said, "And *I sought for a man* among them, that should make up the hedge, and stand in the gap before me for the land, that I should not destroy it: *but I found none*" (Ezek. 22:30). All that had changed; God had provided a Savior for Israel. During the Old Testament years, God had been FOR His people; now in the Person of His Son, God would be *WITH* them. "...and they shall call his name Emmanuel, which being interpreted is, God with us" (v. 23b).

## GOD'S PROMISE

"Now all this was done, that it might be fulfilled which was spoken by the Lord by the prophet, saying, Behold, a virgin shall be with child" (v. 23a). This prediction came from the writings of Isaiah 7:14; "Therefore the Lord himself shall give you a sign; Behold, a virgin shall conceive, and bear a son, and shall call his name Emmanuel." It should be noted again that one of the key statements found in this Gospel is "that it might be fulfilled which was spoken of the Lord by the prophet." Matthew hoped the Jews would see, as he saw, that Jesus was the fulfillment of all that had been promised.

## GOD'S PRESENCE

"Emmanuel...God with us." God was no longer the inscrutable Deity in the sky; He was not even the awesome Jehovah of Mount Sinai. God had descended to earth in the form of a baby. Did Joseph realize the implications of what was taking place? We may never know, but surely, when in after years Matthew wrote these words, his soul was thrilled. Maybe his face became wet with tears, as he remembered he had been permitted to walk and talk with God. He never forgot that privilege, for even when he was completing his Gospel, he quoted the promise of his Master: "Go ye therefore, and teach all nations...and lo, I am with you always, even unto the end of the world. Amen" (Matt. 28:19-20).

**Then Joseph being raised from sleep did as the angel of the Lord had bidden him, and took unto him his wife and knew her not till she had brought forth her firstborn son: and he called his name JESUS (vv. 24-25).**

When Joseph awakened from sleep, two words filled his thoughts. *Jesus*, which meant Savior, and *Emmanuel*, which meant God with us. United, they had one thrilling message: God had come to be with His people and to save them from sin. The closing verses of the chapter suggest three simple, but vital facts. (1) *His Compliance.* He did as the angel had commanded...he took his wife. (2) *His Consecration.* He knew her not till she had brought forth her firstborn son. Tatian, an ancient writer said, "He lived together in holiness with her." (3) *His Cooperation.* "...and he called his name JESUS."

Throughout the church age, much has been said about the mother of the Lord but little about her husband. This is to be regretted, for

Joseph was a prince! It is extremely doubtful if other men would have accepted the situation with which he was confronted. His complete confidence in the truthfulness of the angelic message; his continuing care for his wife; the physical restraints which governed his life, and the soon-to-be flight into Egypt demonstrated that Joseph was indeed God's man!

HOMILY

Study No. 1

### NAOMI AND RUTH... Who Came Home to Bethlehem

They stood together on the road, two lonely, determined women, whose hearts had been united by the common bond of sorrow. Far back across the years, Naomi still saw the failing crops, the prolonged droughts, and the distressing seasons which had suggested the removal of her family from Bethlehem. Her husband, Elimelech, had been driven almost to the point of despair, and he had been firmly convinced that Moab alone offered relief from the famine which threatened the home. The little family had moved to the new land, only to discover that hardship knew no frontiers. Her husband and two sons had died before the resolve to return home had triumphed. Orpah, the other daughter-in-law, had been persuaded to rejoin her people, but Ruth had steadfastly refused to follow her example. In reply to Naomi's suggestion, she answered, "Entreat me not to leave thee...thy people shall be my people, and thy God my God. Where thou diest, will I die, and there will I be buried: the LORD do so to me, and more also, if ought but death part thee and me" (Ruth 1:16-17). And so hand in hand, they came home to Bethlehem.

### THE WORLD NEEDS TO WALK THAT PATHWAY IN ORDER TO FIND PEACE

It is worthy of note that these two women were very different. Racially and religiously, they once had nothing in common. Naomi was a Jewess, steeped in the traditions of her people; Ruth was a Gentile, a maiden of Moab, and one of a people classed as Israel's enemies. The power of love had overcome their scruples, and any feelings of animosity had been banished by their mutual affection. They were no longer Jew and Gentile, they were mother and daughter, united in sorrow, in fellowship, and in the common purpose to allow nothing to separate them. And so they came to Bethlehem. The world needs to follow their sublime example. When Jew and Gentile, European and Asiatic, East and West, can forget their differences and join hands in friendship and love; when all can tread the path to the holy place, then the problems of the world will be solved.

## THE BACKSLIDER NEEDS TO WALK THAT PATHWAY IN ORDER TO FIND PEACE

Bethlehem was known as "The House of Bread" but God had permitted famine to threaten the securities of the district, and alas, one family at least had been unequal to the time of testing. The prosperity of Moab had appeared to be more desirable than the difficulties of the promised land. So they moved to Moab, where attendance at the sanctuary of God was impossible; where the songs of Zion were seldom heard. Probably they made money, for they felt equal to the task of supporting two daughters-in-law. Yet, disaster overtook them. The story seems to be very modern. Every backslider journeys to Moab, where the famine is of another type, and where the grave-diggers are always busy. Wise men realize that a loaf of bread in Bethlehem is far more satisfying than a sumptuous repast in Moab.

## THE SINNER NEEDS TO WALK THAT PATHWAY IN ORDER TO FIND PEACE

Naomi had known the fellowship of Bethlehem, but Ruth was a complete stranger to its charms. Naomi was a child of Israel; Ruth was a child of heathenism. Probably, some lessons about the true God had been taught to her by her mother-in-law. The daughter's admiring eyes had seen fortitude in sorrow, and had come to appreciate that divine help was a reality in the experience of her lonely relative. Happy indeed must be every Naomi who can attract others to her God. When Ruth exclaimed, "Thy God shall be my God," her testimony provided the greatest compliment ever paid to the value of Naomi's influence. Naomi had won a convert, and, "they two went until they came to Bethlehem." Soon everything came right, for God worked on their behalf in an amazing fashion. Wedding bells filled their souls with gladness, and the laughing eyes of a baby boy removed all sorrow from their hearts. And probably, even God smiled, for in the fullness of time Ruth became the great-grandmother of David (see Ruth 4:21-22). (Reprinted from the author's book: *Bible Pinnacles*, pp. 35-36.)

# The Second Chapter of Matthew

THEME: *The Events Connected with the Birth of Jesus*

OUTLINE:
   I. The Experiences of the Wise Men (Verses 1-12)
   II. The Enquiry of the Wicked Monarch (Verses 3-8 and 16)
   III. The Efficiency of the Warning Messages (Verses 12-13 and 19-23)
   IV. The Exasperation of the Weeping Mothers (Verses 16-18)

## INTRODUCTION TO CHAPTER TWO

### THE GOD OF COMMUNICATIONS

A careful study of the second chapter of Matthew's Gospel reveals the genius of its author. At first glance, the casual reader might be tempted to believe Matthew was only thinking of the birth of his Master when he wrote these verses, but that was not so. It should never be forgotten that he adored his Lord, and was dedicated to the task of proving Jesus to be the Messiah. Yet, the way in which he approached the task of convincing Jewish readers commands attention.

Matthew begins by mentioning the birth of his Lord, but then, apparently finds more interest in describing its repercussions. If we may be permitted to liken Jesus to a very beautiful diamond, then this author, having shown his gem, begins to place it in a setting of beautiful filigree. The theme of this chapter could be described as *The God of Communications*. Within the limited space of twenty-three verses, Matthew mentions four fulfilled prophecies, four sensational dreams by which the Baby was protected from His enemies, and tells how God provided a special star to guide men in their search for the infant King.

To revert to our earlier illustration, the diamond is always there in the mind and writings of Matthew, but with great skill the author intertwines around it the most artistic, the most beautiful of heaven's decorative work. Nothing could ever make Jesus more attractive, but because of Matthew's God-given ability, Jewish readers would see more clearly the fact that the promised One had arrived.

Again, let it be stressed, Matthew wrote his Gospel to impress, and if possible, to convince Jewish people, who, at first, would have little if any desire to read what had been written. Had he bluntly stated Jesus of Nazareth was the Messiah, most of the hearers would have scoffed and turned away. Had he written this in a book, the volume would not have been read. Matthew knew exactly what he was doing! He was a Jew himself, and was aware of the way his people thought. Any sensational facts would instantly command their attention; they would be fascinated, intrigued, captivated. Let us summarize the evidence and note his methods.

1. God had placed a brilliant star in the heavens, and this had been an unerring guide through a journey of considerable length. Other people had seen the star; the story was irrefutable.

2. Matthew indicated that at least four prophets had spoken concerning the One to whom the star had brought the wise men from the East. These were Micah, Hosea, Jeremiah, and Isaiah. To be mentioned by one prophet would be an honor of inestimable worth, but to be mentioned by four prophets was nothing short of sensational. A Jewish reader of such details would instantly desire additional information.

3. Matthew mentioned four occasions when God sent dreams to prevent the early assassination of the child, Jesus. All Jews believed in dreams and recognized that God had used them throughout history to communicate with people. They believed that Jacob, Joseph, and many other patriarchs had often had such experiences, in which God had given explicit directions to dreamers. Understanding the workings of a Jewish intellect, Matthew described how dreams had baffled the king, changed the traveling plans of the wise men from the East, sent a young family on a journey to a foreign land, and ultimately changed the course of history. Any intelligent reader of these descriptions would be compelled to ask, ''For whom did God do all these things?''

Thus did Matthew weave his web of words; in this amazing way, he entwined his golden filigree around his precious diamond, until the child of Bethlehem shone forth in superlative loveliness. Matthew probably believed that if he could persuade Jews to read his book, the end would never be in doubt. If the prophets wrote of Jesus, and God protected Him throughout many dangers, then, if they continued reading about the Savior, even Jews would ultimately adore Him. Judged by any standard, the second chapter of this Gospel was a brilliant masterpiece carefully planned to achieve a very definite result.

## SECTION ONE

*Expository Notes on the Arrival of the Wise Men From the East*

**Now when Jesus was born in Bethlehem of Judaea in the days of Herod the king, behold, there came wise men from the east to Jerusalem, saying, Where is he that is born King of the Jews? for we have seen his star in the east, and are come to worship him (vv. 1-2).**

The story of the wise men who came seeking Jesus is one of the most intriguing accounts in the Bible. There is so much we wish to know and so few sources of information. These illustrious scholars should be mentioned in the *Guinness' Book of Records,* for, of all people, they traveled the farthest to see Jesus.

*THEIR IDENTITY...Who were they and where did they live?*

They were known as "The Magi" from the Greek word *magoi.* "The Magi first appear in history as a tribe of the emerging Median nation in the seventh century before Christ. Within this tribe there was a strong tradition which favored the exercise of sacerdotal and occult powers within the frame of their religious system, on the part of those who were capable of such activity. The Magian priesthood dressed in white robes and wore tall, somewhat conical hats made of felt which had long side flaps covering their cheeks as far as the chin. They carried small bundles of divining rods known as barsoms with which they officiated at sacrifices; these rods also were utilized in divining and soothsaying by arranging them in various patterns on the ground while chanting their incantations" (*The Zondervan Pictorial Encyclopedia of the Bible,* Volume 4, p. 31).

The Old Testament suggests that Arabia was "the land of the East" and Arabians were "the people of the East" (see Gen. 25:6 and Judg. 6:3). It therefore seems apparent that the men who traveled to find the infant Christ were scholars, probably Gentiles, who were men of eminence in the kingdom of Persia or Arabia. The study of astronomy was common among their people, and their ability to read or interpret signs in the sky was no cause for amazement. We do not know at which place in their country they lived, but a study of the maps of that part of the world suggests the men traveled at least one thousand miles before they reached Bethlehem.

Most of the ancient records infer that the Magi, the priests in the kingdom of Persia, were soothsayers, politicians, and oftentimes insurrectionists. It has been suggested that the wise men came because they were part of the invasion plans of their king; they came to prepare the way for intruding armies. In all honesty, it is difficult to believe this interpretation when we consider the adoration displayed when they found the Babe. Tradition informs us that at first, the number of visiting men was twelve; later, this figure was decreased, and today, millions believe that three wise men journeyed to see the Lord. With the passing of time, they became known as Caspar, Melchior, and Balthasar, and were recognized as kings. There is no biblical evidence for any of these details. Someone has said, ''The Wise Men came in search of Jesus, and all wise men ever since have done the same thing!''

*THEIR INFORMATION...What did they know and why did they come?*

The possibility exists that after the Babylonian captivity, many Jews of the dispersion refrained from returning to Palestine, and settled in other parts of the world. The ancient Magi might have heard from these Hebrews, news of their religion and prophetical expectations. Daniel had predicted the time of the Messiah's appearance, and Micah had mentioned the place where He would be born. If the wise men learned from these sources, they would be aware of the significance of their times. It was commonly believed by their people that the appearance of any exceptionally bright star was the indication of the birth of a king; and, therefore, when they saw the star shining magnificently in the sky, they reached the conclusion that somewhere, something amazingly wonderful had happened. All this is easily understood, but we are left with problems. Why did these men leave their homes and start on a long, hazardous journey? What did they expect to find? Later, lepers came hoping to be cleansed, and blind men came praying to be given sight. The wise men had no such desires. They came to find, to see, to give, and as soon as those immediate aims had been reached, they departed. They came in through the front door of Israel and started a national commotion, and then, unobtrusively, slipped out through the back door to proceed into oblivion. Doubtless, their gifts were costly and unusual, but they received nothing in return except a smile on a baby's face, and a warm handshake from a carpenter called Joseph. They had endured a long arduous journey across desert sands and had to return to their home with nothing but memories. Commercially, their trip was a loss; physically, the journey might have endangered their lives. Did they ever regret going to Bethlehem? Probably not; the memory of that Child in the arms of Mary restored their youthfulness even when they were old.

Werner Keller, in his entrancing book, *The Bible as History*, supplies in detail the conferences and research endeavoring to identify the Star of Bethlehem. In chapter two on "Jesus of Nazareth," pp. 345-354, he cites reports from all over the world, and quotes from the writings of ancient authors to suggest the Star of Bethlehem was the result of the proximity of Jupiter and Saturn in the constellation of Pisces. This phenomenon occurred and could be seen in Mediterranean areas prior to the time of the Savior's birth. Keller may or may not be correct in his deductions, and for most Christians that would not be an important issue. God, in His sovereign wisdom, communicated with the wise men, and they were wise in that they obeyed the dictates of their conscience.

We do not know what brilliant star these ancient Magi saw. Many suggestions have been made. Halley's comet was visible shooting brilliantly across the skies about 11 B.C. Four years later there was a brilliant conjunction of Saturn and Jupiter. In the years 5-2 B.C. there was an unusual astronomical phenomenon. In these years, on the first day of the Egyptian month, Mesori, *Sirius,* the dog star, rose at sunrise, and shone with extraordinary brilliance. Now the name *Mesori* means "the birth of a prince" and to those ancient astrologers such a star would undoubtedly mean the birth of some great king. None of us knows what star the Magi saw; but we know it was their profession to watch the heavens, and some heavenly brilliance spoke to them of the entry of a king into the world.

*THEIR INSPIRATION...What did they bring and why did they disappear?*

It would seem that the men from the East had knowledge of the writings of Isaiah, for their statement, "We have seen his star in the East, and are come to worship him" (v. 2) appears to be a reference to Isaiah 60..."And the Gentiles shall come to thy light, and kings to the brightness of thy rising" (v. 2). Probably this verse led to the belief that the wise men were three Gentile kings from Arabia. They brought gifts from their homeland, but even these were strange. The obvious present for a king would be gold; but the frankincense and myrrh were hardly suitable for a baby. Frankincense was used by priests, and myrrh was an ingredient necessary in the embalming of bodies. It was expensive, but since the wise men were present to celebrate a birth, it seemed bewildering that they should offer something emblematic of death (see the later notes on verse 11). That they were obedient to the will of God is evident. Their lines of communication were open to heaven. That God should make them dream a precise dream, and that they were able to understand its message, indicates that God was aware of everything taking place. Happy and wise are they who experience no difficulty either in speaking to, or listening to, their heavenly Father.

## SECTION TWO

*Expository Notes on King Herod's Interest in Jesus*

**When Herod the king had heard these things, he was troubled, and all Jerusalem with him. And when he had gathered all the chief priests and scribes of the people together, he demanded of them where Christ should be born. And they said unto him, In Bethlehem of Judaea: for thus it is written by the prophet, And thou Bethlehem, in the land of Judah, art not the least among the princes of Judah; for out of thee shall come a Governor, that shall rule my people Israel. Then Herod, when he had privily called the wise men, inquired of them diligently what time the star appeared. And he sent them to Bethlehem, and said, Go and search diligently for the young child; and when ye have found him, bring me word again, that I may come and worship him also (vv. 3-8).**

### THE TROUBLED PEOPLE

"Herod...was *troubled, and all Jerusalem with him*" (v. 3). To understand this statement, it is necessary to remember that Herod was a despot; a megalomaniac, haunted by fears. Terrified by a crippling sense of insecurity; suffering from an inferiority complex, he asserted himself in despicable ways. He had already murdered five Maccabean princes and princesses, and among the slain was his favorite wife, Mariamne. When Herod became suspicious of anyone, the offender, whether innocent or guilty, was executed. The entire nation had become the habitat of fear.

Josephus wrote, "The people everywhere talked against him, like those who were still more provoked and disturbed by his procedure, against which discontents, he greatly guarded himself, and took away the opportunities they might have had to disturb him, and enjoined them to be always at work. Nor did he permit the citizens, either to meet together, or to walk, or to eat together, but watched everything they did, and when they were caught, they were severely punished. Many there were who were brought to the citadel Hyrcania, both openly and secretly, and were there put to death. And there were spies set everywhere: both in the city and in the roads, who watched those that met together; nay, it is reported, that he did not himself neglect this part of caution, but that he would oftentimes himself take the habit of a private man, and mix among the multitude, in the night time, and make trial what opinion they had of his government...and indeed a great part of the people, either to please him, or out of fear of him, yielded to what he required of them" (*Josephus* Book XV. Chapter XI, Paragraph 4).

Today, in Soviet Russia, the same conditions exist, and all tourists tell the same story. They are not allowed to travel alone; they are closely supervised in all their movements, and public religious gatherings are strictly forbidden. Open-air demonstrations are not permitted unless they are sponsored by the totalitarian officials. The same conditions existed in Nazi Germany, where people at any time, in any place, could be arrested. Freedom ceased to exist, and men and women lived in the shadow of terror. Flavius Josephus might have been describing conditions then, but they are still known in certain parts of our world today. It is not possible to understand fully the significance of "Herod was troubled...and all Jerusalem with him" unless the words be considered against the political backdrop of Herod's kingdom. When the wise men from the East reached the borders of Palestine, they entered into a place of jeopardy. Herod's spies would have been aware of the strange caravan approaching from the desert, and would have been prepared for any eventuality. They questioned the travelers at the border, and ascertained the purpose of the visit. The news that the illustrious visitors were in search of a newly-born king would have been relayed to Herod within a matter of hours. Every movement of the visitors would have been watched, and spies were always close at hand to overhear anything said. Herod, fearing insurrection, would be greatly troubled, but the citizens were even more disturbed. They knew the tantrums of their monarch, and appreciated the fact that, in the final analysis, they would suffer most if Herod went on a murderous rampage. On the flimsiest of pretenses, they could be dragged to the citadel and executed.

## THE TESTIFYING PRIESTS

The statement, "Then Herod, when he had privily called the wise men" (v. 7a) indicates the feverish excitement and fear which gripped the monarch's mind. He could no longer trust his spies; he personally had to interview the visitors. It is said that when eventually they left Herod and continued their journey, they saw the star and "rejoiced with exceeding great joy" (v. 10). That statement begets questions. Had the star ceased to shine? They had followed it across the desert and had seen it many times; it seems strange therefore, that to see it again caused surging happiness. Did God black out His star in order to make the wise men enter the city to ask their question? Was this part of the Lord's program, so that all men should be made aware of the good news? God moves in mysterious ways His wonders to perform.

When panic disturbed his soul, Herod hastily summoned scholars able to supply information concerning the birth of the Messiah. The chief priests were those who had retired from active office; the scribes were the theological scholars of the day; together they represented the aristocracy of the nation. It was their business to study the Scriptures, and Herod was justified in expecting to receive from them the answer to his question. They said that according to the prophecies of Micah, the Messiah would be born in the city of Bethlehem. One would almost expect those religious leaders, having heard the news that the Messiah had been born, to start running in the direction of the nearby birthplace. Alas, Matthew was unable to record that event. The priests who knew so much did so little! They cared nothing for a baby king; they were more concerned with the adult monarch who could line their pockets with gold, and adorn their future with favors.

Once again, we are confronted by the terrible possibility that a man may have much religious knowledge in his head, while his heart remains bankrupt. Religious adornments can so easily be the facade on the front of a derelict soul. Addressing these people at a later date, Jesus said, "Ye hypocrites, well did Esaias prophesy of you, saying, This people draweth nigh unto me with their mouth, and honoureth me with their lips; but their heart is far from me. But in vain they do worship me, teaching for doctrines the commandments of men" (Matt. 15:7-9). Stars are easily seen when the night is dark. The amazing wonder of the Christ child was easily discerned against the blackness of the world into which He was sent. Indisputably God chose the correct moment for the Incarnation; maybe, *maybe,* had Jesus arrived later, He might have been too late!

## THE TRUTHFUL PROPHET

Five centuries before the birth of Jesus, Micah wrote: "But thou, Bethlehem Ephratah, though thou be little among the thousands of Judah, yet out of thee shall he come forth unto me that is to be ruler in Israel; *whose goings forth have been from of old, from everlasting*" (Mic. 5:2). It is worthy of attention, that the high priests omitted to mention the most important part of Micah's prediction, and Matthew also did not quote it fully. Probably, he thought it best not to antagonize his readers at that early part of his manuscript. His chief aim was to get Jews acquainted with the Master; once that was accomplished, the Lord would press His own claims.

Most Christians seem to be unaware of the fact there were two Bethlehems in Palestine, and that it was necessary for Micah to identify which would become the birthplace of the Messiah. He wrote "Bethlehem...though thou be little among the thousands of *Judah....*" There was a second Bethlehem, a town in Zebulon which was in all probability, the burial place of Ibzan, an early judge in Israel (see Judg. 12:8). It should be remembered that this is the first of four references to fulfilled prophecies; that each one is significant, in that extraordinary details were predicted and fulfilled. Unfortunately, many people have no interest in the Scriptures, but every Jew living in the time of Christ, firmly believed the prophets had been the inspired messengers of God. Their word was authentic, reliable, and an inspired prediction of future events. Matthew stressed the importance of every prediction, knowing this to be the only method by which to attract the attention of readers. Wise are those preachers who find their materials where the prophets found their facts.

## THE TERRIBLE PREDICAMENT

The wise men from the East did not become foolish when they arrived in the West. The skillful men of the desert did not become simpletons of the city! They were aware of the world of intrigue into which they had entered; the smiles of an evil king did not bewitch them. They had not traveled many miles to become pawns in the hands of a villain. They knew of the spies which followed them everywhere; and it is not too much to believe they were careful not to betray the whereabouts of the One they sought. We may never know how they eluded the spies, and went unobserved to lay their gifts at the Lord's feet. Perhaps there is more here than at first appears, for any one of the spies would have been generously rewarded by Herod if he could have led the king to Jesus. The wise men had watched carefully, and listened attentively to all that had been spoken; they were indeed confronted by a terrible predicament. One false movement on their part could have brought disaster upon the apparently defenseless Baby. What then could they do? They found consolation in the fact that God was still with them. They may not have known what to do, but God did, and they were not disappointed. ''And being warned of God in a dream that they should not return to Herod, they departed into their own country another way.'' We are reminded of the words of a dying Christian astronomer. Knowing he had only moments to live, he exclaimed, ''They who live with the stars do not fear the night.'' He would have made an excellent additional wise man!

**When they had heard the king, they departed; and, lo, the star, which they saw in the east, went before them, till it came and stood over where the young child was. When they saw the star, they rejoiced with exceeding great joy. And when they were come into the house, they saw the young child with Mary his mother, and fell down, and worshiped him: and when they had opened their treasures. they presented unto him gifts; gold, and frankincense, and myrrh. (vv. 9-11).**

*THE SHINING GUIDE*

''...the star, which they saw in the East, went before them...'' (v. 9b). The text seems to imply that the guide in the sky had brought them safely across the desert, but had disappeared when they arrived in Jerusalem. Its reappearance after the interview with Herod caused great joy. The *Amplified New Testament* renders the text: ''When they saw the star, they were thrilled with *ecstatic joy.*'' If this interpretation be accurate, then the disappearance of the star suggests vital questions. (A) Did God deliberately black out His star in order that the travelers might go into the city and publish the purpose of their journey? The presence of such august visitors in the country was no longer a secret, but the reason for their coming was something not yet revealed to ordinary people. Men could hardly worship the King if they remained unaware of His existence. (B) Did God use this unusual method in order to instruct the wise men they could best serve God by using the wisdom already given to them? The disappearance of their guide might have caused panic. Was God trying to teach them the disappearance of the star did not mean He had deserted them. He would be at their side as they went to make inquiries in the city. When our trusted helpers apparently fail us, we should trust increasingly in Him whose continuing presence is assured. (C) Did God smile when He saw the ecstasy in the souls of His servants? *Great joy* flooded their beings when they recognized the heavenly guide had returned. Did the Lord whisper, "Dear children, did you really think I would bring you so far and then forget you?" Are there times when He might express the same thoughts to us when our faith suffers a setback?

## THE STRANGE GOD!

"...they saw the young child with Mary, his mother, and fell down, and worshiped him" (v. 11a). It is interesting to note *they did not worship Mary!* "They worshiped *him."* Were they shocked to find the Baby in a stable-cave? They came to pay homage to a king, but royal babies ordinarily would be found in a bed covered with the choicest silks and satins. The tiny pillow would be soft and beautiful and certainly not made of straw! Trained nurses would maintain a careful watch, and expert physicians would be present to monitor every heartbeat. The wise men found animals keeping watch, and a weary, though happy husband, sitting near his wife and child. It would appear that sufficient time had elapsed to permit the family to leave the stable and enter the hostel, but even then, the accommodations supplied would not befit a King! The innkeeper undoubtedly ushered the visitors inside, and then respectfully withdrew to his own quarters. The wise men stood in ecstatic wonder; their faces radiant. Men pay homage to a king; but this was no ordinary king. This was a royal King; this was the Son of God. Momentarily, the visitors lost sight of the adoring parents; they knelt to worship. Never before in the entire history of mankind had people seen an infant Deity! That Baby was God incarnate; the eternal Word had been made flesh to dwell among men. The wise men indisputably respected and honored both Joseph and Mary, but for a time, the parents were forgotten. God was resting in the arms of a beautiful young mother; "...and they worshiped him."

Perhaps it would be beneficial to consider another baby. Centuries earlier, a child had been found by a princess of the house of Pharaoh. A young Hebrew mother had placed her child in an ark of bullrushes. There, the baby had been found by a lady destined to be the foster mother of Moses (see Exodus, Chapters 1 and 2). Coming events were already casting their shadows before. Long afterward the Babe of Bethlehem was discovered by princes from the East. His life also was threatened, but no one can destroy what God is determined to preserve.

## THE SUGGESTIVE GIFTS

"...they presented unto him gifts; gold, and frankincense, and myrrh" (v. 11b). To say the least, this was the strangest collection of gifts ever offered to a baby! There were no rattles, no toys, no stuffed animals. There were no pretty baby clothes, no pacifiers, and nothing really useful in the care of an infant. Even the most inexperienced bachelor would be too wise to offer such gifts. We are therefore compelled to ask why these *WISE* men seemed to be stupid!

*Gold* was the usual gift brought to a king. Jesus at that period of His life had no use for wealth of any kind, but His parents had need of financial assistance. They had left their home and occupation; they had encountered the additional expense of childbirth; and very soon, would be hurrying to a foreign land, to which they had had no intention of going. The gold brought by the wise men enabled them to stay out of debt!

*Frankincense* was a scent or perfume derived from the tree *Boswellia*. It is mentioned fourteen times in the Old Testament and twice in the New Testament. "The Hebrew and Greek words used for this substance mean 'white'. This is presumably because when the gum first exudes from the bark it is of an amber color; later, when removed from the tree, the resin produces a white dust on its surface. The gum, when warmed and burned, produces a sweet, pleasant odor. The children of Israel imported frankincense from Arabia — this was produced near Saba or Sheba" (*The Zondervan Pictorial Encyclopedia of the Bible.* Volume 2, p. 606). Frankincense was used mostly by the priests and was part of the sacrificial service. It was costly and rare, and we must ask why such a gift would be given to a newly born child? There are occasions when in every household the air needs to be freshened, but this is not done with very expensive deodorants imported from a foreign land. There must have been a special reason for this extraordinary gift, but that may be more easily understood when we consider the third gift of the Magi.

*Myrrh.* "It is generally agreed that this came from Somaliland, Ethiopia, and Arabia. The trunk and branches of the tree *Commiphora myrrha* exude a gum which produces the delicious fragrance. The *C. myrrha* is related to *C. kataf.* Both are small trees, often called thorny shrubs, and both bear small plum-like fruits. Though the gum exudes naturally from the branches, any artificial incision will, of course, produce an immediate supply. The sap as it first oozes out is oily, but as it drops onto wooden squares or stones on which it is collected, it solidifies'' (W.E. Shewell-Cooper in *The Zondervan Pictorial Encyclopedia of the Bible*. Volume 4, p. 326). Myrrh is mentioned in John 19:39 as being part of the embalming substances brought to the grave of Jesus by Nicodemus. As we review the entire scene, we see the wise men seemingly recognized three vital facts. The baby King was indeed the King of Kings, who would eventually become the High Priest of His people. At the right hand of the majesty on high, He would make intercession for those who trusted Him. Yet that remarkable ministry would never become possible, until He consummated His plans by dying to redeem men and women from the power of sin. The wise men apparently recognized Royalty, Representation, and Redemption in the One they saw cradled in Mary's arms. "And they worshiped him." All wise men follow that example.

## SECTION THREE

### *Expository Notes on the Efficiency of God's Warning Systems*

**And being warned of God in a dream that they should not return to Herod, they departed into their own country another way. And when they were departed, behold, the angel of the Lord appeareth to Joseph in a dream, saying, Arise, and take the young child and his mother, and flee into Egypt, and be thou there until I bring thee word: for Herod will seek the young child to destroy him. When he arose, he took the young child and his mother by night, and departed into Egypt: And was there until the death of Herod: that it might be fulfilled which was spoken of the Lord by the prophet, saying, Out of Egypt have I called my son (vv. 12-15).**

### *THE DREAM OF REDIRECTION... Go to Arabia*

The twelfth verse of this chapter contains an interesting word. This is *chreematisthentes* and it is translated by the *Amplified New Testament* "*And receiving an answer to their asking,* they (the wise men), were divinely instructed and warned in a dream, not to go back to Herod; so they departed to their own country by a different way.'' According to Thayer, there are two Greek words closely associated. They are: *chreematizo* which means "to transact business; to advise or consult with one about public affairs; *to make answer to those who ask for advice, to give a response to those consulting an oracle.''* The other word is:

*chreematismos* which means "a divine response." The account as given by Matthew strongly suggests the men were wise enough to know their wisdom had limitations! Knowing the dangers by which they were surrounded, they asked God for directions, and it was in response to their prayer that God sent the dream. Someone has said that the only knowledge worthwhile is that which comes after a man knows it all! The story of these men reminds all that without God's help, even the wisest people may become foolish. As Herod awaited the return of his visitors, they were safely, secretly going home along a different road through the desert.

## THE DREAM OF REPRISALS...Go to Egypt

"Behold, the angel of the Lord appeareth to Joseph in a dream, saying, Arise, and take the young child and his mother, and flee into Egypt...for Herod will seek the young child to destroy him" (v. 13). Had Joseph known earlier that he would not see his carpenter's shop for many months, and possibly years, he would have been exceedingly worried. How could he possibly afford to pay for a vacation in a foreign land? The steps of a good man are ordered by the Lord; God never gives December grace in June; He never imparts strength to climb a mountain when the path runs through flat prairies. He had promised, "As thy days, so shall thy strength be." Joseph the carpenter had a very efficient organizing secretary! The gold brought by the wise men was more than enough to meet his needs as he walked and talked with God. He quickly discovered that his job was to protect a baby and his mother; God's task was to care for the entire family. Happy and wise are they who have a similar working arrangement with the Almighty. The Lord knew every thought that entered the mind of Herod, and the warning systems for His servants were the most efficient known to man. Later in life, Jesus would say what Joseph learned earlier, "But seek ye first the kingdom of God, and his righteousness; and all these things shall be added unto you. Take therefore no thought [be not unduly anxious] for the morrow: for the morrow shall take thought for the things of itself..." (Matt. 6:33-34).

## THE DREAM OF REASSURANCE...Go to Israel

We have not been told how long Joseph and his family remained in Egypt. Matthew says "but when Herod was dead," Joseph was instructed to return to his homeland. Did he become anxious? Was he a little apprehensive as to what had happened to his carpenter's shop? Was he fretful? If he were like us, then he was very worried, but since he had evidence of God's continuing care, probably that wonderful man enjoyed "the rest of faith." He knew that in the fullness of time, the God who had sent him to Egypt would recall him. Joseph probably found consolation in the words of the Psalmist: "Teach me thy way, O LORD, and lead me in a plain path, because of mine enemies. Deliver me not over unto the will of mine enemies: for false witnesses are risen up against me, and such as breathe out cruelty. I had fainted, unless I had believed to see the goodness of the LORD in the land of the living. Wait on the LORD; be of good courage, and he shall strengthen thine heart: wait, I say, on the LORD" (Psa. 27:11-14).

Once again Matthew referred to fulfilled prophecy, and his reference came from Hosea 11:1, considered by Jews to be a Messianic prediction. There is something thought-provoking about the simple statement "When Herod was dead." Love always outlives hatred; faith remains when fear has gone; goodness is eternal, whereas evil is sure to perish. During the horror of World War II, a German Jewish Christian visited my church in Wales, and I shall never forget his statement. He mentioned all those who had persecuted the Hebrew race, and then very pointedly asked, "What happened to them? They all died, but my people continued to live." Then he paused for a few moments, and finally said, "Just as God dealt with all our enemies, He will deal with Hitler. Just be patient and you will know that my words are true." They were! The most effective way of committing suicide is to fight against God.

## THE DREAM OF RE-EVALUATION...Go to Nazareth

"And [Joseph] arose, and took the young child and his mother, and came into the land of Israel. But when he heard that Archelaus did reign in the room of his father Herod, he was afraid to go thither: notwithstanding, being warned of God in a dream, he turned aside into the parts of Galilee: And he came and dwelt in a city called Nazareth: that it might be fulfilled which was spoken by the prophets, He shall be called a Nazarene" (vv. 21-23). It is significant that here we have again the word *chreematistheis*. Joseph asked for assistance, and the dream was God's response to his request. Long-term arrangements are often useful, but in dealing with God it is better to move on a day-to-day basis. Most business executives on a journey telephone their office several times daily to ascertain what has taken place in the business world. Joseph had a similar arrangement with God, and his immediate response to the instructions issued, led him to reside in the city of Nazareth. This new direction was providential, for it permitted Joseph and Mary to return to where they had once belonged (see Luke 1:26-27 and 2:4). At first the term ''Nazarene'' seems difficult to trace in the prophetic writings. The name means a branch or the separated one, and this possibly is a reference to Isaiah 11:1-2 which reads: ''And there shall come forth a rod out of the stem of Jesse, and a Branch [a separated one] shall grow out of his roots; and the spirit of the LORD shall rest upon him.'' Matthew never lost an opportunity to draw attention to the fulfilment of Messianic predictions: he was convinced his Messiah had arrived!

Josephus had much to write about Archelaus, the despotic son of Herod. ''He was the son of Herod the Great by a Samaritan woman, Malthace'' (*Wars of the Jews*. Book 1; Chapter 28, paragraph 4). ''After Herod's death, he ordered his soldiers to attack the Jews in the temple. As a result of this infamy, three thousand Jews perished. He governed his kingdom with such ferocity that, in the ninth or tenth year of his reign, he was dethroned, deprived of his possessions, and banished to Vienna'' (*Antiquities of the Jews*, Book 17; Chapter 13, paragraph 2). In the light of these facts, it is not difficult to understand Joseph's reluctance to go into Judea. To do so would have been to expose Jesus to the brutality known throughout the earlier reign of Herod.

## SECTION FOUR

*Expository Notes on the Slaughter of the Children*

**Then Herod, when he saw that he was mocked of the wise men, was exceeding wroth, and sent forth, and slew all the children that were in Bethlehem, and in all the coasts thereof, from two years old and under, according to the time which he had diligently inquired of the wise men. Then was fulfilled that which was spoken by Jeremy the prophet, saying, In Rama was there a voice heard, lamentation, and weeping, and great mourning, Rachel weeping for her children, and would not be comforted, because they are not (vv. 16-18).**

### UNRESTRAINED MADNESS

''Then Herod...slew all the children...from two years old and under'' (v. 16b). History has a strange way of repeating itself. When another Savior was born in Egypt, the forces of evil unleashed a terrible attack against the babies of Israel. "And the king of Egypt spake to the Hebrew midwives... And he said, When ye do the office of a midwife to the Hebrew women, and see them upon stools; if it be a son, then ye shall kill him: but if it be a daughter, then she shall live. But the midwives feared God, and did not as the king of Egypt commanded them, but saved the men children alive" (Exod. 1:15-17). Herod and Pharaoh had something in common; they were assassins. Yet as God protected Moses, so He protected Jesus. As Moses grew to be the deliverer of his people, so it was said of the Babe of Bethlehem, "...thou shalt call his name JESUS: for he shall save his people from their sins" (Matt. 1:21).

## UNREQUITED MISERY

"...Rachel weeping for her children, and would not be comforted, because they are not" (v. 18b). This is a quotation from Jeremiah 31:15, but at first glance, it is a difficult passage to interpret. It would seem there was nothing Messianic about Jeremiah's statement. The prophet was merely repeating what God had said, and however foreboding the statement might sound, it is but a small dark cloud in a very blue sky! Jeremiah's chapter is very thrilling, for he quotes promises by which Israel was assured of restoration to greatness. Students should read the whole of the thirty-first chapter of Jeremiah. God spoke of the downfall of the nation and of the approaching captivity in Babylon, but the people were promised ultimate deliverance. "Hear the word of the LORD, O ye nations, and declare it in the isles afar off, and say, He that scattered Israel, will gather him, as a shepherd doth his flock" (Jer. 31:10). The statement concerning the sorrow of Rachel was a reference to the captivity of God's people. The prisoners taken by the Babylonians would be marched past Rachel's tomb, and this would be cause for the mother of the nation *to weep!* Today, when something terrible happens, we say, "It is enough to make a person *turn in his grave!*" This is only to be understood in a figurative sense. Doubtless, the Hebrew mothers in Egypt wept as did the mothers in Bethlehem and its surrounding villages. Matthew saw a similarity in the events, but the true meaning of the text must be found in our third suggestion.

## THE UNSURPASSED MAJESTY

The Lord, after speaking about the tears of Rachel, said, "Refrain thy voice from weeping, and thine eyes from tears: for thy work shall be rewarded, saith the LORD; and they shall come again from the land of the enemy. And there is hope in thine end, saith the LORD'' (Jer. 31:16-17). The tears of the night were to be followed by joy in the morning. This would never have comforted the mothers of Bethlehem, and possibly that was the reason why Matthew refrained from completing his citation of the prophecy. Nevertheless, that was the true setting of the prediction, and we are forced to consider its implications. What Herod did was completely inexcusable, but his onslaught on innocence would only hasten his own death. Right would triumph in the end, and what the Babe of Bethlehem would accomplish would make possible a world in which tears, tragedy, and death would be eternally outlawed. Modern Herods may appear to win battles against goodness, but the final victory rests with God. We must never forget that great truth.

HOMILY

Study No. 2

### THE WISE MEN...Who Looked Through a Starry Window

The Bethlehem story is the greatest in literature, and yet how different is man's conception of it from that which actually took place. Two thousand years ago, in a hastily prepared cave and without any medical assistance whatsoever, a young woman gave birth to her son. There were no picturesque surroundings and twinkling lights such as those so ornamentally presented on Christmas cards. The only illumination present came from a simple lamp, and the light of motherhood just beginning to shine in Mary's eyes. Yet in spite of the unpretentious birthplace, the story of His coming will never grow old.

*GOD REVEALING THE SON*

As we consider the manger scene, three vital truths become obvious. (a) *God is never indifferent to human need.* Four centuries had passed since the appearance of a prophet, and there were those in Israel who were tempted to believe God had forsaken His people; that their suffering and prayers were meaningless to Him. God's response to this problem was found in the Bethlehem story. (b) *The Lord Jesus is God's answer to human need.* In the fullness of time God sent His Son to be born of a woman, and since this was His only begotten Son, should He fail, there could be no other. The divine remedy for human ill is the Savior.

(c) *If God sent His Son, the implications of such an act are far too great to escape attention.* The God responsible for such a gift must at least make known the glad story. How futile would be the coming of Christ, if the world remained ignorant of the fact.

## GREATNESS RECOGNIZING THE SON

Since the gospel was first to the Jew, it was perfectly reasonable that the initial announcement of His coming should be made to the shepherds. Yet the tidings of God's love can never be confined within the narrow limits of one nation. Thus, far away in the East, an astronomer looked intently at the sky, for to his practiced eye, the appearance of a new comet revealed great mystery. He and others of his type read in the brilliance, the news that somewhere a king had been born. It is not for us to speculate how they arrived at this conclusion; it is sufficient to know God is able to speak every man's language. We are not told how many of these eminent men made the pilgrimage to Bethlehem; nor do we know if they all came from the same district. Yet other things are known. (a) *They saw grace in the sky.* God had graciously revealed His purposes. (b) *They saw guidance in the star.* This logically follows, for of what use would it be to tell men of the Christ unless some means be found by which they could be led to Him? (c) *They saw God in the Son,* and placed their choicest treasures at His feet. The memory of that glorious vision enriched them forever.

## GUILT RESISTING THE SON

Unerringly, the star led them over the hills and through the valleys, but as they drew near to the city of Jerusalem, their guide suddenly disappeared. The wise men were thereupon obliged to seek information regarding the birthplace of the new King, and thus the news reached Herod and his people. We must ask the reason for this break in the sequence of guidance. Surely the star could have led the pilgrims until they finally reached their destination. Why should there be a delay in Jerusalem? It is God's will that all men should hear of Christ. He cannot make men yield to the Lord Jesus, but His is the responsibility of carrying the message to them. After their visit to the palace the wise men rejoiced, for the star reappeared to guide them on the final stage of their journey. King Herod sat alone with his problems, and the tragic stages of his increasing sinfulness are clearly defined. (a) *His Fear.* The coming of another king meant a new challenge to his own throne. God's King would never take second place. (b) *His Faith*. He sought information in the Scriptures, and by so doing increased his condemnation. He would never be able to plead ignorance as an excuse for his sin. (c) *His Folly*. Thwarted, he fought grimly against the advent of the child Jesus, and in so doing, he sealed his fate. He died, a poor broken sinner, having lost the glorious opportunity of writing his name in history. He might have been known as the additional wise man.(Reprinted from the author's book, *Bible Cameos*, pp, 83-84.)

# The Third Chapter Of Matthew

THEME: *The Ministry of John the Baptist*

OUTLINE:
  I. The Strange Servant (Verses 1-4)
  II. The Successful Service (Verses 5-6)
  III. The Striking Sermon (Verses 7-12)
  IV. The Submissive Son (Verses 13-17)

## INTRODUCTION TO CHAPTER THREE

### THE SILENT YEARS

Even the most casual reader of Matthew's Gospel must be aware of the immense gap existing in his records. Between the end of the second and the beginning of his third chapters is a period extending over nearly thirty years, and of this, the author said nothing. This obvious omission suggests questions. Was Matthew unaware of what had happened during the early years of the Savior's life, and if so, why did he not research the facts as did Luke? A comparison of the Gospels reveals interesting details.

Mark begins his writings with an introduction to John the Baptist, and never mentions anything about the childhood years of his Savior. He was thrilled with thoughts of Jesus, and as quickly as possible introduced Him to the readers. John, the theologian, used fourteen verses to reach and describe the advent of John the Baptist, and completely ignored the details of the birth and childhood of the Lord. To him, they seemed unimportant. He saw Jesus as the One who had inhabited eternity, and to visualize Him among angels was more thrilling than to see Him as a child in a carpenter's shop. Luke, the beloved doctor, was fascinated by the perfection of Christ's humanity. He researched every aspect of the birth of Jesus, and Mary described to him even the most intimate details of her pregnancy. When he desired additional information, she told him of the incidents in the temple, both at the Lord's circumcision, and when, twelve years later, His questions and answers astounded the doctors of the law. Luke was careful to include these facts in the introductory sections of his Gospel, but then, for some inscrutable reason, ignored the following eighteen years.

Let it be candidly admitted, we would like to know more. Did Jesus attend the school of a rabbi, and if so, did He become an outstanding student? Did He become an expert carpenter as year after year  Joseph taught Him? What was the Lord like when He became a teenager? After the death of Joseph, did Jesus become the fix-it man for the city of Nazareth? Did He ever have awkward customers, and did some of them try to cheat Him? Did He ever have farmers who refused to pay their bills, and if so, how did He handle that test of patience? When He became aware of His greater mission to preach to multitudes of people, how did He harmonize the surging desire in His soul, with the obvious responsibility of remaining at home to support His family? How did He maintain the delicate balance between duty and delight? When the call to minister to needful people began to stir His soul, did He have to restrain Himself for months or years? When eventually He went away preaching, did He miss the warmth of home life? Yes, let it be admitted, we would like to know more about the Lord's silent years. Luke's brief accounts only whet our appetite. Matthew, Mark, and John tell us nothing! We would like to say, "Shame on you," but maybe, if they were able to speak to us, they could explain satisfactorily the glaring omissions in their records. We are only concerned now with Matthew, and perhaps we should ask a few questions, and consider his possible answers.

*"Matthew, why did you refrain from mentioning nearly thirty years of the Lord's life?"*

"My brethren, I had to! When I wrote my Gospel, I was anxious to present the King, and of course, I sought the aid of the Holy Spirit, so that I could do the best job possible. I wished to convince my Jewish readers that the Messiah had come; that they should meet, listen to, and love Him. I fully realized they would not be interested in a boy working in a carpenter's shop; they would consider that to be beneath the dignity of any king! I knew they would not be interested in the exploits of a twelve year-old who seemed a little smarter than other children. Child geniuses were not unknown in those days. My people looked for a real king and therefore as soon as I attracted their attention to the wise men, I thought it opportune to present my Master."

*"Matthew, did you ever have regrets because you never mentioned the details of the early life of the Lord?"*

"Did I ever have regrets? Well, not really. The man who knows everything, knows very little. My first aim was to please God; my second, that with His help, I might be able to convince my readers that Jesus was the fulfillment of all their hopes. I also knew that God had commissioned three other men to write their Gospels. I was not the 'only pebble on the beach;' Mark, Luke, and John were as important as I. Together, we were meant to present a complete, composite picture of the Lord. I was told to portray the Royal Aspect of the Master; my brethren had their stories to tell, and they did a very good job. If the first four chapters of a book were identical, the volume would be ignored! Men love surprises, and the greatest of authors generally keep theirs until the closing section of their story. My brothers and I were different. We desired to show the way to the greatest treasure ever known to man, so we prepared a map to help seekers! I supplied one quarter of it; Mark, Luke, and John supplied the rest. What one of us failed to record, the others did in detail. The very fact that I omitted certain information encouraged seekers to look elsewhere. Your question to me now, only proves we succeeded in capturing your attention. That is precisely what God instructed us to do; evidently He was wise."

We cannot argue with Matthew, but his replies cannot quench our thirst for knowledge. Maybe, if we look more closely at what is available, we might find something to help us penetrate those years of silence.

"And he went down with them, and came to Nazareth, and was subject unto them....And Jesus increased in wisdom and stature (age), and in favor with God and man" (Luke 2:51-52). These verses present three things for consideration. Let us take them in order.

1. *He was "subject unto them." He Listened!* There is always a tendency with growing children to think they know everything! Later in life, they invariably wonder how they could have been so stupid. Jesus must have been a model child, for He listened to, and observed all His parents said and did. There was never a tantrum, rudeness, nor selfishness. He did what the law commanded — He honored His father and mother, but alas, for other reasons, "His days were not long upon the earth."

2. *"And Jesus increased in wisdom." He Learned!* There are great mysteries connected with the Incarnation. Sometime, in eternity, God

might reveal what now is unknown, but at least we can consider the simple facts behind the learning processes of the child Jesus. He had been present at the creation of the world, had designed every flower, and composed the music of the birds. Yet it is inconceivable that He was conscious of this as a baby. Deliberately, He laid aside the robes of His magnificence, and had chosen to become human. As a child, He became subject to our limitations. As He grew, His mind opened gradually to His surroundings, and sometime later, full realization came to His developing intellect. Then He knew and understood all things. This had already taken place when as a boy of twelve, He amazed the doctors of the law in the temple (see Luke 2:46-47). All the potentialities of a gorgeous flower may be found in a tiny seed planted in the ground. Similarly, all the inscrutable knowledge of the godhead was, in embryonic form, within the child of Bethlehem; and it was destined to bloom into the most beautiful flower ever seen by man. Perhaps that fact was expressed when men called Him, "The Lily of the Valley" and "The Rose of Sharon."

3. *"And Jesus increased in favour with God and man."* It becomes evident that as God looked upon the growth of the boy Jesus, He was pleased and proud. He loved what He saw! This verse in the sacred record is a searchlight, illuminating every part of the Savior's life. It was the prelude of a later statement to be made at the Jordan, when God said, "This is my beloved Son, *in whom I am well pleased."* The captivating beauty of the carpenter was such that all His customers admired and appreciated Him. To increase in favor with God is wonderful, but when the love of God is so evident that it thrills neighbors, *that* is supremely marvelous. We now understand, that from the departure of the wise men, until the day John the Baptist preached his first sermon, these developing characteristics were appearing in the life of Jesus, the carpenter. "And there are also many other things which Jesus did, which, if they should be written every one, I suppose that even the world itself could not contain the books that should be written" (John 21:25).

## SECTION ONE

*Expository Notes on the Appearance of John the Baptist*

**In those days came John the Baptist, preaching in the wilderness of Judaea, and saying, Repent ye: for the kingdom of heaven is at hand. For this is he that was spoken of by the prophet Esaias, saying, The**

**voice of one crying in the wilderness; Prepare ye the way of the Lord, make his paths straight. And the same John had his raiment of camel's hair, and a leathern girdle about his loins; and his meat was locusts and wild honey (vv. 1-4).**

The arrival of John the Baptist was nothing less than sensational. He was much more than a voice crying in the wilderness. He was a trumpet sounding at sunrise, a crier shattering the silence of the night, and a spiritual agitator whose voice could not be silenced. One day he was virtually unknown; the next, all Israel was aware of his presence. He was a phenomenon, a man sent by God to do something which for four centuries had not even been attempted. He was God's man, sent at God's time, to do God's work, and he did it well.

The four verses which comprise the opening statement of this chapter divide into three sections. (1) His Stirring Preaching — How fearless. (2) His Sublime Purpose — How faithful. (3) His Simple Provision — How fortunate. Let us consider them in that order.

*HIS STIRRING PREACHING...How Fearless*

John was not a polished, refined speaker, trained in the art of homiletics; he was not a practical psychologist who carefully, gently approached a problem. This wilderness evangelist was not a psychiatrist who asked many questions prior to forming a conclusion. John was a heaven-sent surgeon who instantly recognized the symptoms of a fatal disease and proceeded to challenge it with a scalpel called repentance. This word was the first to be uttered by John, and as long as the church continues its ministry, that must be the initial word in its message.

John challenged the king, the Pharisees, the Scribes, the Romans, the common people, and all who came within the sound of his voice. This tremendous preacher made no distinction between people, to him their status within the nation was meaningless. John saw sinners, and believed that a dead king would be just as lifeless as a dead laborer. He saw enemies destroying the beauty of God's vineyard, and with an outburst of devastating energy, resembled an indignant husbandman attacking those destructive forces. Each time he cried, "Repent ye," his words, with the cutting edge of a scythe, attacked the complacency which had hindered God's cause for four hundred years. When John stood before King Herod, he ordered the monarch to repent. When Pharisees presented themselves for baptism, he called them vipers and told them to repent. Yes, John was much more than a voice crying in the wilderness; he was an outraged reformer denouncing what he saw in his nation. Yet the most amazing thing about the man was his uncanny effect upon people. Instead of becoming offended, thousands of men and women attended his services, and "were baptized of him in Jordan, confessing their sins" (v. 6).

Is it too much to claim that each time a revival has awakened the church, that type of preacher was prominent, and the same message was the foundation upon which spiritual achievement rested? Each time the church denounced the sinfulness of the world in which it ministered, God signally honored His word and blessed His servants. When the church compromised and ministers ceased being prophets, slowly but surely the fires of devotion died upon the altars of God's cause. It is better to be a voice crying in the wilderness than a corpse in a religious morgue!

## HIS SUBLIME PURPOSE...How Faithful

"For this is he that was spoken of by the prophet Esaias, saying,...Prepare ye the way of the Lord, make his paths straight" (v. 3). The word translated "straight" is *eutheias,* and this means "to make level; to make straight; to make passable; to make usable." Doubtless it referred to the roads known as The King's Highway. Most of the thoroughfares in Palestine were made of hard, trampled earth. They were very uneven and bumpy. To travel along them was always an adventure, but often a nightmare! How true was that Eastern proverb which stated, "There are three states of misery — sickness, fasting, and travel!" The word translated "paths" is *tribous* and this according to Thayer means "a worn way" — a path needing repair. Philo states the word means "a carriage-way," and hence the reference would be to the paved, or stone highways leading to Jerusalem. Josephus speaks of a causeway of black basalt stone, and adds that Solomon made this "to manifest the grandeur of his riches and government." Often, after constant use and inclement weather, some of the stones along the edge of the highway slipped, and made parts of the causeway dangerous. Whenever the king planned to travel, messages were sent ahead commanding the people to pay attention to the road so that the journey would be uneventful.

Matthew, following his pattern of proving his Master was the Messiah, quoted this passage from Isaiah 40:3, and claimed that John was the important forerunner preparing the royal highway for the coming of the King. He was not calling attention to himself; he thought only of the Messiah, and reminded listeners of their duty to repair the road along which the King desired to travel. John doubtless knew of the black asphalt stone, but he was far more concerned with the other highway which led to the coronation place within human hearts. That road was in a state of disrepair, and required urgent attention, for the arrival of the King was imminent. It was for this reason the wilderness preacher cried, "Repent ye: for the kingdom of heaven is at hand" (v. 2). Never on any occasion did John seek publicity. He said quite firmly, "He must increase, but I must decrease" (John 3:30). John probably realized that he was sent in the spirit of Elijah; that he was at best, the forerunner of the King of Kings, and throughout his short but dynamic ministry, he never lost sight of the importance of his mission. He was completely, unwaveringly faithful.

*HIS SIMPLE PROVISION...How Fortunate*

"And the same John had his raiment of camel's hair, and a leathern girdle about his loins; and his meat was locusts and wild honey" (v. 4). John the Baptist was a man who lived "off the land." Apparently, he had little if any need of money; he never went shopping, and since he owned no home, probably slept in a cave somewhere in the vicinity of the valley where he preached. 2 Kings 1:8 reveals that this was precisely the same kind of attire worn by Elijah. The leather probably came from the skin of a sheep or a goat, and the locust diet was exactly what the Bible permitted. "Locusts have been used for food in the east from the remotest times until now. Four kinds are permitted in Lev. 11:22. 'The wings and legs are torn off, and the remainder is sprinkled with salt, and either boiled or even roasted' (Meyer). They are mentioned in the Talmud as being sold after preservation in wine. The word *akrides* forbids the identification of these locusts with the pods of the carob, or locust tree, such as the Prodigal Son would have eaten" (*The Pulpit Commentary*, Matthew, p. 69).

John's requirements were few, and since locusts and wild honey were easily obtained, this tremendous preacher was completely independent of everybody except God. He never begged nor appealed for financial assistance. He could not be bribed, for the treasures of earth were meaningless to him. John received nothing from the hands of men, and therefore never feared hurting them by the directness of his remarks. He lived to please God and prepare the way for God's Son. Nothing else was important. This evangelist ministered on earth, but his citizenship was in heaven.

It is refreshing to read about John the Baptist, for he was different from all others who followed in his footsteps. We have grown accustomed to passionate orations heard in the television programs. We have almost become immune to the emotional appeals for financial assistance, without which, so we are told, specific programs will be discontinued. Listeners are made to feel guilty should the cherished dreams of reformers fail to be realized. Their stinginess might destroy the great programs initiated by the Spirit-filled television speakers! With this in mind, we consider John the Baptist. Would his ancient methods work today? John never saw his name in a newspaper; he was never mentioned on the radio, and never appeared on any television program. He never had a trained choir; did no advertising, and never made any special provision for the continuation of his ministry. He had no trained counselors. Some men became disciples, but apart from their company, John apparently was a man who lived, moved and had his being in the presence of God. He began his ministry alone, and, after a very short time, he died alone in the execution room of a king's palace. Yet, all through his short stay on earth, he enjoyed the most excellent company. He walked and talked with God and, if all the details were known, we might be enthralled with the account of his heavenly escort from the death chamber of Herod's palace to the everlasting glories of the city, "which hath foundations, whose builder and maker is God."

John possessed nothing, but he inherited everything, and bequeathed to us a priceless legacy. He taught us how to live, to preach, to pray, and, if we have eyes to see, his glorious example should teach us how to die. That strange man in the Jordan Valley baffled the forces of evil. The secret of his amazing success is easily recognized. He never forgot that he was God's man!

### SECTION TWO

*Expository Notes on the Extraordinary Scenes in the Jordan Valley*

**Then went out to him Jerusalem, and all Judaea, and all the region round about Jordan, And were baptized by him in Jordan, confessing their sins (vv. 5-6).**

This small section of the third chapter of Matthew's Gospel appears to be insignificant, but a close examination reveals it to be a treasure house for all students. There are four areas of thought, and each has its own distinctive teaching. They are (1) The Unsurpassed Compulsion.

(2) The Unanswerable Communication. (3) The Unexpected Contrition. (4) The Unchallenged Confession. Let us consider them systematically.

*THE UNSURPASSED COMPULSION...The Extent of His Parish*

"Then went out to him Jerusalem, and all Judaea, and all the region round about Jordan." John's first sermon might have been preached to a caravan party resting alongside the dusty highway. He was a man who came out of the wilderness of Judaea, and readily seized any opportunity to address listeners. That this small audience quickly grew in size, until many thousands of people thronged the meetings, calls for investigation. It should be remembered that outside of Jerusalem, the most populated area of the country was in the vicinity of the Jordan Valley. The Decapolis cities, ten in number, were within a day's journey, but the valley itself was filled with many homes. Strabo, describing the plain bordering on Jordan, said, "It is a place of a hundred furlongs, all well watered, and full of dwellings." The appearance of this strange preacher would arouse much curiosity; even his garments indicated he was an unusual person. Nevertheless, the fact that within a few weeks thousands of people walked miles to hear him requires an explanation. His weird appearance was quickly forgotten as multitudes listened to his message. John had no need to seek an audience; people came from near and far, and stayed as long as they were able. A thrilling compulsion energized their every movement. They were fascinated, challenged, and sometimes indignant with what they heard, but they were reluctant to leave. They came from all over the area; they picnicked on the river bank, but when John began to preach, everyone listened eagerly. These were no ordinary meetings; the Jordan Valley had become an open-air cathedral.

When we compare this phenomenon with modern, twentieth-century crusades, we marvel that the Jordan crusade ever became possible. We have grown accustomed to intensive advertising; we expect vast organizations to prepare the way for the nationally known speakers. To invite an unknown evangelist would destroy the effort even before its birth. When a man's face has been seen on television, and his services shared with innumerable viewers in many cities, his appearance in any community is sure to draw friendly listeners. Many of these will have already volunteered their services to make the revival meetings a success. John had none of these advantages. He was completely unknown, and had never delivered a sermon in his lifetime. He suddenly appeared on the stage of a national theater, unannounced, and apparently ill-equipped to play even a minor role in the spiritual awakening of his nation. John had no financial resources; his shabby clothing could not compare with the expensive well-tailored suits of modern evangelists. The Baptist made no appeals for money; he had no musical talents to add spice to his services; and yet, somehow, that strange man attracted people by their thousands. He never told funny stories, and the content of his message suggests he never made his audience laugh; yet, every day, increasing numbers of people came from distant places just to see and hear him. This preacher had a greater parish than any priest in the nation, and yet, every night, he placed his head on a pillow of ferns, for he had no home to which to retire.

*THE UNANSWERABLE COMMUNICATION...The Eloquence of His Preaching*

Perhaps the greatest testimonial John ever received is recorded in John 10:41: "And many [people] resorted unto Jesus, and said, John did no miracle: but all things that John spake of this man were true." It is most thought-provoking that the wilderness preacher possessed none of the qualities considered indispensable by modern evangelists. Even today, if a man commenced performing miracles in the middle of a desert, the highways would be thronged with sick people making their way to his meetings. Yet John the Baptist never performed miracles, and never spoke about them. He was not a trained orator. His methods and possibly his message would be criticized in every theological seminary in the world. He was apparently destined for defeat, for he only spoke of the need for repentance and the imminent arrival of the King for whom the highways should be repaired. When the elite of the nation presented themselves for baptism, he called them vipers, and suggested they were as snakes fleeing before a prairie fire. He inferred that once the threat of danger subsided, they would return to their wicked ways. He called the most respected people hypocrites, and yet in those initial meetings, few people argued with the preacher. We do not know how often he preached, we only know that each time he did, he spoke of sin and the coming King. His outstanding success never changed his appearance nor his heart! Even at the height of his spiritual achievements, John said, "...he that cometh after me is mightier than I, whose shoes I am not worthy to bear..." (Matt. 3:11). Humility and happiness are twin sisters; they live together!

*THE UNEXPECTED CONTRITION...The Evidence of His Power*

"And were baptized of him...*confessing their sins*" (v. 6). John's success was made possible by one irrefutable fact. The hand of God unceasingly rested upon him. He had no recognizable talents, and this fact demonstrated the truth expressed in Zechariah 4:6. "Not by might, nor by power, but by my spirit, saith the LORD" By every human standard John was one of the "foolish and weak things of the world," yet as Paul expressed in 1 Corinthians 1:27-28: "God hath chosen the foolish things of the world to confound the wise; and God hath chosen the weak things of the world to confound the things which are mighty; And base things of the world, and things which are despised, hath God chosen, yea, and things which are not, to bring to nought things that are: *That no flesh should glory in his presence.*" A man's gift of oratory may excite the mind and command a degree of admiration, but when the power of the Holy Spirit flows through a preacher's soul and message, hearts may be broken and healed at the same moment. When all has been complete, the most that can be truthfully said is: "This is the Lord's doing, and it is marvellous in our eyes" (see Matt. 21:42).

*THE UNCHALLENGED CONFESSION...The Expressiveness of His Practice*

"They were baptized of him in Jordan, confessing their sins" (v. 6). It is worthy of note that even John's enemies never questioned his act of baptism. Had this been some strange, new innovation, they would have criticized the rite. They would have claimed that since Moses had never endorsed the practice, it was heresy for any unordained preacher to introduce something contrary to the law. Later, the Pharisees opposed John's preaching, but they never criticized his methods. Throughout the centuries, priests observed the ordinance of baptism each time they welcomed a Gentile convert into the family of Judaism. They taught that this alone was a true confession of faith; that proselytes were forsaking, or dying, to their former life of heathenism, and with real determination, planned to live in accordance with the principles taught in Israel. Every Jew knew that baptism was the expression of a resolve to abandon one way of living in favor of another. The only thing *new* about John's baptism was that he baptized JEWS. This, apparently, had never been done; the children of Israel were already considered to be the chosen people of Jehovah. John insisted that sin in a Jewish heart was just as detestable as evil in a Gentile's soul. All men, irrespective of race, creed or color, needed to repent of their sins, and the true evidence that this had been done was the unashamed baptism in water.

The practice was by immersion; it signified burial, and the burial of the dead was never accomplished by sprinkling dirt upon the head of a corpse! It cannot be overstressed that true repentance preceded baptism, whether it were by pouring, sprinkling or immersion. It is possible for immersionists to condemn those who sprinkle and at the same time not to live according to the standards set by their own faith. It is possible for those who practice the method of sprinkling, to ridicule those who immerse, and at the same time to ignore the requirements of the message they preach. If true repentance must precede the ordinance, then it is foolish to baptize a baby who has no knowledge of sin. Any religious ordinance is vain and a waste of time, if the soul is unprepared for the realities of the spiritual life to which it belongs. It is only after cleansing from sin that complete identification with Christ can be accomplished. (see the further notes on this subject in the author's book, *Luke's Thrilling Gospel* p. 87-88.)

## SECTION THREE

### *Expository Notes on John's Brief Sermon*

**But when he saw many of the Pharisees and Sadducees come to his baptism, he said unto them, O generation of vipers, who hath warned you to flee from the wrath to come? Bring forth therefore fruits meet for [befitting] repentance: And think not to say within yourselves, We have Abraham to our father: for I say unto you, that God is able of these stones to raise up children unto Abraham (vv. 7-9).**

## A STRANGE DESIRE

To say the very least, it seems strange that the Pharisees and Sadducees should desire to be baptized by John. That must rank as one of the greatest surprises in the New Testament. They were the religious leaders of the nation, experts in the interpretation of the law, and considered to be examples for all the pious citizens of the country. Luke wrote: "Then said [John] to *the multitude* that came forth to be baptized of him, O generation of vipers..." (Luke 3:7). Matthew states these words were spoken to *the Pharisees and Sadducees.* Probably both were correct in their descriptions. The leaders stood among the great throng that had presented themselves for baptism, and in addressing them, John spoke to everybody. But it leaves a problem. Had the leaders come to be baptized or to witness what was taking place? Some commentators suggest the religious dignitaries were actually seeking baptism, but this is not a safe assumption. If they desired to be baptized, we must believe, in the light of John's indictment, that they were seeking to become leaders in a popular movement; that they were desirous of remaining in the spotlight of public attention; and that their profession of faith was shallow, meaningless, hypocritical.

## A STARTLING DENUNCIATION

John had neither fear nor respect for the men before him. That he called them vipers fleeing from danger had certain connotations. "The simile not only expresses the thought that, behind their smooth exterior, the outward legal strictness of the Pharisees, and the worldly decorum of the Sadducees, lay hidden malice and venom, but that also this is due to their very nature. It may have directly implied that they belonged in a true sense to the seed of the serpent (Gen. 3:15)" *(The Pulpit Commentary*, Matthew, p. 71).

"It should be noted carefully, that this multitude did not come to *hear* John; they came to be *baptized.* Yet, John, who might have been overwhelmed with delight, looked at the people and called them vipers. Observance of any ordinance, if not accompanied by true repentance is only a sham. The word suggests snakes hurrying from a prairie fire. They were actuated only by terror which threatened their existence. Extinguish the flames and they would return whence they came. The evangelist was quick to detect this, and his scathing words of condemnation made bare their souls. When compared with other scriptures, the statement 'offspring or generation of vipers' becomes pregnant with meaning. The evil one, Satan, is called the serpent (Rev. 12:9 and John 8:44). John the Baptist was saying, in actual fact, that the people who had come to his baptism were in reality the children of Satan; that before he could baptize them, they would need to show evidence of true repentance" *(Luke's Thrilling Gospel*, p. 89).

## A SERIOUS DEMAND

"Bring forth therefore fruits meet for repentance" (v. 8). The only real evidence of genuine repentance is deep contrition. Any profession not accompanied by a change of life-pattern is deceiving. We are accustomed to great revival crusades in which large numbers of converts profess faith in Christ; yet, alas, few of these ever seek membership in churches where their faith may be strengthened, and their souls fed with the bread of life. Unfortunately, this makes their confession of faith suspect. The same Bible which commanded them to be baptized, also suggests they forsake not the assembling of themselves together (see Heb. 10:25). When a man responds to an invitation in an evangelistic service, and has no intention of remaining at the disposal of Christ and His cause, then the convert is either unenlightened or disobedient. Experience teaches it is better to plough deep than wide! Isaiah spoke about the value of "taking root downward, and bearing fruit upward" (see Isa. 37:31). If the church were more concerned with tears on faces than signatures on cards, baptism would have increased meaning, and converts would last longer! Sensational statistics in a church handbook may be pleasing to read, but if they do not represent the true growth of a church, the figures are misleading and false. John the Baptist was a very wise man; modern pastors should sit at his feet and listen.

## A SPECIAL DISCERNMENT

This wilderness preacher was an excellent mind reader. He looked at his listeners and knew exactly what they were thinking. They considered themselves to be as good as anyone, and far better than most! All this talk about religious ethics was commendable in its place, but it did not apply to them; they were the descendants of Abraham; they were the chosen of God. Often, when I ask people if they are Christians, I receive a variety of answers! "I am a Presbyterian." "I am a Catholic." "I have belonged to the church since I was a baby." Let no one misunderstand, the church, in spite of her imperfections, is the best institution in the world; to attend its services is a privilege; to serve Christ beneath its banner is something for which there can never be an adequate substitute. It has been my privilege to meet and work with people, both Catholic and Protestant. I have lived with folk from every denomination, and seeing in them a real love for Christ, have recognized them to be my brothers and sisters. Yet, to be merely identified with a religious group is no guarantee that I belong to the family of God. Even if I worked incessantly, I could never be more religious than the Pharisees, and never more studious than the scribes and Sadducees. Religious observances are but the polished veneer on the outside of a temple; that which neighbors behold. The radiance of communion with God is the quality that thrills the soul and transforms every aspect of life. This is what God sees, and without it, I am bankrupt!

John the Baptist saw all this when he looked into the faces of some who came to his meetings. He knew that in the final analysis, they would trust in their religious accomplishments rather than in the message preached. Therefore, even before they could criticize, he laid "his axe to the root of their tree," and destroyed the sanctuary of confidence in which they might have endeavored to hide. What Elijah was to Israel, John became to the people of his generation. It would be very wonderful if God could send both these men to shatter the complacency of our modern world. When John referred to the ability of God to raise up children he probably pointed to the boulders alongside the Jordan River. If God, at the beginning, had been able to make man from the dust of the ground, He would have had no problem in replacing the Pharisees. What they claimed, therefore, was meaningless; what they might have become was something of eternal value.

**And now also the axe is laid unto the root of the trees; therefore every tree which bringeth not forth good fruit is hewn down, and cast into the fire. I indeed baptize you with water unto repentance: but he that cometh after me is mightier than I, whose shoes I am not worthy to bear: he shall baptize you with the Holy Ghost, and with fire; whose fan is in his hand, and he will thoroughly purge his floor, and gather his wheat into his garner; but he will burn up the chaff with unquenchable fire (vv. 10-12).**

Here we have the conclusion of John's message, and once again, it covers three areas of thought. (1) The Warning of Judgment. (2) The Witness of John. (3) The Work of Jesus. Let us consider them in that order.

## THE WARNING OF JUDGMENT

"The axe is laid unto the root of the trees" (v. 10a). The *Amplified New Testament* translates this statement: "The axe is lying at the root of the trees." This appears to be the correct interpretation of the term. If the axe had already been applied to the tree, any attempt at saving it would have been abandoned. Since John had already advised his hearers to repent, it was, obviously, not too late for them to receive God's forgiveness for their sin. However, the time for repentance was fast running out. The axe, the threat of judgment, was already visible. Decaying or diseased trees were only fit for burning. Every farmer in Palestine was aware of this fact, and since Israel was considered to be the garden of Jehovah, it was evident the time for examination had arrived. It is never the anger of God that swings the axe. Wisdom and care unite in removing the dying trees; only thus can the safety of the remaining trees be assured. John's insistence on repentance was the most timely message ever heard by the Pharisees; alas, they were too foolish to accept his advice.

## THE WITNESS OF JOHN

"He that cometh after me is mightier than I, whose shoes I am not worthy to bear" (v. 11b). There is always the danger that a successful evangelist might forget that he is basically nothing. Sometimes, overwhelming success leads to an inflation of the preacher's ego, and the final result is disaster. John never forgot that his mission in life was to introduce and exalt the Lord. At best, John was only a forerunner going ahead of the King. Probably, in the final analysis, his humility outshone the splendor of his preaching. When he said, "...he shall baptize you with the Holy Ghost and with fire" he was probably inspired by Malachi's statement: "Behold, I will send my messenger, and he shall prepare the way before me: and the Lord, whom ye seek, shall suddenly come to his temple, even the messenger of the covenant, whom ye delight in: behold, he shall come, saith the LORD of hosts. But who may abide the day of his coming? and who shall stand when he appeareth? for *he is like a refiner's fire*" (Mal. 3:1-2). The baptism with water signified the candidate's desire to forsake sin and become holy. The baptism with fire indicated the divine Spirit would come upon and dwell within the candidate, giving to him the power to make his dreams come true.

## THE WORK OF JESUS

"He will thoroughly purge his floor" (v. 12b). I shall never forget the first time I saw an Arab farmer winnowing his harvest. He held a large shovel, and, with untiring energy, continued throwing grain into the air. As he did this, a gentle breeze blew away the chaff as the grain fell to the ground. Eventually, he carefully carried the grain away to a building in which it could be safely stored. Some customs never change in the Middle East. Even David knew of the practice, for in the first Psalm he wrote: "The ungodly...are like the chaff which the wind driveth away." John warned his hearers that the coming King would never tolerate hypocrisy; he would sift, shake, and winnow that harvest until only that which was pleasing in his sight remained. John emphasized reality instead of profession, righteousness instead of vanity. He stressed the importance of self-examination, so that people would not be condemned in the day of judgment. Later, when the Lord cleansed the temple, it became evident He was the fulfilment of all that had been predicted. As He was then, so will He be at the end of the age; for it is written: "When the Son of man shall come in his glory...before him shall be gathered all nations; and he shall separate them one from another, as a shepherd divideth his sheep from the goats: And he shall set the sheep on his right hand, but the goats on the left" (Matt. 25:31-33).

## SECTION FOUR

*Expository Notes on the Baptism of Jesus*

**Then cometh Jesus from Galilee to the Jordan unto John, to be baptized by him. But John forbad him, saying, I have need to be baptized of thee, and comest thou to me? And Jesus answering said unto him, Suffer it to be so now; for thus it becometh us to fulfil all righteousness. Then he suffered to him (vv. 13-15).**

## THE GREAT PROBLEM

The baptism of John, was "unto repentance," that is, it was the unashamed confession that the candidate was openly confessing personal sin, and a desire to begin living a life pleasing to God. The baptism of Jesus, therefore, gave rise to serious questions. Since the Lord was sinless, why did He submit to a baptism designed for sinners? This question was debated in the early church, and several of the ancient authors made reference to the subject. Some of them suggested the Lord was only baptized to please the other members of His family. One of the early church manuscripts known as the Gospel according to the Hebrews, says: "Behold, the mother of the Lord and His brethren said to Him, 'John the Baptist baptizeth for the remission of sins; let us go and be baptized by him.' But He said to them, 'What sin have I committed, that I should go and be baptized by him?'" Even the early churchmen had difficulty in appreciating the Lord's reasons for submitting to that ordinance. The Lord could not repent of nonexistent sins; He could hardly confess a desire to return to the paths of righteousness since He had never left them. Why then was Jesus baptized?

## THE GRACIOUS PARTICIPATION

*Wycliffe's Version of the New Testament* says of John, "He protested strenuously when Jesus presented Himself for baptism." Thayer translates the Lord's reply as being "Permit it just now, for this is the fitting way, for both of us, to fulfill all righteousness — that is, to perform completely whatever is right." The Lord was identifying Himself with the greatest spiritual movement known in Israel for centuries. After generations of apathy, a long silence had been broken, and John the Baptist was leading a crusade to bring men back to God. He needed all the support possible, and by His presence and submission, Jesus told everyone "I believe in what this man is saying. I espouse his cause and support his every statement. Listen to him, obey his commands, even as I do." Many theologians suggest that since the Lord came to bear the sins of the world, He made this clear when, by baptism, He literally took the place of a sinner, thus providing an example which all should follow. That John became indignant and argued vociferously against the Lord's proposal, indicates the preacher in the wilderness was one of the first to recognize the intrinsic purity of Jesus, the Son of God.

## THE GLORIOUS PURPOSE

The attestation which came from heaven was both informative and inspiring. It was a searchlight bringing into bold relief every detail of the Lord's life. Even God could detect no blemish; Jesus had neither done nor said anything displeasing in His Father's eyes. The Lord was not only a perfect specimen of humanity; He was the true representative of that other world where God was all and in all. We are intrigued with the voice which Jesus heard at His baptism. "This is my beloved Son," it said, "in whom I am well pleased." That sentence contains two quotations. "This is my beloved Son," is a quotation from Psalm 2:7. Every Jew accepted that Psalm as a description of the coming Messiah, God's mighty King. "In whom I am well pleased," is a quotation from Isaiah 42:1, which describes the Suffering Servant, a description which culminates in Isaiah 53. Two certainties came to Jesus in the baptism — that He was that chosen One of God, and that the way in front of Him was the way of the cross. In that moment, He knew that He was chosen to be King, but He also knew that a cross would precede His throne. In that moment, He knew He was destined to be a conqueror, but His only weapon would be the power of suffering love. In that moment, He knew that He was chosen to be King, but He also knew that a cross would precede His throne. In that moment, He knew He was destined to be a conqueror, but His only weapon would be the power of suffering love. In that moment, there was set before Jesus both His task and the only way to the fulfilling of it.

HOMILY

Study No. 3

### "I AM NOT WORTHY"

Someone has said that until a man strikes rock bottom, he has little chance of reaching the Rock of Ages! Here, as nowhere else, it becomes possible to differentiate between the truly penitent man and an imposter. The one man is adamant in affirming he is as good as anybody; the other insists he is not good at all. And that leads to the study of the text which spans the ages. It introduces four of the greatest Bible characters; it reaches into the past, embraces the present, and even touches the heart of God.

*THE SCHEMER... Jacob (Gen. 32:10)*

Jacob was a schemer; he lived by his wits. He did not mind who was pushed down as long as he climbed; he closed his eyes to the suffering of others, content in the fact that he had no pain. He stole his brother's birthright; he deceived his ailing father, and later, outwitted his father-in-law. Perhaps his wrestling match with the angel revealed the real state of his soul. He was always willing to fight, fiercely, for what he desired. However, a schemer can always be certain that sooner or later he will meet another of his type more skillful in the art of deception. That Jacob should be swindled out of his desired bride makes exciting reading, although it is completely incomprehensible. Surely, he was very drunk the night before his wedding. When Jacob became homesick, he encountered his greatest problem. His past had overtaken him. The fear of his outraged brother haunted him, and it was only then, he reached rock bottom. He knelt to pray and said, "I am not worthy." It was at that moment his groping hands touched the Rock of Ages.

*THE SAINT...John the Baptist (John 1:27)*

John was the exact opposite of Jacob; he was not a schemer, he was a saint. We know he was a sinner, but there is no mention of sin in his record. He was called by the Holy Spirit even from birth. He was the only student ever to graduate from God's University in the wilderness. Recognizing this outstanding brilliance, Jesus declared that of all who had been born of women, none was greater than the famous Forerunner. Yet when John thought of the coming Christ, he insisted he was unworthy even to carry the shoes of the Savior. A man cannot be nearer to God than when he considers himself to be nothing.

## THE SOLDIER...The Centurion (Luke 7:6)

This Roman was probably one of the greatest Gentiles in Palestine; from every angle, he could only be considered the most worthy of all the enemies of Israel. (1) He loved a slave child, and this was almost beyond the bounds of comprehension. (2) He had built a synagogue for the Jews, and as a result, the elders went to the Lord to ask aid for their benefactor. They admitted the man was worthy of assistance. (3) He had been honored by his supervisors, for they had made him a captain in the occupying army. (4) He had such amazing faith that even the Savior expressed surprise, saying, He had not found its equal "not even in Israel." Yet, when this great man heard that Jesus was coming to his home, he rushed into the street saying, "I am not worthy." At that moment, he was very close to the Rock of Ages.

## THE SON...The Prodigal (Luke 15:21)

The story of the boy who left home in order to seek his fortune in the great cities is known worldwide. He had been unable to appreciate the affection of his father, had ignored the comforts of home, and had become destitute in a distant land. His impoverished condition, his bleak outlook, the terrible conditions in which he tried to exist sickened his soul, and slowly, a desire for home promoted action. He came to his senses when the father's encircling arms went around his shoulders. He hardly knew what to do, but he said everything, when he exclaimed, "I am not worthy." For the first time in his life, he was speaking the truth.

## THE SAVIOR...Who is Worthy! (Rev. 5:9)

The only effective antidote for the unworthiness of the creature is the surpassing excellence of the Creator. He loved us with an everlasting love, and died that we might be forgiven. The Lord Jesus is worthy of the highest praise, and this will become increasingly evident when

"...ten thousand times ten thousand, and thousands of thousands; [will say] with a loud voice, Worthy is the Lamb that was slain to receive power, and riches, and wisdom, and strength, and honour, and glory, and blessing....And every creature...heard I saying, Blessing, and honour, and glory, and power, be unto him that sitteth upon the throne, and unto the Lamb for ever and ever" (Rev. 5:11-13). Until a man reaches rock bottom, he has little chance of reaching the Rock of Ages. Yet, once he does reach that blessed shelter, he remains safe forever (see also "Sermons From the Sky." *John's Wonderful Gospel*, pp. 271-273).

# The Fourth Chapter of Matthew

THEME: *The Testing and Triumph of the King*

OUTLINE:

> I. An Increasing Danger (Verses 1-11)
> II. An Important Decision (Verses 12-17)
> III. An Invitation to Discipleship (Verses 18-22)
> IV. An Inspiring Development (Verses 23-25)

## SECTION ONE

*Expository Notes on the Temptations of Jesus*

**Then was Jesus led up by the Spirit into the wilderness to be tempted [tested] by the devil. And when he had fasted forty days and forty nights, he was afterward an hungered. And when the tempter came to him, he said, If thou be the Son of God, command that these stones be made bread. But he answered and said, It is written, Man shall not live by bread alone, but by every word that proceedeth out of the mouth of God (vv. 1-4).**

It is difficult to read Matthew's account of the temptation of the Lord without asking why it was ever permitted. God certainly knew its outcome, for He sees from the beginning. A long period of time was spent in fasting without any public service whatsoever, and since Palestine was filled with needy people, was not the forty days and nights a waste of precious time? Apparently, at first glance, it accomplished little. We might be inclined to think the Lord could have more profitably used the time healing the sick, giving sight to the blind, and spreading His gospel throughout the land. Hence the question: "Why was the time of temptation ever permitted?"

In seeking an answer to the question, we must first give attention to the Greek word translated "tempt." It is *peirazein*. Unfortunately, the English word is used to indicate something evil. When a man is tempted, we infer that some agency is endeavoring to seduce him into illegal actions. He is tempted to steal, to kill, to do something of which, later, he may be ashamed. Let it be understood that, had Satan been successful in luring Jesus into any of these immoral byways, he would have won a great victory. Nevertheless, that was not the primary reason for the Savior's temptation. The word *peirazein* basically means "to test, to prove, to ascertain capability of endurance." The same truth is implied in Genesis 22:1 where we are informed that "God did tempt Abraham." It is completely inconceivable that God should ever try to entice anyone into ways of evil. God's purpose is to prevent moral laxity, and not to push people into quicksands of sin from which escape is sometimes impossible. The text should read that "God tested Abraham." The patriarch had already demonstrated the most admirable spiritual qualities, but one important test remained. Isaac was the delight of Abraham's life, but the Lord wished to prove the adorable boy could never dethrone God in the sanctity of that father's soul. God's faith in His servant was vindicated when the saint took his son to Mount Moriah with the avowed intention of sacrificing the lad upon an altar. The patriarch passed his test magnificently.

Jesus went into the wilderness *to be tested*. It should nevertheless be clearly understood that, throughout the terrible ordeal, the powers of evil tempted the Savior, and continuously tried to find penetrable places in His spiritual armor. There was much at stake in this phase of the spiritual conflict, destined to continue throughout the Lord's sojourn on earth. The devil was entitled to nothing, but within the concept of divine justice, even Satan had to be given the chance of "trying out" his enemy. He needed the opportunity to become acquainted with the strength of his adversary, so that he would never be able to say, "I was never given a real chance." If we may be permitted to borrow a modern illustration, then let us say that God's Man and hell's man entered the arena together. Jesus seemed to say, "Here I am. Look me over and discover what you need to know." The temptations of Jesus were heaven's challenge to Satan. Heaven's David was face to face with hell's Goliath, but the end of the conflict was never in doubt.

When seen from God's viewpoint, the outlook was different. Heaven was about to commit its greatest instrument to the battlefield of time. Ere the true conflict would begin, that instrument had to be subjected to the severest test possible. The world has grown accustomed to the bravery of test pilots risking their lives to test fighter planes of every type. If there is weaknesses of construction anywhere in the machine, it becomes the duty of the test pilot to discover those flaws, before the machine be irrevocably committed to combat. Automobiles, computers, elevators, are all tested prior to public use, for only thus can the manufacturers promote their products, confidently. God thought it necessary to permit the testing of His Son. This should provide illumination and understanding, as we approach the more detailed study of the Lord's experiences in the wilderness.

## THE TEST OF SELFLESSNESS

**Then was Jesus led up by the Spirit into the wilderness to be tempted [tested] of the devil. And when he had fasted forty days and forty nights, he was afterward an hungered [hungry] (vv. 1-2).**

Luke 4:1-2 corroborates Matthew's statement: "And Jesus...was led by the Spirit into the wilderness. Being forty days *tempted [tested] by the devil.* And in those days He did eat nothing." Luke's statement is a searchlight shining into a very foggy area. Beyond the range of vision was a battlefield where a very intense struggle was taking place. We are not aware of the type of testing endured by the Savior; we remain uninformed of the ferocity of that experience. It might have been that throughout the entire period, all desire for physical sustenance was forgotten. When, ultimately, defeated and frustrated, Satan temporarily discontinued his attacks, it became evident that someone later would be able to write: "For we have not an high priest which cannot be touched with the feelings of our infirmities; but was in all points tempted like as we are, yet without sin" (Heb. 4:15). After almost six weeks of being engulfed by the insidious powers of evil, the conflict appeared to end. When the Lord momentarily relaxed, He became aware of intense hunger; His body yearned for nourishment. When Jesus looked around, He saw the small round stones, resembling in shape the cakes of bread, popular among the peasants of the country; and suddenly His soul was troubled. Once again, He sensed the presence of the evil one.

**And when the tempter came to him, he said, If thou be the Son of God, command that these stones be made bread. But he answered and said, It is written, Man shall not live by bread alone, but by every word that proceedeth out of the mouth of God (vv. 3-4).**

Danger always follows unprecedented triumph. A man enduring overwhelming problems clings to any hand outstretched to help. A boxer, elated and filled with confidence, sometimes lowers his guard, and is shattered by an unexpected onslaught from his opponent. Jesus had just won a tremendous victory; Satan appeared to be retreating in defeat, but alas, the Devil is an expert at fighting back, when we are unprepared for another phase in the conflict. Sir George Adam Smith described the territory where the temptation took place. He wrote, "It is an area of yellow sand, of crumbling limestone, and of scattered shingle. It is an area of contorted strata, where the ridges run in all directions, as if they were warped and twisted. The hills are like dust heaps; the limestone is blistered and peeling; rocks are bare and jagged; often the very ground sounds hollow when the footfall or the horse's hoof falls on it. It glows and shimmers with heat like some vast furnace. It runs right out to the Dead Sea, and then, there comes a drop of twelve hundred feet, a drop of limestone, flint and marl, through crags and corries, and precipices down to the Dead Sea. In that wilderness, one could be more alone than anywhere else in Palestine."

When a man stands alone, he should look to the hills from whence cometh aid (Ps. 121:1). If he be in the depths of despair, he should pray. When he is riding high on waves of triumph, he should be exceedingly careful. Danger abounds. It is dangerous when an experienced surfer has to fight for his life against deadly undercurrents threatening his existence. When Satan suggested to the Lord the advisability of using miraculous powers to meet a genuine need, Jesus quoted the Word of God from Deuteronomy 8:3. His need was not to please self and appease His appetite but, in absolute trust, to obey the Word of God. An obedient saint can never starve to death as long as God has feathered friends trained to be waiters in God's Universal Restaurant (see the ministry of the birds in 1 Kings 17:6).

## THE TEST OF SELF-CONFIDENCE

**Then the devil taketh him up into the holy city, and setteth him on a pinnacle of the temple, And saith unto him, If thou be the Son of God, cast thyself down: for it is written, He shall give his angels charge concerning thee: and in their hands they shall bear thee up, lest at any time thou shalt dash thy foot against a stone. Jesus said unto him, It is written again, Thou shalt not tempt the Lord thy God (vv. 5-7).**

We are not told whether this was a battle of the mind or whether Satan actually escorted Jesus from the wilderness to the crowded city of Jerusalem. Luke suggests that Satan took Jesus to the pinnacle of the temple (see Luke 4:9), but it is difficult to decide whether he was taken in thought or literally. If a man cast himself from the pinnacle of the temple, there would be many witnesses to testify of his stupidity. If he descended gradually through the air to land, gracefully, on the ground below, his act would be miraculous and within days, immense crowds would be requesting a repeat performance. Anything sensational commands attention. Satan's suggestion was very subtle. Since the Savior was Lord of creation, there can be no doubt that had He so desired, He could have descended, unharmed, from the elevated place on the temple walls. Had He done as the Devil suggested, the Lord would hardly have been identified with the people He came to save. The laws of gravity would have ordinarily broken the body of Jesus, as it crashed upon the jagged rocks in the Kidron Valley. A premature death could have ruined the plans of God. Either way, to do it, or not to do it, would have been disastrous. Had the Lord complied with Satan's suggestion, immense crowds would have gathered, and Jerusalem would have been overflowing with excited, shouting, demanding people, desiring another circus act.

Anything ostentatious is dangerous, when it appears within the church. A professed faith healer never lacks an audience, but sometimes, his act leaves much to be desired. That God is able to heal the sick, no Christian can ever doubt or deny. Nevertheless, true healing is given according to the will of God, and is never the result of the strange antics of the man who demands that every kind of ailment be banished from the bodies of suffering people. When God heals the sick, He does so because such is His will, and not because the would-be deliverer is half strangling his victim. Furthermore, when God heals a man or a woman, the effect is permanent. It can hardly be claimed that a man has been healed, when relatives bury his body the following week. Let no reader question my motives nor doubt my sincerity. I am quite certain that God can heal the body, for He healed mine — in a moment of time. God did it, not because I was screaming and yelling for heaven's attention, but because, with the simple faith of a small child, I believed He could and would answer my prayer. Had the Savior fascinated a temple crowd by demonstrating His mastery of gravity, they would have claimed He was a genius, but every day would have asked for more and greater demonstrations of His uncanny ability. When finally, they had seen enough, they would have returned to their homes unchanged. Jesus came to earth to save people and not to entertain them. He was aware of the statement in Psalm 91:11-12: "For he shall give his angels charge over thee, to keep thee in all thy ways. They shall bear thee up in their hands, lest thou dash thy foot against a stone." Christ also knew true faith is never the enemy of wisdom. When God said, "*All* thy ways," He was not referring to *some* of those ways. When it is the will of God to stay on safe ground, climbing to the pinnacle of any temple is an absurdity. Even the Devil is an expert at quoting Scripture — out of context.

## THE CHALLENGE OF SUCCESS

**Again, the devil taketh him up into an exceeding high mountain, and showeth him all the kingdoms of the world, and the glory of them; And saith unto him, All these things will I give thee, if thou wilt fall down and worship me. Then saith Jesus unto him, Get thee hence [begone], Satan: for it is written, Thou shalt worship the Lord thy God, and him only shalt thou serve. Then the devil leaveth him, and, behold, angels came and ministered unto him (vv. 8-11).**

There is reason to believe that this might have been the most dangerous of all the Devil's suggestions. He was fully aware of the Lord's intention to rescue a sinful world, but he also knew the cost which would be paid ere the final triumph was won. Jesus would have to endure crucifixion; His followers would become martyrs for their cause, and long before the task of evangelizing was completed, millions of souls would die in their sin. Every part of the world would become a battleground, and every inch would be contested. Satan would never withdraw without a fight. Jesus had decided to walk the most difficult road ever known to man, and then, suddenly, Satan offered to make the task very easy and simple. He suggested there was no need for the cross; for struggle, and pain. "Jesus, thou Son of God, listen to me. I have a master plan. Why struggle to win the world? I will give it to Thee. It can be Thine in a few moments of time. All You need to do is bend Your knee and worship me. Do that, and I will withdraw my opposition."

This was a battle within the Lord's thoughts; there is not a mountain anywhere from which all the nations of the world may be viewed. The Savior's mind resembled a television screen, and as He watched, Satan brought pictures before Him. He saw the heathenism and witchcraft in the heart of Africa; the avarice and greed in the business houses of the world; the filthiness and lust of an apparently respectable humanity. Jesus saw the prisons, the hospitals, the mental homes, and the cemeteries. He saw a world in the grip of evil, and as He watched and wondered, Satan whispered, "You can change all that in a moment. I will withdraw my power; I will instruct my servants to cease work, and all this shall be Your territory — today — now. Jesus, Son of God, just bow the knee and worship me."

Jesus surely sighed deeply; it would have been marvelous to bring instant deliverance to a world in great need. Then, slowly, He shook His head, for He knew such a victory would have been the prelude of eternal disaster. Had He succumbed to that insidious temptation, Africa would have remained in deeper bondage, and the world would have lost hope of gaining deliverance. There was a way by which deliverance would come, and that way had been planned in heaven. The victory to be won at the Cross would eternally break the power of Satan and set free those who sat in the shadow of death. Cheap success was never attractive; that which is gained easily is of little value.

Satan has never lost the ambition which long ago led to his expulsion from heaven. As an important angel, he had conspired to make himself like God, and had fallen from grace through the pride which dominated his thoughts (see Isa. 14:12-15). During the final days of time, once again through the Antichrist, he will insist that all men worship him (see Rev. 13:15). The same principles can be seen today in the multitude of devil-worshiping communities now existent throughout the world. To walk in those paths is tantamount to suicide. Jesus knew this, and preferring death with honor to success with shame, He dismissed His adversary with yet another statement from the Scriptures, "Thou shalt worship the Lord thy God, and him only shalt thou serve" (see Deut. 6:13). "...and, behold, angels came and ministered unto him" (v. 11b). God's ministering angels are never far away from a saint in trouble. They watch and wait and, when victory has been achieved, hasten to help God's faithful servant. Compare this text with Luke 22:42-44. Sometimes we are tempted to believe that God has forgotten us, or at least, that His help will arrive too late. That can never be the case. God waited until the last moment ere He delivered Isaac from the death planned by Abraham. He waited a long time before delivering Jonah, but even the delay was beneficial, for the fish was getting closer to land. There would be no fear of death by drowning, for Jonah was delivered up "on dry ground."

> Ye fearful saints, fresh courage take:
> The clouds ye so much dread,
> Are big with mercy and will break
> In blessing on your head.

"Godet thinks that *this place of temptation* was either *Solomon's Porch,* which was situated on the eastern side of the temple platform, and commanded a view of the gorge of the Kidron, or the *Royal Porch* built on the south side of this platform, and from which, as Josephus says, 'the eye looked down into an abyss' (Godet, *Commentary on Luke*, p. 140).

When the first attacks were defeated by reference to the Word of God, Satan changed his tactics when he also referred to the Scriptures. Nevertheless, he omitted the most essential part of the quotation from Psalm 91:11, 'For he shall give his angels charge over thee, to keep thee *in all thy ways.*' The fact that divine help was keeping Christ *in all His ways,* was the reason why Jesus could never compromise with His enemy. It is a strange but solemn fact that practically every movement under the sun, will from time to time, utter quotations from the Bible. Yet when these quotations are examined, they are either misquotations, or they are removed from the setting to which they belong. The fact that men quote the Scriptures is no guarantee that they are sent by God. Even Satan had the Word of God in his mind, but, unfortunately, it never reached his heart. When the Lord said, 'Thou shalt not tempt the Lord thy God', He claimed to be divine. The careful student will know that NEVER on any occasion did an evil spirit deny the deity of Christ — only men did that.

What might have happened to Christ had He cast Himself down from the pinnacle of the temple? Faith in God is not a license for irresponsibility. If without reason I place an arm into a fire, not even the omnipotence of God can prevent a burn. There is calm, prevailing sanity about which Christians live. The body of Jesus would have been destroyed by a senseless leap from a pinnacle of the temple. God would hardly be justified in breaking the laws of gravity, because fanatical faith dared any man to take a death plunge. Behind all the evil suggestions was the cunning mind of the tempter whose one desire was to prevent Christ from reaching His cross. The marvelous way in which the Lord Jesus overcame every attempt to undermine His sinlessness, suggests strength of character, hard to describe. The battle was over; the campaign would continue. Satan never yields an inch of the battleground until he must. When utterly defeated, the Christian should pray; when oppressed on all sides, he should pray even more; but when conscious of glorious triumph, the saint should pray most of all: for then his danger is greatest. It is well to remember that Satan's vacations are always short." (Reprinted from the author's commentary, *Luke's Thrilling Gospel*, pp. 101-102.)

## SECTION TWO

*Expository Notes on the Fulfillment of an Ancient Prophecy*

**Now when Jesus had heard that John was cast into prison, he departed into Galilee; And leaving Nazareth, he came and dwelt in Capernaum, which is upon the sea coast, in the borders of Zebulun and Nephthalim: That it might be fulfilled which was spoken by Esaias, the prophet, saying, The land of Zabulun and, of Nephthalim, by the way of the sea, beyond Jordan, Galilee of the Gentiles [nations]; The people which sat in darkness saw great light; and to them which sat in the region and shadow of death light is sprung up. From that time Jesus began to preach, and to say, Repent: for the kingdom of heaven is at hand (vv. 12-17).**

These verses represent an important turning point in the life of the Savior. Over a period of almost twenty years, He had lived in the sleepy town of Nazareth, to which Joseph and Mary had taken Him that He might be protected from the wrath of King Herod. There, He had managed a carpenter's shop, and in all probability had been the main economic support of His family. Everything had now changed; the battle lines had been drawn, and the news of the imprisonment of John the Baptist gave warning that the peaceful years spent in a quiet community had ended. The Lord realized the time had come to reside in the seaside city of Capernaum, which at that time, represented the hub of the world. Although this section is very brief, there are, nevertheless, five areas of thought awaiting exploration.

## THE IMPRISONED PREACHER

Eastern potentates held within their hands the power of life and death, and, therefore, they were seldom criticized. John the Baptist was no ordinary man. He recognized evil for what it was, and whether the sin were in the life of the monarch or in the heart of a peasant, it remained sin. Later in his Gospel (Chapter 14), Matthew describes the sin denounced by the wilderness preacher; here, to mark a point in time, Matthew only makes a casual reference to the obvious change taking place in the spiritual climate of the nation. Hitherto, John's message had at least been tolerated; now it was openly rejected. John had been compelled to leave his wilderness pulpit and instead, to occupy a dungeon in the basement of Herod's castle. Apprehension spread throughout the land, and the common people were afraid to express their feelings; there were other cells vacant in the castle of Machaerus! When Jesus heard the news of John's incarceration, He knew the time had come to leave Nazareth. The voice of the Baptist had been silenced; but his message would still be heard, for the Lord Himself would continue John's ministry.

## THE ISOLATED PREDICTION

Matthew, in his search for evidence to prove Jesus was the Messiah, doubtless explored the Scriptures daily. His Gospel is filled with references to ancient predictions, but the one we are now to consider was perhaps the least known of the many included in his manuscript. Isaiah 9:1-2 vaguely refers to Galilee of the Gentiles, but obviously Matthew was firmly convinced this had a bearing on the Lord's change of residence. The prophet had said, "Nevertheless, the dimness shall not be such as was in her vexation, when at the first he lightly afflicted the land of Zabulun and the land of Nephthalim, and afterward did more grievously afflict her by the way of the sea, beyond Jordan, in Galilee of the nations. The people that walked in darkness have seen a great light: they that dwell in the land of the shadow of death, upon them hath the light shined." The closing section of Isaiah's statement was truly pertinent, for the Light of the World did indeed shine upon that part of the nation.

When the Savior moved His residence to Capernaum, it was tantamount to a declaration of war against the powers of evil. Never again did He reside in Nazareth; that part of His life had closed forever. Did Mary and the other members of the family accompany Him to the new home? Did the brothers establish a new business to support the family? Probably they did, for never again did Jesus earn money in a carpenter's shop. Not much has been written about this change of residence, but it became clear that in His ongoing ministry, it was necessary to move closer to the world He desired to reach.

## THE INTERESTING PLACE

Unlike Nazareth, where everything remained quiet and unattractive, Capernaum stood at the pulsating heart of an economic world. Galilee was approximately fifty miles from north to south and, at the most, about twenty-five miles across, but it was surrounded by important countries. Vital highways ran through its territory, and Capernaum was the center in which taxes were paid by travelers. Constantly, caravans went in all directions, and anything happening in Galilee would eventually be known in all parts of that section of the world. If Jesus desired to send His message near and far, He could not have chosen a better place in which to establish headquarters.

Galilee was the most populated area outside of Jerusalem. The ten important cities of Decapolis were situated around the lake, but the most illuminating information comes to us from Josephus, who was himself, at one time, governor of the area. In his writings he states that there "existed two hundred and four villages, each with a population of at least fifteen thousand people." When Jesus moved His residence to Capernaum, He was within reach of over three-and-one-half million people. If somehow He could light a fire in Galilee, its warmth would be felt throughout the known world of His day. Each caravan, with its occupants, would become acquainted with the message of the gospel, and even if they were not sympathetic to the cause of Christ, they would, unwittingly, become the Lord's first missionaries!

## THE INFLAMMABLE PEOPLE

Once again, we are indebted to the historian, Josephus, for the information regarding the Galileans. He writes: "They were ever fond of innovations, and by nature disposed to changes, and delighted in seditions. The Galileans have never been destitute of courage.... Cowardice was never a characteristic of the Galileans.... They were ever more anxious for honor than for gain." Obviously, if they believed in a cause, they would fight for it. This should help us appreciate why the earliest of the disciples were men of this caliber. Believing the gospel, they would carry it to earth's remotest end; they would succeed in their mission, or at least they would die trying to accomplish their goals. They would never quit. The Gospels tell us that James and John were "sons of thunder"; that they were anxious to cremate the inhabitants of a certain Samaritan village because of their opposition to the Lord. Those fiery disciples were representatives of an explosive race of people, among whom Jesus went to reside. He resembled a very wise general, preparing His soldiers for an assault on the citadels of evil.

## THE IDENTICAL PURPOSE

"From that time Jesus began to preach, and to say, Repent: for the kingdom of heaven is at hand" (v. 17). Matthew 14:1-2 tells us that when later, King Herod heard of Jesus and the message He preached, he said, "This is John the Baptist; he is risen from the dead: and therefore mighty works do show forth themselves in him." That conclusion was justified, for the message preached by John and the Savior was identical. Both the forerunner and the Lord said, "Repent for the kingdom of heaven is at hand." God's message can never be silenced. When God buries His servants, He raises a successor. After Moses came Joshua; after John the Baptist came Jesus of Nazareth. Satan may appear to win occasional victories, but the ultimate triumph belongs to God. The preaching of both John and Jesus was so simple; they never used a word hard to understand; they never wasted precious time with unnecessary circumlocutions; they always came straight to the heart of a matter by saying, "Repent." This was, and ever will be, the hallmark of God-inspired evangelism. Men need to turn from their wicked ways and, with great determination, to walk the way of righteousness: the highway that leads to the heart of God.

## SECTION THREE

### *Expository Notes on the Call of the First Disciples*

**And Jesus, walking by the sea of Galilee, saw two brethren, Simon called Peter, and Andrew his brother, casting a net into the sea: for they were fishers. And he saith unto them, Follow me, and I will make you fishers of men. And they straightway left their nets, and followed him. And going on from thence, he saw two other brethren, James the son of Zebedee, and John his brother, in a boat with Zebedee their father, mending their nets; and he called them. And they immediately left the ship, and their father, and followed him (vv. 18-22).**

I shall never forget my first sight of the Sea of Galilee. The coach in which I was traveling with a party of tourists, slowly climbed a steep highway, and suddenly, as we reached the top and commenced the descent, we saw an expanse of peaceful, blue water which seemed to be a mirror. That unforgettable scene is perhaps best described by W. M. Thomson who wrote: "Seen from any point of the surrounding heights, it is a fine sheet of water: a burnished mirror, set in a framework of rounded hills and rugged mountains, which rise and roll backward and upward to where Mt. Hermon hangs the picture against the blue vault of heaven." Early one morning, to be exact, just after dawn, I drove along the shore and suddenly found two young men selling their fish to the local people. I paused to speak with them, and their friendliness won my heart. Their sister was handling the money, but as we conversed, suddenly I remembered that other morning when Jesus did as I did; He was walking by the sea of Galilee, and as He went, He saw and called four young men to be the first disciples. His choice was admirable.

## A DISCERNING CHOICE

Jesus saw Simon, called Peter, and Andrew his brother; James, the son of Zebedee, and John his brother. Had He searched for months, the Lord could not have found four men more suitable for the tasks ahead. They resembled an arrowhead. The striking point was Simon Peter. James and John, the big, brawny formidable ''sons of thunder'' were his bodyguards; and coming up behind, possibly the underlying strength of the others, was Andrew, without whom little would have been accomplished. Peter was the impulsive preacher who had something to say. Often he spoke first and thought later! He made many mistakes, but if anything had to be said, Peter said it while the others were taking a breath. James and John were formidable men; they were ready to substantiate what Peter said. If any adversary planned an assault on Simon, he thought twice before he started. The ''sons of thunder'' who desired to cremate an unfriendly village, would have throttled anybody who interfered with brother Simon. Andrew, the quiet one, listened as Simon preached; watched as James and John flexed their muscles, and all the time planned how their ministry could be made more effective (see ''Andrew...the Patron Saint of Personal Workers'' in the author's book, *John's Wonderful Gospel,* p. 47). At a later time, Jesus called other disciples, but for the moment these were all He needed. Peter would take the gospel message into the surrounding areas; James and John would encourage him in all his efforts, but Andrew would quietly make certain the zeal would never die within the heart of his evangelistic brother!

## A DISTURBING CALL

Luke supplies additional details of the early contacts made with these men, and his accounts make exciting reading. Matthew is content to emphasize the sacrifice made immediately by the four men. That Simon and Andrew were *casting their nets* seems to be indicative of their calling. They were evangelists and were expert at getting fish into the nets. That

James and John were *mending their nets* suggests they were more concerned with keeping the fish in the nets — they were a different breed. John, at least, became the pastor of the churches. He retained the fish that Peter caught! (See the author's notes and homily in *Mark's Superb Gospel,* pp. 81-94.) One wonders what were the reactions of Zebedee, for within minutes he lost his two best helpers. Mark 1:20 speaks of the hired men; the surprised father was not left helpless. It would be interesting if we had a recording of the explanation given to his wife when Zebedee returned home. He had lost two sons — or had he? We should not underestimate the sacrifice made by those four men. When they left their boats on the beach; when they deserted their nets and their calling, they were embarking upon a career of which they knew nothing. They had no theological training, no guarantee of financial support, and Peter, at least, had the moral obligation to support a wife, a mother-in-law, and a home. Yet those indomitable men left their boats and probably never looked back. Jesus had promised to make them fishers of men, and whatever that meant, they were willing to do their best at the new occupation. They did not know they were to become famous; they were completely unaware of what lay ahead, but had they failed to respond to the call of Christ, the nations would have been impoverished.

## A DEFINITE CHALLENGE

Everybody now knows that Jesus took the foolish things of this world and, with them, confounded the mighty. Christ took the raw talents of these rough fishermen and, when He completed their training, they had become polished instruments of heaven. During my numerous visits to the Sea of Galilee, I have watched the types of fishing still practiced there. Things have dramatically changed within Israel's fishing industry. I was told that the movements of fish in the lake have been scientifically studied; that it is now known where the shoals may be found at any time of the day or night. A salt-water fish from the Mediterranean Sea has been placed in the fresh water of Galilee, and is increasing enormously. Nevertheless, the three ancient types of fishing can still be seen daily. (1) A man can fish with a rod and line. (2) A man may throw a drop-net, which falls like a tent upon unsuspecting fish. A slip-cord threaded through the edge of the circular net is then pulled and the whole thing is either pulled to the shore or to the boat from which the net was cast. (3) There is a much larger net usually operated from one or two vessels. This goes much deeper into the waters and is used by commercial fishermen. Early one morning as I came from my hotel, I was amazed to see men landing their huge catch. The fish were pinky-red, and each one weighed twelve to fifteen pounds. To some extent, the art of catching fish in Galilee has been made easy, but we must remember things were different when the four disciples earned their living in that area. They had developed instincts which were of incalculable worth as they prepared to follow Christ.

Those fishermen needed *patience* to wait for the fish either to bite or to be trapped. Fish do not always cooperate, and the fishermen, who prematurely abandoned their quest, would be unsuitable for service in God's fishing fleet! They needed *courage* to face the storms at sea, for the weather sometimes would be threatening. It would be stupid to spend time praying when the mast and the sails urgently required attention. Faith without works would be deadly, especially in a small fishing boat. They needed *endurance,* for the storms might last a long time. In a very literal sense that text would apply "He that endureth to the end, the same shall be saved." When Jesus called the men to follow Him, He did not promise them a picnic, nor a bed of roses upon which to lie. He was aware of storms, hardships, problems, and heartaches awaiting His servants. He needed men who would never turn back, and surely He found four of the type when He walked alongside the Sea of Galilee.

## SECTION FOUR

### *Expository Notes on the Lord's First Missionary Journey*

**And Jesus went about all Galilee, teaching in their synagogues, and preaching the gospel of the kingdom, and healing all manner of sickness and all manner of disease among the people. And his fame went throughout all Syria; and they brought unto him all sick people that were taken with diverse diseases and torments, and those which were possessed with devils, and those which were [epileptics], and those that had the palsy; and he healed them. And there followed him great multitudes of people from Galilee, and from Decapolis, and from Jerusalem, and from Judaea, and from beyond Jordan (vv. 23-25).**

## *THE CONTINUING FAME*

"And his fame went throughout all Syria" (v. 24a). This, apparently, resulted from three very important features. (1) He taught in their synagogues. (2) He preached in the open air. (3) He healed all who came to Him. Synagogues were in every Jewish community; they were the center of social life, and the place in which elders taught the children. Often there was no resident pastor or rabbi, and after the introductory parts of the service, which consisted of prayers and readings from the Law, any visitor was given the opportunity to address the congregation. If he had something interesting to say, the people listened attentively; if he were boring, the audience did whatever came to their minds. I remember attending a service in a synagogue in South Africa, and I was appalled to see members of the congregation reading their newspapers as the rabbi delivered his oration. In all honesty, let me hasten to admit, the newspaper could easily have been more interesting than the speaker! The important thing about the preaching of the Lord was that the local synagogue was the ideal place in which to launch His crusade. His teaching ministry enlightened hearers on matters often beyond their comprehension. The address was always followed by questions and answers, and no one could possibly doubt the ability of Jesus to enthrall those who heard His words.

Throughout the countryside, the Lord often held open-air meetings, when in the power of the divine Spirit, He proclaimed the glad tidings of His gospel. There, with absolute assurance, He bluntly stated truths connected with the need for repentance and faith. The Lord wisely combined the ministries of both pastor and evangelist. Yet, in addition to the proclamation of His message, Jesus healed the sick. The blind were made to see; the lame to walk; and day after day, the Savior demonstrated His power to meet the need of all who came to His meetings. To do these three things should be the ambition of every church. Continuing study of the Scriptures should promote the teaching; enthusiasm should enhance the effectiveness of the preaching, and prevailing prayer should make healings of body and mind gloriously possible.

## THE CONCERNED FRIENDS

It is interesting to note that, as the Lord's fame spread throughout Syria, certain people "brought unto him" their sick friends. As we shall see in the next part of this study, there were others who were content just to watch the daily proceedings; they were completely self-centered. It was always a thrilling experience to listen to the Savior, but it was even more wonderful to watch as a loved one was healed. If we may borrow modern terms, there were many soul winners among the Syrians. If the modern church were filled with such people, the entire world would soon be evangelized. Alas, the Good Shepherd's flock is filled with overfed sheep. They need exercise, not new pasture. The greatest joys ever known to Christ came when He saw grateful people leading others to His feet. I had a friend in the Shetland Islands who recognized a need in a certain district where there was no church. Although he was about to retire from business, he took all of his savings and built a Gospel Hall. One Sunday afternoon, he said, "Brother, when I saw the first convert: a man kneeling at that front pew, I knew my sacrifice had been justified. That was the happiest moment of my life." Happy and privileged are they who "bring their sick to Jesus."

## THE CASUAL FOLLOWERS

"And there followed him great multitudes of people from Galilee, and from Decapolis, and from Jerusalem, and from Judaea, and from beyond Jordan" (v. 25). Perhaps some of these were genuine seekers after truth, but the possibility exists that others were sensationalists; superficial hearers, and doubtless, if they were too lazy to work, were "waiting for the crumbs which fell from the Master's table." The challenge facing Jesus was how to transform those casual listeners into vitally concerned disciples. The same problem confronts the modern church. Faith healers always attract crowds; dynamic evangelists never lack an audience. Emotional appeals for personal commitment often are followed by many decisions, but unfortunately, the enthusiasm of the converts sometimes ends with the special services. Jesus said, "If any man will come after me, let him deny himself, and take up his cross, and follow me" (Matt. 16:24).

> Lord, lay some soul upon my heart,
> And win that soul through me.

# The Fifth Chapter of Matthew

THEME: *The Commencement of the Messages on the Mount*

OUTLINE:
    I. The Delights of the King's Citizens (Verses 1-12)
    II. The Description of the King's Citizens (Verses 13-16)
    III. The Distinction Among the King's Citizens (Verses 17-20)
    IV. The Demands on the King's Citizens (Verses 21-26)
    V. The Determination Within the King's Citizens (Verses 27-37)
    VI. The Devotion of the King's Citizens (Verses 38-48)

## AN INTRODUCTION TO THE SERMON ON THE MOUNT

The fifth, sixth, and seventh chapters of Matthew's Gospel are known throughout the world as "The Sermon on the Mount." There is reason to believe this idea is wrong. Unfortunately, a theologian of an earlier age thought this to be an apt title, and his definition remained throughout the centuries. However, nothing can change the fact that, although these verses have inspired innumerable preachers, they are not a sermon and never even resembled one.

Matthew 5:1,2 says: "And seeing the multitudes, Jesus went up into a mountain: and when he was set his disciples came unto him: And he opened his mouth, and taught them...." Matthew 8:1 says: "When he was come down from the mountain, great multitudes followed him...."

Between these verses is a period of time the length of which remains unknown. Describing this interval, Matthew wrote 109 verses. Some of these have no connection with the others. For example, he described how Jesus spoke of the need for prudent speech; the readiness to forgive neighbors; divorce proceedings; the advisability of loving enemies; the need for sacrificial giving, praying, and fasting. He warned against the dangers of false prophets, and then He announced that some preachers would be condemned in the day of judgment. Throughout the three chapters, there is only one illustration, and that story described how two men built houses: one on the rock, the other on the sand.

Even the casual reader must wonder why there is no development of a theme, and why Matthew, with startling abruptness, goes from one subject to another. Let it be candidly admitted that, if a modern preacher delivered a similar three-chapter sermon, his listeners would either leave before its conclusion or fall asleep!

This was never meant to be a sermon and no amount of reasoning can prove it to be one. It would be helpful if we knew the duration of the Lord's stay on the hillside. Moses went into the mountain of God and remained there forty days and forty nights, during which God gave to him the Ten Commandments. Probably the Lord's stay was much shorter, but it is obvious the disciples returned with much more than did Moses. Some theologians suggest the Savior and His followers remained on the mountain for a week or even longer, and that this resembled a retreat, arranged by Jesus for the edification of the disciples.

Moses was given instructions which governed living within the kingdom of Israel. The disciples were given new laws which indicated the requirements of daily conduct within the kingdom of God. On another occasion Jesus said to His disciples, ''Come ye apart and rest awhile,'' and it was for a similar reason; He led them into the mountain to instruct them in the ideals of kingdom life. Luke in his sixth chapter announces this teaching, following the selection of the twelve apostles. Therefore, the messages on the hillside were a course of study. Having appointed His representatives, the Lord proceeded to instruct them what kind of message they should preach both by life and lip. The contents of the so-called ''Sermon on the Mount'' would be better described as ''The Messages on the Mount,'' for it is probable that the 109 verses are a resume of what Jesus taught throughout the entire retreat. No man could retain in his memory all the amazing details of those discourses, had he listened only once to a very long sermon.

Remember Matthew was the bookman; he was accustomed to making notes! Therefore, when at intervals Jesus continued His instruction, Matthew wrote what he heard. That happened day after day, and when the party descended from the hilltop, he had a collection of the sayings of Jesus. Those notes helped him remember what had been said, and when, many years later, he compiled his Gospel, the sayings of the Lord found an important place in Matthew's manuscript.

Some theologians emphasize that, whereas Matthew placed these verses together in a three-chapter group, Luke quotes them at odd times in strange places. The beloved physician, instead of grouping the statements as did Matthew, reports them as having been made at different times during the Lord's ministry. For example, the thought that the disciples were the salt of the earth is mentioned in Matthew 5:13 and in Luke 14:34-35. Another example may be found in the Lord's references to prayer. Matthew reports these in chapter 7:7-12; Luke reproduces them in Luke 11:9-13. This comparison explains why some teachers insist Matthew's "Sermon on the Mount" is actually a compendium of all the teachings of Jesus; that they were placed in chapters 5-7 because Matthew considered this to be a convenient place to bring them together.

This interpretation is quite unnecessary. Any statement of value will be repeated often. If it is unworthy of repetition, it should not have been uttered in the first place. The Lord instructed His followers concerning the qualities of living necessary within the kingdom of God. Afterward in various places and on different occasions, He repeated His words of wisdom. When this happened, the disciples remembered how He uttered identical truths at the mountain retreat. We must forever be grateful to Matthew, for had he not made notes of the Lord's continuing discourses, the entire church would be intellectually impoverished. Doubtless much more was heard during those memorable days, but when, many years later, Matthew wrote his Gospel, the Holy Spirit directed the author to his notes, and it became easy for Matthew to include in his Gospel an account of the Master's messages in the mountain.

We are now able to proceed with a more detailed examination of those Scriptures known throughout the church as "The Sermon on the Mount."

## SECTION ONE

*Expository Notes on the Beatitudes*

**And seeing the multitudes, he went up into a mountain: and when he was seated, his disciples came unto him. And he opened his mouth, and taught them, saying, Blessed are the poor in spirit; for theirs is the kingdom of heaven (vv. 1-3).**

This section of Matthew's Gospel is among the most important parts of the Bible. Here, the King reveals to His students the characteristics to be manifested in the life of every disciple. Jesus, having called His followers, thought it necessary to instruct them; they could hardly teach others if they remained unaware of the requirements of the kingdom. Therefore, at the earliest opportunity, He took them up the mountain to conduct a retreat, which continued for at least seven days. We must try to visualize that resplendent scene.

Many years earlier, Elijah had sought refuge in the mountains of Israel, and his open-air sanctuary had become the most precious place on earth. The ravens brought his food in the morning and evening, and he drank from the brook. When the prophet lay down to sleep and saw stars shining in the sky, he felt he was looking at God's country. Every morning, he stretched his arms and said, "Good morning, Lord," and every night ere he closed his eyes, he thanked God for the blessings of the day. God was his companion in the mountain.

Now, many years later, the disciples felt they were sharing a similar experience. The Lord, knowing what lay ahead, had possibly purchased sufficient food to last for days, and probably the party camped near a mountain stream from which they could drink. Maybe, as was the case with John the Baptist, they found food in the trees and honey in the rocks where the bees had their home. High in the mountains, the air was pure, the vision glorious. The disciples did not know the importance of the occasion, but, in actual fact, they had returned to school, where Jesus was to be their Teacher.

Morning had arrived; breakfast had been eaten; the camp was set in order and the time for the first lesson was at hand. The Lord deliberately seated Himself, at a convenient location, and looked at His students. They were ready, and perhaps a little nervous. What would He say? The theme to be considered was "Life in the Kingdom," and as Jesus prepared to speak, He thought of other kingdoms around the world where men struggled for power. Throughout the kingdoms of earth, men valued material things, and paid high prices to capture positions of eminence. Jesus considered God's kingdom, and recognized the need to reveal to His friends its basic principles. His students would not understand all He wished to tell them, but it was necessary to begin somewhere.

It is said that "when he was seated," His disciples came unto Him. His action was very deliberate; He was like a judge entering a court room, and as everybody stood respectfully, He calmly took a seat on the bench to announce the session was in progress. The theme to be examined was *Characteristics of God's Kingdom.* It was as though He said, "Listen, My Children, I want to introduce you to the greatest virtues possible; I want to instruct you concerning God's kingdom, and tell you what His children should become. This is the first of nine important lessons."

*THE FIRST BEATITUDE...Blessed Are the Poor in Spirit:*
*for Theirs Is the Kingdom of Heaven*

It must be noted that the blessedness mentioned here is not a promise relating to eternal happiness; it is a joyous experience to be known now. This is not a reward to be given for meritorious service; it is a benediction to be bestowed upon faithful servants of God, each and every day of life. Yet, unlike the kingdoms of earth, and in direct contrast to the characteristics of Caesar's empire, those who would be great in the kingdom of heaven would sometimes be considered the least important among men.

The *Amplified New Testament* translates the passage thus: "Blessed [happy, to be envied, and spiritually prosperous, that is with life- joy and satisfaction in God's favor and salvation, regardless of their outward conditions] are the poor in spirit [the humble, rating themselves insignificant], for theirs is the kingdom of heaven" (v. 3). The word translated "poor" is *ptochoi,* and according to Thayer, is a very expressive word meaning "extreme poverty to the point of destitution". The man literally possesses nothing. Commenting on this, someone wrote, "It describes a poverty that has beaten a man to his knees!" A similiar word may be found many times in the Psalms where David likens himself to a *poor* man. "This *poor* man cried, and the LORD heard him, and saved him out of all his troubles" (Ps. 34:6). This first beatitude could be expressed as: "Blessed is the man who is so beaten to his knees, that from this lowly standpoint, he lifts his eyes to the hills from whence cometh aid." The twin truths are, "trouble and trust; problems and prayer; poverty and praise; dependence and deliverance."

Identical truth echoes in Paul's message concerning the churches of Macedonia. He wrote: "Moreover, brethren, we do you to wit [we would like to describe] of the grace of God bestowed on the churches of Macedonia; How that in *a great trial of affliction the abundance of their joy and their deep poverty abounded unto the riches of their liberality"* (2 Cor. 8:1-2). They posssessed nothing, yet they enjoyed unlimited wealth. They were experiencing overwhelming difficulties, yet they were continually happy. They possessed nothing, yet their sacrificial giving enriched all their brethren.

Had a man endeavored to apply this principle within an earthly kingdom, he would have exhibited stupidity, for such ideas would be inoperative wherever greed dictated selfish action. Yet Jesus taught this would be standard procedure within the kingdom of heaven. It would be impossible to outgive God, therefore, whatever was given away, would be returned, in one form or another, a hundred fold. People who graduated from God's academy would be considered worthy to occupy places of importance within God's kingdom. The Lord was expressing a very basic principle when He said, "Blessed [Happy, Privileged] are the poor in spirit, for theirs is the kingdom of heaven" (v. 3).

*THE SECOND BEATITUDE...Blessed Are They That Mourn: for They Shall Be Comforted*

It is not easy to decide the true meaning of these great words! They are constantly quoted at funerals, where grieving people are reminded of comfort found in the faithful promises of God. This truth is in the beatitude, but such an interpretation cannot exhaust the meaning of the text. Cremer, in the *Amplified New Testament,* translates the scripture as "Blessed and enviably happy, [with a happiness produced by experience of God's favor and especially conditioned by the revelation of His matchless grace] are those who mourn, for they shall be comforted!" The word translated "mourn" is *penthountes* and it is a very expressive word signifying a "heartbreaking lament over tragic death." It is the word used in the *Septuagint* version of the Old Testament to signify Jacob's overwhelming grief when he thought Joseph was dead. (See Gen. 37:34.) "And Jacob rent his clothes, and put sackcloth upon his loins, and mourned for his son many days." It expressed deep and prolonged sadness, such as produced Psalm 51 when David had sinned by murdering the husband of Bathsheba. The beatitude might easily mean, "Blessed are they who break their hearts, because of their having sinned before God — they shall be comforted, by the forgiving grace of God." If this is the true interpretation, then the desired characteristics, in every Christian, would be deep penitence for sin, and increasing gratitude to God for His willingness to forgive. To be assured of pardon is to know genuine comfort within the soul. To receive God's mercy should lead to obedience, when He commands "Go and sin no more." The beatitude implies a close examination of a disappointing past, and a clear indication that in seeking comfort, the soul looks to God for the forgiveness He alone can supply.

We are told that after Bathsheba had given birth to David's child, "The LORD struck the child that Uriah's wife bare unto David, and it was very sick. David therefore besought God for the child; and David fasted, and went in, and lay all night upon the earth. And the elders of his house arose, and went to him, to raise him up from the earth: but he would not, neither did he eat bread with them. And it came to pass on the seventh day, that the child died.'' Later, when David heard the distressing news, He ''arose from the earth, and washed, and anointed himself, and changed his apparel, and came into the house of the LORD, and worshiped.'' His attitude mystified the servants who asked for an explanation. Then David said, ''While the child was yet alive, I fasted and wept; for I said, Who can tell whether GOD will be gracious to me, that the child may live? But now he is dead, should I fast? Can I bring him back again? *I shall go to him,*, but he shall not return to me. And David comforted Bath-sheba his wife'' (see 2 Samuel 12:15-24.)

The gospel is the most wonderful message ever preached. Death is often the harbinger of sorrow, but when the soul can say, ''I shall go to him,'' there is certainty of reunion and loss is only temporary. This glorious fact enables the believer to say, ''O death, where is thy sting? O grave, where is thy victory?'' (1 Cor. 15:55). These Scriptures are stars shining against the background of human sorrow. These promises of God can turn the blackness of the sky into a thing of beauty. The citizens of the kingdom of heaven will be recognized by this type of comforting joy. Jesus knew this and said, ''Blessed are they that mourn: for they shall be comforted'' (v. 4).

*THE THIRD BEATITUDE...Blessed Are the Meek:*
*for They Shall Inherit the Earth*

The word ''meek'' according to the dictionary means, ''gentle, mild of temper, patient, easily imposed upon, unresenting, spiritless, modest, piously humble.'' It is definitely a little-big word with many meanings. Therefore, it is necessary that we proceed slowly as we seek to understand the third beatitude. Unfortunately, the word is often used to express spinelessness; a person with very little backbone! Obviously, such a meaning has no connection with the thought Jesus expressed. The Bible says, ''Now the man Moses was very meek, above all the men which were upon the face of the earth'' (Num. 12:3). Moses did not fit into the mold of the modern interpretations of the word ''meek.'' He could be angry, and was never susceptible to imposition. Moses was the greatest leader Israel ever had; he was a figure of towering strength, and the splendor of his personality struck terror into the hearts of sinful men. Yet, he was described as the ''meekest man on earth.'' Obviously, we must seek the true meaning of this important beatitude.

The Greek word used here is *praeis;* it comes from *praotees* and has several usages. It was often used to express humility; and an absence of anger. It expressed docility, gentleness of character, and sometimes mildness of speech. Probably, its best usage can be found in that it described an animal that had been domesticated, such as a dog trained to respond to the command of its master, or a horse which had been broken. These illustrations may seem strange, but they provide word pictures of meekness. A sinful man can be an untamed animal, a dog to bite, or a horse which throws its rider. Yet, when the grace of God tranforms the sinner into a saint, turbulent passions are tamed and brought into submissiveness to the Lord. The man who formerly lived to please himself, learns to respond when the Holy Spirit gently pulls on the reins! The angry soul which loved to snap and bite, becomes the willing servant of its trainer. A dog will hunt, warn, protect, and do anything the master orders. Instead of being savage and unrestrained, the domesticated dog plays with children and is a delight to an entire family. To the ancient Greeks, this was "being gentle or meek." It denoted a person who had come into contact with a greater power; a dynamic which had transformed an untrustworthy animal into a beloved companion.

Probably the Lord had this in mind when He delivered the beatitude. Such people, instead of losing the battles of life, would emerge as victors. Loving others they would be loved; serving others they would make many friends; giving of their time, talents, and wealth, they would be enriched immeasurably and would inherit the earth. These were the principles operative within the kingdom of heaven. Jesus did not come to make things better, He came to make things new, "Therefore, if any man be in Christ, he is a new creature: old things are passed away; behold, all things are become new" (2 Cor. 5:17).

*THE FOURTH BEATITUDE...Blessed Are They Which Do Hunger and Thirst After Righteousness: for They Shall Be Filled*

This commentary is being written in the year 1985, when the world has become aware of the famine devastating Ethiopia. The pictures shown on television are appalling; it is sickening and frightening to see the emaciated bodies of small children destined to die prematurely. They are slowly starving to death, whereas in America, much food is wasted daily. Throughout World War II, the people in Britain were strictly rationed, but there was always sufficient food to keep people alive and, occasionally, a few luxuries became available. When Jesus spoke of "hungering," many of His listeners understood what He meant. Nevertheless, He was speaking of hungering and thirsting after righteousness. However vital it was to have food for the body, it was even more important to obtain nourishment for the soul. The same idea can be found in Psalm 42:1, "As the hart *panteth* after the water brooks, so *panteth* my soul after thee, O God. My soul thirsteth for God, for the living God...." Acute need begat an irrepressible urge for fellowship with the living God. During my stay in Africa, I often saw deer making their way along forest paths, and their need was apparent. The pasture had been destroyed by bush fires; water seemed unobtainable, but with an unerring instinct, those beautiful creatures knew where to go. They were indeed "panting after the water brooks." Their need was not casual nor partial. They longed with an intensity of desire difficult to describe. Did the Lord have such a thought in mind when He said, "Blessed are they who hunger and thirst after righteousness"? Every Christian, to a degree, longs for righteousness, but, frequently the intensity of desire is missing. The only people who are "filled" with God's wonderful sufficiency, are they who hunger desperately for the things heaven alone can supply. Was Paul expressing a similar thought when he wrote: "Yea doubtless, and I count all things but loss for the excellency of the knowledge of Christ Jesus my Lord: for whom I have suffered the loss of all things, and do count them but dung [refuse], that I may win Christ, and be found in him, not having mine own righteousness, which is of the law, but that which is through the faith of Christ, the righteousness which is of God by faith" (Phil. 3:8-9).

*THE FIFTH BEATITUDE...Blessed Are the Merciful:*
*for They Shall Obtain Mercy*

It might be beneficial to consider this beatitude against the background of an Old Testament story. The Book of Judges describes a very strange king who had a peculiar hobby. Whenever he captured another monarch, he cut off the man's thumbs and his great toes, and then let him eat beneath the royal table. The captives were as dogs begging for food. Their hands resembled claws as they tried to seize food thrown down by the king. Eventually, this man whose name was Adoni bezek, was captured by the men of Judah. It is written: "They...caught him, and cut off his thumbs and his great toes. And Adoni-bezek said, Threescore and ten kings, having their thumbs and their great toes cut off, gathered their meat under my table: as I have done, so God hath requited me" (Judg. 1:6-7). This old story is a great example of the truth: "You reap whatsoever you sow."

The Lord also told a story of a man who was forgiven an enormous debt, and yet refused to forgive a fellowservant. Jesus explained that the man was severely punished (see the exposition supplied in Matt. 18:23-35). The New Testament consistently teaches that if we expect forgiveness from God, we must be prepared to forgive our neighbors. When a man refuses to be merciful, he should not anticipate mercy. Mercy begets forgiveness and this is the message of the Christian gospel. Jesus instructed His disciples when they prayed to say, "Forgive us our debts, as we forgive our debtors." Paul, writing to the Ephesians said, "And be ye kind one to another, tenderhearted, forgiving one another, even as God for Christ's sake hath forgiven you" (Eph. 4:32). An embittered, unforgiving person is the most unlovely, unattractive soul in the world. They repel, but never attract.

*THE SIXTH BEATITUDE...Blessed Are the Pure in Heart: for They Shall See God*

When the Lord uttered these words, He might have been thinking of David's words, "Who shall ascend into the hill of the LORD? or who shall stand in his holy place? He that hath clean hands, and a pure heart; who hath not lifted up his soul unto vanity, nor sworn deceitfully" (Ps. 24:3-4). The Greek words are *katharoi tee pardia* which mean "clean in heart." The phrase is used throughout the ancient writings and indicates "washed clothes." It may also be found expressing cleansed wheat, where the grain has been separated from chaff, etc. It is even used in a military sense, indicating a body of soldiers purged of cowards. The whole idea is that the undesirable elements have been removed in order to improve efficiency.

The Bible teaches that without holiness, no man shall see the Lord (Heb. 12:14). Therefore, as a woman washes clothes to remove dirt; as a farmer winnows grain to remove chaff; and as a general diligently examines the credentials of his soldiers, so we must give attention to our souls. The thought permeating all these illustrations appears to be careful examination. Clothes do not cleanse themselves; a harvest is not gathered without workers; soldiers without discipline are of little use. Quality is always better than quantity. Obviously, Christians should be the best possible in the service of the King. Heroes are they who do valiantly on the field of battle — they meet the King. Cowards are dishonorably discharged from the fighting forces. We are reminded "we wrestle not against flesh and blood, but against principalities and powers"; we are at war with evil. If we please God, when the conflict has terminated, we shall see the King in His beauty.

*THE SEVENTH BEATITUDE...Blessed Are the Peacemakers:
for They Shall Be Called the Children of God*

Peace has always been the most elusive thing in the world. Nations persist in going to war with each other; countries have been divided by factions; churches split by dissension, and even individuals have been made aware of their shortcomings. Peace is the elusive bubble which floats beyond a man's reach. Yet, Jesus insisted the peace of God would be the outstanding characteristic of kingdom life. Discord, strife, and enmity are not the attributes of holiness. A correct relationship with men may often be the prelude to a similar relationship with God. Indirectly the Savior taught this when He said, ''Therefore if thou bring thy gift to the altar, and there rememberest that thy brother hath aught against thee; Leave there thy gift before the altar, and go thy way; first be reconciled to thy brother, and then come and offer thy gift'' (Matt. 5:23-24).

It was Christmas day, in 1917, when a British chaplain climbed out of a muddy trench on the battlefield in France. Slowly, he walked toward the German trenches, and every onlooker expected him to be shot at any moment. Reaching the enemy lines, he reminded the Germans that it was Christmas day, and that in their land and his, families would be singing Christmas carols. He suggested a truce. Both British and Germans climbed out of the mud to attend to the needs of the wounded and to bury their dead. No shots were fired until January 3rd when the ruling powers decided it was time ''to get on with the war.'' That British chaplain received the military medal for his bravery. Probably that was the best Christmas of his life; he knew the reality of Christ's words: ''Blessed are the peacemakers; for they shall be called the children of God.''

It is never easy to bring bitter enemies together; but it is tragic if the attempt is never made. Some people are specially gifted with tact, wisdom, and courage, to intercede in difficult situations. Their patient endeavors; their tactful persuasion, their manifested love for fellow human beings, often bridge what appears to be unbridgable chasms. Blessed indeed are the peacemakers, for these share the desires of the Almighty; they shall be called His children.

*THE EIGHTH BEATITUDE...Blessed Are They Who Are
Persecuted for Righteousness' Sake: for Theirs Is the Kingdom of
Heaven*

Probably, this was the most applicable of all Christ's beatitudes; to follow Christ was to walk the most lonely pathway in the world. It was never easy for anyone to become a Christian, but for the saints of the first three centuries, it was extremely difficult. Historians tell us that Christians had to suffer things beyond description. We have heard of the Christians who were flung to the lions or burned at the stake; but those were kindly deaths. Nero wrapped the Christians in pitch and set them afire, and used them as torches to light his gardens. He sewed them in the skins of wild animals, and set his hunting dogs upon them to tear them to death. They were tortured on the rack; they were scraped with pinchers; molten lead was poured hissing upon them. There were other kinds of torture These things are not pleasant to think about, but these are the things for which a man had to be prepared when he took his stand for Christ.

We are reminded of the words in Hebrews 11:36-38, "And others had trial of cruel mockings and scourgings, yea, moreover of bonds and imprisonment: They were stoned, they were sawn asunder, were tempted, were slain with the sword; they wandered about in sheepskins and goatskins; being destitute, afflicted, tormented...they wandered in deserts, and in mountains, and in dens and caves of the earth...." But — and let it be emphasized, THEY DID IT. Correctly was it said, "Of them, the world was not worthy."

The early Christians saw families turn against them; they lost their employment, were falsely accused of heinous crimes; they heard their faith slandered, twisted, ridiculed. They were compelled to worship Caesar, and when they refused, were sacrificed on the altars of idols. YET THEY ENDURED. Their blood became the seed of the church, and theirs indeed was the kingdom of heaven. Their faith meant so much, they sealed the testimony with their blood. Alas, today, the gospel means so little. We surrender readily that for which our forefathers died. The blessedness of this beatitude is something many people never experience.


*THE NINTH BEATITUDE...Blessed Are Ye, When Men Shall Revile You, and Persecute You, and Shall Say All Manner of Evil Against You Falsely for My Sake. Rejoice, and Be Exceeding Glad; for Great Is Your Reward in Heaven: for so Persecuted They the Prophets Which Were Before You.*

This is the last of the beatitudes. Three areas await investigation. (1) A Great Pleasure. (2) A Glorious Promise. (3) A Gracious Privilege. Let us consider them in that order.

*A GREAT PLEASURE...* "*Rejoice, and be exceeding glad*" (v. 12a).

Jesus never lured disciples with false hopes of grandeur. He promised them suffering, persecution, and a cross. Nevertheless, He also indicated that increasing joy would be their continuing experience as they learned to walk with God. The *Amplified New Testament* translates these verses, "Be glad and supremely joyful, for your reward in heaven is great, (strong and intense)." Happiness among men and women is an experience based upon happenings! If events be adverse, the outcome tends to be sad, discouraging, and miserable. If everything goes according to plan, people feel pleased, satisfied, and glad. Christianity does not work in that way. Joy is not really affected by adverse circumstances. Christians rejoice in success, but they trust when things are contrary. Joy depends upon fellowship with God and not on circumstances to be endured. Happiness may be destroyed in moments; true joy is eternal.

*A GLORIOUS PROMISE...* "*Great is your reward in heaven*" (v. 12b).

There are at least three reasons for the joy of the Christian. Jesus said (Luke 10:20) "Rejoice, because your names are written in heaven." He also says His disciples should rejoice in anticipation of the reward for meritorious service. John in Rev. 22:4 indicates we shall see the Savior's face, when the severity of persecution will fade into insignificance.

> It will be worth it all
> When we see Jesus,
> Life's trials will seem so small,
> When we see Christ.
> One glimpse of His dear face
> All sorrow will erase,
> So bravely run the race
> Till we see Christ.

*A GRAND PRIVILEGE...We Follow in the Prophets' Footsteps*

"So persecuted they the prophets which were before you" (v. 12c). Saints who suffer for righteousness' sake are in good company! Maybe we are being watched. "Since we have such a huge crowd of men of faith watching us from the grandstands, let us strip off anything that slows us down or holds us back, and especially those sins that wrap themselves so tightly around our feet, and trip us up; and let us run with patience the particular race that God has set before us'' (Heb. 12:1. *The Living Bible*)

Thus did Jesus terminate this part of His teaching on the mount. His disciples would soon commence their crusade. They should be ready to preach their message; exhibit the grace and love of God, and should it become necessary, lay down their lives in support of their cause. Doubtless these precepts were reiterated many times during the Lord's incomparable ministry, but Matthew, with rare skill, preserved these sayings for posterity in that remarkable document known as ''The Sermon on the Mount.''

## SECTION TWO

*Expository Notes on Christ's Description of His Followers*

**Ye are the salt of the earth; but if the salt has lost its savour, wherewith shall it be salted? It is thenceforth good for nothing but to be cast out, and to be trodden under foot of men. You are the light of the world. A city that is set on a hill cannot be hidden. Neither do men light a candle [lamp], and put it under a bushel, but on a candlestick [lampstand]; and it giveth light unto all that are in the house. Let your light so shine before men, that they may see your good works, and glorify your Father who is in heaven (vv. 13-16).**

The Lord informed His followers they were the salt of the earth, and today, the statement has become part of our language. Any person considered to be good, helpful or valuable is often described as ''the salt of the earth.'' Salt is known for three things. It purifies, preserves, and permeates. Doctors urge patients to gargle with salt water to cleanse and purify the throat. A mild solution inhaled through the nostrils and expelled through the mouth opens nasal passages, enabling sufferers to breathe freely. During my stay in the Shetland Islands, I often watched girls packing fish into barrels destined for export. The fish were buried in salt, which acted as a preservative during the long journey to the consumers' market. The people in Central Africa would, at times, give anything they possessed for bars of salt. Salt prevents deterioration; it also permeates and flavors cooking to prevent a meal from becoming insipid.

When Jesus told His followers they were to be the salt of the earth, He probably had these thoughts in mind. The church should be a cleansing agency in a sick world. The advent of the gospel into any heart is the forerunner of spiritual health. The presence of Christians should prevent the deterioration of society, and preserve qualities necessary for the prosperity of citizens. Christians in a home, hospital, college, factory, or any other place, should "flavor" the surroundings in which they live. The world is disappointingly evil, but one wonders what it would be like if there were no church, no Sunday schools, no Christian hospitals. Every blessing of Western civilization came through the church, its ministers, and its message. I never heard of communists leaving their homes to nurse lepers in foreign lands. I have known of people who became terrorists, but they were well paid for their efforts, and were able to quit whenever they desired. On the other hand, I knew of a very brilliant doctor who left fame, fortune, and comfort, to help needy people in Africa. He did not quit when things were difficult; he stayed, and ultimately died joyfully at his hospital. It behooves every Christian to be attentive to the high and holy calling, for when, perhaps through negligence, the salt loses its savor, it becomes useless.

The illustration about being cast out and trodden under the feet of men came from a common occurrence in the Middle East. I watched an open-air baker cooking scones for a nearby restaurant. His oven had a base of tile, beneath which was a layer of salt to increase and maintain heat. When the salt loses its potency, it is thrown on the street where pedestrians tread it into the ground.

Christ also said His disciples were the light of the world; that is, they should be as He was, for He said, "I am the light of the world." A light can do many things. First, *it shines* in the darkness; it is meant to be seen. Second, *it may guide,* as it does on the runway of an airport. An incoming pilot knows where to direct his plane, for the avenue of illumination charts his course. Without lights, industry, hospitals, and every home would continue in darkness. Blind men, alas, manage to do certain things, but their actions are severely limited. The same truths apply to the church and its members. Christians should be shining lights in a world of darkness; their testimony must reveal to men and women how to travel, and how "to make a safe landing." Their presence and influence in every walk of life should be invaluable in helping souls to live. The words of Jesus were not only a superlative compliment, they constituted the greatest challenge ever given to disciples.

SECTION THREE

*Expository Notes on the Importance of the Word of God*

**Think not that I am come to destroy the law, or the prophets: I am not come to destroy, but to fulfil. For verily I say unto you, Till heaven and earth pass, one jot or one tittle shall in no way pass from the law, till all be fulfilled. Whosoever therefore shall break one of these least commandments, and shall teach men so, he shall be called the least in the kingdom of heaven: but whosoever shall do and teach them, the same shall be called great in the kingdom of heaven. For I say unto you, That except your righteousness shall exceed the righteousness of the scribes and Pharisees, ye shall in no case enter into the kingdom of heaven (vv. 17-20).**

## A STARTLING DECLARATION

To understand this statement, it is necessary to be aware of what is meant by the law. The Bible refers to (1) The Law of God and (2) The Laws of Moses, but they also mention two others. The Law of God was contained in the Ten Commandments given to Moses in Mount Sinai. They were inscribed on tablets of stone, and became the basis of every legal matter in Israel. The Laws of Moses related to the thousands of lesser commandments to which local judges referred. Later, Moses and the prophets became interrelated, and the term ''The Law and the Prophets'' became familiar in the nation. This covered the entire period from Moses to Malachi. Finally, since printing presses were unknown, and every detail had to be preserved for posterity, the various commandments either had to be written by hand or given orally to generation after generation.

## A STRICT DEFINITION

The scribes were responsible for the preservation of the records, but as years passed, they added all kinds of ideas, some of which were ludicrous. This became the prevailing standard of law throughout Israel, and the thousands of demands made upon the people were so burdensome, they became obnoxious. Ancient records reveal that scribes and lawyers would argue for days about the legality of a man going out on the sabbath wearing artificial teeth, or whether it were a sin if a tailor went out with a needle in his robe. The weightier matters of the real law were obscured by the stupidity of those who professed to be its interpreters. It was this kind of teaching which Christ opposed. The scribes and Pharisees accused Him of violating the law, when in actual fact, they were only protecting ideas which they had inculcated. Jesus emphasized the importance of the Real Law; the true Word of God given to Moses.

In our study of various authors on the customs of ancient Israel, we learned that *to write* was to work on the Sabbath. But writing had to be defined. It was said that he who wrote two letters of the alphabet with his right or with his left hand, whether of one kind or of two kinds, if they were written with different inks or in different languages, was guilty. Even if he were to write two letters from forgetfulness, he was guilty, whether he had written them with ink, or with paint, red chalk, vitriol, or anything which made a permanent mark. But if anyone wrote with dark fluid, with fruit juice, or in the dust of the road or in the sand, or in anything which did not make a permanent mark, he was not guilty.'' The Savior considered all these bewildering and unnecessary dictates to be an abomination, and thus He was in continuous conflict with the scribes.

## A SERIOUS DEFICIENCY

"Except your righteousness exceed the righteousness of the scribes and Pharisees, ye shall in no case enter the kingdom of heaven" (v. 20). There are three types of people in these verses. (1) The least in the kingdom, (2) The great in the kingdom, and (3) The people who will not be in the kingdom. With all their protestations of piety, the scribes were rejected because their piety was based on law; it was the result of what they did. The righteousness which is of God by faith rests upon what God accomplished through the death of Christ (see Phil. 3:9). There are still teachers who insist that salvation depends entirely upon a man's observance of law. They affirm that faith is secondary to obedience. Paul said the law was but a schoolmaster bringing us to Christ. Since graduation we have been subject to a higher law — "the Spirit of Life" in Christ Jesus.

## SECTION FOUR

*Expository Notes on the Need for Prompt Action*

**Ye have heard that it was said by them of old time, Thou shalt not kill and whosoever shall kill shall be in danger of the judgment; But I say**

unto you, That whosoever is angry with his brother without a cause,
shall be in danger of judgment: and whosoever shall say to his brother,
Raca, shall be in danger of the council: but whosoever shall say, Thou
fool, shall be in danger of hell fire (vv. 21-22).

It is hardly possible to read these verses without becoming aware of
the higher standard of moral laws introduced by Jesus. Under law, a
man could think what he wanted without legal guilt. Public condemnation
was only justified when his conduct violated a God-given commandment.
He could only be charged with murder when he had slain a human being.
He could only be charged with adultery when he had intercourse with
another man's wife. Yet, Jesus taught that if a man *thought* such things,
he was as guilty as if he had committed the actual sin. Such truth had
never been taught. The Lord contrasted murder with anger, and indicated
that one was as bad as the other. Uncontrolled anger led to killing;
therefore, the cause was as heinous as the offense.

There are three stages of judgment in the verses. Jesus spoke about
(1) In danger of judgment. That was the village council of elders
responsible for civil law within a parish. (2) In danger of the council.
That was the Sanhedrin; the Supreme Court of the nation. (3) In danger
of hell fire. That was a direct reference to the Valley of Hinnom in
which all the refuse of Jerusalem was dumped, and where fires smoldered
perpetually. It was considered to be the embodiment of all evil; the place
of destruction, where worms fed on refuse to be destroyed in the city's
incinerator. The statement "angry... without a cause" is misleading;
that phrase is not found in the original Greek. Anger is sin and should
not be found in the life of any follower of Jesus.

If a man allowed himself to be controlled by a vicious temper, he
ran the risk of being accused before the local tribunal. When a man
called his neighbor "Raca," he was expressing an unpardonable insult
and could be accused before the highest court in the land. The term
"Raca" implied moral laxity; the accused was said to be quilty of the
worst crimes possible, and for this there was neither excuse nor pardon.
He was considered to be as abominable as the refuse taken to the fires
in the Valley of Hinnom. He could anticipate nothing but total
destruction. The entire emphasis in these verses was upon the need for
continuing carefulness in daily conduct. It would be better to critize
oneself and be merciful to the neighbor; to look for the good things
in other people and to exercise constant watchfulness over the sanctity
of one's own soul.

**Therefore if thou bring thy gift to the altar, and there rememberest that thy brother hath aught against thee; leave there thy gift before the altar, and go thy way; first be reconciled to thy brother, and then come and offer thy gift. Agree with thine adversary quickly, whiles thou art in the way with him; lest at any time the adversary deliver thee to the judge, and the judge deliver thee to the officer, and thou be cast into prison. Verily I say unto thee, Thou shalt by no means come out thence, till thou hast paid the uttermost farthing (vv. 23-26).**

Restitution, unfortunately, is a word which has almost disappeared from the vocabulary of the church. Nevertheless, it governed the conduct of all Jews contemplating offering a sacrifice to God. It was fervently believed that offerings were unacceptable if the suppliant bore grudges against an associate. Basically, God was not willing to accept any man unless the relationship between him and his fellow men was healthy. To draw near to God, one needed to be holy, and this was not possible if the human mind entertained evil thoughts against a neighbor. Therefore, a worshiper standing before the priest was reminded his sacrifice would be useless unless it were offered "by clean hands."

That the Lord Jesus gave added emphasis to this fact becomes obvious when we remember He said, *"If thou...rememberest* that thy brother hath aught against thee" (v. 23a). To be clean, forgiving, kind, would be insufficent to gain the approbation of God. Even if the other man were guilty, an attempt had to be made to remove the bitterness. The health of the church should be considered invaluable and every attempt made to preserve it. The Savior seemed to be saying, "What needs to be done, do it immediately. Do not procrastinate; tomorrow may be too late." A man who delays action may be too late. A small, neglected wound in the leg might easily fester, and could result in amputation. Jesus was recommending constant watchfulness. Christians should remember that a painful incision is better than a sealed casket.

## SECTION FIVE

*Expository Notes on Christ's Comments About Divorce*

**Ye have heard that it was said by them of old time, Thou shalt not commit adultery: But I say unto you, That whosoever looketh on a woman to lust after her hath committed adultery with her already in his heart (vv. 27-28).**

Here we see the lines of demarcation between the old and new systems.

108 MATTHEW'S MAJESTIC GOSPEL

The Mosaic law stated men were blameless of adultery unless they had intercourse with another man's wife. Jesus enunciated greater doctrines when He affirmed a man was guilty even if he only contemplated the deed. According to the new standard of spiritual law, a man could drive his automobile down a crowded street, and without stopping his vehicle, commit adultery twenty times before he had gone a hundred yards! Therefore Jesus stressed it was important to have clean thoughts; to keep the mind protected from evil intrusions; to consider those things which were lovely, wholesome, and pure (see Col. 3:1-2, and Eph. 6:17).

> **And if thy right eye offend thee, pluck it out, and cast it from thee: for it is profitable for thee that one of thy members should perish, and not that thy whole body should be cast into hell. And if thy right hand offend thee, cut it off, and cast it from thee: for it is profitable for thee that one of thy members should perish, and not that thy whole body should be cast into hell (vv. 29-30).**

The word translated "offend" is interesting in that it means "to stumble." It is the Greek word *skandalizei* which has connections with *skandaleethron*. This supplies a word-picture depicting "a baited trap; a lure set on, or in the ground" (Thayer). It represents anything which might snare or trap the human spirit. It could be a covered hole in the ground such as used by hunters in Africa. An animal unsuspectingly might walk over a camouflage of branches and leaves only to discover the pit into which it falls.

Jesus was suggesting that such snares lay in the path of every disciple; each one should walk with extreme care. Anything which led to slavery should be avoided. If the eye became lustful, the soul would surely fall into the abyss. If the hand reached for the illegitimate, the heart would be overwhelmed with evil. It would be better to suffer the loss of temporary satisfaction, than to experience remorse eternally. Nothing could be as important as spiritual health, therefore every effort should be made to maintain it.

> **It hath been said, Whosoever shall put away his wife, let him give her a writing of divorcement: But I say unto you, That whosoever shall put away his wife, saving for the cause of fornication, causeth her to commit adultery: and whosoever shall marry her that is divorced committeth adultery (vv. 31-32).**

Divorce is one of the most difficult problems confronting the church, and unfortunately, the unrelenting attitude of some clergymen has increased the suffering of innocent people. There have been occasions when God was kinder than His representatives. To understand completely the teaching of Jesus, one must be aware of the conditions existent in the ancient world. The sanctity of the marriage bond had been violated in all kinds of unforgivable ways, and union with another had degenerated until it had become an ordinance of convenience. When the Lord was upon earth, God only permitted divorce proceedings in cases of fornication and adultery.

God, speaking through the prophet Malachi, said, "Let none deal treacherously against the wife of his youth. For the LORD, the God of Israel, saith that He hateth *putting away* [divorce]" (Mal. 2:15-16). Nevertheless, the action to which He referred was something far removed from what we know today. Formerly, people were joined in marriage "till death us do part," but as time passed, all kinds of reasons were allowed to disannul a marriage. These were condemned by Christ. One leading teacher in Israel taught "a man could divorce his wife if she spoiled his dinner by placing too much salt in his food; if she went in public with her head uncovered; if she talked with men in the streets; if she were a brawling woman; if she spoke disrespectfully of her husband's parents in his presence; or if she were troublesome or quarrelsome." One rabbi taught that "a man could divorce his partner if he found another woman more attractive than his wife." Throughout the world, marriage was only a bond of convenience. Today, in some lands of the Far East, it is commonplace for a husband to have mistresses. A wife is responsible for the management of her home, and in exchange, enjoys a degree of security. She bears children who carry the father's name, but even she condones her husband's illicit relationships with other women. Such conditions existed throughout the ancient world, and it was to be expected that once the gospel reached those people, pastors would be asked to offer counsel regarding marriage relationships. The Lord gave such guidance to His disciples, and this was communicated to their converts. The selfish, unprincipled rejection of a partner was evil, unforgivable, and foreign to the will of God.

Nevertheless, it should be remembered that in cases of *fornication* divorce was permitted, *and the remarriage of the innocent party was permissible according to the laws of God.* Deut. 24:1-2 says, "When a man hath taken a wife, and married her, and it come to pass that she find no favor in his eyes, because he hath found some uncleanness in her: then let him write her a bill of divorcement, and give it in her hand, and send her out of his house. And when she is departed out of his house, *she may go and be another man's wife.*" The law clearly taught that if that husband married again, *HE* not *SHE* was guilty of adultery. To condemn such a woman to continuing loneliness, and her children to a life without a father, was foreign to common sense and bore no relationship to the revealed love of God.

> Again, ye have heard that it hath been said by them of old time, Thou shalt not forswear [perjure] thyself, but shalt perform unto the Lord thine oaths: But I say unto you, Swear not at all: neither by heaven; for it is God's throne: nor by the earth; for it is his footstool: neither by Jerusalem; for it is the city of the great King. Neither shalt thou swear by thy head, because thou canst not make one hair white or black. But let your communication be Yea, yea; Nay, nay: for whatsoever is more than these cometh of evil (vv. 33-37).

Jesus seems to have stressed the irrelevance of unnecessary speech, and the desirability of godly living. We have grown accustomed to court proceedings where witnesses are required to tell the truth. More often than not they acquiesce, but there is no guarantee they will be truthful. New Year vows generally last a short time. Verbal contracts are often disowned, and the result is chaotic. This should be abhorrent to all Christians whose word should be binding and final. Josephus writing of the ancient Essenes, said, "They are eminent for fidelity and are ministers of peace. Whatever they say also is firmer than an oath. Swearing is avoided by them, and they esteem it worse than perjury. For they said that he who cannot be believed without swearing is already condemned."

The Savior thus indicated His followers should be men of character, esteemed so highly by their fellow men, that their word would become their bond. One of my friends, a diamond merchant from Johannesburg, once explained to me that among his associates, drawn-up agreements were unknown and unnecessary. When two men shook hands over a contract, that remained binding as long as they lived. This suggests character, esteem, worthiness, and reliability; they should be the hallmarks of every follower of the Savior.

## SECTION SIX

*Expository Notes on Christ's Comments About Attitudes*

Ye have heard that it hath been said, An eye for an eye, and a tooth for a tooth: But I say unto you, That ye resist not evil: but whosoever shall smite thee on thy right cheek, turn to him the other also. And

**if any man will sue thee at the law, and take away thy coat, let him have thy cloak also....And whosoever shall compel thee to go a mile, go with him twain. Give to him that asketh thee, and from him that would borrow of thee turn not away (vv. 38-42).**

All students should be aware of Christ's continual claim to authority. "Ye have heard"..."But I say unto you...." This statement is found in verses 21-22; 27-28; 33-34; 38-39. What they had heard from any source, was now to be superseded by what He would say. His doctrines would be the guiding principles in all service. His word was final. The old idea of a tooth for a tooth worked well among sinners; it should not be tolerated among saints. The disciples would never win converts by punching them in the nose! They would never influence communities by being vindictive in the law courts. Ordinary men could be expected to live according to these standards, but Christians should never be ordinary people! They should be recognized by their willingness to go the extra mile to help those among whom they lived. If men and women practiced these principles, wars would cease, crime would disappear, and the earth would be filled with the glory of the Lord, as the waters cover the sea.

**Ye have heard that it hath been said, Thou shalt love thy neighbour, and hate thine enemy: But I say unto you, Love your enemies, bless them that curse you, do good to them that hate you, and pray for them which despitefully use you, and persecute you; that ye may be the children of your Father which is in heaven; for he maketh his sun to rise on the evil and on the good, and sendeth rain on the just and on the unjust. For if ye love them which love you, what reward have ye? do not even the publicans so? Be ye therefore perfect, even as your Father which is in heaven is perfect (vv. 43-48).**

Sometimes a good illustration supplies more illumination than an hour of theological exposition. The following account explains what is implied in that statement. Some years ago, I was a guest speaker at a Russian church where the congregation was rejoicing over a letter which had just been smuggled out of Russia. It told a grim, but wonderful, story. A number of Christians had been severely beaten by the commandant of a prison. One day, they were huddled together in their dirty cell when the door opened. The prisoners were amazed when officials threw the commandant among them. He too, had been beaten unmercifully. The Christians hastened to attend to the man's wounds, and after a while, he was able to give his testimony.

He told how he had been seated in his office when a gentle tap on his door announced a visitor. He arose, opened the door, and saw a boy of eleven years standing with a single rose grasped in his hand. The boy was invited to enter, and as he stood by the commandant's desk, said, "Herr Commandant, it is my mother's birthday, and I always gave her a rose on her birthday, but today I would like to give it to you." The communist official thanked the lad, and then asked, "Son, why do you bring it to me. If this is your mother's birthday, why don't you give the rose to her?" The boy replied, "Sir, I cannot, because you killed her, and you also killed my father. They were Christians, but when she was alive, she always taught me to love my enemies. Herr Commandant, I would like you to give this rose to your wife as a gift from me." The commandant was overwhelmed by the sincerity and simplicity of an eleven-year-old boy. He surrendered himself to Christ, but when his superior officers discovered what had taken place, they beat him unmercifully, and threw him into the prison. That young Russian boy was the living example of what Jesus meant when He said, "Love your enemies, bless them that curse you, do good to them that hate you, and pray for them which despitefully use you, and persecute you....For if ye love them which love you, what reward have ye?"

# The Sixth Chapter Of Matthew

THEME: *The Continuation of the Messages on the Mount: The Warnings and Wisdom of Jesus*

OUTLINE:
  I. Give Graciously (Verses 1-4)
  II. Pray Privately (Verses 5-13)
  III. Forgive Freely (Verses 14-15)
  IV. Fast Faithfully (Verses 16-18)
  V. Trust Triumphantly (Verses 19-34)

## SECTION ONE

*Expository Notes on the Value of Conscientious Giving*

**Take heed that ye do not your alms before men, to be seen of them: otherwise ye have no reward of your Father which is in heaven. Therefore when thou doest thine alms, do not sound a trumpet before thee, as the hypocrites do in the synagogues and in the streets, that they may have glory of men. Verily I say unto you, They have their reward. But when thou doest alms, let not thy left hand know what thy right hand doeth: that thine alms may be in secret: and thy Father which seeth in secret himself shall reward thee openly (vv. 1-4).**

This section of the chapter may be summarized under three headings. (1) *The danger of a false profession.* (2) *The desirability of a firm privacy.* (3) *The delight of a Father's praise.* Let us consider them in that order.

## THE DANGER OF A FALSE PROFESSION

Religion can be a highway to the heart of God, a road along which the faithful travel, or it can be a stage upon which insincere worshipers display their virtue. Alas, many of the Pharisees were great showmen. They valued the praises of men more than the commendation of the Almighty. They had no real objection to giving to God, as long as adequate publicity announced their sacrificial deeds. They were the kind of people who would give lavishly to any worthy cause, as long as their names were printed in large type at the top of the list of donors. They loved to be recognized by beneficiaries, praised by the city's leaders, and welcomed with ovations at any function they chose to attend. They inquired diligently about the dividends to be gained before they invested in any cause. As Jesus indicated, "They loved the praise of men," and professed to worship God because that was a means to the desired end. Most of the beggars along the street were willing to give that recognition, because they were anxious to receive "the crumbs which fell from the rich man's table." The pompous almsgiving was a thin veneer covering the hypocritical souls of proud men.

The Lord demanded better things from those who would represent Him on a mission of evangelism. He said, "Take heed — be careful — that ye do not your alms (parade your righteousness) before men, *to be seen of them.*" "Your mission will be to present the Son of God and not to advertise yourselves. If you do as the Pharisees, there will be no reward awaiting you in heaven." The ostentatious behavior of the religious leaders was planned to draw attention to men, not God. The Pharisees would scatter coins in the street, but not until important citizens were present to watch what was being done. The wealthy man was always willing to place an offering in the temple treasury, but he enjoyed himself much more when other worshipers gasped with surprise at the amount given. As Jesus suggested, he would have used a trumpet to summon viewers, had that been considered proper. I once knew of a rich politician, in Britain, who donated twenty-thousand pounds (at that time, eighty-thousand dollars) to a certain cause, but begrudged every cent of it. His rival had given half that amount, and the miser wanted to outgive his neighbor. The widow woman who cast two mites into the treasury in the temple outgave both of them. The disciples were told to practice what they preached, otherwise they would be unfit for their appointed tasks.

## THE DESIRABILITY OF A FIRM PRIVACY

"But when thou doest alms, let not thy left hand know what thy right hand doeth: that thine alms may be in secret; and thy Father who seeth in secret himself shall reward thee openly" (vv. 3,4). I remember a wealthy man who revelled in sending gifts to people; his letters were always signed Mr. Anonymous. He loved to do this because everybody was aware of his identity. During the difficult days in Britain, when the Second World War enforced a very strict rationing of all food supplies, I often wondered who left bags of groceries at certain doors — but I never did discover the identity of the unknown donor. It meant that I looked with gratitude upon everybody, and yet I never felt embarrassed in the presence of anyone. When a man gives secretly, he does not expect praise, but he knows the indescribable joy of having helped someone; and this promotes a satisfaction difficult to obtain anywhere else.

## THE DELIGHT OF A FATHER'S PRAISE

"...thy Father which seeth in secret himself shall reward thee openly" (v. 4b). I shall always remember a famous Welsh preacher known throughout the country as one of the greatest orators of the nation. There was a day in London when he was being honored by the greatest dignitaries of the church, and to the illustrious gathering came the little old-fashioned mother of the man to be honored. Her dress was unattractive when compared with the elegant garb of the great men and women of society. No one would have noticed her, but when the enthusiasm was at its greatest, that wonderful minister went among the audience, took his mother by the hand, and slowly, carefully, led her to the platform. She seemed a little ill-at-ease, but, proudly, the son indicated he owed everything to the little lady, whose sacrifice had put him through college, whose encouragement had sustained him when the problems of life had been overwhelming, and whose love had cheered him when, discouraged, he was tempted to abandon his work. It was a marvelous moment when that huge audience rose to give the mother a standing ovation. Maybe, even the angels clapped their hands when they saw a great man who was not ashamed of the lowly place from which he had arisen. That same man will always be remembered in Wales for the enthusiasm with which he received news of his acceptance into the college. He jumped upon the kitchen table, and, with a cry of joy, kicked a lamp through the window!

It will be equally thrilling when, in the presence of angels, God will honor those who were faithful to their high calling. Yet there is nothing to suggest that God's rewards will be kept until we leave this world. Constantly, life is proving to be the most surprising and joyous thing imaginable. The Bible says, "But seek ye first the kingdom of God, and His righteousness; and all these things shall be added unto you" (Matt. 6:33). There are many and varied ways by which God honors and blesses His servants, even in the midst of their earthly labor. In point of fact, "No good thing will he withhold from them that walk uprightly" (Ps. 84:11).

## SECTION TWO

*Expository Notes on the Lord's Teaching His Disciples How to Pray*

**And when thou prayest, thou shalt not be as the hypocrites are: for they love to pray standing in the synagogues and in the corners of the streets, that they may be seen of men. Verily I say unto you, They have their reward. But thou, when thou prayest, enter into thy closet, and when thou hast shut thy door, pray to thy Father which is in secret; and thy Father who seeth in secret shall reward thee openly (vv. 5-6).**

Let it be recognized that within the borders of Israel and throughout the other countries of the Middle East, prayer is considered to be the most sacred ordinance on earth. It ill behooves Christians to criticize Jews and Moslems, for often they put us to shame by the sincerity of their prayer life. I have seen Jews standing in the aisles of crowded airplanes when their prayer time arrived. It mattered not that the stewardesses had to move around them, and that the entire procedure meant increasing inconvenience. When the time for prayer arrived, the Jews stood to pray, irrespective of what any person thought or said. I have seen Moslems kneeling in crowded streets when the call from the minarets announced it was time to pray. Many Christians would pray silently and proceed to their destination. The Jews loved to pray, but sometimes their motives were impure.

## THE SECRET PLACE

Some Pharisees stood on the corner of the street — that is, they paused at a place where people approaching from two or more directions could see what was being done and praise the man who was doing it. Jesus said that such men were anxious *to be seen.* Talkative onlookers would broadcast the news that the "man who prayed" was a holy man, and thus his reputation among the influential of the community would be greatly enhanced. This was not true prayer and was never recognized by God. It was for this purpose that Jesus advised His followers to enter into their closets, and to close the door, and to pray secretly. If they did as He commanded, then only God and they would be aware of the prayer. Worship is the experience enjoyed when a man sits at God's feet, asking nothing. He confesses how much he loves his Lord. Prayer is the straight line between two points — the need of man and the sufficiency of God.

## THE SPECIAL PRAYER

"Pray to thy Father" (v. 6b). True prayer gives God work. Prayer is asking for something which only God can give. There is a story which strikingly illustrates this principle of directness in prayer. A prayer meeting was being held in a Yorkshire Chapel, and a few people were there who knew what prayer meant. There wandered into that meeting a man from the city, who had very little understanding of the force, fire, and fervor of true prayer meetings. He had the most terrible habit of *making prayers,* and he made a prayer in that meeting which consisted of beautiful sentences, in which he gave God all sorts of information which the Lord knew long before the man was born. For nearly twenty minutes he prayed. At last he said, "And now, Lord, what more shall we say unto Thee?" One old man, who knew his way into the Secret Place, and who was weary and tired of this exhibition, cried out, "Call Him Feyther, mon, and ax for summat" (Quoted from Dr. G. Campbell Morgan's book on Matthew, p. 60). Prayer is taking hold of the bellropes and pulling so hard that all heaven becomes aware that someone on earth is needing assistance.

## THE SPIRITUAL POWER

"Thy Father...shall reward thee openly" (v. 6d). There are many ways in which this may be accomplished. God is able to flood the suppliant's soul with joy inexpressible; the man or woman who makes time to pray in secret will emerge from the meeting entirely radiant. Moses, after prolonged communion with God, came down from the mountain unaware that the skin of his face shone. The Lord may signally anoint His servant with unique power for service. Simon Peter and the other disciples spent ten days in prayer, and then emerged equipped to meet the need on the day of Pentecost. Their combined efforts at that time brought thousands of souls to the Savior's feet. There might be a sense in which another Scripture verse could be quoted in support of this assertion. When Christians stand at the judgment seat of Christ, their works will be tried in the fires of God's scrutiny; and what abides the test will be rewarded. There, in the presence of an innumerable host, faithful workers will be rewarded openly, and their gains will last forever. The superficial Pharisees drew attention to themselves; the dedicated Christian draws attention to the Lord, but, in so doing, earns the immortal gratitude of all helped by his endeavors.

> **But when ye pray, use not vain repetitions, as the heathen do: for they think that they shall be heard for their much speaking. Be not ye therefore like unto them: for your Father knoweth what things ye have need of, before ye ask him. After this manner therefore pray ye: Our Father which art in heaven, Hallowed be Thy name. Thy kingdom come. Thy will be done in earth, as it is in heaven. Give us this day our daily bread. And forgive us our debts, as we forgive our debtors. And lead us not into temptation, but deliver us from evil: For thine is the kingdom, and the power, and the glory, for ever. Amen (vv. 7-13).**

## A NEEDLESS EXHIBITION

Years ago in the southern counties of England, the people told of a strange incident which happened in one of their country churches. A pastor's son had been accepted as a student into the denominational seminary and, after one semester, had returned to his home for a short vacation. The church members thought it would be proper to invite the young man to take part in the Sunday morning service. The minister thereupon suggested that his son should offer the prayer. Unfortunately, the student had learned new words with which the country people were not familiar. The young man began his prayer by saying, "Lord God Almighty! What shall we call Thee? Omnipotent? Omniscient? Omnipresent? Lord, God Almighty! What shall we call Thee?" Suddenly one old elder sitting close to the pulpit, looked up and said, "Son, call Him Heavenly Father." The next part of the story, which I cannot guarantee to be accurate, went on to describe how the people were amazed that same evening, when the minister announced his text "Lord, look upon my son for he is a lunatic, and sore vexed!"

As a lad in my home church, I became accustomed to the two prayers said at every service. They were known as the long and the short prayers. When the pastor prayed the long prayer, he continued for twenty-five minutes and prayed for everyone from Dan to Beersheba. During that time, several of the elderly members slept. The short prayer was just a three-to-five minute oration in which the pastor begged the Lord to bless the meeting! At that time, it all seemed so strange to me, for I was just beginning to learn the strange things to be found in organized religion.

The Jews had very many prayers, some of which were to be recited at special times and in special places. The whole system became a tiresome ritual; something to be endured, not enjoyed.

## A NOTEWORTHY EXAMPLE

Luke, in his eleventh chapter, tells how the Lord's Prayer was given in answer to the request of a disciple (11:1). Matthew is content to tell how the Lord replied. Actually, this should be called "The Disciples' Prayer." The Lord's prayer is found in the seventeenth chapter of John's Gospel. It is significant that the personal pronoun "I" is never found in this marvelous prayer, suggested by Jesus. The example divides into two sections. The first ascribes glory to God the Father, and the second expresses the needs of the people who pray.

"First, the disciples are reminded of the *Majesty of God.* HALLOWED BE THY NAME. The Almighty is to be addressed as a Father, and, to say the least, this was the introduction of a new relationship. The God whose power had shaken Mount Sinai, whose laws made the people tremble, could hardly have been addressed in this manner. The coming of the Lord Jesus had unveiled new characteristics in the Godhead. It was still true that God was holy, but the approach to His throne should be that of love for a parent, and not fear for a Creator. It was the constant consideration of this important fact that produced, within the suppliant, the right frame of mind in which prayer could be offered. Secondly, the prayer suggests the *Purposes of God.* It was true that the suppliant desired certain things, but the will of God always has priority in the hearts of true believers. Shortly, the praying soul will ask for certain commodities, but the fact that this request had precedence was a confession that if God desired something else, even the prayers to follow could be forgotten. This was another instance of the Lord teaching His followers to say, 'Not my will, but Thine be done.' Nevertheless, if the purposes of the Almighty could be fulfilled, and at the same time, these other requests find favor with the Father, then it was the desire of the believer to ask for certain things. These requests are divided into three categories. (1) Food for the body. (2) Forgiveness for the soul. (3) Fortitude for the spirit" (Reprinted from the author's commentary on *Luke's Thrilling Gospel,* p. 266). See the supplement on "The Lord's Prayer" at the end of this chapter.

In this prayer, when we ask for *food* for the body (bread to sustain our earthly lives) our thoughts are directed to God, *the Father,* Creator and Sustainer of life here and eternally. When we request *forgiveness,* our thoughts center on *God, the Son,* who provided for our forgiveness and cleansing, and adoption into the family of God. Asking for *strength* to yield not to temptation, reminds us of *God, the Holy Spirit,* the Illuminator, Strengthener, Comforter, Guardian, and Guide for our new life in Christ.

## SECTION THREE

*Expository Notes on the Need for a Forgiving Spirit*

### A NEW EXHORTATION

> **For if ye forgive men their trespasses, your heavenly Father will forgive you: But if ye forgive not men their trespasses, neither will your Father forgive your trespasses" (vv. 14-15).**

The Lord not only commanded His followers to pray; they were told not to expect from God what they were unwilling to share with others. Perhaps this is a truth which should be preached more often among the churches. Jesus spoke of a man who was forgiven ten thousand talents (263 million dollars) but who was unwilling to forgive his neighbor one hundred pence (seven dollars and fifty cents) (Matt. 18:23-35). See notes on this incident in chapter eighteen. An unforgiving spirit is a cloud to eclipse the sun; continuing animosity is a cancer threatening the life and usefulness of any Christian. Jesus urged His followers to pray, but if the prayer was not offered from a kind and sensitive heart, the supplication was a waste of time.

## SECTION FOUR

*Expository Notes on the Virtue of Secret Fasting*

> **Moreover when ye fast, be not, as the hypocrites, of a sad countenance: for they disfigure their faces, that they may appear unto men to fast. Verily I say unto you, They have their reward. But thou, when thou fastest, anoint thine head, and wash thy face; That thou appear not unto men to fast, but unto thy Father which is in secret; and thy Father, which seeth in secret, shall reward thee openly (vv. 16-18).**

### THE IMPORTANCE OF FASTING TO A JEW

It is extremely difficult for any citizen of the Western world to appreciate the importance of fasting to a man in the East. Very few Christians include fasting in their pattern of life, and most of them forget that it was a valued part of the daily experience of the founders of the church. I shall never forget watching a "holy man" as he sat cross-legged in an Indian temple. He was absolutely motionless, and remained in that attitude for many hours. He might have been in some kind of a self-imposed hypnotic trance, but he was regarded with awe by all the Hindus who saw him. When I quietly asked about his identity, I was informed he was a well-known holy man fasting before his god. During my stay in South Africa, I was a privileged guest at a Moslem Feast of Ramadan, and I was amazed by the enthusiasm with which thousands of worshipers celebrated the event. No food of any kind was consumed between sunrise and sunset; everybody practiced self-restraint. However, the fast was followed by an immense banquet in which everybody ate far more than was needed. Their religious ecstasy surpassed anything I had ever witnessed among Christians. To them fasting was of supreme importance. This applies throughout all the countries of the Middle East.

All Jews considered fasting to be a sacred duty; it was vitally connected with every phase of life. Actually there was only one mandatory fast and that was linked with the Day of Atonement. Speaking of those observances, Moses said, "For on that day shall the priest make an atonement for you, to cleanse you, that ye may be clean from all your sins before the LORD. It shall be a sabbath of rest unto you, *and ye shall afflict your souls,* by a statute for ever" (Lev. 16:30-31). One of the Hebrew laws insisted that "On the Day of Atonement, it is forbidden to eat, or to drink, or to bathe, or to anoint oneself, or to wear sandals, or to indulge in conjugal intercourse." That day was considered to be most holy, and nothing was permitted to defile it.

Nevertheless throughout the centuries, the practice of fasting spread to other aspects of life; it became an expression of repentance for sin or of grief over the death of a family member. I had a great friend who resided in Israel, but on one of my visits to Tel-Aviv, I failed to recognize him. He had grown a bushy beard which completely covered his face. When he approached, I thought he was a complete stranger, and said so. He smiled and explained that his mother had died, and according to Jewish custom, he had to refrain from shaving for a certain number of days. Some ardent worshipers would actually scourge their bodies to impress upon God the genuineness of their remorse for sin. Fasting could be seen in every facet of Jewish national life. Jesus never condemned the practice, for in some senses it was beneficial. He denounced the hypocrisy that sometimes accompanied it. He drew attention to the disfigurement of their faces, their sad expressions, and the obvious intent to enhance their religious prestige. They wanted people to believe they were good, when, in actual fact, they were evil.

## THE IDEAL FASTING TO JESUS

"But thou, when thou fastest, anoint thine head, and wash thy face; That thou appear not unto men to fast, but unto thy Father which is in secret"(vv. 17,18b). True fasting is the soul speaking to God; it is the practical side of intercession; it is the evidence that the supplicant means business! Fasting designed to influence onlookers is poor advertising! Many of the Pharisees belonged to this category. Remember the man who went up into the temple to pray, thought it necessary to remind God that he fasted twice every week (see Luke 18:11-12)? Apparently he considered God to be uninformed or forgetful, and he was extremely anxious that God should be brought up-to-date! Probably he also made sure that his neighbors were informed! Christ's followers had to be different. They were to fast secretly, and be joyful before their audiences.

The church has probably made two great mistakes. (1) We confine this teaching to matters of physical sustenance, and insist that to fast means to go without food. (2) We forget that fasting had a place in New Testament practice, and therefore refrain from it in any form. Americans, accustomed as they are to abundance, have developed a terrible habit of overindulgence. What they want, they get. Alas, if their bodies are the temples of the Holy Spirit, they have gone to extremes to make sure He has sufficient space in His house! Medical science affirms that excessive eaters deprive God of thirty percent of the time which normally might be given in active service for His kingdom. This is sin, and no amount of argument can make it anything else.

Fasting implies self-restraint. Food may be the least of my worries. Some people have poor appetites, and it would impose no hardship for them to miss a dozen meals. Self-restraint could apply to time; illegitimate pleasure; excessive love of money; unholy ambitions, and hours spent viewing harmful programs on television. True fasting teaches that a man is willing to sacrifice the most desirable thing in his life, in order to experience God's blessing. What we possess is nothing; what He can give is indispensable. To receive and know heaven's benediction should be the great desire in life. No price is too great to pay for what God alone can give.

## THE INDISPENSABILITY OF FASTING TO JOY

"Thy Father...shall reward thee openly" (v. 18c). The Father's commendation indicates that we are pleasing in His sight; that He has recognized the value of our labor. His rewarding of our actions not only indicates successful service, but a promise also that "no good thing will he withhold from those that walk uprightly" (Ps. 84:11). To know these facts is to experience a degree of happiness unobtainable elsewhere. Jesus said, "My joy I give unto you, that your joy may be full." This is the experience of working together *with* God. He is not only pleased with our efforts, He also finds pleasure in participating in our endeavor. He will give *rewards* unobtainable elsewhere. This is the visible evidence that God is on our side, and "if God be for us, who can be against us?" (Rom. 8:31). Here is confidence, peace, and overflowing joy. When God is first; that is, when God is the head of the firm, He becomes responsible for every detail of business transacted in His name. He becomes the guarantee that my health, future, and well-being will never be overlooked. The workman could never have a better "Boss"!; the servant could never have a more kindly Master; the trusting child could never have a more reliable Father. Jesus was merely trying to inform His followers that God pays excellent wages to His workmen.

### SECTION FIVE

*Expository Notes on What It Means to Trust in the King of Kings*

**Lay not up for yourselves treasures upon earth, where moth and dust doth corrupt, and where thieves break through and steal: But lay up for yourselves treasures in heaven, where neither moth nor rust doth corrupt, and where thieves do not break through nor steal: For where your treasure is, there will your heart be also (vv. 19-21).**

During the time when our Lord was upon earth, banking institutions were unknown. If a man possessed wealth, he had to be his own banker. As we shall discover when we study the parable of the treasure hid in the field (Chapter 13), most men hid their wealth in an obscure place. They often buried it. As an alternative, some people invested surplus money in material things such as property, clothing, and cattle. We are reminded how the servant of Elijah asked Naaman for *two changes* of garments (2 Kings 5:22). Alas, Achan also coveted "a goodly Babylonish garment" and *paid for it with his life* (see Josh. 7:19-26). When the Lord gave advice to His disciples, He described three word pictures with which they were familiar. Moths, rust, and thieves were the common enemies of all homes and, alas, many householders quickly discovered it was easier to lose their possessions than replace them.

If moths were allowed to stay among clothing, the result was always disastrous. Even the most costly fabric could be ruined. The Greek word used for rust is *brosis,* and according to Thayer, means to "eat away." That was precisely what moths and rust did to clothing and other articles of value. The third classification of enemies, cited thieves who "broke through and stole." This picture was also easily understood, for the dwellings of the peasants were made of mud walls; a kind of plaster over a framework. It was not difficult for a thief to break through a back wall and gain admittance to the dwelling. The Lord was supplying a vivid contrast between temporal and eternal values. He stressed the fact that earthly things would fade into insignificance, whereas the things of real worth were immortal. Earthly pleasures and treasures could end overnight; the treasures of heaven were timeless and of incalculable worth. Elsewhere, He stressed the identical truth when He compared and contrasted two men who erected houses. One man built upon sand; the other upon the rock. The one builder saw his treasure disappear quickly; the other lived safely within the house which no storm could destroy (see Matt. 7:24-29). The Savior appeared to summarize all His teaching when He said, "For where your treasure is, there will your heart be also." If a man's interests are centered in earthly things, all his talents, affections, and pleasures will be focused on his immediate present; eternity will not attract him. On the other hand, if a man has recognized the importance of eternal verities, his entire life will be lived with that thought in mind. He will ever be mindful of the truth: "Live for self, you live in vain; live for Christ, you live again."

> **The light [lamp] of the body is the eye: if therefore thine eye be single [healthy], thy whole body shall be full of light. But if thine eye be evil, thy whole body shall be full of darkness...No man can serve two masters: for either he will hate the one, and love the other; or else he will hold to the one, and, despise the other. Ye cannot serve God and mammon [money] (vv. 22-24).**

The Greek word for "single" is *haplous,* and its corresponding noun is *haplotees.* In Bible translations, these words mean "generous" and "generosity." James speaks of God who gives liberally (James 1:5) and the adverb he uses is *haplos.* Similarly in Romans 12:8, Paul urges his friends to give liberally (*haplos*). To get the real meaning of this we must translate *haplous,* not "single," but generous; it is the *generous eye* which Jesus is commending. In the *Authorized Version* the word translated "evil" is *poneeros*. Although it is the normal meaning of the word, both in the New Testament and in the Septuagint, *poneeros* regularly means "reluctantly" or "grudgingly." In Deuteronomy we read of the duty of lending to a brother who is in need. The matter was complicated by the fact that every seventh year was a year of release when debts were cancelled. Consider the possibility that if the seventh year were near, a cautious lender might refuse to help, lest the person helped might take advantage of the seventh year never to repay his debt. So the law lays it down: "Beware that there be not a thought in thy wicked heart, saying, The seventh year, the year of release, is at hand; and thine eye be evil *(poneeros)* against thy poor brother, and thou givest him nought" (Deut. 15:9). Clearly *poneeros* there means "reluctantly, grudging, and ungenerous." It is the advice of the proverb, "Eat thou not the bread of him that hath an evil eye" (Prov. 23:6). The real meaning of the passage is clear when we translate *poneeros* not "evil," but "grudging" and "ungenerous." So Jesus is saying, that generosity gives a clear and undistorted view of life and of people; the grudging and ungenerous spirit distorts your view of life and of people.

Obviously the Lord was indicating that the eye was the gateway to the soul; that what it saw, influenced the mind and heart of the beholder. The eye was the camera, feeding to the television screen of the soul, holy or unholy scenes, which in turn could make the sanctuary into a holy place or a scene of regrettable filth. A kindly eye could produce a very unselfish, generous soul; a lusting eye could defile the temple of the mind. If a man focused on questionable things, his entire life could degenerate until he became self-centered; miserly and unresponsive to needs around him. If he saw only the overflowing love of God for all men, he would likely become one of God's messengers helping to solve the oppressing problems of humanity.

The Lord also raised the question of choice. In His estimation, it was impossible to serve two masters at the same time. We are living in days when economic situations compel some people to work at two jobs. That often is necessary even if it be not desirable. The Savior was speaking of other things. It is not possible to serve God and Satan at the same time. It is only possible for one being to occupy the throne of one's affection. Either we dethrone self in order to enthrone Christ, or we forget the claims of the Lord and pursue our selfish desires.

**Therefore I say unto you, Take no thought for your life, what ye shall eat, or what ye shall drink; nor yet for your body, what ye shall put**

on. Is not the life more than meat [food], and the body than raiment? Behold the fowls of the air; for they sow not, neither do they reap, nor gather into barns; yet your heavenly Father feedeth them. Are ye not much better than they? Which of you by taking thought can add one cubit unto his stature? And why take ye thought for raiment? Consider the lilies of the field, how they grow; they toil not, neither do they spin; And yet I say unto you, That even Solomon in all his glory was not arrayed like one of these. Wherefore, if God so clothe the grass of the field, which today is, and tomorrow is cast into the oven, shall he not much more clothe you, O ye of little faith? (vv. 25-30).

Once again we have four areas of thought inviting investigation, and each one is rich in content. Here we find the Savior instructing His followers about the necessity of exercising faith in their heavenly Father.


## THE FRAIL SKILLS

"Behold the fowls of the air.... Consider the lilies of the field" (vv. 26,28). The Savior was an expert teacher who found in ordinary things the most extraordinary truths. It would be untrue to say the birds have no wisdom, and it is unsafe to affirm that the flowers had no controlling motivation in life. Even the greatest scientist would have difficulty making a bird's nest with the same skill exhibited by a thrush or a linet. There are flowers which possess a strange kind of wisdom which enables them to trap an invading insect. Yet, they seem so helpless and valueless when compared with humans. The prevailing thought expressed in the Lord's instruction was the necessity to avoid being burdened with anxiety and worry. There are realms into which we cannot penetrate; we do not know if birds ever worry about future events; we cannot tell if flowers are ever filled with dread. Apparently, they function in life, fulfilling their purpose, and their Creator attends to the other necessities. The same God who made the birds also planned that bushes and trees would produce berries to feed them. The flowers may not endure forever, but throughout their short life-span they exhibit beauty unsurpassed in God's great universe. No flower designs its own excellence; no bird creates its own distinctive song. These characteristics are inherent in the creature, because God in His wisdom ordained them. And yet at their best, they are but birds and flowers. After one or two days the wild flowers begin to die and the colors to fade. Then, to kindle a fire within the stoves, the housewife gathers the dry materials and they are "cast into the oven." If God should exercise such interest and care in the lesser things of life, it becomes obvious that He will never forget nor forsake the man whom He made in His own image.

## THE FAITHFUL SUPPLIER

"Wherefore, if God so clothe the grass of the field..." (v. 30). If God feeds the birds who never build storage barns, who never sow nor reap harvests, then He will not be slow to aid those who are very precious in His sight. The world has known many calamities during which birds have been destroyed and the grass deprived of sustenance, but more often than not, this has been the result of human interference with the laws of nature. There were birds, flowers, and grass in the time of Adam, and without any supervising overseer except God, these have continued throughout the ages. To create something and then to abandon it would be foolish. Similarly, if God abandoned what He made; if the Creator forsook the created, then He would only demonstrate that He was wrong in the first place. God has always been faithful to those who trusted Him, and to doubt or question the continuance of His care would be to exhibit stupidity.

## THE FABULOUS SPLENDOR

"...even Solomon in all his glory was not arrayed like one of these" (v. 29). Dr. G. Campbell Morgan, writing of this passage of Scripture, says, "Take that flower, that huleh lily, gorgeous and beautiful in its coloring, and put it by the side of Solomon in his magnificence, in his robes of gold and silver and splendor — the lily is more beautifully clothed than Solomon. Take the finest fabric that monarch ever wore, and submit it to microscopic examination, and it is sackcloth. Take the lily and submit its garment of delicate velvet to microscopic examination and investigation, and the more perfect your lens, the more exquisite the weaving of the robe of the lily will be seen....No garment loomed to the finest and softest texture is anything but rough sackcloth when placed by the side of the drapery with which God clothes the lilies. Christ says: 'Open your eyes, My children, and look at the lilies scattered over the valleys and mountains, growing among thorns, and know that when God makes the lily, kings desire and cannot obtain such a robing. Looking at the flower, and seeing all its decking, know this: He who clothes the lilies will clothe His children too.' There is not a flower and not a petal which, in exquisite finish and delicate perfection, would not put all the robes of a king to shame" (*The Gospel According to Matthew*, p. 69).

## THE FORTUNATE SAINTS

"Shall he not much more clothe you, 0 ye of little faith...your heavenly Father knoweth that ye have need of all these things" (v. 30,32). Remember that these sayings of Jesus were spoken during His messages on the mountain. Eventually, the disciples descended to the valley to begin their greatest task. They were to proceed without visible means of support; they were not to be overanxious about material possessions, nor disturbed by threats against their lives. The Lord who commissioned them would not forget them. Their trust should be unfaltering; their eyes focused on one single goal — to please their Master. Each day they were to rest in the glorious fact that God, who used the ravens to feed Elijah, would supply their needs, whatever they might be. They were extremely fortunate and should always remember that God who held the universe, would have no difficulty holding them.

**Therefore take no thought, saying, What shall we eat? or, What shall we drink? or Wherewithal shall we be clothed? (For after all these things do the Gentiles seek:) for your heavenly Father knoweth that ye have need of all these things. But seek ye first the kingdom of God, and his righteousness; and all these things shall be added unto you. Take therefore no thought for the morrow: for the morrow shall take thought for the things of itself. Sufficient unto the day is the evil thereof (vv. 31-34).**

When Dr. Lionel Fletcher, that great and wonderful preacher of the last generation, was visiting South Africa, he spoke at a meeting held in the city of Cape Town. It was a service specially convened for women, and the topic was "Women's Greatest Sin." Everybody began to speculate what this might be, and when the time arrived, the great hall was packed to capacity. Dr. Fletcher stood on the platform, smiled, and said, "You are all expecting something sensational. Probably you have thought of sexual relationships, vanity, and many other possibilities. No, women's greatest sin is WORRY." Many listeners were disappointed for they had anticipated something more spicy in the affairs of daily living, but Dr. Fletcher was correct. Many women are perpetual worriers. If they see a fly crawling up a wall, they are apt to worry lest the tiny creature suffers a heart attack before it reaches the top! Worry may not be a sin in the estimation of some folk, but it is certainly a depressant. One cannot have true faith in God and have a heart filled with worry. If God be for us, who can be against us? The disciples were commanded to banish worry from their souls. They were to advance into their spiritual battles realizing their heavenly Father was well acquainted with their needs. He could not instruct them to complete a task and at the same time withhold the tools necessary for the work. If they constantly sought the kingdom of God, and remained firm in their resolve that His righteousness should be their goal, failure would be impossible. That did not mean they were to abstain from making plans for the future. It did not mean they were to live only for the moment, believing tomorrow would never come. God honors wise planning, and the complacent people who never use their brains always discover, too late, that something has gone wrong. Jesus was trying to teach that today should not be ruined by anxious dread of what might come tomorrow. If God could protect His children today, He would also be able to repeat the performance tomorrow. They were not to be overwhelmingly frightened by any possibilities. They were to live for the present, enjoy it to the fullest, do the best possible for their Master, and today's experiences would strengthen them for whatever the morrow had in store. I have often been asked by young ministers what they should do, or what rules they should follow as they begin their work. My answer has always been the same, ''Do the best you can for Christ; don't worry, and leave the rest to God.''

## A SUPPLEMENT TO THE STUDY OF
## THE LORD'S PRAYER (MATT. 6:9-13)

*THE MIRACLE WITH GOD…Our Father Which Art In Heaven Hallowed Be Thy Name*

''And it came to pass, that, as he was praying in a certain place, when he ceased, one of his disciples said unto him, Lord, teach us to pray, as John also taught his disciples. And he said unto them, When ye pray, say, Our Father….'' (Luke 11:1-2). The Lord's response opened a new world to the eyes of the disciples; they were presented with a pattern prayer which thrilled their souls. The idea that the God of Mount Sinai could become their heavenly Father surely astounded them. The rabbis, the Pharisees, the scribes, had never taught such truth; it was amazing. God was far away; the austere, the mystical One, whose manifestations of power often terrorized the nation. Their ancestors had been warned not to touch the Holy Mountain; to disobey would have been fatal. God was Someone to be held in awe, to be kept at a distance; proximity to the Holy One was fraught with peril. He had the ability to seek out faults in His people, and, as with Achan, to be found guilty was to be sentenced to death by stoning. God was to be feared, not loved. Jesus shattered the old conceptions and indicated that God could be as a Father, waiting to put arms of love around a returning prodigal. He taught that God was like Himself; that God could lift little children into His arms and cuddle them to His breast. God could love the outcast, touch the unclean leper, and do even more than the most precious earthly parent. "Yes," said Jesus, "When you pray, call Him FATHER. That is exactly what He desires to be. Yet, on the other hand, never lose the sense of His holiness. When you pray say, 'Our Father...Hallowed be thy name.'" God was still God, but somehow, He seemed to be a lot nearer. Perhaps they had come closer! A miracle had been performed in heaven — or in them — or in both.

*THE MANIFESTATION OF GOD...Thy Kingdom Come.*
*Thy Will Be Done In Earth As It Is In Heaven*

Their first request was to be completely selfless. That God desired to reign upon earth was understood; all the prophets had expressed that fact. True worship is the cooperation of a trusting soul with the expressed will of the Father. What He desired should always take preference over what man might want. If a disciple learned how to subject his desires to the revealed will of God, then his prayers would be answered, for in the fulfillment of the eternal purposes would come that for which the human soul longed. Alas, sometimes, prayer can be an expression of selfish thinking. We desire something for our own enjoyment. We ask, but often forget to say, "Thy will, not mine, be done." If God does not understand and approve of our petitions, we hope He will discover some way of cooperating with us. It must be noted that the personal pronoun "I" is not found throughout this pattern prayer. The praying man must ever be conscious of the needs of other people, and therefore it is permissible to say "us," as that identifies the soul with men and women with similar needs. True prayer is the channel by which we communicate our adoration and love to a heavenly Father, and, at the same time, it becomes the return highway along which God answers His people. The man who thinks more of himself than of the people among whom he lives, has never truly appreciated the value of interceding with God. If God wishes to establish His kingdom upon earth, then His people should not only pray for it, but they should dedicate all their talents to make the divine dream come true. If we expect God to work on our behalf, we should be anxious to work on His behalf, by helping to establish that kingdom within the hearts of our neighbors. "Thy kingdom come," is always more important than "Lord, help me."

## THE MANNA FROM GOD...Give Us This Day Our Daily Bread

This is the first legitimate request made on behalf of human needs. It should be recognized that it was for *needs* not *luxuries*! Bread was necessary for the maintenance of life; food was necessary for the strengthening of the body; without its aid, continuing service for the kingdom would become an impossibility. Alas, we often ask for what we do not need. Babies often want to play with knives or matches, and the wise parent refuses to cooperate. Often we ask for things which might be harmful, and we are disappointed when God refuses to grant our requests. No person can be wrong when asking for bare necessities. When God is pleased to grant additional supplies, we should be profoundly grateful; but true prayer is confined to what we need, and not to the ever-lengthening list of what we might like to possess. When the children of Israel were hungry in the wilderness, God sent them manna from heaven (see Exod. 16). He also provided additional food, but Jesus seemed to be emphasizing that the unchanging God could and would send the daily manna to His servants. If it ever became necessary, He would perform miracles on their behalf. At other times, He would provide jobs and give strength to perform those bread-earning tasks. Prayer should never be the evidence of laziness. Muscles that are never used are apt to become useless. Even Paul, to earn his daily bread, became a maker of tents. It is good sense never to ask God to do something we can do ourselves. As a very young evangelist in South Africa, I said to a very old minister, "We must pray about that project." His answer, born of long experience, shocked me. He said, "That's fine, but God is very, very busy; perhaps you should try to do it yourself." The old man helped with my spiritual education.

## THE MERCY OF GOD... And Forgive Us Our Debts
## As We Forgive Our Debtors

God is never pleased with stingy people. As He shares His mercy with us, we must be willing to share with others. The Lord's pattern of giving is to "give...good measure, pressed down, and shaken together, and running over" (see Luke 6:38). God had made special provision whereby His sinful people might be pardoned. Jeremiah had written: "It is of the LORD's mercies that we are not consumed, because his compassions fail not'' (Lam. 3:22). Nevertheless, the Lord said, "Freely ye have received; freely give." This applied to every walk of life. If a man expects God to pardon his sins, then he should also be willing to pardon any person who has offended him. After Adonijah had tried to seize the throne of Israel, King Solomon was determined to execute vengeance upon the criminal. Adonijah, realizing he had no hope elsewhere, ran to cling to the horns of the altar. His action saved his life. When Solomon heard that his enemy had sought sanctuary at the altar, he gave orders that the man should be pardoned. Probably as the king thought of the altar of forgiveness, he realized that in God's sight he might seem as guilty as Adonijah. Therefore, as Solomon expected to be forgiven by God, he felt obliged to share that forgiveness with his greatest enemy. All this had a bearing on the teaching of the disciples. They should not expect God to forgive their sins unless they were willing to share the blessing with other people. "As we forgive our debtors" should never be empty rhetoric; it must be the pattern for daily conduct. An unforgiving spirit closes God's outlet of blessing. Even Paul wrote: "And be ye kind one to another, tenderhearted, forgiving one another, even as God for Christ's sake hath forgiven you" (Eph. 4:32).

*THE METHODS OF GOD...And Lead Us Not Into Temptation, But Deliver Us From Evil*

Throughout this Gospel, there is a difference between temptation and testing. There is implied evil in temptation; someone is trying to seduce us; it speaks of moral and spiritual dangers against which the soul must be on guard. Testing is not necessarily evil. Bridges must be tested with weighty burdens prior to public use. Steel girders must be subjected to stress and strain above the normal degree to be expected daily. Every kind of machinery must be tried and proved reliable ere the products are offered for sale. This procedure is certainly not evil; it is necessary and beneficial. Both ideas might be incorporated in the disciple's prayer. By constant dependence upon God it would be possible to fill the mind with thoughts of virtue, and to prevent evil from invading mental territory. To avoid a fall is infinitely better than to recover from one. A fence on the edge of a cliff is more to be desired than an ambulance at the bottom. If a stitch in time saves nine, then prompt action on behalf of the believer might prevent disaster. A man can hardly succumb, if his thoughts are centered on the God of his salvation.

If the soul is to be tested, it is always healthy to be conscious of one's inability or weakness. A man is never as weak as when he feels tremendously strong. A man is never so ignorant as when he thinks he knows everything! The prayer might be paraphrased: "Lord, I am so weak, do not burden me with something beyond my strength. Please be sure that I shall not let You down when used for public service. Let me be the best possible; always dependable, useful, and pleasing in Thy sight. And Lord, since I am no match for the devil, please deliver me from his power. I know that my greatest strength lies in looking to Thee for help, so I am asking, please surround me with Thy protective care, and deliver me from the evil one.''

*THE MAJESTY OF GOD...For Thine Is the Kingdom, and the Power, and the Glory, For ever. Amen*

It should never be forgotten that this prayer begins with God and ends with Him. He is the Alpha and the Omega of everything. We begin by addressing Him as OUR FATHER; we finish by remembering that He is the absolute Lord of everything and every person. The miracle of His Fatherhood is appreciated only when we consider that, although He is so great, His loving condescension brought limitless resources within reach of the most undeserving of His children. The kingdom is His; His power cannot be overthrown; His inscrutable glory may never be completely understood, and yet it is something in which redeemed sinners will share eternally. We stand in awe when we see His amazing power in the world around us. When we read of His infallible goodness and unspeakable holiness, we bow in reverence. Yet, when we consider His marvelous love exhibited in the death of His Son, speech fails to express the hidden depths of our souls, and we can only say with the poet:

> Amazing Love, How can it be
> That Thou my God should'st die for me?

The prayer which Jesus taught to His disciples covered every aspect of life. There was nothing left to say, and probably that was the reason why the Lord finished with the glorious word — AMEN — So let it be.

# The Seventh Chapter of Matthew

THEME: *The Conclusion of the Messages on the Mount*

OUTLINE:
    I. The Need to Be Considerate... *"Judge Not"* (Verses 1-6)
    II. The Need to Communicate... *"Ask, Seek, Knock"* (Verses 7-12)
    III. The Need to Be Converted... *"Enter Ye In"* (Verses 13-14)
    IV. The Need to Be Careful... *"Beware of False Prophets"* (Verses 15-23)
    V. The Need to Be Concerned... *"The House Fell"* (Verses 24-29)

## SECTION ONE

*Expository Notes on the Need for Personal Holiness*

**Judge not, that ye be not judged. For with what judgment ye judge, ye shall be judged: and with what measure ye mete, it shall be measured to you again. And why beholdest thou the mote that is in thy brother's eye, but considerest not the beam that is in thine own eye? Or how wilt thou say to thy brother, Let me pull out the mote out of thine eye; and, behold, a beam is in thine own eye? Thou hypocrite, first cast the beam out of thine own eye, and then shalt thou see clearly to cast the mote out of thy brother's eye. Give not that which is holy unto the dogs, neither cast ye your pearls before swine, lest they trample them under their feet, and turn again and rend [lacerate] you (vv. 1-6).**

The Lord was aware that soon His disciples would begin their evangelistic crusades. He was anxious that they should succeed in their mission, but He was concerned lest their endeavors be ruined by unfair criticism. He knew that a critical spirit poisons the life of any believer. Hence He said, ''Judge not, that ye be not judged.'' That was one of the most severe warnings ever given by the Lord. Throughout the church age, more damage has been done by unfair assessment of others than by anything else. It is easy to criticize others, when actually, we may be guilty of worse things. It is never safe to pass judgment on anyone prematurely, for we may be unaware of the circumstances compelling people to act as they do.

The story has been told of D. L. Moody who criticized one of his church members. The man always came into the Sunday morning service, entered the back seat, and promptly went to sleep. Moody became irritated with this behavior and finally expressed his disappointment and anger to the offending brother. The man was crestfallen, and apologized profusely, but Moody became ashamed when the man said, "Pastor, I am an engineer, and I have to drive my train all through Saturday night. I should be in bed, but I hate the thought of my pastor having to preach to my empty seat on Sunday mornings. Everybody tells me I should not come to church, but I cannot stay away. I am so sorry, but when I get into the warm building, my eyes get heavy, and I fall asleep." Moody placed his hand on the man's shoulder, and said, "My brother, it is I who am sorry. You come to church and sleep all you want to. It will be fine with me."

There appears to be an interesting play on words in the Lord's statement, and it is possible that when He uttered these things, His eyes reflected mirth. He said, "And why beholdest thou the mote (*karphos* — chip) that is in thy brother's eye, but considerest not the beam (*dokon* — plank) that is in thine own eye?" No man has the authority to criticize others, unless he himself is above reproach. Millions of Americans have grown accustomed to watching ball games. It has been thought-provoking to watch baseball managers being expelled from games, because they were unable to control their fiery tempers. Many have wondered if any manager has the right to control players, if he is unable to control himself. How can anyone expect from others what he is unwilling to provide?

I shall never forget an angry woman in Devonshire, England, who stormed into the church after we had enjoyed a testimony meeting. One lady had given a brief testimony in which she praised God for His goodness to her. The other, as she listened became infuriated, and later came to express her bitter disapproval of what she had heard. She was very vindictive as she denounced the testifier. I listened patiently as she said, "Sir, you are a stranger in this town; you do not know the people. That woman who stood up is the biggest hypocrite in Bideford. I know, because I live here." Her denunciations came to a halt when she literally ran out of breath! I replied, "Well, well. She is the biggest hypocrite in town. Then she must be going to hell." The critic seemed shocked for a moment, but then with added venom in her voice, said, "Well, so she is." I waited a moment and then asked, "Do you want to go with her? You don't seem to like her very much. If you go to hell with her, you will be together for all eternity. Would you like that?" She replied instantly, and in a very loud voice, "NO! I don't want to be in hell or any other place with her." "Then," I said, "you had better get saved," and I led her to Christ. When she returned the following evening, her face was glowing; her attitude had changed. She said, "Oh, Sir, I am so happy. Isn't God kind to forgive sinners like me?" She never mentioned the woman whom she had so vehemently criticized. Possibly the other lady was doing her best to follow Christ, and sometimes failing to reach the high standards expected of her. It is necessary for every Christian to remember that each moment spent in criticizing other people is a moment lost forever. The time could be better used talking to Christ, or speaking for Him to the people among whom we live.

The statement about giving holy things to dogs and casting pearls before swine presented problems to theologians, but the meaning should be easily discerned. Solomon said there is a time to speak and a time to remain silent. It hardly seems wise to present the treasures of God's Word to people who ridicule and reject the gospel. One evening, prior to my meeting in the First Baptist Church of Vancouver, British Columbia, Canada, a man came to speak with me. I invited him to sit down and explain his problems. He was a very good actor, and directed my attention to places in the Old Testament where sex acts have been recorded. Slowly, very slowly, but with deliberation he stressed certain details, and I began to suspect his motives were impure. Eventually, I excused myself and asked him to leave. Suddenly, his facial expression completely changed, and I thought I was looking into the face of a demon — perhaps I was! He snarled, "Now that I have filled your mind with filth, go and try to preach!" Momentarily, I was filled with both anger and pity. Had I tried to preach to him at that moment, I would have been casting God's pearls before swine. Christians need to be as wise as serpents and as harmless as doves.

### SECTION TWO

*Expository Notes on Christ's Evaluation of Prayer*

**Ask, and it shall be given you; seek, and ye shall find; knock, and it shall be opened unto you: For every one that asketh receiveth; and he**

that seeketh findeth; and to him that knocketh it shall be opened. Or what man is there of you, whom if his son ask bread, will he give him a stone? Or if he ask a fish, will he give him a serpent? If ye then, being evil, know how to give good gifts unto your children, how much more shall your Father which is in heaven give good things to them that ask him? Therefore all things whatsoever ye would that men should do to you, do ye even so to them: for this is the law and the prophets (vv. 7-12).

## THE PERSISTENCE IN PRAYER

Real prayer *changes the person* who prays, and brings to pass things earnestly desired. Yet, of far more importance is the fact that all who come forth from the presence of God do so with "the skin of their faces shining." Moses lingered forty days and nights, and came from the mountain with a revelation which helped change the world. Sometimes it is not possible to receive God's complete revelation in forty seconds. There is need to linger in God's presence. That may be the reason why the Savior divided the prayer experience into three categories. *Asking* means Petitioning. *Seeking* means Persistence. *Knocking* means Perseverance. If at first you don't succeed, try, try again. God likes to know that His children mean business! A casual prayer which seems to say, "0 God, this is what I want, but if You don't give it, I will ask for something else," is a prayer that only reaches a ceiling. A man who is convinced he is asking aright, pulls hard on the bell ropes, and heaven becomes aware that somebody is "on the line." The continuing intercession announces the answer has not been received.

## THE PRIVILEGE OF PRAYER

The Lord said, "Your *Father* which is in heaven." He did not say, "Your God." The Lord emphasized the loving relationship existing between a heavenly Father and children whom He loved intensely. They were not to approach Him with fear and apprehension. Their Father was a multimillionaire and was exceedingly generous. If earthly parents knew how to give gifts to their offspring, God also knew how to reward His children. No father would feed scorpions to his family; no person would offer stones instead of bread. A parent's attitude is governed by love and wisdom. Knowing what is best for the children, the parent exercises care in bestowing gifts or medicine, so that the recipient is helped and not harmed. These facts should enable the disciple to be trusting and grateful: grateful for what is received, and trusting when God says "No."

Let us remember, the disciples were receiving these words of wisdom prior to embarking on their life's work. Soon they would be preaching to crowds of people. Their preaching would be impotent without the power gained through prevailing prayer. They should kneel before God prior to standing before listeners. Then, and only then, would they be true prophets.

## THE PATTERN FOR PRAYER

Matthew says, "If ye then being evil, know how to give good gifts unto your children, how much more shall your Father which is in heaven, give *good things* to them that ask him?" Luke's version is different. He says: "...how much more shall your heavenly Father give *THE HOLY SPIRIT* to them that ask him?" (Luke 11:13). It is almost certain that Luke is correct, and that this might have been one of the sayings often made by the Lord throughout His ministry. Possibly, remembering these occasions, Matthew added the words to his collection of quotations, and incorporated them in his "Sermon on the Mount."

The second of the two versions is by far the more important. To receive *good things* is wonderful; but to receive *the Holy Spirit* is infinitely better. A good thing is inanimate; the Holy Spirit is a living Person, able to accompany, help, and sustain when all else fails. If I possess the Holy Spirit, or better still, *if He possesses me,* I am certain to receive the best heaven can bestow. A good thing is something limited; the Holy Spirit is the Person through whom endless supplies of divine sufficiency reach the trusting soul.

Sometimes prayer can be selfish: there are times when a heavy burden might strengthen muscles; when apparently insoluble problems deepen the prayer experience. "All sunshine makes a desert." This was, indeed, advanced teaching for students about to graduate from Christ's college. A spirit-filled experience enables people to live victoriously before fellow men. They set the example by which, more often than not, they are treated by neighbors. "Give, and it shall be given unto you," is a precept which leads to happiness in every walk of life.

## SECTION THREE

*Expository Notes on Christ's Evangelistic Appeal*

**Enter ye in at the strait gate: for wide is the gate, and broad is the way, that leadeth to destruction, and many there be which go in thereat:**

**Because strait [narrow] is the gate, and narrow [hard] is the way, which leadeth unto life, and few there be that find it (vv. 13-14).**

The inevitability of choosing is something unavoidable. At the gas station, men choose which kind of gas their car requires; in the supermarket customers choose between various brands of every commodity. Life has almost become burdensome because of the necessity of making choices. Nevertheless, if everything were identical, existence would become monotonous.

The texts now to be considered present choices; the Lord Jesus was an excellent evangelist. He mentions *two roads; two decisions; two companies* and *two destinations.* All soul winners should learn from His message. There is a broad, attractive, welcoming road where progress is easy and entertaining. There is a road which is difficult to travel and hard to find. It runs through hostile territory, but it leads to a glorious destination.

There are *two decisions,* and every traveler must choose one, for no person can walk in two directions at the same time. Either he walks the broad road to destruction or the narrow road to life. No one compels him to go either way, but life teaches the impossibility of remaining motionless in regard to eternal realities. Each day we proceed in one direction or the other. There is a difference between a pilgrim and a tramp. One man wanders aimlessly; the other sets his eyes on a desired goal.

There are *two companies.* Many people travel the broad highway; few travel the narrow one. If a man loves noise, revelry, and worldly amusement, he is more likely to be satisfied amid the glamorous, gawdy, paraphernalia which decorates the road to destruction. If a man desires peace, select company, and fellowship of the deepest and best kind, he must search elsewhere. The broad highway does not cater to those seeking blessedness. The true church has nothing in common with the revelry of the worldlings who hasten toward their own funerals.

There are *two destinies.* Jesus said the broad road led to destruction; the narrow way led to life. These differing destinations are far removed from each other. Men who continually travel downhill, will never reach a mountain top; and sinners who persist in refusing to climb the hills, can never reach the celestial city. Jesus therefore insisted that men and women should choose the direction in which to travel. There never was a roundabout way to God's country. The path is very straight; often difficult, and always leads to a hill called Calvary. Jesus said, ''I am the way, the truth, and the life: no man cometh unto the Father, but

by me'' (John 14:6). The inevitability of choice is something all must
face. Even Pilate recognized this when he said, ''What then shall I do
with Jesus?''

> What will you do with Jesus?
> Neutral you cannot be;
> Some day your heart will be asking,
> ''What will He do with me?''

## SECTION FOUR

*Expository Notes on the Danger of False Prophets*

**Beware of false prophets, which come to you in sheep's clothing, but
inwardly they are ravening wolves. Ye shall know them by their fruits.
Do men gather grapes of thorns or figs of thistles? Even so every good
tree bringeth forth good fruit; but a corrupt tree bringeth forth evil
fruit. Every tree that bringeth not forth good fruit is hewn down, and
cast into the fire. Wherefore by their fruits ye shall know them (vv.
15-20).**

False prophets have been known in every generation. Constantly
throughout the Old Testament ages, reference was made to their ministry.
Jesus referred to them, and John and the other apostolic writers warned
their hearers of the danger forthcoming from these deceitful emissaries
of evil. The religious world is still plagued by these people, but they
are easily recognized.

1. Their self-esteem is obvious. They believe and preach that they
alone are correct in matters pertaining to religious doctrine. It is always
easy to recognize a false minister, for he constantly asserts that unless
a man joins his church, he will be rejected by God. I have never known
the leader of any false sect confessing his sin and weeping before the
Lord. Apparently, he never became conscious of his need.

2. Often the emphasis is on money, and never on the Cross. Many
of the exponents of false doctrine believe their followers should live
by faith and suffer hardships, while they themselves live in luxury! It
is worthy of note that Christ and His disciples never appealed for financial
assistance; the false prophets seldom do anything else!

3. False prophets are often eloquent, but their message does not
accurately express Bible teaching. Texts are taken from their setting
(context), and then misinterpreted. It would be refreshing to meet any
false prophet, if he were kind, gracious, consecrated, and like Jesus.

Alas, so often, they are cynical, bitter, unattractive, and appear to be self-made gods worshiping at their own shrine.

4. False prophets love to feed their egos. Some men prefer to be the first citizen of a very small village than to be second in an empire. They prefer to be the pastor of a congregation of twelve, rather than the assistant minister in a congregation of five thousand. They love to have the preeminence among men. They say they love the Bible, but are not attracted by the text which says, "He that is least among you all, the same shall be great" (Luke 9:48).

Jesus said, "Wherefore by their fruits ye shall know them." Oranges do not grow on apple trees; neither do strawberries grow on almond trees. A man who speaks about holiness should be holy, and a person who recommends generosity should be exceedingly generous. A preacher who talks about the body of Christ, should be willing to love his brethren, even if they do not belong to his particular church. A Christian who advocates missionary endeavor, and even supports the cause with liberal offerings, should also be willing to evangelize his neighbor, workmates, and all with whom he comes into contact. When men say they are Christians, they should be like Christ.

**Not every one that saith unto me, Lord, Lord, shall enter into the kingdom of heaven; but he that doeth the will of my Father who is in heaven. Many will say to me in that day, Lord, Lord, have we not prophesied in thy name? and in thy name have cast out devils? and in thy name done many wonderful works? And then will I profess unto them, I never knew you; depart from me, ye that work iniquity (vv. 21-23).**

Religion is not righteousness; preaching is not proof of godliness. A man may be a minister because the vocation provides a means of sustenance. He may be following in his father's footsteps. He may value the prestige which accompanies the calling, and he may devote all his energy to the task of reaching the highest pinnacle in his religious order. Jesus affirmed they might be blind leading the blind. Long ago, God had prophets; today He has ministers, but these are not religious ornaments adorning a church, and they do not spend all their time in recreational pursuits, nor political activities. True prophets have one hand on the throne of God, and the other on the hearts of needy men and women. God's real servants receive their message from God, and deliver it faithfully. Great orations, sensational miracles, and the approval and acclamation of multitudes, are not evidence of divine approbation. Jesus said that many speakers will be rejected on the Day of Judgment.

People who scoff at this exposition might be wise to ask a question. If Christ says, "depart from me," what destination awaits the rejected sinners? If they are not WITH Christ in eternity, where will they be? These were the injunctions given to the earliest preachers destined to become the prototype of all God's evangelists. Pastors of all denominations should assess their qualifications against these standards. If the ministry be not in accordance with the instructions supplied by Jesus, the pastor is not a true representative of Christ. He is only an official in an organization, and he has no assurance of being accepted in the presence of God.

## SECTION FIVE

*Expository Notes on the Two Men Who Built Houses*

**Therefore whosoever heareth these sayings of mine, and doeth them, I will liken him unto a wise man, which built his house upon a rock. And the rain descended, and the floods came, and the winds blew, and beat upon that house; and it fell not: for it was founded upon a rock. And every one that heareth these sayings of mine, and doeth them not, shall be likened unto a foolish man, which built his house upon the sand: And the rain descended, and the floods came, and the winds blew, and beat upon that house and it fell: and great was the fall of it. And it came to pass, when Jesus had ended these sayings, the people were astonished at his doctrine: For he taught them as one having authority, and not as the scribes (vv. 24-29).**

This illustration was given at the end of the discourses on the mountain, where the Lord, over a period of several days, had given instructions to His disciples. He compared and contrasted His teaching with the commandments of the law, and the line of demarcation had been drawn between the ancient and modern precepts. That the Pharisees and many others would remain hostile was fully expected they would reject His words, and denounce the Teacher. Therefore, Christ concluded His messages with an illuminating illustration. He spoke of two men who erected houses; one on the rock and the other on sand. He did this with great authority, stating anyone who rejected His words would be as foolish as the man whose house fell.

I shall never forget the years I worked in Southern Africa. During the summer, dry river beds were an ideal spot for picnics. Children played in the sand; there were neither thistles nor weeds, and the presence of snakes could easily be detected. Yet, I was warned continually never to yield to the temptation to enter those attractive areas. I was informed that when torrential rains fell in the distant mountains, a wave of water, six feet high, rushed down the canyons, and anyone in the river bed would be swept away and drowned. I was nearby when this almost happened. A small family was enjoying a wonderful time, when the alert father listened intently to a roaring sound in the distance. He managed to get his family to the top of the river bank, but in so doing, he nearly lost his life. As he climbed the last few feet to safety, the angry wave was swirling around his knees. If any man had foolishly erected a home on the sands in that river bed, his house would have been destroyed instantly.

This illustration was easily understood by the people in Christ's audience, for there were many canyons in the nearby mountains. They would have scoffed at any builder who risked his home and family in such a situation. This story is among the most used, but many people fail to understand its truth. Rejection of Christ's message is the perfect example of the stupidity which destroys a man's eternal hopes! A lifetime of effort would be useless if the devastating floods of God's judgment ruined all a man had accomplished. The builder who erected his house on sand was sincere, but sincerity was insufficient when storms battered on the walls and destroyed the foundation. It is better to own a cottage erected on a rock than to possess a mansion resting on sand. Earthly communities appoint inspectors in an effort to prevent the tragedy described by Jesus. A wise man conforms to the standards of a safe building code. Any person building for eternity should seek the approbation of heaven's Inspector; only then will his house endure.


HOMILY

Study No. 4

### THE DIVINE LAWYER...and the Dramas In the Court House

There are two Bible words which, pregnant with meaning, offer the most suggestive word pictures. Dr. Strong declares that the Hebrew word *doon,* translated ''to strive,'' really means ''to struggle to resist a charge of murder.'' Liddel and Scott maintain that the Greek word *agonizomai,* which is also translated ''to strive,'' means precisely the same thing. Therefore, in order to appreciate the full significance of these Scriptures, one must endeavor to see a law court where a desperate lawyer anxiously examines the records, sifts each piece of evidence, and does everything possible to gain an innocent verdict on behalf of the accused.

## THE CASE THAT WAS LOST...Genesis 6:7

The courthouse was in the open air and possibly near the forests which lined the sides of a mountain. In the valley stood the skeleton of a huge ship, and not far away was the ancient sawmill, alongside of which were huge piles of sawdust. Nearby stood a strange old man, who always refused to work on the Sabbath. His name was Noah. His ship was truly fantastic, but his preaching was even more so. All the people knew him, and probably thought he was mad. When he insisted that God would pour judgment upon the nation, they laughed him to scorn. What right had Noah, or even God, to interfere in their pleasure? They loved to do that which Noah condemned; he should mind his own business.

They failed to understand they were figures in a court of law. The judge was God; the prosecuting counsel was righteousness; the counsel for the defense was the Holy Spirit; the junior counsel was Noah; the accused was a guilty world. Possibly a rowdy meeting had just ended when God said, "My Spirit shall not always *strive* with man." The word used was *doon*. It might be translated: "My Spirit shall not always struggle desperately to save the lives of sinful people." (A) *How righteous are the laws of God.* The Holy Spirit acted as the counsel for the defense, yet when no righteous escape could be found, love yielded to law and the sentence was passed. (B) *How wonderful is the love of God.* That He should even try to save such people reveals a compassion beyond degree. (C) *How persistent is the Spirit of God.* He continued year after year, and only gave up the struggle when to continue was virtually impossible.

## THE CASE THAT WAS WON...Luke 22:41-44

Once again the courthouse was in the open air, where, beneath starlit heavens, the Son of God lay prostrate. Describing the scene, Luke wrote, "And being in an *agony* he prayed more earnestly: and his sweat was as it were great drops of blood falling down to the ground" (Luke 22:44). The word translated "agony" is the Greek equivalent of the Hebrew word *doon,* and again suggests the desperation to offset a capital charge. Man was in danger; the forces of righteousness were about to pass sentence; the time was very short; but Christ was making a supreme effort to discover a loophole, whereby the guilty could be saved from death. This was the climax of an epic struggle which had continued throughout the Savior's life. Continually, the forces of evil had tried to defeat this great Lawyer; but when victory seemed to be within their grasp, He seized the sin of the accused, suffered in his stead, and satisfied every requirement of divine justice. The Savior of men died in His own courthouse, and the prisoner went out free.

## THE CASE THAT IS STILL IN DOUBT...Luke 13:24

There was a day when the disciples asked the Lord, ''Are there few that be saved?'' (Luke 13:23). His reply presented them with another word picture. They saw a city on a hilltop; the sun was setting, and the gates would soon be closed. Certain travelers who were late were struggling desperately to reach the gate before it closed for the night, and some were finding difficulty climbing the hill. They were hurrying; they were breathless, but to enter in time was a matter of supreme importance. The disciples were still visualizing the scene when Jesus said, ''Strive [agonize] to enter in at the strait gate: for many, I say unto you, will seek to enter in, and shall not be able'' (Luke 13:24).

The same desperation exhibited in Noah's day and in Christ's sacrifice in the Garden of Gethsemane, should be found in man's untiring effort to enter the kingdom of God. There is much at stake; there is no time to lose. This case may be either won or lost, and we shall be the deciding factors. ''What shall it profit a man if he gain the whole world and lose his soul?'' (Homily reprinted from the author's book *Bible Highways*, pp. 9-10. )

# The Eighth Chapter of Matthew

THEME: *The Continuation of Christ's Ministry*

OUTLINE:
    I. Saving the Suppliant (Verses 1-4)
    II. Surprising the Soldier (Verses 5-13)
    III. Serving the Savior (Verses 14-17)
    IV. Sifting the Superficial (Verses 18-22)
    V. Stilling the Storm (Verses 23-27)
    VI. Subduing the Spirits (Verses 28-34)

## SECTION ONE

*Expository Notes on the Cleansing of the Leper*

**When he was come down from the mountain, great multitudes followed him. And, behold, there came a leper and worshiped him, saying, Lord, if thou wilt, thou canst make me clean. And Jesus put forth his hand, and touched him, saying, I will; be thou clean. And immediately his leprosy was cleansed. And Jesus saith unto him, See thou tell no man; but go thy way, show thyself to the priest, and offer the gift that Moses commanded, for a testimony unto them (vv. 1-4).**

## THE CHARM OF THE MOUNTAIN

"When he was come down from the mountain." Alas, the retreat was over; the vacation had terminated; the meetings were things of the past. It was regrettable this had to happen. Life consists of hills and valleys, but always the mountains are preferable to the lowlands. The air is purer; the vision more expansive; the scenery more attractive. Valleys can easily fill with smog, dirt, and undesired tasks. The children of Israel were warned prior to their entrance into the promised land, "The land, whither ye go to possess it, is a land of hills and valleys" (see Deut. 11:11). Life is just the same. We climb into our heavenly experiences only to discover that, when our ecstasy terminates, the problems of the valley remain. We appreciate the sentiments of Simon, who said on the Mount of Transfiguration, "Lord, it is good for us to be here: if thou wilt, let us make here three tabernacles; one for thee, and one for Moses, and one for Elias" (Matt. 17:4). He probably added, "We can sleep on the ground; Lord, this is wonderful, we never wish to see that valley again." It all seemed so desirable, but the fact remained that service for Christ was impossible on the mountain. The need was in the valley to which they were about to return. We must learn to appreciate our mountaintops but, at the same time, remember it is only the place where we charge our batteries! Having done that, we descend to needy people that our light might shine into the darkness of their souls. It is overwhelmingly thrilling to climb the heights; to sit at the feet of Jesus, and gain a fresh vision of the eternal city. Yet, even those glories cannot compare with the thrill of seeing Christ touch the outstretched hand of a leper, or lift a burden from the heart of a despairing parent.

## THE CRY OF THE MAN

"And, behold, there came a leper and worshiped him, saying, Lord, if thou wilt, thou canst make me clean" (v. 2). Yes, the party was over; real work was about to commence. To see a leper is to experience something unforgettable. I shall always remember watching a missionary nurse in the Central Highlands of New Guinea. Lepers had come down from the hills to obtain treatment at the mission hospital, and the nursing sister carefully, gently administered treatment. Outside of one of the oldest churches in Norway, I stood and listened as a guide explained the purpose of the small peep holes in the side wall of the sanctuary. He told us this was the place where, centuries ago, the lepers were allowed to stand, watch, and listen to the gospel. Leprosy was, and in some part of the world, still is, the foulest of all diseases. It was the scourge of Palestine during our Lord's lifetime, and the pitiful cry, "Unclean, Unclean," was often heard as a leper waited for an opportune moment to cross a road. Lepers were banned from all public places, and contact with clean people was totally prohibited. People with the dreaded disease were banished to isolated areas, and life, while it lasted, was a nightmare.

In the ancient world, leprosy was the most terrible of all diseases. E.W.G. Masterman writes, "No other disease reduces a human being for so many years to so hideous a wreck." It might begin with the loss of all sensation in some parts of the body; the nerve trunks are affected, the muscles waste away; the tendons contract until the hands are like claws...then comes the progressive loss of fingers and toes, until in the end, a whole hand or a whole foot may drop off. The duration of that kind of leprosy is anything from twenty to thirty years. It is a kind of terrible progression in which a man dies by inches.

The law enumerated scores of different contacts which could defile. If a leper put his head inside a house, that house became unclean even to the roof beams. Even in an open place it was illegal to greet a leper. No one could come closer to a leper than four cubits (eighteen inches). If the wind were blowing from a leper toward a person, the leper was required to stand at least one-hundred cubits away (37 1/2 feet). One rabbi would not even eat an egg bought in a street where a leper had passed by. To a Jew there could be nothing more amazing then the New Testament simple sentence, "And Jesus put forth his hand, and touched [the leper]" (v. 3).

As we read about the exploit of this unfortunate man, we see that he was (1) Destitute, (2) Desirous, (3) Devoted, (4) Delivered, (5) Delighted, (6) Disciplined. Somewhere, he had heard people speaking about the uncanny powers of the Preacher from Nazareth, and as he considered the reports, faith filled his soul. Probably he was afraid to climb into the hills, and had waited patiently until he saw Jesus returning to the valley. It is suggestive that he came "worshiping." The Greek word is *proskunein* and this was never used except in the worship of the gods. It might be a matter of conjecture if we tried to ascertain how this outcast learned so much in such a short time. It is also noteworthy that primarily he did not come to beg; in fact, he never asked for cleansing. He confessed his faith, worshiped his Lord, and then in absolute confidence, left the matter in the hands of Jesus. Can any writer overstate the greatness of such a suppliant. Naturally, the most desired thing in the world for that man would be deliverance from the scourge of leprosy. He risked his life by drawing close to Jesus — he was so close that Christ could touch him. Had nothing happened, the law could have sentenced him to death by stoning. The man probably considered he would die in any case — unless a miracle were performed. When he saw the Lord, something stirred within his soul, and he knew he was in the presence of One greater than man. He was kneeling before his Maker. He worshiped Him.

*THE COMPASSION OF THE MASTER*

"And Jesus...touched him" (v. 3). Probably tears filled the eyes of the sufferer, for no one had touched him since the day he became a leper. His neighbors seemed to be a million miles away; he was an outcast, unloved, undesired. When Jesus stretched forth His hand, there was life in the touch! The laws of Moses would condemn the Lord for that act. He was running the risk of being defiled; there was danger of being contaminated with the dreaded disease. The Savior might become a leper and, if that were the case, His entire mission to earth would be ruined. Jesus touched the man. He saw not the loathsome disease but a human being in desperate need. He was not appalled nor frightened by the spectacle before Him; He was moved with tremendous compassion; He was the Great Physician approaching a desperate patient. Perfect love casts out fear and, had Jesus not responded, the stones on the roadway might have cried out! This has always been the perfect example for those who claim to be Christians. No man is beyond the reach of God's outstretched arm. However low a man may fall, the grace of God can lift him from the depths of shame and defeat. David described how the Lord lifted him from the miry clay and set his feet upon a rock. David and the leper would have had much in common.

## THE COMMAND OF MOSES

The law recognized the possibility that a leper might become clean, and the fourteenth chapter of the Book of Leviticus explains the laws regulating such an unlikely event. They included a compulsory examination by a priest, the observance of certain ritualistic events, a shaving of certain parts of the body, and a waiting period of at least seven days. If all were done satisfactorily, the priest would issue a certificate authorizing the man to resume his place in society. Should any observer become critical, the document issued by the priest was binding; the leper was no longer unclean. The possibility exists that something of this kind had happened with Simon of Bethany (see Matt. 26:6). He had been cleansed, probably by the Lord, but to distinguish him from the other Simons in the locality, this one carried to his grave the nickname, "Simon the leper."

When the Lord told the man to offer the things commanded by Moses, He considered many possibilities. Had He failed to issue these suggestions, He Himself could have been criticized for breaking the law. Had the man not done as he was told, his future could have been in jeopardy. At any time of the day or night, he could have been arrested by the authorities. If anyone doubted the accuracy of his testimony of cleansing, he could have been accused of being a menace to other citizens of the community. Maybe there was a deeper reason for this act of conformity to the law. If God loved the world, then He also cared for the priests, even though they were obnoxious. They too needed to hear the gospel. Maybe it was difficult for them to attend meetings in which Jesus preached; their leaders would be watching their every movement. The arrival of a cleansed leper, a convert to the faith, would be a more effective witness than a thousand sermons. They would know that the greatest proof of Christ's effectiveness was His power to change men. Behind the closed doors of their homes they discussed these matters, and possibly this was one of the details which led to the triumph recorded in Acts 6:7: "And the word of God increased...and a great company of the priests were obedient to the faith."

## SECTION TWO

*Expository Notes on the Healing of the Centurion's Servant*

**And when Jesus was entered into Capernaum, there came unto him a centurion, beseeching him, And saying, Lord, my servant lieth at home sick of the palsy, grievously tormented. And Jesus said unto him, I will come and heal him (vv. 5-7).**

"The two versions of this event, Matthew 8:5-13, and Luke 7:1-10, should be read and studied together, for either account has something to contribute to the other. When Christ had finished preaching to the multitude, He proceeded to Capernaum, and soon a deputation of Jewish elders arrived to present a special request. The fact that the elders (*presbuterous*) were willing to swallow their pride, and ask a favor of One whom they were already criticizing, indicates the greatness of their esteem for this unknown Gentile. A slave boy was critically ill in the centurion's home, and there were fears that unless the Healer could do something quickly, the lad's life might be lost. Luke uses the Greek word *doulos* which means 'a slave'; Matthew uses another word *pais* which means 'a child, a boy or girl'; and in a secondary sense, 'a servant or slave'. There must have been special reasons why this slave boy had captured the affections of the Roman captain. The word *entimos*, translated 'was dear unto him,' offers a different shade of meaning. Dr. Thayer says it means, 'held in honor, prized, precious.' The *Amplified New Testament* renders the passage, 'Now a centurion had a bond servant.' The lad, who might have been liberated, had chosen to remain with his master; either one was intensely precious to the other.

This youth, therefore, was sick, and the anxious centurion, hearing of the approach of Jesus, sent the elders of the Jews to ask Him to heal his servant. It is possible that this man heard of the healing of the nobleman's son (John 4:46-54), for this miracle had also taken place within the city of Capernaum. Encouraged by what he had heard, but conscious of the fact that he was a Gentile, this centurion sought the help of the elders of the synagogue — the place for which he had been responsible. The use of the definite article — 'for he loved our nation, and the synagogue he built...' suggests at that time, there was only one synagogue in Capernaum, and this had been made possible by the centurion's generosity.'' (Reprinted from the author's commentary on *Luke's Thrilling Gospel*, pp. 162-163.)

## A GREAT GRACE

It should be remembered that slaves could be purchased very cheaply in the market place; they were considered to be *things* — of less value than sick cattle. The only difference between a slave and an animal was that the slave had the ability to speak. A master could ill-treat him, and even kill him, and was never accountable to the law. It was nothing short of astounding that this wealthy centurion had completely lost his heart to this young slave. He loved him as much as he would have loved one of his own family. This surely indicates the abounding grace which filled the noble master.

## A GREAT GENEROSITY

The man was aware of the bitter animosity of the people among whom he served. The Jews detested the Romans and, had they the power, would have driven them into the sea from whence they had come. Their inability to go to war forced them to remain subjects of Caesar, and their frustrations were expressed clearly in their hostile attitude toward every Roman. Confronted by this prevailing bitterness, the centurion had gone to work to conquer it by love. Recognizing that the Jews had no permanent building in which to worship their God, he built a synagogue from his own financial resources and gave it to the Jews. Due to the fact that the centurion probably worshiped pagan gods, this gift was of great significance.

## HIS GRIEF

The sickness of the slave-child devastated his soul; with every passing moment he became increasingly desperate. Recognizing that as a Gentile he had no real claim on the Stranger, the Roman sought assistance from the Jewish elders, believing they would have greater influence in persuading Jesus to render assistance. Blessed are they who can feel the hurt of suffering people; wise are they who, motivated by love, seek the help of the Son of God. The arrival of Jesus means hope for anyone, in any circumstances, in any place.

## HIS GREAT GESTURE

A comparison of the two accounts suggests that, although the elders did as they were requested, the approach of the Lord worried the man, for he felt unworthy to receive the Healer into his home. That he ran into the street to prevent the suggested visit provides food for thought. What he said to Jesus, and what he did, revealed he was a man with extraordinary vision. The centurions mentioned in the New Testament are depicted as gentlemen, but of them all, this captain was the greatest.

**The centurion answered and said, Lord, I am not worthy that thou shouldest come under my roof: but speak the word only, and my servant shall be healed. For I am a man under authority, having soldiers under me: and I say to this man, Go, and he goeth; and to another, Come, and he cometh; and to my servant, Do this, and he doeth it. When Jesus heard it, he marvelled, and said to them that followed, Verily I say unto you, I have not found so great faith, no, not in Israel (vv. 8-10).**

When the officer expressed unworthiness, there were many people who justifiably could have argued with him on that subject. Actually, when judged by human standards, that soldier was probably the worthiest of all the people present. (1) The superior officers in Caesar's army had evidently considered him to be worthy of promotion. He was not an ordinary soldier; he was a centurion in charge of one hundred men. He was one of the regular officers in the army of occupation, and these were the backbone of military prowess of Rome. (2) The Jewish elders considered him to be worthy, and said so. "And when [the elders] came to Jesus, they besought him instantly, saying, That *he was worthy* for whom he should do this" (Luke 7:4). (3) His banker would have thought him worthy, for if the centurion could afford to build a synagogue, and then give it to the local people, he must have been a wealthy man. (4) His home, said to be unworthy, was probably one of the most expensive in the city. A man who had so much money would hardly live in a shack! Had the Lord entered that dwelling, He would have enjoyed a luxury far above average. (5) His vision was truly astounding, for he recognized that Jesus was the representative of an empire far greater than the domain of Caesar. He likened his own servants to the angels hastening to obey their king. Even the Lord admitted He had not found such great faith, "not even in Israel." (6) The neighbors, friends, and especially the sick child, would have been unanimous in proclaiming the worthiness of that centurion, for his kindness and affection beggared description. They knew, as we should know, there has never been a substitute for love.

Nevertheless, this great man hastened to intercept Jesus, and to prevent what he thought would be an unwise action. He felt utter contempt for himself, and would have been overwhelmed with shame had Jesus crossed his threshold. This is one of the irrefutable laws of life. A man is never as tall as when kneeling before God; to reach the highest and best experiences in life, he must first bow in submission to the Lord. When men boast of their greatness, they confess their inadequacy; when the publican smote upon his breast exclaiming. "God be merciful to me a sinner," he was already halfway to heaven!

**And I say unto you, That many shall come from the east and west, and shall sit down with Abraham, and Isaac, and Jacob, in the kingdom of heaven. But the children of the kingdom shall be cast out into outer darkness: there shall be weeping and gnashing of teeth. And Jesus said unto the centurion, Go thy way; and as thou hast believed, so be it done unto thee. And his servant was healed in the selfsame hour (vv. 11-13).**

*A DEFINITE STATEMENT*

"...Many shall come from the east and west, and shall sit down with Abraham, and Isaac, and Jacob, in the kingdom of heaven" (v. 11). The Jews sincerely believed that when the Messiah arrived, the occasion would be celebrated by a huge banquet, but never for a moment did they expect Gentiles to be present at the festivities. In their estimation, these privileges were reserved exclusively for the children of Israel. They had apparently forgotten or ignored the statement in Malachi 1:11: "For from the rising of the sun even unto the going down of the same my name shall be great among the Gentiles; and in every place incense shall be offered unto my name, and a pure offering: for my name shall be great among the heathen, saith the LORD of hosts." It is interesting to note the assurance with which Christ made His statements. The Sadducees denied the existence of life beyond the tomb. They taught that death terminated existence. When Jesus spoke clearly about the patriarchs participating in the great feast at the end of time, He reaffirmed once again His belief in survival.

## A DELIGHTFUL SUPPER

"Many...shall sit down...in the kingdom of heaven" (v. 11). Jesus definitely referred to innumerable Gentiles who would be enthralled and won by the proclamation of the gospel. He plainly stated there were no boundaries to the love of God; that the Gentiles were just as precious in His sight as the Jews, who had long proclaimed they alone were the people of God. Is this a veiled reference to that future event when the marriage of the Lamb will become a reality? The Book of Revelation describes the intense joy of the "ten times ten thousand and thousands of thousands" as they sing, "Worthy is the Lamb." Obviously, for Christians, the best is yet to be, and the anticipation of that glorious event should carry us through every trial until we see Christ face to face.

## A DISASTROUS SURPRISE

"But the children of the kingdom shall be cast out into outer darkness: there shall be weeping and gnashing of teeth" (v. 12). It should not be difficult to imagine the amazement with which the Jews listened to these remarks. It was almost inconceivable. It was tantamount to blasphemy to suggest that the Gentiles should take pride of place over the children of Abraham. This Teacher was absurd, stupid, ridiculous. God would never, under any circumstances, reject His chosen people! They were so wrong. Favor with God never depended upon race, creed, or color. Faith within a man's heart is of more value than the pigmentation of his skin. He may be clothed in shabby clothing, and yet in the sight of God, still be clad in white robes which are the righteousness of saints. On the other hand, a man may be elegantly dressed, and beautifully groomed, but if beneath the glittering surface lurks blatant, filthy sin, what he appears to be is inconsequential. God has already passed sentence on the righteousness of sinners; it is *filthy rags*.

Therefore, there can be no cause for amazement in the preaching of the Savior. The true children of the kingdom are not those born of Abraham, but those who, through faith, are born of God. Within God's family there is neither Jew nor Gentile, rich nor poor, black nor white. Those who have been cleansed from their sin by the atoning death of

Christ, recognize others to be brothers and sisters. Within the shadow of Calvary's cross, people of all races become the true children of a heavenly Father. This fact alone provides admittance to the marriage of the Lamb, and privileged indeed are those people who can say, "Thank God, I shall be there."

## A DELIVERED SERVANT

"And his servant was healed in the selfsame hour" (v. 13b). This was the most fitting climax possible to the message delivered by the Lord. A Gentile captain had asked for help; he had received it. We do not know the nationality of the slave-child; possibly the lad was of Jewish ancestry, and had become the slave of the centurion. There remains the possibility, however, that he could have been an Arab child, who had been left unwanted and unloved in a hostile world. There is no authentic way of knowing all the details of his life. Yet, if he were a Jewish lad, the bonds of love uniting the Gentile master with the Hebrew child would be indicative of the ultimate aims of God to bring all together into the unity of one family. If the child were a Gentile, then fresh evidence was being provided that Gentiles could find favor with God when Jews were too blind to recognize whence it came, and too stubborn to receive it when God offered it to them.

## SECTION THREE

*Expository Notes on the Healing of Peter's Mother-in-law*

**And when Jesus was come into Peter's house, he saw his wife's mother laid, and sick of a fever. And he touched her hand, and the fever left her; and she arose, and ministered unto them. When the even was come, they brought unto him many that were possessed with devils: and he cast out the spirits with his word, and healed all that were sick: That it might be fulfilled which was spoken by Esaias the prophet, saying, Himself took our infirmities, and bare our sicknesses (vv. 14-17).**

We have already seen that Matthew in his continuing search for materials to enhance the claim that Jesus was the Messiah, seized every piece of evidence he could find in the Old Testament writings. Well-known and even obscure texts were quoted, yet sometimes, things thought irrelevant were neglected or overlooked. To gain an adequate understanding of some of these incidents, it is necessary to compare and contrast all the accounts found in the synoptic Gospels. For example, Mark tells us that the healing of Peter's mother-in-law happened after a synagogue service. He explains that when Jesus and four of His disciples entered into the house, they were told, possibly by Peter's wife, of the illness of the older woman. Matthew omits the incident in the synagogue, preferring to mention the miraculous healing of the centurion's slave. It is only when we consider the three versions together, that we are able to obtain a composite picture of all the events which took place on that memorable sabbath.

## THE DELIVERING LORD

We have been informed in the Gospels, that when the Lord healed the woman who touched the hem of His garment, "virtue went out of him." When Jesus gave life to others, His own strength diminished. It is therefore certain that when He arrived in Peter's home, He was exhausted. The Savior had delivered a man in the synagogue, and had rescued a slave child from certain death. The home of Simon Peter offered sanctuary where He could rest, and yet as soon as He stepped inside the door, He was confronted by another person in need. It might be well to consider that equally as great as what He did, was what He did not do. Others might have become irritable with frustration; they might have exclaimed, "No, not another," but the Lord, with absolute serenity, approached the sick woman, and stooping, touched and healed her. Jesus was never too busy to respond to the needs of people, and never too preoccupied to embrace the children brought to Him.

## THE DEVOTED LADY

Matthew tells how the Lord left Nazareth and established new headquarters in Capernaum. Yet there is no record of the Lord ever owning or renting a home. Later, Jesus admitted He had no place to lay His head, and because of these details, the assumption has been made that, whenever the Lord visited Capernaum, He stayed in the hospitable home of Simon Peter. If that were the case, He was already known to the two devoted ladies who resided there. Little is known of Peter's wife, but she must have been a very wonderful lady. Legend states that she traveled with her husband as he went through various countries preaching the gospel. Clement of Alexandria wrote stating that Peter and his wife were martyred together; that the apostle was made to watch as his wife preceded him to the place of execution. He also stated that as she walked to her death, Peter, calling her by name, said, "Remember thou the Lord." Admittedly this could be but a legend, but the story may be true. Surely, she was a very great Christian who loved to share her home with the Lord. Possibly she was the one who told Jesus her mother was sick with a fever.

Church historians tell us there were three kinds of fever prevalent in Palestine, but the most annoying was malaria. Swamp lands at both ends of the Sea of Galilee, where the Jordan River entered and left the sea, provided excellent breeding grounds for the malarial mosquitoes. Consequently, this kind of affliction was known throughout the entire area. It was often accompanied by jaundice and ague, and was distressing to those who suffered from it. Peter's mother-in-law had this great fever, and her sickness had disrupted the household. This was most unwelcome on that Sabbath, for special guests were expected for lunch. When Jesus arrived, they told Him of her. It is thought-provoking to read that, as soon as she was healed, "she arose and ministered unto them." If someone said, "Take it easy! You need to rest or you might have a relapse; do not get in a draught. Sit down, lady, and let us help you," she firmly pushed the speaker aside, and walked toward the kitchen. She had a job to do; a debt to repay; a Friend to serve, and nothing would be permitted to interfere with what she considered a duty and a privilege. She provided a glorious example for all Christians to follow. Professed converts who have no desire to serve their Savior resemble still-born babies!

## THE DELIGHTFUL LIBERATION

"When the evening was come, they brought unto him many that were possessed with devils: and he cast out the spirits with his word, and healed all that were sick" (v. 16). It should be remembered that this happened on a Sabbath day when strict laws governed the movements of citizens. According to the law, which forbade all work on the Sabbath day, it was illegal to heal on the Sabbath. On the Sabbath, medical attention might only be given to those whose lives were actually in danger. Steps could be taken to prevent a man from getting worse, but no steps could be taken to make him better. Further, it was illegal to carry a burden on the Sabbath day, and a burden was anything which weighed more than two dry figs. It was therefore illegal to carry a person from place to place on a stretcher, or in one's arms or on one's shoulders, for to do so would have been to carry a burden. Officially, the Sabbath ended when two stars could be seen in the sky, for there were no clocks then to tell the time. No doubt, for this reason the crowd in Capernaum waited until the evening time to come to Jesus for the healing which they knew He could give. It is thrilling to note there were no cases too hard for Jesus to handle; He healed them all.

## THE DISTINCTIVE LESSON

''That it might be fulfilled which was spoken by Esaias the prophet, saying, Himself took our infirmities, and bare our sicknesses'' (v. 17b). This quotation came from Isaiah 53:4 and supplied additional evidence that all the time Matthew was writing his Gospel, his predominant thought concerned the Messianic claims to be advanced regarding his Master. To Matthew, it was enthralling that all history had been pointing forward to the coming of the King; to us it is equally as exciting that all subsequent history points back to the same Jesus. He stands at the center of everything of worth. His cross defines this truth more than all else. There is a part that points upward to the heart of God; another part reaches down to the place upon which we stand in our need; there are two arms flung wide to welcome all who would hear His invitation: ''Come unto me, all ye that labour and are heavy laden, and I will give you rest'' (Matt. 11:28).

### SECTION FOUR

*Expository Notes on the Two Young Men*
*Who Volunteered to Follow Jesus*

**Now when Jesus saw great multitudes about him, he gave commandment to depart unto the other side. And a certain scribe came, and said unto him, Master, I will follow thee whithersoever thou goest. And Jesus saith unto him, The foxes have holes, and the birds of the air have nests, but the Son of man hath not where to lay his head. And another of his disciples said unto him, Lord, suffer me first to go and bury my father. But Jesus said unto him, Follow me; and let the dead bury their dead (vv. 18-22).**

Matthew now proceeds to mention two men who enthusiastically asserted they would accompany the Lord on His crusades, if certain conditions could be fulfilled. It is interesting to note that in describing the same incident, Luke mentions three men (see Luke 9:57-62). When considered from a human standpoint, it might appear as if Matthew had run out of patience! He was so enthusiastic about the privilege of following Christ, that when he recorded the disappointing attitude of these men, he considered enough was enough! He described the reactions of the two men, and chose to leave the third unmentioned. Here in these verses the claims of discipleship are clearly set forth. There is always danger in false enthusiasm. When riding on the crest of an emotional wave, people are apt to make commitments which do not endure. Their promises are superficial; their profession is disappointing and unreliable. Such followers only do harm to the cause of Christ. It is never safe to count the number of true converts by cards signed, hands raised, or people walking to the front after an evangelistic meeting. It is far easier to recognize them by the number still in the church, working hard for the Lord, twelve months after the termination of the revival services.

### DISCIPLESHIP DEMANDS PERSEVERANCE...Christ always!

When the scribe asserted his willingness to become a follower of Jesus, the Savior issued a warning, saying: "The foxes have holes, and the birds of the air have nests; but the Son of man hath not where to lay his head." Whether or not the man followed the Lord is unknown, but it becomes clear that Jesus never encouraged superficial decisions. He never promised an easy pathway to glory, nor did He bribe listeners with predictions of increasing fame and fortune. Jesus warned people that although "the way of the cross led home," it nevertheless led first to pain, suffering, and self-sacrifice. Even the foxes of the field had lairs to which they could retire, when the weather was inclement. The birds of the air, similarly, had nests in which they could rest and rear their young, but the true disciple could expect more difficulties. When the devastating storms of life descended, they would often have no refuge but the promises of God. When persecution arose, sometimes help would be apparently denied. They would be ridiculed, beaten, stoned, and asked to renounce their faith, or suffer the penalty of death. Jesus seemed to be reminding the scribe of the need to count the cost, before embarking upon a career which would afterward be regretted. If modern evangelists followed their Lord's methods, their popularity might wane and the number of converts decrease, but those who responded to the claims of Christ would set the world alight with the power of their glorious gospel.

*DISCIPLESHIP ASSERTING PRIORITIES...Christ first!*

"And another of his disciples said unto him, Lord, suffer me first to go and bury my father. But Jesus said unto him, Follow me; and let the dead bury their dead" (vv. 21,22). One of the most sacred duties of any Jew was to be present at and, if he were the eldest son, to arrange for and supervise the burial of his father. This obligation prevails to this day. I remember speaking to a young Jew and recommending that he enjoy a tour to Israel. Financially, he was well able to do this, but his reply reminded me of the words spoken long ago to Jesus. That young man said to me, "I have obligations at home. First, I must attend to my parents' needs." Probably the man who spoke with the Lord had a father in the best of health; a father who might enjoy many more years of living. The disciple in question was telling Jesus that he would follow Him *some day.* He believed in the Lord, and would gladly support any project He sponsored, but at that precise moment he could not become a permanent follower because he had other things to do! Many of that man's descendants are still with us! Someone has said, "If Christ be not Lord of all, He is not Lord at all." Tomorrow never comes! Jesus demands that we follow Him now. Procrastination is the thief of time.

*DISCIPLESHIP NEEDING PREPAREDNESS...Christ now!*

Matthew omitted mentioning the third man of the group, but Luke tells us how "...Another also said, Lord, I will follow thee; but let me first go bid them farewell, which are at home at my house. And Jesus said unto him, No man, having put his hand to the plough, and looking back, is fit for the kingdom of God" (Luke 9:61-62). Lot's wife looked back and her action proved to be fatal (Gen. 19:26). Peter, who escaped to the porch, looked back, and his action led to further denials of his Lord (Mark 14:68). A ploughman who constantly looked back would produce very unsatisfactory ploughing. A young sailor climbing the mast for the first time is always urged to look up and not down. Converts should always have their eyes focused on the Lord; just as sheep watch their shepherd and follow him to green pastures and still waters. It is never wise to linger; discipleship demands immediate action. No person can be sure of another day; the only certainty in life is its termination! "It is appointed unto men once to die, but after this the judgment" (Heb. 9:27). How can we say, "Tomorrow," when the Savior says, "Today"?

*Expository Notes on the Stilling of the Storm*

**And when he was entered into a ship, his disciples followed him. And, behold, there arose a great tempest in the sea, insomuch that the ship was covered with the waves: but he was asleep. And his disciples came to him, and awoke him, saying, Lord, save us: we perish. And he saith unto them, Why are ye fearful, 0 ye of little faith? Then he arose, and rebuked the winds and the sea; and there was a great calm. But the men marvelled, saying, What manner of man is this, that even the winds and the sea obey him? (vv. 23-27).**

## THE GREAT STORM

The Sea of Galilee is one of the most treacherous bodies of water in the world. The weather is unpredictable, and although the surface of the water may be unruffled at one moment, within minutes it can become a raging tempest. For many years, critics ridiculed the descriptions supplied in the Bible, but their statements have long since been exposed as ridiculous. Similar storms still occur, and these are explained by the nature of the hills surrounding the sea. The people of the land always referred to this water as a sea, but it is interesting to note that Luke, who had traveled widely, referred to it as a lake! Actually that is precisely what it is — a lake, about thirteen miles long and, at its widest place, about eight miles from east to west. There is nothing to cause alarm, except for the terrible gorges in the hills. On the east bank are the Golan Heights, and on the west side are mountains with gullies which resemble funnels. When a storm builds, the wind is compressed in these narrow valleys, and almost as if the powers of nature had become intensely infuriated, the wind descends upon the lake with uncontrollable energy. The placid waters are so agitated that fishermen taken unawares have to fight for their lives. Fortunately, modern science is now able to provide weather forecasts, and tragedies are thereby averted.

Describing his experiences on the shores of the Sea of Galilee, W. M. Thomson wrote: "On the occasion referred to, we subsequently pitched our tents at the shore, and remained for three days and nights exposed to this tremendous wind. We had to double-pin all the tent ropes, and frequently were obliged to hang with our whole weight upon them, to keep the quivering tabernacle from being carried up bodily into the air...The whole lake as we had it, was lashed into fury; the waves repeatedly rolled up to our tent door, tumbling over the ropes with such violence as to carry away the tent pins. And, moreover, those winds are not only violent, but they come down suddenly, and often when the sky is perfectly clear. I once went to swim near the hot baths, and, before I was aware, a wind came rushing over the cliffs with such force that it was with great difficulty, I could regain the shore.'' It was this kind of storm that suddenly threatened to sink the boat in which the Lord and His disciples were crossing the lake.

## THE GREAT SAVIOR

To read that Jesus slept through that terrible tempest is something difficult to understand. The wind was shrieking through the rigging, the waves were so high that the boat was tossed about as if it were a cork. Each time it descended between the waves, it seemed it would be swamped. The continual slapping on the sides of the boat; the terrified cries of the disciples; all this, one would think, would be sufficient to arouse the dead! Yet, no accumulation of noise could awaken Jesus. After hours of very exacting work, the Lord was utterly exhausted. Jesus was not a machine. Although He was the Son of God, He had chosen to come in the likeness of man, and was subject to the laws of fatigue that every human knows. This is a thrilling truth, for we are assured He understands when we are overcome with weariness; when our spirits are willing, but alas, the flesh is weak. He knows; He cares; He understands. It was truly remarkable that, what the storm could not do, the anguished cry of a frightened disciple did, in a moment. The five simple words of their prayer ''Lord, save us: we perish,'' stirred His loving heart, and He arose and rebuked the winds and the sea.

''The word translated 'rebuked' is *epetimeesen,* and this is both strong and suggestive. The *Amplified New Testament* renders the passage: 'And He, being thoroughly awakened, *censured and blamed and rebuked* the wind and the raging waves...' It is impossible to censure an insensible thing; to scold, as it were, an inanimate object. To blame the wind for blowing would be ludicrous, and therefore we are obliged to give added consideration to this text. Could it have been that the Lord recognized, in the unfriendly elements, the handiwork of His greatest enemy, Satan? Was this another attempt to kill Him; this time, by drowning? Throughout the itineraries of the Lord, the devil constantly tried to end Christ's life prematurely. This text suggests the Lord rebuked not the storm itself, but the hand which controlled the elements. Maybe it is with good reason that Satan is called, 'The Prince of the Power of the air.'" (Quoted from the author's commentary on *Luke's Thrilling Gospel*, pp. 193-194.)

## THE GREAT STILLNESS

"...and there was a great calm" (v. 26b). The disciples were gasping with relief and astonishment. What they had witnessed was unbelievable. Their Master was able to control the forces of the universe and, for a few moments, they wondered if they were dreaming. As the boat ceased to rock; as a wonderful calm came to the sea and their souls, they exclaimed, "What manner of man is this, that even the winds and the sea obey him?" Doubtless, we echo the same sentiments, but we would be foolish if we did not pause to consider the implications of that astonishing event. That Christ did this during His sojourn on earth will forever command our attention but, alas, what He did then, can hardly cheer modern people, when they are being swamped by other storms which do not subside. There are tempests of doubt, difficulty, passion, economic stress, fear, and physical ailments which threaten existence. A Christ of two thousand years ago is of little help unless He can somehow quiet our storms. These thoughts for us can be summed up thus — Wherever Jesus is, the storms of life become a calm. In His presence there is peace, whatever storms may blow.

## SECTION SIX

*Expository Notes on the Expulsion of the Demons*

**And when he was come to the other side into the country of the Gergesenes, there met him two possessed with devils, coming out of the tombs, exceeding fierce, so that no man might pass by that way. And, behold, they cried out, saying, What have we to do with thee, Jesus, thou Son of God? art thou come hither to torment us before the time? And there was a good way off from them an herd of many swine feeding. So the devils besought him, saying, If thou cast us out, suffer us to go away into the herd of swine. And he said unto them, Go. And when they were come out, they went into the herd of swine: and, behold, the whole herd of swine ran violently down a steep place into the sea, and perished in the waters. And they that kept them fled, and went their ways into the city, and told every thing, and what was befallen to the possessed of the devils. And, behold, the whole city came out to meet Jesus: and when they saw him, they besought him that he would depart out of their coasts (vv. 28-34).**

## *THE STRANGE PERSUASION*

No one can deny that the people of Christ's day were ardent believers in the existence of demons. Ancient writers suggest there existed seven-and-a-half million spirits who loved to inhabit tombs, cemeteries, and other places where water was not found. Apparently water was considered fatal to the spirits! They could also be found in deserts or uninhabited places. They were believed to be hostile to travelers by night; to women about to give birth, to newly-married couples, and the children who stayed out after dark. It was said they constantly sought ways to harm human beings. Their presence was always associated with mental illness, and epilepsy was one of the favorite methods of undermining a man's control. Demons were feared far more than people, and anyone who considered himself a victim of these hostile powers believed he was doomed forever. One of the strangest ideas which has reached us from antiquity is the belief that demons gained entrance to a man's body at meal times. The demon, so it was believed, would jump onto the food, and so enter the man as he ate his meal. It all seems strange to modern readers, but this is what the ancients believed. Once again, I quote from Thomson's *Land and the Book* in which the author says, "There are some very similar cases at the present day, furious and dangerous maniacs who wander about the mountains and sleep in caves and tombs. In their worst paroxysms, they are quite unmanageable, and prodigiously strong. And it is one of the most common signs of this madness that the victims refuse to wear clothes. I have often seen them naked in the crowded streets of Beirut and Sidon. There are also cases in which they run wildly about the country and frighten the whole neighborhood."

## *THE SUDDEN PANIC*

When the afflicted men saw Jesus, they instantly recognized His identity, and this ability would be very hard to explain, unless they were inhabited by powers of evil. How could ordinary men, meeting Jesus for the first time, become suddenly aware that He was no ordinary man? The demons obviously believed they would eventually be punished, but the sudden appearance of Jesus frightened them into believing their time of destruction had arrived prematurely. Hence the question, "Art thou come hither to torment us *before the time?*" (v. 29b). It is worthy of consideration that no evil spirit ever questioned the Lordship of Christ, nor failed to recognize from whence He had come. Demons always obeyed the commands of God's Son.

## THE SAVIOR'S PERMISSION

When the evil spirits sought permission to enter into the nearby herd of swine, it was granted; "and, behold, the whole herd of swine ran violently down a steep place into the sea, and perished in the waters" (v. 32b). Modern theologians have criticized this particular Scripture.

Present-day writers express the liberal interpretation as "It is almost certain that Jesus did not in fact deliberately destroy the herd of pigs. The men were shouting and shrieking and were so convinced they were possessed by demons, that nothing in this world could have rid them of that conviction other than visible demonstration that the demons had gone out of them. Something had to be done, which to them would be unanswerable proof. Probably what happened was that their shouting and shrieking alarmed the herd of pigs; and in their terror, the animals took to flight and plunged into the lake. Thereupon, Jesus seized the chance which had come to Him. 'Look,' He said, 'Look at these swine; they are gone into the depths of the lake, and your demons have gone with them forever.' Jesus knew that in no other way could He ever convince these two men that they were in fact cured."

This seems to be an admirable way to explain the phenomenon of the deliverance, and would prove Jesus to be an expert psychologist. Oftentimes when theologians rationalize, they destroy anything miraculous in the Bible story. If the above sample of liberal explanation is the final word in interpretation, then perhaps the writers of the Gospels should be reprimanded for misleading readers! It is written that Jesus gave permission to the demons to vacate their human premises, and that only as a result of that permission, were they permitted to enter into the swine. The animals had more sense than the people; preferring suicide to bondage, they rushed to their death in the water at the bottom of the precipice.

## THE SWINE PERISHING

Let it be understood that the destruction of that herd of swine, two thousand in number (Mark 5:13), represented the loss of considerable wealth. That morning, one of the citizens had been a very wealthy farmer; that evening he was bankrupt. It is thought-provoking, however, that since the inhabitants of the country considered swine flesh to be unclean, their interest in pigs must have been stimulated by a great love of money. Probably they thought it mattered not to whom they sold the animals, as long as they abstained from eating swine flesh. Actually, the Lord was indirectly teaching that when He enters, unclean things should be expelled. That truth still applies, for goodness and vice cannot live together.

## THE STUPID PEOPLE

"And, behold, the whole city came out to meet Jesus: and when they saw him, they besought him that he would depart out of their coasts" (v. 34). Doubtless they would have made Him a freeman of the city had He ceased meddling in their affairs. Why did He not mind His own business? It had taken a long time for that herd to be increased to two thousand. Who would compensate the farmer for his astounding loss? What if Jesus continued as He had commenced? Whose swine would be sacrificed next? Delivered men could not compensate for drowned swine. This Jesus was likely to become a menace to their existence. They were unanimous in the request for His departure. Unfortunately, they never inquired the cost to themselves of asking Him to leave. Had they possessed true wisdom, they would have considered another text, "For what is a man profited, if he shall gain the whole world, and lose his own soul? or what shall a man give in exchange for his soul?" (Matt. 16:26).

# The Ninth Chapter of Matthew

THEME: *The Diversified Ministry of Jesus*

OUTLINE:
    I. Removing a Distressing Guilt (Verses 1-8)
    II. Reclining With Dubious Guests (Verses 9-13)
    III. Replying to Doubtful Grievances (Verses 14-17)
    IV. Raising a Dead Girl (Verses 18, 23-26)
    V. Reaching a Definite Goal (Verses 19-22)
    VI. Restoring a Departed Gift (Verses 27-31)
    VII. Responding to a Discerning Group (Verses 32-34)
    VIII. Revealing a Delightful Grace (Verses 35-38)

## SECTION ONE

*Expository Notes on the Healing of the Palsied Man*

**And he entered into a ship, and passed over, and came into his own
city. And, behold, they brought to him a man sick of the palsy, lying
on a bed; and Jesus seeing their faith said unto the sick of the palsy;
Son, be of good cheer; thy sins be forgiven thee. And, behold, certain
of the scribes said within themselves, This man blasphemeth. And Jesus,
knowing their thoughts said, Wherefore think ye evil in your hearts?
For whether is easier, to say, Thy sins be forgiven thee; or to say, Arise,
and walk? But that ye may know that the Son of man hath power on
earth to forgive sins, (then saith he to the sick of the palsy,) Arise, take
up thy bed, and go unto thine house. And he arose, and departed to
his house. But when the multitudes saw it, they marvelled, and glorified
God, which had given such power unto men (vv. 1-8).**

"And he entered into a ship, and passed over, and came into his own
city" (v. 1). We are reminded again from Matthew 4:13 that Jesus had
left Nazareth and had established new headquarters in Capernaum. It
was to this place He returned when the Gadarenes asked Him to leave
their shores. We should not overlook the somber truth enshrined in this

verse. The people of Nazareth had watched the Lord growing from childhood to manhood. Many of the citizens had been His customers, but their familiarity bred contempt, and the incident in the synagogue clearly revealed they had no intention of allowing the Lord to preach to them. They were opposed to His mission, and their bitterness was obvious when, intent on His murder, the congregation pushed Him to the precipice from which they hoped to throw Him to His death. Whatever they had heard or witnessed during thirty years of His residence in the city, they remained unimpressed. Their rejection was complete. It was therefore no cause for amazement when, similarly, He rejected them. This was one of the warnings which He repeated continually. Had He not sought a new home, His actions would have contradicted His doctrines. God had already said, "My spirit shall not always strive with man," and the Lord's action in leaving Nazareth suggested, that for that city, the time of rejection had come.

## THE MAN'S SECRET SIN

Sickness is not always the result of personal guilt. There are teachers who maintain that any kind of infirmity is caused directly by sin, and that under no circumstances should Christians be afflicted. This is wrong! Writing to Timothy (2 Tim. 4:20), Paul said, "Erastus abode at Corinth: but Trophimus have I left at Miletum sick." The apostle had the ability to heal infirmities, and both he and his trusted servant knew how to confess their shortcomings. Had that sickness been the result of sin, there would have been no need to leave Trophimus behind. His sin could have been forgiven, and his body healed. Probably the Lord realized His servant needed rest, but the only way to persuade him of the fact was incapacitation. Some preachers permit their enthusiasm to run away with their brains. If the Lord did not place a restraining hand upon them, they would self-destruct! Yet, on the other hand, some sicknesses are caused by sin, for a guilty conscience can easily destroy a man's health. This was so with the man who suffered from the palsy.

During World War II, I was the pastor of a church near one of Britain's greatest air bases. One of the chaplains there, visiting my church, told a story concerning a young airman. He explained that, unlike the other young people who drifted away in couples as soon as a service ended, this boy remained to collect the hymnbooks and to replace the chairs. The fellow was most helpful, and yet there was something strange about his behavior. He was always sick, yet when the doctor examined the boy, he found nothing wrong with him. Finally, the young airman was sent to the psychiatrist, for it was feared he was becoming mentally deranged.

That doctor was very clever, for as soon as the boy arrived, he began to sympathize with him, stating that he also was "fed up with the war and everything connected with it." The unsuspecting lad was gradually led into a conversation about civilian life. The doctor seemed to confide in his patient, and reciprocating, the airman spoke of his experiences before he enlisted. As the conversation developed, the psychiatrist appeared utterly casual, but suddenly the young man mentioned an incident for which the doctor had been searching. Then, with seemingly brutal directness, he pounced on the boy's confession, and in a moment became, once more, the professional doctor. "What about this?" he asked, and the boy, realizing he had been trapped into revealing something he had hidden for years, cried out, "O God, what am I to do?" Very slowly the psychiatrist answered, "You had better see the chaplain; he believes in the forgiveness of sin, but that is his job not mine." That airman had been sitting, as it were, on a time bomb. At any moment, so he believed, it could destroy him, and as day after day he worried about the matter, his health deteriorated, causing all kinds of problems.

## THE MAN'S SERIOUS SICKNESS

The man who was sick with the palsy was one of that type; somewhere in his past he had committed sin, and this had destroyed his health. One thing led to another, until finally, he was helpless. His plight was further accentuated by the fact that Jews believed sin to be the cause of disease. One of their famous rabbis taught, "No sick person is cured from sickness, until all his sins are forgiven" (Rabbi Chija ben Abba). However strange this sounds to modern readers, it nevertheless was the belief of the people among whom the Lord labored. Therefore, there was no problem regarding Christ's diagnosis of the cause of the man's infirmity. The Pharisees and others present believed the man's indiscretion was the cause of his problem. Nevertheless, they vehemently opposed the Lord's claim to be able to forgive that sin. Had Jesus prayed and asked God to forgive the man, there would have been no objection. Probably, the critics would have applauded the prayer. Jesus did not ask God to grant forgiveness; He gave it to the sinner, and it was this act which aroused the anger of the Jewish leaders. Having heard the Lord's remarks, they said, "This man blasphemeth" (Matt. 9:3). "Who can forgive sins, but God alone?" (Luke 5:21)

It is very important that we recognize this fact. This was no slip of the tongue; the Lord knew exactly what He was saying, and the resultant miracle amplified what He was trying to tell His audience. He claimed to be equal with God, and acted as though He were God manifest in flesh. The Jews fully understood what He said, but instead of examining the claims of Christ they formulated a charge against Him, saying He was worthy of death, because He made Himself equal with God. It is thought-provoking to compare their soul-sickness with the disease which had almost destroyed the sufferer. Christ could and did heal the palsied man; alas, He could do nothing for the sickness of the Pharisees; they refused all treatment.

## THE MAN'S SUBLIME SAVIOR

Matthew, Mark, and Luke report this incident, and all agree the sufferer never asked for anything. This fact has been cited by many teachers to support an assertion the man was mute. Obviously, he shared the faith of his friends, for otherwise he would have been unwilling to allow the decision to break up the roof of a neighbor's home. Matthew says, "And Jesus seeing their faith said unto the sick of the palsy; Son, be of good cheer; thy sins be forgiven thee." The Lord gave to the man (1) Pardon, (2) Peace, and (3) Power. The strength supplied by the Savior enabled the sufferer to demonstrate to everybody he was able to triumph over the thing that had held him. Dr. G. Campbell Morgan used to say, "A man, with Christ to help, can trample under feet the things by which, formerly, he was trampled down." The arrival of Jesus emphasized the fact that earth's greatest opportunity had arrived. He who created the world was perfectly able to solve its problems, lift its burdens, and bring peace to troubled hearts. The only prerequisite for heaven's blessing was a cooperative spirit. Alas, the Pharisees remained sinful and stubborn; they missed the greatest blessing the Almighty could provide. (For further notes and homilies, consult the author's commentary on *Mark's Superb Gospel*, Chapter 2:1-12; and *Luke's Thrilling Gospel*, Chapter 5:17-26.)

## SECTION TWO

*Expository Notes on Matthew's Response to the Call of Christ*

**And as Jesus passed forth from thence, he saw a man, named Matthew, sitting at the receipt of custom [tax office]: and he saith unto him, Follow**

me. And he arose, and followed him. And it came to pass, as Jesus sat at meat in the house, behold, many publicans and sinners came and sat down with him and his disciples (vv. 9-10).

## GREED IN HIS HEAD

The publicans, or tax gatherers, were the most detested people in the Jewish nation. They had accepted employment from the Roman invaders, but to make matters worse, they had used their official position as a means to obtain from their own people, exorbitant taxes. Anything extra which could be obtained from the taxpayers, went into the pockets of the wealthy publicans. Yet, it should not be assumed that all publicans were evil men; there were good and bad people in every walk of life. Luke describes in his nineteenth chapter how Zaccheus met Jesus. He tells how the tax gatherer said to the Lord, "Behold, Lord, the half of my goods I give to the poor and if I have taken any thing from any man by false accusation, I restore him fourfold" (19:8). This can hardly be taken as a promise to be generous; it was the normal procedure for this tax gatherer to be kind to the folk among whom he lived. This could have been the same with Matthew. The possibility exists that he also might have been a man of kindness but, if this were not so, then we must assume that his response to the call of Christ wrought immediate changes in his money-loving soul.

## GRACE IN HIS HEART

All the synoptic Gospels describe the feast in Matthew's house, but it is interesting to note the omissions in Matthew's account. For example, he states that "Jesus sat at meat in *the* house." Luke informs us that "Levi made him a great feast in *his own house*" (Luke 5:29). The converted publican was always more anxious to present his Lord than to advertise his own virtue. Luke emphasized the fact that "[Matthew] made Him a great feast," that is; he planned and paid for it. The tax gatherer never mentioned this important fact. Mark (2:15) inferred that many publicans sat eating with Jesus; Matthew was content to say the additional guests were sitting nearby. He seemed reluctant to say anything good about himself, and this surely indicated the greatness of his character. If indeed he had been the despicable man many say he was, we can only conclude that great changes had occurred in a hurry! The evidence seems to prove that Matthew was an extraordinary man; generous in giving, knowledgeable as a student of the Scriptures, and firm in his faith that the Messiah had arrived.

## GENEROUS IN HIS HOSPITALITY

"Matthew-Levi was indisputably a man of rare discernment. His feast suggests three vital things. (1) He desired more of the *presence of Christ;* therefore he took the Lord to his own home. (2) He desired to increase the *pleasure of Christ,* and therefore, planned the greatest feast possible. He gave the best that he had. 'It was a great feast.' (3) He desired to assist the *purposes of Christ,* and therefore provided a congregation to hear the Teacher. This was a wonderful occasion, and it is not difficult to imagine the excitement which prevailed during the time of preparation. This was Levi's first missionary effort; it would have been a marvelous beginning had he been able, with one effort, to bring all of his friends to Christ. He had no idea what their reactions would be; he had no way of knowing what would happen at the supper, but at least he was determined that his associates should meet the Master. This set a pattern for modern disciples. When special revival meetings are now arranged, Christians consider the occasion to be a time for feasting, rather than an opportunity to bring others to Christ." (Reprinted from the author's commentary on *Luke's Thrilling Gospel,* p. 134-135).

## GLORIOUS IN HIS HOPE

**And when the Pharisees saw it, they said unto his disciples, Why eateth your Master with publicans and sinners? But when Jesus heard that, he said unto them, They that be whole [well] need not a physician, but they that are sick. But go ye and learn what that meaneth, I will have mercy, and not sacrifice: for I am not come to call the righteous, but sinners to repentance (vv. 11-13).**

When the Pharisees criticized Jesus for His association with sinners, it became evident their religion was a thing of the head, not the heart. They observed commandments, but never exhibited love for other people. When the Lord said, "They that be [well] need not a physician, but they that are sick," He was emphasizing that consciousness of physical need is often halfway to being healed. When a man is not aware of need, he is unlikely to consult a physician. The Pharisees were assured they were pleasing to God; there was no need to repent; they were already the chosen people of God! Matthew, realizing this fact, quoted from the writings of Hosea: "For I desired mercy, and not sacrifice; and the knowledge of God more than burnt offerings" (Hos. 6:6). Again we see the author producing evidence to prove Jesus was the fulfillment of Messianic predictions. It must not be forgotten that *God* was speaking through Hosea; Jesus was speaking for Himself. He had come to call sinners; He desired mercy and not sacrifice. His was a new conception of truth, in which sincere tears of remorse were more important that observance of any Mosaic law. He realized they had no knowledge of these precepts, therefore He said, "Go and learn what that meaneth." Obviously, He believed a man could be well educated and yet understand little of the greatest facts in life. (See the special notes on the call of Levi and the homily, "Matthew...The Master's Man," in the author's commentary on *Luke's Thrilling Gospel*, pp. 134-140.)

## SECTION THREE

*Expository Notes on Christ's Answer Concerning the Wine and the Bottles*

**Then came to him the disciples of John, saying, Why do we and the Pharisees fast oft, but thy disciples fast not? And Jesus said unto them, Can the children of the bridechamber mourn, as long as the bridegroom is with them? but the days will come, when the bridegroom shall be taken from them, and then shall they fast. No man putteth a piece of new cloth unto an old garment, for that which is put in to fill it up taketh from the garment, and the tear is made worse. Neither do men put new wine into old bottles [wineskins]: else the bottles break, and the wine runneth out, and the bottles perish: but they put new wine into new bottles, and both are preserved (vv. 14-17).**

This is one of the least used parts of the New Testament, and yet for all preachers, the verses are a goldmine! Once again, there are four areas awaiting exploration, and the careful seeker will find many valuable nuggets of truth in these remarkable words of the Lord.

## THE UNDENIABLE PLEASURE

When the disciples of John asked the reason for the disciples abstaining from fasting, they expressed a measure of disapproval, because the actions of Christ's followers appeared to be negligent. They had either forgotten, or were unaware, that fasting was a practice connected with the Day of Atonement, when Israel confessed their sins before God. That fasting had become a part of the daily routine of the Pharisees, and was now the result of traditions and customs imposed upon people throughout the generations. The rite had begotten burdens too heavy to be carried. Christ was not improving the old regime, He was replacing it. Having fulfilled the requirements of the law, Jesus introduced something joyous, wonderful, and lasting. When He spoke of the friends of the Bridegroom, or the children of the bridechamber, He was obviously thinking of the ultimate goal of His mission. It was the purpose of God to call from the nations a people to be known as "The Bride of Christ." God had planned a wedding, and now that the fulfillment of that plan was to be made possible, sadness, fasting, and problems were to be banished from the minds of the disciples. They were to be radiant; the Bridegroom was in their midst!

## THE UNAVOIDABLE PASSION

"The days will come, *when the bridegroom shall be taken from them*, and then shall they fast" (v. 15b). Even at that early stage, the Lord was aware of coming events. He would be delivered into the hands of cruel men who would mock, scourge, and crucify Him. Yet, in this strange manner, the plans made in heaven would be consummated, and the marriage of the Lamb made possible. The Lord saw clearly that the path to the eternal city would first go through the valley of the shadow of death. When those unavoidable days arrived, and the disciples' sky became temporarily overcast, then would be the time to mourn. At that time, fasting would be what it should have been throughout the ages — the sincere expression of sorrowful, penitent hearts. It would be a spontaneous desire arising from within sincere worshipers, and not necessarily an edict imposed by dictatorial leaders. Probably the most thought-provoking detail about these words was the clear indication that He was looking ahead, and not back. The Pharisees looked back through the ages to Mount Sinai to hear words of law; Christ was looking ahead to Mount Calvary to hear words of grace. The bondage inflicted by legalism promoted sorrow; the pardon given by a heavenly Father would promote everlasting joy and peace. The Savior then gave two illustrations which all His listeners would understand.

## THE UNSHRUNKEN PATCH

The Greek word translated "new" is *agnaphou* and this means, "unmilled, unfilled, undressed, unshrunken." To patch an old garment with a piece of unshrunken cloth would be folly. If the garment became wet, the patch would shrink and pull away from the material in the garment, thus causing damage. "The last state of the garment would be worse than the first." Actually, there could be no affinity between the old and the new cloth. It was imperative that old garments be patched with old cloth, or that new garments similarly be patched with new cloth. The Lord's teaching was unmistakable. The old garment, the old dispensation, had served its purpose; but it had come to the end of its life. It belonged to the past, and for all intent and purpose it should be left there. The new teaching, enunciated by Jesus, was not something to be added to the old garments of ritualism. They were completely incompatible and, in time, either would do the other harm. Circumstances would dictate problems; the requirements of the Gospel would apparently be in conflict with the demands of the law, and with no flexibility in operation, the results would be disastrous. The Lord was suggesting that the disciples be gratefully appreciative of what had been, and yet joyously apprehensive of the new laws about to be enunciated by the king.

## THE UNCONTROLLABLE PRESSURE

The Greek word translated "old" is *palaios,* and this means "old" or "ancient." Since the Lord was referring to water or wine containers, He was obviously speaking of skins generally used for the transportation of liquids. An old skin would have lost its elasticity and would resemble a piece of worn leather; that is, it would not stretch. New wine would automatically ferment, and the gas thus generated would exert pressure on an unyielding, unresponsive skin. The end result would be an explosion; a tearing of the container. Obviously, new wine should be placed in new skins, so that expansion would be possible. It is worthy of attention that, on the Day of Pentecost, men mocked and said of the disciples, "These men are full of new wine." Peter replied, "Ye men of Judaea, and all ye that dwell at Jerusalem, be this known unto you, and hearken to my words: For these are not drunken, as ye suppose, seeing it is but the third hour of the day. But this is that which was spoken by the prophet Joel" (Acts 2:14-16).

The "new wine" of the gospel could hardly be contained in the *old, worn-out* Pharisees and Sadducees, whose capabilities of being controlled by the Holy Spirit were, at the time, non-existent. The church would extend its borders until the known world heard the truth, and people everywhere would rejoice. If such an explosive message had been miraculously placed within the cold, critical Pharisees, they would have burst! The new wine needed new bottles; the new message needed new men and women to preach it. Thus did the Lord draw the lines of demarcation between the old and the new regimes. "If any man be in

Christ, he is a new creature: old things are passed away; behold, all things are become new'' (2 Cor. 5:17). (See also the comments on the parallel passage in *Luke's Thrilling Gospel*, pp. 136-137.)

SECTION FOUR

*Expository Notes on the Raising of Jairus' Daughter*

**While he spake these things unto them, behold, there came a certain ruler, and worshiped him, saying, My daughter is even now dead; but come and lay thy hand upon her, and she shall live. And Jesus arose, and followed him, and so did his disciples (vv. 18-19).**

Matthew, Mark, and Luke mention this incident, but Matthew omits the fact that the man was a ruler of the synagogue (see Mark 5:22 and Luke 8:41). To obtain a complete picture of this incident, it is necessary to read all three accounts. Mark informs us that the man's name was Jairus. He had been elected to high office by the "board of elders," and was in charge of all the administrative details connected with the synagogue. He was responsible for the order of public service and for the people who participated in it. He presided over every business meeting, and he was responsible for the upkeep and maintenance of the school and library. When heresy threatened the authority of the leaders, he became responsible for the condemnation of the heretic. He held a very important position, and in times of emergency, the entire congregation looked to him for guidance. It was surprising that such as he should ever make a public appeal for help to One he had often condemned. Only a very personal crisis in the man's life could have begotten such action. Probably every doctor in the city had been consulted, but to no avail; the child had died. Desperately, the bereaved father thought of Jesus and, knowing there was no hope elsewhere, came, hoping the Teacher would help. The word translated "worshiped" is *prosekunei* and should be rendered "did homage"; that is, Jairus respectfully bowed before Jesus as though he were bowing before a king, or some extremely important person. Mark states the man said that the daughter "lieth at the point of death." Luke, the doctor, wrote, "she lay a dying." Matthew reports the father as having said, "My daughter is even now dead." The *Amplified New Testament* translates the words, "My daughter has just now died." All these details are of tremendous interest as the new section will reveal.

**And when Jesus came into the ruler's house, and saw the minstrels and the people making a noise, he said unto them, Give place: for the maid is not dead, but sleepeth. And they laughed him to scorn. But when the people were put forth, he went in, and took her by the hand, and the maid arose. And the fame hereof went abroad into all that land (vv. 23-26).**

The Jews had strange customs relating to mourning for the dead; they turned a house of grief into a circus! Professional mourners were hired to make as much noise as possible, and their weird performances made the burden of death unbearable. Ancient writings attest the fact that professional mourning included three main characteristics: Music supplied by flute players, the tearing of garments, and the incessant, loud wailing over the body. Throughout the Middle East some of these customs still remain, and to say the least, they are strange when seen through Western eyes.

The death chamber was turned into a scene of hysterical pandemonium, when strangers displayed their art. Concerning the tearing of garments, there were thirty-nine different rules and regulations how garments should be torn. The tear was to be made while you were standing, torn to the heart so that the skin was exposed. For a father or a mother, the rent was exactly over the heart; for others it was on the right side. It must be large enough for a fist to be inserted into it. For seven days the tear must be left gaping open; for the next thirty days, it must be loosely stitched so that it could still be seen; only then could it be permanently repaired. Because it would have been improper for women to tear their garments in such a way that the breast was exposed, a woman must tear the inner garment in private. She must then reverse that garment, so that she wore it back to front; and then in public she must tear her outer garment.

Many other requirements were expected from the mourning relatives and, unless these were supplied, the entire family was criticized by their neighbors. When Jesus arrived in the house, He entered a place of pandemonium! His statement that the girl was only sleeping instantly changed the hysterical screaming to cynical mirth, "they laughed him to scorn." "But when the people were put forth, he went in, and took her by the hand, and the maid arose" (v. 25). Luke adds: "And her spirit came again, and she arose straightway: and he commanded to give her meat. And her parents were astonished: but he charged them that they should tell no man what was done" (Luke 8:55-56).

This passage of Scripture has aroused much debate within theological circles. The question has often been asked, "Was the child dead or in a deep coma?" Attention has been focused on two Greek words, *koimasthai* and *katheudein*. Scholars insist that both words mean "to sleep," and that the daughter of Jairus was not dead, but in a deep coma. Archaeological discoveries have revealed that, unfortunately, people were often buried alive, because ancient doctors were unable to ascertain whether or not life had ended. People who were thought to be dead were, in fact, only in a "deep sleep." Theologians claim the miracle in the home of Jairus was one of "divine diagnosis," which prevented a girl being buried alive. The evidence cited is interesting but not conclusive.

The girl's father admitted his daughter "had just now died." Dr. Luke stated "her spirit came again." This would hardly have been the case if her *spirit had not already departed.* It is correct to assert that both the Greek words primarily mean "to sleep." Thayer says *koimasthai* means to "cause to sleep; to put to sleep." He also says of *katheudein* that it means, "to fall asleep; to drop off to sleep." Both words are also used to express a "state of death." There is another word which means "to sleep"; it is found in John's Gospel. "Our friend Lazarus sleepeth" (John 11:11). The word is *kekoimeetai* from *koimao*. Dr. Thayer says it means "to cause to sleep; to still, to calm, to quiet." It also is used to express "a state of death." There is an interchange of words throughout the Greek Testament, and *all* of those mentioned are used to express "a state of being dead." For example, in 1 Thessalonians 4:15 we have "we which are alive and remain unto the coming of the Lord shall not prevent them which are asleep." *Tous koimeethentas* is translated "those who are fallen asleep." It is the same word, and we cannot believe that when the Lord returns he will bring with Him all those who have been reposing in a deep coma! The danger with all liberal interpretations of the Bible is that everything supernatural is often destroyed. Human rationalization rules out anything which suggests miraculous intervention in the affairs of men. There are times when it is easier to accept the Bible as it is, than to believe the interpretations offered by sincere, but illogical, theologians. If the daughter of Jairus were only in a deep coma, we still have to explain how the Lord could awaken her with a word, and how the change was so amazing that she was able to eat a meal immediately. "He commanded to give her meat." It is extremely difficult to avoid the conclusion that modern commentators often strain at a gnat and swallow a camel! (See also the expository notes and homilies on the parallel passages in the author's commentaries on Mark and Luke.)

*Expository Notes on the Woman Who Touched Christ's Garment*

**And, behold, a woman, which was diseased with an issue of blood twelve years, came behind him, and touched the hem of his garment: For she said within herself, If I may but touch his garment, I shall be whole [well]. But Jesus turned him about, and when he saw her, he said, Daughter, be of good comfort; thy faith hath made thee whole. And the woman was made whole from that hour (vv. 20-22).**

It is interesting to note how Matthew groups together four miracles and almost passes them nonchalantly. It might appear he was not interested in them. He resembles a flower-child tossing beautiful blossoms to spectators along the route of a parade. Matthew is thrilled to be following the King; his eyes are constantly upon his Master, but as he follows the route through the Gospels, here and there, he tosses to the crowd his gorgeous flowers in the form of miracles. He devotes a few verses to each one, and then they are apparently forgotten. The other Gospel writers give more time to each account. For example, Matthew only needs three verses to describe how a woman touched the hem of Christ's garment; Mark needed ten verses, Luke tells the story in six verses. As we shall see in the new section, Matthew takes only five verses to describe how two blind men received their eyesight; John takes a whole chapter (9) to tell how one blind man was given his sight. It would seem that, to Matthew, miracles were incidental; they were secondary in importance. Matthew was only concerned with the presence of the Grand Marshal! His eyes were always focused on the King. This story of the woman is one of his greatest accounts.

## HER CONTINUING DISEASE AND DISTRESS

"And, behold, a woman, which was diseased with an issue of blood twelve years" (v. 20a). Throughout twelve, seemingly endless years, this unfortunate woman had suffered humiliation, hard to describe. Her continuing hemorrhaging not only endangered her life, it meant deep embarrassment. She was always reluctant to move among people, for at any moment her affliction could promote problems. To make matters worse, the law and the traditions of the fathers had combined to make her life a misery.

The law outlined several things which could be done to alleviate her sufferings, but some of the traditional requirements were based on superstition. One suggestion stated she had to carry the ashes of an ostrich egg in a linen bag in summer, and in a cotton bag in winter. Another stated it was beneficial to carry a barley corn, which had been found in the excrement of a white she-ass.

The severest judgment against her was the restriction placed upon her spiritual activities. The law stated: "And if a woman have an issue of her blood many days out of the time of her separation, or if it run beyond the time of her separation; all the days of the issue of her uncleanness shall be as the days of her separation; she shall be unclean. Every bed whereon she lieth...and whatsoever she sitteth upon shall be unclean...And whatsoever toucheth those things shall be unclean" (see Lev. 15:25-27). This woman was considered to be dangerous; contact with her excluded people from worship within the sanctuary; they were deprived of things considered to be essential and invaluable. Mark 5:25-26 tells us she had consulted innumerable doctors who had been unable to help. She had spent all her money and was now desperate. It might be interesting if we could discover why she went to doctors before she came to Christ. If we could know the answer to that question, we might be able to understand why people still make the same mistake.

*HER CALCULATED DECISION AND DANGER*

She "came behind him, and touched the hem of his garment" (v. 20b). She was either very brave, very desperate, or very foolish. If the crowd had known of her affliction, they would have felt contaminated by her presence and would have insisted on her punishment. Ignoring these possibilities, she pressed forward, and reaching out her hand, touched the tassel which hung from the bottom of his shawl. Numbers 15:37-41 and Deuteronomy 22:12 describe how Jews were instructed to wear fringes on the hems of their garments. From historians, we learn that the fringes consisted of four threads passing through the four corners of the garment, and meeting in eight. One of the threads, longer than the others, was twisted seven times round the others, and a double knot formed; then eight times; then eleven times; then thirteen times. The thread and the knots stood for the five books of the law. The idea of the fringe was two-fold. It served both to identify a Jew as a Jew, as a member of the chosen people, no matter where he was; and to remind a Jew, every time he put on or removed his garment, that he belonged to God.

The woman stood in the crowd and watched the Lord. He was wearing the conventional Jewish clothing and, somehow, her attention got focused on the hanging fringe. She thought, "If I can only touch that tassel, it will be enough." Certain theologians identify this with heathen superstition, but it is difficult to accept that interpretation, in view of the Lord's commendation of her faith. Deep within her soul, she believed Jesus could do, in a moment, what the doctors had been unable to do in twelve years. She had become so desperate that, for her, it was all or nothing! If He did not respond, or if her faith had been misplaced, the crowd might stone her. Probably she considered immediate death preferable to more years of humiliation and embarrassment.

## HER COMPLETE DELIVERANCE AND DELIGHT

"He said, Daughter, be of good comfort; thy faith hath made thee whole. And the woman was made whole from that very hour" (v. 22). Language is inadequate to describe, effectively, all the woman thought and experienced, when the life-giving power of the Savior began to reach her body. He never touched her; at first, He never even looked at her. There was neither ordinance nor ritual. The only link between her need and His healing sufficiency was a stretched-out arm of faith. It bridged the gap, and she went away healed. That was a glorious pattern for all faith healers. The poet wrote, "Only believe, only believe; All things are possible, Only believe." When the woman's hand touched the Lord's garment, a thrilling power began to move through her veins; she knew that healing was taking place; it was unbelievable! When He turned, looked into her eyes, and spoke words of encouragement, she knew everything was all right. Probably tears of joy streamed down her cheeks but, forever, she remembered her Benefactor. Her Savior would always be the most wonderful Person she had ever met.

> Oh, touch the hem of His garment,
> And thou too shalt be free.
> His saving power, this very hour,
> Shall give new life to thee.

### SECTION SIX

*Expository Notes on the Giving of Sight to Two Blind Men*

**And when Jesus departed thence, two blind men followed him crying, and saying, Thou Son of David, have mercy on us. And when he was come into the house, the blind men came to him: and Jesus saith unto**

**them, Believe ye that I am able to do this? They said unto him, Yea, Lord. Then touched he their eyes, saying, According to your faith be it unto you. And their eyes were opened; and Jesus straitly charged them, saying, See that no man know it. But they, when they were departed, spread abroad his fame in all that country (vv. 27-31).**

This account is peculiar to Matthew's Gospel, and is increasingly interesting when compared with Matthew 20:30-34. In both instances Matthew speaks of two blind men. This one appears to be an incident mentioned only in the first Gospel. There are four areas which we might profitably explore. These are: (1) Their sincere desire…"they cried out." (2) The strange delay…"He was come into the house." (3) The searching demand… "Believe ye that I am able to do this?" (4) Their sudden disobedience… They celebrated and "spread abroad his fame." Let us consider these carefully.

## THEIR SINCERE DESIRE

Blindness was, and still is, one of the major medical problems in the Middle East. It is occasioned by poor hygiene and negligence. During my visits to Arab countries, it was appalling to see crowds of children upon whose eyelids flies were crawling. Apparently the boys and girls were accustomed to these intruders, for no attempt was made to drive the pests away. Germs are transmitted freely, and eventually many of those children become blind. Their only hope of survival is to beg, and it is quite impossible to walk along an eastern street without being apprehended by beggers asking for money.

The two men mentioned by Matthew did not ask for money; they wanted sight. Their cry "Son of David," might even infer they considered Jesus to be the long-awaited Messiah. It also suggests they were Jews, for such a title would have been meaningless to Gentiles. They realized the Lord might be able to do for them what others had found impossible. There is always hope for people, when they are aware of personal need.

## THE STRANGE DELAY… "He was come into the house" (v. 28).

It is interesting to read that Jesus proceeded into the house; He could easily have performed the miracle in the street. It would appear "as though he heard them not" (compare Matt. 15:23 and John 8:6). Why the delay? The fact that this temporary postponement of healing was followed by a searching question, suggests the Lord was making sure the men were genuine. It is not difficult to make decisions when crowds of people are supportive. Every man can advance on the crest of a wave of emotion. When he stands or kneels alone before his Maker; when he is not motivated by cries of encouragement from people around him; his sincerity is beyond dispute. It is better to be alone in the secret place of the Most High, than to be influenced by any crowd. Jesus delayed the miracle to bring out of those men their best qualities. A person who kneels before God has no difficulty standing before crowds — even if the people be hostile.

*THE SEARCHING DEMAND... "Believe ye that I am able to do this?" (v. 28b).*

There is no record that the men were told to follow Christ into the house. They had come so far, it seemed unwise to turn back! They might have traveled miles to reach that home; they would have been foolish to allow a door to keep them from a priceless blessing. They could not see Jesus, but inner senses warned them He was looking in their direction. "Do you believe I am able to restore your sight?" Their voices may have quivered when they replied, "Yea, Lord!" They are to be commended for their brevity. Some men would have taken thirty minutes to tell Jesus what He already knew. They came straight to the point with one single word "YEA." Then they added another illuminating word "LORD." We are told elsewhere that no man can call Him Lord but by the Holy Spirit. It would therefore seem that the divine Spirit was already operating on their souls, even before the Great Physician began removing their blindness. When this happens, the end result is never in doubt. These suppliants were there, not for handouts; a deep yearning within their beings cried aloud for the living God. No crowds urged them on; they were alone with Jesus.

*THEIR SUDDEN DISOBEDIENCE... "They spread abroad his fame" (v. 31b).*

"Jesus straitly charged them, saying, See that no man know it. But they... spread abroad his fame in all that country" (vv. 30,31). It is difficult to criticize them; exuberance filled and overflowed their hearts. They had been delivered and everybody should know it. Their actions in other circumstances would have been commendable. They could have become successful evangelists. The time for aggressive evangelism had not yet arrived. Excessive enthusiasm could incite people to insurrection against the Roman invaders and, since the opposition was growing stronger, their testimony might have been dangerous (compare John 12:10-11). Fiery testimonies have always thrilled the church, but fire is harmful if it be not controlled. Blessed are they who are courageous in speaking when God so directs, but wise are they who know how to remain silent, when the Lord forbids speech. Abraham Lincoln said, "It is better to remain silent and be thought a fool, than to speak and remove all doubt."

SECTION SEVEN

*Expository Notes on the Giving of Speech to the Mute*

**And as they went out, behold, they brought to him a dumb man possessed with a devil. And when the devil was cast out, the dumb spake; and the multitudes marvelled, saying, It was never so seen in Israel. But the Pharisees said, He casteth out devils through the prince of the devils (vv. 32-34).**

This passage of the Scriptures is interesting because it contrasts four types of people. First, we have the man who was unable to speak; then we have the multitudes who wished to see a miracle; the Master who was able to save, and the critics who remained stubborn. Let us consider them in that order.

*THE MAN WHO COULD NOT SPEAK... How silent*

The Lord and His disciples were walking away, when suddenly the people pushed a mute man before the Savior. It would be informative if we could know their motives. Were they trying to help an unfortunate man, and if so, why did not the man come unassisted to seek help? Was he too embarrassed, fearing he would appear to be foolish as he stood silently before Jesus? Could he not have written his request and placed the paper into the hands of Jesus? On the other hand, were the people sympathetic, understanding the man's predicament and fears? Did they render real assistance asking for the man what he could not request personally? Yet there is no mention of any request having been made. There exists the possibility that they were presenting a challenge. Would this case be too hard for Jesus to handle? Would failure embarrass Him? There are all kinds of possibilities hidden in the text; there are questions which cannot authoritatively be answered. Nevertheless, there is one important truth evident to all Christians. The best thing to do with any problem, whether it be centered in people, circumstances, or things, is to bring the difficulty to Jesus. If He cannot help, nobody can.

*THE MULTITUDES WISHING TO SEE... How suggestive*

The Lord had already performed numerous miracles, yet they wanted Him to repeat His actions. Was this an act of love or a seductive challenge? Was their faith always to be dependent upon supernatural signs? Could they not believe without miracles? It should be remembered how the Lord said to Thomas, "Because thou hast *seen* me, thou hast believed: blessed are they that have not seen, and yet have believed" (John 20:29). True faith knows how to walk in the dark; alas, many people require the crutches of sensationalism before they take a step. If the multitude were testing or challenging the Lord, they were exhibiting stupidity. Their devotion could thrive during revivals, but they would be conspicuous by their absence as soon as the miracles disappeared. If a man's faithfulness depends upon whether God answers prayer affirmatively, then his worship and requests are questionable. A consecrated man is content to leave things in the hands of a heavenly Father, saying, "Thy will, not mine be done."

*THE MASTER ABLE TO SAVE... How superb*

"And when the devil was cast out, the dumb spake" (v. 33a). It is comforting to know that Jesus was equal to every demand legitimately made upon Him. "He is able," should be a favorite text in the life of every Christian. Testifying for Jesus should be a priority in daily conduct. If we have a story to tell, our friends will be deprived of blessings if we fail to speak. The *Amplified New Testament* translates the verse as follows, "...and the crowds were stunned with bewildered wonder, saying, Never before has anything like this been seen in Israel." It was a day to be remembered!

*THE MEN WHO REMAINED STUBBORN... How stupid*

"But the Pharisees said, He casteth out devils through the prince of devils" (v. 34). There were none so blind as the people who did not wish to see! The Pharisees had decided already that no good thing could come out of Nazareth: whatever the Lord did or said, their attitude would remain unchangeable. They were content to remain as they had always been; the law was God's final word; any addition was unacceptable. Any person who detests the light welcomes darkness; any individual who hates truth encourages a lie. There is no neutral position. Jesus said, "If a man be for me, he cannot be against me, and if he be against me, he cannot be my disciple." It is written that every knee must bow, and every tongue confess that Jesus is Lord (see Phil. 2:9-11).

## SECTION EIGHT

### *Expository Notes on Christ's Words*
### *Concerning the Need for Laborers*

**And Jesus went about all the cities and villages, teaching in their synagogues, and preaching the gospel of the kingdom, and healing every sickness and every disease among the people. But when he saw the multitudes, he was moved with compassion on them, because they fainted, and were scattered abroad, as sheep having no shepherd. Then saith he unto his disciples, The harvest truly is plenteous, but the labourers are few. Pray ye therefore the Lord of the harvest, that he will send forth labourers into his harvest (vv. 35-38).**

## A TRAVELING EVANGELIST

"And Jesus went about all the cities and villages" (v. 35a). The Lord not only commanded His disciples to go forth preaching the gospel of the kingdom; He showed them how to do it. Day after day, week after week, He moved slowly, gracefully, from place to place, and His arrival was like spring sunshine after winter storms. The seeds of faith within human hearts felt the warmth of His compassion, and germinated to produce fruit of the most delightful kind. The synagogues provided His meeting places, but the open air became His cathedral. The people welcomed Him with open arms, and followed Him when He left. The Lord realized that Calvary's cross awaited the termination of His journey, but temporarily, the horror of the crucifixion was ignored. Jesus loved and healed people; He hugged the children to His breast, and thrilled audiences with His glorious gospel. He was wonderful and they knew it. He worked while it was day, knowing the night was coming when work would be impossible.

## A TOUCHING EMOTION

"He was moved with compassion" (v. 36a). The word translated "compassion" is *esplagchnisthee*. It is derived from *splagchna* which, according to Thayer "means the bowels, or the depths of one's being." Jesus was very deeply moved when He saw the restlessness of the people. They appeared to be as sheep without a shepherd, and they had no idea where to go or what to do. The *Interlinear Greek Testament* translates the sentence, "He was filled with tenderness." The *Amplified New Testament* renders the passage, "He was moved with pity and sympathy for them, because they were bewildered — harassed, distressed, dejected and helpless, like sheep, without a shepherd." These are translations of the Greek statement: *heesan eskulmenoi kai eppimmenoi* "they were distressed and prostrate. They were in a state of extreme fatigue." Jesus saw them, loved them, and helped them.

## A TRUE EVALUATION

"The harvest truly is plenteous, but the labourers are few" (v. 37b). Elsewhere He said, "Say not ye, There are yet four months, and then cometh harvest? behold, I say unto you, Lift up your eyes, and look on the fields; for they are white already to harvest" (John 4:35). The Lord looked upon the small company of disciples, but realized that if the harvest of precious souls were to be reaped, there would be need for increased workers in the fields. Jesus required volunteers; He needed them then, and He needs them now. The opportunities had increased; alas, the workers had diminished. That the Lord urged the disciples to pray this prayer, for increased numbers of workers, suggests they would not be easy to find. There would be need for divine assistance. Satan would resist every movement to extend the kingdom of God. Jesus urged His men to pray, for only thus would they enjoy being laborers together with God. They should never forget heaven also was interested in reaping the harvest. The Lord bequeathed to the disciples a message which should never be forgotten. If the task seemed hopeless, the worker should never despair. He should plead his case before the throne of grace, and assistance would be forthcoming. For additional notes and homilies, consult the comments on the parallel passages found in the author's commentaries on the Gospels of Mark and Luke.

# The Tenth Chapter of Matthew

THEME: *The Call and the Commissioning of the Twelve Apostles*

OUTLINE:

    I. The Privilege of the Preachers... *"He called them"* (Verses 1-4)

    II. The Power of the Preachers... *"He gave them power"* (Verses 5-8)

    III. The Preparation of the Preachers... *"Provide nothing"* (Verses 9-15)

    IV. The Persecution of the Preachers... *"They shall deliver you up"* (Verses 16-23)

    V. The Persistence of the Preachers... *"Fear not"* (Verses 24-31)

    VI. The Promise to the Preachers... *"I will confess you"* (Verses 32-33)

    VII. The Problems of the Preachers... *"They of his own household"* (Verses 34-38)

    VIII. The Payment to the Preachers... *"A Prophet's Reward"* (Verses 39-42)

## SECTION ONE

*Expository Notes on the Call of the Twelve Apostles*

**And when he had called unto him his twelve disciples, he gave them power against unclean spirits, to cast them out, and to heal all manner of sickness and all manner of disease. Now the names of the twelve apostles are these; The first, Simon, who is called Peter, and Andrew his brother; James the son of Zebedee, and John his brother; Philip, and Bartholomew; Thomas, and Matthew the tax publican; James the son of Alphaeus, and Lebbaeus, whose surname was Thaddaeus; Simon the Canaanite, and Judas Iscariot, who also betrayed him (vv. 1-4).**

Every person is called to discipleship, but not everyone is called to the ministry. Unless a man is certain of this call, he should avoid it in every way possible. There is nothing glamorous about becoming a pastor, and the mission field has never been a fairyland. Some enthusiastic young people have been fascinated by the apparent charm of adventurous service and, on the spur of the moment, decided this had to be their vocation in life. They started out like a house-on-fire, only to find the flames were easily extinguished. A charming young lady once asked my advice concerning her intense desire to become an overseas missionary. She seemed bewildered when I strongly urged her to forget it. I said, "Lady, run for your life; become anything or anyone, but never volunteer to become a missionary." When she continued asking for my reasons, I replied, "Run for your life, and if, after six months, you discover that you cannot outrun God; that your desire has become too heavy a burden to be carried; that the urge persists day and night, THEN, AND ONLY THEN, can you be sure that GOD has called you. The mission field can be a place of loneliness where hearts sometimes break. If that happens, you can wander along a forest path and quietly remember God called you, not to occupy a place in fairyland, but to be His chosen witness among circumstances, which at times may be overwhelmingly difficult." A middle-aged man overheard what I said, and it was interesting to hear his comment. "Sir, I have been a missionary in India for the last twenty-three years, but I wish before God that I had met you before I went out there." Jesus called the men that He desired, but without that experience, they would have failed at every task.

To say the least, the Lord's choice of disciples was astounding; a more less-promising crowd of students it would have been hard to find. For example, He chose Simon the Zealot and Matthew the publican, and that in itself supplies food for thought. The Zealots were a small political band of outlaws! They were ardent nationalists, who considered the liberation of their country the most important thing in life. They detested the occupying Romans, and would have gladly surrendered their lives to expel the hated oppressers Any compromise with the army of occupation was considered to be treason, and any attack launched against people who assisted the enemy was considered justifiable. Thus, for Simon the Zealot to live with, and help Matthew the publican, was in itself a miracle. Matthew had sold himself to the Romans and, worse than that, had become one of those detestable men who made Jews pay the taxes which Zealots considered illegal. Matthew was a traitor; a man who betrayed his own people and, in former days, Simon would have considered it a privilege to execute the tax collector. Their love for Christ had united the extremists, and instead of harming each other, they became brothers. The warmth of God's love can melt the most icy conditions.

Then consider Thomas and Simon Peter; more diversified disciples could not be found. Peter was the man of enthusiasm. He acted first and thought later. He was the impulsive man who would knock down a building and later, when looking at the wreckage, wonder why he had done it. Thomas was the steady man, the thinking man, who carefully contemplated every action. Peter would burn down a building, while Thomas looked for a match. Peter would have sailed his boat across Galilee, while Thomas was making up his mind if the weather would be suitable for sailing. Peter was an expert at keeping his foot on the accelerator pedal; Thomas constantly held the brake. Those two men, ordinarily, would have driven each other crazy, but somehow the love of Christ united their hearts, and they also became brethren.

Andrew, the go-getter disciple, was a strange companion for Judas Iscariot. Andrew desired to bring people to his Lord; Judas lived to take money from the treasury. Andrew never counted the cost of his dedicated services, yet Judas probably believed he was underpaid. Andrew and the others might have been excused had they said, "Get out of the way, Judas, you are a pain in the neck!" Judas might have replied, "Mind your own business. You do your job, and I will attend to mine." That strange collection of men could have quarreled any day of the week, but somehow, the Savior took the useless, the foolish things of the world, and made them into a striking force for God's crusade. (For more detailed notes on the individual characteristics of each of the apostles, see the author's commentary on *Mark's Superb Gospel*, Chapter 3:14-19)

While I was the evangelist for the Baptist Church in Australia, many soldiers returned from the war. They were filled with intense hatred for the men against whom they had fought. Unfortunately, they had been made to watch as some of their comrades had been killed by the enemy. Australians had been spread-eagled, and nailed on doors, and as they slowly died, the Japanese used them for practice in mock bayonet attacks. Language of any kind was insufficient to describe the deep antagonism of the survivors. They hated their former enemies with intense bitterness. Their philosophy was expressed in one statement, "The only good Jap is a dead one." Yet, after the war, the pilot who led the raid on Pearl Harbor became a Christian, and it was truly remarkable to see the reception he received from some of the Australian Christians. When former enemies stand in the shadow of Calvary's cross, the end result will never be in doubt. If both men tell how they were introduced to the Son of God and confess their unworthiness of the grace bestowed upon them, they cease being Australian and Japanese and become brothers in the family of God. The Savior is still calling and commissioning the strangest people, and just as a potter molds and remakes even a marred vessel, so Christ can make the least promising person fit for the kingdom of God (see Homily No. 6, "Jordan Management Consultants" at the end of Section 8).

## SECTION TWO

*Expository Notes on the First Instructions Given to the Disciples*

**These twelve Jesus sent forth, and commanded them, saying, Go not into the way of the Gentiles, and into any city of the Samaritans enter ye not: But go rather to the lost sheep of the house of Israel. And as ye go, preach, saying, The kingdom of heaven is at hand. Heal the sick, cleanse the lepers, raise the dead, cast out devils: freely ye have received, freely give (vv. 5-8).**

The word which is used in the Greek for Jesus "commanding" His men is very interesting and illuminating. It is the word *paraggellein*. This word has four usages: (1) It is the regular word for a military command. Jesus was like a general sending commanders out on a campaign, briefing them before they went. (2) It is used when calling friends to help you. Jesus was like a man with a great ideal, who summoned His friends to make that ideal come true. (3) It is used by a teacher giving rules and precepts to his students or disciples. Jesus, like a teacher, sent His students out into a world, equipped with His teaching and with His message. (4) It is the word which is regularly used for an imperial command. Like a king, Jesus dispatched His ambassadors into the world to carry out His orders and to speak for Him.

These four areas of thought should impress every reader with the importance of Christ's commission. That He forbade their going to the Gentiles presents no insoluble problem. His mission was to the entire world, but the methods necessary to reach that goal demanded careful and precise planning. All tourists to the Middle East are aware of similar restrictions imposed by the wise planning of a tour leader. There exists a bitter animosity between certain nations and the Israeli people. If a traveler desires to visit both Israel and the adjacent countries of the Arab world, it is wise to leave Israel until last. When an Israeli stamp is found inside a passport, the traveler is sure to have problems with Arab officials. The problem is partially overcome by having the Israeli stamp placed on a separate piece of paper. When the visit to Israel has been completed, the passport can then be presented "unblemished" to foreign officials. There is no trouble at any Israeli Port of Entry, for with the exception of known criminals, the Israelis welcome everybody.

Something of the kind must have been in the thoughts of Jesus when He issued His commands to the disciples. However, the problems were in reverse. The arrogant Jews desired no contacts with the uncircumcised heathen, and the Gentiles were not too enamored with the Hebrews. The incident of the Samaritan villagers who refused to welcome Christ, because He was intent on visiting Jerusalem, provides insight into the situation existing in those days. The possibility existed, that if the gospel were considered something associated with Gentiles, the Jews would reject it, even before they heard the message. Anything associated with Gentiles was considered tainted. The Lord loved Israel, and although He realized the nation would ultimately desire His crucifixion, they too had to be given the opportunity to hear the truth. That the Gentiles would eventually get their opportunity to hear, believe, and live, was never open to conjecture. Jesus knew they would still be there when Israel had rejected His message. A brief postponement of the Gentile opportunity could do no harm, especially when it was part of the divine plan by which all men would learn of the Savior.

There was something gloriously positive about the method of proclamation of those early itinerant evangelists. They did not "beat about the bush"; they came straight to the point and said, "The kingdom of heaven is at hand." The Jews believed firmly in the forthcoming establishment of the kingdom of God, and the announcement that the moment had arrived was the most startling statement they had heard in years. They might have shunned and rejected the heralds of the King, but amazing miracles endorsed each word uttered. Within the land where hospitals were unknown, and doctors few and far between, the miracles performed by the visiting preachers could only be viewed as blessings sent by God. However, it should be carefully noted that the disciples were only able to dispense what they had first received from their Master. He had said, "Freely ye have received, freely give" (v. 8b). It is hardly possible to give away something not possessed. Every minister of the gospel should gaze into the face of the Lord before seeing faces in a congregation. Unless we receive the Bread of Life from Christ, we shall never satisfy the hunger of those to whom we are sent. An appointment with Christ should always precede an appearance in a church. Unless we charge our batteries in His presence, our light will never effectively shine in the communities we visit.

Our provision must be adequate. Some specially gifted men may be able to perform miracles, but most of God's servants are not as richly endowed. Yet even the least should be able, with Christ's help, to heal those who are sick in soul. It should be possible to release men from the bondage of sin.


## SECTION THREE

*Expository Notes on the Strange Lack of Equipment*


**Provide neither gold, nor silver, nor brass in your purses, Nor a scrip for your journey, neither two coats, neither shoes, nor yet staves; for the workman is worthy of his meat. And into whatsoever city or town ye shall enter, inquire who in it is worthy; and there abide till ye go from thence. And when ye come into an house, salute it. And if the house be worthy, let your peace come upon it; but if it be not worthy, let your peace return to you. And whosoever shall not receive you, nor hear your words, when ye depart out of that house or city, shake off the dust of your feet. Verily I say unto you, It shall be more tolerable for the land of Sodom and Gomorrha in the day of judgment, than for that city (vv. 9-15).**


## THEIR COMPLETE DEPENDENCE

It is difficult to imagine the arrival of these preachers in any town; a more unpresentable collection of men it would have been hard to find. They were totally without visible means of support; they had no change of apparel; they had no homes in which they were sure of a welcome, and to say the least, their immediate future seemed ominous. Their arrival in a community would resemble the coming of a group of hippies to beg in a very respectable town. And yet, the situation was not as bad as might be thought. The Jews were accustomed to itinerant rabbis, who practiced the identical things commanded by Jesus. The clothing worn by Easterners was limited. Men wore a simple loincloth as an undergarment, and a long flowing robe which hung from their shoulders to cover the entire body. The undergarment could easily be washed and would take only moments to dry in the fierce heat of an Eastern day. The purse, to which Jesus referred, was a belt worn around the waist. It had two pockets in which valuables could be carried. The bag might have been the kind usually owned by a wandering minstrel, who accepted an offering after giving a street performance. Every listener should be convinced immediately of the genuineness of the preachers, who were not interested in material things, but only in the proclamation of their message.

Jewish law said, "No one is to go to the Temple Mount with staff, shoes, girdle or money, or dusty feet." The sanctuary was not the place in which to discuss business or make money. The people who gathered there should only think about worshiping God. It was believed that poverty developed increasing trust in the Lord. This common faith encouraged all citizens to feed a rabbi or any holy men as they continued their pilgrimages. Jesus was merely following lines of conduct already established within the nation. The attitude of the disciples would instantly identify them as holy men, and their food would therefore be assured. It is not an established fact that these methods would operate successfully today, but we must remember we are considering a different culture in an age far removed from the twentieth century.

## THEIR CAREFUL DECISION

"And into whatsoever city or town ye shall enter, inquire who in it is worthy; and there abide till ye go from thence" (v. 11). Years ago when I was to preach in a certain British town, the local Christians made reservations for my hospitality in a well-known establishment. It was more like a hotel. However, a few days prior to my arrival, a set of circumstances made it necessary to change my accommodation. I was therefore sent elsewhere. We did not realize at the time how God had miraculously intervened to save me from very embarrassing moments. A week later, when my meetings were gaining momentum, the place in which I was to have stayed was raided by the police. The owners were charged with running a house of prostitution, and the people staying beneath that roof were all apprehended for complicity in illegal practices.

When the Lord gave strict instructions concerning the choice of a place in which to stay, He was aware of things which could make or break their mission. His recommendation, that the chosen home should be their place of residence throughout the stay in the city, was wise. I have often been entertained in homes from which I would have loved to escape, but discretion promoted extreme caution. If a preacher left a cottage in order to be more lavishly entertained in a palace, the action would contradict his testimony. His leaving might crush the spirit of the sincere folk who at least had offered their best to God's servant. During the depression in Lancashire, England, a man said to me, "Sir, I am a coal miner, and we have all been on strike for a long time. The wife and I do not have much, but if you will come home with me, we will gladly share what little we have." I reminisce with gratitude and joy. That was one of the happiest nights of my life. We did not have a sumptuous meal, but the fellowship surpassed anything I had known in a long time. Every preacher should embrace everything helpful; shun every possible hindrance, and be very careful deciding which is which!

## THE CANDID DECLARATION

"And whosoever shall not receive you, nor hear your words, when ye depart out of that house or city, shake off the dust of your feet" (v. 14). This was the most severe indictment that could be made against any Jewish community. When Jews traveled in Gentile countries, they considered themselves as having been defiled. It was customary, on their return to Palestine, to stop at the border and shake off the dust of the accursed Gentile world. It was a confession that the traveler had nothing in common with the pagans; that he was glad of the opportunity of becoming clean again. That Jesus should use the common practice of the Jews to teach the importance of His message was of extreme importance. To reject the message of the kingdom was to be as unclean as the detested Gentiles; to be filthy in the sight of God, and totally unworthy of any blessing He could send. It inferred that the chosen people were no longer what they had been; they were rejected by God, and unfit to enter into the kingdom of heaven. Thus did Jesus send forth His missionaries on what was virtually the first evangelistic crusade. That His Spirit went with them became obvious, for when they returned they reported all kinds of amazing things had taken place. They said, "even the devils are subject unto us through thy name" (Luke 10:17).

*Expository Notes on Christ's Warning of Approaching Problems*

**Behold, I send you forth as sheep in the midst of wolves: be ye therefore wise as serpents, and harmless as doves. But beware of men: for they will deliver you up to the councils, and they will scourge you in their synagogues; And ye shall be brought before governors and kings for my sake, for a testimony against them and the Gentiles. But when they deliver you up, take no thought how or what ye shall speak. For it is not ye that speak, but the Spirit of your Father which speaketh in you (vv. 16-20).**

## THE URGENT WARNING

The Lord never enticed followers with promises of easy conquests. He warned them of approaching trials, and indicated opposition would come from royalty, religion, and relatives. They would be brought before governors and kings; the strongest powers in the world would be arrayed against them; their testimony would be refuted by the cleverest of earth's lawyers. The most bigoted religious authorities would scourge them; their backs would be bleeding; they would be as sheep among ravenous wolves. The battlefield would be no place for cowards; the faint-hearted should turn back immediately. Yet, for those who dared, a special kind of wisdom would be imparted, and the outcome of the persecution would be a thrilling testimony reaching the entire world. The privilege being bestowed upon the disciples would rank as one of the greatest ever given by God. They should be aware of these possibilities, but if a man put his hand to the plough and then looked back, he would be unfit for the kingdom of God.

## THE UNIQUE WITNESS

Overwhelming academic distinction would be arrayed against them, but an apparent lack of educational ability should not worry them. Throughout any crisis, the answers, wisdom, and needed strength would be miraculously given to them. They would know what to say and to do, for the Holy Spirit would be present to help in every time of need. That promise was never a license for laziness. God never meant for men to be supernaturally controlled robots. Man had been given the capacity to think, to plan, to be wise. The disciples should do all within their power to become good soldiers of Jesus Christ, but they were never to forget that the Holy Spirit would be their commanding officer. He would direct, protect, and supervise each detail of the offensive being planned in heaven. When special help became necessary, the Lord would impart to their minds the words to be spoken, and to their lives the power which would make them invincible.

## THE UNEXPECTED WICKEDNESS

Their greatest opponents would be those of their own households. "And the brother shall deliver up the brother to death, and the father the child: and the children shall rise up against their parents, and cause them to be put to death" (v. 21). Similar conditions prevailed throughout Germany during World War II. The fanaticism of Nazi doctrines destroyed family ties, and indoctrinated children betrayed their parents, believing their duty to the state superseded filial devotion. This was slavery of the most detestable kind, when love was sacrificed upon altars of nationalism, and honor, truth, and goodness became features found only in history books. The disciples were warned that this situation would confront them; that families would be split; that hatred would supersede love. Discipleship demanded courage of the highest order and sacrifice unlimited. History attests that the men chosen by Jesus were more than equal to their task.

## THE UNFINISHED WORK

The followers of Christ would be hated of all men, but a conqueror's crown awaited those who endured to the end. Faithful servants would have true joy when acclaimed as spiritual heroes; they enter the palace of their King. The apostles would sit upon twelve thrones, governing the twelve tribes in an eternal kingdom. Their work should be continued at all costs; there were many needy places awaiting the gospel message. It would be impossible to reach all the cities of Israel before their Master would return; their work would never be completely finished. Many cities were awaiting the arrival of the gospel preachers, therefore the task of evangelism had the highest priority

### SECTION FIVE

*Expository Notes on The Need for Faith and Courage*

**The disciple is not above his teacher, nor the servant above his lord. It is enough for the disciple that he be as his master, and the servant as his lord. If they have called the master of the house Beelzebub, how much more shall they call them of his household? Fear them not**

therefore: for there is nothing covered, that shall not be revealed; and hid, that shall not be known. What I tell you in the darkness, that speak ye in light; and what ye hear in the ear, that preach ye upon the housetops. And fear not them which kill the body, but are not able to kill the soul: but rather fear him which is able to destroy both soul and body in hell. Are not two sparrows sold for a farthing? and one of them shall not fall on the ground without your Father. But the very hairs of your head are all numbered. Fear ye not therefore, ye are of more value than many sparrows (vv. 24-31).

## THE GLORIOUS PRIVILEGE

"It is enough for the disciple that he be as his master, and the servant as his Lord" (v. 24). If the enemies had slandered the Lord, it was to be expected they would do likewise with those who represented Him. If they would crucify the Son of God, it would be no cause for amazement when they ill-treated His messengers. Their highway would be one of suffering and heartache; they should find comfort in their Companion who would never leave them. Paul later called this "the fellowship of his sufferings," and confessed it was one of his greatest ambitions to be identified with the Lord, and to walk at His side all the way to the gloryland (see Phil. 3:8-10). However, it should be remembered that enjoyment of this kind is only known by those who graduate from God's school of consecration. It depends upon three things: (1) Complete commitment to Christ. (2) Constant closeness to Christ. (3) Consuming consecration to Christ. To walk with and to learn of the Savior, is to grow in grace and godliness. Perfect love for Him should expel all fear from the disciple's soul, and every situation in life should be confronted in the absolute assurance that God was still on His throne. Emblazoned upon their banners should be, "Fear them not." There can be no secrets with God. He knows the hidden depths of every heart and, in the fullness of time, everything will be made clear for all to understand.

## THE GOOD PREACHING

"What I tell you...speak ye...what ye hear in the ear, that preach [proclaim] ye upon the housetops" (v. 27). The source of the message must always be God. He plans to use His preachers and bless His Word. When the herald spends time in the secret place, God whispers the great truths related to salvation. The preacher, however eloquent, is but an amplifier announcing words spoken in heaven's broadcasting station. He should follow the script written indelibly on his mind, and never express personal ideas, nor advocate political policies. A minister's job is to introduce Christ to everybody who will listen. The devil will use every device possible to turn God's servants from their divinely appointed task. Every land needs reformers; every community needs courageous orators to denounce the decadent tendencies of the times, but the preacher's job is to proclaim Christ. Alas, some great preachers have a tendency to become reformers; they spend time with the lesser things of life, and eternal verities are sometimes pushed into the background of their activities. Paul's advice to the young pastor, Timothy, is as valid today as it was at the beginning of the church age: ''PREACH THE WORD'' (2 Tim. 4:2).

## THE GREAT PRICE

''And fear not them which kill the body, but are not able to kill the soul'' (v. 28a). During the Spanish Civil War, Pastor S. Vila, a Baptist minister from Barcelona, visited my church in Wales and thrilled the congregation with his account of what happened in a Spanish prison. A Baptist pastor had been thrown into what was, in actual fact, a filthy dungeon. Each day a guard came to the door and read aloud a list of prisoners to be executed that morning. Consequently fear overwhelmed the prisoners, and they were running around shrieking, and scribbling obscenities on the walls. One man in a frenzy wrote, ''Death to Franco; death to the Pope.'' The Baptist pastor felt troubled that he had not written something more beneficial. He thereupon took a piece of chalk and wrote, ''Fear not them which kill the body; but are not able to kill the soul. For God so loved the world, that He gave His only begotten Son, that whosoever believeth in Him should not perish but have everlasting life.'' When the prisoners read the message, they advanced on the pastor shouting, ''He is one of them; let us kill him.'' Then a schoolmaster intervened saying, ''Men, he is with us, and his name may be announced tomorrow morning.'' His words quieted the mob, and afterward this schoolmaster sat with the pastor and asked how he could be so calm, when he also faced death. The Christian expounded the Bible passage we are now studying and explained that the death of Christ had destroyed fear for all true believers. Two mornings later when his name was called, the teacher marched to the door, paused to look back at his friend, and said, ''Thank God, I met you. Everything is fine; I know where I am going.'' We would be unaware of this incident, except for the fact that intervention from high political and international circles succeeded in obtaining the release of the pastor who, afterward, related the account to his people.

Matthew tells us that two sparrows were sold for a farthing; the smallest of all British coins. Actually, it was the tenth part of a Roman penny, but Luke 12:6 informs us that five sparrows were sold for two farthings. If a man were willing to spend two farthings, *one extra bird was given*. These small birds were almost worthless, and yet Jesus indicated that not one of them fell to the ground anywhere, unobserved by His Father. He also reminded His disciples that they were of more value than many sparrows. Accentuating His statement, He said, "The very hairs of your head are all numbered." To know the number of hairs on one's head is of little consequence to men, but if God can be interested in such minor details, He surely cares for the man beneath the hair! It was imperative that each outgoing missionary should remember this important fact.

## SECTION SIX

*Expository Notes on Christ's Confession in Heaven*

**Whosoever therefore shall confess me before men, him will I confess also before my Father which is in heaven. But whosoever shall deny me before men, him will I also deny before my Father which is in heaven (vv. 32-33).**

This probably is one of the most potent of all the sayings of Christ. The disciples were to preach the gospel but, always, the Lord should be the theme of their message. Everything should revolve around Him. Men's moral character; church affiliation and reputation might be important, but these would have little influence upon eternal values. Every listener was to be confronted with Jesus of Nazareth. His words were to be of preeminent importance; His Cross the gateway to a new life; His gift of salvation was either to be accepted or rejected. Men had to be informed that, as they treated the Son of God, so would they be judged when they appeared before God. The salvation of their souls was of paramount importance; it would affect their eternal existence. If they truly confessed the Savior, then He would confess them; if they rejected Him, they had no hope for eternity. That precisely was His message, and it matters not how theologians and others might dilute the message; that was, and still is, the message given by Christ. He described two decisions and two destinies, either irrevocably connected with the other.

The disciples were to go forth into the highways and byways of life preaching this message, and constantly were to watch for four things: (1) Contrition, (2) Conversion, (3) Confession, (4) Consecration. If any one of these important features were not seen in the life of the convert, then his profession of faith was suspect. Contrition without confession only led to continuing misery. Conversion which did not produce consecration, could be as meaningless as the acceptance of dead dogma. Conversion meant turning from something to Someone, and if the professed convert did not desire to serve the Lord, then, obviously, there was something wrong, either with his eyesight, or with his soul. Good works would never be sufficient unless they were preceded by repentance and regeneration. The entire gospel preached by the disciples revolved around these facets of truth, and even today the same spiritual laws apply.

It is an attractive sight when many people respond to the appeals of an enthusiastic evangelist, but sometimes all that glitters is not gold! Converts are counted, not by the number of decision cards signed, nor by the number of people walking down an aisle. True converts are only numbered by those working hard to win others twelve months after the special meetings terminate. Happy and wise are they who measure up to these standards. Jesus promised that as they confessed Him on earth, they would be confessed before the throne of God. The acceptance of His promise should enable a convert to say triumphantly, (1) I am saved, (2) I am safe, and (3) I am satisfied.

If Christ confesses my name before the Father in heaven, and He promised so to do, then I have no need to question my acceptance. I have turned from empty religious systems; I have renounced my self-righteousness which is likened unto filthy rags; and my complete dependence is upon Christ, the Lamb of God. Christ never misled His followers with false promises. He meant exactly what He said and, if the Lord admits I am one of His followers, I should cease worrying about my unworthiness, and rather rejoice that He has made Himself responsible for my citizenship in God's country. I must be saved if *He* says so. Happiness depends on how I cling to Him; safety depends on how He clings to me. I may lose my grip, but the Lord said, ''I give unto them eternal life; and they shall NEVER perish, *neither shall any man pluck them out of my hand*'' (John 10:28). Surely the Lord meant what He said. It follows that all who become sheep in His flock are not only saved, they are safe. Unless there is something wrong in the convert's conception of eternal promises, he should be completely satisfied as he continues to serve his Lord. If these things are true, and they are, then it also follows that the opposite is also true concerning those who reject Christ. The Lamb of God was the very best that God could offer. If Christ, the eternal Son, cannot save sinners, they remain lost. This was the New Testament gospel, and since it was authorized by the Lord, only unwise people question His statements. To possess Christ is wonderful; to be possessed by the Lord is even better.

## SECTION SEVEN

*Expository Notes on the Strangest Message Jesus Ever Preached*

**Think not that I am come to send peace on earth: I came not to send peace, but a sword. For I am come to set a man at variance against his father, and the daughter against her mother, and the daughter-in-law against her mother-in-law. And a man's foes shall be they of his own household (vv. 34-36).**

Viewed from one angle, the gospel of Christ must be considered the most revolutionary message ever brought to man. Peace, the most elusive treasure in the world, has always been linked with the Savior; it is impossible to have peace without the Prince of Peace. Isaiah predicted the Messiah's name would be "The Prince of Peace" (Isa. 9:6). Micah said that when Messiah arrived, every man would be able to sit at peace beneath his own fig tree (see Mic. 4:4). When the Lord came to earth, the angels said, "Glory to God in the highest, and on earth peace, good will toward men" (Luke 2:14). The disciples, believing their Master would establish the Messianic kingdom, anticipated the day when peace would be enjoyed in Israel. When the Lord predicted that families would be irrevocably divided, their preconceived ideas were ruined. That the message of Christ should create discord within family circles was unbelievable. Yet, such results were unavoidable. The cutting edge of the gospel, its transforming power in the lives of converts, could not fail to cause division and pain. Within a home where idolatry was practiced, the conversion of a member of that family would inevitably lead to tension. If a daughter or a son objected to the family practice, refusal would lead to argument and strife; peace would be impossible. Then each young Christian would have to choose between conformity to ancestral custom and faithfulness to the Savior (see the special homily at the end of this chapter).

*Expository Notes on the Rewards Given to the Preachers*

**And he that taketh not his cross, and followeth after me, is not worthy of me. He that findeth his life shall lose it: and he that loseth his life for my sake shall find it. He that receiveth you receiveth me, and he that receiveth me receiveth him that sent me. He that receiveth a prophet in the name of a prophet shall receive a prophet's reward; and he that receiveth a righteous man in the name of a righteous man shall receive a righteous man's reward. And whosoever shall give to drink unto one of these little ones a cup of cold water only in the name of a disciple, verily I say unto you, he shall in no way lose his reward (vv. 38-42).**

When the Lord had completed instructing His disciples, He reminded them that God always pays high wages for services faithfully rendered. Every action; every vestige of work would be assessed, and the very difficulty of their tasks only enhanced the possibility of higher rewards. Nothing would be forgotten and no sacrifice overlooked.

## GOD'S REVELATION

"He that findeth his life shall lose it: and he that loseth his life for my sake shall find it" (v. 39a). This is one of the most remarkable facts of life. Dr. Frank Boreham, addressing a meeting in Melbourne, Australia, said, "If you possess something without which you cannot live, give it away." That minister was a very wise man. Anything that is completely indispensable is apt to become dangerous. It is infinitely better to remain poor with God at your side, than to be a millionaire and journey through life alone. Poverty can be turned to wealth in the presence of the Lord; riches can quickly become memories when death approaches. There are things money cannot buy; happy are the people who invest their time and talents in eternal realities.

## GOD'S RECKONING

"He that receiveth you, receiveth me, and he that receiveth me receiveth him that sent me" (v. 40). The faithful preachers would become part of God's lifeline, reaching out to a dying world. Identification with Christ meant union with God. The faithful witness would become an integral part of an eternal redemptive plan. God, the Father; the Lord

Jesus Christ, the Son; the Holy Spirit and the believer, would be intimate partners in the greatest endeavor ever undertaken on earth. The Father would plan each operation; the Savior would operate the venture, and the Holy Spirit would accompany each preacher. The Christian would be given the inestimable privilege of becoming a worker WITH God. The preacher would be lending his voice, his mind, his body to the Lord of the universe, and this would be a privilege beyond description. That was the way in which the Savior described the tasks awaiting His chosen apostles. If they remembered the most mundane task was being specially performed for God, then even the trivial jobs would become resplendent with ineffable glory.

## GOD'S REWARDS

Jesus seemed to emphasize that God pays great wages! No one is ever underpaid, and yet, rewards had to be earned; there would be nothing cheap about the life of service upon which they were about to embark. The Lord cited (1) A prophet's reward, (2) A righteous man's reward, (3) A special reward given for assistance offered to "one of these little ones." To receive a prophet was equal to doing the work of a prophet. A man may not have the outstanding ability to proclaim, eloquently, the message of the Lord, but even if he only offered the preacher a bed and a meal, God would assess this as though the man had been a prophet himself. God's computers work in strange ways. It may not be as simple to explain the righteous man's reward, for such a man would seldom find a welcome in the abode of an unrighteous person. Does it mean that if a householder found pleasure in sheltering a godly man, and if this became a habit, something of the good man's righteousness would eventually produce a similar righteousness in the life of the host? God is aware of the most insignificant gifts, and finds pleasure in rewarding the offering of a cup of water to a thirsty soul. Thus did Jesus teach that every kind of dedicated action is blessed by His Father, and no sacrifice for Him will ever be made in vain. At the conclusion of a life of service would come "pay day," when the Lord's servants would be rewarded for their consecrated efforts. These promises would be a great incentive to serve faithfully, but there is reason to believe that the greatest motivating power in the lives of the itinerant evangelists was not the promise of future rewards, but their overwhelming love for the Master who had commissioned them to preach. Every true missionary would gladly exclaim, "If He rewards me, that will be wonderful; if He does not, I'll do it anyway — just for His sake."

HOMILIES

Study No. 5

### The Savior's Strangest Utterance

The coming of Christ stirred the hearts of Israel as they had never previously been stirred, and from all parts of the country crowds rushed to hear the new Teacher. Every miracle gave promise of greater things to come, and the fact that He gave peace to innumerable sufferers, seemed to guarantee that soon He would be able to bring peace to the troubled nation. Then to the consternation of His followers, He said, "Think not that I am come to send peace on earth: I came not to send peace, but a sword. For I am come to set a man at variance against his father, and the daughter against her mother....And a man's foes shall be they of his own household" (vv. 35,36).

*THE SWORD THAT WOUNDS*

The Bible has three things to say of the usefulness of a sword. In the first place it is able to wound. The Savior came to act as a great surgeon  and, knowing the need of His patients, endorsed a gospel destined to be a two-edged sword. Recognizing the deep-seated need of sinners, the Lord Jesus did not hesitate to hurt them, for only by so doing could He bring healing to their sick hearts. He also warned His disciples that the forceful presentation of the gospel message would arouse resentment, for the sword of truth would penetrate into the secret places of the conscience, to reveal things that most people would prefer to remain hidden. He said, "Woe unto you, when all men shall speak well of you" (Luke 6:26). Holy warfare must always precede the healing of souls, for until sin is ruthlessly exposed and overcome, spiritual healing will be an impossibility.

*THE SWORD THAT SEPARATES*

"For I am come to set a man at variance against his father, and the daughter against her mother" (v.35a), and we might add "a friend against his friend." The incoming of the gospel message leads to a complete transformation in the outlook of men. The convert's former associates will probably misunderstand his motives; they might even persecute him in his new faith. In order to follow the Lord Jesus, the Christian may have to renounce his old delights and forsake many of his former friends. The business man may find it necessary to revise all his ideas of trading, and if this should lead to serious financial loss, his partners will probably have a great deal to say in the matter. A wife who has accepted Christ as her Savior may find it impossible to accompany her husband in the ways of sin, and her refusal to cooperate may lead to domestic unpleasantness. The sword of the gospel will sever ties that might have been in existence for years and, instead of creating peace, will prove to be the harbinger of discord. The early history of the Church provided ample evidence of the truth of Christ's prediction.

## THE SWORD THAT MINISTERS

The inspired Old Testament prophet recognized another use for the sword, and embodied his vision in his thrilling utterance concerning the coming of the King. ''And he shall judge among the nations, and shall rebuke many people: and they shall beat their swords into plowshares, and their spears into pruninghooks: nation shall not life up sword against nation, neither shall they learn war any more'' (Isa. 2:4). The prophet saw that the coronation of the Messiah would transform the steel weapons of war and make them to serve a new purpose in the production of food. People who had been hurt by the sword would suddenly be fed by the new instrument. And in like manner, this is true concerning the gospel of Christ. The message of redemption will hurt, and then separate the sinner from the ways of sin. Yet, when this operation has been completed, and Christ occupies the throne of a man's affection, the Bible suddenly becomes the greatest book in the world. Within its pages the Christian discovers the true source of the bread of life. It will minister to his deepest needs and satisfy his hungry soul. The universal coronation of the Lord Jesus will lead to a new world, and the greatest proof of this sublime fact is found when a similar transformation takes place within the kingdom of a man's heart. (Reprinted from the author's book, *Bible Pinnacles*, pp. 85-86.)

Study No. 6

## THE JORDAN MANAGEMENT CONSULTANTS

To Jesus, Son of Joseph
Woodcrafters Carpenter's Shop
Nazareth, 25922

Dear Sir,

Thank you for submitting the résumés of the twelve men you have for management positions in your new organization. All of them have now taken our battery of tests; and we have not only run the results through our computer, but also arranged personal interviews for each of them with our psychologist and vocational aptitude consultant. The profiles of all tests are included, and you will want to study each of them carefully. As part of our advice and for your guidance, we make some general comments, much as an auditor will include some general statements. This is given as a result of staff consultation and comes without any additional fee.

It is the staff opinion that most of your nominees are lacking in background, education, and vocational aptitude for the type of enterprise you are undertaking. They do not have the team concept. We would recommend that you continue your search for persons of experience in managerial ability and proven capability. Simon Peter is emotionally unstable and given to fits of temper. Andrew has absolutely no qualities of leadership. The two brothers, James and John, the sons of Zebedee, place personal interest above company loyalty. Thomas demonstrates a questioning attitude that would tend to undermine morale. We feel that it is our duty to tell you that Matthew has been blacklisted by the Greater Jerusalem Better Business Bureau. James, the son of Alpheus, and Thaddeus definitely have radical leanings, and they both registered a high score on the manic-depressive scale. One of the candidates, however, shows great potential. He is a man of ability and resourcefulness, ambitious, and responsible. We recommend Judas Iscariot as your controller and right-hand man. All of the other profiles are self-explanatory.

Sincerely Yours,

Jordan Management Consultants
Jerusalem. 26544 (Copied from Pulpit Helps).

# The Eleventh Chapter of Matthew

THEME: *Christ's Testimony Concerning John the Baptist*

OUTLINE:
    I.  A Great Concern (Verses 1-6)
    II.  A Gracious Compliment (Verses 7-19)
    III.  A Grievous Condemnation (Verses 20-24)
    IV.  A Glorious Communion (Verses 25-27)
    V.  A Godlike Compassion (Verse 28)
    VI.  A Gentle Companion (Verses 29-30)

## SECTION ONE

*Expository Notes on the Question Asked
by John the Baptist*

**And it came to pass, when Jesus had made an end of commanding his twelve disciples he departed from there to teach and to preach in their cities. Now when John had heard in the prison the works of Christ, he sent two of his disciples, And said unto him, Art thou he that should come, or do we look for another? (vv. 1-3).**

When John sent his disciples to Jesus, the wilderness evangelist had been imprisoned for eighteen months. Things had dramatically changed for the great forerunner of the Messiah. Formerly, he had stood alone against the powers of evil, and had enjoyed outstanding success in every phase of his dynamic ministry. Beneath the blue skies of Galilee he had seen the multitudes gathering to hear God's message, and to him had been granted the inestimable privilege of baptizing many converts. Uncompromisingly, he had denounced the hypocrisy of the religious leaders. He had insisted on their repentance ere they participated in any part of his work. That God had signally blessed his efforts none could deny but, after those glorious days of success, his sky had become overshadowed; the tremendous meetings held in the Jordan valley were but memories. Day after day, week after week, he looked at the cold, damp walls of his prison cell, and realized that any day could be his last. Occasionally, his harassed disciples were permitted to visit him, and they were his only contact with the outside world. Their lives had been disrupted; they knew not what to do. They had been thrilled to assist their leader, but now that John was imprisoned, they seemed at a loss, and life had no meaning. To make matters worse, the Carpenter, whom John had introduced, was so very different from their adorable master. John had denounced sinners; Jesus dined with them, and He seemed to be flirting with the enemy. Their master was imprisoned; Jesus had the privilege of going wherever He desired. It did not seem fair. They knew God had blessed John, but this Jesus presented problems of intense magnitude. They could not understand all the ramifications of the situation, but they expressed their feelings to John, and confessed they were mystified. Could he possibly have been mistaken by suggesting the Carpenter was the Messiah? In their estimation, a more unlikely Messiah there could never be.

John listened to their complaints, then gravely said, "I will tell you what to do. Go to Jesus, and tell Him that I sent you to ask a question.'Art thou He that should come, or do we look for another?'" Matthew informs us they did exactly as their leader suggested. During the long history of the church, theologians questioned John's motives. There are two schools of thought.

The *first* teaches that John, like us, was intensely human. His prolonged incarceration had eclipsed the sun of his confidence and, temporarily, he lost his faith. If this were the case, then John was not alone. The great prophet Elijah, with whom John was compared, had also experienced similar problems. His glorious witness for God on Mount Carmel had thrilled a nation. Idols had been smashed; false teaching destroyed, and a wayward people had confessed, "The Lord, He is the God." A spiritual awakening had come to Israel, and then, alas, Elijah had been threatened by Jezebel. Her anger so scared the prophet that he ran for his life. That foolish act terminated his fiery ministry; he never again preached to Israel. Afterward, when despondency overwhelmed his soul, he said, "...I, even I only, am left; and they seek my life, to take it away" (1 Kings 19:14).

Another great servant of God had a similar experience. Jonah tried to run away from his duty, but when he failed, poor Jonah said, "It is better for me to die than to live" (Jonah 4:8). Even the greatest of God's servants are poor mortals, and that, possibly, was the reason why David wrote, "For he knoweth our frame; he remembereth that we are dust" (Ps. 103:14). We should all be exceedingly grateful that our heavenly Father looks upon our shortcomings with great pity. Jeremiah wrote, "This I recall to my mind, therefore have I hope. It is of the LORD'S mercies that we are not consumed, because his compassions fail not. They are new every morning; great is thy faithfulness" (Lam. 3:21-23). It should be easy to understand John's doubts, and to see in his actions the same failures that haunt us when, like Peter, we begin to sink in the stormy waters of life (see Matt. 14:23-31). However, it must be considered that this may not have been the reason why John sent his disciples to Jesus.

The *second* school of thought insists that John's faith never wavered, and there is strong evidence to support this assertion. John looked at his grumbling disciples and recognized their malady needed the touch of a Master Physician. His own arguments or reasonings would be insufficient to banish doubts from the minds of his followers. What then could he do? He loved his faithful disciples; he could not leave them wallowing in waves of criticism. Then he smiled; Jesus would know how to handle the situation; He alone could restore confidence to his troubled men. So John sent his followers to Jesus, assured that whatever the Lord might say would solve the problems of those beloved men. That Jesus was soon complimenting the Baptist, saying he was not a reed shaken by the wind, suggests John was hardly a man whose faith had been destroyed.

**Jesus answered and said unto them, Go and show John again those things which ye do hear and see: The blind receive their sight, and the lame walk, the lepers are cleansed, and the deaf hear, the dead are raised up, and the poor have the gospel preached to them. And blessed is he, whosoever shall not be offended in me (vv. 4-6).**

Luke and Matthew agree that Jesus referred to the things which the messengers had *seen and heard*. This suggests that, ere the men returned to John, they were privileged to witness miracles. They watched as a variety of healings happened, and were probably dumbfounded, for John never performed a miracle nor even spoke of one. The greatest evidence for Christ is not what men say about Him, but His power that changes lives. One real miracle is worth ten thousand sermons; one demonstration of His power to save is of more importance than the theological training offered by a thousand seminaries. Let no one misunderstand that statement. A wise student will endeavor to receive all the education possible; to train one's mind is as beneficial as the exercising of the body. Nevertheless, academic distinction alone is insufficient to meet the demands of a suffering world. We not only need to tell how Christ helped the people of His generation; we need to demonstrate that, through His servants, He is still able to assist those who desire His help.

Possibly, the greatest part of the Lord's reply was, "And blessed is he, whosoever shall not be offended in me." Miracles are very desirous; but sometimes they are denied. When men live on the strength of sensationalism, they walk an uncertain pathway. Job would have appreciated a miracle to restore his health. Yet, even during his long trial of faith, that wonderful man exclaimed, "Though he slay me, yet will I trust in Him" (Job 13:15). It is easy to have faith in God when all is going well, but "The man worthwhile is the man who can smile, when everything goes dead wrong." It should be remembered that great multitudes followed Jesus. They witnessed His miracles, ate His loaves and fishes, and basked in the sunshine of His warm personality. Yet, when the icy winds of Calvary began to blow upon them; when the expected kingdom seemed as far removed as ever, many of His supporters "went back and followed him no more." It was wonderful to see Jesus performing miracles, but to love Christ without the miracles was even more wonderful. Then, people became fascinated with Jesus Himself. They had time to gaze into His lovely face, to feel the pressure of His hand, and the opportunity to say, "Thou art the Christ, the Son of the living God."

## SECTION TWO

### *Expository Notes on Christ's Testimony*
### *Concerning John the Baptist*

**And as they departed, Jesus began to say unto the multitudes concerning John, What went ye out into the wilderness to see? A reedshaken with the wind? But what went ye out for to see? A man clothed in soft raiment? behold, they that wear soft clothing are in kings' houses. But what went ye out for to see? A prophet? yea, I say unto you, and more than a prophet. For this is he, of whom it is written, Behold, I send my messenger before thy face, which shall prepare thy way before thee. Verily I say unto you, Among them that are born of women there hath not risen a greater than John the Baptist; notwithstanding he that is least in the kingdom of heaven is greater than he (vv. 7-11).**

This section of the chapter suggests five simple, but very potent questions. What? Why? Who? When? Where? Let us consider them in that order.

*WHAT?* After the departure of John's disciples, the Lord addressed the crowd saying, "What went ye out into the wilderness to see? *A reed shaken by the wind?*" The Jordan valley was filled with rushes and weeds, and all reacted to the wind. If it blew from the north; the reeds leaned toward the south. When it blew from the south, the same reeds leaned toward the north. They were not dependable; they were affected by circumstances. That there were, and are, people of that caliber none could possibly deny. There are politicians and other leaders who carefully watch to see which way the wind of popular might blow. When they are convinced of certain characteristics they act to increase their popularity. Colleges offer specialized courses of instruction to prepare men to become successful business managers. It is sometimes called advanced psychology, and gullible students are assured their feet will be placed upon the road that leads to the top of any realm they chose to enter. No true prophet of God ever enrolled in such a college. Prophets were more like pinnacles of rock than swaying reeds. They stood alone, and always pointed to the sky.

*WHY?* Jesus asked why the multitudes had left their homes and gone into the wilderness — was it to see the fulfillment of their dreams? They were hungry for reality; they looked for the kingdom of God, and John seemed the logical man from whom to obtain information. He was unlike the scribes and Pharisees; he had something to say. They had never heard a preacher of his type, and although sometimes they did not like what he said, they knew he spoke the truth.

*WHO?* Jesus said, "For this is he, of whom it is written, Behold, I send my messenger before thy face" (v. 10). The last of the prophets had written: "Behold, I will send you Elijah the prophet before the coming of the great and dreadful day of the LORD; And he shall turn the heart of the fathers to the children, and the heart of the children to their fathers, lest I come and smite the earth with a curse" (Mal. 4:5-6). Jesus knew that the majority of His listeners would be aware of this prediction, and reading their thoughts, he saw the speculation concerning the identity of the Baptist. Could he possibly be the promised Elijah? Jesus affirmed continually that John, at least, had appeared in "the spirit of Elijah," but the reference implied even more. If this were indeed the promised forerunner, then another statement made by Malachi demanded investigation. "Behold, I will send my messenger, and he shall prepare the way before me; AND THE LORD, WHOM YE SEEK, SHALL SUDDENLY COME TO HIS TEMPLE, even the messenger of the covenant, whom ye delight in: behold, he shall come, saith the LORD of hosts. But who may abide the day of his coming?..." (Mal.

3:1-2). If the people considered John to be the appointed forerunner, and since John had introduced Jesus: then consideration had to be given to the unuttered claim of the Savior. He was THE LORD, suddenly coming to His temple.

*WHEN?* "Behold, I send my messenger before THY FACE...." "THE LORD shall suddenly come to his temple." We have already been made aware of Matthew's search for Messianic evidence; but now we must recognize increasing interest in the Lord's testimony concerning Himself. All true Bible students know that the "great and dreadful day of the LORD" did not immediately follow the ministry of John the Baptist. The ultimate fulfillment will come when, at the end of the forthcoming tribulation, Israel will indeed pass through the valley of the shadow of death. That period will also be characterized by the appearance of Elijah, who will be one of the two witnesses to testify to Israel (see Rev. 11:3-13). Christ was crucified, because "he made himself equal with God." Jesus never denied that charge *because it was true.* He claimed to be the fulfillment of all the Messianic predictions made concerning Himself. He had indeed arrived; and all wise men should give attention to that fact.

*WHERE?* The testimony of Jesus concerning John was truly remarkable, but when He said, "...he that is least in the kingdom of heaven is greater than he" (v. 11b), the Lord was enunciating even greater truth. To say that a small child in a Sunday school would be greater than John the Baptist would be ludicrous. John was said to be the greatest born of women, so that not even our most eloquent preachers could compare with him. John was indeed supreme among men, but *he was still outside of the kingdom of heaven.* Jesus had come to establish that society, so how could John belong to something which at that time did not exist? When through the reconciling death on the Cross, the Lord established His church, the gospel was preached among the nations, and God's triumph was declared for all to hear. Then, even the youngest, the most inexperienced child was received into the fellowship of the church, and the least INSIDE that kingdom, was greater than the greatest OUTSIDE the kingdom. Thus did Jesus witness of John and proclaim His gospel at one and the same moment.

**And from the days of John the Baptist until now the kingdom of heaven suffereth violence, and the violent take it by force. For all the prophets and the law prophesied until John. And if ye will receive it, this is Elias, which was to come. He that hath ears to hear, let him hear (vv. 12-15).**

## HOW FAITHFUL AND FEARLESS

It was impossible to misunderstand the Lord's preaching. His statement "from the days of John the Baptist until now," limited the time period to which reference was being made. The Lord's words were being spoken to the people of that generation. They could not blame others for the predicament in which they were; they could not hide behind the failure of their ancestors. Jesus was saying that even during the eighteen months that had elapsed since John ministered in the Jordan valley, the kingdom of heaven had been attacked. The insinuation suggested the people present were responsible. There was a sharp edge to the cutting knife of Christ's message. That He never shirked His responsibility in delivering such a message indicated He was both faithful to His convictions and fearless in His delivery. His statement "the violent take it by force," may seem a little hard to understand. That He was referring to the religious leaders of His day, none can doubt. Their legal requirements; their insistence upon the strict observance of the traditions of men, created burdens too heavy to be carried. They made laws which ruined every concept of freedom; and they were using powers which were neither spiritual nor necessary. As a result, the kingdom of heaven was under seige.

> **But whereunto shall I liken this generation? It is like unto children sitting in the markets, and calling unto their fellows, And saying, We have piped unto you, and ye have not danced; we have mourned unto you, and ye have not lamented. For John came neither eating nor drinking, and they say, He hath a devil. The Son of man came eating and drinking, and they say, Behold a man gluttonous, and a winebibber, a friend of publicans and sinners. But wisdom is justified of her children (vv. 16-19).**

## HOW FICKLE

That man's greatest opportunity had arrived was clear. All the prophets, whom they professed to revere, had ministered until John came; that apparently was their mission. The arrival of the Baptist indicated the close of an era; he was the climax of all that had preceded him. If they had any vision, they could have beheld in this wilderness preacher the forerunner of whom Malachi had spoken. He had delivered his message; the Messiah had arrived! Jesus emphasized, "He that hath ears to hear, let him hear." We might paraphrase that same saying with the words, "If you have ears, use them!" The Lord surely sighed when

He compared His listeners with the children in the marketplace. Frustrated, they were expressing disappointment in the fact that those with whom they played were selfish. Whatever they did failed to elicit a response; the other children had made up their minds they wanted to do things their way; to play their games, and to reject any suggestion made by other boys and girls. Jesus inferred that His hearers were just the same. Whatever God said through His prophets; whatever Jesus Himself might say, the hearers had already decided they had no desire to accept suggestions. "We have piped unto you, and ye have not danced; we have mourned unto you, and ye have not lamented." "What more can be said or done? John was a separated man, who neither ate nor drank with you. He maintained a strict vigilance, and warned people of the approach of disaster. You said he was possessed of a devil. On the other hand, I come to you; to share your time; to eat at your table; to walk along your streets, and you call Me a winebibber, a glutton, a companion of those considered to be evil. Why are you dishonest? Why are you not forthright and say you do not wish to hear anything John or I might say? Indeed, you are like those frustrated boys and girls in the marketplace. If you cannot have things your way, you will have nothing to do with others. You state that we should be one, but you wish to be the one! You are critics not converts; sanctimonious not saintly; disappointing not delightful!"

## HOW FOOLISH

"Wisdom is justified of her children" (v. 19). There might be two ways of interpreting this text. (1) True wisdom is always justified by the conduct of her offspring. Wise people do not need to advertise their brilliance; their wisdom will be obvious to every onlooker. When Solomon passed judgment upon the two women who claimed to be mothers of the same child (1 Kings 3:16-28) "...all Israel heard of the judgment which the king had judged; and they feared the king: for they saw that the wisdom of God was in him, to do judgment." Wise people do not exhibit stupidity! (2) It might be inferred that the opposite view expressed the thoughts of Jesus. When wise counsel is rejected, the resultant failure of those who refused to accept it vindicates the value of wisdom. When the Savior gave words of advice to His hearers, and they rejected His message, their unhappiness in life proved they should have obeyed the instructions given in the first place. If they were condemned in the day of judgment, it would not be anyone's fault but their own. To see and understand the ways of God increases condemnation when people remain disobedient. Knowing the truth increases responsibility. Wisdom is indeed justified of her children.

## SECTION THREE

*Expository Notes on Christ's Denunciation of Three Cities*

**Then began he to upbraid the cities wherein most of his mighty works were done, because they repented not: Woe unto thee, Chorazin! woe unto thee, Bethsaida! for if the mighty works, which were done in you, had been done in Tyre and Sidon, they would have repented long ago in sackcloth and ashes. But I say unto you, It shall be more tolerable for Tyre and Sidon at the day of judgment, than for you (vv. 20-22).**

*THE GREAT PLACES... they were very prosperous*

Chorazin, Bethsaida, and Capernaum were cities at the northern end of the Sea of Galilee; trade flowed in and out of their business houses; the communities were exceptionally prosperous, possessing everything except the peace of God. They were great examples of the old truth, "all that glitters is not gold." There are commodities which are beyond the purchasing power of money, but alas, so few people realize the fact. That the majority of the miracles was performed in the vicinity of these three cities, apparently had no effect upon the privileged citizens. To see one miracle only begat a desire to see another. What Jesus said was of little consequence; the viewers desired something sensational, and even when their wishes were granted, they questioned the Lord's motives and asserted He was assisted by the prince of demons. There are none so impoverished as a wealthy man unable to obtain peace of mind: there are none so stupid as the millionaire who waits to discover there is no space in a casket for anything but a corpse!

*THE GLORIOUS PRIVILEGE...they heard the message of the Lord*

Perhaps we shall never know the reasons why Jesus performed so many miracles in that part of Palestine. Day after day, He labored in the midst of these self-reliant people, whereas, on the other hand, there were places to which He only went once. When He referred to Tyre and Sidon, the cities on the northwest coast, He drew attention to the contrast between their lack of privilege and the many opportunities given to the cities of Galilee. A modern parallel may be seen in the intense revival meetings now being held in the underprivileged nations of the world, and the deadly complacency of those countries in which the gospel has been preached for centuries. There are countries in which people walk many miles to hear the gospel; there are others, in which even the church members are too busy to attend a service. When professing Christians value material things more than eternal verities, their faith becomes suspect. They are automobiles without an engine; boats without oars; bodies without life.

*THE GREAT POSSIBILITY...they were able to decide*

What would have happened, had they been obedient to the Lord's commands? What would their cities have become, had the citizens reverently knelt at the feet of the Savior? God never created robots; He made man with the ability to choose which way he would travel. The word of God describes the highway that leads to blessedness, but the Lord never forces people to walk that road. God may graciously supply a banquet, but men and women are expected to grasp that which has been supplied. As it is now, so it was among the cities of Galilee. They had the power to embrace and love the Savior; that they criticized and rejected Him only proved their hearts were not attuned to the will of God. Those cities might have gained an immortal place in the history of the world, alas, they disappeared into oblivion.

*THE GRIM PREDICTION...they fell*

Jesus spoke of the coming of the day of judgment, and insisted it would be more tolerable for Sodom and Gomorrha in that day, than for the cities of Galilee. He indicated that, had they been given equal opportunity, the people of Tyre and Sidon would have repented. This can only mean that men will be judged according to the light received. God cannot expect of anyone that which is impossible. Men who have never heard the gospel will have an easier time standing before God than the people who often heard the message and rejected it. That there will be a day of reckoning, no serious student of the Bible can deny; each reader should be sure before it arrives, what the verdict in his own case might be. The prediction uttered by Jesus has been fulfilled; today, the cities in Galilee do not exist.

**And thou, Capernaum, which art exalted unto heaven, shall be brought down to hell: for if the mighty works, which have been done in thee,**

had been done in Sodom, it would have remained until this day. But I say unto you, That it shall be more tolerable for the land of Sodom in the day of judgment, than for thee (vv. 23-24).

Today, the ruins of Capernaum, that once mighty city of the East, stand as solemn reminders of the past. The Israeli authorities are trying to restore some of its ancient dignity, in that they insist tourists must be suitably attired before they are permitted to go beyond the entrance gate. The burnt-out remains of the synagogue can still be seen, and on the long stone bench people can sit and think of the fall of the once majestic city. All over the area, ancient farming implements may be seen, and if they were able to speak, they would remind the world of the folly of their former owners. No city is so great that it can safely ignore the Lord; and no city is so small and defenseless but what God can exalt it to prosperity and happiness. Alas, the only hindrance with which God cannot cope, is the folly of arrogant men who believe they are self-sufficient and need nothing (see Rev. 3:14-18).


## SECTION FOUR

*Expository Notes on Christ's Brief Prayer to His Father*

**At that time Jesus answered and said, I thank thee, O Father, Lord of heaven and earth, because thou hast hid these things from the wise and prudent, and hast revealed them unto babes. Even so, Father: for so it seemed good in thy sight. All things are delivered unto me of my Father: and no man knoweth the Son, but the Father; neither knoweth any man the Father, save the Son, and he to whomsoever the Son will reveal him (vv. 25-27).**

Suddenly, the Lord reached the eye of the cyclone! The high winds of emnity had been swirling around His soul; every horizon seemed black with problems, but suddenly in the midst of the unpleasant circumstances, there was calm. When He paused to pray, He looked into the heart of God, and said, "I thank thee, O Father, Lord of heaven and earth...." It is imperative for all Christian workers to remember that, however bleak the outlook, it is always possible to gaze heavenward. Often, when we look back, we are ashamed; when we look ahead, we are scared; when we look within, we are disappointed; when we look around, we are apprehensive, but when we look to God, we are safe.

## THE SERENITY OF COMPLETE CONSECRATION

When the furious tempests of life beat upon us, it is sometimes difficult to retain our composure. Circumstances often dictate attitudes. When things go well, we smile; if things disappoint, we frown. When people applaud, we love them; if people sneer, we detest them. Jesus was so different! When Satan would have introduced unholy tendencies into the life of Jesus, the Lord looked into the face of His Father, and knew that God was still "The Lord of heaven and earth." The unruffled calm within His heart indicated "no earth-born cloud could ever arise to hide Him from His Father's eyes." Let the critics plot His downfall; let adverse circumstances threathen His mission; let hell rage against Him, God was still God, and the final word regarding every matter of life was with Him, and not with the adversaries. That was the secret of Christ's amazing fortitude and peace. It is possible for us to share that experience, if we gaze more at the Lord than at the circumstances by which we are confronted.

## THE SIMPLICITY OF CONTINUING CHILDLIKENESS

"...Thou hast hid these things from the wise and prudent, and hast revealed them unto babes." What a babe lacks in knowledge and strength, it makes up in trust. Ere the child takes a step, it is content to rest in its parents' arms. Babes are miniature treasures; rare diamonds in earthen cases! They do not say much, but they can be heard; they are eloquent in speaking a language understood by a mother's heart. Jesus recognized there were such people within His kingdom. There was, and still is, a great difference between childishness and childlikeness. One indicates a grown adult who remains a child; childlikeness reveals a man who, great as he might be, remembers he came from nothing. A child's mind is open; preconceived ideas have not yet closed the door of understanding. A small child will never try to persuade anyone he knows everything. Alas, some men do not proclaim their greatness; they expect viewers to recognize it! Jesus said, "Except ye be converted, and become as little children, ye shall not enter into the kingdom of heaven" (Matt. 18:3).

## THE SUBLIMITY OF CONSTANT COMMUNION

"All things are delivered unto me of my Father; and no man knoweth the Son, but the Father; neither knoweth any man the Father, save the Son.'' That statement of the Lord enables us to gaze into the inscrutable ages of eternity. Long before a flower bloomed or a meadowlark sang its song; when creation was only a thought in the Creator's mind, the Father and the Son enjoyed an indescribable fellowship. They had planned together, and from their omniscient decisions came a world of exceeding loveliness. Even before time began, the Members of the Triune God enjoyed each other's confidence, and experienced fellowship which finite minds are unable to comprehend. No person, however brilliant, could know the eternal Father as did the Lord Jesus Christ, and by the same token no observer, not even the closest of earthly friends, could explore and know the mind of Christ as did the Father. The relationship existing between the Members of the Godhead was so intimate, so holy, so amazingly wonderful, that even to express its spiritual qualities was impossible. This idea may be recognized in John's description of what he saw in heaven. The apostle described how he was told the Lion of the tribe of Judah was able to open the book, and to loose the seven seals thereof. Yet when John looked for the Lion, he saw the Lamb (see Rev. 5:1-6). Men gazed upon Jesus and saw a Lamb; heaven looked upon Him and saw the Lion. Let us be honest and admit that regarding the person of our Lord, we are as astronauts looking at the immensity of the heavens above. We have just begun to explore its magnitude and to stand in awe, unable to comprehend the immensity of what awaits exploration.

One other remarkable statement was made by the Savior. It is quite impossible for sinners to know God without the assistance of Jesus. ''No one knows the Father except the Son, and *he to whomsoever the Son will reveal Him*'' Sinners are men whose vision has been ruined by cataracts of sin. The Great Physician-Surgeon operates, through grace, to remove the shadows. When the experience has been completed, He carefully removes the bandages, and behold we are able to see the glory of God. Philip had very bad cataracts; his vision was blurred when he said, ''Lord, show us the Father, and it sufficeth us.'' His operation was completed within a few moments, for Jesus answered, ''He that hath seen me hath seen the Father'' (see John 14:6-11). What is God like; whom does He resemble? The answer is ''JESUS.'' What does God have to say to us? The answer is equally simple. ''Listen to Jesus, and He will tell you.'' The Lord is all we need to know about God, for He is God.

*Expository Notes on the Amazing Invitation of Jesus*

**Come unto me, all ye that labour and are heavy laden, and I will give you rest (v. 28).**

## *THE SIMPLICITY OF THE INVITATION...'' Come''*

This glorious invitation of the Lord shines as a star against the blackness of man's sin. There are many wonderful promises within the Bible, but none greater than this one. Throughout the ages, unwise people thought acceptance with God depended upon human merit; that unless they achieved some mighty project, they had nothing to commend them in the sight of the Lord. The ancients were urged to keep the law; heathens ceaselessly worshiped idols, and modern man seeks comfort in all kinds of charitable endeavors. Ardent devotees of one, or many religions, will often make lengthy pilgrimages to famous shrines, in the hope their deed will merit the beneficence of a watching God. Jesus made everything simple. He taught that faith was more to be desired than glittering deeds of accomplishment; that the most wonderful pilgrimage ever undertaken led to Himself. He said, ''Come.'' That is the first word learned by a baby, for even before the sounds of articulation can be recognized, a baby understands the meaning of the outstretched arms of its mother. It is so simple, a child can understand; it is so profound, that even the wisest of men cannot ridicule its message.

## *THE SCOPE OF THE INVITATION...''All Ye That Labour and Are Heavy Laden''*

How thrilling it is to know that Jesus did not say, ''Come unto Me, all ye wealthy.'' Had He done so, most of the world's citizens would have been excluded. Had He said, ''Come unto Me, all ye educated people,'' the illiterate would have had no chance. His glorious gospel was the message of ''the whosoever will, may come,'' and therefore, when He spoke of people who were weary with labor, and distressed with burdens, every person on earth could exclaim, ''Jesus included me.'' Kings and queens, millionaires and scholars, great and small, old and young, in every nation of the world, become burdened with the problems of life. No one is excluded. A man may possess great riches, and yet be faced with an early death. A parent may have a beautiful home, and yet be troubled by children who persist in breaking his heart. A wonderful lady might be all that anyone could desire, but her foolish husband can be a graduate from the school of indiscretion, and as a result of his stupidity, home life can be ruined. All people experience the trials of being heavy laden, and therefore, Jesus asked everybody to respond to His invitation.

## THE SUFFICIENCY OF THE INVITATION... "I Will Give You Rest"

No other person, at any time, or in any age was able to make such a claim. Solomon offered advice; Simon Peter could deliver a stirring sermon; Samson would have been able to carry a load; David might have given financial assistance to the impoverished, but no one ever offered rest! If a modern preacher made such a promise, I would be the first to accept his offer. If he proceeded to give counsel, I would remind him of his statement. A troubled man needs REST not counsel. What business house in the world advertises this product? Where can one go to purchase it, and how much will it cost? On what page, and in what newspaper or magazine, is it advertised? The whole world needs rest, but alas, most people have no idea where to locate it. It is very thrilling to remember how Jesus invited everyone to come for rest, and although two thousand years have passed since the invitation was first given, no man or woman has ever come in vain. The poet expressed the sentiments of millions of people when he wrote:

"I heard the voice of Jesus say, 'Come unto Me and rest;
Lay down, thou weary one, lay down thy head upon My breast.'
I came to Jesus as I was, weary and worn and sad;
I found in Him a resting place, and He has made me glad.''

### SECTION SIX

*Expository Notes on a Beautiful Illustration*

**Take my yoke upon you, and learn of me; for I am meek and lowly in heart: and ye shall find rest unto your souls. For my yoke is easy, and my burden is light (vv. 29-30).**

To appreciate the beauty of this illustration, it is necessary to see a wise old ox, standing patiently beside one side of the projecting arm of a plow. An unbroken, stubborn young animal is to have its first lesson of servitude. With increasing indignation, the foolish youngster looks at the plow, and says, "Never!" Then, after a few moments of thought, the animal continues, "If that farmer thinks I am going to do his dirty work, he is wrong! I was made to roam and graze in these wide open fields, and not to be harnessed to that plough. If he tries to get me hitched to that contraption, I will kick it into the next field." The older, wiser ox calmly replies, "Youngster, don't be stupid! The master's way is better for all of us. If you get your way, your incessant grazing will soon take you to the slaughter house. Your fat old body will attract butchers, and you will soon be a memory! Now, if you have enough brains to understand, you will discover that a little work is good for everybody, including the master. When he knows that you are putting your best into his work, he will treat you like a king. When he sees you pulling the plough, he will not sell you to a butcher. You will have a long and happy life, and even if the grass withers, the master will feed you in the warm barn. If the weather is very bad, you will be able to sleep all day and night. So youngster, stop your bellowing, and come over here alongside me. If you are willing to listen and learn, I will show you how to pull this plough. If you get tired, do not worry, I shall be with you always, and in any case, I will take the heavy end of the load. You and I will live, work, and enjoy life together. Now, come on, let us get on with it."

Jesus, with a radiant smile upon His face, took the place of the wise old ox and, looking at His inexperienced, immature disciples, invited them to share His yoke. "Take My yoke upon you, and learn of Me. I will show you how to work in God's fields; I will take the heavy end of the task; watch Me; learn of Me; you and I will live, move, and have our being together. Disciples, we need each other, so come, and let us get on with God's great work." The entire range of Christian doctrine appears to be summarized in three simple words: *Listen, learn, love.* There have been times when young oxen were better students than the farmers!

# The Twelfth Chapter Of Matthew

THEME: *The Increasing Opposition to the Ministry of Jesus*

OUTLINE:
I. The True Witness (Verses 1-8)
II. The Triumphant Work (Verses 9-14)
III. The Timely Withdrawal (Verses 15-21)
IV. The Terrifying Warning (Verses 22-37)
V. The Three Wonders (Verses 38-42)
VI. The Thrilling Word-Picture (Verses 43-45)
VII. The Troubled Woman (Verses 46-50)

## SECTION ONE

*Expository Notes on the Incident in the Cornfield*

**At that time Jesus went on the sabbath day through the corn [grainfields]; and his disciples were an hungered, and began to pluck the ears of corn, and to eat. But when the Pharisees saw it, they said unto him, Behold, thy disciples do that which is not lawful to do upon the Sabbath day. (vv. 1-2).**

The initial thrills of the ministry of Jesus were beginning to disappear; the Pharisees were becoming hostile. Each miraculous manifestation of power was considered a challenge to their authority, and therefore every chance to criticize Christ and the disciples was welcomed. There was nothing illegal about plucking corn in a neighbor's field. Deut. 23:25 clearly stated, "When thou comest into the standing corn of thy neighbour, then thou mayest pluck the ears with thine hand; but thou shalt not move a sickle unto thy neighbour's standing corn." The objection was based on the simple fact that the disciples had plucked the corn on the Sabbath day, and their action was considered to be work. As we have already seen, the three main avenues of legal expression had been confined to (1) *The Law of God* as represented by the Ten Commandments; (2) *The Laws of God and Moses* as expressed in the

Pentateuch; and (3) *The Message given by The Law and the Prophets* comprising the Old Testament. All the subsequent difficulties were caused by what was known as "The Laws of the Scribes and Pharisees." For many years, the law was transmitted orally from one generation to the next. Eventually, this was considered inadequate, and a special class of writers, known as the Scribes, was commissioned to interpret and write the laws. This led to confusion, because they wrote all kinds of ludicrous commandments which reduced people to bondage.

If a tailor went out on the Sabbath carrying a needle in his clothing, this was considered to be a violation; he was working! Ancient writings reveal that even petty things, such as whether or not a man should go out on the Sabbath wearing false teeth, or using an artificial leg or arm, became lengthy arguments, and the true value of God's law was obscured or destroyed. It is against this background the cornfield incident must be examined. The attitude of Jesus brought Him into conflict with His critics. Jesus never violated any of the authentic laws of Moses, but even from the beginning of His ministry, His actions and teachings appeared to be a declaration of war against the unauthorized requirements of the Scribes.

**But he said unto them, Have ye not read what David did, when he was an hungered, and they that were with him; How he entered into the house of God, and did eat the showbread, which was not lawful for him to eat, neither for them that were with him, but only for the priests? Or have ye not read in the law, how that on the sabbath days the priests in the temple profane the sabbath, and are blameless? (vv. 3-5).**

## JESUS WAS CAREFUL IN HIS CONDUCT

The Lord was aware of the critical attitude of His enemies, and therefore became extremely careful how He answered their questions. He neither condoned nor criticized the actions of His followers. This became the pattern for His entire ministry. He was a Master at replying to questions with one of His own. The inference of the Lord's remarks was that if their ancient heroes had been guilty of a similar misdemeanor, then the disciples could not be blamed for their conduct in the cornfield. Human need was something God not only understood, He sympathized when people acted innocently to meet that need. Jesus reminded them that love was preferable to man-made laws. Their law exposed even small indiscretions and demanded judgment; love covered a multitude of sins.

The Lord quoted two Old Testament scriptures; 1 Samuel 21:1-6 and Numbers 28:9-10. If work were prohibited in every aspect on the Sabbath, then the priests were to be condemned, for they labored on the Sabbath day. The words of Jesus were ironic; He was focusing attention on the ludicrous interpretations given by the scribes. If we might superimpose modern language on an ancient scene, then it was wrong to get out of bed in the morning, unless the person got out on the correct side of the bed!

When David came to Ahimelech the priest, he was given the hallowed bread from the sanctuary, and this appeared to be a violation of law, for that bread was reserved exclusively for the priests. Yet, God did not punish David; in fact, God signally blessed and honored him. Therefore, if David were permitted to eat the consecrated bread from the sanctuary, the disciples were blameless in eating the unconsecrated corn from the field. If the priests were allowed to work at their jobs on the Sabbath, then such deeds were permissible and the Scribes were unjustified in making laws contrary to the will of God. The disciples might be condemned by tradition, but not by God. His listeners recognized the force of His argument, and this enraged them.

## *JESUS WAS CONSISTENT IN HIS CLAIMS*

**But I say unto you, That in this place is one greater than the temple. But if ye had known what this meaneth, I will have mercy, and not sacrifice, ye would not have condemned the guiltless. For the Son of man is Lord even of the sabbath day (vv. 6-8).**

The claims made by Jesus were truly astonishing, and it became obvious that, unless He was what He claimed to be, He was the greatest charlatan of all time. The Sabbath was given to man as a rest day when he could remember his Creator; it became a day for worship. The temple was the appointed place where this could be done. God was said to dwell above the Mercy Seat, but the privilege of drawing near to that awesome place was known only by the high priest. Everything sacred in Israel was linked with the temple and the holy day. Only God could be greater than the sanctuary, and no person could be more important than the Sabbath day, unless He was the One who instituted it. Only a king was able to change a royal edict. The temple, with its magnificent grandeur, was nothing compared with the Lord, who controlled the universe. The

Sabbath was of no importance when compared with God who was supreme before any such day was arranged. With His simple but profound utterances, Jesus was claiming to have been present with God, before the world began. "In the beginning was the Word, and the Word was with God, and the Word was God" (John 1:1).

## SECTION TWO

*Expository Notes on the Healing of the Man in the Synagogue*

**And when he was departed thence, he went into their synagogue: And, behold, there was a man which had his hand withered. And they asked him, saying, Is it lawful to heal on the sabbath days? that they might accuse him. And he said unto them, What man shall there be among you, that shall have one sheep, and it fall into a pit on the sabbath day, will he not lay hold on it, and lift it out? How much then is a man better than a sheep? Wherefore it is lawful to do good on the sabbath days. Then saith he to the man, Stretch forth thine hand. And he stretched it forth; and it was restored whole, like as the other. Then the Pharisees went out, and held a council against him, how they might destroy him (vv. 9-14).**

## THE DESIRE FOR WORSHIP

"He went into their synagogue" (v. 9b). There were three possible reasons why He did this.

1. Maybe He went to worship and to set an example for others. Luke 4:16 informs us that "He came to Nazareth, where he had been brought up; and, *as his custom was*, he went into the synagogue on the sabbath day, and stood up for to read." It is impossible to avoid the conclusion that there were many hypocrites in all the synagogues, but Jesus regularly visited those sanctuaries. It is true that He grasped every opportunity to teach, read, or preach, but during those moments when He sat quietly on a bench, did He bow His head in reverence? Many church members make all kinds of excuses to stay away from the sanctuary, but to follow Christ's example, they should make every effort to attend the services, for their actions publicize their faith in God.

2. Maybe He went to minister to needy people. Invariably, He discovered some desperate soul who needed assistance. It is worthy of attention that the man in the synagogue did not go there expecting to be healed. He had no idea what would take place there that day. He

apparently went to worship, and for him as for everybody, the text was true, "But seek ye first the kingdom of God, and his righteousness; and all these things shall be added unto you" (Matt. 6:33). A man is far wiser to be on his knees in a church than to be on his feet anywhere else!

3. Maybe He went in search of His greatest opportunities. Later, the apostle Paul often went to the synagogues, for it was there the people gathered; it was the obvious place in which to find a ready-made congregation. When the apostle wished to start people talking about the gospel, he began in their sanctuary. The same truth applied throughout the Lord's ministry. It was true that multitudes of people came to Jesus, but it was also true that *He went to them*. The church has always been strongest when this has been the normal procedure. Many churches are content to arrange services in which their pastors minister to a few faithful members. The famous evangelists of the past, Luther, Wesley, and others of their type, took their message into the streets, where ordinary people were made aware that God still lived.

## THE DISPLAY OF WICKEDNESS

Seeing the afflicted man in the service, the Pharisees asked their question, "that they might accuse him." They hoped Jesus would utter words which might be used as evidence against Him. They had neither compassion for the man, nor reverence for the true spirit of worship. Their attitude was a greater violation of the Sabbath than anything forthcoming from the Savior. As the Lord warned earlier, they were trying to find a speck in His eye, and were apparently unaware of "the plank" in their own eye. They were hypocrites; wolves in sheep's clothing. Had they been there to worship, they would have been kneeling before the altar. Oblivious to the presence of God, they only saw a carpenter, whom they considered to be dangerous. It is always to be regretted when men forget God, and are content to watch and criticize other people in church! It is better to look at a sunrise than to gaze at a fog-bank!

## THE DISCRETION OF WISDOM

Again the Lord answered their question with one of His own. When they asked about the legality of healing on the Sabbath, He inquired what they would do if one of their animals, inadvertently, slipped into a ditch. Would it be amiss to liberate a sheep from discomfort; to restore it to the green pasture, and to ensure its safety on a Sabbath day? Perhaps He was also thinking of their reactions to the possibility of financial loss if the animal died. Would they place the sanctity of the holy day above their financial investment in the animal? Which would be of greater importance, the observance of the scribal law or the protecting of perhaps ten shekels? That they did not answer His question revealed the bankruptcy of their souls. He was too careful and too wise to be ensnared by their evil words. Impetuosity was never seen throughout His ministry. His wise answers and serene attitude infuriated them.

## THE DECLARATION OF WAR

"Then the Pharisees went out, and held a council against him, how they might destroy him." They believed the time for argument had passed; the time for action was overdue. The only effective way to stop the accursed Nazarene was to kill Him. When men refuse the light, they are stupid and sinful; when they try to extinguish the light, they are without excuse. The die was now cast; the declaration of war was complete. Henceforth, whatever Jesus did or said, His enemies would be vindictive, treacherous, and diabolical. Jesus was aware of the threatening dangers, so he quietly withdrew Himself from their presence. To continue speaking to them would be casting pearls before swine.

### SECTION THREE

*Expository Notes on the Withdrawal of the Savior*

**But when Jesus knew it, he withdrew himself from thence; and great multitudes followed him, and he healed them all, And charged them that they should not make him known. That it might be fulfilled which was spoken by Esaias, the prophet, saying, Behold my servant, whom I have chosen; my beloved, in whom my soul is well pleased: I will put my Spirit upon him, and he shall show judgment to the Gentiles. He shall not strive, nor cry; neither shall any man hear his voice in the streets. A bruised reed shall he not break, and smoking flax shall he not quench, till he send forth judgment unto victory. And in his name shall the Gentiles trust (vv. 15-21).**

## THE TIMELY PRECAUTION

Fire is helpful, unless it gets out of control; enthusiasm is a stimulating thing, until it is misdirected; then it becomes dangerous. To see the great crowds might have led to a measure of defiance, with which Jesus could have confronted His scheming enemies. The Lord represented the incarnate wisdom of God. When He became aware of the plots against Him, He quietly withdrew from what might have been a conflict. Had the multitude decided to fight for His cause, civil war could have begun. The Romans would have mutilated or massacred many people, and the entire mission of Jesus would have been placed in jeopardy. Discretion is always the better part of valor. The Lord's withdrawal probably saved the lives of many people.

The time — *His hour* — had not yet come. Some might argue that had the Romans attacked the followers of the Lord, His power could have prevented a catastrophe. That conclusion may be justified but, since He desired to redeem sinners, to annihilate them would have been a tragedy. Military commanders believe that sometimes to attack is the better form of defense, but it is also true that "he who lives to run away, lives to fight another day." The Lord knew exactly what He was doing, and every wise man learns from His example.

## THE TRUE PREDICTION

Matthew again seized an opportunity to present his claim that Jesus was the Messiah. His quotation came from Isaiah 42:1-3, but the original message of the prophet expressed much more truth. He wrote, "I the LORD have called thee in righteousness, and will hold thine hand, and will keep thee, and give thee for a covenant of the people, for a light of the Gentiles; To open the blind eyes, to bring out the prisoners from the prison, and them that sit in darkness out of the prison house" (Isa. 42:6-7). It had become obvious to Matthew that the Master was the fulfillment of everything predicted of the Messiah. It seemed inconceivable that the religious leaders were so blind and devoid of understanding.

## THE THRILLING PORTRAYAL

It should not be forgotten that the words spoken by God through Isaiah were repeated at the baptism of Jesus. Nothing had changed except perhaps the scenery! Jesus had been, still was, and ever would be the delight of the Father. He remained the One in whom God was well pleased. The two word pictures which followed were beautiful. "A bruised reed shall he not break." The pens with which scribes wrote were reeds sharpened at one end. This was dipped into the writing fluid, and messages written on parchment or tablets of clay. It was to be expected that continual use would soften the fibrous point, and when the pen became saturated, it would bend and be unfit for further service. The scribe would then crush the softened reed with his fingers and throw it into a container — a waste paper basket! "...smoking flax [a dimly-burning wick] shall he not quench." The lamps used in the time of our Lord were made of clay; they resembled a large desert spoon, with a handle at one end and a hole for the wick at the other. The wick, a piece of string, lay flat on the surface of the very small amount of oil within the lamp. Sometimes when the oil supplies were exhausted, the wick slowly burned until only a pin-point of light remained. Then an offensive odor would be emitted, and an impatient writer instantly extinguished the light by squeezing the wick between his thumb and finger. The prophet said the coming One would be possessed with extreme patience. He would not discard men because they were broken and unreliable, and would not extinguish a light because it had grown dim. The Messiah would replenish the oil and restore backslidden souls to their former usefulness. The coming King would deliver men, and not destroy them.

*THE TRUSTING PEOPLE*

"And in his name shall the Gentiles trust." The Messiah would remove the barriers between Jew and Gentile; He would open the gates into the kingdom of God, so that everyone would have the opportunity to enter. His voice would not be that of a brawler in the streets, nor an agitator promoting insurrection. He would look at a restless world and say, "Come unto me, all ye that labour and are heavy laden, and I will give you rest." What had been exclusively reserved for Jews, would be offered to Gentiles and, unlike the Hebrews, the outcasts of society would believe, receive, and love the Lord.

### SECTION FOUR

*Expository Notes on Christ's Indictment of the Pharisees*

**Then was brought unto him one possessed with a devil, blind, and dumb: and he healed him, insomuch that the blind and dumb both spake and saw. And all the people were amazed, and said, Is not this the son of David? But when the Pharisees heard it, they said, This fellow doth**

not cast out devils, but by Beelzebub the prince of the devils. And Jesus knew their thoughts, and said unto them, Every kingdom divided against itself is brought to desolation; and every city or house divided against itself shall not stand: And if Satan cast out Satan, he is divided against himself; how shall then his kingdom stand? And if I by Beelzebub cast out devils, by whom do your children cast them out? therefore they shall be your judges. But if I cast out devils by the Spirit of God, then the kingdom of God is come unto you (vv. 22-28).

## THE OVERLOOKED MIRACLE

It has often been said, "familiarity breeds contempt." This was true during the Lord's ministry. The thrilling wonder of His miracles had disappeared; they no longer pleased the Pharisees. The case of the blind and dumb man was a repetition of what had transpired earlier (see Matt. 9:32-34). The Pharisees had already made an accusation stating Jesus was assisted by Beelzebub, but afterward they enlarged their argument. Had they been able to discredit Jesus, the common people might have left Him; they were all scared of demons. Doubtless the Lord had considered what to say to His critics, and He was ready when they repeated their insinuation.

## THE OVERCONFIDENT MURMURERS

"But when the Pharisees heard it, they said, This fellow doth not cast out devils, but by Beelzebub the prince of the devils. And Jesus knew their thoughts." We are reminded of the words found in 2 Kings 6:11-12, "Therefore the heart of the king of Syria was sore troubled for this thing; and he called his servants, and said unto them, Will ye not show me which of us is for the king of Israel? And one of his servants said, None, my lord, O king: but Elisha; the prophet that is in Israel, telleth the king of Israel *the words that thou speakest in thy bedchamber*." It is not possible to out-think God, for He sees the end from the beginning. It was no cause for amazement that Jesus was always a step ahead of His critics. He knew what they would say, even before the words were uttered.

## THE OVERWHELMING MESSAGE

"The kingdom of God is come unto you." Once again, any wise men would have recognized the significance of His remarks. The kingdom was near because the King was there. Kneeling at His feet, the Pharisees could have become citizens. They were too blind to see their opportunity and too stupid to seize it. *Their arguments were futile* , for Satan would never oppose himself. *Their statements were foolish*, for if their words were correct, the members of their own families were also in league with Satan. *Their decision was fatal*, for their rejection of the King would inevitably lead to His rejection of them. Their anticipation of future glory would be an illusion, something never to happen.

**Or else how can one enter into a strong man's house, and spoil his goods, except he first bind the strong man? and then he will spoil his house. He that is not with me is against me; and he that gathereth not with me scattereth abroad. Wherefore I say unto you, All manner of sin and blasphemy shall be forgiven unto men: but the blasphemy against the Holy Ghost, shall not be forgiven unto men. And whosoever speaketh a word against the Son of man, it shall be forgiven him; but whosoever speaketh against the Holy Ghost, it shall not be forgiven him, neither in this world, neither in the world [age] to come (vv. 29-32).**

## THE POWER OF CHRIST

The claim made by Jesus was unmistakable. The Pharisees said He was in league with Beelzebub, but Jesus affirmed He was greater than the prince of demons and had, in fact, rendered him impotent. Jesus said, ''How can one enter into a strong man's house, and spoil his goods, except he first bind the strong man?'' That Jesus had expelled demons was irrefutable evidence that in His presence, evil spirits were powerless. Jesus not only had the authority to issue a command; He had the power to enforce it. Charles Wesley expressed this truth when he wrote,

> He breaks the power of cancelled sin,
> He sets the prisoner free;
> His blood can make the foulest clean,
> His blood availed for me.

## THE PEOPLE OF CHRIST

''He that is not with me is against me; and he that gathereth not with me scattereth abroad'' (v. 30). According to Jesus, there is not a neutral position. Either a man is for or against the Savior. To be *with* Jesus implies nearness, affinity, and affection. The evidence of the reality of this experience is found in service. Either I gather with Him, or I scatter abroad without Him. ''By their fruits ye shall know them.'' But there are two sides to this truth. Unfortunately, the modern church has emulated the actions of the scribes. Additional requirements have been added to the words of Jesus, so that today, unless a servant of God conforms to man-made requirements, he is often barred from participating in a communion service. If a man loves the Savior he should be recognized as a brother by all who share his faith. When a woman loves and serves the Lord, she should be beloved by all her sisters in Christ, regardless of the church or assembly to which she belongs. Marriages might have been made in heaven, but denominational barriers were conceived elsewhere.

## THE PREACHING OF CHRIST

"But blasphemy against the Holy Ghost shall not be forgiven unto men" (v. 31b). Throughout the history of the church, this has been one of the most difficult texts to interpret. False teaching has thrived on incorrect versions, and often people have become mentally ill, fearing they have committed the unpardonable sin. It must be stressed that the Bible teaches there is only one unforgivable sin, and that is the rejection of Christ. The Bible has nothing to say about an extension of forgiving grace into the hereafter. Jesus emphasized that if men died unforgiven and unrepentant, they would be rejected in eternity. Speaking to the Pharisees, Jesus said, "...ye...shall die in your sins: whither I go, ye cannot come" (John 8:21).

The Lord emphasized that when the Holy Spirit came into the world, His mission would be to present Christ. To do this, it would be necessary to proclaim the gospel, and the chief agency in doing this would be the Spirit of Truth. "Howbeit, when he, the Spirit of truth, is come, he will guide you into all the truth: FOR HE SHALL NOT SPEAK OF HIMSELF...He shall glorify me: for He shall receive of mine, and shall show it unto you" (John 16:13-14). Any message which does not exalt Christ is uninspired. The work of the Holy Spirit is to exalt Christ; when a person rejects that message, there is no forgiveness, either in this world or the next.

**Either make the tree good, and his fruit good; or else make the tree corrupt: and his fruit corrupt; for the tree is known by his fruit. O generation of vipers, how can ye, being evil, speak good things? for out of the abundance of the heart the mouth speaketh. A good man out of the good treasure of the heart bringeth forth good things: and an evil man out of the evil treasure bringeth forth evil things. But I**

say unto you, That every idle word that men shall speak, they shall give account thereof in the day of judgment. For by thy words thou shalt be justified, and by thy words thou shalt be condemned (vv. 33-37).

The key statement here is "how can ye, being evil, speak good things?" Jesus came to save sinners, but it became increasingly obvious that He detested hypocrisy. When the Lord denounced their empty profession, He used very strong language. He called the Pharisees whited sepulchers, ravenous wolves, hypocrites, and many other things. A broken and a contrite heart He could and did help, but the arrogant, sanctimonious attitude of critical religious leaders, was an abomination in His sight. His appeal for decisiveness should not pass unnoticed. He seemed to be saying, "Either be a healthy tree or be a diseased one. Either produce wholesomeness, or let it be known everywhere that your fruit is inedible." Figs did not grow on apple trees; dates did not grow on citrus trees. According to the fruit, so the tree could be identified. Similarly, righteous trees produced righteousness, and godly trees produced godliness. Evil men produced evil fruit in thought, action, and every other conceivable sense.

Pharisees resembled the church at Laodicea; they were neither hot norcold; they spoke eloquently, but their lives contradicted all they said. Furthermore, they not only did these things, they refused to change their pattern of living. Jesus called them a generation of vipers; they were children of "that old serpent the devil"; their nearness was a threat; their venom could be poisonous to anyone they attacked. His indictment should have warned them but, unfortunately, they were too deaf to hear, and too blind to recognize their need.

## SECTION FIVE

*Expository Notes on Christ's Prediction of the Future*

Then certain of the Scribes and of the Pharisees answered, saying, Master, we would see a sign from thee. But he answered and said unto them, An evil and adulterous generation seeketh after a sign; and there shall no sign be given to it, but the sign of the prophet, Jonas: For as Jonas was three days and three nights in the whale's belly; so shall the Son of man be three days and three nights in the heart of the earth. The men of Nineveh shall rise in judgment with this generation, and shall condemn it: because they repented at the preaching of Jonas; and, behold, a greater than Jonas is here. The queen of the south shall rise up in the judgment with this generation, and shall condemn it: for she came from the uttermost parts of the earth to hear the wisdom of Solomon; and, behold, a greater than Solomon is here (vv. 38-42).

## THE REQUEST FOR A SIGN

"Master, we would see a sign from thee...But he answered...there shall no sign be given...but the sign of the prophet Jonas" (vv. 38,39). It seemed bewilderingly strange that the Pharisees, who had witnessed innumerable miracles, should ask for another sign. Were they not satisfied, or were they seeking a reason for further criticism? Pharaoh had witnessed signs prior to the deliverance of the Jewish captives, but with each manifestation of power his heart became increasingly resistant to the will of God. True faith needs a better foundation than sensationalism. Love is better than legalism. The Lord's reply regarding Jonah provides food for thought.

Except for one detail, Jonah and Jesus were as unlike as it was possible to be. Jonah refused his commission; Jesus gladly accepted His. Jonah tried to run away from God; the Lord submitted to His Father's will, and proceeded to the place in which He was to do God's bidding. Jonah grumbled when people repented in Nineveh; Christ rejoiced when even one sinner saw the error of his ways. Yet, in the midst of the conflicting episodes of life, one glorious detail eternally linked the prophet with the Son of God. "For as Jonas was three days and three nights in the whale's belly; so shall the Son of man be three days and three nights in the heart of the earth." It is thought-provoking to compare and contrast two Scriptures. When Nicodemus, a seeking sinner, asked for help, the Lord mentioned a cross; when hypocritical Pharisees desired a sign, Jesus pointed to His resurrection. There are none so blind as those who have no desire to see (see Luke 16:31).

## THE REMORSE OVER SINS

"The men of Nineveh shall rise in judgment with this generation, and shall condemn it" (v. 41). The words of Jesus suggested a courtroom in which there was a judge, a prosecuting counsel, witnesses, the accused, and finally, a verdict. Jesus believed there would come a Judgment Day, and this He mentioned throughout His entire ministry. The reference to Nineveh reminds us of several key applications concerning this city. (1) *A strange recognition.* It is interesting to note that a large, wicked city renounced its sins after the people had heard only one sermon. Every minister on earth covets similar success.

Doubtless, Jonah carried upon his body the marks of the ordeal through which he had passed. The people of Nineveh worshiped the Fish god, and in their estimation Jonah had risen from the dead! That basically was the cause of their repentance. (2) *A sudden repentance.* That the entire population, including the king, repented in sackcloth and ashes, provides food for thought. Their motivation must have been exceedingly great. (3) *A sure reprieve.* Their city was spared by the Almighty, even though Jonah expressed great displeasure with the mercy of God. He said, "I knew that thou art a gracious God, and merciful, slow to anger, and of great kindness, and repentest thee of the evil" (Jonah 4:2). When Jesus cited this account, and said the men of Nineveh would stand in the judgment to give testimony against the Pharisees, it was an unmistakable indictment of those who had listened to a greater preacher than Jonah.

## THE RESEARCH OF A SOVEREIGN

"The queen of the south shall rise up in the judgment with this generation, and shall condemn it" (v. 42a). The Old Testament reference is 1 Kings 10:1-10. The queen of Sheba had heard reports of the wisdom and grandeur of Solomon and, to corroborate the story, she made a journey to Israel. She did her utmost to discover the truth, and her effort condemned the Pharisees who did nothing but criticize. Jesus said, "Behold, a greater than Solomon is here." The grouping of several texts provides increasing interest. Jesus was greater than *the temple* (12:6), *the Sabbath* (12:8), *Jonah* (12:41), *Solomon* (12:42), *Jacob* (John 4:12). (See "The Witnesses for the Prosecution" in the author's book, *Luke's Thrilling Gospel*, pp. 275-277.)

## SECTION SIX

*Expository Notes on the Cleansing of the Unclean House*

**When the unclean spirit is gone out of a man, he walketh through dry places, seeking rest, and findeth none. Then he saith, I will return into my house from which I came out; and when he is come, he findeth it empty, swept, and garnished. Then goeth he, and taketh with himself seven other spirits more wicked than himself, and they enter in and dwell there: and the last state of that man is worse than the first. Even so shall it be also unto this wicked generation (vv. 43-45).**

"This Scripture belongs to one of the most fascinating of the Lord's sermons. Christ was a great student of human nature, and it is said of Him that He did not commit Himself unto the people because He knew all men. Constantly, He came face to face with all types, and here, in this challenging message, He centers attention on one class — the man who says he could never live the Christian life, even though he tried.

## THE PARABLE

The house was a study in contrasts. It seemed impossible that this could be one home, for its two ends were two extremes. One was as beautiful as the other was ugly. Seen through modern eyes, one end was charmingly decorated, beautifully curtained, and a sight to gladden the heart. The other was bleak, barren, and exceedingly dirty. *But it was one house.* The good householder occupied one portion, and a demon occupied the other. The good man desired to throw out his evil neighbor, but felt unequal to the task. They continued to live side by side. We are reminded of the human heart, where so often the good and bad impulses live together. Paul said, 'When I would do good, evil is present with me.' Studdart Kennedy wrote:

> There's summat that pulls us up,
> And summat that pulls us down;
> And the consequence is that we wobble
> Twixt muck and a golden crown.

If we could be rid of the evil within us, our entire house could be beautiful, according to our noblest desires.

## THE PROBLEM

A great inspiration energized the householder, and in one supreme moment of triumph, he ejected the unwanted demon. Probably he was more surprised than the evil one, but after a little while the demon said, "I will return into my house from which I came out." Then he discovered it to be empty, swept, and garnished; and realizing the householder might expel him once again, he took with him seven other spirits more wicked than himself. Thus, said Christ, "the last state of that man was worse than the first." There is something peculiarly suggestive about this scene. It is obvious that Christ appreciated the difficulties of sincere souls. It seemed so futile to make a decision which, in after days, might return as a boomerang to create dismay. It is easy at times to cry, 'Lord, I will follow Thee whithersoever Thou goest,' and yet to fail when, subsequently, the road is long and steep. In the glorious ecstacy of His presence, we can brave unlimited perils, but alas, we are mindful that the expelled demon might someday return with reinforcements. Our philosophy says, 'Better be content with the presence of one demon than run the risk of his bringing seven others.'

*THE PREACHING*

The weakness of the story seems to be in that, having expelled the demon, *the householder was content to live alone.* If he could have found a companion whose power exceeded that of many demons, he would have had a chance to maintain the freedom of his home. And however imaginative this may seem, it is nevertheless the real fact behind the message. Matthew 12:22-24 tells of the deliverance of a demoniac, and no one can deny the actuality of the miracle. Even the Lord's enemies admitted He had performed the impossible, but they cunningly suggested He was in league with Beelzebub, the prince of the demons. But let us remember that He had established beyond all doubt His superiority over demons. He thereupon proceeded to describe the harassed householder, and to this there can only be one feasible explanation. If such a man *could invite Christ* to live in his heart, he would find security in the new fellowship. And that is the crux of the gospel message. If the Lord tarries with me, His strength will be made perfect in my weakness. How silly it is to live in the shadow of nameless fears. I must seek the companionship of a new Guest.'' (Reprinted from the author's commentary, *Luke's Thrilling Gospel,* pp. 272-274).

## SECTION SEVEN

*Expository Notes on Christ's Comments Concerning His Family*

**While he yet talked to the people, behold his mother and his brethren stood without, desiring to speak with him. Then one said unto him, Behold, thy mother and thy brethren stand without, desiring to speak with thee. But he answered and said unto him that told him, Who is my mother? and who are my brethren? And he stretched forth his hand toward his disciples, and said, Behold my mother and my brethren! For whosoever shall do the will of my Father which is in heaven, the same is my brother, and sister, and mother (vv. 46-50).**

## A WEAKENING FAITH

Mark also records the visit of the Lord's relatives (3:31-35), and supplies additional details which enable us to understand their motives. The Greek text in Mark 3:21, *Hoi par autou ezeethon krateesai auton,* which has been translated "those belonging to him went out to lay hold on him," has been rendered in the *Amplified New Testament*: "And when those who belonged to Him, that is, His kinsmen, heard it, they went out to take Him by force, for they kept saying, *He is out of His mind — beside Himself, deranged* " This is the force of the word *krateesai* — "to seize in order to bring into one's power" (Thayer). The continuing reports of the Lord's sayings had troubled His family, and fearing He was on the verge of a nervous breakdown, or that He might be arrested for what apparently were outrageous statements, they were determined to rescue Him from Himself! Their faith had been undermined, but their motives, at least, can be appreciated.

## A WONDERFUL FAMILY

When Jesus was made aware of the presence of His loved ones, He asked, "Who is my mother? and who are my brethren?" Then, pointing to His followers, He indicated His *real family* consisted of those who did the will of His Father. Thus, within a few moments, He drew the clear lines of demarcation between the family of God and the family into which He had been born. Earthly ties would ultimately be severed; the bonds uniting members of God's family would be eternal. This suggests that there are times when a brother in the faith may be more understanding, more loyal and kind, than brothers and sisters in the flesh. The Lord had already taught that a man's foes would be they of his own household. The sword of the gospel would divide families, setting "fathers against their children." All kinds of circumstances destroy earthly families, but nothing would ever be able to separate Christians from the love of Christ.

## A WELCOMING FATHER

"For whosoever shall do the will of my Father...the same is my brother, and sister, and mother" (v. 50). That glorious statement of the Lord revealed the infallible way by which God's family could increase. Everybody was welcome within the fold of God. Outcasts, sinners, lepers, publicans, anybody could gain admittance, but entry was based upon one unchanging test — *doing the will of the Father*. John 6:29 says, "This is the work [or will] of God, that ye believe on him whom he hath sent." Jesus said, "I am the way, the truth and the life: *no man cometh unto the Father*, BUT BY ME" (John 14:6). Christ is the only door into heaven. With Him, men live; without Him, they die. Blessed is the soul that finds the door and enters — in time!

# Thirteenth Chapter of Matthew

THEME: *The Parables of the Kingdom*

OUTLINE:

    I. The Sower... *Sowing* (Verses 1-23)
   II. The Wheat and Tares... *Spoiling* (Verses 24-30, 36-43)
 III. The Mustard Seed... *Succeeding* (Verses 31-32)
 IV. The Leaven... *Seasoning* (Verse 33)
  V. The Savior... *Speaking* (Verses 34-43)
 VI. The Treasure... *Searching* (Verse 44)
VII. The Pearls... *Sacrificing* (Verses 45-46)
VIII. The Dragnet... *Separating* (Verses 47-53)
 IX. The Citizens... *Sinning* (Verses 54-58)

## INTRODUCTION TO CHAPTER THIRTEEN

This is one of the most interesting, and yet controversial, chapters in the Bible. Its message has divided the church into three schools of thought. It is imperative that this be understood before an attempt is made to explain its message. *First,* there is the dispensational interpretation. It has been claimed that the entire Gospel of Matthew is related to the kingdom, and has no value in any matter related to the church. A spokesman expressing this thought said, "If the first Gospel were removed from the Scriptures, the church would lose nothing. What Matthew said was meant for Jews; the commandments and precepts expressed were Jewish related, and no promise in that Gospel had any message for the daily conduct of the church." Without equivocation, it must be said that such a viewpoint is misleading and senseless. The Lord said in Matthew 11:28, "Come unto me, all ye that labour and are heavy laden, and I will give you rest." That promise has brought blessing to people in all ages since Pentecost and, if the verse has no bearing on today's conditions, then the entire Bible becomes suspect. Furthermore, since much of Matthew's information is also in the Gospels of Mark and Luke, are we to believe their information is also irrelevant?

Nevertheless, in order to be fair and present all the facts, it must be noticed that in the thirteenth chapter of Matthew, are seven parables of the kingdom, and alone, some of them are unimportant. For example, there are the parables of the meal and the treasure hid in the field. Taken from their context, they are almost meaningless, but as the dispensationalists affirm, considered with the other parables of the kingdom, they supply links in the progressive revelation of church and world history. They are compared with the seven churches of Asia mentioned in the second and third chapters of the Revelation. These are also said to be seven progressive pictures of church history, extending from the inception of the church to its completion. When John sent his messages to the churches, some important assemblies were omitted; others, which were almost unknown, were included. This is difficult to explain, unless they were divinely chosen to fit into a special revelation indicating events in later years. It has been claimed by the dispensationalist teachers that the parable of the sower is identical with the church at Ephesus; the parable of the wheat and tares is the equivalent of the church at Smyrna. The third parable of the mustard seed corresponds with the message sent to Pergamos, the fourth, which speaks of the woman and her meal, resembles the church at Thyatira, the fifth, concerning the treasure in the field, equals the church at Sardis, the sixth, which speaks of the pearl, relates to the church at Philadelphia, and finally the parable of the dragnet speaks of the church at Laodicea. It is claimed that in both instances the seven messages are more or less identical, revealing successive stages of church history.

Let it be emphasized that there could be very much truth in this presentation, but when exponents of the view endeavor to make every verse conform to the pattern of their own doctrines, they render a disservice to the message of God. There may be a similarity between the Lord praying in the mountain and His intercessory work as our High Priest in the heavens, but the idea that each incident is a definite type of the other, might be open to debate. To say that every time Jesus descended to the valley was a foreshadowing of His second advent, might be an example of "straining at a gnat and swallowing a camel."

The *second* school of interpretation includes the liberal theologians, who reject every attempt to dispensationalize the message of Matthew's Gospel. They do not accept any doctrine advancing the teaching of the Lord's return, and maintain that, like the other Gospels, Matthew's message relates only to the daily conduct of Jesus and the disciples. They teach that what He said was meant to be an example for everybody, in every age, and should be accepted and believed accordingly.

The *third* interpretation indicates a middle-of-the-road position. There are teachers who believe that "ALL scripture is given by inspiration of God, and is profitable for doctrine, for reproof, for correction, for instruction in righteousness: That the man of God may be perfect, thoroughly furnished unto all good works" (2 Tim. 3:16-17). They dislike what appears to be the arrogant dogmatism of the dispensationalists, but recognize there may be some truth in their affirmations. They believe the Bible to be an unfathomable sea of truth in whose depths treasures of incalculable worth await discovery. They dislike the denial of everything miraculous within the Bible. Having experienced a miracle within their own hearts, they find it easy to believe that God can do anything. They state that any miracle mentioned in the Bible fades into insignificance when compared with the regeneration of men and women. Therefore, without preconceived notions warping their minds, they approach the Scriptures as hungry people approach the dinner table; they come to be fed, and are never disappointed.

Therefore, it should be evident that when we approach the study of the thirteenth chapter of Matthew's Gospel, we must remember the viewpoints of each of the three schools of thought. It is possible to glean knowledge from every expositor of the Scriptures; the teacher who knows everything, generally, has much to learn; the man who has no desire to learn, has lived too long!

## SECTION ONE

### *Expository Notes on the Parable of the Sower*

**The same day went Jesus out of the house, and sat by the sea side. And great multitudes were gathered together unto him, so that he went into a ship, and sat; and the whole multitude stood on the shore. And he spake many things unto them in parables, saying, Behold, a sower went forth to sow; And when he sowed, some seeds fell by the way side, and the fowls came and devoured them up: Some fell upon stony places, where they had not much earth; and forthwith they sprung up, because they had no deepness of earth. And when the sun was up, they were scorched; and because they had no root, they withered away. And some fell among thorns; and the thorns sprung up, and choked them: But other fell into good ground, and brought forth fruit, some an hundredfold, some sixtyfold, some thirtyfold. Who hath ears to hear, let him hear (vv. 1-9).**

*THE NEW PLACE*

Leaving, what in all probability was the home of Simon Peter in Capernaum, the Lord proceeded to the seashore to teach the multitudes. Formerly, Jesus had taught in the synagogues, but now He went to the beach. There were two possible reasons for His action. The rulers of the synagogues had expressed disapproval of His message, so it seemed unwise to continue casting "pearls before swine!" The crowds had become so great, that synagogues could no longer accommodate those wishing to hear the Savior. Maybe His movements were emblematic of greater truths. Was He trying to tell His disciples that what had been for the Jews alone, was now to be told to the Gentiles? The distance from the synagogue to the seashore might have been only a few miles; from the confines of Israel to the Gentile world was almost immeasurable.

*A NEW PATTERN*

"And he spake many things unto them in parables" (v. 3a). Suddenly the style of Christ's teaching changed; He began to express His messages in word pictures. Some of these were based on actual things taking place in the vicinity; others were drawn from memory. Yet, in every instance, His message was simple and easy to understand. Stories are always acceptable, and sometimes they brighten sermons immeasurably. An illustration in a speech is what windows are to a house. Jesus was a master of the art of telling stories, and all preachers should learn from His example.

*THE NEW POWER*

It is written, "The common people heard him gladly" (Mark 12:37). Jesus was always able to attract multitudes of listeners, but as soon as He began to use easily remembered parables, His influence became phenomenal. His messages were so simple that even children understood their meaning, and yet so profound, no one could despise what He uttered. Millions of people have been influenced by His teaching, and it can still be asserted, "Never man spake like this man" (John 7:46).

### THE FIRST PARABLE

"A sower went forth to sow" (v.3b). Possibly, this parable might be better identified as an object lesson, for Jesus might have been describing something taking place in a nearby field. Matthew relates that, because of the intense pressure exerted by the crowd, it became necessary for Jesus to speak from a small boat. Thus, as He sat facing the congregation, He would have been looking toward the hills rising in the background. Everything mentioned in His parable was there to be seen by listeners. Seed was sown in two different ways. It was thrown by hand, or allowed to trickle through small holes in a bag placed upon the back of a donkey.

"The lowlands running up from the sea would be suitable for cultivation; higher, where farming would be somewhat difficult, weeds and thistles abounded. Further up still, where rocky slopes were very prominent, and where the depth of soil was negligible, the production of crops would be impossible. At the top of the cliff, where in all probability a path had been made, the ground would be hard and uncultivated. Any seeds which fell there would be food for the birds. Beyond that higher path would be other fields where crops were sown and harvested. Farmers sowing seeds on such terrain, would be aware that some of the seed would be swept by the wind over the cliff, and would fall on all kinds of ground. When Jesus uttered His parable, and probably indicated the illustration before His eyes, the audience easily understood His sermon. Matthew cited the fruitful increase as 'A hundredfold, sixtyfold, thirtyfold.' Mark cites the same differences but reverses the order. Luke is content to mention the fact that some seeds produced a hundred fold. There are no contradictions here. These varying viewpoints indicate that God was using *men* to tell the Good News, not *robots*. The Lord was speaking through the intellects of humans and not tapping out messages on the keys of typewriters'' (Reprinted from the author's *Commentary on Luke's Thrilling Gospel,* p. 187). (See also the homily: "Christ's…and His Commentary on Preaching" — The Stolen, Starved, Strangled and Successful Seeds. Reprinted from the author's *Commentary on Luke's Thrilling Gospel,* pp. 190-192.)

Some teachers argue that, since the sower was one man, he represented the Lord who came to scatter the gospel seeds throughout the world. They may be correct in their deductions. However, since every disciple receives an identical commission, it might be helpful to consider certain propositions. (1) *Every farmer MUST sow his seed.* If he does not, he will soon be out of business. The good seed is the message of the gospel. If a minister, pastor, or any other type of Christian farmer sows anything else, his harvest will be disappointing. Good wheat does not grow from the seeds of thistles and weeds. If a man does not preach the soul-saving gospel of Christ, he is wasting his time. (2) *A minister should never be discouraged*; some of his efforts might appear to fall on barren land; others might be choked by all kinds of hindrances. When enemies threaten the harvest, the worker must do all within his power to protect his labors, but he should never abandon his task — some seeds will germinate. The sower needs patience. (3) *A farmer should count his blessings, not mourn his losses.* There are always two sides to a picture, and one's happiness often depends on vision. One man might say, "I do not have a cent"; another might add, "Thank God I am not in debt." One pastor might complain of lack of success; another might praise God for the opportunity to make a new start. If God be on our side, we are certain of His help; if He be alongside, we are in very good company. (4) *The pastor-farmer will finally reap a harvest*, if he faints not. If he abandons his task when the job is only half completed, he might be making the greatest mistake of his life. It is always wise to seek more efficient methods of doing our job, but if we leave our ploughs, we are not fit for the kingdom of God.

As we have already considered, there are teachers who believe the "kingdom of heaven" means the whole realm of "Christendom," and this parable of the sower is but the first of seven word pictures depicting its history. This point of view will be the more easily understood if we consider all seven together. This we shall do, later in the chapter.

**And the disciples came, and said unto him, Why speakest thou unto them in parables? He answered and said unto them, Because it is given unto you to know the mysteries of the kingdom of heaven, but to them it is not given. For whosoever hath, to him shall be given, and he shall have more abundance: but whosoever hath not, from him shall be taken away even that he hath. Therefore speak I to them in parables because they seeing: see not; and hearing they hear not, neither do they understand (vv. 10-13).**

There are three things here to be considered. (1) *A Special Gift...*"It is given unto you to know the mysteries of the kingdom of heaven" (v. 11). (2) *A Serious Gesture...*"to them it is not given" (v. 11). (3) *A Saddening Guilt...*"this people's heart is waxed gross...their eyes they have closed" (v. 15). At first glance, the verses are difficult to comprehend. A superficial reading might suggest that God was selective in His choice of people. These Scriptures can be understood only when they are compared with certain old Testament utterances. Isaiah 6:9-10, Jeremiah 5:21, and Ezekiel 12:2 shed light on the Savior's message. He was reminding the people of facts with which they were conversant.

They surely knew WHY God spoke these things through the prophets. The basic cause of their unenlightened minds was rebellious hearts. Israel had killed God's messengers. To waste time teaching their descendants would be "casting pearls before swine." They only listened because they wished to argue; they watched in order to criticize. It is against this background we must consider the Lord's words. He had uttered certain principles of the kingdom. Those whose hearts were receptive to the message would understand; others who were enemies of the faith would hear in parables and, failing to understand, would depart, leaving the disciples in peace.

> **And in them is fulfilled the prophecy of Esaias, which saith, By hearing ye shall hear, and shall not understand; and seeing ye shall see, and shall not perceive: For this people's heart is become gross, and their ears are dull of hearing, and their eyes have they closed; lest at any time they should see with their eyes, and hear with their ears, and should understand with their heart, and should be converted, and I should heal them. But blessed are your eyes, for they see: and your ears, for they hear. For verily I say unto you, That many prophets and righteous men have desired to see those things which ye see, and have not seen them; and to hear those things which ye hear, and have not heard them (vv. 14-17).**

The revelation supplied in these verses was astonishing, for the increasing guilt of men was compared with the inspiring grace of God. Jesus said the Jews had deliberately resisted the efforts of heaven because they had no desire to participate in God's purposes. His message may be divided into three sections. (1) *A Deliberate Sin.* "...their eyes they have closed... lest at any time they should see...." (2) *A Desiring Savior.* "...and should be converted, and I should heal them." (3) *A Delightful Sight.* "...those things which ye see." It is almost incomprehensible that God should continue to love undeserving people. The Jews had consistently rejected His message, stoned His servants, and blasphemed His name, and yet He still desired to save and heal them. Perhaps the best illustrations of this glorious fact may be found in the Book of Judges, where again and again, after the people repented of their sin, God graciously came to their rescue. It almost seemed a wasted effort, for as soon as Israel was pardoned the people sinned again. Yet, throughout the centuries, God's love never diminished. It is a stimulating thought that, since He is unchangeable, the same love is extended toward us.

Could we with ink the ocean fill
And were the skies of parchment made,
Were every stalk on earth a quill
And every man a scribe by trade,
To write the love of God above
Would drain the ocean dry,
Nor could the scroll contain the whole
Though stretched from sky to sky.

The writer to the Hebrews, having mentioned the great men and women of faith, concludes with an important statement. "And these all, having obtained a good report through faith, received not the promise: God having provided some better thing for us, that they without us should not be made perfect" (Heb. 11:39-40). The Lord had similar thoughts in mind when He said the prophets and righteous men desired to see the things which the disciples saw. Were they thinking of miracles or of the One who would perform them? To see anything is a privilege; to see the works of Christ is greater, but to see the Lord in His loveliness is the greatest of all privileges.

**Hear ye therefore the parable of the sower (v. 18).**

"The wicked enemy is Satan. The seed is the Word. The deceitfulness of riches choke the word. They who receive the message and understand it...these are the children of the kingdom."

## THE DANGER FROM A SINISTER ENEMY

Jesus was more aware of the presence of Satan than anyone else on earth. Day after day the Lord's greatest enemy tried to find a flaw in the Savior, and because of this continuing threat Christ was extremely careful in all He did and said. The disciples would similarly be tempted, and should therefore endeavor to sow seed in hearts where the gospel would be appreciated. They should learn how to nourish it with their prayers, and protect it with continuing attention. If they neglected what they had commenced, their labor would be in vain.

## THE DECEPTION OF A SUPERFICIAL EVALUATION

Any immediate success should increase the watchfulness of the sower. Growth without depth is always dangerous. Emotional impulses are not always evidence of deep conviction. Sometimes tears are better than thrills! The fields of Palestine were often unproductive, because only a very thin layer of earth covered the rock. Soil erosion was such that, after every gale, much of the underlying stone was exposed. Seeds, without a bed of soil, sprang up quickly, but perished as soon as the sun shone upon them. Jesus knew it was impossible to grow upward unless the roots first went down into productive soil. His disciples should be more concerned with a true harvest than with immediate results. It would be better to have one steadfast convert, than have hundreds who would leave as soon as danger threatened.

## THE DISTRESS OF A STARVED ENVIRONMENT

Jesus was a superlative teacher. He taught His followers the absolute necessity of separation. This has become a forgotten doctrine within the church. Yet its truth is undeniable. To accept the truth of the gospel is one thing; to promote its healthy growth is another. "The care of this world, and the deceitfulness of riches, choke the word, and he becometh unfruitful." There are many other commodities which could be added to the list. John said, "Love not the world, neither the things that are in the world. If any man love the world, the love of the Father is not in him" (1 John 2:15). Horticultural experts stress that certain plants should be placed in favorable surroundings; some flowers flourish in the shade, others in the sunshine. The followers of Jesus should be equally careful in the cultivation of precious souls. The question whether or not a thing is evil is not the only issue at stake. Some details of life may not be evil, but they may be detrimental to the fruitfulness of the Christian. All weeds should be removed from the garden of a man's soul.

## THE DELIGHT OF A SUCCESSFUL ENDEAVOR

John said, "I have no greater joy than to hear that my children walk in truth" (3 John 4). This statement can be compared with the Lord's words in Matthew 13:23. The seed which fell into good ground yielded a harvest, and nothing could be more pleasing to a farmer than to see the successful culmination of his efforts. "Hearing" and "understanding" are related words. They represent twin truths. Many people *hear* but do not *understand*, and it is impossible to understand unless the words of the gospel are first heard. "How shall they hear without a preacher?" (Rom. 10:14). "So they read in the book in the law of God *distinctly, and gave the sense, and caused them to understand the reading''* (Neh. 8:8). Topical preaching can be useful and interesting, but nothing can ever supersede the value of expository preaching. When the Word of Truth is the foundation upon which a preacher builds his sermon, the edifice is likely to remain. It might be reproduced a hundredfold, or sixtyfold, or twentyfold — but it cannot die. These are some of the lessons to be found in the parable of the sower.

## SECTION TWO

*Expository Notes on the Man Who Sowed Tares Among the Wheat*

**Another parable put he forth unto them, saying, The kingdom of heaven is likened unto a man which sowed good seed in his field: But while men slept, his enemy came and sowed tares among the wheat, and went his way. But when the blade was sprung up, and brought forth fruit, then appeared the tares also. So the servants of the householder came and said unto him, Sir, didst not thou sow good seed in thy field? from whence, then hath it tares? He said unto them, An enemy hath done this. The servants said unto him, Wilt thou then that we go and gather them up? But he said, Nay; lest while ye gather up the tares, ye root up also the wheat with them. Let both grow together until the harvest: and in the time of harvest I will say to the reapers, Gather ye together first the tares, and bind them in bundles to burn them: but gather the wheat into my barn (vv. 24-30).**

This parable was easily understood; tares in Palestine were the most annoying of all weeds. During the early stages of growth these plants were indistinguishable from the grain, and thus to separate wheat from tares was impossible. Archbishop Bench in his *Dictionary of Christian Biography,* Book 1, p. 745, draws attention to the fact that "the first extant exposition of this parable is in Cyprian's successful appeal to the Novationists not to separate from the church" (*The Pulpit Commentary,* Vol. 2, p. 7).

Thomson describes in *The Land and the Book* how he saw these tares *lolium temulentum* in the Wady Hamam. He says: "The grain is just in the proper state of development to illustrate the parable. In those parts where the grain is headed out, the tares have done the same, and there, a child cannot mistake them for wheat or barley; but when both are less developed, the closest scrutiny will often fail to detect them. I cannot do it at all with any confidence. Even the farmers who, in this country, generally weed their fields, do not attempt to separate the one from the other...the roots of the two are so intertwined, that it is impossible to separate them without plucking up both. Both, therefore, must be left to grow together, until the time of harvest.''

From the writings of Levison, we learn as a rule that the separation of the darnel [tares] from the wheat is done after the threshing. The grain is spread on a large tray, and when set before the women, they are able to pick out the darnel. It is a seed similar in shape and size to wheat, but slate gray in color.

Any person guilty of contaminating a neighbor's wheat was severely punished by Roman law. No matter how great the enmity existing between people, it was considered an unpardonable offense to sow tares among wheat. These verses may be divided into four categories.

## THE FAITHFUL SOWER

Primarily, this must be the Son of man. The Lord Jesus came into the world to scatter the good seed of the gospel. He planned to produce a harvest of very precious souls, and since the only way to do this was by the regeneration of men and women, the Lord not only preached the gospel Himself, He commissioned His disciples to go into all the world to do the same. To the Lord, this was of supreme importance. His miracles could not even compare with the transformation He planned for human hearts. Therefore, with untiring effort He scattered seed in every direction.

## THE FOOLISH SERVANTS

''But while men slept, his enemy came and sowed tares'' (v. 25). Probably the men who slept were those appointed to cultivate the fields; that is, to water, guard, and superintend the cultivation of the crop. Within a land where enemies abounded, it was obvious that guards should have been watchful at all times. The inference is that the watchmen had gone to sleep on their job, and the enemy, seizing his opportunity, sowed the tares. The Lord was offering advice to His servants, to whom would be entrusted the task of helping and building the church during the initial stages of growth.

## THE FORBIDDEN SEPARATION

''So the servants of the householder came and said unto him...Wilt thou then that we go and gather them up? But he said, Nay...'' (vv.

27-29). At that time, the wheat and tares were indistinguishable from each other, and workmen could not effectively weed the field. The Lord was telling His servants that it would be unsafe and unwise to make premature judgment in regard to people. One human plant might appear to be a product of the good seed, and yet be a tare. Another might seem to be a weed, and yet be wheat. An observer cannot always decide the quality of the person being scrutinized. Therefore, instead of moving in with a sickle, the disciples should exhibit love and patience as they watched the growing harvest.

## THE FINAL SCRUTINY

"Let both grow together until the harvest: and in the time of harvest I will say to the reapers, Gather ye together first the tares, and bind them in bundles to burn them: but gather the wheat into my barn'' (v. 30). Jesus was quite sure that God's Harvest Day would come. He taught this throughout His ministry. He spoke of wheat and tares; mercy and judgment; heaven and hell. He came to earth to save sinners, because they needed to be saved. We must ask, "From what were they *needing to be saved?*" The final separation of saints and sinners should make individuals consider the destinies mentioned in the Scriptures. There is much at stake; no man can afford to be negligent.

### SECTIONS THREE AND FOUR

*Expository Notes on the Parables of the Mustard Seed
and the Measures of Meal*

**Another parable put he forth unto them, saying, The kingdom of heaven is like to a grain of mustard seed, which a man took, and sowed in his field: Which indeed is the least of all seeds: but when it is grown, it is the greatest among herbs, and becometh a tree, so that the birds of the air come and lodge in the branches thereof. Another parable spake he unto them; The kingdom of heaven is like unto leaven, which a woman took, and hid in three measures of meal, till the whole was leavened (vv. 31-33).**

These two parables have been debated at length throughout the history of the church. The three schools of thought mentioned at the beginning of this chapter have all focused their attention on these words of the Savior.

*HOW SIMPLE HIS STORIES*

Tristram in *The Natural History of the Bible* supplies the following information. ''The Common Mustard Seed of Palestine is *Sinapis nigra* of the order of Cruciferae, the Black Mustard, which is found abundantly in a wild state, and is also cultivated in the gardens for its seed. It is the same as our own mustard, but grows especially in the richer soils of the Jordan valley to a much greater size than in this country. We noticed its great height on the banks of the Jordan, as have several other travelers; and Dr. Thomson remarks that in the Plain of Acre, he has seen it as tall as a horse and its rider.'' The seed of this tree is very small, and is a favorite food for the flocks of finches and linnets which settle in the trees. The connotation of the parable was that something very small became very great, offering rest, nourishment, and safety to those who sought its shelter.

It has been taught consistently that this parable represented the astounding growth of the church which, beginning from almost nothing, became the greatest power in the ancient world. Leaven was a small piece of sour dough which had been allowed to ferment. It resembled yeast which permeated new dough to make it more appetizing. Within Palestine, for the most part, bread was baked in homes, and three measures of meal was approximately the quantity needed for a fairly large family. There exists the possibility that Jesus had often watched His mother doing what He was describing. Unleavened bread was hard and unappetizing. It is the kind of dry biscuit often used in the communion services of churches. Yet, within families, such bread would never be used, unless it were connected with a religious ordinance. On the other hand, bread baked with leaven was very tasty, soft, and spongy. Thus this parable resembles the mustard seed, in that the meal expanded through permeation. The meal increased not only in size but in tastiness; it became a delight. It has therefore been claimed that this represents the transforming power of the gospel. The message of Christ can reach the dry, unattractive sinners and transform them into saints. The Lord was an expert in His choice of illustrations; these parables complement each other.


*HOW SPLENDID HIS SUCCESS*

The expansiveness of the mustard seed, and the invaluable permeation of the leaven in the meal, both indicate the miraculous effect of the gospel as seen in the growth of the church. Within the lifetime of Paul, and largely through his efforts, the message of Christ had been proclaimed throughout the entire Roman Empire. The growth of the church had been phenomenal. Restless, hungry and needy people had flocked to the sanctuary and had found all they needed. Innumerable birds of the air had, indeed, sought the protective branches of the tree, and all had been fed by the bountiful supplies of God's provision. What had been a small persecuted minority in Jerusalem, had increased to such an extent, that even Caesar was worried. Sustained attacks had been made to exterminate what was considered to be a threat to the empire. Yet the blood of the martyrs became the seed of the church.

The same fact was expressed in both the parable of the meal and the leaven. A small piece of truth had produced energy of its own, and unbelievable miracles had been performed in the lives of men and women, throughout the world. Moody men had become confident; cowards had courageously lain down their lives for Christ. A new power had spread throughout the world, turning unattractive, tasteless dough into fresh, appetizing, wholesome bread! With this, dying people were beginning to live; without it, starving people were already dying. The quiet, almost unnoticed permeation of the dry, unresponsive inhabitants of the world was noticeable everywhere. Ephesus was so completely changed that, by the middle of the second century, all its inhabitants were professedly Christian. The disciples were commissioned to go into all the world to preach the gospel, knowing they could not fail. His presence would go with them; His strength would be made perfect in their weakness.

## HOW STRANGE HIS SUGGESTIONS

These interpretations would be absolutely thrilling except for one disturbing feature. Consistently, throughout the Scriptures, leaven has connotations of evil. How then could Jesus refer to it as the greatest good known to man? Prior to the Feast of the Passover, every Jew had to be sure all leaven had been removed from his home. Its presence contaminated the dwelling. Jesus said to His followers, "Take heed and beware of the leaven of the Pharisees and of the Sadducees" (Matt. 16:6). Moses had strictly commanded Israel that no leaven should be found in offerings. "Thou shalt not offer the blood of my sacrifice with leavened bread..." (Exod. 23:18). Throughout the generations of Israel, leaven was forbidden in any act of worship. How then could Jesus use the illustration to indicate the transforming power of the gospel?

The dispensationalist teachers deny that He did this. They state the seven parables of the kingdom represent seven periods of history, and that was the reason why these mysteries were revealed only to the disciples. They say the unfolding of truth in Matthew thirteen is as follows. The parable of the sower supplies the first section of church history when Christ, through His servants, sowed the good seed in the world. The second represents the period when the first love of the church began to disappear; when it became apparent Satan was trying to undermine the efforts of the Son of man. This period continued through the centuries when, like a great mustard tree, the outgoing branches of Christendom reached the entire world. At the beginning of the fourth century, the Emperor Constantine professed to become a Christian, and it became evident the mustard tree had covered the earth. Alas, during the following centuries, the State became dominant and the leaven of false teaching contaminated the church.

The Lord supplied two other word pictures of events to transpire during forthcoming ages. (1) *The treasure hid in the field* is said to be Israel, the chosen people of God, lost amidst the nations. (2) *The pearl of great price* is said to represent the church, formed through suffering, in the depths of the sea. Contrasting the treasure with the pearl, it has been claimed the treasure may be made of many pieces; the pearl is one priceless gem which will adorn Christ's crown throughout eternal ages. The final illustration of the dragnet speaks of the end of the age, when all seven parables of the kingdom reach their appointed climax. The wicked and the good will be separated by judgment. This is the interpretation supplied by dispensational teachers of the Bible. There may be truth in their assertions. Compare these parables with the messages sent to the seven churches of Asia (Rev. 2 and 3), and it might be possible to find twin highways of truth.

## SECTION FIVE

*Expository Notes on Christ's Explanation of His Parable*

**All these things spake Jesus unto the multitude in parables; and without a parable spake he not unto them: That it might be fulfilled which was spoken by the prophet, saying, I will open my mouth in parables; I will utter things which have been kept secret from the foundation of the world. Then Jesus sent the multitude away, and went into the house: and his disciples came unto him, saying, Declare unto us the parable of the tares of the field (vv. 34-36).**

These verses represent an interlude in our Lord's continuing teaching. Having delivered four of His word pictures, Jesus dismissed the people and went into a house. Eventually, He delivered three more parables but, in the meantime, the disciples sought an explanation of the parable of the tares. Matthew's account divides into five sections.

## THE SPECIAL PREACHING

"...without a parable spake he not unto them" (v. 34b). The sermons in which Christ taught the need for repentance and forgiveness were now things of the past; He had become a raconteur; a master of storytelling. The possibility existed that the details of His preaching might be forgotten by His listeners; His illustrations would be remembered forever. His new style of teaching has always been the most effective way of imparting truth.

## THE STRANGE PREDICTION

"That it might be fulfilled which was spoken by the prophet" (v. 35a). The reference was to Psalm 78:2 "I will open my mouth in a parable: I will utter dark sayings of old." *The Living Bible* translates the latter part of the verse, "I will explain mysteries hidden since the beginning of time." This is an intriguing statement, for very special things were planned by God, and then preserved as a secret until the Lord revealed them to the disciples. What were those secrets? The answer must relate to the inclusion of Gentile nations in the family of God.

## THE STIRRING PRONOUNCEMENT

Christ began to reveal that mystery; Paul continued and deepened it, and finally at the end of the age God will complete it. Matthew, however, seized the opportunity to draw evidence from the ancient writings, that Jesus was the true Messiah. To all intent and purpose Jesus was the final Revelation of God. Who else could interpret the divinely-hidden mysteries of eternity, except the One who came from God? The moment of revelation had arrived, for "God, who at sundry times and in divers manners spake in time past unto the fathers by the prophets, Hath in these last days spoken unto us by his Son" (Heb. 1:1-2).

## THE SUDDEN PARTING

The sentence " *Tote apheis tous oxlouseelthen eis oikan ho Ieesous,*"
has been translated by the *Interlinear Greek Testament,* as, "Then having
dismissed the crowds, went into the house Jesus." The Lord apparently
dismissed the people and then deliberately went indoors. His action
suggested all kinds of thought. Opportunities should be grasped
immediately; they might never return. Service of any kind should be
punctuated by recesses; "a candle burnt at both ends is destined for
a short life."

## THE SERIOUS PLEA

"His disciples came unto him, saying, Declare unto us the parable
of the tares of the field" (v. 36b). His simple story had mystified them;
His secret remained a secret! They needed additional information and
asked the Lord to explain His story. It was useless listening to Jesus
if they did not understand what was being taught. They were diligent,
decisive, determined. Happy and wise are all who follow in their
footsteps. No preacher can be a successful soul winner if he is not assured
of the accuracy of his message.

**He answered and said unto them, He that soweth the good seed is the
Son of man; The field is the world; the good seed are the children of
the kingdom; but the tares are the children of the wicked one; The enemy
that sowed them is the devil; the harvest is the end of the world [age];
and the reapers are the angels. As therefore the tares are gathered and
burned in the fire so shall it be in the end of this world [age]. The Son
of man shall send forth his angels, and they shall gather out of his
kingdom all things that offend, and them which do iniquity; And shall
cast them into a furnace of fire: there shall be wailing and gnashing
of teeth. Then shall the righteous shine forth as the sun in the kingdom
of their Father. Who hath ears to hear, let him hear (vv. 37-43).**

These Scriptures divide into four sections, and each one has truth
to impart. Let us proceed carefully.

## THE SIMPLICITY OF THE SERMON

Within the restricted area of six sentences, the Lord placed all the
information required by His followers; there were no unnecessary words.
Even a child would have comprehended what was taught in the parable
of the wheat and the tares. It was exposition at its best! Some men speak

for an hour and say nothing! Jesus spoke for a few seconds and said everything!

## THE SORROW OF THE SINNERS

Jesus taught there existed two kinds of people, and one, obviously, was composed of unrepentant sinners. These were the tares, said to be "the children of the wicked one." Elsewhere, Jesus said some of His listeners were "the children of Satan." "Ye are of your father the devil and the lusts of your father ye will do" (John 8:44). That Jesus also believed there would be a day of judgment was obvious to all who heard His message. He predicted that, at the end of the age, God would gather the tares from the world, and men and women would be judged according to their deeds. Preachers who deny this fact did not graduate from God's University.

## THE SAFETY OF THE SAINTS

"Then shall the righteous shine forth as the sun in the kingdom of their Father" (v. 43a). Their ultimate and final acceptance by the King of kings can never be in doubt. These are the wise people who "received the word into their hearts." They listened, learned, and loved the Lord. Accepting Christ, they were accepted by Him. His promise, "they shall never perish" (John 10:28), will be completely fulfilled. It is strange how liberal theologians amplify this section of the Lord's message, but discredit the rest of it.

## THE SERIOUSNESS OF THE SAVIOR

"Who hath ears to hear, *let him hear*" (v. 43b). It was as though the Lord said, "If you have ears, then listen! Your life might depend upon what you hear and do." It should be remembered that the Savior was speaking to men who were to evangelize the world. They were to broadcast the same message enunciated by their Master. The pathway of instruction to be followed was clearly defined. They were to contrast evil with goodness; religion and righteousness; sanctimoneousness and salvation; hell with heaven. They were entrusted with this message. If preachers did not adhere to the Lord's commandments, they were neither ordained nor commissioned by God. Furthermore, the Bible teaches that if people perish because of the watchman's negligence in broadcasting truth, the blood of those who perish will be required at the watchman's hands. This warning should be included in every ordination service; it might lead to healthier and wiser pastors.

## SECTIONS SIX AND SEVEN

### THE FIFTH AND SIXTH PARABLES

*Expository Notes on the Parables of the Treasure and the Pearl*

**Again, the kingdom of heaven is like unto treasure hid in a field which when a man hath found, he hideth, and for joy thereof goeth and selleth all that he hath, and buyeth that field. Again, the kingdom of heaven is like unto a merchant man, seeking goodly [fine] pearls: Who, when he had found one pearl of great price, went and sold all that he had, and bought it (vv. 44-46).**

These two parables are perhaps among the most interesting parts of the Bible. They are complete in themselves and, whatever dispensational value might be accredited to them, nothing can change the fact they present pictures which, once seen, can never be forgotten. The story of the treasure in the field is based upon the simple fact that, until recent times, banks were unknown in the Middle East. A man's wealth was invested in cattle and land. Afterward, if he had surplus money, he had to be his own banker. Wise people never hid valuables at home, for marauding tribes could unexpectedly raid a village to destroy homes and property. If a man hid his wealth at home, he could suddenly become impoverished. This led to the practice of burying treasure in the fields. It is still possible to see men digging around the remains of old buildings in the hope of discovering hidden coins. The law said that if a man found treasure in purchased fruit, the treasure was his *if he could prove he owned the fruit*. The same law applied to treasure found *in a piece of land*. A few coins could be found and remain undeclared. Larger treasures were more conspicuous. The finders had to rebury the treasure, and then try to obtain exclusive ownership of the land in which the valuables had been discovered. This was common practice during the New Testament era, and therefore the Lord's parable was easily understood by His listeners.

HOMILY

Study No. 7

### THE GOLD DIGGER ... And the Way He Staked His Claim

Again, the kingdom of heaven is like unto treasure hid in a field;

the which when a man hath found, he hideth, and for joy thereof goeth and selleth all that he hath, and buyeth that field'' (v. 44). This text is based upon the fact that in ancient times banks were unknown in the Middle East. During Bible days, men had to be their own bankers.

## THE MAN SEEKING

Probably the finder had first heard about buried treasure when he was a little child. His mother told romantic stories which thrilled his heart, but these tales had been allowed to remain dormant in his mind. Now the boy had become a man, and with increased interest had decided to test the validity of the account so often repeated. Armed with his spade, he went forth to dig, and his first discovery revealed far more dirt than treasure. When he began his work, critics laughed him to scorn. The Lord declared that the kingdom of heaven was like that. God's treasures are not always found on the surface. It would appear that an evil hand had covered them. Enemies of the Christian faith glibly declare that seekers after eternal treasure will be more likely to find hypocrites. Their remarks accentuate the fact that to find spiritual wealth, man needs to look beyond dirt!

## THE MAN SACRIFICING

Ignoring the jibes of the onlookers, the digger proceeded with his task, and suddenly discovered the buried box. Careful investigation revealed this was no hallucination. The story heard from childhood was true. He asked, "How can I make this mine?" Jesus continued, "Which when a man hath found, he hideth, and for joy thereof    goeth and selleth all that he hath, and buyeth that field." We see the man selling his cottage, his clothing, his possessions, and if, at the end of the sale, he required extra money, he earned it with the labor of his hands. Carefully preserving the secret of his motives, the man appeared to be the greatest fool in the village. When he gave all his possessions in exchange for a field, his fellow citizens probably pronounced him to be insane. He merely smiled, for he realized that no sacrifice was too great under these special circumstances. And the Lord said, "The kingdom of heaven is like that!" Let a man discover reality in the gospel, and the criticisms of the crowd will be meaningless.

## THE MAN SUCCEEDING

The business transaction was completed in the presence of the elders, and the news of the purchaser's lunacy became the talk of the community. Perhaps people followed him and wondered what he intended to do with his property. Did the man borrow his neighbor's spade, or did he dig with his hands? The earth was thrown from the hiding place, and once again the treasure was uncovered. The astonished crowd gasped for, while they jested, he had become rich. Within a little while his cottage was replaced by a mansion; his old garments were superseded by those of a prince. And Jesus said, again, "The kingdom of heaven is like that." Let a man ignore the sneers of fellow men; let a man look beyond what appears to be hypocritical dirt; let a man seek wholeheartedly for God and, soon, he will uncover eternal riches. The gold of grace; the pearls of promise; the rubies of redemption, and wealth from an everlasting realm will reward his efforts. The old cottage of mortality will be replaced by immortality; the corruptible will put on incorruption; and from poverty, the finder will be transported to realms of enchanting wonder. Yes, "the kingdom of heaven is like unto treasure hid in a field; the which when a man hath found, he hideth, and for the joy thereof goeth and selleth all that he hath, and buyeth that field." Gold diggers and diamond hunters need excellent eyesight! The entire purpose of their activities might be thwarted if they allow too much dirt to get into their eyes. (Homily reprinted from the author's book *Bible Treasures*, pp. 75-76).

## THE PEARL OF GREAT PRICE

Again, it should be remembered that this word picture was easily understood by the Lord's listeners; pearls were in great demand throughout the ancient world. Cultured pearls were unknown in antiquity, and any kind of pearl was considered to be of great value. These treasures were constantly sought by peddlers, who were assured of great profits when they resold their gems. Nevertheless, this parable was of tremendous interest because of the words used by Jesus. This seeker after pearls was no mere peddler.

## *THE METICULOUS PERSON*

Jesus spoke of a "merchant man, seeking goodly [fine] pearls." According to Dr. Thayer, there were two important words used in this connection. The first was *emporos* which implied "a collector or a dealer of great wealth." No ordinary street peddler, nor even a retailer, he was a wealthy man; possibly a collector of rare gems. The same word is used in Revelation 18:23 where the merchants (*emporoi*) are said to be "the great men of the earth." The second word used was *kapeelos* which meant "a peddler, a dealer, a retailer." The picture thus provided was not that of a money-making dealer, but of a skilled connoisseur; a collector of rare gems with an almost inexhaustible supply of purchasing power.

This has been the one parable about which all theologians agreed. The pearl of great price is the church formed through suffering. The man said to be seeking the treasure is Christ, the Son of God, the Prince of Heaven. Dr. Thayer further states the word *emporos* was used in ancient writings to indicate a man who goes "on a journey, whether by sea or by land, especially for traffic or business." This, of course, was in harmony with the theme of the parable. The Prince of Heaven came to earth to search for, and to acquire something of tremendous value. "He sacrificed all that He had" to obtain His pearl.

## THE MAGNIFICENT PEARL

It should be noted that the seeker was looking for *goodly* pearls. The Greek word used here is *kalous* which means, "beautiful, handsome, excellent, eminent, choice, surpassing, precious, suitable, commendable, admirable, beautiful to look at, shapely, magnificent." *Kalous* is no ordinary word. The seeker was only interested in gems of surpassing excellence. That he only found *one pearl* embodying all these qualities provides food for thought. Pearls are formed through suffering. A small grain of irritating sand creates pain inside the shell of an oyster. The mollusk, "upon this grain of sand, deposits a thin crust of brilliant material. How often this is repeated, no one can tell; one deposit after another is made till at last in the side of the oyster, there is found a most beautiful pearl, a pearl of great price, a pearl in which the colors of the rainbow of the heavens are wonderfully blended together. It is taken up and becomes the well nigh priceless jewel in the crown of some mighty monarch" (Arno C. Gaebelein. *The Gospel of Matthew,* p. 300). The pearl of great price can only be the Christian church created through the sufferings of the Savior. There could only be *one* of this type.

## THE MEMORABLE PRICE

The special collector, as suggested by the Greek word, had to be exceedingly wealthy, but the added detail that "he sold all that he had," suggests great sacrifice. In modern language, the multimillionaire became penniless through one tremendous transaction. Basically, he had nothing left except the acquired pearl, but he obviously considered the purchase worthwhile. There can be no way to measure the love with which he looked at His purchase. The Prince of Heaven, "Who, being in the form of God, thought it not robbery to be equal with God: But made himself of no reputation, and took upon him the form of a servant, and was made in the likeness of men: And being found in fashion as a man, he humbled himself, and became obedient unto death, even the death of the cross" (Phil. 2:6-8). The seeker after the pearl of great price, literally gave all that He had even His life, but obviously, He thought it worthwhile. How greatly Jesus must have loved us!

## THE MATCHLESS PLEASURE

It is difficult to understand completely, the Lord's satisfaction in purchasing the church. Maybe the nearest we can approach to that superlative appreciation is to remember how ten thousand times ten thousand, and thousands of thousands will sing, "Thou art worthy...for thou wast slain, and hast redeemed us to God by thy blood out of every kindred, and tongue, and people, and nation; And hast made us unto our God kings and priests: and we shall reign on the earth" (Rev. 5:9-10). When the Lord Jesus listens to the anthem of His redeemed choir, He will be thrilled, and perhaps might borrow our language and exclaim, "It was worth it all."

### SECTION EIGHT

### THE SEVENTH PARABLE

*Expository Notes on the Parable of the Dragnet*

**Again, the kingdom of heaven is like unto a net, that was cast into the sea, and gathered of every kind: Which, when it was full, they drew to shore, and sat down, and gathered the good into vessels, but cast the bad away. So shall it be at the end of the world [age]: the angels shall come forth, and sever the wicked from among the just, And shall cast them into the furnace of fire: there shall be wailing and gnashing of teeth. Jesus saith unto them, Have ye understood all these things? They say unto him, Yea, Lord. Then said he unto them, Therefore every scribe which is instructed unto the kingdom of heaven is like a man that is an householder, which bringeth forth out of his treasure things**

new and old. And it came to pass, that when Jesus had finished these parables, he departed from thence (vv. 47-53).

## TWO KINDS OF NETS

These verses can be very productive for the thoughtful student. There may be a great amount of truth in the viewpoint of the dispensationalist teachers. They draw attention to the sequence of parables. The treasure in the field, the pearl of great price, and finally the dragnet preceding the establishing of Christ's earthly kingdom. They affirm that during this age, God's peculiar treasure, Israel, is hidden among the nations. Then reference is made to the pearl of great price, the church, which grows until the beginning of the Tribulation. Finally, the parable of the dragnet refers to the separation of saint and sinner immediately before the return of the King to earth (see Matt. 24:29-31). If their viewpoint be correct, then this throwing and retrieving the net refers to the preaching of the gospel of the kingdom during the time of "Jacob's Trouble." That good and bad will be scrutinized and separated, makes it obvious that the bad will be rejected. This cannot refer to the "Gospel Net," for all who truly believe will never be rejected. (See John 10:28-29.)

Two kinds of nets were, and still are, used in the Middle East. The first was a casting net, known as the "amphibleestron." Dr. Thomson in *The Land and the Book* referred to this type of fishing when he wrote, "The net is in shape like the top of a bell-tent, with a long cord fastened to the apex. This is tied to the arm, and the net so folded, that, when it is thrown, it expands to its utmost circumference, around which are strung beads of lead to make it drop suddenly to the bottom." The second net was known as the "sageenee," and was used in trawling. It was a combination of floats and weights, so that the net stood vertically in the water. Cords were attached to each corner, but when the boat began to move the whole thing came together to float like a mammoth sausage in the sea. A large "pocket" existed at the end, and into this all kinds of creatures were swept. Finally, the whole thing was dragged to the beach where fishermen carefully examined the catch. Small fish were returned to the water; undesirable creatures were thrown away, and the good fish often were placed into tanks filled with water, so that they could be delivered fresh to distant customers.

## TWO KINDS OF FISH

Jesus was speaking to men who had used nets daily. These disciples were commissioned to go fishing for men and, therefore, if the parable related to the future ministry of the church, no preacher should abandon his task because of the presence of undesirable "fish" in his net! It would be the responsibility of God's angels to separate the good from the bad. If the disciples did this, they might make mistakes. Their job was to fish, pull the net, then leave the rest to God. Any fisherman who expected his entire catch to be flawless would be disappointed; and every teacher of the Bible would be equally at fault, if he denied the existence of a day of judgment.

## TWO KINDS OF ANSWERS

"Jesus saith unto them, Have ye understood all these things? They say unto him, Yea, Lord" (v. 51). Their answer was very positive; it could have been negative. If they did not understand what Jesus taught, they should have made it the first priority in life to ascertain what He meant. The reference to the instructed scribe, displaying treasures, suggests the enthusiasm of a collector ardently showing his greatest jewels. What he possessed was of such superlative worth, he longed for others to view and admire his exhibits. So should it be with every instructed scribe or minister of the gospel. What he finds in the old and new revelations of God, should be displayed for everybody to see. When Jesus had ended this period of instruction, He left the district.

## SECTION NINE

*Expository Notes on the Unbelief in His Own Country*

**And when he was come into his own country, he taught them in their synagogue, insomuch that they were astonished, and said, Whence hath this man this wisdom, and these mighty works? Is not this the carpenter's son? is not his mother called Mary? and his brethren, James, and Joses, and Simon, and Judas? And his sisters, are they not all with us? Whence then hath this man all these things? And they were offended in him. But Jesus said unto them, A prophet is not without honour, save in his own country, and in his own house. And he did not many mighty works there because of their unbelief (vv. 54-58).**

## THE RETURN OF THE CARPENTER

"And when he was come into his own country" (v. 54a). The Lord had already established new headquarters in Capernaum, and this, of necessity, led to the removal from Nazareth. However, in such a small country, news of His exploits would travel quickly, and the people of Nazareth would hear with interest of all He said and did. Perhaps a few of them had been to the meetings in Capernaum and had seen miracles. The news that Jesus was returning spread throughout the district, and realizing He would be visiting the synagogue, people hastened to attend the services. They were eager, inquisitive, curious. He had lived in their midst for nearly thirty years; had grown up with their children, and had become the village carpenter. Now He was a national hero, and it was only natural they would want to see the village boy who had made good! They had watched Him among the sawdust and shavings, and had done business with Him, but it seemed incomprehensible that their carpenter could do the impossible. What had happened to Him? They remembered He always went to the synagogue on the Sabbath and, expecting to see and hear Him there, they hastened to the sanctuary.

## THE REASON FOR THEIR CRITICISM

It would appear He taught them over a period of days; but even one of His sermons would have been sufficient to promote amazement in the minds of His former customers. They listened to His words, but thought of His upbringing. They looked into His face, but remembered sawdust. They could not forget the poor environment in which His family still lived. Was it jealousy or prejudice which dominated their thinking? Seeing, they saw not, and hearing, they understood nothing! The Bible says "they were astonished, and said, Whence hath this man this wisdom, and these mighty works?" They would have shown greater respect for any visiting rabbi, but it seemed inconceivable that a boy of the village should ever amount to anything! They thought and spoke of His brothers and sisters. They expressed a mild contempt for Mary, the woman who had lived down the street, and suddenly their attitude became obnoxious. They were as people needing surgery, but they despised the greatest surgeon in the land, because they remembered His hands had formerly been those of a village carpenter!

## THE RESULT OF THEIR CONDUCT

"And he did not many mighty works there because of their unbelief" (v. 58). Mark supplied a few more details when he wrote, "And he could there do no mighty work, *save that he laid his hands upon a few sick folk, and healed them*'' (Mark 6:5). The contrast provided was very thought-provoking. Jesus did no *mighty* works, but He did heal a few folk. Mark seems to indicate the healing of a few sick people was nothing compared to what He could have done for the entire region. Had they given the welcome He deserved, every family could have been helped and each home transformed into a haven of delight. Alas, their prejudice erected immovable barriers. The ''Light of the world'' was beginning to shine into their souls, but they preferred darkness. Nevertheless, it must be remembered that He did heal a few folk. Did they seek His help? Did their faith shine as stars against the blackness of the unbelief of the other people? We may never know, but one thing remained obvious. Jesus was able to save, under any circumstances, in any place. The faith of the few in Nazareth resembled that of Bartimaeus who, although he was told by many people to refrain from appealing to Jesus, persisted and received sight. Nothing — nothing, should ever prevent a soul from seeking the Savior's help.

# The Fourteenth Chapter Of Matthew

THEME: *Events Following the Murder of John the Baptist*

OUTLINE:
   I. Jesus Remembers a Worker (Verses 1-12)
   II. Jesus Removes a Worry (Verses 13-21)
   III. Jesus Rescues a Walker (Verses 22-33)
   IV. Jesus Receives a Welcome (Verses 34-36)

## SECTION ONE

*Expository Notes on the Execution of John the Baptist*

**At that time Herod the tetrarch heard of the fame of Jesus, And said unto his servants, This is John the Baptist; he is risen from the dead; and therefore mighty works do show forth themselves in him. For Herod had laid hold on John, and bound him, and put him in prison for Herodias' sake, his brother Philip's wife. For John said unto him, It is not lawful for thee to have her. And when he would have put him to death, he feared the multitude, because they counted him as a prophet (vv. 1-5).**

The history of the Herod family is complex and confusing, but the modern student needs to be acquainted with some of its ramifications. Herod the Great, who was responsible for the slaughter of the children at Bethlehem, was married ten times and had many sons. Only two of these are related to the ministry of John the Baptist, but it helps if we understand the historical background of these men. Prior to his death, and with Roman consent, Herod the Great divided his kingdom into three territories and willed them to three of his sons. To Archelaus, he left Judea and Samaria; to Philip, he bequeathed the northern part of the kingdom, known as Trachonitis and Ituraea; and to Herod Antipas, who eventually killed John the Baptist, he left Galilee and Perea. Luke 3:1 indicates that this Herod had a brother named Philip, who was also a ruler over considerable territories. There was also another Philip, who apparently held no public office. He was very wealthy and was content to live as a private citizen in Rome. Possibly his wealth guaranteed access to every function in Rome, and his acceptance by the leading citizens of the empire was never denied. He was married to his niece, Herodias, who bore him a daughter, Salome.

Historical records show that this Philip had been next in line to succeed Antipas, but because of his mother's unfaithfulness and treacherous behavior, the line of succession was changed by royal decree; and thereafter, Philip disappeared from public life. Everything apparently went well for him until his brother from Galilee decided to visit Rome, and the possibility exists that his hospitality was furnished by Philip. Alas, close proximity to his hostess provided devastating temptation for both Herod and Herodias. Their illicit love affair ruined two households. Herodias left her husband Philip, taking her daughter Salome; Herod banished his wife to make place for his new mistress. This caused consternation in Israel, for Herod violated two cardinal laws of the Hebrew faith. His act of adultery was condemned by Moses, and the taking of a brother's wife, in itself, was a violation of another law. It was not permitted for any man to marry a brother's wife. The entire nation was shocked, but because of the King's tremendous power only John the Baptist condemned the Ruler.

The whole world knows how the wilderness preacher publicly condemned Herod. Matthew reminds us that when the king heard of the continuing ministry of Jesus, he became afraid and said, "This is John the Baptist; he is risen from the dead; and therefore mighty works do show forth themselves in him" (v. 2). There were three possible reasons for his fear.

## THE PERSONAL APPEARANCE

Origen, the Alexandrian theologian who lived at the beginning of the third century, mentioned the fact that Mary and Elizabeth were blood relations. He then cited an ancient tradition which said Jesus and John resembled each other. They might have been thought to be brothers in the flesh. We have no way of ascertaining whether or this were the truth but *if it were*, Herod would have had legitimate reasons for his panic.

## THE PREACHING ABILITY

Prior to John's death, Herod had often listened to John, and was even willing to make concessions if only the preacher would cease criticizing what had transpired. John had been (1) *Faithful to his message,* (2) *Fearless in his manner,* and (3) *Faultless before his Maker,*. There were no other preachers who reached that standard of excellence. Herod knew this, but the appearance of a new preacher from Nazareth filled him with nameless dread. Jesus resembled John in every detail, and the king jumped to the conclusion that his former victim had returned to terrorize him and exact vengeance.

## THE POPULAR ACCLAIM

John had attracted huge audiences, and that in itself was amazing. Religious enthusiasm was at a very low ebb; the dictates of the scribes and Pharisees had made life too burdensome. People only attended the services in the sanctuary when there seemed no way of avoiding the responsibility. John's amazing meetings had been the first in centuries. Yet, the new preacher was attracting even larger congregations. Herod considered the matter, and decided there could not possibly be two such evangelists in one generation. John and Jesus were the same; John was alive once more, and even the thought of this made the king tremble.

**But when Herod's birthday was kept, the daughter of Herodias danced before them, and pleased Herod. Whereupon he promised with an oath to give her whatsoever she would ask. And she, being before instructed of her mother, said, Give me here John the Baptist's head on a platter. And the king was sorry: nevertheless for the oath's sake, and them which sat with him at meat, he commanded it to be given her. And he sent, and beheaded John in the prison. And his head was brought [on a platter], and given to the damsel; and she brought it to her mother. And his disciples came, and took up the body, and buried it, and went and told Jesus (vv. 6-12).**

## THE FATEFUL PARTY

The birthday celebrations were at their height, when the king excitedly announced a surprise for his guests. Murmuring, they retreated, to stand around the walls of the beautifully decorated ballroom. The orchestra played soft music, and through the curtains came the dancing girl. She had been specially trained in the art of seduction. Her movements were graceful, but suggestive, and every man stared in lustful amazement. They had often seen lewd exhibitions, but never had they known a princess to descend to such questionable behavior. She, who hitherto had been protected by the protocol of palace life, was before them, and every line of her beautiful body was accentuated by her lack of clothing. With the ease and skill of a panther she moved around the dance floor, and even the music enhanced the attractiveness of her performance. As the orchestra increased the tempo, as the dance moved toward a thrilling climax, even Herod was overwhelmed by the questionable desires of his heart. Suddenly, as the orchestra ceased, Salome was prostrate at the king's feet; the guests were shouting terms of praise and, on the spur of the moment, Herod promised as a reward anything she desired up to one half of his kingdom. He must have been drunk; had she desired, she could have become co-ruler of the kingdom, and had Herod died, she would have been queen in her own right. Sin and lust can do strange things with a man's mind; they can turn him into a fool.

## A FOOLISH POTENTATE

One half of a kingdom was a very high price to pay for an entertainment which probably continued for five minutes. Alas, Herod paid an even greater price; he lost his soul. The people were screaming approval; they would never forgive the breaking of his word. He knew this was the result of the scheming of Herodias; when he married her, he seized a scorpion by the tail! She hated the Baptist, and even hell had no fury to be compared with that of a woman scorned. Yes, he knew she was responsible for the request, but what could he do? He had promised. I am reminded again of the African boy who, when asked what he would have done had he been in Herod's predicament, replied, "I would have said that John's head belonged to the other half of the kingdom, which I had not promised." Things done hastily, are often repented at leisure. Unfortunately, Herod was soon to learn that he would have eternity in which to consider the immensity of his mistake.

## THE FAITHFUL PROPHET

Within a dungeon in the basement of the royal palace, John sat and probably prayed. This was one of the rare occasions when he was at ease speaking in whispers! We do not know if he could hear the sounds of revelry emanating from the upstairs ballroom. Perhaps he was too intent listening to the music echoing from the palace of the King of kings. His end was near, and it would be inconceivable that he who knew so much, should remain ignorant of the fate awaiting him. He had feared God so much that he never feared anyone else. His race was run; his ministry had ended; he was ready to go home! Then, footsteps were sounding on the cold damp steps, and within a few minutes the floor of his cell was being stained scarlet. Did he die with a smile on his face? Was that serenity still visible when his head was carried into the ballroom to be presented to the princess? John had been faithful unto death, and there is reason to believe a crown awaited him in the palace of God.

## THE FORLORN PEOPLE

"And his disciples came, and took up the body, and buried it, *and went and told Jesus*" (v. 12). They carried his body silently to its last resting place; there was no sound, unless one of the men unashamedly sobbed. The amazing meetings in the Jordan valley now seemed to mock them. Their godly master had died. Wretched, unrepentant sinners were gloating over their dastardly deed, but even God seemed to have forgotten them. Why had He not struck the king in defense of His trusted servant? Sadly, they shoveled the earth over the quickly wrapped body, and when the task was finished, they looked at the grave. With John, they had also buried their hopes. What could they possibly do now? Then one of those disciples surely said, "Let us go and tell Jesus." The rest nodded agreement, and sadly, slowly, they went away. John was dead, but Jesus lived. John could do nothing for them now, but Jesus could and would help them. Their action that day supplied an example which has enriched millions of people. When all else fails; when the outlook is bleak and threatening, troubled people can always tell Jesus about their problems.

> Tempted and tried, I need a great Savior:
> One who can help my burdens to bear;
> I must tell Jesus, I must tell Jesus,
> He all my cares and sorrows will share.
> I must tell Jesus, I must tell Jesus
> I cannot bear my burdens alone.
> I must tell Jesus, I must tell Jesus,
> Jesus can help me; Jesus alone.

## SECTION TWO

*Expository Notes on the Feeding of the Thousands*

**When Jesus heard of it [the death of John the Baptist], he departed**

**thence by ship into a desert place apart; and when the people had heard thereof, they followed him on foot out of the cities (v. 13).**

## A FRUSTRATED DESIRE

The news of the death of John the Baptist must have been distressing to Jesus. He had not only lost a dear friend; He knew coming events were casting their shadows before Him. He also would be rejected by those He wished to help. Feeling the need for solitude and contemplation, Jesus stepped into the small boat, and instructed the disciples to seek a quiet place where He would remain undisturbed. There were, and still are, many such places along the northern shores of the Sea of Galilee, and selecting one of them, the men commenced their journey. The Lord was aware of an intense desire to be alone with God; to share His thoughts, and commune with His Father. There were occasions when, even for Jesus, it was better to be alone with God than to be preaching to multitudes of people. This is a lesson all preachers should learn. Unless our spiritual batteries are charged in the secret place of the Most High, our light shining among men will be dim.

## A FIRM DISCIPLINE

When Jesus saw the crowds had followed Him; that His plans had been thwarted, and solitude was an impossibility, He was moved with compassion, and proceeded to heal their sick companions. Any one of the disciples might have become frustrated, irritable, angry, and critical of the people who appeared to be selfish. "Why couldn't they give the Master a few moments to Himself? They were becoming a nuisance!" The Lord smiled, and approaching the sufferers, stretched out His hand to touch them. There is reason to believe that this response could have been counted among His greatest triumphs. So often with other people, a small disappointment or intrusion into privacy results in spontaneous manifestations of irascibility, which lead to all kinds of unpleasantness. This was never so with the Savior. He was always in command of His words and actions and, because of this strict, never-failing discipline, Satan was unable to penetrate the Lord's spiritual defenses.

## A FRIENDLY DISCERNMENT

"And Jesus…saw a great multitude, and was moved with compassion toward them" (v. 14a). The greatest way to help oneself is to assist other people. The privilege and ability to serve needy people is probably man's greatest blessing. Throughout history, the happiest of all humans have been those who sacrificed everything on the altar of service. When Jesus saw the sick people, His soul was stirred and when, within moments, He saw gladness shining in the eyes of those transformed by His grace, joy filled His heart. He was no longer sad and apprehensive; He had failed to reach His desired rendezvous with His Father, but God, with characteristic grace, had come to help Him. Together they had alleviated suffering and pain; together they rejoiced over what had been accomplished; they were content.

**And Jesus went forth, and saw a great multitude, and was moved with compassion toward them, and he healed their sick. And when it was evening, his disciples came to him, saying, This is a desert place, and the time is now past; send the multitude away, that they may go into the villages, and buy themselves victuals. But Jesus said unto them, They need not depart; give ye them to eat. And they say unto him, We have here but five loaves, and two fishes. He said, Bring them hither to me. And he commanded the multitude to sit down on the grass, and took the five loaves and the two fishes, and looking up to heaven, he blessed, and brake, and gave the loaves to his disciples, and the disciples to the multitude. And they did all eat, and were filled: and they took up of the fragments that remained twelve baskets full. And they that had eaten were about five thousand men, beside women and children (vv. 14-21).**

This must be considered one of the most important events in the life of the Lord. All the gospel writers mentioned the incident in their narratives. It is necessary to read all the accounts to understand the complete meaning of this miracle.

## A PLANNED INTERVENTION

"Christ was careful to have the audience seated before He performed His miracle. Had He neglected to do this, the scene might have beggared description. Had they been standing in a closely packed throng around Him, the startling news of what He was doing might have turned that crowd into a rushing multitude of fanatics. The people would have pressed from all sides to see what was taking place; children might have been injured in the crush, and the whole scene would have become the object of criticism. Therefore, with the aid of the disciples, the Lord arranged that the people be seated in groups of fifty (Matthew) or by double rows of fifty-hundreds (Mark). This exhibited orderliness in the Master's methods; it provided an easy way by which the people could be counted, and each individual was able to see clearly what Christ did. Thus a catastrophe was averted and a benediction rested upon the scene." (Reprinted from the author's commentary, *Luke's Thrilling Gospel*, p. 220.)

## A PLAUSIBLE INTERPRETATION

Liberal theologians, who find difficulty in accepting the literal inspiration of the Bible, constantly endeavor to explain away any supernatural cause for what is described as a miracle. They have focused attention on the feeding of the thousands, and one of the interpretations *suggests* the people were selfish as many had possibly brought a lunch. No one would produce what he had, lest he had to share it, and he would not have enough for himself. Rather than share their scanty provisions, they kept them in their wallets. Then Jesus took the lead. Such as He and His disciples had, He began to share with a blessing and an invitation and a smile. And thereupon all began to share, and before they knew what was happening, there was enough, and more than enough for all. If that happened, this was not the miracle of the multiplication of loaves and fishes; it was the miracle of changing selfish people into generous people at the touch of Christ. In fairness to such it should be pointed out that they write "IF...IF...this happened."

Unfortunately, those authors omit the fact mentioned by John (6:9) that the food shared belonged to a small boy. Jesus did not take food from the bags of the disciples, and so set an example for others to follow. Apparently they had nothing, and a small child overhearing what was being said, volunteered to surrender his lunch in order to help his hero — Jesus of Nazareth. It seems incredible that great scholars should seek ways and means of finding explanations of miracles — explanations foreign to the meaning of the Scriptures. In the beginning, God took a handful of dirt and made man; earlier, He had uttered a command, and the worlds came into being. Did the Son of God have less power? Had His ability diminished? Is it too difficult to believe that had He only possessed one loaf and one small fish, He would have been able to feed that crowd of hungry people? Sometimes it is infinitely easier to believe the Bible than to accept the teaching of those who are supposed to be its interpreters.

## A PERFECT ILLUSTRATION

"He took...he blessed...he gave...and they did all eat, and were filled" (v. 20). Thus did He prepare His followers for their forthcoming mission of carrying the Bread of Life to a hungry world. When the task seemed impossible, they were to look to Him and bring such as they had. Nothing would be impossible if they knew how to believe. He could turn crumbs into a sumptuous repast just as easily as He could turn a mountain of insurmountable problems into a very small mole-hill. Hungry souls should never be turned away nor left to their own resources. The disciples were never to forget they stood between an all-sufficient Savior and a very needy world. What they obtained, they were to dispense to others. They were to be God's servants through whom sustenance would reach dying people. This has, and must ever be, the standard by which to assess the value of the Christian ministry. Christ depends upon His followers. If they fail, He will be disappointed and a world will perish.

## SECTION THREE

*Expository Notes on Peter's Walk on the Sea of Galilee*

**And straightway Jesus constrained his disciples to get into a ship, and to go before him unto the other side, while he sent the multitudes away. And when he had sent the multitudes away, he went up into a mountain apart to pray: and when the evening was come, he was there alone. But the ship was now in the midst of the sea, tossed with waves: for the wind was contrary. And in the fourth watch of the night Jesus went unto them, walking on the sea. And when the disciples saw him walking on the sea, they were troubled, saying, It is a spirit; and they cried out for fear. But straightway Jesus spake unto them, saying, Be of good cheer; it is I; be not afraid (vv. 22-27).**

## AN INSISTENT COMMAND

John 6:15 adds, significantly, to Matthew's version of this incident. The miracle of the loaves and fishes had brought the enthusiasm of the crowd to fever pitch; they wanted to make Jesus their king and so rebel against the Romans. Jesus recognized the danger of the situation and compelled the disciples to leave. Had they remained, they might have offered to become leaders of the revolution. He could better handle the situation alone. Sometimes the best antidote for a false emotional stress is hard work. The night was approaching; a storm was coming, and with great deliberation He constrained His followers to sail across the lake.

## AN INSPIRING COMMUNION

"He went up into a mountain apart to pray: and when the evening was come, he was there alone." It was soon after sunset when Jesus commenced His vigil; it was between three and four o'clock in the morning when He hastened to help the disciples. He had prayed for at least eight hours before He descended to help the storm-tossed men. Probably, He had prayed with His eyes open! He was able to see the Father and, at the same time, see men struggling against a ferocious storm. Why did He wait so long before hastening to their rescue? Probably for the same reason He delays His coming to help us. It often takes a long time to exhaust our resources and to trust implicitly in Him. As long as we can set a sail and pull on the oars of our self-sufficiency, we almost forget to pray. When our boat appears to be sinking, when all hope is gone, we look to Him, and appreciate His nearness. We sometimes forget that He sees us when we cannot see Him. Did the Lord end His prayer with the words, "Father, I must go now; my friends need Me?"

## AN INCREASING CONCERN

"And when the disciples saw him walking on the sea, they were troubled" (v. 26a). The Greek word translated "walking" is *peripaton*, which according to Thayer means " to walk, to walk about, to make one's way, to make progress." The critics have built upon this fact the supposition that Jesus did not actually walk on the water; He was walking about in the surf! For example, one critic suggests this may describe a miracle in which Jesus actually walked on the water. Or, it may mean that Jesus came down from the mountain to help them when He saw them struggling in the moonlight, and that He came walking through the surf of the shore toward the boat. It is extremely difficult to accept this interpretation. If Peter stepped out into the surf, that experienced swimmer was scared, because he was sinking into one, two, or at most three feet of water. Compare this with John 21:7. The Sea of Galilee is about eight miles wide, and according to John (6:19) the disciples had rowed their boat about 25 or 30 furlongs, which, according to Roman measurements, would only be a one-half of the distance across the lake.

Had they been blown to the beach, there was hardly need for concern; these men were skilled fishermen. The beach presented no problems; the shore was sandy not rocky; the *middle* of the lake was deadly at any time during a storm. It would be difficult to decide where was the greater concern — in the hearts of the disciples or in the soul of their Master?

**And Peter answered him and said, Lord, if it be thou, bid me come unto thee on the water. And he said, Come. And when Peter was come down out of the ship, he walked on the water, to go to Jesus. But when he saw the wind boisterous, he was afraid; and beginning to sink, he cried, saying, Lord, save me. And immediately Jesus stretched forth his hand, and caught him, and said unto him, O thou of little faith, wherefore didst thou doubt? And when they were come into the boat, the wind ceased. Then they that were in the ship, came and worshiped Him, saying, Of a truth thou art the Son of God (vv. 28-33).**

## AN IRREPRESSIBLE CONSTRAINT

This was one of the most outstanding events in the life of Simon Peter. He was always an impulsive man; he was accustomed to doing things, but afterward he wondered why he did them. Peter was a man of action. When he saw the Lord approaching, something stirred within his soul, and on the spur of the moment he cried, "Lord, if it be thou, bid me come unto thee on the water" (v. 28b). Jesus did not condemn the request, for He recognized an opportunity to instruct the disciples. Throughout the years of their ministry, they would often be confronted by perils of every type; they would embark on journeys fraught with danger. There was no need for fear. If they kept their eyes focused on Him, they would never be overwhelmed by difficult circumstances. They would be able to walk anywhere, if they continued to watch their Lord. If they lost sight of Him, they would surely sink. Yet, even in those circumstances, He would respond as soon as they requested help. It is better to walk by faith than to fail through foolishness.

## AN INSTANT COLLAPSE

"But when he saw the wind boisterous" (v. 30a). The *Amplified New Testament* renders this passage, "But when he perceived, and felt the strong wind, he was frightened." This was always Peter's weakness. He denied his Lord at the fire because he ceased watching the Master to see a girl. He asked a foolish question on the beach of the Sea of

Galilee, because he saw John, not Jesus. He was later rebuked by Paul, because once again he became more anxious to please Jewish observers than to adhere to the precepts of the new faith (see Gal. 2:11-13). Charles Alexander, the famous gospel singer, sang at a school for the blind. At the end of his performance, he offered to sing anyone's favorite hymn. A blind boy lifted his hand and said, "Please, Sir, sing 'Never Lose Sight of Jesus.'" That blind child had excellent vision!

## AN ILLUMINATING CONCLUSION

"They...worshiped him, saying, Of a truth thou art the Son of God" (v. 33b). Those disciples were wet, scared, tired, and amazed. They had witnessed the impossible; even the storm had subsided; the wind and waves no longer threatened their existence. Obviously, no man could have accomplished what their Master had done. Even the weather was subject to His control. He must be, He had to be the Son of the living God. The boat was now completely still; the lake had become a mill pond. Calmly, the Lord of creation sat in the stern of the boat, a boat which had become a holy place. Slowly, the men, one by one, knelt at His feet; *they worshiped him.* Blessed are they who worship in the sanctuary; but even more thrilled are the people who can find and worship Him anywhere.

> What matters where on earth we dwell:
> On mountain top or in the dell?
> In cottage or a mansion fair,
> Where Jesus is, 'tis heaven there.

## SECTION FOUR

*Expository Notes on Christ's Unexpected Visit to Gennesaret*

**And when they were gone over, they came into the land of Gennesaret. And when the men of that place had knowledge of him, they sent out into all that country round about, and brought unto him all that were diseased, And besought him that they might only touch the hem of his garment: and as many as touched were made perfectly whole [well]. (vv. 34-36).**

This is one of the short interludes of Matthew's Gospel. Ordinarily, a casual reader would let it pass unnoticed. Yet, within these three verses is a picture of the entire purpose of Christ and His church. Doubtless many of the inhabitants of Gennesaret had often seen and heard Jesus. The memory of His exploits could never be forgotten. His unexpected return to their district caused instant enthusiasm, but it is noteworthy that the citizens asked nothing for themselves. They thought only of others, and wasted neither time nor effort to bring their friends to the Lord.

*They recognized Him.* They remembered earlier days when they had seen manifestations of His power. Their memories would never die. *They recommended Him.* "They sent out into all that country round about." His return to their district opened doors of possibility for many of their friends. The men either went or sent messages in all directions; their neighbors should meet the Savior; no time should be lost. That surely was a perfect portrayal of the ministry of the church. Knowing Christ, we should never rest until our friends also meet Him. *They respected Him.* They were not rude; they never imposed upon Him. They had hopes and aspirations, but they remembered He was Lord, and graciously sought His permission to touch the fringes of His garment. *They rejoiced with Him.* "As many as touched were made perfectly whole." Were there some who did not touch Him? Did they come within an inch of blessing only to miss it by a mile? Here we see Christ, the church, and the convert.

HOMILY

Study No. 8

### PETER... Whose Ardor Was Somewhat Dampened!

Simon Peter did many praiseworthy things during the course of his lifetime, but this episode of walking upon the water must rank as one of his greatest. When fear had frayed his nervous energies, and when a seeming apparition had startled the entire crew, the realization that the Savior had drawn near was a little too much for Peter's self-control. In the excitement and relief of the moment, he cried, "Lord, if it be thou, bid me come unto thee on the water." And Jesus said, "Come." And when Peter was come down out of the boat, he walked on the water, to go to Jesus.

*A TRIUMPHANT RESPONSE*

We must never underestimate the greatness of Peter's achievement. Surrounded by obvious dangers, and faced with utter impossibilities,

Peter found strength in his Lord's command, and forgetting all else, stepped into the midst of a noisy tempest. *And he did not sink*. It seems fitting that this should have happened to Peter for, in later days, he was destined to become the evangelist of the church. Few pictures could so aptly reveal the beginning of a Christian journey. When Christ draws near to the tempest-tossed souls of men and women, the sound of His voice brings life's greatest challenge. Eventually, the soul is confronted by the call to leave a comparatively safe boat, in order to step into the unknown. Reason and doubt would shrink from this, but a burning heart, an eager soul, and a waiting Christ are very hard to deny.

## A TERRIBLE REALITY

The story presents no difficulties to the man who has responded to a similar invitation. The facts of Christian experience prove that no man was ever engulfed by temptation while he steadfastly looked at his Savior. Through His enabling grace, it is possible to trample under foot the very waves that would bury us. Yet even the greatest saint is endangered when he loses sight of his Lord. "But when he [Peter] saw the wind boisterous, he was afraid; and beginning to sink..." (v. 30). Frantic despair gripped the sinking man as he cried, "Lord, save me." Possibly, he thought he had been unwise to leave the boat; but in later years, saner judgment admitted that the mistake lay in losing sight of his Lord. When he ceased listening to, and looking at, his Master, dangers overcame him.

## A TREMBLING REQUEST

Peter's prayer is one of the best on record. There are no superfluous words, and no unnecessary finesse of phraseology. It is the quickest, easiest, and most desperate way to reach the heart of God. "Lord, save me." His sudden cry reveals three vital things. (1) *His Predicament*. He sinking, and every moment counted if he were to be saved from drowning. (2) *His Perception*. Christ was near, and was able to save. The ability of the Master more than equalled the demands of the moment. If only He would, He could meet Peter's need. (3) *His Prayer*. There was no time to elaborate on any details, and no time to observe any ceremonial law. One thing mattered, and that was to be saved. It banished all else from Peter's mind, and he cried, "Lord, save me." This modern world would be well advised to emulate Peter's example.

*A TIMELY REPLY*

"And immediately Jesus stretched forth his hand, and caught him, and said unto him, O thou of little faith, wherefore didst thou doubt?" (v. 31). The surging waves gave up their victim, and as Peter instinctively wiped the water from his eyes, he realized that once again he was standing on the sea. The boat was some distance away, but fear had now disappeared. A new calm had settled upon his mind, for he was conscious that Christ still held his hand. His clothing was saturated with water, but every moment increasing elation drove the chill from his soul. Yes, he could walk on the water that would have drowned him. Maybe in after years, Paul gave to Peter a text to fit the occasion. "I can do all things through Christ which strengtheneth me" (Phil. 4:13). The secret of every Christian triumph seems to be expressed in the two words, "through Christ."

> Hold Thou my hand; so weak I am and helpless;
> I dare not go one step without Thy aid.
> Hold Thou my hand: for then, O loving Savior,
> No dread of ill shall make my soul afraid.

# The Fifteenth Chapter of Matthew

THEME: *The Preaching, Patience, and Power of Jesus*

OUTLINE:
I. Christ's Memorable Preaching (Verses 1-20)
II. Christ's Marvelous Patience (Verses 21-28)
III. Christ's Miraculous Provision (Verses 29-39)

## SECTION ONE

*Expository Notes on Christ's Sermon*
*About Sources of Defilement*

**Then came to Jesus scribes and Pharisees, which were of Jerusalem, saying, Why do thy disciples transgress the tradition of the elders? for they wash not their hands when they eat bread. But he answered and said unto them, Why do ye also transgress the commandment of God by your tradition? For God commanded, saying, Honour thy father and mother; and, He that curseth father or mother, let him die the death. But ye say, Whosoever shall say to his father or his mother, It is a gift, by whatsoever thou mightest be profited by me; And honour not his father or his mother, he shall be free. Thus have ye made the commandment of God of none effect by your tradition. Ye hypocrites, well did Esaias prophesy of you, saying, This people draweth near unto me with their mouth, and honoureth me with their lips, but their heart is far from me. But in vain they do worship me, teaching for doctrines the commandments of men (vv 1-9).**

## A PARAMOUNT PROBLEM

It is important that these verses be considered carefully; they describe a major confrontation between Christ and the leaders of the Jewish nation. The emissaries of the Sanhedrin went from Jerusalem to Galilee to interrogate Jesus about the most vital parts of their faith. There is no way to decide if they were antagonistic. There was so much at stake; they could have been genuine in their requests for information. The foundation of their faith was being undermined. This had become a great concern, for if Jesus of Nazareth were correct in His teachings, their scriptures had become meaningless, and everything in which they trusted was open to conjecture.

Worship of Jehovah was the foundation upon which everything of valuerested, but, in order to draw near to God, each worshiper had to be ceremonially clean. If he did not reach the required standard of acceptability, he was denied every form of worship, and was considered a menace to those with whom he came into contact. This idea of cleanness and uncleanness has nothing to do with physical cleanliness or, except distantly, with hygiene. It is entirely a ceremonial matter.

Uncleanness was contracted by touching certain persons or eating certain things. For instance, a woman was unclean if she had an issue of blood, even if that issue of blood was that of the normal monthly period. Also, for a stated time after she had a child. Every dead body was unclean, and to touch one was to become unclean. Every Gentile was unclean.

This uncleanness was transferable; it was, so to speak, infectious. For instance, if a mouse touched an earthenware vessel, that vessel was unclean. Unless that vessel were ritually washed and cleansed, everything that was put into it was unclean. The consequence was that anyone who touched that vessel, became unclean. Anyone who touched the person who had so become unclean, then became unclean. An elaborate system of washings was worked out to combat this uncleanness. These complicated washings came to be used and demanded by the strictest of the orthodox Jews.

To every Jew, these innumerable washings were an integral part of worship; without them, worship was impossible. They not only had to wash before each meal; they were obliged to wash in certain prescribed ways; even the water in which they dipped their hands could be a further cause of defilement. Religion had been reduced to a series of man-made commandments, some of which obscured even the original commandments given by God to Moses. Even today, these practices may be observed as Moslems prepare to enter a mosque. I have often watched ardent worshipers bathing their hands and feet outside of the great Mosque of Omar, in Jerusalem. It is against these facts that we must consider the opening verses in Matthew 15.

The teachings and practices permitted by Jesus were a violation of everything taught in Israel. It seemed as if He were promoting a spiritual revolution, and therefore the scribes and Pharisees felt obliged to investigate His actions.

## A PROTECTIVE PRECAUTION

It should be noted that the Lord parried the initial thrust of their verbal sword. When the critics asked, "Why do thy disciples transgress the tradition of the elders? for they wash not their hands when they eat bread" (v. 2). He replied, "Why do ye also transgress the commandment of God by your tradition?" (v. 3). Immediately, it became obvious that He considered the Word of God to be more important than the requirements devised by and demanded of men. Jesus did not argue for Himself or His followers; He drew attention to their own shortcomings.

It was considered a primary duty of every Jewish son to honor and protect his parents. This was commanded by God through Moses, but the artful scribes had found a way to circumvent this obligation. Unfortunately, there were times when avaricious people tried to dodge family responsibilities. For example, it was legal for a man to enter into a covenant with the synagogue rulers by which his possessions were dedicated to religious purposes. His money would eventually be bequeathed to the synagogue, and, from the dates of the covenant it was said to be "Corban" (see Mark 7:11). If the time came, when his parents needed sustenance or financial assistance, the son could evade his responsibility by declaring his possessions belonged to God, and he was unable to give away that which was not his. This was a hypocritical sham, for the man retained and used all his possessions except for the "commission" paid to the synagogue. There were outstanding leaders in the nation who insisted that once money was so dedicated, it could not be touched or used for any other purpose, except to meet the requirements of the donors. Jesus condemned these practices.

## A PERTINENT PRONOUNCEMENT

"Ye hypocrites, well did Esaias prophecy of you, saying, 'This people draweth nigh unto me with their mouth, and honoureth me with their lips; but their heart is far from me" (vv. 7,8). Then Jesus said, "Ye reject the commandment of God, that ye may keep your own traditions." His reference to the washing of pots and cups was an indictment of the complicated system of worship to be observed each time a person desired to pray. This was a major confrontation from which there was no escape. It was inevitable that the teaching of Jesus should clash with the doctrines of the scribes, and obviously, something had to be done to clarify the situation. Jesus said they had violated the true meaning of the Ten Commandments and therefore were disobeying God. They were hypocrites.

> And he called the multitude, and said unto them, Hear, and understand: Not that which goeth into the mouth defileth a man; but that which cometh out of the mouth, this defileth a man. Then came his disciples, and said unto him, Knowest thou that the Pharisees were offended, after they heard this saying? But he answered and said, Every plant, which my heavenly Father hath not planted, shall be rooted up. Leave them alone; they be blind leaders of the blind. And if the blind lead the blind, both shall fall into the ditch (vv. 10-14).

## THE SHOCKING DECLARATION

The question asked by the disciples has been translated (*The Jerusalem Bible*) in a most interesting way. "Do you know that the Pharisees were *shocked* when they heard what you said?" This is in keeping with the meaning of the Greek word, *eskandulistheesan*. The Pharisees were not only hurt or offended; they were *truly shocked*, for what Jesus taught abrogated much of the Levitical law. Moses had explicitly stated that certain meats were prohibited. Many things itemized in the law were to be considered unclean; and under no circumstances were God's people permitted to partake of forbidden food. When Jesus announced that nothing entering a man could defile him, He was destroying the foundation upon which the religious life of the nation rested. In fairness to the Pharisees, let it be admitted that if the Lord were on earth today, saying the same things, many church people would refuse to accept His teaching. It might be asked, "Is it legitimate to swallow drugs or liquor? Are parts of the Old Testament law not applicable to modern people? Are we to read the commandments of Moses and reject them, believing they no longer apply to our times?" Acts 10:9-15 reminds us that when Peter objected to eating forbidden flesh, he was reprimanded by God, who said, "What God hath cleansed, that call not thou common." Obviously something had happened to change the thinking of men and women. Unaware of this fact, the Pharisees were truly shocked, for in their estimation even the authority of Jehovah was being challenged by the Preacher from Nazareth.

## THE STARTLED DISCIPLES

The followers of Jesus were surprised, because they failed to recognize the underlying motives of their Lord. He was trying to teach that true fellowship with God did not depend upon the observance of dietary laws. What a man *was* exceeded anything he *did* He might do all the legal things, and yet be far removed, in spirit, from what God desired. If a man were truly holy, then what he did would be in harmony with what he was. Religion did not rest on the exacting ordinances made by ritualistic leaders of an organization. Sanctuaries were to be admired, but any true worshiper could, and would, find God when he was far removed from any dedicated building. To observe the details of ecclesiastical requirements might or might not be beneficial, but to deny a person the joys of communing in the synagogue was unjustified. Jesus believed and taught that, whereas man looked upon the outward appearance, God looked upon the heart (see 1 Sam. 16:7). He was insisting that the ancient laws of Moses had been superseded by another and a greater law. The Pharisees were shocked by what appeared to be an outrageous attack on their Scriptures, and, in fairness to them, let us admit we also would be disturbed if someone made a similar attack on our faith.

## THE SIMPLE DESCRIPTION

Jesus said, "Let them alone: they be blind leaders of the blind" (v. 14a). This was a terrible indictment of the Pharisees, for it inferred that in spite of their knowledge, they knew nothing! Although they professed to be able to understand the dictates of the law, they were completely blind. A blind man, unable to see, had to feel his way through impenetrable darkness. To see one of these men trying to lead another blind beggar was truly a pitiable sight. It was no cause for amazement when both stumbled into a ditch. The statement that the honored rulers of the nation were as blind as the people they taught, was insulting. They considered Jesus to be a menace, and their continuing opposition to His work reflected the animosity within their souls.

**Then answered Peter and said unto him, Declare unto us this parable. And Jesus said, Are ye also yet without understanding? Do not ye yet understand, that whatsoever entereth in at the mouth goeth into the belly, and is cast out into the draught? But those things which proceed out of the mouth come forth from the heart; and they defile the man. For out of the heart proceed evil thoughts, murders, adulteries, fornications, thefts, false witness, blasphemies; These are the things which defile a man; but to eat with unwashen hands defileth not a man (vv. 15-20).**

These verses are but an extension of the earlier ones. This was not a parable but a straightforward statement of truth. That Peter failed to comprehend the Lord's words reflects upon his own ignorance. He, as all others in the party, could not grasp the true significance of the Savior's teachings. His preconceived ideas were hard to overcome. They remained even to the time when he was reluctant to eat food supplied by God (see Acts 10:14). The Lord was very patient with His listeners. Slowly, and with characteristic grace, He repeated that anything entering through the mouth went into the stomach, and was ultimately expelled from the body and sent into the drains. This food was planned to meet *physical needs* The observance or rejection of dietary laws had little if anything to do with the growth of a man's soul. What a man felt, experienced, and believed in his inmost being, alone indicated the direction in which his soul desired to travel. Even a stained hand, soiled with honest labor, could receive the Bread of Life, and still be acceptable in the sight of God. The Pharisees who often washed their hands, never removed defilement from their souls.

## SECTION TWO

*Expository Notes on Christ's Only Journey Outside of His Country*

**Then Jesus went from thence, and departed into the coasts of Tyre and Sidon. And, behold, a woman of Canaan came out of the same coasts, and cried unto him, saying, Have mercy on me, 0 Lord, thou Son of David; my daughter is grievously vexed with a devil (vv. 21-22).**

## A STRANGE DEPARTURE

The story of Christ's journey to Tyre and Sidon was, and still remains, one of the most interesting accounts in the Gospel. It describes the only occasion when Jesus left His own country, and that He should even consider doing this amazed His followers. Tremendous meetings had been held in the vicinity of Capernaum; vast crowds had attended the services; and excitement had reached fever pitch. Enthralled, the disciples expected the kingdom to be established at any time, and then, suddenly, the Lord decided to go away. Furthermore, He had never been to Tyre and Sidon, and consequently had few if any friends in that Phoenician territory. Some teachers think the journey was necessary to allow the Lord to enjoy a measure of privacy, in which to prepare for the ordeal of the cross. That conclusion may be justified, for it was impossible to avoid the crowds in Palestine. However, there is much more truth awaiting discovery in this remarkable account.

Tyre and Sidon were two important cities about a hundred miles northwest of Capernaum. The territory was inhabited by Gentiles, and Jews would not follow Him into areas considered to be unclean. Probably the Lord's fame had spread abroad, and we may safely assume that some of the Sidonians had traveled south, in order to see what was taking place in Israel. There was a day when Jesus, addressing the people in Chorazin and Bethsaida, said, "If the mighty works which were done in you, had been done in Tyre and Sidon, they would have repented long ago in sackcloth and ashes." Visitors from the northern cities would have agreed with the Savior's statement. The decision to visit Tyre and Sidon probably filled the disciples with questions. Why should Jesus unnecessarily make such a journey?

> **But he answered her not a word. And his disciples came and besought him, saying, Send her away; for she crieth after us. But he answered and said, I am not sent but unto the lost sheep of the house of Israel. Then came she and worshiped him, saying, Lord help me. But he answered and said, It is not meet to take the children's bread, and to cast it to dogs. And she said, Truth, Lord; yet the dogs eat of the crumbs which fall from their masters' table. Then Jesus answered and said unto her, 0 woman, great is thy faith: be it unto thee even as thou wilt. And her daughter was made whole [well] from that very hour (vv. 23-28).**

## A SUGGESTIVE DELAY

Residing in those northern territories was a Gentile woman whose daughter was said to be demon possessed. Maybe she had heard of the Jewish Preacher, and had wished the Gentiles had one such as He. When she heard Jesus was approaching the city, she conceived a plan which, to say the least, was startling and exciting. The woman was able to speak Hebrew fluently; if it were necessary, she could change her attire, and make herself appear to be a Jewess. She became an amateur actress who deliberately tried to deceive Jesus. When she cried, "0 Lord, thou Son of David," she was using the words which ordinarily would have been used by a daughter of Israel. The lady was a Canaanite, and David would have been one of the greatest enemies of her race. She was acting, and consequently, the Lord apparently ignored her appeal. "He answered her not a word." When the disciples reminded Him that she was becoming a nuisance, He replied, "I am not sent but unto the lost sheep of the house of Israel." His words should have warned her that He was aware of her deception. Yet, with desperation born of love, the mother replied, "Lord, help me." "If You are here to help the children of Israel, then this is Your opportunity. Help me." His likening her to dogs was not as harsh as it sounds. It is important that we remember the word He used was *kunariois*. This signified the young dogs loved by children. He was not referring to the scavenger animals found at refuse dumps. The Lord was thinking of small puppies, and the woman, quick to recognize this fact, said, "Even the puppies eat of the crumbs which fall from their masters' table." This was the first time she admitted being a Gentile dog! Her act had failed; her performance had been unconvincing.

## A SUBLIME DELIVERANCE

Her honesty produced a miracle, for Jesus, recognizing the sincerity of her appeal, said, "0 woman, great is thy faith; be it unto thee even as thou wilt. And her daughter was made whole from that very hour" (v. 28). This was the foreshadowing of a very blessed fact, the gospel was meant for all people. Even Gentiles could be assured of a welcome when, in trust and simplicity, they drew near to God whose love knew no limitations. Nevertheless, it was of paramount importance to remember that no person could deceive the Lord. The woman of Canaan would appreciate the hymn, which reads, "Just as I am, without one plea but that Thy blood was shed for me. And that Thou bidst me come to Thee, 0 Lamb of God, I come."

## A SUDDEN DECISION

Mark tells us (7:31) that after the deliverance of the Canaanite daughter, the Lord, by a circuitous route, made His way toward the cities of the Decapolis. There was no mention of additional miracles in Tyre and Sidon. It is not possible to know how much time was used in solving the woman's problem, but it seems strange that soon after the Lord's arrival He decided to leave again. This procedure was unusual; since Jesus had taken days to get there, why did He leave so soon? Were there not other sufferers awaiting Him in those northern cities? The following homily might be of interest.

HOMILIES

Study No. 9

### THE SYROPHENICIAN... Who Tried to Deceive Christ

"How strange it seems that Jesus went only to certain places, and how suggestive, that always the solitary visit led to something supernatural. For example, He arrived in Nain in time to meet a funeral and heal a broken heart. In Tyre and Sidon, where apparently His voice had never been heard, He — but let the story speak for itself. Somewhere in the vicinity, a Gentile mother lived with her stricken daughter, one possessed with a demon. Periodically, her yearning eyes watched the people going away to the southern towns where the great Healer would be preaching. How she longed to accompany them, but alas, she was needed at home. When the travelers returned, she would ask for news of the meetings, and her eyes would shine with amazement when she heard of the miracles Jesus had performed. 'And Jesus' she would ask, 'is He a Jew?' 'Oh, yes, He always works among the people of the chosen race.' She remembered the existent racial barriers, and sighing, half whispered, 'What a pity He's not a Gentile; then, perhaps I could have gone to Him.'

### HOW GREAT THE LORD'S PERCEPTION

When she heard that Jesus was coming to visit the district, her desires to see Him became irrepressible and, as she remembered Jewish prejudice, she faced her greatest temptation. She could speak Hebrew, and probably looked like many of the Jewish ladies. He might not detect the deception. Anyhow, it was worth trying, and for her daughter's sake she went forth with the cry of a Jewess. '0 Lord, thou Son of David, have mercy on me; my daughter is grievously vexed with a devil. But he answered her not a word.' His indifference must have seemed catastrophic to this misguided little mother, for she had yet to learn that all who come to Christ must be honest. Let us be careful to deal kindly with her. She did not know that, within the circle of God's fatherly care, all racial barriers disappear. The Lord was aware of her dishonesty.

### HOW GREAT THE LORD'S PATIENCE

The embarrassed disciples must have wondered why His attitude was so unsociable; it was contradictory of all they had ever known of Him. The crowd also must have been greatly surprised, and finally, the disciples whispered, 'Send her away, for she crieth after us.' He replied, 'I am not sent but unto the lost sheep of the house of Israel' (v. 24). The patriots would nod approval; but, desperately, the woman fell at His feet, crying, 'Lord, help me.'

'Ah, kindly little soul. You are doing this for the girl's sake; but you are still wrong. You seem to be saying, "If you have come for the lost sheep of the house of Israel, why not help me?"' The Lord Jesus patiently waited for her enlightenment to come. He still does when His people are difficult.

## HOW GREAT THE LORD'S POWER

'It is not right to take the children's bread, and to cast it to dogs' (v. 26). Oh, surely the warmth of His eyes offset the seeming rebuke of His lips. Momentarily shocked, she could only stare at Him but, ultimately, she replied, 'Truth, Lord, yet the dogs eat of the crumbs which fall from their masters' table.' 'I may be a Gentile, a dog; but is there not a portion for me?' 'Of course, little lady, there is a portion for all when they come honestly.' Listen to the Lord's words, '0 woman, great is thy faith: be it unto thee even as thou wilt.' Now hurry home, your little girl is well and waiting for you.

As she went, the Lord turned, and not long afterward His voice was againheard in the familiar haunts of Galilee. But, and this fact must always beremembered, He had been, once at least, to Tyre and Sidon. He did not go invain. Tonight, He might come to us. Let us be ready.'' (Reprinted from the author's book *Bible Cameos*, pp. 91-92.)

### SECTION THREE

*Expository Notes on the Varying Miracles of Jesus*

**And Jesus departed from thence, and came nigh unto the Sea of Galilee; and went up into a mountain, and sat down there. And great multitudes came unto him, having with them those that were lame, blind, dumb, maimed, and many others, and put them down at Jesus' feet; and he healed them: Insomuch that the multitude wondered, when they saw the dumb to speak, the maimed to be whole, the lame to walk, and the blind to see: and they glorified the God of Israel (vv. 29-31).**

## THE EXTENDED TRAVEL

Mark (7:31) informs us that "He came unto the sea of Galilee, *through the midst of the coasts of Decapolis.*" This is exceedingly interesting; the Lord could have used a much shorter route. If we may be permitted to superimpose the Lord's journey on a map of California, we might say that leaving Santa Barbara, Jesus made His way to San Diego, via Fresno. That is, He went northeast in order to reach a southern destination. There are two possible reasons for this extended journey. (1) It permitted additional time to be spent exclusively with His followers. (2) He was able by this circumlocution, to visit areas occupied by Gentiles. For example, the ten cities of the Decapolis were inhabited for the most part by Greeks. Possibly, the multitudes of Jews refrained from following Him to those areas, for they considered contact with Gentiles to be defiling. By comparing Scripture with Scripture, we estimate this journey took almost six months to complete. We know so little about what happened in these six months, but we may be sure that they were the most important months for the disciples. For in them, Jesus deliberately taught and instructed them, and He opened their minds to the truth. It is well to remember that the disciples had six months apart with Jesus before the testing time came.

## THE EXPERT TOUCH

"And great multitudescame unto him, having with them those that were lame, blind, dumb, maimed and many others..." (v. 30a). The news of the Lord's return to the vicinity of the sea of Galilee quickly spread throughout the cities of Decapolis, and soon a vast crowd left their homes in search of Him. They brought with them people suffering from various ailments, and Jesus healed all of them.

Study No. 10

### THE CROWD THAT KNELT DOWN AND REACHED HEAVEN

"The silvery waves were breaking on Galilee's beaches, and the fishermen were mending their nets when Jesus drew near and 'went up into a mountain and sat down there.' Many of the men had already met the great Teacher, and would instantly recognize Him. They left their work, and spreading the news among the homes of the people, brought their sick folk and '[put] them down at Jesus' feet; and he healed them.' The congregation on the ancient hillside seems strangely like the people of today.

## THE BLIND MAN

Somewhere in the village he sat in his world of darkness. He could hear the voices of other people and, to some degree, understood what they were trying to describe. Yet, he was unable to see. On that remarkable morning, someone told him of Jesus and explained that this was the great Prophet who could open the eyes of the blind. He had only to come and, in simple faith, respond to the Teacher's message, and all would be well. Yet, to this man in the dark, the project was not as easy as it appeared to be. He could not see, and he was expected to accept the testimony of other people. Was the story true?

That picture presents the case of every unconverted soul. Friends may bring a radiant testimony of Christ's power to save; they may describe the joy of God's salvation, but, to a poor sinner, this can sound confusing and uncertain. Yet, when he can be persuaded to draw near to Christ and to kneel at the feet of Jesus, his eyes will be opened; and he will joyfully exclaim, 'The half was never told me.'

## THE LAME MAN

Poor fellow! His legs were very troublesome. Once he had walked perfectly, but of late years, he had been obliged to use crutches. His eyesight was good, and he required no explanation of things beyond the reach of his vision. Yet carelessness had probably robbed him of freedom of movement. Unwittingly, he had placed his foot in some place of danger, and, suddenly losing his balance, he had fallen. From that moment, he was lame. He hobbled to the outskirts of the crowd and stood listening to the message of Jesus. His name was Mr. Backslider! No man of his type ever needs persuasion concerning the truth of the gospel message; he knows it already. The trouble is in his feet! Self-confidently, he forgot the injunction, 'Let him that thinketh he standeth, take heed lest he fall,' and, placing his foot in a worldly pot-hole, he lost his balance and has never been the same since. In fact, his life would be most miserable, if he were denied the support of his crutches. He would agree that these are poor substitutes for strong legs, but they are better than nothing. 'Poor backslider! Why don't you kneel at the Savior's feet? He is a marvelous Physician.'

## THE DUMB MAN

How easy it is to recognize this man as he silently stands in the crowd. His eyesight is good, and, because he has exercised care in his daily walk, he is not lame. He is neither the unbeliever nor the backslider; he is the secret disciple, who has never made a public confession of Christ. Let us watch him as he wrestles with his great problem. Should he kneel at the Savior's feet? How would he be able to pray? Would Christ understand, and what would the watching people say? Oh dear! We shall never know what battles had to be fought before this man knelt on the mountainside. Then he quickly discovered the ability of Jesus to hear the unspoken prayer of a man's appealing eyes. 'And the tongue of the dumb was loosed.'

## THE MAIMED AND MANY OTHERS

The maimed, who might have been injured in life's encounters; the many others, who might have included people just like us; they all knelt at the feet of Jesus, and no one came in vain. And the greatest news in the world is that Christ is just the same today. How futile will be all our efforts if we fail to reach this place of blessing.'' (Reprinted from the author's book, *Bible Cameos*, pp. 93-94.)

## THE EXCITING TESTIMONY

"...they glorified the God of Israel'' (v. 31b). The people who saw the miracles of Jesus were probably, for the most part, Greeks. This might be the reason why Matthew mentions the "God of Israel.'' The watching, appreciative Gentiles, recognized their own gods had nothing to do with this miraculous manifestation of power. Jesus, and the One He represented, were responsible for the healing of their friends and, consequently, were worthy of the highest praise. They had seen unbelievable things; if they held their peace, the stones might cry out in protest.

**Then Jesus called his disciples unto him, and said, I have compassion on the multitude, because they continue with me now three days, and have nothing to eat: and I will not send them away fasting, lest they faint in the way. And his disciples say unto him, Whence should we have so much bread in the wilderness, as to fill so great a multitude? And Jesus saith unto them, How many loaves have ye? And they said, Seven, and a few little fishes. And he commanded the multitude to sit**

down on the ground. And he took the seven loaves and the fishes, and gave thanks, and brake them, and gave to his disciples, and the disciples to the multitude. And they did all eat, and were filled: and they took up of the broken pieces that were left seven baskets full. And they that did eat were four thousand men, beside women and children. And he sent away the multitude, and took ship, and came into the coasts of Magdala (vv. 32-39).

This miraculous feeding of the four thousand men and their families has been criticized by liberal commentators. They state there was only one miracle of this type, and this second account with its different details is the result of the failing memory of a gospel writer. They ignore the fact that later, Jesus referred to *both* miracles (Matt. 16:9-10). A careful examination of the records reveals that the Lord fed the five thousand when the grass was green (Mark 6:39). That was in the spring of the year, for at any other time, the grass is either brown or non-existent. When Christ fed the four thousand, He commanded that they be seated on the ground. The word used is *geen* which is translated "ground." Thayer says it means the earth where people might stand. This would be in opposition to ploughed fields, and would fit the picture of a crowd assembled on the slopes of a mountain. Obviously this miracle was performed later in the summer when the relentless heat of the sun had withered the grass. Furthermore, both the location and people to whom the Lord ministered were different. One miracle was performed in an area where the inhabitants were predominantly Jewish; the other, where most of the population was comprised of Gentiles. It seems strange that critics admit the one miracle happened, yet dispute the other. Surely, if Christ were able to feed five thousand people, He would have no difficulty feeding a smaller crowd!

## HIS ABILITY TO UNDERSTAND

"I will not send them away fasting [hungry], lest they faint in the way" (v. 32b). The multitude had been with the Lord for three days. Possibly this means one complete day and the greater part of the other two. They had slept on the ground, probably using their arms as pillows. Such food as they possessed had already been consumed, and, recognizing this, the Lord said, "I pity these people, they've been here with me for three days now, and have nothing left to eat. I don't want to send them away hungry, or they will faint along the road" (*Phillips Modern English Translation*). It is worthy of note that, for an extended period, the Lord had been healing many sick people. Virtue had gone out of Him, and He must have been exceptionally tired. The audience had done nothing but watch. Yet, in spite of extreme weariness, Jesus thought not of Himself, but of the needs of His audience. "Lest they faint along the way" is a window through which we see into the depth of His concern. He saw the hungry children, appreciated the anxiety of the mothers, and understood completely the problems confronting the men.

## HIS ABILITY TO UNDERTAKE

"He commanded the multitude to sit down on the ground" (v. 35). It should be remembered that, in the former miracle, the Lord commanded the people to be seated in groups of fifty and hundreds. That might have been impossible on a hillside, where people would have to search for a suitable place upon which to recline. The presence of small children could have been hazardous, for the excited movements of a crowd might have endangered the safety of mothers and their babies. The Lord commanded the people to sit down, so that no one would be hurt, if people became too anxious to obtain food. Every person would be able to witness what was being done, and all would know there was sufficient food to satisfy every. It is thrilling to know the Lord was always in command of every situation. His wise preventative arrangements often averted possible tragedies. As long as the disciples received instructions from Him, their work continued to be efficient. Probably, Jesus was as much concerned to watch the developing trust of His followers, as He was in feeding the hungry multitude.

## HIS ABILITY TO UNDERWRITE

It should be remembered that Jesus planned to send those disciples on the greatest evangelistic crusade ever known. Soon, they would have the responsibility and privilege of feeding greater multitudes than Jesus ever saw in Palestine. Throughout the entire world, millions of people would become aware of spiritual hunger, and the leaders of the church would be required to answer their request for the Bread of Life. Jesus wanted His friends to know they would never face any situation alone. His promise, "I will be with you, always," should be the mainstay of their confidence. They could not feed the hungry, but He could. They were to continue their mission, confident He would never fail them.

## ANOTHER WAY TO FEED A MULTITUDE

The Rev. H. Merrieweather of the Ceylon and India General Mission, was a devoted missionary who often visited my church in Wales. During a visit to America, he was asked to visit and thank a lady responsible for the support of a missionary. He told how he, reaching her home, was surprised by the ordinary type of house in which she lived. He had expected to find a beautiful home. He explained how, after he had been welcomed by the motherly old lady, his eyes continually examined the room. Everything was neat and clean, but this seemed to be the dwelling of a working class woman struggling against poverty. How could she possibly support a full-time missionary? Ultimately, he explained his problem, and the lady was greatly amused. She replied, "But Mr. Merrieweather, I support four missionaries. I have one in India, one in Africa, one in China, and one in South America. Yes, Sir, I have four people all over the world preaching for me." He was nonplussed, and replied, "Sister, how on earth do you do it?"

Her lovely old face became grave; only her eyes smiled as she told of "the faithfulness of God." She explained she had always given one-tenth of her income to God. Regularly, she had set aside His tithe and this had accumulated. Then someone bequeathed to her a certain amount of property. The rental from this greatly increased her income, and consequently her "Lord's Fund" became larger. Soon she was able to support a missionary. She added, "I also discovered that my own funds were increasing, and eventually I was able to purchase more property. And so it continued. Mr. Merrieweather, come over to the window, and I will show you my houses." She indicated a row of magnificent villas, and said, "What does a poor old body like me want with such big houses? I have all I require in this little home, and the rent from those places supports my missionaries. I knew I would never be able to preach the gospel, so I determined others should do it for me." (Condensed from the author's book, *Bible Windows* pp. 131-132.)

# The Sixteenth Chapter of Matthew

THEME: *The Questions and Answers of Jesus*

OUTLINE:
    I. The Denial of Foolish Desires (Verses 1-4)
    II. The Danger of False Doctrines (Verses 5-12)
    III. The Declaration of a Fervent Disciple (Verses 13-20)
    IV. The Demands of a Faithful Devotion (Verses 21-28)

## SECTION ONE

*Expository Notes on the Request of the Pharisees and Sadducees*

**The Pharisees also with the Sadducees came, and tempting his desired that he would show them a sign from heaven. He answered and said unto them, When it is evening, ye say, It will be fair weather: for the sky is red. And in the morning, It will be foul weather today: for the sky is red and lowering. O ye hypocrites, ye can discern the face of the sky; but can ye not discern the signs of the times? A wicked and adulterous generation seeketh after a sign; and there shall no sign be given unto it, but the sign of the prophet Jonas. And he left them, and departed (vv. 1-4).**

## REQUESTING THE SIGN

The enemies of the Lord were relentless; they had sought a sign earlier (12:38), but now their request was somewhat different. The first request was for a sign of any kind, but now they ask specifically for a sign *from heaven*. They had rejected the Lord's miracles, stating they had been made possible by assistance from Beelzebub, the prince of demons. Now they desired to see something specially sent from God. They had neither faith nor sincerity, and it mattered not what Jesus did or said, they would have contradicted everything. The Savior had already given explicit instructions about the folly of casting pearls before swine, and His refusal to conform to the requirements of His critics set an example for those who were to follow in His footsteps. It is noteworthy that the Pharisees and the Sadducees had joined forces against Him; at other times these people would have had nothing in common.

## READING THE SKY

"O ye hypocrites, ye can discern the face of the sky; but can ye not discern the signs of the times?" (v. 3b). There was a subtle inference in the Lord's statement. These religious leaders were supposed to be brilliant at interpreting the Word of God. The scribes also professed to interpret the law, to explain to listeners what certain things meant. Yet, they were more proficient supplying weather forecasts! They were experts with things irrelevant, and blind concerning the most important things in the world. They were "clouds without rain"; they gave promises without substance. They were more proficient reading the sky than the Scriptures; they were false prophets in sheep's clothing.

## REPEATING THE SCRIPTURE

"...there shall no sign be given...but the sign of the prophet Jonas" (v. 4b). That was precisely what Jesus had told them earlier. His questioners suffered from the same malady; there was no need to change the medicine! The Lord refused to cooperate. He referred them to Jonah, and although they did not understand His reply, He remained immovable in His attitude. He had already said all that was necessary, and there was no need to jeopardize Himself and the cause by entering into arguments. All preachers should learn from His example.

## REJECTING THE SINNERS

"And he left them, and departed" (v. 4c). Matthew's statement was ominous. Jesus had no message for His critics. He had preached to them, had performed miracles in their midst, and had done everything possible to bring the truth to their souls. Nothing more could be done. His departure testified to the terrible fact that, as they had consistently rejected Him, He was rejecting them. They had no intention of yielding to His control; the thought of becoming disciples was abhorrent. Jesus knew this, and probably he considered it a waste of time trying to win people who did not wish to surrender. There comes an end even to the mercy of God, and probably that was the reason why God said, "Come NOW, and let us reason together...though your sins be as scarlet, they shall be as white as snow" (Isa. 1:18).

## SECTION TWO

*Expository Notes on the Danger of False Doctrine*

**And when his disciples were come to the other side, they had forgotten to take bread. Then Jesus said unto them, Take heed and beware of the leaven of the Pharisees and of the Sadducees. And they reasoned among themselves, saying, It is because we have taken no bread. Which when Jesus perceived, he said unto them, O ye of little faith, why reason ye among yourselves, because ye have brought no bread? Do ye not yet understand, neither remember the five loaves of the five thousand, and how many baskets ye took up? Neither the seven loaves of the four thousand, and how many baskets ye took up? How is it that ye do not understand that I spake it not to you concerning bread, that ye should beware of the leaven of the Pharisees and of the Sadducees. Then understood they how he bade them not beware of the leaven of bread, but of the doctrine of the Pharisees and of the Sadducees (vv. 5-12).**

## THE MUTTERED CONCLUSION

When the disciples began speaking among themselves about their lack of bread, it became obvious they had misinterpreted the Master's message. Probably they were already apportioning blame, and excusing themselves for their forgetfulness in obtaining supplies. They were irritable, and their tempers were a little on edge as they looked at each other. Peter, on the offensive, might have blamed Judas, saying that since he held all the money, he should have attended to his business. Judas, on the defensive, might have accused the others of laziness, affirming he was the only one that did anything! Things might have gotten out of control had not the Lord intervened to quell the uprising.

## THE MASTER'S CORRECTION

"O ye of little faith...do ye not yet understand?...I spake of the leaven of the Pharisees and of the Sadducees." There is always danger when impulsive people jump to conclusions; tension increases when folk blame others for something which might have been avoided. Most quarrels result from unimportant details, and when a great amount of damage has been done, the participants hardly remember how they began. It has been said "A stitch in time, saves nine"; it might also be said that a match, not lit, will never cause a fire. The disciples had forgotten to buy bread. Peter might have asked, "So What? We shall not starve to death overnight!" Molehills of dissension become mountains of difficulty when people criticize each other instead of listening to Jesus.

## THE MALICIOUS CONTAMINATION

The doctrines of the Pharisees and Sadducees might be summarized under three simple headings. (1) *Piety without purity*. Their religion was without reality. Both sects had innumerable laws and bylaws which enslaved ordinary people. Their "do's and don'ts" were numbered in thousands. They spoke of God, but they remained strangers to Him. Their doctrines were ideas in the head and not principles of the heart. They were shams not saints, and it was this fact which brought words of condemnation from the Savior. They had become blind leaders of the blind, and yet they claimed to be the appointed representatives of the Most High. They insisted on the rigid obedience to the Ten Commandments, and yet they convened meetings in which they discussed the possibility of murdering Jesus. They were condemned by their own teachings, and were hypocrites. (2) *Precepts without peace*. The Sadducees, for example, taught many doctrines, and among them was the denial of any life beyond the tomb. They believed existence ceased at death, and therefore a man had to enjoy his pleasure as soon as possible. Life for every Sadducee was a short-term investment. If he did not draw his dividends very quickly, he would not have any. Consequently, he lived in a realm of uncertainty, wondering what would happen next. His mind was the prey of nameless fears; peace was beyond his grasp. (3) *Possessions without pardon*. Nearly all the religious leaders were wealthy. They occupied the most important places in society, and held the highest offices in the Sanhedrin. They could all say, "I give tithes of all I possess." They could easily afford to do this. Yet most of them were impoverished beyond description; their possessions would be left for relatives to share. Their money could purchase anything except the blessings of God. Yet, they continued to preach and teach, affirming their way of living was the only one pleasing in the sight of God. Repentance and faith were words never found in their vocabulary; their cheeks were never wet with tears; their hearts remained unresponsive to the promptings of the divine Spirit. Jesus considered them to be enemies of truth and said so.

## SECTION THREE

*Expository Notes on the Confession of Simon Peter*

**When Jesus came into the coasts of Caesarea Philippi, he asked his disciples, saying, Whom do men say that I the Son of man am? And they said, Some say that thou art John the Baptist; some, Elias; and others, Jeremias, or one of the prophets. He saith unto them, But whom say ye that I am? And Simon Peter answered and said, Thou art the Christ, the Son of the living God. And Jesus answered and said unto him, Blessed art thou, Simon Bar-jona: for flesh and blood hath not revealed it unto thee, but my Father which is in heaven (vv. 13-17).**

## AN INTERROGATIVE REMARK

"Whom do men say that I the Son of man am?" (v. 13b). Did Jesus ask this question because He was unaware of the reactions of the multitudes, or was the question a means to an end? The impact of the Lord upon the following multitudes was surely unmistakable; He could not proceed through a market place and not hear the comments of the people. Possibly, He was not concerned with their opinions, but He was vitally interested in any development occurring within His closest friends. Was His question a method of encouraging testimony, of strengthening their convictions and preparing them for future occasions, when their instruction would be necessary in guiding the church? Jesus was clearly revealing that secret faith is insufficient to meet the needs of a world. A man must fearlessly confess to others what he believes. Secret disciples were unknown within the early church. They confessed with their lips, their lives, and by their baptism, in places where onlookers could see clearly what was taking place.

## AN INTERESTING REPLY

"Some say that thou art John the Baptist: some, Elias; and others, Jeremias, or one of the prophets" (v. 14). Here we see clearly what might be called *the inevitability of Jesus*. It is impossible to avoid Him; every man and woman, sooner or later, must be confronted by His claims and challenged by His message. The question, "What think ye of

Christ?'' requires an answer from every individual. It was not a cause for amazement when people compared the Lord with Elijah and John the Baptist. Both these men were fiery denunciators of evil, urging sinners to repent of sins and renounce their wicked ways. The folk who likened Jesus to Jeremiah must have been aware of His sorrow and tears. Jeremiah was the sad preacher who grieved over the state of the nation and urged his listeners to amend their ways. There were others who could not decide what they believed. They readily confessed that Jesus was an extraordinary preacher, but beyond that they would not go. Yet, whatever their answer might have been, they were already condemned. Every prophet was the spokesman of the Almighty, and their words commanded respect and obedience. If Jesus were a prophet, His identity was inconsequential; if He were *a man sent by God*, the multitudes should have obeyed His commands.

## AN INSPIRED RESPONSE

"But whom say ye that I am? And Simon Peter answered and said, Thou art the Christ, the Son of the living God'' (vv. 15,16). Did Peter express the thoughts of the entire group, or was this his personal opinion? Throughout the Gospel, there were others who shared this faith. Even before Lazarus was restored to life, Martha made a similar confession, "I believe that thou art the Christ, the Son of God, which should come into the world'' (John 11:27). When the centurion had seen all that had taken place on Calvary's hill, he exclaimed, "Truly this was the Son of God'' (Matt. 27:54). After Jesus had found the beggar mentioned in John's Gospel, He asked, "Dost thou believe on the Son of God?...and the beggar said, Lord, I believe'' (John 9:35-38). We might ask if these people shared a common experience? Had the Holy Spirit inspired them, and if so, it might be beneficial for students to compare and contrast all the details leading to each confession. To *discover* Jesus, leads to the greatest moments in life.

## AN IMPARTED REVELATION

"Blessed art thou Simon Bar-jona: for flesh and blood hath not revealed it unto thee, but my Father which is in heaven'' (v. 17). Paul said, "It pleased God...to reveal his Son in me, that I might preach him among the heathen'' (Gal. 1:15-16). All true revelation comes from God, and each time He speaks, listeners are directed to Jesus. "This is my beloved Son, in whom I am well pleased; HEAR YE HIM'' (Matt.

17:5). Any preacher who does not present Christ is a false prophet; any cause unrelated to the kingdom of Christ is undeserving of Christian support, and any person who does not love the Lord cannot be a citizen of God's country.

I knew of an evangelist who stayed in a British home where a servant girl was seriously retarded. She expressed interest in the gospel but had not the mental capacity to understand its message. The preacher invited her to say a prayer, "Lord, show me myself." He asked her to repeat this every night. She faithfully did as was suggested, and after some days returned to say she was very unhappy. The minister thereupon gave her a new prayer, "Lord show me Thyself." Again he asked her to say this every night, and she did. A few days later she returned, and appeared to be radiantly happy. When she was asked what had happened, she replied, "I think I have seen Jesus." "Flesh and blood" had given her advice, but it was God who opened her eyes and provided peace. "Blessed art thou, Simon Bar-jona," and blessed indeed are they who follow in his footsteps.

> **And I say also unto thee, That thou art Peter, and upon this rock I will build my church; and the gates of hell shall not prevail against it. And I will give unto thee the keys of the kingdom of heaven: and whatsoever thou shalt bind on earth shall be bound in heaven: and whatsoever thou shalt loose on earth shall be loosed in heaven. Then charged he his disciples that they should tell no man that he was Jesus the Christ (vv. 18-20).**

Let it be candidly admitted, that throughout the centuries these verses have been among the most difficult to interpret. They have caused continuing discussions and false interpretations have supported churches in every country. Today, enormous changes have occurred with the Roman church, but it still remains a mystery how religious scholars could have been so mistaken. Recently, one nationally-known priest was interviewed on a television network, and when asked to explain the new ideas being propagated within his church, he replied, "We have come to understand that certain verses do not mean what we thought they meant." He was to be commended for his honesty. The best way to understand what is meant by the aforementioned verses is to understand, first of all, what they CANNOT mean.

1. Peter was NEVER meant to be the foundation upon which the church would be erected. "For other foundation can no man lay than that is laid, which is JESUS CHRIST" (1 Cor. 3:11).

2. Peter was not even the leader of the apostles. The apostle who presided over the first church council was James. "And after they had held their peace, James answered, saying, Men and brethren, hearken unto me" (Acts 15:13).

3. Peter was not the one who opened the kingdom to the gentile world. That privilege was given to Paul. "And [the Lord] said unto me, Depart: for I will send thee far hence unto the Gentiles" (Acts 22:21). "But the Lord said unto [Ananias], Go thy way; for [Saul] is a chosen vessel unto me, to bear my name before the Gentiles" (Acts 9:15).

4. Peter was not the only apostle to whom "the gift of remitting sins" was granted. "And when [Jesus] had said this, he breathed on THEM, and saith unto THEM, Receive ye the Holy Ghost: Whosoever sins ye remit, they are remitted unto them; and whosoever sins ye retain, they are retained" (John 20:22-23).

It must be recognized that the teaching which claims Peter was the source of apostolic succession, the basis upon which Roman Catholic doctrines rest, is erroneous. To assert that priests, descending from Peter alone, have the right of absolving sin is false, misleading, and wrong. Andrew, Bartholomew, or any other of the apostles could have given birth to his own version of apostolic succession. We are now able to study, systematically, WHAT THE BIBLE DOES TEACH.

*A PLAY ON WORDS*

Arno C. Gaebelein has an interesting paragraph in his exposition of Matthew's Gospel. He writes, "What then does the Lord mean when He says, 'Thou art Peter and upon *this rock* will I build My assembly [church]'? He did not mean Peter or He would have said, 'upon THEE will I build My church.' The word Peter — *petros*, means a part of a rock; that is, a stone. When the Lord says upon what He is going to build His church, He no longer speaks of *petros* — a stone, but uses the word *petra*, which means "a rock". Out of the rock a stone is hewn; in other words, *a stone is a part of the rock*. The word *petra* — a rock, He uses for the first time in Matthew 7:24-25. The house there is built upon a *petra* — a rock, and cannot fall. This rock is Christ Himself. But why this peculiar use of *petros* and *petra* — a part of a rock, and the rock itself? Let Peter answer, 'To whom [Christ] coming, as unto *a living stone*, disallowed indeed of men, but chosen of God, and precious, Ye also *as lively stones*, are built up a spiritual house' (1 Pet. 2:4-6). The foundation of God's building is Christ. Peter's confession said, 'Thou art the Christ, the Son of the living God.'" "Other foundation can no man lay." Peter, a stone hewn from a parent rock, is like any other believer, one of the stones in the spiritual edifice, resting upon the solid rock, the Lord Jesus Christ.

## A PLACE TO WORSHIP

"Upon this rock I will build my church; and the gates of hell shall not prevail against it" (v. 18b). The term "MY CHURCH," refers to that spiritual building which belongs exclusively to the Savior, and any other interpretation is unpardonable. The narrow, confined limits of religious legalism are something to be deplored. Catholic priests still teach that unless a man belongs to their church, he is not within the true fold of God. The leaders of Protestant sects have become equally guilty, for they insist, as they criticize all other bodies of Christians, that their assembly alone is pleasing to God. There are churches where no baptism is recognized except that administered by their own clergymen; any ordinance celebrated elsewhere is classed as alien baptism. They resemble the Scribes and Pharisees who created innumerable regulations not related to the will of the Lord. Thank God, when we reach heaven it will be impossible to find a denominational church. We shall be too wise to argue about details of law. God's true church is an institution erected on the finished work of Christ, and all who love the Savior enjoy its fellowship.

## A PROMISE TO WATCH

"And I will give unto thee the keys of the kingdom of heaven" (v. 19a). A key is something to open that which is closed. The idea that Peter holds the key into heaven is so ludicrous, it hardly deserves mention. Yet unfortunately, all the masterpieces of religious art depict Peter as holding a key, and all who desire entrance into realms of eternal blessedness, of necessity, must seek Peter's assistance. Throughout the ages, unscrupulous men exploited this teaching in order to extort money from anxious suppliants. Attention has already been drawn to the fact that, when Jesus uttered these words, He was speaking not only to Peter, but to ALL THE APOSTLES. The Lord was placing into their hands the means by which they could open doors of understanding, and so make possible the entry of lost sinners into the kingdom of God. The Lord promised to watch from heaven to ratify any decisions made by His church. Matthew 18 describes a proposed meeting of the church to deal with an offensive brother (see vv. 15-20). He speaks of the church; that is the corporate body of believers as found in a local assembly and says, "Whatsoever thou shalt bind on earth shall be bound in heaven: and whatsoever thou shalt loose on earth shall be loosed in heaven." He was asserting the simple fact that, what His church decided would be ratified in heaven; that Christians on earth should be aware they were representatives of the eternal kingdom and should act accordingly. The whole idea of any appointed man being authorized to forgive sins is foreign to the Scriptures, and distasteful to every intelligent human being.

## A PLAN TO WAIT

"Then charged he his disciples that they should tell no man that he was Jesus the Christ" (v. 20). He knew the day would come when His followers would be required to go forth into all the world to broadcast the glorious gospel, but that day had not yet arrived. A premature uprising could bring danger to the cause and the people. For the time being it would be better to remain silent so that the extension of the kingdom would not be threatened. They did not know, at that moment, the strength of the gospel message would be derived from a cross. They needed further training and, until God said, "Advance," they were required to be patient. There are times when it takes more grace to remain motionless than it does to advance. No man should attempt to control others until his own impetuosity has been completely overcome.

## SECTION FOUR

### Expository Notes on Christ's Preparation of His Disciples

**From that time forth began Jesus to show unto his disciples, how that he must go unto Jerusalem, and suffer many things of the elders and chief priests and scribes, and be killed, and be raised again the third day. Then Peter took him, and began to rebuke him, saying, Be it far from thee, Lord: this shall not be unto thee. But he turned and said unto Peter, Get thee behind me, Satan: for thou art an offence unto me, for thou savourest not the things that be of God, but these that be of men (vv. 21-23).**

## HIS CONSTANT AWARENESS

It must have been very wonderful to watch the Lord as He moved closer to the predetermined death on a cross. He knew exactly where He was going, and slowly, inexorably, walked the appointed way. He knew what awaited Him in Jerusalem, but never for a moment did He try to escape from the clutches of the enemy. His knowledge begat constant care; had He made one mistake, enemies would have condemned anything He said or did. The Savior was never impetuous, irritated, nor afraid; and it was this constant watchfulness which helped preserve the sanctity of His soul. Wise workers follow His example.

## HIS CONTENDING ADVERSARY

"Then Peter...began to rebuke him...." Peter was not a good student! That he meant well, none can deny; but had he learned from his Master to think before he spoke, he would not have uttered his foolish words. Within a matter of moments, Peter fell from heights of blessed revelation to depths of foolish ignorance. His mind, which had been illumined by light from heaven, was overcast with clouds of doubt. He meant well, and doubtless would have given his life to help his Lord, but even good intentions can be misleading when they are not in keeping with the will of God. Peter's mind was like a radio set not perfectly tuned to a station. Two voices were coming simultaneously. The voice of God had distinctly spoken concerning the identity of the Master, but suddenly without warning, the other voice spoiled the original reception. "Be it far from thee, Lord, this shall not be." Peter must have been embarrassed when the Lord replied, and yet Jesus was characteristically kind when He blamed — not Peter, but Satan. When He said, "Get thee behind me, Satan," it was obvious that He knew from whence the suggestion had come. When Peter graduated, later, from Christ's school, he also would recognize the need for extreme care when all kinds of thoughts influenced his mind.

## HIS COMMANDING ANSWER

Authoritatively, Jesus commanded the evil one to depart; there could neither be compromise with, nor time for consideration of Satan's suggestions. Christians suffer defeat when they allow the devil a little breathing room! They listen to his suggestions; debate whether or not to accept his ideas, and often before they decide, evil takes possession of their minds. When the thoughts of men are pure, their actions exhibit cleanliness. When a man's mind becomes an art gallery for the display of questionable pictures, the soul is depraved, and happiness destroyed. "Get thee behind me, Satan," is a sentence with which all saints should be familiar; it should become a rule of Christian conduct.

**Then said Jesus unto his disciples, If any man will come after me, let him deny himself, and take up his cross, and follow me. For whosoever will save his life shall lose it; and whosoever will lose his life for my sake shall find it. For what is a man profited, if he shall gain the whole world, and lose his own soul? or what shall a man give in exchange for his soul? For the Son of man shall come in the glory of his Father with his angels, and then he shall reward every man according to his works. Verily, I say unto you, There be some standing here, which shall not taste of death, till they see the Son of man coming in his kingdom (vv. 24-28).**

## THE UNIQUE REQUIREMENTS

The Lord never tried to attract followers with promises of future glory. He preferred to warn them of approaching perils. He said, "If any man will come after me, let him deny himself...." When men expect the worst, they are pleasantly surprised if things are not as bad as anticipated. To be forewarned is to be forearmed! Someone said, "A cross is an 'I' crossed out!" Selfishness of any kind is not compatible with life within the kingdom; a servant who exists to please himself has little affection for the interests of his master. Self-denial is one of the most difficult lessons to learn, but it is the sure way to promotion. The pathway to riches often is the highway to sacrifice. The man with the closed hand never helps anyone, including Christ. Giving, we receive; holding, we lose everything. When the corn of wheat dies, it produces a harvest; when it remains unplanted, it is useless. These are the basic laws of fruitfulness within the kingdom of God.

## THE UNPREDICTABLE REWARDS

"For the Son of man shall come...and then he shall reward every man according to his works" (v 27). Jesus said that even a cup of water given in His name would not go unnoticed; even the most menial gift would bring its reward. The Pharisees, Sadducees, and Scribes must have been shocked when Jesus predicted His return with a host of angels. Unless He was what He claimed, then His predictions were ludicrous.

He invisaged the end of time, the resplendent glory of His return, and the certainty of His ultimate triumph. These were to be sources of inspiration as the disciples evangelized the world. They should never be weary in well doing, for they would reap, if they did not faint. Nevertheless, the greatness of the rewards to be received could never be predicted accurately. This would depend upon the quality of service rendered (see 1 Cor. 3:13-15).

## THE ULTIMATE REVELATION

"There be some standing here, who shall not taste of death, till they see the Son of man coming in his kingdom" (v. 28). This is a tremendous verse, but in order to appreciate its worth, it is necessary to compare it with two others. The term "to taste of death" applies to the end of time, when sinners participate in "the second death" (Rev. 20:14). Hebrew 2:9 asserts that "Christ, by the grace of God should taste death for every man." This can only refer to His sacrificial death on the cross at Calvary. John 8:52 states Jesus said, "If a man keep my saying, he shall never taste of death." This was a promise made to all believers who find joy in serving their Lord. Matthew 16:28 was spoken to critics and others standing in the presence of the Lord. Jesus said that, prior to their being judged, their criticisms would be silenced as they witnessed His ultimate triumph. (See the homily "The Nastiest Taste in the World" in the author's book, *Bible Treasures,* pp. 153-154.)

# The Seventeenth Chapter of Matthew

THEME: *The Radiant Savior*

OUTLINE:
    I. The Shining Face (Verses 1-8)
    II. The Sincere Followers (Verses 9-13)
    III. The Sad Father (Verses 14-21)
    IV. The Strange Fish (Verses 22-29)

## SECTION ONE

*Expository Notes on the Transfiguration of Christ*

**And after six days Jesus taketh Peter, James, and John his brother, and bringeth them up into an high mountain apart [privately], And was transfigured before them; and his face did shine as the sun, and his raiment was white as the light. And, behold, there appeared unto them Moses and Elias talking with Him. Then answered Peter, and said unto Jesus, Lord, it is good for us to be here; if thou wilt, let us make here three tabernacles [booths]; one for thee, and one for Moses, and one for Elias. While he yet spoke, behold, a bright cloud overshadowed them; and behold a voice out of the cloud, which said, This is my beloved Son, in whom I am well pleased; hear ye him. And when the disciples heard it, they fell on their face, and were sore afraid. And Jesus came and touched them, and said, Arise, and be not afraid. And when they had lifted up their eyes, they saw no man, save Jesus only (vv. 1-8).**

It is impossible to overemphasize the importance of the transfiguration experience in the life of the Savior. It was a half-way house on a very difficult journey! From it, Jesus looked back to the cradle and creation, and onward to the cross and the crown. With Him were Moses and Elijah, the prophets, who represented all others whose ministry prepared the world for the Lord's first coming; with Him also were those who would, with their successors, prepare the world for His return. The Mount of Transfiguration was the lookout place from which His vision encompassed the past, present, and future. It was there God testified of Jesus who was to be His Spokesman to a needy world. It was there Jesus stood between God and the men He wished to help. During the hallowed hours spent in the mountain, God said, "Hear ye him," and thus indicated that Christ alone could interpret all that needed to be understood. When mists of doubt, speculation, and uncertainty swirled around the disciples, that tremendous command would be their guiding star, leading onward. When viewed from certain angles, the experience in the mountain was the most amazing thing to take place during the ministry of the Lord. It is with awe and reverence that we try to understand what happened during that memorable night.

## THE SHINING FACE

"...and his face did shine as the sun, and his raiment was white as the light" (v. 2). The word translated "white" is *leuka*, which, according to Thayer means, "light, bright, brilliant, dazzling." Hence, the *Living Bible* translation, "And as they watched, His appearance was changed so that His face shone like the sun, and His clothing became dazzling white" (v. 2). When the watching disciples noticed the change taking place in their Master's body, they were amazed. Resplendence emanated from His inmost being, and slowly but surely, His body began to glow. His face became dazzlingly brilliant, and the disciples probably had to shade their eyes. Even the Lord's garments shone with supernatural radiance. Many years later, Simon Peter still remembered that amazing sight. He wrote, "We...were eyewitnesses of his majesty. For he received from God the Father honor and glory, when there came such a voice to him from the excellent glory, This is my beloved Son, in whom I am well pleased. And this voice which came from heaven we heard, when we were with him in the holy mount" (2 Peter 1:16-18).

The Rev. Lukyn Williams has written concerning the Transfiguration of the Lord, "The Word of God allows, for a brief space His essential glory to irradiate and shine through the form of a servant which He wore. Not that He showed His Divine nature, or laid aside His human body; His bodily nature remained in its entirety, but permeating it was an effulgence which indicated the Godhead. Perhaps it might be said, as an old writer put it, that the Transfiguration was less a new miracle than the temporary cessation of a habitual miracle; for the veiling of His glory was the real marvel; the Divine restraint which prohibited the illumination of His sacred humanity'' (*The Pulpit Commentary. Matthew*, Vol. 2, p. 172).

Perhaps we shall never be able to comprehend all that happened in the mount, but quite obviously the frail barrier of flesh was unable to conceal the ineffable glory of the transcendent Lord. What He had always been, became visible; the glory of the Infinite shone through the limitations of humanity, and the result beggared description. Matthew, Luke, and the others could only say, ''And as he prayed, the fashion of his countenance was altered, and his raiment was white and glistering'' (Luke 9:29). (For additional notes consult the author's commentaries: *Mark's Superb Gospel,* and *Luke's Thrilling Gospel.*)

## THE SUPPORTING FELLOWSHIP

''And behold, there appeared unto them Moses and Elias talking with him'' (v. 3). Luke supplies additional information. ''Who appeared in glory, *and spoke of his decease which he should accomplish at Jerusalem''* (Luke 9:31). This statement suggests questions. Why did Matthew omit such an important announcement? Probably he did so because death was not something to be connected with the arrival of the Messiah. Matthew looked for an unprecedented triumph and not an unpardonable tragedy. The word translated ''accomplish'' is *pleeroun,* and this has a variety of meanings. Thayer says it can be interpreted, ''to fill; to fill up to the brim; to render complete; or when used in matters of duty, to carry through to the end; to perform, to execute; to bring to realization.'' All this information infers that whatever lay ahead had been planned. Jesus was to *complete*; *to fill up to the brim*, that which had been purposed; *to realize a fulfillment of a dream; to bring to perfection something planned, so that nothing more would need to be done.* That this should be the theme of the conversation between Moses, Elijah, and Jesus also begets questions. What were they discussing?

They could not have been telling the Lord something He did not know. Neither could they have been warning Him of dangers to be encountered along the road to the cross. Could it possibly be that they were comforting and encouraging Him? Is it possible that, on behalf of millions of others, they were thanking Him for what He was about to do? Were they praising Him for the love which was about to make redemption a reality and not a dream? Perhaps, it is impossible to understand the detailed complications of this event, but happy are they who render assistance to the Lord, at any time and in any place.

## THE SPEAKING FATHER

"...and behold a voice out of the cloud, which said, This is my beloved Son, in whom I am well pleased; hear ye him" (v. 5). That statement was a searchlight, bringing into bold relief every detail of the Lord's life, and illuminating every moment of His ministry. There had been nothing displeasing to God in anything Jesus had spoken or done. The Scribes and Pharisees might continue to criticize, but God was perfectly satisfied with every facet of His Son's life. If this is the standard of excellence all Christians should reach, then, alas, we have a long way to go.

It must be emphasized that, in calling Jesus "THE SON," God did not infer He was subordinate to the Father; that He was *less than,* or *inferior to God.* The readers of this book are all children of their parents, but that does not necessarily imply they are *less* than their forbears. Educationally, socially, financially, a son may be greater than his father. The term "son" is used to indicate both father and child are of the essence; they share a common life; their blood stream is identical. Jesus was called the Son of God to indicate He belonged to the same family; He was one — by nature — with God. The men who heard this awe-inspiring announcement would be given the responsibility of guiding the early church; to formulate doctrine, answer questions, and supervise the interpretation of theology. They received their first lesson from God as they lay, fearfully, on the hillside.

## THE SUBDUED FRIENDS

"They were sore afraid. And Jesus came and touched them...And when they had lifted up their eyes, they saw no man, save Jesus only. And...Jesus charged them, saying, Tell the vision to no man, until the Son of man be risen again from the dead" (vv. 6-9). The transcendent glory of Jesus had now subsided; the heavenly visitors had departed, and even God's voice was only a memory. Yet, their Master was still with them. That supreme fact was their greatest comfort. Visions can be very stimulating; electrifying moments of spiritual ecstasy may be experiences never to be forgotten. Mountain retreats may lift the soul to unprecedented heights of joy, but, alas, none of these last forever. Life teaches the best things in life may burst upon us like a sunrise, but the initial glory fades into ordinary skies. It must always be remembered that Jesus remains — He never leaves us. Years ago, when the Eskimos were starving to death and cannibalism became a real threat in the northern territories of Canada, the government commissioned a marvelous man, named Andy, to lead the first great collection of reindeers across the top of the world. That expedition took five years, during which blinding blizzards harassed the travelers. The two thousand animals were scattered in all directions, and the men had to dig into the ice to make shelters in which to hide from the fury of the weather. After one such ordeal, when Andy had, unfortunately, broken his compass, one of the men fearfully cried, "We are lost." Andy looked at him and seemingly growled. "You've got me, haven't you? As long as you can see me, you are home." Many storms devastate our outlook, and occasionally, we think the situation is hopeless. Andy's words should be remembered. "If we can see Him, we are HOME!"

## SECTION TWO

*Expository Notes About the Disciples' Problem*

**And as they came down from the mountain, Jesus charged them, saying, Tell the vision to no man, until the Son of man is risen again from the dead. And his disciples asked him, saying, Why then say the scribes that Elias must first come? And Jesus answered and said unto them, Elias truly shall first come, and restore all things. But I say unto you, That Elias is come already, and they knew him not, but have done unto him whatsoever they listed. Likewise shall also the Son of man suffer of them. Then the disciples understood that he spake unto them of John the Baptist (vv. 9-13).**

## THE DEFINITE COMMAND

"Tell the vision to no man" (v. 9). At first glance, this command seems difficult to understand. The three privileged disciples were not to confide in their colleagues in the valley. Possibly the others would not have believed even had they been told, and their unbelief might have had an adverse effect upon their outlook. Had the disciples been argumentative, the unity of the company would have been impaired. For example, Simon Peter and Thomas could have argued for hours about the impossibility of Peter's testimony. Discord is never the harbinger of triumph. Furthermore, the significance of the appearance of Moses and Elias might have been misinterpreted. The Pharisees might have said the prophets had appeared only to give commandments to Jesus, to tell Him what He did not know! Thus any claim to the divinity of the Lord would have been thwarted. That they would be free to tell their story after the resurrection, suggests Christ's conquest of death would have removed all doubts concerning His true identity, and that only then would the significance of the transfiguration experience be fully understood.

## THE DISCIPLES' CONCERN

"Why then say the scribes that Elias must first come?" (v. 10). Probably, the disciples were thinking of the statement made by Malachi, "Behold, I will send you Elijah the prophet before the coming of the great and dreadful day of the LORD; And he shall turn the heart of the fathers to the children, and the heart of the children to their fathers, lest I come and smite the earth with a curse" (Mal. 4:5-6). Obviously, the disciples were puzzled by the statement of the prophet, the teaching of the scribes, and the appearance of Elijah on the mount. They were asking if the appearance of the prophet had fulfilled what Malachi predicted, and if so, would the establishing of the kingdom take place soon. They were genuinely disturbed because all the events seemed contradictory. "Master, was that the real coming of Elijah, or will he come again, or what?" Apparently, they did not consider the closing part of Malachi's statement. It was true that John had ministered, but how could his mission be considered a success when Herod had killed him? What had seemed a promise of true revival, had fizzled out like a dying flame.

## A DISTURBING CONCEPT

"Elias truly shall first come and restore all things. But I say unto you, That Elias is come already, and they knew him not" (vv. 11,12). Jesus did not say John the Baptist was Elijah. That Elijah will come before the great and dreadful day of the Lord is emphasized in Revelation 11:3-6. Furthermore, although John the Baptist exercised a wonderful ministry, he did not accomplish all that was predicted of Elijah. John had come *in the spirit of Elijah*, and had preached repentance with the same enthusiasm seen in the acts of the ancient preacher. John and Elijah were twin souls sharing a common purpose. Nevertheless, it must be remembered that, as John foreran the first appearance of Christ, so will Elijah do, prior to the Lord's return to the earth. That Jesus was completely aware of His approaching end was obvious. He predicted He also would suffer at the hands of unbelieving religious leaders. Probably the chief thought behind this Scripture was that God always does His part, in any age, and under any circumstances, to bring salvation to men. If and when they reject His message, they are responsible for their action. As John the Baptist came in the spirit of Elijah, then in like manner any Spirit-filled preacher might be another "Elias" specially sent to minister to us.

SECTION THREE

*Expository Notes on the Distressed Father
and the Helpless Disciples*

**And when they were come to the multitude, there came to him a certain man, kneeling down to him, and saying, Lord, have mercy on my son: for he is lunatic [epileptic] and sore vexed: for oftentime he falleth into the fire, and oft into the water. And I brought him to thy disciples, and they could not cure him. Then Jesus answered and said, O faithless and perverse generation, how long shall I be with you? how long shall I suffer you? bring him hither to me. And Jesus rebuked the devil; and he departed out of him: and the child was cured from that very hour. Then came the disciples to Jesus apart [privately], and said, Why could not we cast him out? And Jesus said unto them, Because of your unbelief: for verily I say unto you, If ye have faith as a grain of mustard seed, ye shall say unto this mountain, hence to yonder place; and it shall remove; and nothing shall be impossible unto you. Howbeit this kind goeth not out but by prayer and fasting (vv. 14-21).**

## A SERIOUS PROBLEM

During the Lord's stay in the mountain, the disciples who remained in the valley encountered a baffling problem. A distressed father had brought a demoniac child seeking deliverance. Alas, the depleted party had failed to alleviate the situation, and the unsolved problem discredited them in the eyes of a watching audience. The word translated "lunatic" is *seleenlazeetai* which according to Thayer means "to be moon-struck," and in a secondary sense to be "epileptic." Mark 9:26 and Luke 9:42 give graphic details of what happened when the father brought his son to Jesus. It was commonly believed that insanity was related to the moon, hence the term lunacy. Observers had noticed that when the moon was full, the boy's condition became worse, and therefore, every month brought added anxiety to a parent, who could not cope with his son's ailment. The boy became uncontrollable, and constant care had to be exercised, for there had been danger of the lad being burned or drowned. Probably, the father had come unaware that Jesus was absent. He had presented his request to the disciples, and had been dismayed and disappointed when they failed to render the required assistance. To his everlasting credit it must be said that the failure of Christ's representatives only increased the man's desire to meet Jesus, personally. He exhibited wisdom when he obviously looked beyond men to the Master. Unfortunately, today people become disappointed in professing Christians, and never think about seeking aid directly from Christ. The church and other institutions may fail to solve problems, but happy and wise are they who never abandon hope, until they have knelt at the feet of Jesus.

## THE SINCERE PLEA

"Lord, have mercy on my son..." (v. 15). Even as the petition was being presented, the child was groveling in the dust; his fingers had become claws; his face was twisted grotesquely, and the evil spirit seemed to be mocking the desperate parent. The Lord looked at the boy, the father, the crowd of onlookers, and especially at the disciples. Then sadly He said, "O faithless and perverse generation." "O unbelieving, and difficult people. How long must I be with you, teaching you, showing you God's truth? How much longer must I have patience with you." He sighed and asked that the lad be brought closer. His command expelled the demon, and the boy was instantly cured. Alas, for the watching disciples, the ecstasy of that miraculous deliverance was somewhat ruined by their frustrations. They had used the same words of exorcism; they had used an identical ritual, but the demon had been stronger than they. They were ashamed, puzzled, and very disappointed. Perhaps even Peter, James, and John were looking at them with disapproving eyes; they had not maintained the standards of efficiency known on their missionary itinerary (see Luke 10:17).

It was inevitable that they should ask, "Why could not we cast him out?" (v. 19). The Lord's reply indicated that prayer was more important than preaching; that Christians should spend time with God in order to prepare for service among people. Even the message of God's grace can be reduced to empty words, unless the lips of the preacher be touched with a coal from the fires burning on God's altar (see Isa. 6:7-8). The Lord's reference to the removal of mountains was an indication that no problem should ever be too hard to solve; no burden too heavy to remove. It cannot mean anything else, for no Christian has ever had need to command a mountain to remove itself to another part of the planet. If God does not remove our mountain, then perhaps He wants us to climb it. This might lead to a strengthening of our limbs, and in addition, every mountain provides an excellent view of God's glorious handiwork.

## A SPECIAL POWER

The helplessness of the nine disciples suggests a very interesting question. If the desperate father had presented his problem to Peter, James, and John, would they have been able to expel the demon? Alas, they also had slept throughout the transfiguration of the Lord. Perhaps the only difference between the three and the nine was that the men in the valley slept with their eyes open! Their impotence when facing the demon suggested they might just as well have closed them! This was the classic way in which Jesus drew attention to the importance of priorities. The preacher who spends more time playing golf than he does with his Bible, needs to learn more about fasting! The supplicant who stays on his knees long enough to say ''Thank You, Lord,'' has never learned to pray. The gifted orator whose eloquence charms audiences, appears to be suffering from lockjaw when he tries to exorcise demons. All pastors live busy lives, but if they are too busy to pray, they are too busy!

### SECTION FOUR

*Expository Notes on Peter's Strange Fishing Expedition*

**And while they abode in Galilee, Jesus said unto them, The Son of man shall be betrayed into the hands of men: And they shall kill him, and the third day he shall be raised again. And they were exceedingly sorry. And when they were come to Capernaum, they that received tribute money came to Peter, and said, Doth not your master pay tribute? He saith, Yes. And when he was come into the house, Jesus [spoke first to] him, saying, What thinkest thou, Simon? of whom do the kings of the earth take custom or tribute? of their own sons, or of strangers? Peter saith unto him, Of strangers. Jesus saith unto him, Then are the children free. Notwithstanding, lest we should offend them, go thou to the sea, and cast an hook, and take up the fish that first cometh up; and when thou hast opened its mouth, thou shalt find a piece of money: that take, and give unto them for me and thee (vv. 22-27).**

## A SPECIAL COLLECTOR

The first two verses in this section appear to be an after-thought of Matthew. He recalled that throughout the stay in Galilee, the Lord repeated His statement concerning His death and resurrection, and that on hearing the message the disciples were exceeding sorry. They were still immature students struggling to graduate from God's academy. To them it appeared incomprehensible that the King of Israel should become the victim of an enemy. Nevertheless the Lord knew the seeds of truth would ultimately germinate within their minds. His persistence should remind every Christian worker of the old proverb, ''If at first you don't succeed, try, try, try again.''

The laws of Moses made it clear that each man in Israel was responsible for the maintenace of the temple. To operate the many functions of the religious life of Israel was an expensive matter; priests had to be paid; incense robes, and many other commodities had to be purchased; and, without an income, this would have been an impossibility. From writers on this custom, we learn that every male Jew over twenty years of age had to pay an annual temple tax of one-half shekel. (In the days of Nehemiah, when the people were poor, it was one third of a shekel.) One half shekel was equal to two Greek drachmae; and the tax was commonly called the didrachm. The tax was about twenty cents, but in perspective that sum would be two days pay. It brought into the temple treasury at least $100,000 per year, and that represented a great amount of money in Jesus' day.

''The method of collecting was carefully organized. On the first day of the month Adar (March), an announcement was made in all the towns and villages of Palestine that tax time had come. On the fifteenth of the month, booths were set up in each town and village where the tax was paid. Any tax, not paid by the twenty-fifth of Adar, could only be paid directly to the Temple in Jerusalem.''

Capernaum was an important center for the collection of taxes, and obviously the booths had been set up, and specially appointed men were waiting to receive dues. One of these agents saw the approach of Jesus and the disciples, and he naturally wondered if they were about to pay the tax. If and when the Lord walked past the booth, the official was surprised, and later asked if Jesus paid taxes. Some people might suspect an evil intent, but the question might have been expected. The man was there to do his job. Spontaneously, Peter answered affirmatively, but then became worried about the accuracy of his reply.

## A SERIOUS CONSIDERATION

Peter was frowning; he was no longer the ebullient disciple; he was pensive, moody, a man with trouble expressed on his face. Jesus knew something was wrong, and asked what was worrying His friend. The tax in question related to the worship within the sanctuary, and the Lord's reference to the tax-free exemption of a royal family was an endorsement of what He had taught. God could not be expected to pay for His own worship. A monarch would never be asked to pay for the crown which sat upon his head. Furthermore, a king might subject conquered nations to taxation, but victorious nations never paid taxes for something they had achieved. The Lord was saying that, as the Son of God, He was exempt from such demands, and should never even be asked. "Notwithstanding," He continued, "lest we should [cause them to stumble], go thou to the sea, and cast an hook, and take up the fish that first cometh up; and when thou hast opened his mouth, thou shalt find a piece of money: that take, and give unto them for me and thee" (v. 27). The word translated "offend" is *skandalisomen* and as we saw earlier, it means "to place an obstacle in one's path, to cause him to slip, to stumble, to slide". There was no legal compulsion on Christ to pay the tax, but He also could "go the extra mile" in order to prevent offense. There are times when it is wiser to bend than break; sometimes, the longest way around is the shortest way home!

## A SIMPLE COMMAND

The account of Peter's fishing exploit is among the strangest, yet most exciting stories in the Gospel. Alas, it has been challenged, misinterpreted, and denied by liberal theologians. It has been said that Jesus commanded the disciples to return temporarily to their old occupation. Money earned through honest labor would be more valuable than money begged or borrowed. Concerning this viewpoint, during my college years I was privileged to listen to Dr. Pierson, a visiting lecturer; an expert on Palestinian affairs. He had conducted tours to the Holy Land, and was a biblical scholar. He referred to the fishing incident when Peter was told to cast a hook into the sea, and explained how the finding of a coin in the mouth of the fish was *not a miracle*. It was a natural occurrence which happened often on the Sea of Galilee. Once again, in thinking of the liberal theologians, I am reminded of the words of Abraham Lincoln. "Better to remain silent and be thought a fool, than to speak and remove all doubt."

Many evangelical Christians reject this interpretation, considering it to be misleading. If this idea were based on fact, why did not Matthew say so? When this teaching is applied, all miracles become suspect. If the intervening, supernatural power of God be excluded from the amazing events of the New Testament, then perhaps even the death of Jesus could have been an unfortunate occurrence. He might have been the victim of a Jewish mob!

## *A STRANGE CATCH*

It is thrilling to detect there is a two-fold miracle in the story, but it is not in the fact the fish had a coin in its mouth. The Lord knew the coin would be in the mouth of the first fish caught, and He also knew its value. It would be sufficient to pay the tax for two people. Peter was instructed to cast a hook, not a net, into the water. Even this was significant. Had Peter thrown a net, he might have had sufficient fish to pay the taxes for the entire party! Obviously, this was a personal matter between the Lord and His follower. The Lord of creation had been able to see the fish; to know what was in its mouth, and to direct it toward Peter's hook. What would have happened if another fish had struck first? The Lord, who held the world in His hand, was quite sure of His facts. This was additional proof of His omniscience. Thus would He teach us that all problems can be solved, if we are careful to do what He commands.


HOMILY


Study No. 11


### PETER...and his Greatest Fishing Story

Simon Peter was worried. He had a cloud on his mind; a shadow had fallen across his soul. The Master had discovered his problem and had sent him on a fishing expedition. Peter was glad to get away from the searching eyes of the Lord, but his problem remained. Slowly, he went down to the edge of the waves; he baited his hook and, with a dexterous twist of the wrist, sent his sinker skimming over the water. Thoughtfully, he watched the splash, and allowing the line to slip through his fingers, waited until its slackness told the sinker was at the bottom. Slowly he wound in the line until it was moderately taut, and then he waited. Eventually, the telltale wriggle of the handline informed him that the bait had been attractive, and with long steady pulls he hauled in his fish. Peter gripped it with his free hand, and then loosing the hook from its mouth, nonchalantly looked at the coin between the jaws of his captive. As he placed it safely in his pocket, he turned and walked up the beach.

## THE MAN WITH A CLOUD ON HIS MIND

His troubles had begun when the income tax officials had asked him, "Doth not your master pay tribute?" (Matt. 17:24). Spontaneously, Simon answered, "Yes," but afterward he wondered if he had told the truth; if he were guilty of defrauding the authorities and they would investigate the matter, and they could bring punishment upon the disciple band. Finally, his countenance showed evidence of his great concern. When he did not bring his troubles to the Lord, his worry increased. The Lord Jesus recognized the symptoms of anxiety, and realized that something had disturbed His disciple. Easily reading Peter's thoughts, He placed His finger on the cause of the trouble. "What thinkest thou, Simon? of whom do the kings of the earth take custom or tribute? of their own children or of strangers? Peter saith unto him, Of strangers. Jesus saith unto him, Then are the children free" (vv. 25-26).

## THE FISH WITH A COIN IN ITS MOUTH

"Notwithstanding, lest we should offend them, go thou to the sea, and cast an hook, and take up the fish that first cometh up: and when thou hast opened his mouth, thou shalt find a piece of money; that take, and give unto them for me and thee" (v. 27). Peter went to obey his Master, and it was a strange experience when he saw the fulfillment of Christ's prediction. Certain critics ridicule the account, yet missionaries from the Holy Land assure us there was no miracle in the fact the fish had a coin in its mouth. A certain type of fish found in the Sea of Galilee carries its young in its mouth, and when these are old enough to begin their separate existence, the parent fish replaces them with a stone or any suitable object. Even today, fishermen from Galilee show coins taken from the mouths of such fish. Nevertheless, there was *a two-fold miracle* in Peter's exploit. The Lord knew the coin would be in the mouth of the first fish to be caught; and secondly, He knew its value, and said it would be sufficient to pay for both Peter and Himself. "That take, and give unto them *for me and thee*"

*THE CHRIST WITH A CHARM IN HIS MESSAGE*

Christ had wonderful ways of imparting truth. (1) *How Great His claim.* If the princes of a royal household are exempt from the taxation demanded by their father, then the Prince of Heaven could not be expected to do as had been suggested. (2) *How Great His concern.* "Lest we should offend them." He knew that if men's hearts were biased against Him, their ears would be closed to His message. He was keen not to erect intellectual barriers which might hinder the proclamation of the Gospel. (3) *How Great His care.* "...for me and thee." We shall never know how many times the Lord met the need of His followers. Yet, here at least is another example of His great kindness. When He paid Peter's debt and delivered him from the requirements of the law, He surely taught, in principle, that in like manner He would soon pay Peter's eternal debt. Christ, the Son of God, had deliberately chosen to be *one with Peter in responsibility*, that Peter might become *one with Him in freedom.* "...for me and thee." (Reprinted from the author's book, *Bible Pinnacles*, pp. 89-90.)

# The Eighteenth Chapter of Matthew

THEME: *Jesus Instructs His Disciples*

OUTLINE:
I. The Importance of a Child (Verses 1-14)
II. The Inspiration of the Church (Verses 15-20)
III. The Illustration of Compassion (Verses 21-35)

## SECTION ONE

*Expository Notes on the Need to be Childlike*

**At the same time came the disciples unto Jesus, saying, Who is the greatest in the kingdom of heaven? And Jesus called a little child unto him, and set him in the midst of them, And said, Verily I say unto you, Except ye be converted, and become as little children, ye shall not enter into the kingdom of heaven. Whosoever therefore shall humble himself as this little child, the same is greatest in the kingdom of heaven. And whosoever shall receive one such little child in my name receiveth me. But whosoever shall offend one of these little ones which believe in me, it were better for him that a millstone were hanged about his neck, and that he were drowned in the depth of the sea (vv. 1-6).**

The above verses divide into four categories, and it is important that each be considered carefully.

## THE DESIRE FOR SUPREMACY

When the disciples asked their question regarding positions of honor to be received within the expected kingdom, they opened a new realm of thought. Had they become envious of each other? Had jealousy disturbed the peaceful relations within the company? Such a conclusion might be an injustice to the disciples. Those men were surrounded by circumstances which might have prompted the question. The Roman empire, by whose legions Palestine had been conquered, had degrees of responsibility among the soldiers. The centurions were leaders over a hundred men; tribunes were in charge of greater numbers, and this rule applied throughout the empire. Officials governed provinces, and Caesar gave to some of these permission to be known as kings. The systems were highly organized and, for the most part, the arrangement was satisfactory to those who sponsored it. On the other hand, the disciples of Jesus were hearing every day about a kingdom to be established by God, and yet were unable to detect any official preparation for its arrival. They had no idea how it could operate. The simple question, "Who would do what?" tormented them every day, and their question could have been legitimate. It was obvious that without some intelligent administration, the kingdom of heaven upon earth would be in serious jeopardy. If appointed officials were necessary for the kingdom to continue, then each disciple could have been forgiven, if he desired for himself some measure of security as he contemplated the future.

## THE DEMAND FOR SIMPLICITY

"Except ye be converted, and become as little children, ye shall not enter into the kingdom of heaven" (v. 3). Some early churchmen believed the child placed in the midst by Jesus was the son of Simon Peter, but no authoritative evidence can be provided to substantiate this theory. It is of little significance, as any child would have been appropriate for the occasion. The disciples had failed to differentiate between God's kingdom, established on love, and the empire of Caesar, based on military power. Love, as such, hardly existed among the soldiers, where obedience was demanded from every man. Disobedience led to reprimand, and repeated reprimands led to execution. The citizens of God's kingdom knew no compelling force except love. They obeyed their Master, because they desired so to do.

The reference to the child, momentarily, must have shocked the disciples. The suggestion that they needed to be converted, that is, "turned around," meant they had been traveling in the wrong direction. Their hopes, longings, and aspirations were ill-conceived. A small child never makes extensive plans for the future, and knows nothing of desires for personal gain. The chief characteristic of little children is implicit trust in a parent. They never worry about supplying meals, for they expect their parents to provide what is necessary. A child knows nothing of the demands of life; of paying income tax; providing clothing and other necessities, for these are the responsibilities of adults. Completely confident in the unfailing care of a devoted parent, a child walks calmly through the adolescent years.

Jesus was trying to teach His followers that such were the characteristics of all citizens of God's kingdom. Within the realms of the eternal, it was better to be a trusting child of God than a scheming adult, lusting for importance.

## THE DISCOVERY OF SERENITY

"And whoso shall receive one such little child in my name receiveth me" (v. 5). It is impossible to overestimate the importance of a child. Children of today are the adults of tomorrow. As an acorn becomes a strong tree, so the immature child has the potentiality of becoming the greatest of earth's citizens. God recognizes this fact, and it behooved the disciples to remember it also. On one important occasion they tried to prevent mothers bringing children to Jesus, and their action brought instant rebuke. The Lord was trying to teach that He could always be found where innocence and trust were prevailing factors among men. He appreciated all whose hearts were filled with these commendable qualities.

Some misguided pilgrims walk thousands of miles in the hope of finding a place where God might be discovered, and shrines offering such rewards are popular throughout the world. Jesus never went on any such pilgrimage. His own personal heaven surrounded Him. To feel the clutch of a child's hand reminded Him of His Father's care, and to see the sparkle of delight in youthful eyes was a reflection of heaven's happiness. This was true serenity.

## THE DISPLAY OF STUPIDITY

"But whoso shall offend one of these little ones which believe in me, it were better for him that a millstone were hanged about his neck, and that he were drowned in the depth of the sea" (v. 6). The Lord had now widened the scope of His message. He could not have been referring to small children, but to others whose childlike faith indicated they had become the children of God. Jesus said that rejection and persecution of His followers meant He also was being rejected. Such actions were unpardonable, and death by drowning was preferable to continuing guilt.

Let us note that the Jew feared the sea; for him heaven was a place where there would be no more sea (see Rev. 21:1). The man who taught another to sin would be better to be drowned far out in the sea, the most lonely of places. Furthermore, the very picture of drowning held terror for the Jew. Drowning was sometimes a Roman punishment but never a Jewish method. To the Jew it was the symbol of utter destruction. When the rabbis taught that heathen and gentile objects were to be utterly destroyed, they said they must be "cast into the salt sea." Josephus has a terrible account of a Galilean revolt in which the Galileans took the supporters of Herod and drowned them in the depths of the Sea of Galilee ( *Antiquities of the Jews*, 14:15:10). The very phase to the Jews would paint a picture of utter destruction and annihilation. Jesus' words were carefully and deliberately chosen to show the fate that awaits a man who taught another to sin.

> **Woe unto the world because of offences! for it must needs be that offences come; but woe to that man by whom the offence cometh! Wherefore if thy hand or thy foot offend thee, cut them off, and cast them from thee: it is better for thee to enter into life lame or maimed, rather than having two hands or two feet to be cast into everlasting fire. And if thine eye offend thee, pluck it out, and cast it from thee; it is better for thee to enter into life with one eye, rather than having two eyes to be cast into hell fire (vv. 7-9).**

*THE SEVERE DIFFICULTIES... "It must be that offences come."*

Sometimes God's choicest blessings arrive in disguise! The followers of Jesus were never promised unending happiness; they were warned that difficulties would need to be overcome, and dark days of depression endured. They who look for the rising sun must be prepared to watch through cold nights. They who would enter into the eternal city must be prepared to climb steep hills and walk along difficult highways. To endure to the end would be to gain a crown of glory. The disciple should never forget that God could and would make all things work together for good to those who were called according to His purpose (see Rom. 8:28). Nevertheless, the people who provided hindrances and persecution would be extremely foolish. To hinder a saint would be tantamount to hurting the Savior. Men were urged to consider this important fact.

*THE SPECIAL DIRECTIONS*

"If thy hand or thy foot offend thee, cut them off...if thine eye offend thee, pluck it out" (vv. 8,9). These words of Christ were a very serious warning. At first glance the casual reader would suspect Jesus to be encouraging amputations! If the words were literally interpreted and obeyed, hospitals would be too small to accommodate maimed people. There is need for improvement in every Christian, but if the causes of our imperfections were removed by surgery, the world would be filled with amputees. We are obliged therefore to seek a deeper interpretation of the Savior's message. Jesus stressed the fact that man's supreme desire should be to enter fully into the kingdom of heaven. Compared with this achievement, other earthly goals faded into insignificance. Therefore, every hindrance should be avoided. Undesirable companions should be shunned; unholy pleasures sacrificed, and everything said or done by the disciple should be in harmony with the will of God. There would be no need to remove a lusting eye if the object of lust be avoided. There would be no need to amputate legs taking a walk into quicksands of evil if the person were truly converted and made to walk in another direction.

> **Take heed that ye despise not one of these little ones; for I say unto you, That in heaven their angels do always behold the face of my Father, which is in heaven; For the Son of man is come to save that which was lost. How think ye? if a man have an hundred sheep, and one of them be gone astray, doth he not leave the ninety and nine, and goeth into the mountains, and seeketh that which is gone astray? And if so be that he find it, verily I say unto you, he rejoiceth more of that sheep, than over the ninety and nine which went not astray. Even so it is not the will of your Father which is in heaven, that one of these little ones should perish (vv. 10-14).**

*THE SURPRISING DISCLOSURE "...their angels do always behold the face of my Father."*

It must be remembered that during the time of our Lord's sojourn upon earth, the Jews firmly believed in the ministry of angels. It was an accepted fact that angels were appointed by God to superintend many functions in life. Probably, the same thought was expressed in Hebrews 1:14 where angels were said to be "ministering spirits, sent forth to minister for them who shall be heirs of salvation." The Lord, knowing the current belief of those He was addressing, indicated that according to their teaching, each child was under the care of a guardian angel, whose privilege it was to have instant audience with the Almighty. Jesus was trying to accentuate the importance of any child whose "angel" had instant access to the throne of grace. This thought is even more pronounced in John 14:16, "And I will pray the Father, and he shall give you another Comforter, *that he may abide with you forever.*" The trusting child of God is in excellent company and in good hands! The Holy Spirit abides with him here, and the risen Lord intercedes for him in heaven. It should therefore be understood that every soul is intensely precious to God. It would be unwise and unsafe for an enemy to hinder or persecute one of God's precious children.

## THE SUPREME DELIGHT

It may seem a little surprising to us that these words should be found among the sayings of Christ, but we have already discovered that Matthew was a meticulous scribe. Within his mind, he filed away events and statements, and when an opportune moment arrived he placed his facts where he thought they would be of most value within his manuscript. Jesus likened the potential "little ones" to a lost sheep wandering upon the mountains. He had come to earth to seek lost sheep, and His greatest joys were experienced when His efforts were successful. The disciples who were soon to be sent on a similar mission should learn the art of soul winning and thus become acquainted with heaven's joys. Pastors would know the wisdom of feeding sheep within the fold, but not even that could equal or surpass the joy of bringing back a lost soul. It was this glorious fact which inspired the great commission, "Go ye into all the world, and preach the gospel to every creature" (Mark 16:15).

### SECTION TWO

*Expository Notes on the Inspiration and Authority*
*of the Local Church*

**Moreover if thy brother shall trespass against thee, go and tell him his fault between thee and him alone: if he shall hear thee, thou hast gained thy brother. But if he will not hear thee, then take with thee one or two more, that in the mouth of two or three witnesses every word may be established. And if he shall neglect to hear them, tell it unto the church: but if he neglect to hear the church, let him be unto thee as an heathen man and [tax collector]. Verily I say unto you, Whatsoever ye shall bind on earth shall be bound in heaven: and whatsoever ye shall loose on earth shall be loosed in heaven (vv. 15-18).**

This is one of the most interesting of all the Lord's commandments, for He saw clearly the arising of the church and endorsed the authority of its elders. He saw the need for responsible people commissioned to rule authoritatively in all matters of law and order within the assembly. Fully aware of the dangers to beset the church, He gave explicit advice to the disciples who would try to keep the church above reproach. Once again, we discover these verses cover four areas of thought.

## A SACRED DUTY

As termites are able to destroy a building, so internal discord can ruin an assembly. If the kingdom of heaven were to be established on love, then the same element should prevail in every aspect of church life. Any threat to unity should command instant attention. If a stitch in time saves nine, then wise, instant action might prevent never-ending trouble. Problems would arise, for there would be irresponsible brothers completely incapable of detecting fault in themselves. The injured or slandered member should never be embittered. The offender should be made aware of his indiscretion, and every attempt made to heal a wound before it became infested. Those aware of God's forgiving grace should have no difficulty forgiving others within the family of God. It was to be the sacred duty of every church member never to tolerate the continuance of anything threatening the sanctity of the church.

## A SPECIAL DISCRETION

Jesus recognized that men might remain argumentative and stubborn, and therefore instructed that should this prove to be the case, the peace-desiring member should seek the assistance of others within the assembly. Their influence might have an effect upon the obstinate listener. If two heads are better than one, then three would be better than two! There might arise the need for verification of what was said during the interview, and the presence of trustworthy witnesses might be of incalculable worth if the problem increased.

## A STERN DISCIPLINE

As a last resort, if all attempts at conciliation failed, the brother had to be brought before the elders of the church. If he remained adamant and unyielding, they were authorized to excommunicate him. Afterward, he was to be considered as a heathen or as a publican. This was an exercise of serious discipline, but evidently Jesus considered the health of the church to be more important than the exclusion of one individual. He believed it was better and wiser to remove a thorn from a finger than to procrastinate until an arm needed amputation.

## A STIMULATING DECLARATION

The oneness of Christ with His church was never seen to better advantage than in these verses. The decision of the church in any matter regarding the spiritual health of the assembly would be ratified in heaven. They were never to be fearful in acting on any urgent matter relating to the work of the kingdom; the Holy Spirit would preside at their church councils; His guidance should be sought before any binding decision was made, and afterward God's people should know their action was in alignment with the will of God. Alas, the modern church appears to have lost or forgotten this important truth. Invariably, an adverse decision made by a church council leads to a split in the assembly, and unfortunately many of today's churches are filled with people who failed to live at peace in earlier churches which they helped to erect. Sometimes, even in church matters, it is better to be a gracious loser than to succeed and become an arrogant winner.

**Again I say unto you, That if two of you shall agree on earth as touching any thing that they shall ask, it shall be done for them of my Father, which is in heaven. For where two or three are gathered together in my name, there am I in the midst of them (vv. 19-20).**

Dr. Frank Boreham, my very famous friend in Australia, once described this text as "The most misunderstood text in the Bible." He said, "Even a blind man would know when the attendance at a meeting was poor. Sooner or later someone would pray and say, 'Lord, it is alright, for You promised that where two or three gathered together, You would be in the midst.'" It is interesting to note that when this text was first given by the Savior, He was not thinking of poorly attended services. This utterance was made because Jesus was speaking about the need for forgiveness within the church. Furthermore, as we shall see, the following verses also dealt with the same. (See the special homily at the end of the chapter.)

### SECTION THREE

*Expository Notes on the Parable of the Unmerciful Servant*

**Then came Peter to him, and said, Lord, how oft shall my brother sin against me, and I forgive him? till seven times? Jesus saith unto him, I say not unto thee, Until seven times: but, Until seventy times seven (vv. 21-22).**

## AN INTERESTING SUGGESTION

It must be emphasized that the entire theme of these verses is the need for forgiveness. Peter recognized this fact and asked his question. Perhaps his inquiry may be more appreciated if we paraphrase it. "Lord, if my brother blacken my eye, how much am I expected to take before I strike him? Do I endure seven black eyes? Must I wait until he is about to strike me the eighth time, and then will I be free to retaliate?" Let it be admitted this was extremely gallant for a man of Peter's fiery disposition. Others might have been unwilling to receive a second black eye! The strangely expressed philosophy of the old negro can be understood and appreciated. He said, "If I be kicked in de pants once, it is a big pity. But if I be kicked in de pants de second time by de same shoe, dat be my fault for bending over."

Jesus listened attentively to Peter's question and then gave His immortal answer, "I say not unto thee, Until seven times: but, Until seventy times seven." He probably realized that His follower would not have sufficient patience to continue counting until the number reached four hundred and ninety. It would be far easier for a man of Simon's disposition to keep on forgiving. This thought-provoking reply becomes even more interesting when we consider the illustration which followed. When Jesus said, "THEREFORE," it became obvious the story He was about to tell was the direct result of Peter's question.

**Therefore is the kingdom of heaven likened unto a certain king, who would take account of his servants. And when he had begun to reckon, one was brought unto him, who owed him ten thousand talents. But forasmuch as he had not [nothing] to pay, his lord commanded him to be sold, and his wife, and children, and all that he had, and payment to be made. The servant therefore fell down, and worshiped him, saying, Lord, have patience with me, and I will pay thee all. Then the Lord of that servant was moved with compassion, and loosed him, and forgave him the debt (vv. 23-27).**

## AN INTRIGUING STORY

In all probability we should never have received this immortal illustration, but for the fact that Peter had questioned the Lord about the necessity of forgiving a brother's indiscretion. The Savior's story was most unusual. He spoke of a man who owed his master ten thousand talents. Throughout the ages theologians tried to compute the size of the debt. One teacher suggested it equalled $262,800,000. Another states that a talent was the equivalent of 240 British pounds, and that the entire debt would have been 2 million, four hundred British pounds. When he made that computation, a pound and also the American dollar were worth very much more than they are today. Yet under any circumstances the debt was immense, and the offending man must have enjoyed a position of great eminence within a kingdom. The inference was that he had been a Minister of Finance who embezzled a great amount of money. An examination of the royal books revealed the fraud, and the day of reckoning arrived for the offender. Somewhere we read that "the total revenue of even a wealthy province like Galilee was only 300 talents. Here was a debt which was greater than a king's ransom." The embezzlement made by this high official of state was enormous, and yet when he and his family were faced with slavery, his desperate request for clemency was granted, and the guilty man was pardoned.

> **But the same servant went out, and found one of his fellowservants, which owed him an hundred pence [denarii]: and he laid hands on him, and took him by the throat, saying, Pay me that thou owest. And his fellowservant fell down at his feet, and besought him, saying, Have patience with me, and I will pay thee all, And he would not: but went and cast him into prison, till he should pay the debt. So when his fellowservants saw what was done, they were very sorry, and came and told unto their lord all that was done (vv. 28-31).**

The hundred pence owed by the servant was less than five dollars, and it seems incredible that he who had been forgiven so much should be reluctant to cancel such a small debt. Even the language used by the Lord indicates the vicious character of this unforgiving man, for *he took his victim by the throat* as if to strangle him. We must remember that Peter had spoken of the possibility of forgiving seven times, and had been told by Jesus that seventy times seven would be a more appropriate figure. If we superimpose these facts upon the illustration given by Jesus, we discover the enormity of the offense of the unforgiving dignitary. Having been forgiven a sum of money in excess of millions of dollars, he refused to forgive a debt which was very insignificant. Had he been more gracious, he would have recognized his need to forgive — not seventy times seven, but at the very least, *three hundred thousand times seven*. It might have been even more, for it is difficult to know fully how great had been his own debt.

These staggering figures were really not of overwhelming importance. It was the thought behind the story which became paramount. Jesus was reminding His disciples that God had already forgiven them many millions of dollars worth of sins! His unfailing mercy had cancelled their debt. If they had been forgiven so much, they should be more than willing to forgive any brother or sister whose debt was minimal. Peter needed a computer to unravel all the suggested financial problems, but the prevailing fact was obvious. It would be easier to continue forgiving everybody. A lifetime of perpetual pardoning would be too short for Peter to forgive others what God had already forgiven him.

**Then his lord, after that he had called him, said unto him, O thou wicked servant, I forgave thee all that debt, because thou desiredst me; Shouldest not thou also have had compassion on thy fellowservant, even as I pity on thee? And his lord was wrath, and delivered him to the tormentors, till he should pay all that was due unto him. So likewise shall my heavenly Father do also unto you, if ye from your hearts forgive not every one his brother their trespasses (vv. 32-35).**

## AN IGNORED STATEMENT

The last verse of the eighteenth chapter of Matthew is frightening! When Jesus had described the fate awaiting the unforgiving steward, He proceeded to say, "So likewise shall my heavenly Father do also unto you, if ye from your hearts, forgive not every one his brother their trespasses." It is problematical how far we can go in trying to harmonize this statement with other New Testament verses, but however much we reason or debate, the text remains when talking has ceased. Sometimes Christians take too much for granted! They rejoice in the redemptive work of Christ, and proclaim the wonder of His forgiving grace, and yet their treatment of fellow Christians leaves much to be desired. First John 1:7 says, "*But if we walk in the light, as he is in the light*, we have fellowship one with another, and the blood of Jesus Christ his Son cleanseth us from all sin." Unfortunately, many Christians rejoice in the final section of that remarkable verse, but completely ignore the initial statement. It is true the precious blood of Christ actually *goes on* cleansing from sin, but the paramount condition is that men *walk in the light*. John said, "IF — IF — we walk in the light," we have fellowship and cleansing. When a man refuses to walk in the light of God's revealed word, and carries grudges against others within the family of God; when his spirit remains unforgiving, fellowship becomes an impossibility and sin remains unforgiven. This is truth which the church needs to remember and teach. It is possible for a Christian to be an expert theologian, a very enthusiastic speaker, and still be bankrupt in his soul.

HOMILY

Study No. 12

## CHRIST IN THE MIDST OF HIS PEOPLE

Matthew gave to the church a text which in all probability has been more quoted than any other of the Lord's utterances (v. 20). It has become known as "The Prayer Meeting Text," for always, sooner or later, at every prayer meeting a person reminds the Lord of His promise to be with the twos and threes gathered in His name. It is thought-provoking to remember that when the words were first spoken, they had no reference to attendance at a church service. This delightful little text provides food for thought.

### CHRIST AMONG THE FORGIVING

This marvelous verse is set in the thought of forgiveness. The Lord had spoken about the problem of an awkward brother, and had told a story about a man greatly forgiven, who in turn refused to forgive another fellowservant. The two gathered in Christ's name might have been argumentative brethren, and the third, the peace-maker, through whose instrumentality the antagonists were reconciled. Jesus was obviously encouraging His followers to live peacefully, and at the same time assuring them of His presence, should they ever have cause to meet in a conciliative manner. The Bible says, "Where the brethren dwell together in unity, there the Lord commandeth the blessing."

### CHRIST AMONG THE FAMILY

Tertullian, one of the early church fathers, had his own interpretation of this text. Asking the question, "What is the most natural thing in the world?" he went on to emphasize the importance of the marital relationship instituted by God. When a young man takes a bride, the couple should sanctify their home by inviting Jesus to become the head of the household. When their first baby arrives, the two become three, and the promise of Jesus to be with the two or three becomes truly operative in their marriage. Tertullian correctly taught that the strength of the church lay in consecrated, dedicated families, and with that thought in mind, stressed the importance of family devotions. It is an inestimable privilege to be able to attend the Lord's house, but it is even better to welcome Christ into our own home.

## CHRIST AMONG THE FOLLOWERS

The Lord was very wise when He sent out His followers, two by two, to preach the gospel. Loneliness is one of the most saddening qualities in the world. On the other hand, the fellowship of the saints is one of the most delightful experiences known to believers. Either one of the two missionaries would be able to encourage his partner and to share his problems and successes. When God promised that the preaching of His Word would not return void, He guaranteed that sooner or later, the preachers would win a convert. When this happened the two became three, and as they knelt in prayer, Christ would meet with them.

## CHRIST AMONG THE FAITHFUL

Alas, a crippling apathy has overwhelmed the church, and the prayer service is the most poorly attended of all meetings. Young people hurry to hamburger stands; argumentative members attend business meetings, but unfortunately only the faithful church members pray for the well-being of the assembly. Even Bible classes have more participants, for there people get something! At a prayer service saints come to give to the Lord; to speak with Him; to listen to His suggestions. The prayer meeting used to be, and still should be, the pulsating heart of every church. When a person has a weak heart, death can be expected at any moment. I shall never forget a Canadian minister who glibly said to me, ''Ha! prayer meetings and Bible classes went out of my church ten years ago.'' I quietly replied, ''I know, but now the church is praising God that you are leaving in two weeks.'' Startled by my words, he said, ''How do you know?'' I may not have been very wise, but at least I was truthful when I said, ''Your deacons told me. You have stayed long enough to preside at the funeral of this church.'' Cancers are never cured by compliments!

# The Nineteenth Chapter of Matthew

THEME: *Jesus Answers Questions*

OUTLINE:
1. Jesus Explains the Law (Verses 1-12)
II. Jesus Exhibits Love (Verses 13-15)
III. Jesus Expounds About Life (Verses 16-26)
IV. Jesus Examines Losses (Verses 27-30)

### SECTION ONE

*Expository Notes on the Sanctity of Marriage*

**And it came to pass, that when Jesus had finished these sayings, he departed from Galilee, and came into the coasts of Judaea beyond the Jordan. And great multitudes followed him; and he healed them there. The Pharisees also came unto him, testing him, and saying unto him, Is it lawful for a man to put away his wife for every cause? And he answered and said unto them, Have ye not read, that he which made them at the beginning made them male and female, And said, For this cause shall a man leave father and mother, and shall cleave to his wife: and they twain shall be one flesh? Wherefore they are no more twain, but one flesh. What therefore God hath joined together, let not man put asunder (vv. 1-6).**

The advisability and legality of divorce has always been the sharpest thorn in the flesh of the church. From time immemorial, religious leaders have argued about the pros and cons of marital separations, and probably it would be true to say that more heartaches have been caused by this topic than any others arising within Christian assemblies. Originally, the laws of God given through Moses were simple to understand and easy to interpret. Throughout the earliest history of the human race there was no mention of divorce; men and women were married and remained together until death brought separation. Much later, when many families formed a nation and lived in close proximity, problems arose, and it was obvious that laws were necessary to deal with continuing changes within communities. Many kinds of circumstances made it extremely difficult for some married people to remain together, and this became one of the gravest issues in Israel. Most people agreed that a lifetime union was the best in principle, but when sickness, adversity, and lust desecrated matrimonial vows, people needed guidance as to their course of action.

The first basic guidelines regarding divorce were expressed in Deuteronomy 24:1-4. Moses said, "When a man hath taken a wife, and married her, and it come to pass that she find no favour in his eyes, because he hath found some uncleanness in her: then let him write her a bill of divorcement, and give it in her hand, and send her out of his house. And when she is departed out of his house, she may go and be another man's wife. And if the latter husband hate her, and write her a bill of divorcement, and giveth it in her hand, and sendeth her out of his house; or if the latter husband die, which took her to be his wife; Her former husband, which sent her away, may not take her again to be his wife, after that she is defiled; for that is abomination before the LORD: and thou shalt not cause the land to sin, which the LORD thy God giveth thee for an inheritance. ''

## A DIRECT TEMPTATION

The first basic law regarding divorce was that *it was not wrong for a divorcee to remarry.* Any person who denied this fact did so without the authority of Moses. The Scripture was very clear on this point. Moses said, "And when she is departed out of his [her husband's] house, she may go and be another man's wife." It was legal for a divorcee to remarry, and when a man was willing to take her, a new marriage was arranged and consummated. There must have been many of these weddings in Israel. It must be recognized that the only grounds upon which divorce was granted was that the husband "had found some uncleanness in her," and that meant adultery. When this was proved, the husband could write a bill of divorcement, give it to his wife, and from that moment the marriage was annulled. It should be remembered that only the man could do this. Except in very special cases, the woman had no power to divorce her husband. We must consider also that Mark 10:11-12 appears to contradict this statement. The law practiced by *Gentiles* was totally different, and we can only assume that Jesus was looking beyond the boundaries of Israel, and speaking truth applicable to the Gentiles among whom the gospel would soon be preached.

## A DEVISIVE TEACHING

It was inevitable that among sinful people the original statement of Moses would be challenged. Hebrew law stated, "A woman may be divorced with or without her consent, but a man can be divorced only with his consent." It must be remembered that under certain conditions, a woman could appeal to the judges who, if they thought her appeal were justified, could bring pressure to bear on the husband, making him divorce his wife. It was considered grounds for divorce if a man refused to consummate his marriage. When a woman remained childless, she was considered to be "under a curse." If a man refused to father her child, or if he were impotent, that also was a justifiable reason for seeking annulment of the marriage. If a man became a leper, or if he were engaged in any occupation considered to be unclean, the wife could seek authority to leave her partner. All these details further complicated what was already a vexing question among the Jewish religious leaders.

During the early years of Israel's history, divorce proceedings were an extremely simple affair involving a one-sentence statement, but as time passed, the procedure became increasingly difficult. Men who were only concerned with satisfying their personal desires, debated the interpretation of the statement made by Moses, "Because he hath found some uncleanness in her." There arose in Israel, two schools of thought. The strict, unrelenting fundamentalists were led by a man called Shammai, who declared divorce was only to be granted when a partner was guilty of adultery. The more liberal school was led by a man called Hillel, and naturally, his teachings had a much wider acceptance among men who considered old fashioned laws to be restrictive. Hillel obviously was a man-pleaser; his teachings were sure to please those whose personal desires were considered beyond the condemnation of ancient commandments. The "defilement found in a woman," was interpreted as meaning anything which displeased the husband. Hence, if she spoiled his dinner, or spoke so loudly that the neighbors could hear her voice; if she spoke to a man in the street, or criticized her husband's people, even if she had failed to braid her hair, her man could sue for divorce. A certain Rabbi Akiba went so far as to teach that if her husband found another woman more pleasing than his wife, then even that could be included as something unclean discovered in his legal wife. Consequently, these two schools argued ceaselessly about the legality of divorce, and when Jesus was asked for His opinion, the Pharisees were merely trying to entangle the Lord in one of the most vital controversies of that age. Whatever He said guaranteed that the opposition would criticize His reply, and this would only intensify the bitterness of the forces arrayed against Him.

## A DEFINITE THOUGHT

It will be easily understood that the arrival of Jesus in the midst of such fiercely debated issues provided an opportunity for theologians to involve Jesus in discussions which could only increase the anger of those whose viewpoint He did not support. The wisdom of Jesus became apparent when He sidestepped the thrust of their verbal sword, and directed their attention to the irrefutability of God's ideal marriage arrangements for Adam and Eve. Perhaps the most important feature about the ministry of Jesus was the wisdom with which He continued to direct attention to the infallibility of God's Word. It became increasingly difficult for anyone to accuse Him of being a lawbreaker. There were days when He appeared to be walking along a tightrope, but He never fell. Wise are they who think before they answer any question!

> And said, For this cause shall a man leave father and mother, and shall cleave to his wife: and they [two] shall be one flesh. Wherefore they are no more [two], but one flesh. What therefore God hath joined together, let not man put asunder. They say unto him, Why did Moses then command to give a writing of divorcement, and to put her away? He saith unto them, Moses because of the hardness of your hearts suffered you to put away your wives: but from the beginning it was not so. And I say unto you, Whosoever shall put away his wife, except it be for fornication, and shall marry another, committeth adultery, and whosoever marrieth her which is put away doth commit adultery (vv. 5-9).

## A SUBTLE SCHEME

God never planned nor made concessions for any disgruntled, unhappy partner in a marriage. This was obvious, for Adam and Eve were alone in the world; marriage to another would have been impossible. This union of two people was ordained by God to be a long-range investment in marital bliss. They belonged either to the other until death intervened. Long afterward, when everything had changed upon the earth, man-made regulations were introduced which altered the structure of married life. The entire purpose of marriage was dedicated to the raising of families, but if after ten years a couple remained childless, divorce became compulsory whether the man and his wife loved each other or not. Reflecting on early conditions, someone says, "Desertion was never a cause for divorce. If there were desertion, death had to be proved. Nor was insanity. If the wife became insane, the husband could not divorce her, for she then would have no protector in her helplessness. If the husband became insane, divorce became impossible, for, in that case, he was incapable of 'writing a bill of divorcement,' and without such a bill, initiated by him, there could be no divorce." The question could have been asked by sincere people, but since Matthew says, "The Pharisees also came unto him, tempting him," we are compelled to believe their motives were sinister.

## A SUBLIME SAVIOR

"Wherefore they are no more twain, but one flesh." When this difficult question was asked of the Lord, He exhibited great wisdom in the manner in which He replied. The act of marriage was not exclusively relegated to acts of sexual intercourse. Marriage was ordained and blessed by God, not that participants should do *one* thing together, but rather that they should do *all* things together. They were to be one flesh. They were to share continually love, talents, responsibilities, successes, failures, health, and sickness. Marriage was meant to be the joyous union in which either complemented the other. Childbearing was but a part in the continual development of marital bliss.

## A SINCERE STATEMENT

We are left to reflect upon the tragedies to be found in our modern society. Divorce is never to be desired, but the fact remains that, for a variety of reasons, some marriages have no hope of succeeding. When the help of doctors, counselors, clergy, and churches fails to alleviate the problem; when matters continue to deteriorate, is it wise and mandatory that two people obviously unsuited to each other, must continue to live in misery until death intervenes? Are ministers justified in consigning such people to unending tragedy, of excommunicating them from the assembly, of refusing to welcome them into what should be the comforting arms of the church? Alas, God is often kinder than ministers who claim to represent Him. On the other hand, people who only enter a church to get married, should never try to disguise a churchless existence with a robe of respectability worn only on the occasions of repeated marriages. There is a prevailing sanity about all

God's acts. Ministers should consider carefully the Lord's loving example before proceeding with harsh treatment, to destroy the last remaining vestiges of happiness within hearts capable of being broken. It must be recognized that Christ's remarkable answer to the question asked by the Pharisees made Him to be One *with* God and not *against* Him.

The Pharisees were more concerned with selfish desires than sanctified decisions. When they asked, "Why did Moses then command a writing of divorcement, and to put her away?" they were endeavoring still further to entangle the Lord in their dastardly schemes. They were accusing Him of denying the authority of Moses. The patriarch had received the law from God, and if Jesus taught anything contrary to the commandments, He would be assuming more authority than God Himself. If they could successfully bring this charge against Him, their insinuations could destroy the Preacher. Jesus recognized their evil intentions, and with superb confidence continued to expound the Scriptures.

Unruffled, undismayed, He proceeded to say the commandments given by Moses were an expression of the *permissive* will of God. It would be senseless to impose perfect requirements upon imperfect people. It was impossible to fly without wings! God, through Moses, had graciously condescended to alleviate human misery by permitting something not originally envisaged. To meet the crucial needs of a changing society, God in grace had done His utmost to lift burdens and solve the problems of suffering people. Nevertheless, and on this point Jesus was adamant, human reasoning and carnal desire could never change vice into virtue. When God permitted divorce, He never abandoned nor forgot His original desires. "Therefore," said Jesus, "I say unto you, Whosoever shall put away his wife, except it be for fornication, and shall marry another, committeth adultery."

**His disciples say unto him, If the case of the man be so with his wife, it is not good to marry. But he said unto them, All men cannot receive this saying, save they to whom it is given. For there are some eunuchs, who were so born from their mother's womb: and there are some eunuchs, who were made eunuchs of men: and there be eunuchs, which, have made themselves eunuchs for the kingdom of heaven's sake. He that is able to receive it, let him receive it (vv. 10-12).**

The disciples were amazed and depressed by the words of Jesus. His teaching was contrary to the doctrines of the rabbis, and His views appeared to be restrictive and prohibitive leading to a life of frustration and unhappiness. The teachings of Hillel provided many escape hatches if married life became undesirable. Peter and the other men concluded it would be better to remain free bachelors than to become frustrated husbands. The Lord replied, "Maybe, but not for all men." Many people fail to recognize that marriages truly made in heaven never end in hell! Marriages of convenience seldom end anywhere else!

Jesus taught that some men would be incapable of entering such a relationship, and contrary to the teaching of the scribes, they should be sympathetically understood rather than harshly condemned. Jesus mentioned three types of eunuchs included in this category. (1) There were men physically incapable of becoming fathers; they were impotent. (2) Others were made eunuchs by men. This referred to customs freely recognized in ancient times. A typical example would be the rulers who deliberately castrated all men connected with the royal harem. The act might have been the result of a king's jealousy, or an attempt to safeguard women from the vicious attacks of rapists. (3) Some men voluntarily remained single "for the kingdom of heaven's sake." This did not imply the need for physical surgery, but the sacrificial abstinence from all marital relationships, so that the purposes of heaven might be completely served. This may be seen in the vows of celibacy practiced within the Roman Catholic church. I knew of a young doctor who went to serve in a leper colony. He was never married, because he thought it unfair to expect a bride to share his danger. Many young ladies became nuns. They believed that by remaining free from marital relationships, they could be "married to Jesus." Such sacrifice should never be *demanded* by anyone; it must be the sincere desire of individuals, whose devotion desires complete and absolute surrender to Christ. No religious institution should *impose* such laws. It is important to remember that Simon Peter, who was claimed to be the leader of the early church, was a married man. It has been written,"Peter's wife's mother lay sick of a fever" (see Mark 1:30).

## SECTION TWO

*Expository Notes on Mothers Bringing Children to Jesus*

**Then were there brought unto him little children, that he should put his hands on them, and pray: and the disciples rebuked them. But Jesus said, suffer little children, and forbid them not, to come unto me; for**

**of such is the kingdom of heaven. And he laid his hands on them, and departed thence (vv. 13-15).**

We cannot help but wonder if Matthew deliberately placed this insignificant incident in its position in his manuscript. Did the Holy Spirit direct him to do so, for these three verses resemble a glorious spring morning after a very bleak winter. The chilling winds of argument and criticism had been replaced by the radiance and warmth of a rising sun.

## THE INSISTENT MOTHERS

Mothers "brought unto him little children, that he should put his hands on them, and pray." There was something very attractive and noteworthy about those ladies. They were surely aware of the animosity of the Pharisees, and knew of the plots to destroy Jesus. Nevertheless, they thought only of their babies and desired that Christ would bless their offspring. They were not troubled about the possibility of repercussions from the synagogue, for they believed one touch from the hand of Jesus would mean continuing benediction for their children. Blessed are they who are cradled in the arms of believing mothers; privileged are they who are touched by the hands of Christ — whether or not they are aware of it.

## THE IMPATIENT MEN

"And the disciples rebuked them." We must not judge these men harshly; their actions were probably prompted by concern for their Master. The Lord was tired and needed protection from those who would unthinkingly intrude into His privacy.

I once admired a famous baseball player who paused on the field to sign a child's autograph album, but my admiration turned to concern when he was suddenly surrounded by hundreds of eager children who came from all parts of the ground to make a similar request. The overwhelmed player ran from the playing area, and insensitive reporters were merciless in their criticism of his action.

When my wife and I first went to Hollywood, we were permitted with many others to fill a large studio where a very famous television personality was about to film his weekly show. At the conclusion of the screening, I tried to approach the man to thank him for the great pleasure I had experienced during the three years I had watched his programs in Canada. I was disappointed and frustrated when a paid attendant almost manhandled me out of the building. Had all who wished to approach the performer been permitted to do so, he would have seemed lost in a sea of humanity. When the disciples tried to prevent women bringing their children to Jesus, they probably thought they were rendering great service to their Leader.

## THE IRRESISTIBLE MASTER

When Jesus welcomed the children and enfolded them in His outstretched arms, He provided a picture which every artist desired to paint. I once saw a picture in which Jesus was depicted playing tug-of-war with a small group of children. Boys and girls from Africa, China, Japan, Britain, America, and other parts of the world were trying in vain to pull Jesus in their direction. With delight shining in His eyes, the Lord was leaning back on His end of the rope, enjoying every moment of the contest. The indescribable charm of Jesus made Him irresistible to children. As Solomon wrote, "My beloved is...the chiefest among ten thousand...He is altogether lovely" (Song of Sol. 5:10-16).

### SECTION THREE

*Expository Notes on the Rich Young Ruler*

**And, behold, one came and said unto him, Good Master, what good thing shall I do, that I may have eternal life? And he said unto him, Why callest thou me good? there is none good but one, that is, God; but if thou wilt enter into life, keep the commandments. He saith unto him, Which? Jesus said, Thou shalt do no murder, Thou shalt not commit adultery, Thou shalt not steal, Thou shalt not bear false witness, Honour thy father and thy mother: and, Thou shalt love thy neighbour as thyself. The young man saith unto him, All these things have I kept from my youth up: what lack I yet? (vv. 16-20).**

Matthew, Mark, and Luke mention this incident, but a careful analysis of their records reveals minor differences. Matthew (19:20) informs readers that the questioner was young. Luke (18:18) says the man was a ruler. Mark (10:17) describes the enthusiasm of the suppliant by saying, "There came one *running* and kneeled to him." The complete account of the incident can only be obtained by considering the three versions together. Another account was available to the early church; it was known as "The Gospel according to the Hebrews." The men who compiled the canon of the New Testament rejected this manuscript as uninspired, and therefore it was excluded from the recognized Scriptures. Nevertheless, many scholars are inclined toward accepting the manuscript as authentic, believing it contains valuable information. The additional quotation reads as follows: "The second of the rich men said to him, 'Master, what good thing can I do and live?' He said unto him, 'O man, fulfill the law and the prophets.' He answered him, 'I have kept them.' He said unto him, 'Go sell all that thou ownest, and distribute it unto the poor, and, come, follow me!' But the rich man began to scratch his head, and it pleased him not. And the Lord said unto him, 'How sayest thou, I have kept the law and the prophets? For it is written in the law: Thou shalt love thy neighbor as thyself; and lo, many of thy brethren, sons of Abraham, are clad in filth, dying of hunger, and thine house is full of many good things, and nought at all goeth out of it unto them.'" To say the least, it is difficult to harmonize this statement with others in the three Gospels.

## A SERIOUS DESIRE

Obviously, the arrival and preaching of the man from Nazareth had shattered the complacency of the ruler. He who possessed everything suddenly became aware of insufficiency. He who had the ability to purchase everything was made aware that the greatest of all possessions could not be bought with money. Did the ruler attend many meetings? Were his theological conceptions shattered? That eventually, "he came running," indicates anxiety, determination, and desire. There was something he needed to learn, and obviously Jesus was a very capable Teacher. He asked, "What good thing shall I do — DO — that I may have eternal life?" *The Amplified New Testament* translates the statement, "Teacher, what excellent, and perfectly and essentially good deed must I do to possess eternal life?" Apparently, this man thought the most excellent deeds were required to please God, so that ultimately He might be willing to impart eternal life. It would seem at first glance that Jesus was considered to be only a very wise Teacher, capable of answering a theological question. Apparently, the ruler was completely unaware of Christ's ability to give eternal life to any suppliant, at any time, and in any place. Faith, and not deeds was the key to heaven's treasure house.

**Jesus said unto him, If thou wilt be perfect, go and sell that thou hast,**

and give to the poor, and thou shalt have treasure in heaven: and come and follow me. But when the young man heard that saying, he went away sorrowful: for he had great possessions. Then said Jesus unto his disciples, Verily I say unto you, That a rich man shall hardly [with difficulty] enter into the kingdom of heaven. And again I say unto you, It is easier for a camel to go through the eye of a needle, than for a rich man to enter into the kingdom of God. When his disciples heard it, they were exceedingly amazed, saying, Who then can be saved? But Jesus beheld them, and said unto them, With men this is impossible, but with God all things are possible (vv. 21-26).

## A SUGGESTIVE DISTINCTION

It is interesting to note that when the Lord replied to the ruler's question, He made a special choice of commandments. When a lawyer asked a similar question (Luke 10:25-28), Jesus emphasized the importance of loving God with all one's heart, soul, and strength. Yet when He spoke to the young ruler, He directed attention to the second section of the decalogue which concerned attitude toward people. The Lord was emphasizing it was impossible to love God, *if that love did not also embrace God's children*. If this were the case, then Jesus was only stressing the truth mentioned in John's first epistle. "But whoso hath this world's good, and seeth his brother have need, and shutteth up his bowels of compassion from him, how dwelleth the love of God in him?" (1 John 3:17). The Lord appreciated the ruler's sincerity but was endeavoring to deepen the man's understanding of what it truly meant to keep the commandments.

## A STARTLING DIRECTION

"...go and sell that thou hast, and give to the poor, and thou shalt have treasure in heaven: and come and follow me" (v. 21). The Lord was testing the man's priorities. It was essential that the ruler recognized the absolute necessity of crowning Christ Lord of his life. Was he willing to give up everything for Jesus? Did the possession of eternal life offer more pleasure than the enjoyment and acquisition of increasing wealth? Was the ruler's initial request for guidance indicative of genuine, sincere resolution, or was this a superficial, soon-to-end enthusiasm emanating from an immature young man? Obviously the ruler had deified wealth, and this friendly attractive monster was already enslaving the nobler instincts within the suppliant's soul. Would the ruler be willing to dethrone wealth in order to follow an itinerant Preacher? It was upon this level the man was forced to make his momentous decision. It should be obvious to everyone that nothing has really changed. "If Christ is not Lord of all, He is not Lord at all." Any person who persists in enthroning earthly pleasures, gain, popularity, or anything else, has little if any chance of entering the kingdom of God.

## A SORROWFUL DECISION

"...he went away sorrowful: for he had great possessions" (v. 22). Actually, it might be said, "He had no possessions; *they had him*." Jesus was sad, for He had come face to face with a man in danger of losing his soul. There are two interpretations to the text which refers to the "eye of a needle." The "eye of a needle" was the name given to a small door within a larger door or gate. When the large gate of a city closed at sunset, the smaller door remained open for pedestrians. Sometimes, a cameleer arriving late, tried to squeeze his animal through the small doorway. Certain prerequisites were necessary to make this possible. (1) The camel had to kneel. (2) Its burden had to be removed. (3) The beast, somehow, had to proceed on its knees. It was always a difficult procedure, but it could be done. The same laws applied to any wealthy person seeking entrance into the kingdom of God. Humility promoted kneeling; wisdom demanded off-loading, and intense desire encouraged progress.

Some theologians draw attention to another explanation. The Greek word for camel was *kameelos*. The word for a ship's cable was *kamilos*. There was hardly any phonetical difference between the two pronounciations, and the possibility exists, so we are told, that the writers of the Gospels misinterpreted the Lord's message. The theologians suggest that Jesus might have been saying, "It is easier to thread a needle with a ship's cable than for a rich man to enter into the kingdom of God." This is unacceptable. To thread a needle with a ship's cable would be *impossible*, not difficult. It was possible for a wealthy man to enter into the kingdom of heaven. The disciples were astonished by the Lord's answer, but His reassuring words gained an abiding place in the consciousness of His followers. (For additional interpretations and homilies, consult the author's commentaries on *Mark's Superb Gospel*, Chapter 10:17-31, and *Luke's Thrilling Gospel*, Chapter 18:18-30.)

*Expository Notes on the Lord's Reply to Simon Peter*

**Then answered Peter and said unto him, Behold, we have forsaken all, and followed thee; what shall we have therefore? And Jesus said unto them, Verily I say unto you, That ye which have followed me, in the regeneration when the Son of man shall sit on the throne of his glory, ye also shall sit upon twelve thrones, judging the twelve tribes of Israel. And every one that hath forsaken houses, or brethren, or sisters, or father, or mother, or wife, or children, or lands, for my name's sake, shall receive an hundredfold, and shall inherit everlasting life. But many that are first shall be last; and the last shall be first (vv. 27-30).**

## A SIMPLE PLEA

There was something natural, and yet conspicuously awful, about Peter's question. He had witnessed the departure of the young ruler, and had heard the Master's words concerning him. Suddenly, Peter compared himself to the departing young man, and began to contrast himself with the ruler. He had been unwilling to forsake his possessions; Peter and his brethren had left everything. Actually, were they any more fortunate than he? If there were any justice and reward in following Jesus, they should be generously compensated! Today, millions of people would gladly forsake everything to know the privilege enjoyed by those disciples. To live with the Lord; to behold His marvelous miracles, and to listen to His incomparable messages would mean endless joy. That in itself would more than compensate for any sacrifice made. Alas, Peter thought only of material rewards. Throughout the Lord's ministry these contrasts became noticeable. Jesus spoke of the Bread of Life from heaven; His followers thought only of loaves and fishes! Jesus spoke of "living water" which could fill and overflow a man's soul; the disciples thought only of ordinary water to quench their thirst. They appeared to be unable to comprehend that Jesus lived in fellowship with God, where mundane, earthly values were trivial compared with eternal verities.

## A SUPERB PREDICTION

"Ye also shall sit upon twelve thrones, judging the twelve tribes of israel." That one statement of Jesus resembled the beam of a searchlight piercing the darkness of an unknown future. The Lord was quite sure that, in spite of their sin, Israel would survive, for no power could kill what God intended to keep alive. He was also convinced that His followers, rough as they seemed to be, would survive any attack made upon them; they would die in various ways, but death would never prevent their entering into the everlasting kingdom of God. Their sacrifices would never pass unnoticed; they would be remembered and rewarded, and finally given places of emminence in the kingdom of their Lord. No person can work for God and go unrewarded. The tiny seed of sacrifice germinates to produce a great harvest. The man or woman who invested time in the work of extending the kingdom would be rewarded a hundred-fold. Judged by any standard, ancient or modern, that represented a phenomenal return on the original deposit.

## A SURPRISING PRONOUNCEMENT

"But many that are first shall be last; and the last shall be first" (v. 30). "The Lord may have had in view the case of Judas, who was an early apostle, and had the care of the bag, and fell by reason of covetousness; and that of one like St. Paul, who was called late, and yet labored more abundantly than all that were before him. The application may be made with perfect truth to many professors of religion" (*The Pulpit Commentary, Matthew*. Vol. 2, p. 253).

## SURPRISES...The Result of Overconfidence

Confidence is a valuable asset for anyone attempting to extend the kingdom of Christ. It might even be called faith. Yet too much confidence leading to apathy can be extremely deadly. When a man feels he has done enough; that God should assume responsibility for all that remains, he may be walking along a road leading to disaster. Yogi Berra, the Yankee baseball player, was made famous not merely by his achievements on the playing field, but also for some pertinent remarks made at various stages of his games. Perhaps his most outstanding statement was, "It's never over 'til it's over." That represented Yogi's determination never to quit when the going was tough. At the end of his brilliant career, Paul was able to write, "I have fought a good fight, *I have finished my course*, I have kept the faith: Henceforth there is laid up for me a crown..." (2 Tim. 4:7). Alas, of the Galatian Christians, it was said, "Ye did run well; who did hinder you?" (Gal. 5:7). An athlete, who unwisely slackens his pace near the finishing line, may be overtaken. Perhaps one of the major surprises at the Judgment Seat of Christ will be the decisions of the Judge, who will examine every participant in the earthly race. Our race can never be over until it is over!!

## *SORROW...The Remembrance of Overindulgence*

"But many that are first shall be last." The eternal rewards given by God must be earned. Many of earth's glamorous leaders may have to take second place, as others, unimportant on earth, are invited to take precedence over everybody else. It is possible to be overindulgent in time, pleasures, food, drink, and many things. Anything which becomes more important than doing the will of God, should always be suspect. To the church at Smyrna, the Lord said, "...be thou faithful unto death, and I will give thee a crown of life" (Rev. 2:10). Yet to the church at Philadelphia, the Lord sent a warning, saying, "Behold, I come quickly: hold that fast which thou hast, that no man take thy crown" (Rev. 3:11).

Christian service is the greatest privilege given to man, and as long as a lost soul remains in our vicinity, work can never be finished. When Cecil Rhodes, the great pioneer in Africa, lay dying, he thought of his country and sighed, saying, "So much to do, and so little time in which to do it." When the venerable Bede was approaching the end of his life, he worked ceaselessly to finish his translation and writing. He wanted to complete that which he had commenced. Sickness or age may terminate our time of service, but when the attractiveness of other pursuits dim our vision of a God-appointed duty, life ends in sadness and regret.

## *SATISFACTION...The Reward for Overwork*

"...and the last shall be first." When the Lord had healed a man in the home of one of the chief Pharisees, He told a very wonderful parable and then said, "For whosoever exalteth himself shall be abased; and he that humbleth himself shall be exalted" (Luke 14:11). Humility is the most commendable of all qualities. The man who considers himself to be great has never recognized himself. The man who sincerely believes he is without talent, has yet to learn that "God hath chosen the foolish things of the world to confound the wise; and God hath chosen the weak things of the world to confound the things which are mighty" (1 Cor. 1:27). God has a strange but wonderful way of estimating the worth of a man's effort. If we may use a modern saying, "It is not whether we win or lose that matters, but *how we play the game.*" God did not say, "Be thou successful unto death and I will give thee a crown"; He said "BE THOU FAITHFUL." There is reason to believe that when God examines the records of His servants, the little old lady who sat in the back pew of the church to pray, might have a greater reward than the pastor who stood in the pulpit to preach. It will be much more pleasing to hear Christ saying, "Well done, thou good and faithful servant" than to blush as He says, "Ye did run well. What hindered you?"

# The Twentieth Chapter of Matthew

THEME: *The Wisdom and Work of Jesus*

OUTLINE:
    I. The Men and Their Money (Verses 1-16)
    II. The Master and His Message (Verses 17-19)
    III. The Mother and Her Mission (Verses 20-28)
    IV. The Multitude and the Miracle (Verses 29-34)

## SECTION ONE

*Expository Notes on the Parable of the Vineyard*

For the kingdom of heaven is like unto a man that is an householder, who went out early in the morning to hire labourers into his vineyard. And when he had agreed with the labourers for a penny [denarius] a day, he sent them into his vineyard. And he went out about the third hour, and saw others standing idle in the marketplace, And said unto them; Go ye also into the vineyard, and whatsoever is right I will give you. And they went their way. Again he went out about the sixth and ninth hour, and did likewise. And about the eleventh hour he went out, and found others standing idle, and saith unto them, Why stand ye here all the day idle? They say unto him, Because no man hath hired us. He saith unto them, Go ye also into the vineyard; and whatsoever is right, that shall ye receive. So when even was come, the lord of the vineyard saith unto his steward, Call the labourers, and give them their hire, beginning from the last unto the first. And when they came that were hired about the eleventh hour, they received every man a penny. But when the first came, they supposed that they should have received more; and they likewise received every man a penny. And when they had received it, they murmured against the goodman of the house, Saying, These last have wrought but one hour, and thou hast made them equal unto us, which have borne the burden and heat of the day. But he answered one of them, and said, Friend, I do thee no wrong: didst not thou agree with me for a penny? Take that thine is, and go thy way: I will give unto this last, even as unto thee. Is it not lawful for me to do what I will with mine own? Is thine eye evil, because I am

**good? So the last shall be first, and the first last: for many be called, but few chosen (vv. 1-16).**

The parable of the laborers in the vineyard is one of the greatest of the Lord's illustrations. It is recorded only by Matthew, but it has tremendous meaning for all workers for the Savior. However, ere we begin studying this Scripture, it is necessary to understand certain basic facts. Some expositors have gone to extremes in trying to discover new meanings in an old story; they have strained at a gnat and swallowed a camel!

It must be remembered that this parable is a continuation of the preceding chapter. A wealthy young ruler had refused to leave his wealth and follow Jesus, and Peter knowing this, asked what rewards he and his brethren could expect, since they had left everything to become disciples. Jesus immediately promised that all who sacrifice anything for the kingdom of heaven's sake would not go unrewarded. Yet He warned His listeners that "...many that are first shall be last; and the last shall be first" (19:30). Then He proceeded to give His parable, and in 20:16 used the same words. "So the last shall be first, and the first last." It must therefore be obvious that chapter twenty is the continuation of chapter nineteen, and the theme in this opening section is the remuneration given to workers in the vineyard of Jesus. It is very important that this fact be recognized in view of the following interpretations.

Throughout the centuries, teachers have likened the man hired at the eleventh hour to the dying thief who responded to Christ when his life was ending. The penny, or denarius, mentioned in the story is compared with eternal life, and whether a man comes at the beginning or end of his life, the reward is the same. This does not harmonize with other Scriptures. Salvation is not a reward given for faithful service, it is the gift of God (Rom. 6:23) made possible through the merits of the Lord Jesus Christ. It is "not of works, lest any man should boast" (see Eph. 2:9). If the penny given to the man who was hired at the eleventh hour represents salvation, then grace has nothing to do with redemption.

Others teach that the story covers God's *dispensational day.* They believe each party of men hired represents different ages, and the man who came late into the employ of the husbandman represents the church which responded last and received the greatest blessing. Such explanations spoil the beauty of the teachings of Christ. When men ignore the obvious, and go to great lengths to discover something new and sensational in a very simple story, they do an injustice to the Word of

God. It must always be remembered that Jesus was speaking primarily to Peter and the other disciples. What He said, had nothing to do with eternal life; it referred to the quality of the service they were about to render within the kingdom of heaven. With that thought in mind, we can now proceed to the consideration of this remarkable story.

*HIRING THE MEN*

First, notice this was the normal way of hiring servants to work on any farm or vineyard during the harvest. In Palestine, the grape harvest ripens toward the end of September, and then close on its heels the rains come. If the harvest is not ingathered before the rains break, then it is ruined; and so to get the harvest in is a frantic race against time. Any worker is welcome even if he can only give an hour to the work. Any British reader would recognize this scene, for dock workers often gather at the beginning of each working day hoping to find employment. Jesus spoke of the husbandman who "went out early in the morning to hire labourers into his vineyard." It should be noted that before they consented to work, they had to be assured of their rate of pay. If the hirer offered good wages, they were willing to work for him; if they considered the remuneration insufficient, he could go elsewhere looking for men! The forum, or market place, was the equivalent of our modern employment exchange. It is interesting to recognize that the employer made five different trips to the market place on that memorable day. This in itself is thought-provoking. Was he a stingy employer expecting few men to do the work of many? (See the special homily at the end of this section.)

*HINDERING THE MISSION*

Later, about nine o'clock in the morning, the employer again approached would-be workers, and this time the men were content to work without any agreement regarding wages. They were more anxious and less independent than the first employees. The same thing happened at midday and three o'clock in the afternoon, and again, the men did not insist on any written or oral agreement. They were willing to work for whatsoever the master offered. Did they all begin their task with enthusiasm? Is it possible the first workers persuaded the late-comers to slacken their speed, in order to save some of the harvesting for another day? If the grape-gathering could be spread over a whole week, there would be no need to stand daily in the market place. Did the master recognize this go-slow policy and was this the reason for his five visits to the market place?

## HELPING THE MASTER

"And about the eleventh hour," which was the equivalent of 5 o'clock in the afternoon, or one hour before the end of the working day, he "found others standing idle...He saith unto them, Go ye also into the vineyard; and whatsoever is right, that shall ye receive." Once again we are presented with an inescapable question. Why had the men lingered so long — probably eleven hours — in the unrelenting heat of the day? Wisdom would have suggested retirement to their home, and an early start the next day. Were they desperate? When they arrived at the vineyard, probably only forty-five minutes of working time remained, for according to Jewish law, the wages had to be paid before sunset (see Deut. 24:15). Moses recognized that poor men could not wait a week to receive wages; they needed to be paid daily in order to meet the needs of hungry children. It was quite impossible for the last of the hired men to fill as many baskets as those who had worked throughout the day. If a man meandered along at one mile per hour, even then he would have walked 12 hours in the day. On the other hand, those who started very late, however fast they walked, would hardly walk twelve miles an hour. Both the employer and the men would be aware of this undeniable fact, but it seems that a mutual trust existed in their hearts. The employer was not committed to paying high wages; but the men trusted him to do what was just. They went into the vineyard *to work*; and the other workmen ignored them. The owner was not unaware of what was taking place in his vineyard. Some of the men were only going through *the motions of working*; the late-comers *were working*!

## HEARING THE MURMURERS

At the end of the day, the husbandman commenced paying the workmen, beginning with those he had hired at five o'clock. When he gave to them wages for a whole day's work, the eyes of the other men became alight with hope. They expected more than they had been offered. Yet, when they received that for which they had agreed to work, their smiles were replaced by scowls; their expectation gave place to criticism. "But he answered one of them, and said, Friend, I do thee no wrong: didst not thou agree with me for a penny? Take that thine is, and go thy way: I will give unto this last, as even unto thee." It was as though the master said, "Friend, I have honored my word to you. Now I can do as I please with my money. Must you be jealous because I am generous?" "So the last shall be first, and the first last: for many be called, but few chosen." Anybody may be called to work in the vineyards, but few are chosen for special rewards. Some workers fill fewer baskets because they spend too much time looking at their watches! Students should find help in the consideration of the following important homily.

HOMILY

Study No. 13

### THE HUSBANDMAN...Who Paid Strange Wages!

You are a most interesting character, Mr. Unknown Husbandman, and your delightful ways have caused a great amount of discussion. A man whose actions are always unpredictable is always a source of interest, but you succeeded in surprising a world. Many of us would have liked to accompany you that morning when you went into the market place in search of laborers. Your first employees were sent into the vineyards at six a.m. After you had eaten your breakfast, you visited the workmen and decided it was necessary to employ more men. These commenced their belated shift at 9 a.m. This unusual procedure was repeated at 12 noon, and again at 3 p.m. Your method of seeking workmen seems totally foreign to western ways, and we have often wondered why you did not save time and trouble by hiring sufficient men when you first visited the market place. Yet at 5 p.m. you asked others to go and work for one hour, and at the end of the day, they received a full day's wages. In the attempt to explain this unexpected generosity, we have asked several questions. Mr. Husbandman, we wish you were here to answer them.

*Why hire so few men at 6 a.m.?*

We rejected the idea that you were stingy, and expected a few men to do the work of many. Your magnificent gesture toward the last batch of men outlaws any suggestion of stinginess. We also asked if you were inexperienced in assessing the number of men required for the completion of the task. The successive hirings denote that had such been the case, you were very slow at learning your trade. When a business man has to be taught the same lesson four times in one day, there is obviously something wrong with his business. We decided, therefore, that the fault was in the workmen. They had a go-slow policy to lengthen the time of their employment. And since you were anxious to get the job done on that particular day, it became necessary to increase the number of your workmen. The late arrivals worked well for a time, but were eventually influenced by their leaders.

*Why did the five o'clock men wait so long?*

It was a very trying experience to wait eleven hours in a market place. As the day began to pass away, and the shadows of night gathered, common sense would suggest a homegoing with a promise to return early the following morning. It must have seemed unlikely that a man would engage labor at such a late hour, yet these would-be employees continued their weary vigil. Husbandman, were they desperate? Were they anxious to obtain food for their families? Were their prayers answered when you appeared on the scene? How we would love to obtain replies to all these thought-provoking questions. Yet one thing needs no explanation. These men worked conscientiously when they entered your vineyard. They put their best endeavors into the task, and while they could not equal the number of baskets filled by the men who had slowly worked for twelve hours, they at least did their best.

*Why did you pay them a full day's wages?*

Obviously you were very pleased with their efforts. They had fewer boxes of grapes to place at your feet, but they had more perspiration on their brows. It seems to us that you were more concerned with the way they had worked than with the results achieved. They had done their utmost at the job, and you revealed your appreciation in the magnificent wages which left them speechless with surprise. Mr. Husbandman, we heard about you because Jesus of Nazareth introduced you as the theme of one of His outstanding sermons. When thinking of eternal rewards, Simon Peter said, "Behold, we have forsaken all, and followed thee; what shall we have therefore? And Jesus said, ...And every one that hath forsaken houses, or brethren, or sisters, or father, or mother...for my name's sake, shall receive an hundredfold, and shall inherit everlasting life" (Matt. 19:27-29). It seems quite clear to us now, that the Lord Jesus realized He would have many followers who would be half-hearted and unenthusiastic. He therefore desired to teach that, when He returns at the end of life's day to reward His servants, His awards will be given, not to those expecting them, but to faithful people who did their utmost in His service." (Reprinted from the author's book, *Bible Pinnacles*, pp. 91-92.)

SECTION TWO

*Expository Notes on Christ's Third Warning*
*of His Impending Death*

**And Jesus going up to Jerusalem took the twelve disciples apart on the way, and said unto them, Behold, we go up to Jerusalem; and the Son of man shall be betrayed unto the chief priests and unto the scribes, and they shall condemn him to death, And shall deliver him to the Gentiles to mock, and to scourge, and to crucify him: and the third day he shall rise again (vv. 17-19).**

## HE WAS MARVELOUSLY INSISTENT

"And Jesus...took the twelve disciples apart...." The roads leading to Jerusalem were filled with people about to attend the Passover. Everybody was delighted with the prospect of attending the feast, and privacy was almost impossible. Mark tells us "Jesus went before them" (10:32); it becomes obvious then, that He paused until they had overtaken Him, and then quietly, unobtrusively, led them from the crowded highway to a quiet place to rest and listen. Continuing noise and unceasing distraction can be harmful when the Lord would share secrets with His followers. The crowded roadway may be an ideal place for confession, but more often than not, it is unsuitable for communion. The Scripture had already said, "Be still, and know that I am God," but this becomes difficult when crowds and circumstances jostle the soul. Jesus had already predicted the events to take place in Jerusalem (Matt. 16:21 and 17:22-23), but His words had fallen on deaf ears. The disciples were now expecting the Passover crowds to crown their Master, King of Israel. The Lord realized the greatness of the disappointment about to challenge the faith of His followers, and therefore quietly insisted that they accompany Him to the secret place. If we do not recharge out batteries in the stillness, our lights will be dim in the streets. His invitation, "Come...apart...and rest awhile," is as important to us now as it was to the disciples then (see Mark 6:31).

## HE WAS MINUTELY INFORMED

(A) He knew that He would be betrayed into the hands of His enemies. (B) He knew that the Jewish rulers would condemn Him. (C) He knew the Jews would deliver their Prisoner to the Gentiles, for a death sentence could only be carried out by the Romans. (D) Jesus knew that the Gentiles would mock, scourge, and finally crucify Him. (E) The Lord also knew that the final triumph rested in the hands of God; death would be conquered, and Jesus would be raised from the dead (see Rom. 1:1-4). The Savior was completely aware of everything that threatened Him, and had He so desired, could have refrained from attending that Passover feast. That He went to Jerusalem is evidence that *He desired to go there*; He was not taken unawares, nor surprised by His enemies. He saw clearly the pathway planned by God, and with calm deliberation walked it to the end. Jesus was perfectly capable of managing His future, but obviously the disciples needed a little more instruction. Therefore, He led them back to His open-air classroom that they might hear again His greatest lessons.

## HE WAS MAJESTICALLY INSPIRED

''...and the third day he shall rise again.'' His vision was focused on the glorious coronation day and not on the shadowy valley preceding it. He saw the resplendent sunrise and not merely the darkness heralding the dawn. ''Jesus...who for the joy that was set before him endured the cross, despising the shame, and is set down at the right hand of the throne of God'' (Heb. 12:2). The disciples, however, were not as far advanced in their knowledge; they needed to be taught a little more. Without this, they would be overwhelmed by disappointment and incapable of fulfilling their commission. Yes, He would tell them once more, and then perhaps, in the hour of their approaching sorrow, they would remember His words. Jesus knew that although the corn of wheat of His teaching might appear to fall into their forgetful minds to die, it would nevertheless germinate, and eventually bear fruit. How great His CARE — CONFIDENCE — CONQUEST. We shall never be able to estimate the value of that final period of instruction given to the disciples.

## SECTION THREE

*Expository Notes on a Mother's Request to Jesus*

**Then came to him the mother of Zebedee's children with her sons, worshiping him, and desiring a certain thing of him. And he said unto her, What wilt thou? She saith unto him, Grant that these my two sons may sit, the one on thy right hand, and the other on the left, in thy kingdom. But Jesus answered and said, Ye know not what ye ask. Are**

**ye able to drink of the cup that I shall drink of, and to be baptized with the baptism that I am baptized with? They say unto him, We are able. And he saith unto them, Ye shall drink indeed of my cup, and be baptized with the baptism that I am baptized with: but to sit on my right hand, and on my left, is not mine to give, but it shall be given to them for whom it is prepared of my Father (vv. 20-23).**

This passage of Scripture is exceedingly interesting, because the accounts supplied by Matthew and Mark appear to be at variance. Mark insists that the special request for seats of honor within the kingdom was made by James and John (see Mark 10:35-45). Matthew tells us it was their mother who asked this favor of Jesus (see Matt. 20:21). This fact has attracted attention in all ages. Some theologians state that Matthew was reluctant to criticize the apostles, because at the time he wrote his Gospel, James and John were among the most revered of the church leaders. Therefore, Matthew refrained from stating anything detrimental to these men, and more or less, blamed their mother for this selfish request. Mark, who had written his gospel much earlier, did not have this problem and stated the case as it had happened. It might be nearer the truth to say all three of the family were present when the request was made. Did the brothers place the original idea into the mind of the mother or did she covet places of eminence for her children? We may never know the answer to that question, but it is evident they all shared the desire.

It has been suggested that James and John were closely related to Jesus. Matthew, Mark and John all give lists of the women who were at the Cross when Jesus was crucified. Mary Magdalene is named in all the lists found in Matthew 27:56, Mark 15:40, and John 19:25. Mary, the mother of James and Joses, must be the same person as Mary, the wife of Cleophas; therefore the third woman is described in three different ways. Matthew calls her *the mother of Zebedee's children*; Mark calls her *Salome*; and John calls her *Jesus' mother's sister*. So, then, we learn that the mother of James and John was named Salome, and that she was the sister of Mary the mother of Jesus. That would mean that James and John were almost certainly full cousins of Jesus, and it may well have been that they felt their close relationship to Jesus entitled them to a special place in His Kingdom.

## A DANGEROUS CONCEPT

It is difficult to avoid the conclusion there was something sneaky and underhanded about the request. The mother did not immediately state her request, but endeavored to exact a promise without stating what she desired. Obviously the time had been well chosen, for the other disciples were not present when the request was made. The earlier lessons concerning childlikeness had been ignored; the men and their mother coveted special privileges. The fact that they made certain the other disciples were absent, suggests they already feared the unpleasant repercussions that would come. The harmony of the entire party, the true spirit of fellowship, and the desirability of humility were of little concern to them. They thought only of selfish ambition. Jesus had already taught that he who desired preeminence should be the servant of all. That teaching was unwelcome. The disciples had more faith in the concept "God helps those who help themselves!"

## A DIVERSIFIED CUP

"But Jesus answered and said, Ye know not what ye ask. Are ye able to drink of the cup that I shall drink of, and to be baptized with the baptism that I shall be baptized with? They say unto him, We are able." It is interesting that James and John were told they would indeed drink of the Lord's cup of suffering. James became the first apostle to become a martyr (see Acts 12:2). Yet John was permitted to live until he was almost a hundred years old. The problems encountered by James were soon ended, and he went to be with his Lord; John, however, was left to be the father of the churches, to shoulder burdens, offer guidance, and frequently to become weary with inconsistencies. If we were asked which of the two apostles had the heavier cross to carry, it would be difficult to supply an answer. It might be wiser to ask which of the two leaders enjoyed the greater privilege? To serve Christ in any capacity, in any place and at any time supplies a serenity with which earth's pleasures cannot be compared.

## A DELIGHTFUL CHRIST

It is well to remember that however selfish and ill-conceived the request made by the two men, there remained, nevertheless, something pathetically wonderful about their desire. They had just been informed that their Master was going to Jerusalem to be crucified, and yet somehow they could not abandon their original belief that Jesus would still become the King of Israel. Nothing could destroy that faith. They could not understand how this would be accomplished, but nevertheless, remained convinced His kingdom would be established, and they would be there with Him. Jesus knew they were confused, but He never chastised nor criticized them. With infinite patience He listened to their request, and calmly directed their thoughts into higher and nobler channels. He said, "To sit on my right hand, and on my left, is not mine to give, but it shall be given to them for whom it is prepared of my Father." The Savior can offer many things, but eternal rewards must be earned through faithful service.

**And when the ten heard it, they were moved with against the two brethren. But Jesus called them unto him, and said, Ye know that the princes of the Gentiles exercise dominion over them, and they that are great exercise authority upon them. But it shall not be so among you: but whosoever will be great among you, let him be your minister; And whosoever will be chief among you, let him be your servant: Even as the Son of man came not to be ministered unto, but to minister, and to give his life a ransom for many (vv. 24-28).**

The anger within the ten disciples was at least understandable. The brethren had been deceitful, and had conspired to obtain privileges which every one of the twelve secretly desired. When Jesus called the dissentients unto Himself, and quietly directed their attention toward the qualities expected from every follower, He exhibited true wisdom. An unwise action, an impetuous word of rebuke might have turned the spark of discontent into a raging fire of antagonism. His carefully chosen words extinguished the blaze before it could destroy the unity of the party.

## THE POWER OF THE RULERS OF THE GENTILES

Every ambitious man yearned for prestige and power. Promotion within the ranks of the Roman army not only increased the soldier's pay; it provided superiority over other men. Every centurion had a hundred men who obeyed his commands. Each governor exercised authority over lesser officials; all potentates were surrounded by slaves ready to do their bidding. Nevertheless, authority alone was insufficient to encourage affection. Men feared their rulers; sometimes they respected those in command, but they obeyed only because there was no safe alternative. A monarch who visits a hospital might gain the respect and admiration of the patients, but an understanding, sympathetic nurse is far more likely to gain appreciation and love. When Jesus compared and contrasted the gentile empire with the kingdom of heaven, the lines of demarcation were clearly seen. The chief characteristic of God's trusted leaders was love and not authority; service, and not the ability to issue commands. Beggars appreciated gifts from wealthy men, but those who tended their wounds and shared their needs and sorrows won the hearts of suffering people. There have been occasions when a warm handshake was more likely to succeed than an eloquent sermon. Sometimes, a loving embrace and a sympathetic tear are more effective than hours of academic counseling.

## THE PRIVILEGE OF THE REPRESENTATIVES OF GRACE

Within the kingdom of God, the greatest instruments of blessing are nearly always inconspicuous. The disciples distributed the loaves and fishes, but an unknown boy made it all possible. A man's speech may be dramatic and his features very beautiful, but the unseen members of his body are responsible for everything he says and does. Without a heart, lungs, blood vessels, bones and sinues, nothing would function through his lifetime. Great ships are driven by powerful engines, airplanes carry hundreds of men and women into the skies, but in both instances the secret of success rests in the oil can held in the hands of an unknown mechanic. Man thinks that God's BIG PEOPLE are famous speakers, wealthy sponsors, and popular artists able to command great audiences. Such folk may be invaluable to the work of the church, but God has the ability to find greatness even in unlikely places. His diamonds are produced from obscurity; His whitest lilies emerge from the dirtiest ponds. Jesus saw the attributes of the rulers among the Gentiles, and said, "It shall not be so among you: but whosoever will be great among you, let him be your minister." "If you would reign with Me, be the servants of My people!" Human recognition may never excite the soul nor brighten the future, but humility and sincerity are found in all to be honored when God establishes His everlasting kingdom.

## THE PATTERN SET BY THE REDEEMER FROM GOD

"And whosoever will be chief among you, let him be your servant: Even as the Son of man came not to be ministered unto, but to minister, and to give his life a ransom for many." Jesus taught that the disciples should follow His example; no other standard of excellence was acceptable. If the Son of man stretched out a helping hand to lepers and others in desperate need, the disciples should never, under any circumstances, be unkind to anyone. There are ways by which men may behold the attributes of God. They may see the wonder of His creativity in the world He made; they may recognize His love for colors, special designs, and even His architectural brilliance in the hills whose summits point to heaven. Nevertheless, the beauty of Jesus can only be seen as it shines through His followers. Christ's amazing love is expressed in the one supreme statement, "The Son of man came...to give his life a ransom for many." Jesus exchanged the glories of heaven for the agony of the Cross, because in His estimation, the greatest privilege in the world was the helping of needy men and women.

During my ministry in Australia, I met a man who was affectionately known as "Mr. Bott." His name actually was Mr. Bottomley and his testimony will live forever. A derelict, sleeping with eleven others of his type on the cement floor of a basement in a condemned building, this unfortunate man was discovered by the Rev. McKibbin, a very wonderful Methodist minister, and ultimately placed in the back room of a church no longer used for services. To kill time, Mr. Bott used some of his pension to buy flower seeds, and soon had a small garden filled with colorful plants. When children paused to look at the strange old man, they were given bunches of flowers to take to their teachers. Soon, all the citizens of Camdenville were aware of the old man in the church, and one day they asked if he would start a Sunday school. His work became so successful that the church reopened with Mr. Bott as the unofficial pastor. Reporting the news, the local newspaper printed a long article, part of which I now reprint.

"At sixty years of age, Mr. Bottomley was a human derelict drifting along the roads, carrying his few belongings, and often drinking to forget. At seventy years of age, when many men have given life away, Mr. Bottomley started to build a new life for himself, quite different from the existence of the previous ten years. Now, at seventy five, he is one of the busiest men in Newtown, because he has adopted more than a hundred children, teenagers, young men and women. The little church in Laura Street, Camdenville, which was closed and empty five years ago, is now the center of busy social life and youthful activity. Mr. Bottomley runs a cricket team and a vigaro team, which compete with other teams in Sydney. He sees that his adopted charges go to gymnasium and handicraft classes, and every Sunday his children crowd the church for Sunday-school."

I shall never forget the moment when this wonderful old man said, "I have to be careful of what I do or say, for not very long ago, a little girl put her arms around my neck and said, 'I love you, you are God.'

I did not want to break her faith, so I explained that I wasn't God, but that *I was trying to be like Jesus.*"

> Let the beauty of Jesus be seen in me;
> All His wonderful passion and purity!
> O Thou Spirit divine, all my nature refine,
> Till the beauty of Jesus be seen in me.

## SECTION FOUR

*Expository Notes on the Giving of Sight to Two Blind Men*

**And as they departed from Jericho, a great multitude followed him. And, behold, two blind men sitting by the wayside, when they heard that Jesus passed by, cried out, saying, Have mercy on us, O Lord, thou Son of David. And the multitude rebuked them, because they should hold their peace: but they cried the more, saying, Have mercy on us, O Lord, thou Son of David. And Jesus stood still, and called them, and said, What will ye that I shall do unto you? They say unto him, Lord, that our eyes may be opened. So Jesus had compassion on them, and touched their eyes: and immediately their eyes received sight, and they followed him (vv. 29-34).**

## A DESCRIPTION OF THE REGION

Jericho, as we know it today, is a very pretty oasis in a surrounding desert. Fruit stands line the roadway, and everywhere huge pipes may be seen carrying water from the inexhaustible springs of Elisha. The is always warm and humid, and many tourists arrive daily from all parts of the world. The Jericho mentioned in the New Testament was a place of magnificence and beauty. It is necessary to appreciate this fact before we try to understand the accounts supplied by the writers of the Gospels. Dr. Geikie, in his great book writes about Jericho (*The Life of Christ,* Volume Two, p. 384), "...the road led down to the sunken channel of the Jordan, and the 'divine district' of Jericho. This small but rich plain was the most luxuriant spot in Palestine. Sloping gently upwards from the level of the Dead Sea, 1350 feet under the level of the Mediterranean, to the stern background of the hills of Quadrantana, it had the climate of lower Egypt, and displayed the vegetation of the tropics. Its fig trees were preeminently famous; it was unique in its growth of palms of various kinds; its crops of dates were a proverb;

the balsom plant, which grew principally here, furnished a costly perfume, and was in great repute for healing wounds; maize yielded a double harvest; wheat ripened a whole month earlier than in Galilee. Innumerable bees found a Paradise in the many aromatic flowers and plants...which filled the air with odors and the landscape with beauty. Rising like an amphitheatre from amidst this luxuriant scene, lay Jericho, the chief place east of Jerusalem, seven or eight miles distant from the Jordan, on swelling slopes seven hundred feet about the bed of the river. Its gardens and groves were thickly interspersed with mansions, and covering seventy furlongs from north to south, and twenty from east to west, were divided by a strip of wilderness. The town had had an eventful history. Once the stronghold of the Canaanites, it was still in the days of Christ, surrounded by towers and castles. A great stone aqueduct of eleven arches brought a copious supply of water to the city, and the Roman military road ran through it. The houses themselves, however, though showy, were not substantial, but were built mostly of sun-dried bricks, like those of Egypt; so that now, as in the similar case of Babylon, Nineveh, or Egypt, after long desolation, hardly a trace of them remains.'' With this description in hand, we can now proceed to the second part of our consideration.

## A DIFFERENCE IN THE RECORDS

It is impossible to read carefully the accounts of miracle as presented in the first three Gospels without becoming aware of discrepancies. Matthew says that *two* blind men came to Jesus as He was leaving (Matt. 20:29-30). Mark says that *one* beggar, a man named Bartimaeus, came to Christ as the Lord was about *to enter* the city (Mark 10:46). Luke apparently agrees with Mark (Luke 18:35), but infers the incident happened "as he was come nigh unto Jericho." This could have been at the entrance gate, or at some other place in close proximity to the city. Josephus stated that over three million people attended the Passover, and it is certain that very many of these pilgrims passed through Jericho. This was the greatest time of the year for beggars, and probably there were dozens of these along the highway. Many of them made more money at that period of the year than they did at any other time. People were in the right frame of mind to give, and every beggar would take advantage of the situations. St. Augustine in his writings suggested this account in the Gospel was really a few incidents joined together. He even inferred that the blind beggar first approached the Lord some distance from the city, but was discouraged by the attitude of the crowd.

Later, probably the next day, he came again with another beggar, and received sight. Some other church leaders taught that Bartimaeus became one of the best-known members of the early church, and by the time Mark wrote his Gospel, had gained spiritual notoriety! Let it be admitted that however attractive these ideas might appear to be, there is no historical evidence to support the suggestions.

There need be no contradictions in the various narratives. Jericho was a great city, around which went a highway specially built by the Romans to the movement of their armies. All cities of major significance were surrounded by walls, and for the purpose of expediency, gates were provided allowing access from all directions. Probably a million and a half pilgrims, at least, came to Jerusalem from the direction of Jericho, and it is very difficult to conceive these struggling to get through a very overcrowded city when the Romans had provided a very accessible bypass. The gate facing that military highway provided an easy way by which people desiring entrance to Jericho could achieve their purpose, but for all others, not wishing to enter the city, they could easily stay on the highway. Thus that particular gate became both an arrival and a departure point for travelers. This idea appears to be expressed by Mark, for he described the incident with thought-provoking words: ''And they came to Jericho: and as he went out of Jericho.'' Thus in two simple sentences, Mark described the Lord's arrival and departure. It would have been easy for a second beggar to be attracted by the first, and thus be mentioned in the Gospel.

## THE DETERMINATION IN THE REQUESTS

Luke says: '''And they which went before rebuked him, that he should hold his peace: but he cried so much the more, Thou Son of David, have mercy on me' (Luke 18:39). The *Amplified New Testament* renders the passage: 'They told him, Jesus of Nazareth is passing by. And he shouted saying, Jesus, Son of David, take pity and have mercy on me. But those that were in front, reproved him [telling him] to keep quiet; *yet he screamed and shrieked* so much the more, Son of David, take pity and have mercy on me.' This translation rests upon the fact that Luke uses two different words. *Eboeesen* translated 'shout' or 'he cried' means: 'to lift up one's voice and cry aloud.' *Ekrazen* , the word used in verse 39, and translated 'he cried so much the more', is a much stronger word. Thayer says it means: 'to cry out; to cry aloud; to vociferate particularly of inarticulate cries.' It is also used to express a croak, hence a scream or desperate screech. The first cry of the beggar, or perhaps the beggars, was born of intense desire; the second by deepening despair. The first was produced by a longing for help; the second by the fear they would not get what was needed. And when we recall that in the earlier chapters, Luke emphasized the value of prayer, this incident adds to the quality of the manuscript '' (condensed from the author's commentary, *Luke's Thrilling Gospel,* p. 391.)

## THE DELIVERANCE IN THE RESPONSE

''And Jesus stood still, and called them'' (v. 32). Above all the noise made by the crowd, Jesus heard the cry of the beggars. Similarly, above all the noise made by the storm in Galilee, He heard the desperate cry of the disciple who said, ''Lord, save us: we perish'' (Matt. 8:25). It is stimulating to remember that in spite of all the demands made upon Him, He still has the same characteristics. He is never too busy to hear the cry of anxious people. The rebuke given by the crowd might be explained in two ways. All rabbis going to the Passover had their own congregation of people who followed in the hope of hearing words of wisdom. It might have been that the desperate shrieks of the beggars made it difficult to hear what Jesus was teaching. On the other hand, it might have been that the listeners failed to understand how Jesus could be interested in two insignificant blind men. That the suppliants disregarded the advice or commands issued, indicated ''they meant business.'' This alone is *true prayer.* Jesus said, ''Men ought always to pray, and *not to faint.*'' It is interesting to note the men first asked for *mercy*; when Jesus called them and asked what they desired, they were far more specific. They said, ''Lord, that our eyes may be opened.'' They who are truly aware of the urgency of their need never waste time nor words! ''So Jesus had compassion on them, and touched their eyes: and immediately their eyes received sight.''

## THE DISCERNMENT IN THEIR RESOLVE

''...and they followed him.'' Let us not neglect to see the significance of their action. As has already been said, Passover was the one tremendous opportunity when beggars could reap a financial harvest. There were always Pharisees and others who loved to give ostentatiously so they could gain the praise of men. There were always travelers passing to and from, but this was the only time in the year when millions of people were passing by, and furthermore, their preparation for the feast promoted generosity. They wished to gain favor with God, and believed

He would take into consideration almsgiving. If they gave, they would be blessed; God would give to them. Every beggar at Passover time had a chance to become wealthy. Probably, at that time, begging was the most lucrative occupation in Israel. There is reason to believe that even people with eyesight feigned blindness in order to take advantage of the generosity of pilgrims. When the beggar left everything to follow Jesus, he was probably making the greatest sacrifice of his life. He never hesitated; he abandoned his quest for coins; he had discovered a goldmine. (See the special homily, ''The Man who could See without Eyes.'' The author's commentary on Luke's Gospel, pp. 392-394.)

# The Twenty-first Chapter of Matthew

THEME: *Jesus Reaches Jerusalem*

OUTLINE:
    I. The Arrival of the King (Verses 1-11)
    II. The Anger of the King (Verses 12-17)
    III. The Action of the King (Verses 18-22)
    IV. The Answer of the King (Verses 23-27)
    V. The Announcements of the King (Verses 28-46)

## SECTION ONE

*Expository Notes on Christ's Arrival in Jerusalem*

**And when they drew nigh unto Jerusalem, and were come to Bethphage, unto the mount of Olives, then sent Jesus two disciples, Saying unto them, Go into the village over against you, and straightway ye shall find an ass tied, and a colt with her: loose them, and bring them unto me. And if any man say aught unto you, ye shall say, The Lord hath need of them; and straightway he will send them. All this was done, that it might be fulfilled which was spoken by the prophet, saying, Tell ye the daughter of Sion, Behold, thy King cometh unto thee, meek, and sitting upon an ass, and a colt the foal of an ass. And the disciples went, and did as Jesus commanded them, And brought the ass, and the colt, and put on them their clothes, and they set him thereon (vv. 1-7).**

## THE SPECIAL EXPECTANCY

Jesus was now commencing the final and most important phase of His life. He was to visit Jerusalem for the last time, and had no illusions about the outcome. We can only wonder and worship as we recognize the serenity of His soul, and the calm orderly way in which He managed His affairs. "Bethphage is an Aramaic name meaning 'the house of unripe figs.' It was a small place on the mount of Olives, on the way from Jerusalem to Jericho, and close to Bethany. It was a Sabbath's day's journey from Jerusalem. No trace of it now remains. It is never mentioned in the Old Testament'' (*Unger's Bible Dictionary*, p. 141). It is possible that when the disciples went to fulfill the Lord's command, the Savior took advantage of the opportunity to visit His friends in Bethany. The detailed description of what the men were expected to find in seeking the donkey suggests Jesus had already made arrangements with one of His friends.

Matthew tells us there were two donkeys; an ass and her colt, but Mark and Luke only mention the colt. Probably Matthew was correct; obviously the younger animal had never been broken, and its mother was in close proximity to her offspring. Mark and Luke apparently were more concerned with the fact that the unbroken colt never resisted the Lord; that the ensuing ride was miraculously peaceful. Matthew, however, describes a scene which would be perfectly normal. When the men took away the colt, the mother naturally followed. The statement, ''The Lord hath need of them,'' seemed to be the prearranged password by which the owner of the animals would know they were not being stolen. His willingness to comply with the Master's command suggests gratitude, affection, and possibly discipleship. Obviously Jesus was not a stranger to this unknown friend.

## THE SEETHING EXCITEMENT

Aware that the prophet had predicted this event, the disciples brought the animals, and thrilled by an increasing excitement, took off some of their garments and placed these on both animals. At that moment they did not know which beast would carry Jesus. The word translated ''clothes'' is *himatia* which means upper garment or coat or cloak. Using these as a saddle, they prepared to follow Jesus to what they hoped would be a public recognition of His kingship. Zechariah had written: ''Rejoice greatly, O daughter of Zion; shout, O daughter of Jerusalem: behold, thy King cometh unto thee: he is just, and having salvation; lowly, and riding upon an ass, and upon a colt the foal of an ass'' (Zech. 9:9). Believing the time for the fulfillment of this prediction had arrived, the elated disciples were ready for anything; their enthusiasm was contagious, for as the procession proceeded along the streets, enormous crowds appeared to join in the celebrations, and the streets were soon filled with ecstatic cries, ''Hosanna to the Son of David: Blessed is he that cometh in the name of the Lord; Hosanna in the highest.''

That resplendent scene was perfect except for one detail. Kings always road on horses; the symbols of royalty and power. Donkeys or asses were only used by judges and governors when they embarked on peaceful missions. (See Judges 5:10 and 10:4.) Had the Lord ridden upon a horse, His action might have fanned patriotic flames into a raging inferno of rebellion, and this inevitably would have led to violence. It is not without interest that the presence of two animals on that memorable occasion has engaged the attention of many theologians. For example, Jerome offered a mystical explanation. He believed the ass represented the Jewish people, which had long borne the yoke of the law; the colt represents the Gentiles; as yet unbroken. Jerome believed that by the triumphant entry, Christ proclaimed He was destined to be Lord of the entire world.

**And a very great multitude spread their garments in the way; others cut down branches from the trees, and strawed them in the way. And the multitudes that went before, and that followed, cried, saying, Hosanna to the Son of David: Blessed is he that cometh in the name of the Lord; Hosanna in the highest. And when he was come into Jerusalem, all the city was moved, saying, Who is this? And the multitude said, This is Jesus the prophet of Nazareth of Galilee (vv. 8-11).**

## THE STRANGE EXCLAMATION

"And when he was come into Jerusalem, all the city was moved, saying, *Who* is this?" The *Amplified New Testament* translates this verse: "And when he entered Jerusalem, all the city became agitated, and trembling with excitement said, *Who* is this?" It seems a little strange that after three-and-a-half years of the most sensational ministry ever known among men, that any person should ask such a question. Perhaps the statement reflects the fact the Lord had spent most of His time in Galilee. If the citizens had asked, " *What* is this?" the question would not present problems. Continuing noise in the streets; increasing crowds, almost beyond control, would naturally arouse curiosity, and the citizens would have asked, "What is happening today?" Yet the people in Jerusalem did not inquire concerning the events taking place; they looked at the central Figure, and apparently had no idea as to His identity. Although Jesus had spent most of His time elsewhere, He had nevertheless preached in Jerusalem and had performed miracles in the area. Why then did they not recognize Him? Possibly the addage was as true then, as it is now: "None are so blind as they who have no wish to see." Such people still exist. They explain answers to prayers as coincidences and miracles as natural phenomena. Every aspect of faith is subjected to scientific scrutiny, and by the time the investigation is completed, nothing remains but argument and dead dogma. Many of the critics walked in darkness because to them the light was unattractive.

## THE SURPRISING EXPLANATION

"And the multitude said, This is Jesus the prophet of Nazareth of Galilee." At first glance, this testimony seems inspiring, fascinating, and wonderful. Yet it fell short of what might have been expected. Everything about the scene suggested royalty; the King had arrived. It has been claimed that silence, sometimes, is more eloquent than words. That Matthew did not write "This is the king of Israel" reflects upon the inadequacy of the testimony. The crowds were willing to go so far, and no farther. The Prophet of Nazareth might perform miracles and preach sermons; at least they were anticipating such events. Yet, if He were "THE KING OF ISRAEL" they would be expected to fall at His feet; do homage, and honor Him whom God had sent. Apparently they were more concerned with what He might do *for them*, than with anything they might do *for Him*. It is wise to remember that even these strange people were among the number for whom "The Son of man...gave his life a ransom for many..." (20:28).

SECTION TWO

*Expository Notes on the Cleansing of the Temple*

**And Jesus went into the temple of God, and cast out all them that sold and bought in the temple, and overthrew the tables of the moneychangers, and the seats of them that sold doves, And said unto them, It is written, My house shall be called the house of prayer; but ye have made it a den of thieves. And the blind and the lame came to him in the temple; and he healed them. And when the chief priests and scribes saw the wonderful things that he did, and the children crying in the temple, and saying, Hosanna to the Son of David; they were so displeased, And said unto him, Hearest thou what these say? And Jesus said unto them, Yea; have ye never read, Out of the mouth of babes and sucklings thou hast perfected praise? And he left them, and went out of the city into Bethany; and he lodged there (vv. 12-17).**

This is a very interesting and vital story in which there are at least five areas of thought awaiting investigation. We must proceed slowly and carefully, for there is much to be learned from this account of the cleansing of the temple.

## THE DENIAL OF SACRED PRIVILEGES

When God spoke concerning the Gentiles who would come to His house He said: "Also the sons of the stranger, that join themselves to the LORD, to serve him, and to love the name of the LORD....Even them will I bring to my holy mountain, and make them joyful in my house of prayer...for mine house shall be called an house of prayer for *all people*" (Isa. 56:6-7). Unfortunately, the Pharisees had placed severe restrictions on the fulfillment of the ancient promise. The outer court, which was one of several courts connected with the temple, was "the open area extending from the inner side of the porticoes....It was here that Jews and Gentiles were free to mingle, but beyond the *Soregh*, only Jews were permitted to go. This outer court was paved with variegated stones" (*The Zondervan Pictorial Encyclopedia of the Bible*, Vol. 5, p. 652).

It should be remembered that the selling and sacrificing of animals were essential to the temple ritual, but it is worthy of attention that this feature was confined to that part of the temple visited by Gentiles. The Jews would never have permitted filth of any kind to desecrate their portion of the sacred house. In addition to this, a thoroughfare ran through this part of the temple grounds; it was a short cut by which travelers and others could avoid going a roundabout way to their destination. Since the Gentiles were not permitted to proceed further, their prayers had to be said in that outer court, and the noise, smells, and other distractions made meditation extremely difficult. Gentiles were forced to worship God amid intolerable conditions, and this was a violation of the promises of God. That in itself would have aroused the indignation of Jesus.

## THE DENUNCIATION OF SINFUL PRACTICES

The only type of currency acceptable within the temple precincts was that issued by the religious authorities. No coin bearing the inscription of a heathen monarch was acceptable, and thus worshipers from foreign lands were obliged to change their money. The moneychangers cheated all their clients, and it has been estimated that Caiaphas, the high priest, made over three million dollars per year from these detestable transactions. Mark supplies an interesting detail (Mark 11:11). "And

Jesus entered into Jerusalem, and into the temple: and *when he had looked round about upon all things*...he went out unto Bethany with the twelve." The cleansing of the temple was not produced by a sudden, spontaneous burst of anger. Jesus had thought all night about the disgusting scenes witnessed in the sanctuary, and His subsequent action was the product of deliberate planning. These money-making hypocrites were erecting barriers along the highway which led to the heart of God. They were making a mockery of the most sacred things in existence, and their actions were completely reprehensible.

## THE DISPLAY OF SPECIAL POWERS

"And the blind and the lame came to him in the temple; and he healed them." The moneychangers had gone; the Lord was alone. Then, aware of movement, He looked toward a door to see a lame man leading a blind friend. Doubtless they had heard of Christ's exploits, and knowing He was inside the temple, came hoping for healing. What Jesus did that day echoed around the world. He was preaching one of His greatest sermons. When He has been able to cleanse a human heart, thus making it the true temple it was always supposed to be, anything becomes possible. There will never be need to wander in darkness nor stumble amidst the problems of life. He had taught this lesson earlier (John 2:13-17) but unfortunately, the moneychangers were slow learning their lessons. Alas, we also make the same mistake. The poet knew this for he wrote:

> Cleanse me from my sin, Lord;
> Put Thy power within, Lord,
> Take me as I am, Lord,
> And make me all Thine own.
> Keep me day by day, Lord:
> Underneath Thy sway, Lord;
> Make my heart Thy palace,
> And Thy royal throne.

## THE DISPLEASURE OF STUPID PEOPLE

"And when the chief priests and scribes saw the wonderful things that he did, and the children crying in the temple, and saying, Hosanna to the Son of David; they were sore displeased." This means *they were very indignant*. "The wonderful things that he did" must refer to the healing the blind and lame; the Lord's critics could be infuriated even by acts of mercy. The statement perhaps also refers to the noise made by the children, and this has created debate within the church. The term "children" was often applied to adults, and some think the reference was to disciples whose enthusiasm had gotten out of control. The audience, more or less, had become a noisy, hysterical crowd, and the priests considered this a defilement of the sanctuary. It has been claimed that had the children been out of control, the temple police or guards would have removed them from the building. The evidence does not support this interpretation. At that moment many unusual things were happening within the sanctuary. People were running here and there; excitement was tremendous, and everyone wished to see the men who had been healed. Even the guards would have been spellbound, and under such pressure, would have been oblivious to children's behavior. It seems inconceivable that any one could be critical, when the temple had suddenly become a house of praise. During the Feast of Tabernacles songs were permitted, but during Passover, the priests preferred silence to praise. The dignity of the house was more to be desired than miracles which liberated people.

## THE DEPARTURE WITH SIGNIFICANT PURPOSE

"And he left them." It is always a solemn occasion when Christ leaves anyone! And yet, the question might be asked, "What more could He have done?" He had already advised against casting pearls before swine, and obviously the temple authorities had no intention of listening to His message. They loathed Jesus, and resisted any interference. To continue preaching to people who had closed their minds to the truth was to increase the condemnation of those who rejected the message. Difficult as the statement might sound, the departure of the Lord from such folk was evidence of His mercy. To continue preaching the gospel to those whose hearts are hardened increases the condemnation of sinners. There are degrees of punishment in eternity (see Matt. 10:15; 11:22-24). Christ sometimes leaves people in order to *decrease* judgment on their guilty souls. It is worthy of consideration that under all circumstances, Christ always did the utmost for undeserving men and women.

And Jesus "went out of the city into Bethany; and he lodged there." Some teachers believe that Jesus spent the night in one of the many booths erected for pilgrims during the Passover week, but this idea is not conclusive. The whereabouts of the disciples were always known to the Lord's friends in Bethany. When the home and hearts of His best friends were ready to welcome the Lord, it would have been inconceivable that He would spend the night in any other place.

## SECTION THREE

*Expository Notes on the Cursing of the Fig Tree*

**Now in the morning as he returned into the city, he hungered. And when he saw a fig tree in the way, he came to it, and found nothing thereon, but leaves only, and said unto it, Let no fruit grow on thee henceforward for ever. And presently the fig tree withered away. And when the disciples saw it, they marvelled, saying, How soon is the fig tree withered away! Jesus answered and said unto them, Verily I say unto you, If ye have faith, and doubt not, ye shall not only do this which is done to the fig tree, but also if ye shall say unto this mountain, Be thou removed, and be thou cast into the sea; it shall be done. And all things, whatsoever ye shall ask in prayer, believing, ye shall receive (vv. 18-22).**

Throughout the centuries, many questions have been asked concerning this immortal incident. There is reason to believe that the cursing of the fig tree was among the Lord's most provocative actions.

## A STRANGE PROBLEM

''Now in the morning as he returned into the city, he hungered'' (v. 18). ''Things were happening within the temple area which were an insult to the name of God, and Jesus knew He would be obliged to take action against those who were responsible for the evil deeds. Having looked at the despicable scene, He returned to the vicinity of Bethany. Some expositors think He stayed two days, and that during this time, He visited Martha, Mary and Lazarus, and enjoyed a supper in the home of Simon, the leper. If this were so, He would have had sufficient time in which to meet all His friends. However, it appears that at least for the final night, Jesus did not sleep in the home of His friends. Probably He spent those hours in prayer and fasting, gleaning the strength necessary to challenge the religious authorities within the temple. It is written that 'he was hungry.' Obviously, Martha had not supplied breakfast that morning'' (reprinted from the author's commentary, *Mark's Superb Gospel*. See the notes on Mark 11:10-14). No one can be dogmatic in attempting to interpret this Scripture. It is quite inconceivable that the Lord would have been in the vicinity of Bethany without visiting His friends. Yet, He could easily have explained to them the necessity for being alone to prepare for His immediate future. He could have warned them of His intention to rise early from bed, and that because of this fact, He would be making an early departure. Perhaps He instructed Martha not to prepare breakfast. On the other hand, as has been suggested, Jesus might have spent the entire night on the hillside, but would we be justified in assuming the disciples followed His example? Either way, it is understandable why, after an indeterminate number of hours, "he hungered."

## A STRANGER PROBLEM

When Jesus came to the barren fig tree and found no fruit, He cursed the tree, and ultimately it died. Mark adds the intriguing statement, "he found nothing but leaves; *for the time of figs was not yet.*" Mark also implies that the tree did not die immediately. It was on the morning of *the following day* that Peter said, "Master, behold, the fig tree which thou cursedst is withered away" (Mark 11:21). Matthew appears to be at variance for he wrote (21:19): "And presently." "And the fig tree withered up at once" (*The Amplified New Testament*). The Greek word translated "presently" is *parachreema* which according to Thayer means: "immediately; forthwith; instantly." I see no problem in what appears to be conflicting texts. Probably when the Lord uttered His condemnatory words, the fig tree immediately began to die. As Mark stated "it dried up from the roots." The process of dying began immediately, but the following morning when the disciples saw the tree again, the tree was completely dead. It suggests to many readers that since the Lord cursed the tree "for the time of figs was not yet" (Mark 11:13), He was acting hastily, expecting a tree to bare fruit out of season! It must be remembered that in Eastern countries, the figs often appear *before* the leaves. Jesus was perfectly justified in expecting to find fruit, but alas, the tree, like the Jewish leaders, was famous for empty profession. W. E. Shewell-Cooper has written an illuminating paragraph explaining this scripture. "In the East the fig tree produces two definite crops of figs per season. The normal winter figs ripen in May and June and the summer figs in late August and September. Sometimes, one crop overlaps the other. The baby fruit buds are usually seen in February before the leaves appear in April each year. It is possible to pick figs over nine or ten months of the year in Palestine...."

Our Lord condemned a fig tree at Passover time on Mount Olivet (Matt. 11:13; Matt. 21:19). This tree should have borne early, ripe figs.

The Lord would have known whether the tree should have been cropping. Moses had said that fruit borne on trees by the wayside could be picked by passers-by. A fig tree produces masses of large green leaves and gives ample welcome shade in a hot country. "The fig tree was cursed not for being *barren* but for being *false!*" The statement, "for the time of figs was not yet," can only mean, "For the time of *fruit gathering* or *the time of harvest*, was not yet" (quoted from *The Zondervan Pictorial Encyclopedia of the Bible*, Vol. 2, p. 534).

## THE STRANGEST PROBLEM

"If ye have faith...ye shall say unto this mountain, Be thou removed, and be thou cast into the sea; [and] it shall be done." The other, earlier problems fade into insignificance when compared with this one. Jesus was standing on the Mount of Olives, and at first glance it would seem He was teaching the possibility of lifting the hill from its foundations and casting it into the ocean. At the risk of offending some of the more ardent readers let it be said that this cannot supply a satisfactory exposition of the text. If any man or woman, completely filled with faith, can remove a mountain from its place, we must conclude there has never been such a person. No mountain has ever been flung through space to land with a splash in any sea. A demented person might *think* himself capable of such an act, but if he tries, the end result advertises his stupidity. Someday, an earthquake will split the Mount of Olives (Zech. 14:4), but even then, it will not be cast into the sea. We must therefore seek an explanation elsewhere.

The Lord immediately spoke about the value of prevailing prayer, and indicated that "...whatsoever ye shall ask in prayer, believing, ye shall receive." Let no one accuse me of "tampering" with the Word of God. There is a prevailing sanity about all God's dealings with men and women. If, perchance, I were able to cast the Mount of Olives into the sea, I would only succeed in spoiling God's handiwork, and the resultant gash in the earth would cause disaster, pain, and death. A mountain falling into the sea would create a major tidal wave which would devastate all lands adjacent to the Mediterranean Sea. Yet, if in simple faith, I can look at my mountainous problems, and banish them from mind, that surely would be in keeping with the promise of Christ. If I truly believe that God will never fail nor forsake me, whatever my circumstances might be, then I can enjoy peace that passeth understanding. Sometimes a prospector examining drab stones in a river bed discovers golden nuggets. This is true for those who carefully examine the "problem texts" of the Bible. Often, in the most unlikely places, it is possible to find promises capable of removing all our mountains. These discoveries supply happiness of incalculable worth.

## SECTION FOUR

*Expository Notes on the Way Christ Confounded His Critics*

**And when he was come into the temple, the chief priests and the elders of the people came unto him as he was teaching, and said, By what authority doest thou these things? and who gave thee this authority? And Jesus answered and said unto them, I also will ask you one thing, which if ye tell me, I in like wise will tell you by what authority I do these things. The baptism of John, whence was it? from heaven or of men? And they reasoned with themselves, saying, If we shall say, From heaven; he will say unto us, Why did ye not then believe him? But if we shall say, Of men; we fear the people; for all hold John as a prophet. And they answered Jesus, and said, We cannot tell. And he said unto them, Neither tell I you by what authority I do these things (vv. 23-27).**

## A DANGEROUS CHALLENGE

The chief rulers of Israel were worried; their influence was being undermined; their authority was being challenged by the ministry of Christ. Earlier, when John was preaching in the Jordan Valley, the rulers had sent their representatives to question the evangelist concerning his identity, authority, and work (John 1:19). This kind of interrogation had been avoided regarding Jesus. Most of the Lord's ministry had been exercised in Galilee, and the confrontation with Jesus, which was inevitable, had been postponed as long as possible. His arrival in Jerusalem, where great crowds listened to His teaching, brought, so to speak, the conflict into the backyard of the Sanhedrin. The challenge of the Nazarene could no longer be ignored; something had to be done quickly. Vast multitudes were already in the city, and in the days immediately before Passover, people were eager to see or hear anything exciting. The presence of the famous Preacher from Nazareth added zest to the enthusiasm, and the Pharisees were becoming extremely nervous. Somehow, somewhere, this menace from Galilee had to be discredited before the multitudes, and the need was urgent. Therefore, "...the chief priests and the elders of the people came unto him as he was teaching, and said, By what authority doest thou these things?" (Matt. 21:23).

## A DISCERNING CHRIST

"And Jesus answered and said unto them, I also will ask you one thing....The baptism of John, whence was it? from heaven, or of men?" The Lord was both wise and extremely careful for "Jesus did not commit himself unto them, because *he knew all men*...he knew what was in man" (John 2:24-25). The rulers were already planning how to terminate Christ's ministry! Doubtless they planned to entangle Him in His words. "Jesus," they asked, "Who gave You authority to act in this fashion? By whose permission have You brought Your teaching and deeds into the sacred confines of this city? Who authorized You to interfere with the normal business procedures of the temple? We are in charge here, and we did not tell You to take the law into Your own hands. Who are You?" Calmly the Lord looked at them, knowing their evil intentions. Had He replied, "I do this by my own authority," He could have been arrested for blasphemy. Had He claimed authorization from God, they could have brought a similar charge against Him. Yet, had He ignored their question, the crowd of listeners might have misunderstood His silence. He was not obliged to answer any question. His works alone were sufficient justification for any claim He made. Sometimes, "fools rush in where angels fear to tread." Men of lesser stature might have argued and caused an uproar. Assessing the dangers enshrined in the question, Jesus proceeded to ask a question of His own. There are times when the longest way around is the shortest way home!

## A DELIBERATE CONSIDERATION

"They reasoned with themselves, saying, If we shall say, From heaven; he will say unto us, Why did ye not then believe him? But if we shall say, Of men; we fear the people; for all hold John as a prophet. And they answered Jesus, and said, We cannot tell." Their reply was astonishing, for they were scholars responsible for interpreting legal matters within the nation. They were admitting limitations in their knowledge; but their hypocrisy was recognized by all who heard the reply. John the Baptist, who had never performed a single miracle, and Jesus who performed miracles constantly, were both rejected by the Jewish leaders. They alone, so they believed and taught, were the sole vicegerents of the Almighty, and no other person could be permitted to trespass on the holy ground, where they alone walked and talked.

## A DEFINITE CONCLUSION

"Neither tell I you by what authority I do these things." Confounded and dismayed, the critics ceased questioning Jesus. They could not blame Him for refusing to answer their question; they had been the first to refuse. Jesus had outwitted them and alas, the common people had recognized their discomforture. Preachers and teachers should learn from the Lord's example. Basically, they need not defend the gospel nor answer questions designed to baffle ministers. Charles Haddon Spurgeon once said, "There is never need to defend a lion; let the animal out of its cage, and the beast will defend itself!" Similarly, we are hardly commissioned to defend the message of Christ; our job is to preach it. God is capable of looking after His own affairs.

## SECTION FIVE

### Expository Notes on the Illustrations of Jesus

**But what think ye? A certain man had two sons; and he came to the first, and said, Son, go work today in my vineyard. He answered and said, I will not: but afterward he repented, and went. And he came to the second, and said likewise. And he answered and said, I go, sir: and went not. Whether of them twain did the will of his father? They say unto him, The first. Jesus saith unto them, Verily I say unto you, That the publicans and the harlots go into the kingdom of God before you. For John came unto you in the way of righteousness, and ye believed him not: but the publicans and the harlots believed him: and ye, when ye had seen it, repented not afterward, that ye might believe him (vv. 28-32).**

## THE CONFLICTING DECISIONS

It must be remembered that this illustration told by Jesus was spoken to the same people who had already questioned the authority of the Lord. This section of the chapter is the continuation of the earlier discussion. When the Jewish leaders seemed dumbfounded by the adroitness of the Lord, He began to present *a disguised sermon!* He spoke of a father who had two sons. Both boys had glib tongues and strange personalities! The one boy was very rude and abrupt and refused vehemently to work in the father's vineyard. Yet afterward he had a change of heart and did what previously he had refused to do. The second son, receiving the same commission, respectfully acquiesced in his father's plan, but for reasons unknown, refrained from doing what he had promised. "He answered and said, I go, sir: and went not." It might have been that he had every intention of fulfilling his promise to the father, but something hindered him. On the other hand, he could have been hypocritical, promising to do something he had every wish to avoid. Jesus was aware of the fact that in a country where vineyards abounded, the scene described would be easily recognized by His hearers.

Some theologians teach that Christ had both the Jews and Gentiles in mind when He told this story. The Gentiles who served pagan gods had no desire to worship Jehovah, but afterwards became His most untiring workers. The Jews who *professed* to be the servants of God had no intention nor desire to obey Him. This interpretation may be feasible, but primarily, Jesus was thinking of publicans and harlots, who by their life style confessed unwillingness to serve the Lord. Later, when they were converted they became the most ardent workers in His vineyard. The Jews who resisted Christ continually, in spite of their professed piety, were unwilling to observe anything He suggested.

## THE CONSPICUOUS DEVOTION

When Jesus asked, "Whether of the twain did the will of his father?," the listeners replied, "The first," and it would appear that they did not know He was describing them. It was for this reason He continued to say, "Verily I say unto you, That the publicans and the harlots go into the kingdom of God before you." He was comparing Mary Magdalene, Zaccheus, and others with the proud haughty rulers from the temple. They appeared to be consecrated people but were not. The publicans, sinners, and harlots appeared to be sinful, and they were, but their desire for sin was destroyed by devotion to the Savior. The teaching of Christ was almost revolutionary, for He taught realities. God was concerned only with what men were; holiness was better than theological precepts; repentance was far more to be desired than empty profession. The law taught man's actions were paramount, but Christ said a man's character was more important. To occupy places of prominence in religious assemblies could be meaningless unless the official exhibited holiness. To be a converted outcast, sincerely trying to reach higher standards of morality, always had precedence over the disappointing profession of religious leaders.

## THE CONTINUOUS DENIALS

Jesus remembered how the questioners asked concerning the

authenticity of John's ministry, and deliberately mentioned the dynamic ministry of the wilderness evangelist. He said, "For John came unto you in the way of righteousness, and ye believed him not: but the publicans and the harlots believed him: and ye, when ye had seen it, repented not afterward, that ye might believe him" (v. 32). It was as though Jesus said, "You ask about John, but ignore his message. You inquire about his doctrine, but at the same time close your minds against it. You criticize and condemn the outcasts, and yet they are closer to God than you have ever been. Furthermore, although you have had many opportunities to repent of your sins, you prefer to remain unchanged, and have no inclination toward repentance of any kind! How then can you be the representatives of Him whose temple you occupy?" Jesus had come to Jerusalem to die; His hour was approaching; there was no time to lose. What He had to say, was said regardless of any unpleasant repercussions. There might be reason to add that if He were here today, His message would be the same as it was two thousand years ago. Many people within the church pray for revival, and are anxiously waiting for God to do something spectacular. Perhaps God is waiting for them to remember the words of Jesus and learn how to be worthy of the blessing requested!

**Hear another parable: There was a certain householder, which planted a vineyard, and hedged it round about, and digged a winepress in it, and built a tower, and let it out to husbandmen, and went into a far country: And when the time of the fruit drew near, he sent his servants to the husbandmen, that they might receive the fruits of it. And the husbandmen took his servants, and beat one, and killed another, and stoned another. Again he sent other servants more than the first: and they did unto them likewise. But last of all he sent unto them his son, saying, They will reverence my son. But when the husbandmen saw the son, they said among themselves, This is the heir; come, let us kill him, and let us seize on his inheritance. And they caught him, and cast him out of the vineyard, and slew him. When the Lord therefore of the vineyard cometh, what will he do unto those husbandmen? They say unto him, He will miserably destroy those wicked men, and will let out his vineyard unto other husbandmen, which shall render him the fruits in their seasons (vv. 33-41).**

*THE PARABLE ABOUT GOD*

This parable, in all probability, was the most outstanding message spoken by Jesus. A parable has been defined as an earthly story with a heavenly meaning, but sometimes all the meanings of the story are not easily discerned. This commentary supplies numerous examples of the fact that occasionally, a parable may be interpreted in several ways, and frequently, commentators differ in their expositions. There is only one way to explain this parable of the wicked husbandmen. What the Lord inferred was so clear that even the chief priests and Pharisees "perceived that he spake of them." Every listener that day knew that the vineyard was Israel. God, through His servant Isaiah had made this perfectly clear. "And now, O inhabitants of Jerusalem, and men of Judah, judge, I pray you, betwixt me and my vineyard. What could have been done more to my vineyard, that I have not done in it? wherefore, when I looked that it should bring forth grapes, brought it forth wild grapes" (Isa. 5:3-4). The scene described by Jesus was perfectly normal even to the plotting against the son of the owner. Economical unrest was evident throughout Palestine, and disgruntled workers were angry with people who exercised authority over them. It was common practice for absentee owners to make an agreement with workers by whom the vineyards were rented. The rent or payment was nationally recognized, and could be made in any of three ways. First, the husbandmen could pay in cash the amount upon which the owner and the men had mutually agreed. Secondly, they could give a percentage of the annual crop, whatever that might be. Finally, if the owner were willing, they could rent the vineyard in exchange for a fixed amount of fruit. The remuneration was given after the harvest. It was also customary for the absentee owner to send his representative to collect dues. The parable was easily understood by all who listened to Jesus.

*THE PEOPLE OF GOD*

The passage already quoted from Isaiah indicated that God's vineyard was the work place for "the inhabitants of Jerusalem and for the men of Judah." When the Pharisees recognized that Jesus had spoken against them, they were associating themselves with the people mentioned by the prophet. The work of God's vineyard had been entrusted to them, and the subsequent details of the story made this fact increasingly clear. Their actions were likened to the deeds of their forefathers who had stoned and killed the messengers sent by God. The prophets had been "...stoned, they were sawn asunder, were tempted, were slain with the sword..." (see Heb. 11:37). Yet, however abhorrent those deeds had been, they were no worse than the actions of the Pharisees who were daily rejecting the Savior. The husbandmen in the parable had disregarded the commands of the owner, and had worked in the vineyard only to enrich themselves. This indictment was very serious, for it inferred the rulers of the nation had become hypocrites.

## THE PROVISION OF GOD

Isaiah had asked, "What more could have been done to my vineyard?" Jesus said the owner had "hedged it round about, and digged a winepress in it, and built a tower..." (Matt. 21:33). The hedge represented safety — it denied entry to marauding animals and robbers. The winepress represented success, for in it, the grapes would have been pressed beneath the feet of the winepressers. It was generally two basins carved in stone, or built of stones. The juice ran from the higher elevation to the lower basin where it was easily collected. The tower provided a lookout point from which the property could be seen, and during storms or nights, provided shelter for the workmen. The owner of the vineyard had gone to great lengths to supply every comfort for his employees. Similarly, God had spared no expense in providing everything needed by His chosen race. He had redeemed them from the bondage of Egypt; had preserved them throughout many generations, and although other nations had tried to annihilate the Hebrews, God had preserved them in all kinds of ways. That they could turn away from such a munificent Benefactor was unthinkable.

## THE PATIENCE OF GOD

"Again, he sent other servants more than the first...But last of all he sent unto them his son." Here we are able to obtain one of the best word pictures ever painted. The sending of God's prophets had covered a period of thousands of years, during which His patience and mercy had been inexhaustible. At any period in history, God could have abandoned His people, leaving them to perish; but instead, He taught them through suffering, helped them in difficulties, and forgave them whenever they asked for help. The laws of Moses suggested an austere God; the teaching of Jesus was completely different. He described God as a Father waiting to welcome a returning prodigal. Nevertheless, it is hard to comprehend the scope of God's love, for in spite of the treatment afforded to the prophets, God decided to send His own Son finally. We might ask, Why did He do this when He already knew the fate awaiting Him? Possibly even John had the same problem when he wrote: "For God SO loved the world, that he gave his only begotten

Son.'' We can only exclaim, ''Amazing Grace: How can it be that Thou my God shouldst die for me?''

## THE PROPHETS OF GOD

''The husbandmen...beat one, and killed another, and stoned another....'' It is difficult to assess the complete number of prophets sent by God to Israel, but we do know of the sixteen whose writings are included in the Bible. We must remember that these did not include Moses, Elijah, Elisha, and John the Baptist. There were also many lesser-known men whose fiery denunciations shattered the complacency of their listeners. Throughout the entire age of the Old Testament God, with unfailing regularity and faithfulness, did His utmost to turn Israel from their wicked ways. He made of them a great nation; He allowed their enemies to overwhelm the nation; He gave blessings; He withheld blessings; God tried every measure known to Him, and yet the people remained unresponsive. Finally, as a last desperate measure God sent His Son, but as we now know, even that amazing gesture had little effect upon those who rejected the message sent from heaven. Had Isaiah been present to express an opinion, once again he would have said, ''What could have been done more to my vineyard, that I have not done it?''

## THE PAIN OF GOD

A well-known skeptic once tried to discredit the Word of God by asking a very potent question. He recited some of the sufferings of Christ and then sneeringly asked, ''Where was God when His Son needed Him most? What father would permit a beloved son to suffer such anguish and not lift a finger to help him?'' A person standing near answered, ''I know where God was at that moment. He 'was in Christ, reconciling the world unto himself''' (2 Cor. 5:19). It has often been claimed that when a mother sees her suffering child, the pain in her heart exceeds the pain in her child's body. When David in mourning for Absolam said, ''O my son Absolam, my son, my son Absolam! would God I had died for thee, O Absolam, my son, my son!'' (2 Sam. 18:33), his anguish of soul greatly exceeded any suffering endured when his son was hanging from the branch of a tree. Perhaps in the deepest and most unfathomable manner, we shall never comprehend what the death of Christ meant to God, for when Jesus died, God died with Him! He was in very deed and truth, reconciling the world unto Himself.

## THE PUNISHMENT FROM GOD

"When the Lord of the vineyard cometh, what will he do unto those husbandmen?...He will miserably destroy those wicked men..." When the Pharisees answered the Lord's question they condemned themselves. If there be any meaning in the Savior's parable, there must of necessity be a day of judgment when justice will be administered to those who rejected and killed God's Son. That the vineyard has already been taken away from its ancient custodians or workmen has become obvious. Israel, the nation through which God sent His word to the world, has already been superceded by the church, which is now responsible for God's efforts to reach a sinful world. There remains one other area in which this text is of vital significance. Every man must be the guardian of his own vineyard! God has permitted us to live, and has placed within human breasts the capacity to respond and serve Him. He has every right to expect us to be faithful to our obligations. His word reminds us of the relationship which should exist between our souls and His loving heart. If we spurn His message, and reject His advances, "there remaineth no more sacrifice for sins, But a certain fearful looking for of judgment and fiery indignation, which shall devour the adversaries" (Heb. 10:26-27).

**Jesus saith unto them, Did ye never read in the scriptures, The stone which the builders rejected, the same is become the head of the corner: this is the Lord's doing, and it is marvellous in our eyes? Therefore say I unto you, The kingdom of God shall be taken from you, and given to a nation bringing forth the fruits thereof. And whosoever shall fall on this stone shall be broken: but on whomsoever it shall fall, it will grind him to powder. And when the chief priests and Pharisees had heard his parables, they perceived that he spake of them. But when they sought to lay hands on him, they feared the multitude, because they took him for a prophet (vv. 42-46).**

## THE REJECTED STONE EXALTED

These verses uttered by Jesus bring His sermon to its dynamic conclusion. They were clear and concise, and left no room for doubt in regard to what He was teaching. The wicked husbandmen had killed the son who visited the vineyard; the Pharisees would do their utmost to destroy God's Son who at that moment was standing in their midst. Yet, God would take His Son and exalt Him to the highest place in heaven. He Who would become the object of derision and scorn, would occupy the most illustrious place in eternity. The quotation came from Psalm 118:22, and became one of the most cited of all the Old Testament scriptures. Simon Peter used the statement when he testified before the council in Jerusalem (Acts 4:11). Paul indirectly mentioned it when he wrote his letter to the church in Ephesus, and Peter again used it when he wrote his first epistle (1 Peter 2:7).

"Dean Plumptre says, 'In the primary meaning of the Psalm, the illustration seems to have been drawn from one of the stones, quarried, hewn, and marked, away from the site of the temple, which the builders, ignorant of the head architect's plans, had put on one side, as having no place in the building. It was found afterward to be that on which the completeness of the structure depended, that on which, as the chief corner stone, the two walls met, and were bonded together'" (*The Pulpit Commentary,* Matthew, p. 356). Such a huge stone, though marred, may still be seen in one of the ancient quarries of Egypt. There is no ambiguity about the remarks made by Jesus. He knew that death awaited His arrival in Jerusalem, but was aware also that beyond the Cross lay His crown. Nothing could prevent the coronation which had been planned before the world began.

## THE REBELLIOUS SINNERS EXAMINED

"Therefore say I unto you, The kingdom of God shall be taken from you, and given to a nation bringing forth the fruits thereof." Here we find two extremes brought together in one verse. The exaltation of the Son of God is considered in conjunction with those people who tried in vain to prevent it. The kingdom of God, where He was supposed to be the absolute Ruler, and where the Jewish people were His special representatives, would be eternally changed. The Jews would be removed from their special place; their privileges would be bestowed upon others, who unlike the wicked husbandmen in the story, would render to God that which was rightfully His. There has been a great amount of discussion regarding these words of Jesus. Did He mean the Gentiles; particularly the church, which would inherit what the Jewish leaders lost, or was Christ referring to another generation of Jews who would ultimately become faithful servants? It is wiser to reflect on the issue and decide whether or not we are pleasing to God in the part of the vineyard entrusted to our care.

## THE REJECTED SOULS EXPELLED

"And whosoever shall fall on this stone shall be broken: but on whomsoever it shall fall, it will grind him to powder." There are teachers who affirm that this statement refers to penitents falling before the Rock of Ages, but it is difficult to accept this exposition. The statement refers only to judgment. It is the natural sequence to the murderous efforts of the husbandmen. It is thought that the reference to "falling upon the stone" refers to the ancient custom of flinging known criminals from the edge of a precipice, so that their bodies would be broken on the rocks below. This was attempted at Nazareth when the mob unsuccessfully tried to throw the Lord to His death. It was even included in the temptations of the Lord (see Luke 4:9-12). When Jesus mentioned the stone falling upon the guilty, He was obviously thinking of the message given by Daniel 2:34-35.

Once again we are given the basic facts of the gospel. (1) Man is a responsible creature placed on this earth to do the will of God. (2) There will be a final day of reckoning when each person will stand before God to be judged according to those things written in God's records. (3) Those who are found guilty will be rejected and banished eternally from the presence of the Judge. The word translated "shall grind him to powder" is *likmeesei* and according to Thayer means: "to winnow; to cleanse, that is, to completely separate from the wheat; to scatter; to grind to powder, that is, to destroy completely." It is incomprehensible how teachers can misinterpret this message. (4) Possibly, this is the most important detail in the story. In view of the impending doom awaiting the unrepentant sinners, it is imperative that the gospel message be brought to these people as quickly and as effectively as possible. As we have previously considered, the owner of the vineyard sent many servants, and finally his son, in a supreme endeavor to turn the workmen from their wicked ways. If the church realized the seriousness of the world's situation, they would make New Testament evangelism their greatest priority.

To see the light, and to prefer walking in darkness, is inexcusable. The Pharisees realized the Lord had spoken directly to them, but even then would have seized and rushed Him to His death. Their dread of the reactions of the multitude overshadowed their fear and respect for the God they professed to represent. Again it must be emphasized that none are so blind as those who have no desire to see. (See the special homily: "The Rock of Ages." The Stone of *Stumbling; Strength; Shelter; Smiting* and *Splendor.* The author's commentary, *Luke's Thrilling Gospel,* pp. 416-419.)

# The Twenty-second Chapter of Matthew

THEME: *Jesus Offsets the Attacks of His Enemies*

OUTLINE:
    I. The People at the Lovely Wedding (Verses 1-14)
    II. The Presence of the Listening Witnesses (Verses 15-22)
    III. The Problem of the Lonely Widow (Verses 23-32)
    IV. The Power of the Lord's Words (Verses 33-46)

## SECTION ONE

*Expository Notes on the Royal Wedding*

**And Jesus answered and spake unto them again by parables, and said, The kingdom of heaven is like unto a certain king, which made a marriage for his son, And sent forth his servants to call them that were bidden to the wedding: and they would not come. Again, he sent forth other servants, saying, Tell them which are bidden, Behold, I have prepared my dinner: my oxen and my fatlings are killed, and all things are ready: come unto the marriage. But they made light of it, and went their ways, one to his farm, another to his merchandise: And the remnant took his servants, and entreated them spitefully, and slew them. But when the king heard thereof, he was wroth: and he sent forth his armies, and destroyed those murderers, and burned up their city (vv. 1-7).**

There are two accounts of this parable. Luke's version is found in Luke 14:16-24, and on certain details, he appears to be at variance with Matthew. Matthew says little about the reasons for the guests refusals and mentions the king's wrath in sending forth emissaries of judgment. Luke elaborates on the refusals and makes no mention of armies sent to punish offenders. There may be no contradictions in the differing versions. There is always the possibility that Jesus gave this illustration on more than one occasion. Matthew might have been describing one of the incidents and Luke the other. Many things which Jesus said and did were never reported in writing (see John 21:25). It might be helpful and informative to remember that by the time Matthew was writing his Gospel, the Roman legions had destroyed Jerusalem, and Matthew, recalling the Lord's words, was able to see the fulfillment of what had been predicted. As we shall discover in the story, the message had unmistakable dispensational truth; the rejection by the Jews led to the invitation being given to the Gentiles. When the original guests refused to accept their king's request, the outcasts in the streets were given the chance to participate in the wedding feast. Luke, on the other hand, was not too interested in the outpouring of judgment; he was more concerned in describing the stupidity of men who missed the greatest privilege ever offered. To repeat what has been said, Jesus could have given this illustration several times, and Matthew and Luke might have been describing the same account viewed from different angles.

## THE ROYAL REQUEST

It is essential to remember that throughout Eastern countries, particularly in Bible times, the sending of invitations to a wedding was somewhat different from the practices known in Western nations. Today, the invitation to, and the date of, the proposed wedding are mentioned together, and guests are required to notify the sender of their ability to attend the celebrations. Weddings are now solemnized within a very short time. It was not always so easy. When wedding celebrations lasted a week great preparations were required. When a royal marriage was planned, very extensive preparations had to be made, and guests were given ample warning of the forthcoming event. Invitations were dispatched weeks ahead of the time, so that prospective guests were able to make arrangements to leave their businesses, farms, or whatever occupation claimed their time. Later, when everything was in readiness, the final summons was issued, and the invited people were expected to respond immediately. Jesus was now preparing to lay down His life, and knew His time for preaching was limited. This parable was important because it opened new vistas of thought. Jesus had already said the kingdom was to be taken from the Jews; the vineyard was to be given to others. Now, in much more detail, He emphasized what God intended to do. He would take the kingdom from the Jews and *offer it to the Gentiles*. The parable was easily understood. The King was God; the prepared celebrations were to honor His Son; the invited guests were the Jews. The invitations had been issued throughout Old Testament ages when the prophets had been authorized to speak concerning future events. God had now finished His preparations, and the time to honor the Son had arrived.

## THE REPEATED REFUSAL

The king "sent forth his servants to call them that were bidden to the wedding: and they would not come. Again, he sent forth other servants, saying, Tell them which are bidden, Behold, I have prepared my dinner: my oxen and my fatlings are killed, and all things are ready: come unto the marriage. But they made light of it, and went their ways." Once again we are able to recognize the prevailing thought in these parables of Jesus. The husbandmen were privileged to work in the Master's vineyard; the guests were invited to attend the marriage celebrations. They all refused to do what was expected of them, and finally were punished. That Jesus was describing the attitude of the Jewish nation and its rebellion against God, none could deny. "They made light of it." If we can superimpose Luke's account on the record given by Matthew, then it becomes obvious that anything seemed more important than doing the will of God. Matthew says that one man found attraction on his farm, and another in his business. Both were anxious to make money, and nothing Christ offered could compensate for the loss of earthly gain. The Greek word translated "they made light of it" is *ameleesantes* which means "to be careless; to neglect; not caring for what had been said." The inference was that the king was wasting time; the people considered him to be a bore! They were only concerned about material gains. They had no intention of listening to, or accepting, any invitation even though it came from God. This was a terrible indictment against the rulers who claimed to be God's sole representatives among the Jewish nation.

## THE RIDICULOUS REBELLION

"And the remnant took his servants, and entreated them spitefully, and slew them." Compare this with the description of how the husbandmen took the son and killed him, and there can be no misinterpretation of Christ's message. Fully aware of His impending crucifixion, Jesus plainly stated that the responsibility for the crime would be placed at the feet of the people to whom He was then speaking. Jesus had been the greatest Benefactor ever to walk in their cities. He had healed the sick, fed the multitudes, cleansed the lepers, and raised their dead. He had preached about peace and holiness, and had glorified God. Yet, because His message exposed hypocrisy, the priests hated Him, and rejoiced when He was crucified. They had no desire to consult God about any of these matters. They could decide for themselves, and were willing to say, "His blood be on us, and on our children" (Matt. 27:25).

## THE REQUIRED RETRIBUTION

"But when the king heard thereof, he was wroth: and he sent forth his armies, and destroyed those murderers, and burned up their city." Luke omits this part of the story, and many commentators believe Matthew only inserted it because he was writing after the fall of Jerusalem, and could see before his eyes the fulfillment of the Lord's prediction. This might have been the fact, but there can be no doubt Christ uttered these words. Unpunished sin is a violation of the law of God. Righteousness demands retribution. When grace begets forgiveness, God is able to accept a sinner. If, however, a person rejects grace, God, according to His own laws, must punish the offender. That truth not only applied to the Jews of the first century, it applies even more to the people of the twentieth century. The Hebrews did not possess a complete Bible, nor the benefit of two thousand years of Christian activity. There is reason to believe that in the day of judgment some of those unfortunate people might have a better chance than those who heard the gospel and rejected it.

**Then saith he to his servants, The wedding is ready, but they which were bidden were not worthy. Go ye therefore into the highways, and as many as ye shall find, bid to the marriage. So those servants went out into the highways, and gathered together all as many as they found, both bad and good: and the wedding was furnished with guests. And when the king came in to see the guests, he saw there a man which had not on a wedding garment: And he saith unto him, Friend, how camest thou in hither not having a wedding garment? And he was speechless. Then said the king to the servants, Bind him hand and foot, and take him away, and cast him into outer darkness; there shall be weeping and gnashing of teeth. For many are called, but few are chosen (vv. 8-14).**

## THE GREATER INVITATION TO THE GENTILES

The dispensational aspect of this parable is unmistakable. When the Jews refused to accept what God was offering in Christ, the identical message went out to the Gentiles who responded gladly to the gospel. The second part of this Scripture supplies the foreshadowing of events to follow Pentecost. Then those other servants went out into the highways of the world to summon people to honor the King's Son. This also was the fulfillment of an ancient prediction, for Isaiah had said: "I will also give thee for a light to the Gentiles, that thou mayest be my salvation unto the end of the earth" (Isa. 49:6). "And the Gentiles shall come to thy light, and kings to the brightness of thy rising" (Isa. 60:3). It was God's plan that the gospel should be proclaimed throughout the entire world. This probably was the worst thing that could be mentioned to the Pharisees, for they considered all but Jews to be unworthy of even the least of the blessings of God.

## THE GUARDED INVESTIGATION OF THE GUEST

To appreciate the importance of this incident, it is necessary to be aware of an ancient Eastern custom. The Rev. A. Lukyn Williams writing in the *Pulpit Commentary, Matthew,* p. 358, draws attention to an Oriental practice. "It is said to have been an Oriental custom to present each guest invited to a royal feast with a festive robe to be worn on the occasion, as nowadays persons admitted to the royal presence are clothed with a caftan. "A caftan, also spelled kaftan, is an undercoat having long sleeves and a sash, worn in Eastern Mediterranean countries" (*The Readers Digest Encyclopedic Dictionary*). It seems possible that Jesus had this custom in mind when He told His story. Obviously the monarch had his own color scheme for the feast, and at great expense provided what he desired. The inference, of course, was that God desired all His guests to be clothed with the garments of righteousness, which He provided at great expense through the death of His Son. The fact that a stranger appeared without the offered garment aroused immediate attention. Consider the homily at the end of this section.

## THE GHASTLY INDEFENSIBILITY OF THE GUILTY

"And he was speechless." Whatever arguments might have been made elsewhere, the man had no comment to make when he stood before the king. It would have been impossible to gain admittance except by one of the doors where an attendant would have offered the costly garment. It is not too much to believe that every beggar would have accepted the gift gladly, in order to hide his rags. It would seem that this guest was completely satisfied with his appearance. He must have been dressed in his finest garments and believed there was no need to be beholding to the king for anything. He reminds us of modern people who are proud of their righteousness; they say, as did the people of Laodicea, "I am rich, and increased with goods, and have need of nothing" (Rev. 3:17). Their robes of self-righteousness are outstanding, and they scoff when a preacher mentions the garments of salvation bought by the precious blood of Christ. Their attitude proclaims, "We are as good as anyone!" They say with the wealthy young ruler, "All these commandments have I kept from my youth," but, unfortunately, they never ask, "What lack I yet?" Such people have no place in the kingdom, and no hope for eternity. This was the message Jesus preached centuries ago and it remains unchanged. A. M. Toplady expressed great wisdom when he wrote:

> Nothing in my hand I bring;
> Simply to Thy cross, I cling!
> Naked, come to Thee for dress;
> Helpless, look to Thee for grace:
> Foul, I to the fountain fly:
> Wash me, Savior, or I die.

HOMILY

Study No. 14

### THE GUEST...Who Refused a Wedding Garment

When the Lord Jesus spoke about the king who made a marriage for his son, He gave to the world one of His most comprehensive parables. The far-reaching implication of this message went beyond the immediate circumstances of His day, and embraced the entire age of grace. In speaking of the people who openly spurned the invitation to the wedding, Christ undoubtedly referred to the Jewish rejection of God's proffered grace. Yet, out of this tragedy came a greater invitation to a wider audience. "Then saith he to his servants, The wedding is ready...Go ye therefore into the highways, and as many as ye shall find, bid to the marriage. So those servants went out into the highways, and gathered together all as many as they found, both bad and good: and the wedding was furnished with guests'' (Matt. 22:8-10).

## THE GLAD REQUEST

It is significant that class distinction was unknown in this great message. The earlier invitation to the privileged few had been superseded by a far greater declaration — ''Whosoever will may come.'' The ''casting away of them'' resulted in ''the reconciling of the world'' (Rom. 11:15). Thus, the servants of the great king went out in every direction to seek guests for the wedding, and probably the scenes which took place beggared description. It seemed a fantasy that a king should welcome tramps and hoboes to his palace. Yet, the messengers of the royal household assured everyone that this was the king's intention. It was indeed a great request, and nothing else could so adequately describe the wonder of the gospel message. God is determined to honor His Son, and sinners of all nations are invited to the marriage supper of the Lamb.

## THE GLORIOUS RAIMENT

An Eastern wedding was always a most colorful affair, but a royal wedding was a scene of brilliant magnificence. Every guest was clothed in special garments provided by the king, and the entire scene became one of unprecedented splendor. The cost of supplying this raiment was very great, but no expense was ever spared in the matter of honoring a king's son. Bought at great price, the garments were offered free to all the guests. Therefore, when the servants brought the poor, the wretched, the filthy, and the unlovely to the wedding, the colorful garments offered by the attendant seemed in strange contrast to the rags of the people. A quick wash to remove the dirt, a putting off of rags, and a glad acceptance of the offered garment, were sufficient to turn a beggar into a prince. Probably this was the Savior's best illustration of the garments of salvation. Provided at the greatest cost, they are offered free to sinners. We discard the rags of our self-righteousness, and reaching forth the hand of faith, accept the garments of grace, and stand clothed in the righteousness of Christ. Glorious raiment indeed!

## THE GREAT REFUSAL

"And when the king came in to see the guests, he saw there a man which had not on a wedding garment: and he saith unto him, Friend, how camest thou in hither not having a wedding garment? And he was speechless" (Matt. 22:11-12). The king was perfectly justified in asking the question, for he had made ample provision to meet the needs of all his guests. Surely, this particular person could not have been clad in rags, or he would have readily seized the chance to hide his poverty. Perhaps his garments were new, and he was proud of them. Maybe he was a Pharisee and said, "I am not as other men are...or even as these publicans." He therefore refused the offer of the garment, believing he was perfectly presentable for the king's banquet.

## THE GHASTLY RESULT

"Then said the king to his servants, Bind him hand and foot, and take him away, and cast him into outer darkness; there shall be weeping and gnashing of teeth" (v. 11). An expression of penitence at that late hour would have been totally unacceptable. The arrogant man had refused the king's offer; he had done so deliberately and had spurned a king's grace and dishonored a prince. He was exceedingly guilty and responsible for his misfortune. This was a tragedy which might easily have been avoided. "Who hath ears to hear, let him hear."

## SECTION TWO

### *Expository Notes on Christ's Encounter*
### *With the Pharisees and Herodians*

**Then went the Pharisees, and took counsel how they might entangle him in his talk. And they sent out unto him their disciples with the Herodians, saying, Master, we know that thou art true, and teachest the way of God in truth, neither carest thou for any man: for thou regardest not the person of men (vv. 15-16).**

## THE SLY REMARK...A Dubious Compliment

When the Lord arrived in Jerusalem, He began to denounce the atrocious things which the Pharisees did under guise of religion. It was to be expected that they would retaliate, but the way in which they did so was extremely clever. The plan was probably suggested by an astute lawyer in the Sanhedrin who said, "Gentlemen, you will never thwart the purposes of this Nazarene unless you use your heads! He is too clever for you. If you denounce Him publicly, you arouse the animosity of the foolish crowds; they think He is a prophet. Oppose Him, and they will turn on you. The only way to upset that meddlesome Man is by using guile. Catch Him off guard; make Him appear stupid; concoct some idea which will annoy the Romans, and He will be discredited. Furthermore, I know how to do this. He does not like us anyhow, so we must form a coalition with our enemies. We must unite our forces and should there be any unpleasant repercussions, maybe, our collaborators will be blamed. Listen to my suggestions."

The Herodians and Pharisees were opposed on almost every political matter. The former were the ardent supporters of King Herod, who curried favor with Caesar, and paid tribute to his sponsor. The Pharisees hated Roman domination, and detested everything done within their occupied country. Consequently, the two parties were argumentative on every issue. It was strange that enemies should unite in an attempt to defeat the Savior. The same thing happened when Pilate and Herod were reunited in friendship when Jesus was brought to trial (see Luke 23:12). The Herodians gladly accepted the invitation to join forces with the Pharisees, and thus they came together to do what the lawyer had suggested. They were smiling when they approached to say, "Master, we know that thou art true, and teachest the way of God in truth...." "You are not beholding to any man; You are not afraid of people. We like that; You are very wise. Master, we have a problem concerning the tribute demanded by Caesar. Should we pay this or not?" The Lord was justified in calling them hypocrites. If they believed He taught the way of God truthfully, why then had they not accepted His doctrine?

**Tell us therefore, What thinkest thou? Is it lawful to give tribute unto Caesar, or not? But Jesus perceived their wickedness, and said, Why tempt ye me, ye hypocrites? (vv. 17-18).**

*THE SUBTLE REQUEST...A Deceitful Conspiracy*

Historical records indicate there were three regular taxes which the Roman government exacted. There was a *ground tax* which a man was required to pay to the government one tenth of the grain, and one fifth of the oil and wine which he produced. There was an *income tax*, which was one per cent of a man's income. There was a *poll tax* which had to be paid by every male person from the age of fourteen to the age of sixty-five, and by every female person from the age of twelve to sixty-five. This amounted to one denarius — that is what Jesus called the tribute coin, and was the equivalent of about twelve cents, the average amount paid for a day's labor in the vineyard. The tax in question here is the poll tax.

The apparently simple question was dangerous. If the Lord had replied that it was correct to pay the tax, the common people would have been incensed, for everyone hated paying taxes to the heathens. Caesar was acclaimed as one of the gods, and demanded worship from his subjects. Every Hebrew considered it sacrilege to worship any God except Jehovah. If Christ had endorsed the paying of taxes, He would have become embroiled in one of the fiercest debates within Israel. Yet, if He had opposed taxation, the Herodians present would have informed Herod and the Romans, and this would have led to the Lord's arrest. Whatever He said, so they thought, there would be sufficient evidence to cause trouble, and the discredibility of Jesus would lead to the termination of His ministry.

**Show me the tribute money. And they brought unto him a penny [denarius]. And he saith unto them, Whose is this image and superscription? They say unto him, Caesar's. Then saith he unto them, Render therefore unto Caesar the things which are Caesar's; and unto God the things that are God's. When they had heard these words, they marvelled, and left him, and went their way (vv. 19-22).**

*THE SUPERB REPLY...A Definitive Christ*

History records that the first order given by a new Caesar authorized the issue of new coinage bearing the image of the ruler. This caused one of the chief complaints made by Jews against foreign currency. It was unlawful to bring the "blasphemous" money into the temple, for each coin announced the deity of the person whose image and superscription it carried. The Lord easily read the motives of His questioners, and avoided the pitfall into which they hoped He would fall. Jesus said, "If this coin belongs to Caesar, then give it to Him. There are other things which should be given to God." Thus did He teach that every man has a duty to perform to the country in which he lives. Even the Romans brought blessings to Palestine; they erected houses and made roads. They built aqueducts to supply water, and if the Jews enjoyed these amenities, they should have been willing to pay a share of the cost. The Roman legions preserved Israel from invasions made by war-like neighbors, and the rule of law and order offered protection against thieves and other criminals. These services were expensive to provide, and all Jews should have been willing to help carry the financial burden.

Many people stress the fact they are citizens of heaven, and therefore have no responsibility for anything in this world. They abstain from taking part in elections; they never exercise their right to vote, and yet they are the first to criticize the decadence of their political leaders. No onlooker has the right to be critical unless he is willing to do what is possible to correct the situation. If men desire good government, they should work to place good people in office. If they wish for safe communities, they should help to elect officials who share their views. The man who has no interest in this world should not be in it! Any citizen who is not willing to pay his share of taxation should not use the public highways; he should be deprived of heat, light, and water, and should be alone on a distant island where he could be king over himself! Even now, we must render to Caesar that which belongs to Caesar, and to God the things which belong to God. Paying taxes to Caesar does not mean worship at his feet.

## SECTION THREE

*Expository Notes on the Problem of the Lonely Widow*

**The same day came to him the Sadducees, which say that there is no resurrection, and asked him, Saying, Master, Moses said, If a man die, having no children, his brother shall marry his wife, and raise up seed unto his brother. Now there were with us seven brethren: and the first, when he had married a wife, deceased, and having no issue, left his wife unto his brother: Likewise the second also, and the third, unto the seventh. And last of all the woman died also. Therefore in the resurrection whose wife shall she be of the seven? for they all had her. Jesus answered and said unto them, Ye do err, not knowing the scriptures, nor the power of God. For in the resurrection they neither marry, nor are given in marriage, but are as the angels of God in heaven. But as touching the resurrection of the dead, have ye not read that which was spoken unto you by God, saying, I am the God of Abraham, and the God of Isaac, and the God of Jacob? God is not the God of the dead, but of the living. And when the multitude heard this, they were astonished at his doctrine (vv. 23-33).**

## THE CONFUSING SITUATION

To understand the problems connected with this incident, it is necessary to consider the theological arguments of the Pharisees and Sadducees. "For the Sadducees say that there is no resurrection, neither angel, nor spirit, but the Pharisees confess both" (Acts 23:8). The Sadducees were, for the most part, very wealthy, and occupied the chief religious positions in Israel. They were the aristocracy of the nation, and were liberal in their interpretation of Scripture. They believed in the Pentateuch, that is, the five books of Moses, but rejected all else. They insisted there was no evidence in the books of Moses to prove there was life beyond the grave, and it was this fiercely contested argument which caused continued trouble in Israel. The matter was further aggravated by the strange beliefs of the Pharisees.

They not only believed in survival, but went to great lengths to propagate their doctrines. They claimed that any man who denied the resurrection was excommunicated from God, and had no part whatsoever in the divine plan. The Sadducees fiercely resented this suggestion, and the hostilities between the two parties seemed endless. The Pharisees debated whether or not people would rise again clothed or naked. If clothed, would they rise in their old clothes or new? If new, where and how were the new garments obtained? They often quoted the incident when the witch of Endor apparently raised Samuel to life, and from it, tried to prove that after death the deceased still retained the same appearance as during his lifetime. Some of their teachings were ludicrous, for they claimed that all Jews would be resurrected in Palestine, the blessed land, but they were concerned about the Hebrews who died in distant lands. How could these be resurrected in Palestine when their graves were elsewhere? Some rabbis believed that tunnels existed beneath the ground, and that dead bodies passed through these to reach the promised land, where on the day of resurrection, they would be raised with those who had never left their homeland. These teachings were obnoxious to the elite Sadducees, they laughed the ideas to scorn, asserting that the stupidity of the suggestions revealed the immaturity of the people who made them. When the Sadducees heard how Jesus had confounded the Pharisees, they probably considered the time opportune to exhibit their own cleverness in being able to succeed where the Pharisees had failed.

## THE CONSPIRING SADDUCEES

Referring to the commandments of Moses, they proceeded to explain their difficulty. A woman had been married to each of seven sons, and had eventually been left without husband or children. If there were such a thing as the resurrection, which of the seven brethren would claim the lonely widow? Some rabbis taught that the first husband would have a prior claim, but it would be interesting to discover what Jesus thought. The commandment of Moses to which they referred is found in Deuteronomy 25:5-10. This was called the Levirate law, but it was seldom, if ever, observed during the time of the Lord's sojourn on earth. Formerly, if a man were unwilling to meet his obligation to the sister-in-law, she could bring him before the elders and disgrace him by spitting in his face. Doubtless this often happened, for some men preferred indignity to abandoning another woman whom they loved. The Sadducees stated '' *there were with us* seven brethren.'' This may not have been literally true; it is more likely that they were citing a hypothetical case in order to set a trap for Jesus. They had probably decided already that they were greater intellectually than Jesus could ever be; they had formulated a problem which Christ could not solve. If He denied the resurrection, then the Pharisees would be enraged, and people would become disillusioned with the Nazarene. Then, the Sadducees would emerge as victors where their counterparts had failed.

## THE CONFIDENT SAVIOR

The Sadducees were very unwise antagonists. When they pitted their puny intellects against the mind of Christ, they advertized their stupidity. ''Jesus answered and said unto them, Ye do err, not knowing the scriptures, nor the power of God.'' This is generally the case with people intent on criticizing others. Most of the false teachers in the world know only portions of the Bible and quote the verses to express their own brand of doctrine. Like the Sadducees, they reject what they do not believe, and only accept certain parts of the word of God which, taken from their context, express an alien point of view.

With assurance Jesus spoke of the resurrection, and emphasized details of the life which they denied. Marriage was instituted by God so that births could compensate for deaths. It was necessary that cradles took the place of coffins; otherwise this planet would have become uninhabited. Throughout the eternal ages, death will be abolished; there will be no need for replacements, and marriage will be a thing of the past. What God has prepared to take its place remains to be discovered. Probably everybody will love everybody, and all will love God.

It is interesting to recognize how Jesus referred to the Scriptures unconditionally accepted by His questioners. He said, "But as touching the resurrection of the dead, have ye not read that which was spoken unto you by God, saying, I am the God of Abraham, and the God of Isaac, and the God of Jacob? God is not the God of the dead, but of the living." Jesus did not say, "God WAS the God of the patriarchs; He said GOD IS THE GOD of Abraham, Isaac and Jacob." If there were no resurrection, He would have been the God of dust and skeletons! When the people heard this statement, they were astonished. They had never heard such wisdom, and even the Pharisees must have been excited when they saw the embarrassment of their traditional antagonists.

## SECTION FOUR

*Expository Notes on the Discussion With the Pharisees*

**But when the Pharisees had heard that he had put the Sadducees to silence, they were gathered together. Then one of them, which was a lawyer, asked him a question, tempting him, and saying, Master, which is the great commandment in the law? Jesus said unto him, Thou shalt love the Lord thy God with all thine heart, and with all thy soul, and with all thy mind. This is the first and great commandment. And the second is like unto it, Thou shalt love thy neighbour as thyself. On these two commandments hang all the law and the prophets (vv. 34-40).**

## THE STRANGE TRADITIONS

Once again it is necessary to compare two versions of the same account. Matthew says a lawyer came *tempting* Jesus; Mark reporting the same incident, calls the questioner a scribe, and paints a different picture of the Pharisee. He says "...when Jesus saw that he answered discreetly, he said unto him, Thou art not far from the kingdom of God" (Mark 12:34). It would appear therefore that after the Lord had silenced the Sadducees, the Pharisees gathered in their counsel to discuss what had happened. They probably decided they could do better, and appointed one of their skillful lawyers to interview Jesus. Matthew says the man came to tempt Jesus, and this probably reflects the attitude of the commissioning Pharisees. The emissary himself had no sinister motives, but came to ask a question about a very complex situation. He said,

"Master, which is the great commandment in the law?" It does not necessarily mean that he could not decide which of the Ten Commandments was the greatest.

The real foundation upon which all legal and religious matters rested was the Ten Commandments, but these were insufficient to meet the requirements of Israel. The books of Leviticus, Numbers, and Deuteronomy mention many additional laws which became guidelines for the judges before whom various law suits were brought. To add to the confusion, throughout succeeding centuries the scribes added innumerable extra laws in which were included "the traditions of the fathers." Ultimately, the true law had been obscured by the ridiculous requirements written by scribes and doctors of the law. The Talmud, to which reference is often made, expressed the "body of Jewish religious and civil law (with related commentaries and discussions), not included in the Pentateuch, and commonly identified with the Mishna and Gemara" (*Reader's Digest Dictionary*). The Mishna was the first part of the Talmud, consisting of a collection of early rabbinical traditions and decisions compiled chiefly by Rabbi Judah he-Nasi born about A.D. 150. According to the teaching of the rabbis, there were more than six hundred precepts in the law, and these were divided into two sections, named *the heavy and the light commandments*, to express that some were more important than others. They said that if a man were truly concerned with keeping some of the heavy commandments, he could be excused if he neglected the lighter ones. This led to confusion in many areas.

"The Jews made many distinctions about the commandments of God, calling some 'light,' others 'weighty,' others 'little,' others 'great.' According to their estimating, therefore, some commandment must be 'greatest.' Some of them contended that the law of the sabbath was the greatest commandment, some the law of sacrifice, some that of circumcision, and some pleaded for the wearing of phylacteries...The Talmud reckons the commandments at six hundred and thirteen; of which three hundred and sixty-five are negative and two hundred and forty-eight affirmative; but our Lord's enumeration is two, for that all the Law is fulfilled in love to God and man" (Rev. J. A. Macdonald. *The Pulpit Commentary. Matthew*, pp. 386-387).

The scribe who came to ask the question about the prior commandment could have had these problems in mind. Believing Jesus to be an expert Teacher, he desired to know the Lord's opinion on those things, and was amazed when the Savior ignored man-made laws and stressed the importance of God's work spoken to Moses.

*THE SUBTLE TEMPTATION*

The aims of the Pharisees remained unchanged; they hoped to embroil Jesus in the theological arguments disrupting the nation. If Jesus supported any one of the many interpretations, He would automatically enrage people who had other ideas. The twenty-second chapter of Matthew is filled with repeated efforts to entangle Jesus in His words; to make Him contradict Himself, and arouse opposition of any kind. A verbal war had been declared, and there appeared to be no cessation in the counterattacks being made by the Pharisees, Sadducees, and Herodians. Every sect within the nation was antagonistic to the Lord whose preaching exposed their shortcomings. Jesus had to exercise constant care; one false word or action would have led to disaster. To safeguard against these insidious attacks, Jesus often rose early in the morning to climb the mountain and be alone with God. To be aware of need is halfway to winning the ensuing battle.

*THE SUBLIME TRUTH*

It should be considered that whereas the lawyer asked about one commandment, the Savior mentioned two. ''Jesus said unto him, Thou shalt love the Lord thy God with all thy heart, and with all thy soul, and with all thy mind. This is the first and great commandment. *And the second is like unto it*, Thou shalt love thy neighbour as thyself.'' A profession of love for God will always be suspect if that love is not directed toward neighbors. The essence of true religion is to serve others, for this is the will of our heavenly Father. God never directed any of His servants to become hermits. To live alone is to die alone. Love imprisoned within a soul is meaningless; love must be expressed. There is no greater privilege than to lift a burden from the shoulders of weary travelers, and bring light to those who sit in darkness and the shadow of death. If a man never helps another, he has outlived his usefulness in a world of need.

**While the Pharisees were gathered together, Jesus asked them, Saying, What think ye of Christ, whose son is he? They say unto him, The son of David. He saith unto them, How then doth David in spirit call him Lord, saying, The Lord said unto my Lord, Sit thou on my right hand, till I make thine enemies thy footstool? If David then call him Lord, how is he his son? And no man was able to answer him a word, neither durst any man from that day forth ask him any more questions (vv. 41-46).**

*AN INADEQUATE TITLE*

Every Jew fervently believed in the coming of the Messiah, and referred to Him as "The Son of David." The blind beggar at Jericho said, "Jesus, thou Son of David, have mercy on me" (Luke 18:39). The woman of Canaan used the same title (Matt. 15:22). Yet, this in itself was insufficient to describe the true nature of Jesus. It should be remembered that on several occasions the Lord forbade people to testify concerning Him, and had discouraged the disciples to broadcast His Messianic claims. Things had now changed. The Lord, knowing He would soon be crucified, was emphasizing those claims and making sure His audience had no illusions about His message. All His enemies had been silenced; they were embarrassed by their ignominious failure to discredit Jesus before the people. They were about to leave Him, when Jesus, seeing the crowd in the temple, asked a question.

*AN INSPIRING TRUTH*

The Lord said to the Pharisees: "What think ye of Christ? whose son is he?" He knew the answer they would give, and planned to make it an introduction to one of the greatest claims He would ever make concerning Himself. They replied, "The Son of David." Jesus then quoted from Psalm 110:1 which all Jews recognized to be Messianic in its implications. He said, "The Lord said unto my Lord, Sit thou at my right hand, until I make thine enemies thy footstool." This same verse was often used by the apostles and the church (see Acts 2:34-35 and Heb. 1:13). It was to be expected that Jesus would be an expert expositor of His own word, but this was one of the most momentous lessons He ever taught. The Pharisees were dumbfounded when He asked, "How could David call his own son Lord?" "The Lord said unto my Lord" indicates that David was thinking of two Lords. The first Lord said unto the second Lord, "Sit thou on my right hand, til I make thine enemies thy foot stool." David had many sons, but this statement could not have been made concerning any of his children. The princes were never invited to sit on the right hand of God. Therefore the Messiah had to be infinitely more than David's son. He had to be THE SON OF GOD who would be invited to occupy the most illustrious seat in eternity. This was the strongest claim ever made by Jesus. As it is often said, "Jesus must have been what He claimed to be, or He was the greatest charlatan that ever walked the earth."

## AN IRREFUTABLE TEACHER

''And no man was able to answer him a word, neither durst any man from that day forth ask him any more questions.'' At last the critical Pharisees, Sadducees, Herodians, and priests admitted their inability to win an argument against the man from Nazareth. They were able to appreciate the testimony of the officers who were sent to arrest Jesus. When the men returned without the prisoner, they said: ''Never man spake like this man'' (John 7:46). The remarkable feature about the Savior's ministry was His ability to meet every challenge, and defeat every attempt to undermine His influence. As far as we know, He never attended any school nor sat at the feet of any professor. He never studied a textbook except the Scriptures. He was never a graduate of any earthly institution, and had no degrees after His name. Yet the world is filled with books written about Him, and the earth's greatest scholars reverently kneel at His feet. He never had a bank balance, but He held the world in the hollow of His hand. Jesus never owned a house and yet He inhabited eternity. The Lord never possessed any real estate, but He died on one of the trees He made. We can only exclaim with the disciples: ''What manner of man is this?'' The answer comes to us from the sign of the fish, the insignia of all New Testament Christians. He was Jesus, the Son of God; our Savior.

# The Twenty-third Chapter of Matthew

THEME: *Christ Condemns His Critics*

OUTLINE:
   I. The Importance of Being Nothing (Verses 1-12)
   II. The Danger of Knowing Everything (Verses 13-32)
   III. The Awfulness of Being Condemned (Verses 33-36)
   IV. The Tragedy of Being Lost (Verses 37-39)

## SECTION ONE

*Expository Notes on Christ's Indictment of the Rabbis*

**Then spake Jesus to the multitude, and to his disciples, Saying, The scribes and the Pharisees sit in Moses' seat: All therefore whatsoever they bid you observe, that observe and do; but do not ye after their works: for they say, and do not. For they bind heavy burdens and grievous to be borne, and lay them on men's shoulders; but they themselves will not move them with one of their fingers. But all their works they do for to be seen of men: they make broad their phylacteries, and enlarge the borders of their garments, And love the uppermost rooms at feasts, and the chief seats in the synagogues, And greetings in the markets, and to be called of men, Rabbi, Rabbi. But be not ye called Rabbi: for one is your Master, even Christ; and all ye are brethren. And call no man your father upon the earth: for one is your Father, which is in heaven. Neither be ye called masters: for one is your Master, even Christ. But he that is greatest among you shall be your servant. And whosoever shall exalt himself shall be abased; and he that shall humble himself shall be exalted (vv. 1-12).**

This is one of the most depressing chapters in Matthew's Gospel. It is impossible to read its message without gaining the impression that Christ had abandoned hope of winning His listeners. The scribes and Pharisees had hardened their hearts, and were determined to reject every advance made by Jesus. Matthew, in recording the outcome, cites a series of woes mentioned by His Master. Verses 13, 14, 15, 16, 23, 25, 27, and 29 all begin with the warning,·"Woe unto you." The scribes and Pharisees had rejected God's offered grace, spurned His Son, and alas, their house was now "left unto [them] desolate."

## A FEEBLE INTERPRETATION

The Lord was not criticizing the dictates of Moses when He said, "The scribes and the Pharisees sit in Moses' seat." He was publicly recognizing the fact that these men were occupying the seat of authority; they were in the place where Moses would have been had he been living on earth at that time. The original laws of God were excellent as a foundation upon which to build a legal system necessary for the growth of a nation. Yet, the custodians of the records had added thousands of new regulations which enslaved people and in some instances dishonored God. When they spoke according to the decalogue, their message was mandatory, for what Moses said had been the expression of the will of God. Additional commandments had been written as a cover for the evil and selfish practices of the men who wrote them. A scribe could write any law permitting whatever he desired. Afterward, should anyone criticize his deeds, the man cited his own law as justification for his questionable behavior. The fine line of demarcation between that which was right and wrong can be seen in verse three. "All therefore whatsoever they bid you observe, that observe and do; *but do not ye after their works: for they say, and do not .*" Maybe this refers to *the second son* mentioned in Matthew 21:30. "And he answered and said, I go, sir: and went not." There was nothing wrong with the commandments of God, but alas, the life-giving water of God's Word was being polluted by dirty channels. Jesus condemned the scribes and Pharisees because of their insensitiveness to the sufferings of other people. The thousands of unnecessary requirements made life unbearable, and yet, the legal experts "would not move a finger" to lighten the load carried by suffering people.

## A FALSE IMPORTANCE

The phylacteries were amulets or tassels worn on the outermost garment. "The tephillin, or the prayer-fillets, as they were called, were either strips of parchment or small cubes covered with leather, on or in which were written four sections of the Law, viz, Exodus 13:1-10; 11-16; Deuteronomy 6:4-9, and 11:13-21. They were worn fastened either to the forehead, or inside the left arm, so as to be near the heart. Their use arose from a literal and superstitious interpretation of Exodus 13:9; Deuteronomy 6:8 and 11:18. Their dimensions were defined by rabbinical rules, but the extra pious formalists of the day set these at naught, and increased the breadth of the strips or of the bands by which they were fastened, in order to draw attention to their religiousness and their own strict attention to the least observances of the law. These phylacteries are still in use among the Jews. Thus in a 'Class Book for Jewish Youth' we read: 'Every boy, three months before he attains the age of thirteen, commences to make use of the tephillin, which must be worn at least during the time of the morning prayers. The ordinance of the tephillin is one of the signs of the covenant existing between the Almighty and ourselves, that we may continually bear in mind the miracles God wrought for our forefathers''' ( *The Pulpit Commentary. Matthew.* Vol. 2, p. 396).

The ostentatious display of amulets; the desire to occupy the chief seats in the synagogue, and the wish to be recognized by people in the streets and market, indicated the plaudits of men were more desirable than the approbation of God. These professors of religion were shams and hypocrites. The cloak of religion was worn to influence onlookers and was no indication of a consecrated life. It was against such people that Jesus directed His eight "woes."

## A FAVORED INSIGNIFICANCE

The Lord looked at His disciples and said, "But be not ye called Rabbi: for one is your Master, even Christ; and all ye are brethren. And call no man your father upon the earth: for one is your Father, which is in heaven." Jesus emphasized that the disciples were required to be the exact opposite of the scribes and Pharisees. They professed piety but were impious; the disciples should never advertise their holiness, their acts would be self-explanatory. Jesus said, "But he that is greatest among you shall be your servant." Humility is the foundation upon which true holiness rests. Love recognizes that even the most insignificant of human beings is precious in the sight of God, and any service rendered to them is a service to God. It was this attribute which made Christianity different from all other religious movements. Love can always be recognized by its desire to give and not to get. An open hand can do many things, but a closed hand becomes a fist and can never be attractive in the sight of God. The Savior stressed the fact that to walk this path in life was to traverse a select highway leading to the heart of God. They who knelt to wash the feet of others would someday receive a crown.

## SECTION TWO

### *Expository Notes on the Eight Warnings of Christ*

**But woe unto you, scribes and Pharisees, hypocrites! for ye shut up the kingdom of heaven against men: for ye neither go in yourselves, neither suffer ye them that are entering to go in. Woe unto you, scribes and Pharisees, hypocrites! for ye devour widows' houses, and for a pretence make long prayer: therefore ye shall receive the greater damnation. Woe unto you, scribes and Pharisees, hypocrites! for ye compass sea and land to make one proselyte, and when he is made, ye make him twofold more the child of hell than yourselves (vv. 13-15).**

### *THE FIRST WOE...A Warning Against Flagrant Perversity*

This frightening series of denunciations resemble thunder claps during an intense storm. Robinson describes this chapter as '' the rolling thunder of God's wrath.'' The storm clouds had been gathering for a long time but finally the outburst became deafening when Jesus enumerated the successive woes expressed in this chapter. The word translated ''woe'' is *ouai* which has dual meanings of grief and denunciation. The Lord was exceedingly angry, and yet intense pity echoed in His voice. It is therefore difficult to find an English word which adequately expresses what Jesus said. Furthermore, as we have already seen, the word translated ''hypocrite'' originally was used for *an actor*; ''one who played a part.'' The scribes and Pharisees were pretending to be godly, but their hearts contradicted what they said. They were false, unreliable, and evil. They had heard about the kingdom of heaven, but were determined never to enter. Furthermore, they were doing their utmost to prevent other people from entering, and there was danger that precious souls would be lost because of the evil example set by those detestable men. Their actions were premeditated. They were without excuse.

### *THE SECOND WOE...A Warning Against Futile Prayers*

**Woe unto you...for ye devour widows' houses, and for a pretence make long prayer (v. 14).**

The word picture behind this statement was unmistakable. The women who had lost husbands became prey for these covetous men. The religious leaders pretended to be genuinely concerned about the widows' grief. They offered long prayers to impress the listeners, and by devious ways endeavored to extract payment for their services. Their continuing efforts led to the decimation of the widows' property. It is interesting to note that in Luke's Gospel, this denunciation is followed by the account of the widow placing her very small gift in the treasury (see Luke 20:47; 21:1-4). The inference is that the widow was poor because the Pharisees had taken all her money! This practice became infamous during the Middle Ages when priests charged exorbitantly for intercessions which were supposed to get people out of purgatory. It was against these practices Martin Luther rebelled, and ultimately nailed his theses to the church door in Wittenberg. Any man, be he priest, minister, or layman, who hides a covetous heart beneath a cloak of religion, is worthy of the greatest condemnation.

*THE THIRD WOE...A Warning Against Fatal Pursuits*

**...for ye compass sea and land to make one proselyte, and...make him twofold more the child of hell than yourselves (v. 15).**

There was a certain attractiveness about the Jewish teaching, and even in Old Testament times some Gentiles were drawn closer to the Hebrew faith. The converts or proselytes were generally divided into two categories. Those men who submitted to the rite of circumcision were known as *proselytes of rightousness*; others were called *proselytes of the gate*. The word translated "proselytes" is *proseelutos* and according to Thayer means: "one who has drawn near; a stranger; a newcomer." When people attracted to Israel entered into commitments to observe certain laws, they were considered to be "converts." Many of the Pharisees were untiring in their attempt to proselytize strangers. They were the forerunners of sectarianism, a curse which was to discredit the church for centuries. Alas, this kind of menace may still be seen. Some churches are more concerned with protecting their ordinances than extending their influence. Their leaders spend more time building a fence around their kingdom than in trying to win precious souls for the Savior. Often they are embittered, unyielding, and cynical. Their man-made prohibitions destroy the attractiveness of the gospel they claim to preach. It is wise to remember that any professing Christian without love is a Pharisee without Christ.

*THE FOURTH WOE...A Warning Against Fickle Promises*

> **Woe unto you, ye blind guides, which say, Whosoever shall swear by the temple, it is nothing; but whosoever shall swear by the gold of the temple, he is a debtor! Ye fools and blind: for whether is greater, the gold, or the temple that sanctifieth the gold? And, Whosoever shall swear by the altar, it is nothing: but whosoever sweareth by the gift that is upon it, he is guilty. Ye fools and blind: for whether is greater, the gift or the altar that sanctifieth the gift? Whoso therefore shall swear by the altar, sweareth by it, and by all things thereon. And whoso shall swear by the temple, sweareth by it, and by him that dwelleth therein. And he that shall swear by heaven, sweareth by the throne of God, and by him that sitteth thereon (v. 16-22).**

It is difficult to appreciate the forcefulness of this denunciation without an understanding of the complex way in which the Pharisees regarded vows. Formerly, as with the case of Jepthah (Judg. 11:30-40) the honoring of a vow made to God was considered to be of the utmost importance and honor. When a man made a vow, he was expected to keep his promise. The Jews of later generations became expert evasionists, and created special loopholes by which they could avoid responsibilities. The legalists differentiated between vows which included God's name, and vows which did not. They affirmed that the sacrifice placed upon the altar was of more importance than the altar itself. Therefore, if a man did not wish to honor a promise, he vowed by the altar, believing he would be justified later if he failed to honor his solemn promise. If, on the other hand, he swore by the sacrifice, it was not as easy to avoid his obligations. Thus the nation recognized different degrees of responsibility, and no one considered what God might think of the strange procedure. Jesus attacked the very core of the religious structure of Israel when He denounced the perpetrators as "blind guides and fools." He taught that any promise made to God, in any place and at any time, was sacred. Worshipers should never make vows to the Almighty unless they were determined to honor their commitments.

*THE FIFTH WOE...A Warning Against Forgetting Priorities*

> **Woe unto you, scribes and Pharisees, hypocrites! for ye pay tithe of mint and anise and cummin, and have omitted the weightier matters of the law, judgment, mercy, and faith: these ought ye to have done, and not to leave the other undone. Ye blind guides, which strain at a gnat, and swallow a camel (v. 23-24).**

Tithing was a basic part of the religious life of Israel and was practiced in obedience to the command found in Deuteronomy 14:23. It is significant that Jesus mentioned mint, anise or dill, and cummin. Mint was one of the ingredients of the sauce of bitter herbs used at the Passover feast (see Exod. 12:8). It was also hung in the synagogue, for its fragrance was very attractive. Anise was used for medicinal purposes and by housewives for seasoning. Cummin was a plant used for food, flavoring, and medicine. These were not large crops grown for commercial purposes. Every householder had small quantities in his garden, and it is significant that the law of tithing had been applied to such small commodities. The Pharisees taught that the tithe concerned even the stems and leaves of these plants. This was ridiculous as the amount to be tithed was very small. Yet in contrast the same men neglected the more important features of the law. Their judgment was biased, their mercy questionable, and genuine faith unknown.

When Jesus mentioned the gnat and the camel, He was bringing together extremes considered to be unclean. The gnat was very small and insignificant; the camel was large and awkward. The word translated "strain" is *diulizontes*, which according to Thayer means: "to defecate; to cleanse from dregs or filth; to filter through; to strain thoroughly; to pour through a filter; to rid wine of a gnat by filtering; to strain out." Jesus was referring to the common practice of straining wine through linen. The Pharisees were meticulous about avoiding the least impurities and yet openly and unashamedly "they swallowed a camel." Their inconsistencies were blatantly disgusting.

*THE SIXTH AND SEVENTH WOES...A Warning Against False Professions*

**Ye make clean the outside...but within are full of extortion....Ye are like unto whited sepulchres, which indeed appear beautiful outward, but are within full of dead men's bones, and of all uncleanness. Even so ye also outwardly appear righteous unto men, but within ye are full of hypocrisy and iniquity (v. 25-28).**

The Jewish laws regarding defilement were so complex, they had become ridiculous. An earthen vessel which was *hollow* became unclean only on the inside and not on the outside; and it could only be cleansed by being broken. Certain earthen vessels could not become unclean at all — a flat plate without a rim, an open coal shovel; a grid iron with holes in it for parching grains of wheat. On the other hand, a plate with a rim, or an earthen spice box, or a writing case could become unclean. Of vessels made of leather, bone, wood, and glass, flat ones did not become unclean; deep ones did. Any metal vessel which was once smooth and hollow could become unclean; but a door, a bolt, a lock, a hinge, a knocker could not become unclean. The regulations seem to us fantastic, and yet these are the very regulations the Pharisees religiously and meticulously kept.

It was inexcusable that men who were so fastidious about trifling matters should be vicious in their dealings with Jesus, and whose consciences condoned murder. The outward appearance suggested piety, virtue, and godliness, and yet their desires were motivated by evil. At Passover all roads leading to Jerusalem were signposted in regard to the locations of graves. Once a year, about the middle of the month of Adah, all tombs were whitewashed partly out of respect for the dead, but also to give warning to travelers that tombs were in the vicinity. Contact with the dead meant defilement, and this barred pilgrims from participating in the Passover feast. It would have been disastrous if pilgrims who traveled great distances were accidentally prevented from taking part in the annual celebration. Therefore all tombs along the highways were clearly marked to warn travelers of danger. Referring to these graves, Jesus compared them with the Pharisees. He stated that their external beauty hid internal corruption. This was His strongest indictment of the religious leaders of His day.

*THE EIGHTH WOE...A Warning Against Foolish Pride*

**Woe unto you, scribes and Pharisees, hypocrites! because ye build the tombs of the prophets, and garnish the sepulchres of the righteous, And say, If we had been in the days of our fathers, we would not have been partakers with them in the blood of the prophets. Wherefore ye be witnesses unto yourselves, that ye are the children of them which killed the prophets. Fill ye us then the measure of your fathers (vv. 29-32).**

Probably when Jesus uttered these words, He pointed to some of the carefully preserved tombs in the vicinity. He indicated that, whereas the Pharisees condemned the murders of ancient prophets, they remained proud of their ancestors who committed the crimes. They said they would not have participated in the stoning of God's servants, but yet at the same time, were trying to emulate the deeds of their forefathers. "Stier quotes a striking passage from the Berlenberger Bibel: 'Ask in Moses' times, "Who are the good people?" They will be Abraham, Isaac, and Jacob; *but not Moses, he should be stoned*! Ask in Samuel's times, "Who are the good people?'' They will be Moses and Joshua, *but not Samuel*! Ask in the times of Christ, and they will be all the former prophets with Samuel, *but not Christ and His apostles*''' (*The Pulpit Commentary. Matthew*. Vol. 2, pp. 404-409).

The Pharisees were filled with foolish pride; yet they failed to realize that pride and penitence never live together. They were proud of ancestors, traditions, and historical events; they boasted of their heritage and associations with God, but never exhibited anything indicative of fellowship with the Almighty. They were whited sepulchres, blind guides, and abominable hypocrites. When Jesus said, ''Fill ye up then the measure of your fathers,'' He seemed to be saying, ''Alright, do as you please; fill to the brim the cup of your fathers' evil example. They killed the prophets; you plan to kill Me. Do it and you will discover the stupidity of your act. No man can fight against God and survive.''

SECTION THREE

*Expository Notes on Christ's Condemnation of Hypocrites*

**Ye serpents, ye generation of vipers, how can ye escape the damnation of hell? Wherefore, behold, I send unto you prophets, and wise men, and scribes: and some of them ye shall kill and crucify; and some of them ye shall scourge in your synagogues, and persecute them from city to city: That upon you may come all the righteous blood shed upon the earth, from the blood of the righteous Abel unto the blood of Zacharias son of Barachias, whom ye slew between the temple and the altar. Verily I say unto you, All these things shall come upon this generation (vv. 33-36).**

*THE UNANSWERABLE CHALLENGE*

''How can ye escape the damnation of hell?'' The question could not be answered, for there was no escape! It must be obvious to every sincere reader that Jesus believed there existed ''the damnation of hell''; otherwise He was misleading listeners by mentioning an impossibility. The writer to the Hebrews asked a similar question: ''How shall we escape, if we neglect so great salvation...?'' (Heb. 2:3). The Savior was very explicit when He said, ''I am the way, the truth, and the life: no man cometh unto the Father, but by me'' (John 14:6). Simon Peter was equally emphatic when he preached, saying: ''Neither is there salvation in any other: for there is none other name under heaven given among men, whereby we must be saved'' (Acts 4:12). The Christian church was founded upon the great precept that sinners needed to repent and yield themselves to Christ. Throughout the centuries that message was preached among the nations, and millions of souls, responding to its challenge, were brought to Christ. There is evidence in our age that the church has lost its influence in the world. Liberal theologians teach that every religion is a way by which sinners may come to God. Their conclusions are not supported by the teachings of Jesus. He alone can save sinners. Paul was correct when he wrote to Timothy, saying, ''For there is one God, and one mediator between God and men, the man Christ Jesus'' (1 Tim. 2:5). Any message which fails to emphasize this important truth is a perversion of the true gospel.

## THE UNMISTAKABLE CLAIM

''Wherefore, behold, I send unto you prophets, and wise men, and scribes: and some of them ye shall kill....'' This statement must be considered against the background of the Lord's earlier teaching. He had spoken of a lord who sent servants to gather the fruits of the vineyard; of a king who sent servants to bid guests attend a marriage, and of God who had sent prophets to warn Israel. Now Jesus said, ''I SEND UNTO YOU PROPHETS, AND WISE MEN, AND SCRIBES.'' The Lord was now representing Himself as God; He and He alone would be responsible for the commissioning of special missionaries, many of whom would be persecuted by those to whom they were sent. Jesus had no illusions about the outcome of their mission. His disciples would be as important as Moses, Elijah, and all the ancient prophets. They would deliver a message already endorsed by God, and people who rejected it would be as guilty as the forefathers who murdered the prophets. Yet, in spite of the fierce persecution to be encountered, those missionaries would go from city to city, until the whole world would be aware of the good news of the gospel. Nothing would prevail against the power of God; even emperors would be unable to prevent the extension of the kingdom of heaven.

## THE UNAVOIDABLE CONCLUSION

''That upon you may come all the righteous blood shed upon the earth, from the blood of the righteous Abel unto the blood of Zacharias...whom ye slew between the temple and the altar.'' The story of the murder of Abel is well known to all readers of the Bible; the account of the death of Zacharias may only be known to a few. It is found in 2 Chronicles 24:20-22. It is interesting to note that in the Hebrew Bible, *Genesis* is the first book as it is in ours; but, unlike our order of the books, 2 Chronicles is the last book in the Hebrew Bible. It has been wisely observed that the murder of Abel was the first murder in the Bible story, and the murder of Zacharias was the last. From the beginning to end, the history of Israel is the rejection, and often the slaughter, of the men of God. As in ancient times, men still scoff at the idea of retribution, and insist they can do as they please. Yet the same laws given by Moses continue to operate within modern societies. If men commit murder they are penalized accordingly. The same Bible which communicates to us the laws of the patriarch, also states that after death men will be judged according to their records. Jesus insisted this would be a reality, and any teacher who believes to the contrary is to be condemned.

## THE UNSURPASSED CALAMITY

Jesus said, "Verily I say unto you, All these things shall come upon this generation." Doubtless, the Lord was able to see beforehand the events to take place during the Roman siege of Jerusalem. To the Jews it was unthinkable that any calamity should befall their famous city; God would surely protect His property. They had no understanding that the true temple of God was within human hearts; that stones and timber could never be as important as a contrite spirit and a dedicated soul. Within forty years of Christ's prediction, Jerusalem fell before the onslaught of Caesar's legions. Josephus describes how, during the sacking of the city, rivers of blood flowed through the gates. He adds that as far as it was possible to see, in every direction there was no sight but that of crucified Jews. The impossible came to pass; the grandeur of Israel was destroyed. All that Jesus predicted was fulfilled, and this in itself should encourage people to give increasing attention to the other predictions made by the Son of God. Surely, He knew what He was talking about!

## SECTION FOUR

*Expository Notes on Christ's Lament Over Jerusalem*

**O Jerusalem, Jerusalem, thou that killest the prophets, and stonest them which are sent unto thee, how often would I have gathered thy children**

together, even as a hen gathereth her chickens under her wings, and ye would not! Behold, your house is left unto you desolate. For I say unto you, Ye shall not see me henceforth, till ye shall say, Blessed is he that cometh in the name of the Lord (vv. 37-39).

## LOVE PERSISTING..."How Often Would I Have Gathered Thee?"

We have already considered that most of the Lord's ministry had been exercised in Galilee. That He visited Jerusalem can never be questioned, but for some inscrutable reason, the evangelists only mention a few of those occasions. It may be safely assumed that Jerusalem was seldom, if ever, out of His thoughts. The "how often" of the text suggests that constantly His heart yearned for the opportunity to embrace the Jewish people. In spite of their blatant rebellion and antagonism, Jesus continued to love them, and would have done anything for the privilege of helping His enemies. Alas, "He came unto his own, and his own received him not" (John 1:11).

## LOVE PROTECTING..."Would I Have Gathered Thy Children Together, Even as a Hen Gathereth Her Chickens Under Her Wings."

The story has often been told of the chicken who gathered her chicks beneath her wings to protect them from an approaching prairie fire. When the fire had passed, the farmer saw a charred mass, and gently moving it, was amazed to see small chicks emerging from what remained of the incinerated mother. Love is gentle and kind; love never faileth. That Jesus should liken His desires to those of a mother chicken indicates the surging emotions which filled His soul. Love frustrated is the harbinger of disappointment and tears. There is reason to believe that had the nation accepted His entreaties, God would have protected the city, and Jerusalem would never have been conquered by the Romans. "If God be for us, who can be against us?" Yet without God, even the strongest of men and nations become vulnerable.

## LOVE PRONOUNCING..."Your House is Left Unto You Desolate."

The Lord probably had tears in His eyes when He made this fateful announcement. It was then too late to do anything. To quote the prophet: "The summer had ended, and Israel was not saved." The days of opportunity had passed; the outlook had become bleak. God had spoken in the days of Noah saying that His Spirit would not always strive with men, and He meant what He said. This had become obvious. There was no more hope; the citizens of Jerusalem were dead already! Nevertheless, Jesus continued to love those people, but the reason for this will probably remain eternally incomprehensible.

*LOVE PREDICTING... "Ye Shall Not See Me Henceforth, Till Ye Shall Say, Blessed is He That Cometh in the Name of the Lord."*

It has been claimed that every cloud has a silver lining, and the prediction made by Jesus seems to support the suggestion. The Lord looked beyond His disappointment, and rejoiced in the distant future when things would change. He foresaw the time when God's chosen people would recognize Him to be, and accept Him as, the Messiah. They had acclaimed Him when He rode triumphantly into the city, and they would do this again using identical phraseology. Etched against the blackness of the approaching storm, the realization of ultimate triumph must have been extremely comforting to the Lord. What He had yearned to do for the people of His time, He would ultimately do, not only for Israel, but for the entire world. He would not die in vain! It was this realization which made the writer to the Hebrews exclaim, "...let us run with patience the race that is set before us. Looking unto Jesus the author and finisher of our faith; who for the joy that was set before him endured the cross, despising the shame, and is set down at the right hand of the throne of God" (Heb. 12:1-2).

# The Twenty-fourth Chapter
# of Matthew

THEME: *The Return of Christ*

OUTLINE:
    I.  Be Warned...*"Not Yet."* (Verses 1-13)
    II.  Be Wise...*"Listen."* (Verses 14-28)
    III.  Be Watchful...*"Look."* (Verses 29-35)
    IV.  Be Waiting...*"Any Moment."* (Verses 36-44)
    V.  Be Workers...*"Constantly."* (Verses 45-51)

## SECTION ONE

*Expository Notes on Signs of the Latter Days*

**And Jesus went out, and departed from the temple: and his disciples came to him for to show him the buildings of the temple. And Jesus said unto them, See ye not all these things? verily I say unto you, There shall not be left here one stone upon another, that shall not be thrown down. And as he sat upon the mount of Olives, the disciples came unto him privately, saying, Tell us, when shall these things be? and what shall be the sign of thy coming, and of the end of the world? (vv. 1-3).**

The Lord had already said, "Behold, your house is left unto you desolate"; He was now leaving the temple for the last time. Mark tells us that as Jesus was departing, one of the disciples drew His attention to the magnificent stones in the structure, and that later, from a vantage point on the mount of Olives, Peter, James, John and Andrew inquired about the signs to precede the end of the age (Mark 13:1-4). Dr. Edersheim describing the scene, wrote: "A sudden turn in the road, and the sacred building was once more in full view. Just then, the western sun was pouring its golden beams on tops of marble cloisters, and on the terraced courts, and glittering on the golden spikes on the roof of the holy place. In this setting, even more than in the rising sun, the vast proportions, the symmetry, and the sparkling sheen of this mass of snowy marble and gold stood out gloriously. And across the black valley, and up the slopes of Olivet, lay the dark shadows of those gigantic walls built of massive stones, some of which were nearly twenty-four feet long. Even the rabbis, despite their hatred of Herod, grow enthusiastic, and dream that the very temple walls would have been covered with gold had not the variegated marble, resembling waves of the sea, seemed more beauteous. It was probably as the disciples gazed on all this grandeur and strength, that they broke the silence imposed on them by gloomy thoughts of the near desolateness of that house which the Lord predicted.''

As the Lord made His final departure from the temple precincts, the disciples mentioned the outstanding features of the ornate sanctuary, and to their amazement, Jesus answered, ''There shall not be left here one stone upon another, that shall not be thrown down.'' It should be remembered that some of the disciples had been fishermen in Galilee, and their occupation would have denied to them the privilege of going often to Jerusalem. Even they must have been thrilled by the grandeur of the temple; their shining eyes had looked with awe and wonder upon the sights which attracted millions of visitors annually. The terrible prediction concerning the complete destruction of Jerusalem amazed them. Many years later they were to remember what Jesus said.

Describing the fulfillment of the Lord's prediction, Josephus wrote: ''While the house was on fire, everything was plundered that came to hand, and ten thousand of those that were caught were slain; nor was there any commiseration of any age, or any reverence of gravity, but children and old men, and profane persons and priests, were all slain in the same manner; so that this war went round all sorts of men, and brought them to destruction...those that made supplication for their lives, as those that defended themselves by fighting. The flame was also carried a long way, and made an echo, together with the groans of those that were slain; and because this hill was high, and the works at the temple were very great, one would have thought that the whole city had been on fire. Nor can one imagine anything either greater or more terrible than this noise; for there was at once the shout of the Roman legions who were marching all together, and a sad clamour of the seditious, who were now surrounded with fire and sword...One would have thought that the hill itself on which the temple stood, was seething hot, as full of fire on every part of it, that the blood was larger in quantity than the fire, and those that were slain more in number than those that slew them. The ground did nowhere appear visible, for the dead bodies that lay on it, but the soldiers went over heaps of those bodies as they ran upon such as fled from them'' ( *The Wars of the Jews*. Chapter Five. Paragraph One).

Josephus further describes the activities of the frenzied Romans as they dismantled the temple stone by stone. A group of Jews made their final resistance within the temple, but when they realized the futility of their efforts, they set the temple alight and died in the conflagration. The walls in the building became so hot that even the plundering Romans could not approach the ruins for several days. Only when the stones cooled, could they be touched, and it was then in their search for molten gold, the besiegers took them one at a time from the walls. With but one exception, the prediction of Jesus was literally fulfilled. That exception attracted attention throughout the ages. What is now called "The Great West Wall" (formerly called The Wailing Wall) is said to be the only surviving part of the temple. That section of the wall was not dismantled. It is believed that when the Israelis build their new temple, those stones will be incorporated into the structure, and if this takes place, once again the world will be reminded of the veracity of the Word of God. It is worthy of attention that when the disciples asked their question upon the Mount of Olives, their doubts had disappeared; they firmly believed their Master was correct in His assessment of the future. The reply to the question, "What shall be the sign of thy coming, and of the end of the world?" supplied the introduction to some of the most remarkable prophecies in the Bible.

**And Jesus answered and said unto them, Take heed that no man deceive you. For many shall come in my name, saying, I am Christ; and shall deceive many. And ye shall hear of wars and rumours of wars: see that ye be not troubled: for all these things must come to pass, but the end is not yet. For nation shall rise against nation, and kingdom against kingdom: and there shall be famines, and pestilences, and earthquakes, in divers places. All these are the beginning of sorrows (vv. 4-8).**

These verses contain four areas of thought (1) *Carefulness*. "Jesus said, "Take heed that no man deceive you." There would be many pretenders whose ministry might undermine the confidence of men not "rooted and grounded" in the faith. Eloquence and even a knowledge of the Scripture would not be guarantees of divine ordination. John at a later date warned his readers to "try the spirits [and prove them] whether they be of God" (see 1 John 4:1-3). (2) *Constraint*. The Lord not only predicted events to come, He urged His friends to remain calm whatever happened. Peace of mind would rest upon the soul's ability to be confident in the sovereignty of God. At the appointed time, and not before, a satisfactory climax would be reached. Until then, the disciples should remain untroubled. (3) *Commotions*. Jesus warned that throughout history, international discord, widespread famines, devastating diseases among humans and plants, and earthquakes of enormous proportions would shatter the tranquillity of mankind. Sometimes the outlook might be bleak, but the disciples should never forget God was still on His throne; that ultimately, His perfect will would be accomplished. (4) *Courage*. "All these are the beginning of sorrows." The phrase "the beginning of sorrows" comes from the Greek words *archee odinon* which means "birthpangs." The difficulties of the future would not be evidence that God had abandoned His people; they would suggest that in spite of the nation's sin, He would create a new world in which righteousness would be dominant. Jesus was simply saying that although Satan might win some battles, the final victory would be won by God.

> **Then shall they deliver you up to be afflicted, and shall kill you: and ye shall be hated of all nations for my name's sake. And then shall many be offended, and shall betray one another, and shall hate one another. And many false prophets shall rise, and shall deceive many. And because iniquity shall abound, the love of many shall wax cold. But he that shall endure unto the end, the same shall be saved (vv. 9-13).**

When the Lord sat upon the mount of Olives, answering the questions of the disciples, He not only saw the immediate future, His vision reached to the end of time. Four areas of thought await investigation.

## THE DISTRESS OF DELIBERATE PERSECUTION

"Then shall they deliver you up to be afflicted, and shall kill shall many be offended, and shall betray one another, and shall hate one another." Jesus realized the formation of the Christian church would bring unprecedented happiness to His followers, but alas, the road they traveled would be steep and stony. Many of the disciples would be required to sacrifice their possessions, and some would become martyrs. The best of the Roman emperors, constrained by fear of their gods, would do their utmost to annihilate the church, and three centuries of terrible persecution would test the faith of the most ardent followers. Christians would be fed to ravenous beasts; others would be burnt to death to provide entertainment for the guests of Caesar. The problems occasioned by suffering would disturb the saints, and many might ask why God permitted such things to happen.

## THE DANGERS FROM DECEPTIVE PROPHET

Jesus knew the teachers of Judaism would challenge the authority of the church, and Paul, aware of this fact, said to the elders of the Ephesian church, "For I know this, that after my departing shall grievous wolves enter in among you, not sparing the flock. Also of your own selves shall men arise, speaking perverse things, to draw away disciples after them" (Acts 20:29-30). When John wrote his epistles, he had much to say about the false teachers who had become a menace within the assemblies (see 3 John 9-10). The warnings issued by Jesus, Paul, and John are still important. This world is filled with strange, pernicious sects which misinterpret the Scripture, ensnare young converts, and menace the ongoing work of the kingdom of God. Referring to these prophets, Jesus said, "Not every one that saith unto me, Lord, Lord, shall enter into the kingdom of heaven...Many will say to me in that day, Lord, Lord, have we not prophesied in thy name? and in thy name have cast out devils? and in thy name done many wonderful works? And then will I profess unto them, I never knew you: depart from me, ye that work iniquity" (Matt. 7:21-23).

## THE DIFFICULTY FROM DISTURBING PROBLEMS

"And because iniquity shall abound, the love of many shall wax cold." *Phillips* translates this passage: "Because of the spread of wickedness the love of most men will grow cold." It is to be eternally regretted that many of the early followers of Jesus turned away, and ultimately lost their zeal for righteousness. This was repeated on innumerable occasions during the history of the church, when people allowed unpleasant circumstances to eclipse the sun of their faith. They could not reconcile the spread of lawlessness and its consequent suffering with the patience and longsuffering of a heavenly Father. They asked, "Why did God permit this to happen?," and when no satisfactory answer was forthcoming, became embittered backsliders. It is wise to consider that any vehicle is able to run downhill; it takes one with an engine to climb steep highways. "The man worthwhile, is the man who can smile, when everything goes dead wrong."

## THE DELIGHT FROM A DEFINITE PROMISE

"But he that shall endure unto the end, the same shall be saved." It has been claimed that no Christians perished in the downfall of

Jerusalem, for obeying the Lord's commands, they fled to the mountains (v. 16). They did not capitulate, commit suicide, nor doubt the accuracy of the Lord's predictions. They endured, and lived to tell their story. There may be a wider sense in which the text could apply to any person convicted of sin. To endure against all opposition and fear, and faithfully adhere to the principles enunciated by Jesus, will always be the means by which to enjoy life everlasting. It should never be forgotten that under all circumstances, in every place, the promises of God are the only foundation upon which to rely.

### SECTION TWO

*Expository Notes on Christ's Predictions Concerning the End of the Age*

**And this gospel of the kingdom shall be preached in all the world for a witness unto all nations; and then shall the end come. When ye therefore shall see the abomination of desolation spoken of by Daniel the prophet, stand in the holy place, (whoso readeth, let him understand:) Then let them which be in Judaea flee into the mountains: Let him which is on the housetop not come down to take any thing out of his house: Neither let him which is in the field return back to take his clothes....But pray ye that your flight be not in the winter, neither on the sabbath day: For then shall be great tribulation, such as was not since the beginning of the world to this time, no, nor ever shall be. And except those days should be shortened, there should no flesh be saved: but for the elect's sake those days shall be shortened (vv. 14-22).**

The parenthesis "whoso readeth, let him understand" might be the most important statement in this Scripture. Matthew was obviously referring to Daniel 12:11 where the prophet mentioned "the abomination that maketh desolate." Having made his reference, he seemed to say to his readers," You will understand what I am trying to tell you." Similarly the Lord also used this method when, after telling His parables, He said, "Who hath ears to hear, let him hear" (Matt. 13:43). Jesus was saying, "Since you have ears, use them!" It might be helpful to know what the Scripture CANNOT mean.

Toward the end of the second century before Christ, a Syrian king, Antiochus Epiphanes, captured Jerusalem and defiled the temple by erecting an altar to Zeus in the temple court. Upon this abomination, he sacrificed swine flesh, and the private rooms of the priests were made into brothels. This was a deliberate attempt to destroy the Jewish faith.

Doubtless Jesus knew of this atrocity, but His prediction recorded in this chapter cannot possibly mean the act of the Syrian monarch, for that had been performed many years earlier.

Later, about the year A.D.135, an insurrectionist named Barcochebas, tried to destroy the partially rebuilt Jerusalem. He wished to abolish the old name of the city and history describes how he erected a temple to Jupiter on the site of the holy place, and placed a statue of the emperor upon the foundation of the altar. (See *The Pulpit Commentary. Matthew*. Vol. 2, p. 435.) The Lord could not have been referring to this event, for at that time, the Gospel "had not been preached for a witness unto all nations." Jesus emphasized that the end could not come until the world had been evangelized (see Matt. 24:14).

We are therefore obliged to accept the fact that the Savior was referring to the end of time, when the Jews would be threatened by the forces of the Antichrist.   Paul also mentioned this when he wrote "Let no man deceive you by any means: for that day shall not come, except there come a falling away first, and that man of sin be revealed, the son of perdition; Who opposeth and exalteth himself above all that is called God, or that is worshiped; *so that he as God sitteth in the temple of God, shewing himself that he is God*" (2 Thess. 2:3-4). Similar events taking place earlier must be regarded as *partial fulfillments* — evidence that sometimes "coming events cast their shadows before."

No one can deny that some of the warnings given by Christ were applicable to the fall of Jerusalem in the year A.D. 70. His advice that people should flee immediately to the mountains went unheeded, and this contributed to the gravity of the disaster. Believing the Almighty would protect His house, the Jews refrained from obeying the command of Jesus, and instead, sought refuge in the doomed sanctuary. They did not understand that even the most ornate temple was only a building when deprived of the indwelling presence of God. Josephus, who shared the terrible experience of watching the destruction of the temple, stated that ninety-seven thousand people were captured and taken into slavery, and one million, one hundred thousand died during the siege of the city. That the final onslaught on Jerusalem will resemble this pattern should fill every person with dread. Yet, against the blackness of that terrible sky, a star of promise shone. Jesus said, "And except those days should be shortened, there should no flesh be saved: but for the elect's sake those days shall be shortened." The mercy of God is one of His outstanding attributes. Not even the sinfulness of man can destroy divine love; happy indeed are they whose eyes are able to see!

Then if any man shall say unto you, Lo, here is Christ, or there; believe it not. For there shall arise false Christs, and false prophets, and shall show great signs and wonders; insomuch that, if it were possible, they shall deceive the very elect. Behold, I have told you before. Wherefore, if they shall say unto you, Behold, he is in the desert; go not forth: behold, he is in the secret chambers; believe it not. For as the lightning cometh out of the east, and shineth even to the west; so shall also the coming of the Son of man be. For wheresoever the carcase is, there will the eagles be gathered together (vv. 23-28).

## BE WISE AND CAREFUL

The Lord was careful in warning the disciples that false Messiahs would appear; that their teaching and miracles would ensnare, if that were possible, even the most ardent of His followers. His words concerning their going into the desert or to some secret meeting place in order to find Him, were partially fulfilled during the siege of Jerusalem. Seditionists spread the lie that the Messiah was recruiting an army in the desert and would soon be marching to deliver the besieged city. Many fanatical Jews, believing the report, went out to seek Him, and fell into the hands of the Roman legions. It is thought provoking that throughout the centuries, strange men have claimed to be the Messiah, and always were able to obtain adherents to their cause. Jesus affirmed that even the performance of miracles should not be regarded as evidence of a divine commission. God had spoken through His Son, and what He said would be repeated by His devoted disciples. There would be no other infallible source of information (see Rev. 22:18-19). Any church, sect, or movement which has more faith in books other than the Bible, must be suspect. Mormons trust the *Book of Mormon*; Muslims trust the *Koran*; Christian Scientists study the works of Mary Baker Eddy. Jews rely on their books of law, and various other types of people believe implicitly in literature produced by revered founders of their faith. Let it be stressed continually that Christians have the Bible, and recognize it to be the unerring Word of God.

## BE WISE AND CONTENT

Jesus taught that there would be many inscrutable mysteries connected with His return to earth, but doubt should never exist in the minds of His disciples. He would return, and all His followers should live in a constant state of readiness. His coming would be as sudden as a flash of lightning, and within moments the entire world would become aware of the event. He also stated that the time of His return would be known only to God, and therefore any speculator who announced specific dates for His appearing would be foolish. Certain signs would appear in the heavens and earth, and when these became visible, men would know the return of the Lord would be "near, even at the doors." With this thought in mind, they should be watchful, wise, and content.

## BE WISE AND CONSIDERATE

"'For wheresoever the carcass is, there will the eagles [vultures] be gathered together.' Let it be candidly admitted that this has always been a difficult verse to interpret. "Bishop Ryle in *Expository Thoughts on the Gospels* mentions fifty-six writers who hold different views in regard to the interpretation of this mysterious verse....Throughout the Bible vultures are often mentioned in regard to their gathering around a carcass — a dead body — the place of putrefaction. Maybe Christ was thinking of the sinners of that future time; people who would be unacceptable to God. If that were the case, then the vultures might represent the angels of judgment whose task it will be to separate 'the wheat from the tares....'" (Reprinted from the author's book, *Luke's Thrilling Gospel,* p. 369.)

"Sometime ago, reports began to circulate that the vulture population of the Middle East was increasing enormously. It was claimed by teachers that this was a sign of the approach of the end of the age. Then came denials asserting that what had been publicized was untrue. I did not wish to say things which would be false, and therefore, the next time I visited Israel, I asked my guide, Mr. Ari Cohen, if the reports circulating in America could be authenticated. He smiled and said, 'You have surely asked the right person. I belong to the Bird Watching Society of Israel. What you heard is certainly true. We cannot explain it, but for the first time in history, those birds are increasing enormously.'" (Reprinted from the author's book, *What in the World Will Happen Next?* pp. 130-131.)

In the light of this important fact, it might have been that Jesus, knowing what would take place in the end times, cited the fact that, when the rottenness of human greed and evil approached its climax, the vultures, literally, would gather to participate in what the Bible calls, "The supper of the great God" (Rev. 19:17).

*Expository Notes on the Signs to be Seen Before Christ's Return*

> **Immediately after the tribulation of those days shall the sun be darkened, and the moon shall not give her light, and the stars shall fall from heaven, and the powers of the heavens shall be shaken: And then shall appear the sign of the Son of man in heaven: and then shall all the tribes of the earth mourn, and they shall see the Son of man coming in the clouds of heaven with power and great glory. And he shall send his angels with a great sound of a trumpet, and they shall gather together his elect from the four winds, from one end of heaven to the other (vv. 29-31).**

These verses are among the greatest prophetical utterances ever made, and deserve very careful and minute study. It should be remembered that "as [Jesus] sat upon the mount of Olives, the disciples came unto him privately, saying, Tell us, when shall these things be? and what shall be the sign of thy coming, and of the end of the world (age)." We are now to consider the answers to those vital questions and it might be helpful if we ask certain questions of our own. When? What? Where? and Why?

*WHEN?...The Statements in the Scriptures*

The references to the signs to be seen in the heavens have always intrigued man. For many years the statements of the prophets appeared to contradict each other, and only in recent times did facts become available to harmonize the apparently conflicting texts. Isaiah (30:26) said, "Moreover the light of the moon shall be as the light of the sun, and the light of the sun shall be sevenfold, as the light of seven days, *in the day that the LORD bindeth up the breach of his people, and healeth the stroke of their wound.*" If the sun suddenly became seven times more brilliant, then the moon correspondingly would be seven times more luminous, for it receives its light from the sun. The prophet insisted that this would happen when God healed the wounds of His people. The Bible teaches this will occur when Christ returns to establish His kingdom. Joel expressed another view when he said (2:31), "The sun shall be turned into darkness, and the moon into blood, *before the great and the terrible day of the LORD come.*" The Lord apparently agreed with Joel, for He said: "Immediately after the tribulation of those

days shall the sun be darkened, and the moon shall not give her light...."
At the end of the great Tribulation, these signs may be expected.

*WHAT?...The Signs in the Sky*

During recent years famous international scholars "expressed concern
over the possible 'death of the sun.' They said the sun ' is a small star
in a back alley of space, and is in danger of undergoing a nova.' They
claimed that when a star reaches the end of its life, it glows with great
intensity for a period of eight to fourteen days and then subsides into
darkness. It was once thought that the heat-energy output of the sun
would last forever, but in recent years scientists have reappraised their
ideas. Some think the sun — as a small star — has already used half
its hydrogen, and this is always followed by a nova. All the Scripture
passages agree on the timing of the events — they are to happen at the
end of the tribulation when the Lord returns with power and great glory.
We now know that Isaiah, Joel, and Jesus were merely describing a
nova — or the death of our sun-star. To repeat and to emphasize the
important point in all these deliberations — we may not know the precise
moment these events will occur, but we do know HOW they will happen
when the time comes. Surely it is thought provoking that when all the
signs of Christ's return are appearing on the earth, attention is being
drawn to possibilities in the sky. Can this be a coincidence? Are these
details unimportant? Is it not possible that we are living in the most
exciting days the earth ever knew?'' (Quoted in part from the author's
book *What in the World Will Happen Next?* pp. 127-129.)

*WHERE?... The Splendor of the Sun*

"And then shall appear the sign of the Son of man in heaven: and
then shall all the tribes of the earth mourn, and they shall see the Son
of man coming in the clouds of heaven with power and great glory.''
Once again we must remember the quotation already given. "If Jesus
was not what He claimed, He was the greatest charlatan ever to walk
the earth.'' When the Lord predicted this amazing event, He was either
speaking as the infallible Son of God or revealing mental incompetence.
Another detail intrigues the thoughtful reader. If the return of Christ
is to take place over Jerusalem, how shall all the tribes see the event
and mourn at His arrival? When Jesus uttered those words it would
have been a physical impossibility for the nations of the world to view
the event at the same moment. Television has changed our capabilities.

What once was considered to be impossible is now easily performed. We have become accustomed to watching events as they happen at the other side of the world.

*WHY?... The Selection of the Saints*

"And...his angels...shall gather together his elect...from one end of heaven to the other." The terrible period of trial to be endured during the Tribulation will produce faithful people who, resisting all threats from the Antichrist, will endure to the end and be saved. Many enthusiastic but unwise teachers categorically deny this fact, believing that after the Holy Spirit has been withdrawn (2 Thess. 2:7-8) no person will be accepted by God. This interpretation is erroneous. Describing the end times, John wrote "And I saw thrones, and they sat upon them, and judgment was given unto them; and I saw the souls of them that were beheaded for the witness of Jesus, and for the word of God, and *which had not worshiped the beast, neither his image, neither had received his mark upon their foreheads, or in their hands*; AND THEY LIVED AND REIGNED WITH CHRIST A THOUSAND YEARS" (Rev. 20:4). When Christ returns, these saints will be gathered from all directions to meet the Lord. They will be "the second crop of God's great harvest!" His first crop, if we may use the term, will have been gathered at the Rapture of the church. (See 1 Thess. 4:16-18.)

> Now learn a parable of the fig tree; When his branch is yet tender, and putteth forth leaves, ye know that summer is nigh. So likewise ye, when ye shall see all these things, know that it is near, even at the doors. Verily I say unto you, This generation shall not pass, till all these things be fulfilled. Heaven and earth shall pass away, but my words shall not pass away (vv. 32-35).

It must be remembered that the Lord indicated the exact date of His appearing would remain unknown. Nevertheless, it would be possible to detect early signs of His coming. The buds on a tree are the harbingers of spring and summer, and correspondingly, the appearance of predicted signs in the sky and upon the earth should inform God's people of the imminent return of their Savior. The statement "This generation shall not pass, till all these things be fulfilled" presents problems not easily solved. There are two possible solutions.

Matthew was a collector of the sayings of Jesus, and many of his quotations are grouped in chapters 24 and 25 of his Gospel. Does this statement refer to the return of Christ, or to the destruction of Jerusalem?

If Jerusalem's destruction be the case, there is no problem, for within forty years of Christ's prediction the Romans sacked Jerusalem and many people who heard Jesus witnessed the devastation which came in the year A.D.70. Secondly, if the first suggestion be unacceptable, we are confronted by the problem that "that generation" seemingly passed away long ago, and the return of Jesus had not taken place. We are therefore obliged to ask another question. To what and to whom was Christ referring when He spoke of "this generation?" It is important to remember that sometimes the words of Jesus indicated He was speaking "to the present, but thinking of the future." For example, in Matthew 16:28 He said, "There be some standing here, which shall not taste of death, till they see the Son of man coming in his kingdom." Obviously we have the same problem there as in the Scripture now being considered. The people to whom Jesus spoke died centuries ago, yet the kingdom of heaven upon earth has yet to be established. Read again the notes on chapter 16, and consider that "tasting death" refers to the eternal tragedy, when sinners stand to be judged before God's great white throne. Jesus seemed to be saying, "You may reject My teaching and blaspheme My Name now, but before you are lost eternally, you will see with your own eyes the fulfillment of all I predict. Then you will know that I spoke the truth." Did the Lord have similar thoughts in mind when He said: "This generation shall not pass till it has seen the fulfillment of what I now predict"? If this be the case, it is easy to understand His additional statement, "Heaven and earth shall pass away, but my words shall not pass away."

## SECTION FOUR

*Expository Notes on Christ's Warnings Concerning His Coming*

But of that day and hour knoweth no man, no, not the angels of heaven, but my Father only. But as the days of Noe were, so shall also the coming of the Son of man be. For as in the days that were before the flood they were eating and drinking, marrying and giving in marriage, until the day that Noe entered into the ark, And knew not until the flood came, and took them all away; so shall also the coming of the Son of man be. Then shall two be in the field; the one shall be taken, and the other left. Two women shall be grinding at the mill; the one shall be taken, and the other left....Watch therefore: for ye know not what hour your Lord doth come. But know this, that if the goodman of the house had known in what watch the thief would come, he would have watched, and would not have suffered his house to be broken up. Therefore be ye also ready: for in such an hour as ye think not the Son of man cometh (vv. 36-44).

## THE PROFOUND PROBLEM

Matthew quotes the Lord's statement as follows: "But of that day and hour knoweth no man, no, not the angels of heaven, but my Father only." Mark expands the statement, saying, "But of that day and that hour knoweth no man, not the angels which are in heaven, *neither the Son*, but the Father." The differing versions have always created problems for the church. As early as the end of the third century after Christ, Arius, a Greek theologian from Alexandria, divided the church with his doctrine that Christ was not of one substance with the Father. The fierce debate which followed led to a special council in which the churches discussed the heresies expressed in the doctrine of the religious agitator. The attacks made then disturbed the assemblies, but the conflicting variations of the Gospels remained. Arius maintained that if Jesus were God, He would know everything; if He did not, then He could hardly be equal with One who did.

There can hardly be shame in admitting that our finite minds may not be able to grasp some of the mysteries enshrined within the Word of God. Life is an ever-learning process, and our spiritual education will never be completed. There will always be something to discover; limits can never be set in regard to what God has prepared for His people. Can it be that the answer to our problem is found in the amazing fact that Jesus, the Son of God, voluntarily took upon Himself our flesh, and in so doing became subject to the laws governing humanity? Did God the Father reserve for Himself certain pertinent details relative to eternal events? Did God formulate plans concerning the final moments of time, and did Christ *by His own volition* abstain from acquainting Himself with such details, so that in every possible sense He could remain the Man He wished to be? Someday, when mysteries will be banished forever, we shall be even more amazed how "He [who] was rich...became poor, that ye through his poverty might be rich" (see 2 Cor. 8:9).

We may find it difficult to understand the details of the text, but one fact should be obvious. Since the exact timing of the Lord's return is a divinely preserved secret, only very foolish people attempt to set a specific time for the Savior's reappearing.

I remember a very famous Christian in Britain who, for some inscrutable reason, ignored the warning enshrined in the text. He claimed to have received a special revelation from God, and predicted Christ would return on a certain date. The newspapers carried leading articles, and the country was made aware of the man's statement. Alas, the day came and went, and the mistaken prophet was overwhelmed by confusion. The media laughed at his mistake, ridiculed his faith, and poured contempt on his church. The disillusioned prophet disappeaed from public life, and the loss was immeasurable, for he had truly been a very dedicated preacher. His mistake should be a warning to all others who try to gain publicity through sensationalism.

## THE POWERFUL PREACHING

Jesus said, "As it was...so shall it be." There was a period in which critics ridiculed the story of Noah and the flood, but the archeologists discredited the criticisms and the world now recognizes the validity of the story in the book of Genesis. Jesus was drawing attention to the fact that love for materialism and forgetfulness of the greatest issues in life can never be justified. The situation in the days of Noah was (1) Sinful; (2) Serious; (3) Sudden; (4) Sad. The people perished in the waters of the flood because they had rejected the preaching of the wise old ship-builder. Jesus claimed that similar events would be repeated in the end times. Men would be lovers of pleasure more than lovers of God; their judgments biased by selfishness. The world of the twentieth century is far removed from the times of Noah, but some things never change. Technology has captivated the mind of modern man; computers seem to solve all the problems of the mind but, unfortunately, the distresses of the soul remain untouched. People hear God's word, reject its message, and die in ignorance just as they did in the times of Noah. Men today are much wiser than the patriarch, but it is extremely doubtful if the superior knowledge will be of value when death terminates life.

## THE POIGNANT PLEA

The Savior said, "Watch therefore: for ye know not what hour your Lord doth come." His words were so important that He repeated and emphasized His message. He said, "Therefore be ye also ready: for in such an hour as ye think not the Son of man cometh." His reference to the indolent householder reflected His thoughts. Men who ignored the dangers of burglary were foolish. Disciples who ignored the warning would be without excuse when disaster overwhelmed them. Just as two women working in the field, and two others grinding corn at the mill were suddenly parted so, said Jesus, would people be separated when the Lord returned. Disciples ought to be constantly vigilant. The Savior was aware of a truth enshrined in the ancient proverb: "A stitch in time saves nine."

SECTION FIVE

*Expository Notes on the Additional Warnings of Jesus*

**Who then is a faithful and wise servant, whom his lord hath made ruler over his household, to give them meat in due season? Blessed is that servant, whom his lord when he cometh shall find so doing. Verily I say unto you, That he shall make him ruler over all his goods. But and if that evil servant shall say in his heart, My lord delayeth his coming; And shall begin to smite his fellowservants, and to eat and drink with the drunken; The lord of that servant shall come in a day when he looketh not for him, and in an hour that he is not aware of, And shall cut him asunder, and appoint him his portion with the hypocrites; there shall be weeping and gnashing of teeth (vv. 45-51).**

Matthew ends this section of his writings by describing the Lord's message concerning two extremes in personal service. This was a natural conclusion, for if the Lord promised to return, His servants should be prepared for the event. The verses to be considered divide into two sections; both with three subdivisions.

## THE GREAT COMMISSION

Jesus asked, "Who then is a faithful and wise servant?" and immediately supplied an answer to the question. He said,"The servant whom his lord hath made ruler over his household to give them meat in due season." The word picture described a master who commissioned a special servant to become responsible for the care of his household. The story describes the lord's absence and his confidence in the trustworthy servant. The text clearly indicates the thoughts in the mind of Jesus. He was about to leave His disciples, and the care of the kingdom to be established was the responsibility of the men left behind. The Lord expected them to be trustworthy in performing the tasks committed to their care.

## THE GRACIOUS CONDUCT

"Blessed is that servant, whom his lord when he cometh shall find so doing." The Greek text is interesting: *makarios ho doulos ekeinos.* This means "happy or blessed is that bond slave." This implies more than casual service. A bond slave was one who by his own volition chose to remain in the service of his master, even when at the year of liberation, he might have become a free man. To be a bond slave meant devotion both to the master and the work. The man was not working to obtain money; he worked because he loved his lord. He found happiness in his work and in the pleasure seen on the master's face. This was the type of service Jesus expected from His disciples. They were not to remain ordinary laborers; they were to be bond slaves, utterly trustworthy, and unceasingly active.

## THE GLORIOUS CONSEQUENCES

"Verily I say unto you, That he [the lord] shall make him ruler over all his goods." Every wise and appreciative Master found joy in rewarding deserving servants. Thus did Jesus teach that no man can outgive God. What is conscientiously done for Him, not only supplies immediate pleasure; it also guarantees that when God assesses the value of Christian service, His rewards will be dispensed among faithful servants (see 1 Cor. 3:11-15). Malachi expressed a similar truth when he wrote: "Then they that feared the LORD spake often one to another: and the LORD hearkened, and heard it, and a book of remembrance was written before him for them that feared the LORD, and that thought upon his name. And they shall be mine, saith the LORD of Hosts, in that day when I make up my jewels; and I will spare them, as a man spareth his own son that serveth him" (Mal. 3:16-17).

## THE GRAVE CONCLUSION

"But and if that evil servant shall say in his heart, My lord delayeth his coming." Jesus was fully aware that some servants would be disappointing; the quality of their service would leave much to be desired. He had already said that "because iniquity shall abound, the love of many shall wax cold" (Matt. 24:12). There would be disciples who would falter before oncoming times of persecution. Some would scoff at the promise of Christ's return, and the emptiness of their profession would be made obvious by their conduct. Jesus affirmed that men should maintain a constant watch of expectancy; their eyes should never become dim. Nothing should ever be permitted to create doubt in their minds. Writing to the Galatians, Paul said, "And let us not be weary in well doing: for in due season we shall reap, if we faint not" (Gal. 6:9).

## THE GUILTY CONDUCT

"If that evil servant...shall begin to smite his fellowservants, and to eat and drink with the drunken...." It was inconceivable that disciples could fall to such low levels of morality, but history has demonstrated the reliability of the word of Jesus. He was aware that many tares would grow among the wheat. Ideas could easily be changed, and if Christian service were not the result of a life-changing experience, a man's future would be in jeopardy. Unfortunately, there are vast numbers of religious people who have become inactive. Some are even antagonistic to the faith they formerly espoused. There should always be intense pity for a person overcome by desires for illegitimate pleasures. Yet for the apostate who blasphemes, for the man or woman whose former experiences and profession were based on a sham, there can only be condemnation. This warning from Christ was spoken to people who professed much but possessed nothing.

## THE GHASTLY CONDEMNATION

"The lord of that servant shall come in a day when he looketh not for him....And shall cut him asunder....there shall be weeping and gnashing of teeth." *Phillips' Modern English Translation* reads: "That servant's master will return on a day which he does not expect, and at a time which he does not know, and will punish him severely, and send him off to share the penalty of the unfaithful — to the place of tears and bitter regret." Some teachers believe this is a reference to an ancient form of punishment when offenders were literally cut to pieces. Be that as it may, the basic truth is unmistakable — those who sin against the truth cannot escape the wrath of the Master. A day of reckoning will come, when the guilty will know the bitterness of eternal remorse. Such a warning coming from the lips of Jesus should be sufficient to make every professing Christian examine the quality of his faith and conduct. Apathy is a cancer which destroys the soul.

# The Twenty-fifth Chapter of Matthew

THEME: *The Return of Christ*

OUTLINE:
    I. The Ten Virgins...*A Great Slumber* (Verses 1-13)
    II. The Ten Talents...*A Great Stupidity* (Verses 14-30)
    III. The Sheep and the Goats...*A Great Surprise*
        (Verses 31-46)

SECTION ONE

*Expository Notes on the Parable of the Virgins*

**Then shall the kingdom of heaven be likened unto ten virgins, which took their lamps, and went forth to meet the bridegroom. And five of them were wise, and five were foolish. They that were foolish took their lamps, and took no oil with them: But the wise took oil in their vessels with their lamps. While the bridegroom tarried, they all slumbered and slept (vv. 1-5).**

## PECULIAR BUT SIMPLE

The three illustrations supplied in this chapter are the continuation and conclusion of the Lord's discourse about His return to earth. The story concerning the ten virgins may seem strange to modern readers, but it was easily understood by the people to whom Jesus spoke. Even today the same type of marriage arrangements are made among the nomadic tribes, where it is common practice for people to go forth "to meet the bridegroom." Edersheim explaining these things says, "The usual marriage customs of the Jews are well known. On the appointed day, the bridegroom accompanied by his friends, proceeded to the bride's house, and thence escorted her, with her attendant maidens and friends, to his own or his parents' home. In the parable, however, the proceedings are somewhat different. Here the bridegroom is not in the town but somewhere at a distance, so that, although the day is settled, the exact hour of his arrival is uncertain. He will come in the course of the night, and the virgins who are to meet him, have assembled in the house where the wedding is to take place. They wait for the summons to go forth and meet the bridegroom, and to conduct him to the bridal-place. When the signal is given that he is approaching, they set forth on the road, each bearing her lamp.''

Dr. J. A. Findlay has described what he saw in Palestine. ''When we were approaching the gates of a Galilaean town, I caught a sight of ten maidens gaily clad and playing some kind of musical instrument, as they danced along the road in front of our car. When I asked what they were doing, the dragman (guide-interpreter) said they were going to keep the bride company till her bridegroom arrived. I asked him if there were any chance of seeing the wedding, but he shook his head, saying in effect, 'It might be tonight, or tomorrow night, or in two weeks' time; nobody ever knows for certain.' Then he went on to explain that one of the great things to do, if you could, at a middle-class wedding in Palestine, was to catch the bridal party napping. So the bridegroom comes unexpectedly, and sometimes in the middle of the night. It is true that he is required by public opinion to send a man along the street to shout: 'Behold! the bridegroom is coming!' but that may happen at any time; so the bridal party have to be ready to go out into the street at any time, to meet him, whenever he chooses to come...Other important points are that no one is allowed on the streets after dark without a lighted lamp, and also that, when the bridegroom has once arrived, and the door has been shut, late-comers to the ceremony are not admitted.'' Many nations observe ancient customs and this is particularly true in the East. Jesus was speaking to people who had often witnessed the scene described in the Parable of the Ten Virgins.

The lamps used in ancient times were made of pottery, and were shallow saucer-like creations in which a very small quantity of oil supplied the lighting fuel. The wick protruded through a hole at the one end. Sometimes, larger lamps of the same type were tied to a long pole and lifted high in the air so that they could be used in processsions. Surplus supplies of oil were carried in a small container attached to a belt worn around the waist. The five wise virgins, remembering the time of the bridegroom's arrival was uncertain, thoughtfully provided additional supplies of oil, but the others neglected to do this; they were careless and thoughtless. The words translated ''slumbered and slept'' are *enustazan* and *ekatheudon*. They tell us that the young ladies became drowsy, and finally fell into a deep sleep. It should be remembered that Jesus was speaking about events to take place immediately before His return to earth. He was inferring that His followers would be divided into two types of people — wise and foolish; those with oil and those without it. It should also be remembered that even the wise virgins fell asleep, and by so doing lost the most precious opportunity of a lifetime. (See the homilies at the end of this section.)

> **And at midnight there was a cry made, Behold, the bridegroom cometh; go ye out to meet him. Then all those virgins arose, and trimmed their lamps. And the foolish said unto the wise, Give us of your oil; for our lamps are gone out [going out]. But the wise answered, saying, Not so; lest there be not enough for us and you: but go ye rather to them that sell, and buy for yourselves. And while they went to buy, the bridegroom came; and they that were ready went in with him to the marriage: and the door was shut (vv. 6-10).**

## PRECARIOUS BUT SUGGESTIVE

The word *spennuntai* translated "gone out" really means "going out." The virgins arose, removed charred pieces from the wicks in their lamps, and lit them. The foolish virgins saw their flickering lights, and suddenly realizing they had no reserve supplies of oil, asked help from their friends. Some teachers, recognizing that oil is a synonym or type of the Holy Spirit, used this Scripture to teach the insecurity of believers in Christ. They insisted that the wise virgins who once possessed oil were eventually rejected by the Bridegroom. This is erroneous. Obviously the foolish virgins had no oil, and therefore cannot represent Christians who fall from grace. They appeared to be ready for the wedding but actually were not. They resemble unconverted church members who are flashlights without batteries!

It is interesting to note that even the wise virgins fell asleep. Had they remained awake and alert, each might have escorted a convert into the marriage celebrations. If there be any Scripture relative to this generation, it must be this one, for unfortunately a deadly apathy has affected the church. This simple fact emphasizes the importance of Christ's command, "Watch therefore, for ye know neither the day nor the hour wherein the Son of man cometh." Jesus was careful to stress that only "they that were ready" were permitted to enter the marriage chamber. It is illuminating to compare this Scripture with the words of John. "And one of the elders answered, saying unto me, What are these which are arrayed in white robes? and whence came they? And I said unto him, Sir, thou knowest. And he said to me, These are they which came out of great tribulation, and have *washed their robes, and made them white in the blood of the Lamb*'' (Rev. 7:13-14). People without a passport can only blame themselves when they are prevented from reaching desired destinations.

**Afterward came also the other virgins, saying, Lord, Lord, open to us. But he answered and said, Verily I say unto you, I know you not. Watch therefore, for ye know neither the day nor the hour wherein the Son of man cometh (vv. 11-13).**

## PREDICTABLE BUT SAD

It must be remembered this message was the conclusion of earlier teachings of Jesus. He had spoken of the anger of the lord of the vineyard (Matt. 21:41) and of the fate of the man without a wedding garment (Matt. 22:13). Here the Savior speaks of the exclusion of unprepared virgins from the marriage celebrations. The whole emphasis of these messages was that people could and would be excluded from the presence of God if they continued to ignore the warnings issued by Jesus. Whatever liberal theologians might say regarding the destiny of unrepentant souls, it remains obvious that Jesus believed sinners could be eternally condemned. If all people, irrespective of preparedness, obtain an abiding place in the presence of God, then the gospel is misleading, and the mission of Christ to earth unnecessary. Jesus said, ''I go my way, and ye shall seek me, and shall die in your sins: whither I go, ye cannot come...ye shall die in your sins: for if ye believe not that I am he, ye shall die in your sins'' (John 8:21-24). ''They that were ready'' went into the marriage; others were excluded. The Savior speaking to Nicodemus said, ''Except a man be born again, he cannot see the kingdom of God...Marvel not that I say unto thee, Ye must be born again'' (John 3:3,7). The Bible teaches the supreme necessity of being ready to meet God.

## HOMILIES

Study No. 15

### THE DISCIPLES WHO HAD SLEEPING SICKNESS

''But Peter and they that were with him were heavy with sleep: and when they were awake, they saw his glory....'' There are three instances of sleeping disciples mentioned in the New Testament, and in each case the time spent in slumber proved to be exceedingly costly. When the Lord Jesus led His faithful followers into the Mount of Transfiguration, they did not realize what amazing events were about to take place. Determined to remain with Him during the night watches, they sat on the ground and were soon asleep. That they awakened just in time to see a transfigured Lord, and then to accompany Him into the valley, seems to suggest they had slept for most of the night. We shall never know how much they missed.

## THEY SLEPT AND MISSED HIS GLORY

"When they were awake, they saw his glory, and the two men that stood with him" (Luke 9:32). Their brief vision left an indelible impression upon their memories, for even after thirty years, the apostle Peter wrote: "...when we were with him in the holy mount" (2 Peter 1:18). The disciples never forgot the soul-stirring vision of the face that shone as the sun, and the garments which were white and glistening. They remembered how God said, "This is my beloved Son; hear him." With awe and amazement they recalled how Moses and Elijah spake of the "decease which he should accomplish at Jerusalem," and probably speculated as to the reason why both the patriarchs were informed about the Messiah's death. The glory of that resplendent scene was indescribable. Radiance emanated from their beloved Master, and He seemed more like the King of angels than the hero of poor fishermen. All this happened just prior to the dawn, and we are obliged to ask what untold revelations might have been received had the disciples remained awake and watchful. Perhaps their slumber caused their subsequent defeat in the valley.

## THEY SLEPT AND MISSED HIS PASSION

There was a strange and eerie silence in the Garden of Gethsemane on the night when Jesus was betrayed. The stillness preceding the breaking of the storm only accentuated the heartbreaks of the Lord Jesus. Fully conscious of His great need, He temporarily withdrew from the crowds and, accompanied by three disciples, "went, as he was wont, to the mount of Olives...And being in an agony, he prayed more earnestly: and his sweat was as it were great drops of blood falling down to the ground. And when he rose up from prayer, and was come to his disciples, he found them sleeping for sorrow" (Luke 22:39-45).

Indeed we are left with a question: If these men were sleeping, who witnessed the sufferings of Christ? Possibly one of the men who had been left outside the garden became a little impatient and came in search of his friends. If this happened, then he arrived in time to witness the indescribable. The love of God's heart was overflowing; the streams of eternal compassion were reaching out to earth's remotest end. Yet, if the disciples had remained awake during those moments of agonizing conflict, their appreciation of the price paid for our redemption might have increased immeasurably. Their sleep in the garden preceded the fear which made them forsake their Lord.

## THEY SLEPT AND MISSED ETERNAL JOYS

When the disciples asked for signs of the Lord's return, He described ten virgins going forth in anticipation of a wedding (Matt. 25:1-13). While the bridegroom tarried, they all slumbered and slept, but when the cry went forth, "Behold, the bridegroom cometh," they arose immediately and went forth to meet him. Thereupon five foolish virgins became instantly conscious of their need, and while they vainly tried to prepare for the future, their moment of opportunity passed by. The five wise virgins entered into the marriage, and had great joy in the presence of the bridegroom. Yet each one of the five should have been accompanied by a convert! The Lord Jesus cited this as an indication of conditions to exist in the world prior to His return. Souls would be perishing while Christendom remained inactive and sleepy. His word has been fulfilled. "Watch therefore, for in such an hour...the Son of man cometh." (Reprinted from the author's book, *Bible Pinnacles*, pp. 107-108.)


Study No. 16

### THE GREAT WEDDING... And the People Who Came Late

"And as he sat upon the mount of Olives, the disciples came unto him privately, saying, Tell us, when shall these things be? and what shall be the sign of thy coming, and of the end of the world [age]?" (Matt. 24:3). By parable and preaching the Lord granted their request, and instructed them regarding His return. He warned them not to be deceived by false prophets; He urged them not to be weary in well-doing; and finally, in short thought-provoking illustrations, He described the church of the future.

## THE CERTAINTY OF HIS RETURN

"Watch therefore, for ye know neither the day nor the hour wherein the Son of man cometh." As the Lord drew near to His death and departure from this world, He constantly repeated the promise of His second advent, and His statement harmonized perfectly with other prophetical utterances. At His birth the promise had been given, "He shall be great, and shall be called the Son of the Highest: and the Lord God shall give unto him the throne of his father David: And he shall reign over the house of Jacob for ever; and of his kingdom there shall be no end" (Luke 1:32-33). It need hardly be said that this promise was never fulfilled during the Lord's ministry on earth. The throne of David was in Jerusalem, where Christ received a cross and not a crown. Messianic prophecies referred to an earthly kingdom, and these predictions have never been fulfilled. The angels repeated the promise immediately after Christ's ascension (Acts 1:10-11), and this teaching became the hope and message of the early Christian church (see 1 Thess. 4:16-18; 1 John 3:2).

## THE CONFORMITY TO HIS REQUIREMENTS

"Then shall the kingdom of heaven be likened unto ten virgins, which took their lamps, and went forth to meet the bridegroom. And five of them were wise, and five were foolish." It has been claimed that this is one of the greatest of Christ's parables. Here two classes are seen in bold relief. All ten virgins believed in the coming of the bridegroom, and hoped to be present at the marriage reception. The entire party waited for the glad event, but in the moment of testing, five virgins were found to be unprepared to meet the bridegroom. Their lamps were going out! It is a cause for regret that hours had been wasted in sleeping, when a few minutes work might have avoided a tragedy. The foolish virgins remind us of a vast host of modern people. Even the wise virgins were content to sit at ease and to slumber, when at their side were people in urgent need. It is not sufficient to believe in Christ's return; we must be ready for His appearing. None can deny that a large proportion of Christendom is filled with dead formalism. There are many custodians of the lamp, but not much light!

## THE CALAMITY OF HIS REJECTION

"And...the bridegroom came; and they that were ready went in with

him to the marriage: and the door was shut. Afterward came also the
other virgins saying, Lord, Lord, open to us. But he answered and said,
Verily I say unto you, I know you not. Watch therefore, for ye know
neither the day nor the hour wherein the Son of man cometh.'' There
is nothing to suggest the door of opportunity was ever reopened. The
people who might have been rejoicing in the presence of the bridegroom
were left to mourn in the shadows of the night. Three thoughts demand
expression. (1) *A belated request.* "Lord, Lord, open to us.'' Had there
been adequate preparation, the need for this request would have been
unknown. Hours of complacent self-confidence had ruined priceless
opportunities. (2) *A bewildering response.* "I know you not.'' Self-
esteem could not become a key to open the closed door. The Lord had
disowned them, and His verdict was final. On another occasion Jesus
spoke of some who would say on the day of judgment, "I have preached
in thy name,'' and again his response was,"I know you not.'' (3) *A
bitter remorse.* "...there shall be weeping.'' Jesus said, "Be ye also
ready.'' Many Bible teachers believe the coming of Christ to be
imminent. They may be correct in their deductions and every Christian
should be attending to his lamp and preparing to attend the Marriage
Supper of the Lamb. When the door of heaven closes, it stays closed
a long time! It is far easier to walk through an open doorway, than to
force a lock! (Reprinted from the author's book, *Bible Treasures,* pp.
83-84.)

SECTION TWO

*Expository Notes on the Parable of the Talents*

**For the kingdom of heaven is as a man travelling into a far country,
who called his own servants, and delivered unto them his goods. And
unto one he gave five talents, to another two, and to another one; to
every man according to his several ability; and straightway took his
journey. Then he that had received the five talents went und traded
with the same, and made them other five talents. And likewise he that
had received two, he also gained other two. But he that had received
one went and digged in the earth, and hid his lord's money (vv. 14-18).**

## AN INTERESTING COMPARISON

Throughout the history of the church, theologians have contrasted
and compared this parable with another found in Luke 19:11-28. Some

teachers claim the two versions are but variations of one account, but this is erroneous. Matthew writes of talents which were measures of weight; Luke speaks of pounds (minas). One pound was equal to the amount earned by a laborer in three months of hard work. There are numerous differences in the two accounts, and thus we may assume the two parables were delivered at different times, in different places. There was no reason why the Lord should not repeat an illustration nor change its details to make it applicable to different people with varying needs.

## AN ILLUMINATING CONCLUSION

It is obvious that this parable is the continuation of the preceding one. The parable of the ten virgins emphasized the importance of obtaining entrance to the marriage feast, that is of getting into the kingdom. This story emphasizes not entrance into the kingdom, but the place of authority and importance which might be gained or lost within the kingdom. Paul taught that service rendered by Christians would be examined in the fires of God's scrutiny, and that saints would either be rewarded or suffer loss according to the results of that examination at the Judgment Seat of Christ (see 1 Cor. 3:11-15 and 2 Cor. 5:10). The parable contrasts the excitement and enthusiasm of the diligent servants with the complacency and content of others who were lazy. Some were "about their master's business"; but the others could not have cared less. Doubtless the Lord was aware of such people even in His day, but no one would deny that in our modern age the church is filled with adherents whose apathy has become obvious. The parable under consideration was part of a series of messages concerning the approach of the kingdom, and was a prediction of conditions to be expected in the end times. Jesus said, "And many false prophets shall rise, and shall deceive many. And because iniquity shall abound, *the love of many shall wax cold*" (Matt. 24:11-12).

## AN IMPORTANT COMMISSION

It must be remembered that in Bible times, slaves could not own anything; they and their possessions belonged to their master. When the departing lord delivered his property to the servants, he was commissioning them to work for him during his absence. He said, "Occupy till I come" (Luke 19:13). "And unto one he gave five talents, to another two, and to another one; to every man according to his several ability...." *The Living Bible* translates this passage as follows: "He gave $5,000 to one, $2,000 to another, and $1,000 to the last — *dividing it in proportion to their abilities*, and then left on his trip." This Scripture is filled with potent suggestions. (1) Every person has a talent given by God. It can, and should be used for His glory. (2) One man appeared to have more talents than his neighbor, but that was inconsequential since the master rewarded faithfulness and not merely *success*. (3) The man who did nothing had no excuse for his indolence. It would have been better to try and fail than to do nothing. Excitement may be found even in the business effort itself; to see the initial investment increasing quickens the pulse and gladdens the heart, but to remain idle is an indication of laziness, complacency, and decline. When Jesus taught this parable, He was issuing warnings not only to His immediate listeners, but to all who believed He would return to establish a kingdom upon earth. We should work while it is day; the night cometh when no man can work!

## AN INEXCUSABLE COMPLACENCY

When we compare this account with another Scripture in Luke's Gospel, the picture becomes increasingly disappointing. "And another came, saying, Lord, behold, here is thy pound, which I have kept laid up in a napkin: For I feared thee, because thou art an austere man; thou takest up that thou layedst not down, and reapest that thou didst not sow" (Luke 19:20-21). It is thought-provoking to notice that the man who did nothing for his master tried to excuse himself by blaming the austerity of his lord. Yet in so doing he condemned himself. If he were aware of the master's expertise in trading, he should have worked ceaselessly, emulating his example. What was the man doing all the time the money lay buried in the ground? Was he keeping a lonely vigil over the hidden talent? Unused limbs lose their flexibility; they become stiff and rigid; talents not used can never increase. It is better to wear out than to rust out!

**After a long time the lord of those servants cometh, and reckoneth with them. And so he that had received five talents came and brought other five talents, saying, Lord, thou deliveredst unto me five talents: behold, I have gained beside them five talents more. His lord said unto him, Well done, thou good and faithful servant: thou hast been faithful over a few things, I will make thee ruler over many things: enter thou into the joy of thy lord. He also that had received two talents came and said,**

Lord, thou deliveredst unto me two talents: behold, I have gained two other talents beside them. His lord said unto him, Well done, good and faithful servant; thou hast been faithful over a few things, I will make thee ruler over many things: enter thou into the joy of thy lord. Then he which had received the one talent came and said, Lord, I knew thee that thou art an hard man, reaping where thou hast not sown, and gathering where thou hast not strawed: And I was afraid, and went and hid thy talent in the earth: lo, there thou hast that is thine. His lord answered and said unto him, Thou wicked and slothful servant, thou knewest that I reap where I sowed not, and gather where I have not strawed: Thou oughtest therefore to have put my money to the exchangers, and then at my coming I should have received mine own with usury [interest]. Take therefore the talent from him, and give it unto him which hath ten talents, For unto every one that hath shall be given, and he shall have abundance: but from him that hath not shall be taken away even that which he hath. And cast ye the unprofitable servant into outer darkness: there shall be weeping and gnashing of teeth (vv. 19-30).

## THE DIVERSITY OF GIFTS

As we have already considered, Matthew mentions talents, which were a measurement of weight; Luke mentions pounds, which were money. The value of the talent was governed by the metal with which it was identified. A talent of gold was much more than a talent of silver or copper. A pound remained unchanged whatever the time or season of the year. Paul in 1 Corinthians 12:8-12 reminded his readers that the gifts of the Spirit are varied; men do not share identical talents. Some are blessed with amazing musical abilities; others who cannot sing a note, may have brilliant business instincts. Some people are skilled organizers; others excel in courage and may become untiring missionaries in hostile countries. Some followers of Christ may appear to have no gifts, but they render faithful service to other people. Jesus said that even this kind of unspectacular service gains its reward; that help given to ordinary men and women was something given to Him. The most important lesson of this parable seems to be that if we use what we have, God will give us more. If we remain inactive, we lose what we have and finish with nothing.

## THE DELIGHTS OF GRACE

This study may be summarized under three headings. (1) *The*

*Excitement of Service*. This has to be experienced to be understood. The men endowed with talents went out to increase their assets. Their efforts brought them into contact with other people, and each night they were able to review the events of the preceding day. They found joy in successful trading. Their minds were active, their plans made, and the thought of success increased the zeal attending their efforts. This is characteristic of all Christians who go into the market places of life to extend the kingdom of Christ. They experience the joy of telling others about the Savior; they are thrilled by every victory won, and if converts are won to the faith, the soul winner's happiness rivals the joy known among the angels in heaven. (2) *The Ecstacy of Seeing*. "And after a long time the lord of those servants cometh, and reckoneth with them." It has been thought that "the long time" was a means by which Jesus tried to correct the belief that His ascension would soon be followed by His return. Jesus knew that a long period of time would elapse prior to His personal return to earth, and yet He never hesitated in affirming that eventually He would return just as He promised. The statement "And they shall see his face" (Rev. 22:4) should be the inspiration of all who work for Christ. To see a smile on the face of Jesus will be sufficient reward for every sacrifice made on His behalf. (3) *The Experience of Serenity*. "...enter thou into the joy of thy lord." This suggests progress. However great the experience of serving upon earth, and seeing Christ at His coming, the privilege of greater participation in eternal bliss will be an additional reward for those who find favor in the Lord's sight. Having experienced the pleasure and privilege of tasting the joy of God's salvation and sharing this with others, the triumphant saints are encouraged to go deeper into the unfathomable blessedness of eternal satisfaction. This is something beyond the expressive power of words. It reminds me of a very old man who belonged to my church. He prayed one evening saying, "Lord! please don't give me any more blessings or I shall burst!"

## THE DISASTER OF GUILT

"Take therefore the talent from him...And cast ye the unprofitable servant into outer darkness: there shall be weeping and gnashing of teeth." Primarily, this parable was spoken against the scribes and Pharisees who abhorred change of any kind. Their talent, which some might interpret as the law and the traditions of the fathers, remained unchanged. It was buried and hidden within their own systems, and any new message was considered an intrusion into privately owned and protected property. It should be remembered that both Peter and Paul encountered great opposition when they tried to bring Gentiles into the fellowship of the church. Jewish teachers followed them everywhere trying to insist on the infallibility of the law. There could be no justifiable addition to "the talent." As it had always been it should remain until the end of time! These arrogant custodians of a legal talent were more concerned with the letter of the word than with the task of introducing all nations to fellowship with God. When they deprived others of the joy of knowing the Lord they lost even that which they had, and ultimately became bankrupt. There are none so blind as the people who have no desire to see!

### SECTION THREE

*Expository Notes on the Separation of the Sheep From the Goats*

**When the Son of man shall come in his glory, and all the holy angels with him, then shall he sit upon the throne of his glory: And before him shall be gathered all nations: and he shall separate them one from another, as a shepherd divideth his sheep from the goats: And he shall set the sheep on his right hand, but the goats on the left. Then shall the King say unto them on his right hand, Come, ye blessed of my Father, inherit the kingdom prepared for you from the foundation of the world: For I was an hungered, and ye gave me meat: I was thirsty, and ye gave me drink: I was a stranger, and ye took me in: Naked, and ye clothed me: I was sick, and ye visited me: I was in prison, and ye came unto me. Then shall the righteous answer him, saying, Lord, when saw we thee an hungered, and fed thee? or thirsty, and gave thee drink? When saw we thee a stranger, and took thee in? or naked, and clothed thee? Or when saw we thee sick, or in prison, and came unto thee? And the King shall answer and say unto them, Verily I say unto you, Inasmuch as ye have done it unto one of the least of these my brethren, ye have done it unto me (vv. 31-40).**

This is the third of the three illustrations regarding the return of Christ to earth. Whether or not they were all spoken in sequence as one lengthy discourse, is of little importance. The entire sermon of illustrations could have been delivered at one time or, as we have considered earlier, this could be another example of the way in which Matthew collected his materials, to reproduce them at a time thought suitable by the author. The Holy Spirit desired them where they are, for together they present a complete picture of what will take place in the end times. The Parable of the Ten Virgins emphasizes *entry into the kingdom*. The Parable of the Talents speaks of *eminence within the kingdom*. The message about the judgment of the nations stresses explanations throughout the kingdom. The whole may be summarized as follows. (1) *What we shall do*; (2) *What we shall be*; (3) *What we shall understand*. It is important to recognize the two interpretations suggested by theologians.

The dispensationalists argue that this Scripture has nothing to do with the church, since it refers to events to take place ''when the Son of man shall come in his glory, and all the holy angels with him....'' These teachers insist that it is wrong to take verses from their original setting, and to make them teach something alien to the original thought. Furthermore, since there is no mention of a resurrection, this judgment cannot be the final day of reckoning mentioned in Revelation 20:11-15. It is believed therefore that at the end of the great Tribulation, when Christ returns to deliver a remnant of the Jewish nation, all other nations will be gathered before the king, to answer for their behavior. God promised Abraham that He would bless them that blessed his seed, and curse those who afflicted them (see Gen.12:3). The judgment of the nations will be evidence that God honors His promises.

## THE DAY OF JUDGMENT

There are other people who believe this Scripture has a much wider application. They accept the dispensational interpretation, but insist the truths enshrined in this remarkable passage relate to every aspect of Christian service. There is reason to believe that their ideas are not without substance. It must be recognized that there is no mention here of the gospel of redeeming grace, nor of the necessity for personal faith in Christ. The grounds of acceptance appears to be kindness to ''the Lord's brethren.'' That phrase apparently is very important. These people must be the Jews — the Lord's brethren in the flesh. The times of terrible persecution to precede the return of Christ will almost destroy the Jewish people, but the Bible mentions nations who will befriend Israel in their time of peril. (See the author's book, *What in the World Will Happen Next?*, Chapter 32.) To such nations Christ will say: ''Inasmuch as ye have done it unto one of the least of these my brethren, ye have done it unto me.'' Whatever interpretation might be acceptable to the readers of this commentary, it must be obvious that all men will be required to answer to God for what they did during their lifetime.

## THE DECISION OF THE JUDGE

The Lord used the common illustration of the sheep and goats. These animals still graze and run together in Israel just as they did when Jesus was upon the earth. The goats are generally black, and the sheep dirty white; they are easily distinguished either from the other. It should be noticed that the decision of the judge was final; there was no court of appeal. It is also interesting to note the King said to the saints, "Come, ye blessed of my Father, inherit the kingdom prepared for you *from the foundation of the world.*" This suggests forethought, planning, and predestination. God knew those for whom preparation was being made. Even from eternity, God was aware of what would happen ages hence, and never at any time was He taken by surprise. Compared with the omniscience of God, man's intellect is as nothing. It should behoove him therefore to consider carefully every message sent by the Almighty.

## THE DELIVERANCE OF THE JUST

Let it be emphasized again, that here there is no mention of redeeming grace, and personal faith in the Savior is not stressed. However, these may be inferred from the actions which gained the commendation of the King. The people or nations which "fed the hungry, clothed the naked, visited the prisoners," must have had great motivation. Are we justified in assuming that they helped God's people because they first loved God? It is worthy of thought that great preaching, generous donations, social importance, and other embellishments are never mentioned by the King. He spoke of mundane things; of unspectacular events often considered unworthy of mention; He never spoke of ostentatious acts of splendor; instead, He spoke of hungry and naked people requiring assistance, sick people needing healing, and lonely prisoners needing comfort. He identified Himself with the most helpless of earth's citizens and indicated service to them was a service to Him. Perhaps in this strange but delightful way He was emphasizing that often "the first things in life would be the last, and the last, first."

**Then shall he say also unto them on the left hand, Depart from me, ye cursed, into everlasting fire, prepared for the devil and his angels: For I was an hungered, and ye gave me no meat...Then shall they also answer him, saying, Lord, when saw we thee an hungered... Then shall he answer them, saying, Verily I say unto you, Inasmuch as ye did it**

**not to one of the least of these, ye did it not to me. And these shall go away into everlasting punishment: but the righteous into life eternal (vv. 41-46).**

There is no need to supply a detailed exposition of these verses, for they are the other side of the picture supplied by earlier verses. This might be an appropriate time to consider the second of the two interpretations already mentioned. That there is a dispensational message in the parable few would deny, but it is equally true to assert this illustration given by Jesus enhanced the beauty of all Christian service. What is done for Him cannot be unimportant, and even a cup of water given in the name of Jesus does not pass unnoticed.

The story is told of Martin of Tours. He was a Roman soldier and a Christian. One cold winter day as he was entering a city, a beggar stopped him and asked for alms. Martin had no money; but the beggar was blue and shivering with cold. Martin gave what he had. He took off his soldier's coat, worn and frayed as it was; he cut it in two, and gave half to the beggar man. That night he had a dream. He saw the heavenly places, and Jesus in the midst of the angels. The Lord was wearing half of a Roman soldier's cloak. One of the angels said to Him, "Master, why are you wearing that battered old cloak? Who gave it to you?" And Jesus answered, "My servant Martin gave it to me." When we learn the generosity which, without calculation, helps men in the simplest things, then we too will know the joy of helping Jesus Himself."

It is interesting to see how Paul also used this standard by which to judge Christian service. Writing to Philemon, he said concerning the slave Onesimus: "If thou count me therefore a partner, receive him as myself. If he had wronged thee, or oweth thee aught, put that on mine account" (vv. 17-18).

# The Twenty-sixth Chapter of Matthew

THEME: *The Events of the Last Night*

OUTLINE:
    I. The Dastardly Goal (Verses 1-5)
    II. The Devotional Gift (Verses 6-13)
    III. The Disgusting Greed (Verses 14-16)
    IV. The Displayed Graciousness (Verses 17-30)
    V. The Denying Guests (Verses 31-35)
    VI. The Dozing Group (Verses 36-56)
    VII. The Detestable Gathering (Verses 57-68)
    VIII. The Disturbing Guilt (Verses 69-75)

## SECTION ONE

*Expository Notes on the Plot to Kill Jesus*

**And it came to pass, when Jesus had finished all these sayings, he said unto his disciples, Ye know that after two days is the feast of the passover, and the Son of man is betrayed to be crucified. Then assembled together the chief priests, and the scribes, and the elders of the people, unto the palace of the high priest, who was called Caiaphas. And consulted that they might take Jesus by subtlety, and kill him. But they said, Not on the feast day, lest there be an uproar among the people (vv. 1-5).**

The end was now in sight! That which had been planned in eternity, was just around the corner. Jesus had arrived in Jerusalem and was aware of the events soon to take place. He arrived possibly on what is now known as Tuesday of Holy Week. He said to the disciples, ''Ye know that after two days is the feast of the Passover, and the Son of man is betrayed to be crucified.'' Throughout the so-called Christian ages, the church taught that Jesus was crucified on Friday, but this cannot be true. We know that the Lord rose from His grave early on the morning of the first day of the week, and that was Sunday. The Bible teaches that His body was in the grave for three days and nights. The Jewish day ended at sunset, and it was somewhere between that point in time and the rising of the sun (Matt. 28:1 and Mark 16:2) that the Lord emerged from the grave. From sunset on Friday to sunset on Saturday would have been one day. From the same time on Thursday to sunset on Friday would have been two days. From sunset on Wednesday to the same time on Thursday would have been three days. Therefore if the Scripture is to be our guide, we must acknowledge the simple fact that our Lord was crucified on Wednesday afternoon, and placed in His tomb before nightfall. If, as He stated, the Passover feast was to begin two days after His statement, then Jesus reached Jerusalem on Tuesday of Holy Week. It appears as if He spent Monday in the company of His friends at Bethany.

## THE MEETING IN THE PALACE

"Then assembled together the chief priests, and the scribes, and the elders of the people, *unto the palace of the high priest* , who was called Caiaphas" (v. 3). Had this been a normal, regular meeting of the Sanhedrin, it would have been held in the hall known as Gazith or "The Hall of Hewn Stones." Under the circumstances this was not permitted, for laymen were excluded from that illustrious place. To understand the importance of this Scripture it is necessary to be aware of the problems associated with the office of the high priest. Originally, when a man was appointed to that position of eminence, he was elected for his entire lifetime. It has been claimed that from approximately 37 B.C. until A.D. 67, there were at least twenty-eight high priests. If the official cooperated with the Romans, he continued in office; if he did not, another more amenable man was appointed to succeed the dethroned leader. Joseph Caiaphas, as he is called by Josephus the Jewish historian, seemed to have mastered the art of pleasing Caesar, and thus continued in office for eighteen years. He was the religious leader of the nation from A.D. 18 until A.D. 36. "Caiaphas had been elevated to his high post by the Romans, who found in him a submissive tool. His father-in-law Annas had been appointed by Quirinius, but after nine years had been deposed; he was succeeded in turn by Ismael, Eleazar son of Annas, Simon, and fourthly by Caiaphas, who superseded his immediate predecessor by favour of the procurator Valerius Gratus, the tenant of the office before Pontius Pilate. The ex-high priest, Annas, was counted still by some rigorists as holding the office, and he appears to have possessed high authority (see John 18:13 and Acts 4:6)." (Quoted from *The Pulpit Commentary. Matthew*. Volume 2, p. 515.)

## THE MALICE OF THE PRIESTS

The urgency of handling the Carpenter from Nazareth appeared to be so important that the most influential people in the nation were hurriedly summoned to the palace of the former high priest. The statement, "they... consulted that they might take Jesus by subtlety, and kill him," indicates the depth of their animosity toward the Lord. It was written, "the common people" heard Jesus gladly; alas, on the contrary, the religious leaders constantly desired to silence His testimony. Why were they continually hostile? Did they resent His increasing popularity? Were they angry because His fearless declaration of truth exposed their hypocrisy? Sometimes it is difficult to understand how people who receive much give little in return. Their decision to murder the Lord was the result of premeditated planning. They considered possible repercussions should the crowd become annoyed with their deeds; and thought of everything except the reactions of God. What He might think of them never entered their discussions. They were so determined to please themselves that even the Almighty was excluded from their thoughts.

## THE MURMURING OF THE PEOPLE

It has been estimated that nearly three million people attended the Passover feasts in Jerusalem. Josephus in his *Wars of the Jews*; Book 6; Chapter 9; paragraph 3, supplies the following details: "Cestius, who being desirous of informing Nero of the flower of the city, who otherwise was disposed to condemn that nation, entreated the high priest, if the thing were possible, to take the number of their whole multitude. So these high priests, upon the coming of their feast which is called the *Passover,* when they slay their sacrifices, from the ninth hour till the eleventh, but so that a company not less than ten belong to every sacrifice (for it is not lawful for them to feast singly by themselves) and many of us are twenty in a company, found the number of sacrifices was two hundred and fifty-six thousand, five hundred; which, upon the allowance of no more than ten that feast together, amounts to two million, seven hundred thousand, and two hundred persons that were pure and holy. As to those that have the leprosy, or the gonorrhea, or women that have their monthly courses, or such as are otherwise polluted, it is not lawful for them to be partakers of this sacrifice; nor indeed for any foreigners neither, who come hither to worship."

A great many of the people who attended the feast came from Galilee where Jesus was considered to be a hero, a prophet, and certainly a man sent by God. If that section of the crowd suspected foul play, their fierce opposition could have incited a riot, and Pontius Pilate, the Governor, would have sent soldiers to quell the uprising. The possibility existed that under these conditions Jesus might be rescued, the Pharisees could be discredited, and their plans ruined. It was therefore thought necessary to exercise extreme caution or their project might fail.

## SECTION TWO

*Expository Notes on the Incident in the Home of Simon the Leper*

**Now when Jesus was in Bethany, in the house of Simon the leper, There came unto him a woman having an alabaster box of very precious ointment, and poured it on his head, as he sat at meat. But when his disciples saw it, they had indignation, saying, To what purpose is this waste? For this ointment might have been sold for much, and given to the poor. When Jesus understood it, he said unto them, Why trouble ye the woman? for she hath wrought a good work upon me. For ye have the poor always with you; but me ye have not always. For in that she hath poured this ointment on my body, she did it for my burial. Verily I say unto you, Wheresoever this gospel shall be preached in the whole world, there shall also this, that this woman hath done, be told for a memorial of her (vv. 6-13).**

The story we are about to consider was recorded also by Mark and John, but for some reason Luke did not mention the incident. However, he did write of another woman who performed a similar act (see Luke 7:36-50). Consider also the expository notes in the author's commentary, *Luke's Thrilling Gospel*, pp. 177-183. Many writers tried to prove the notorious sinner was the same woman mentioned here by Matthew. Their evidence is far from conclusive. The unknown woman who came to the home of the Pharisee was a notorious prostitute; Mary was a saint who sat at the feet of Jesus. Sinners can be transformed into saints by the matchless grace of God, but to suggest this had been the case with Mary of Bethany can only be conjecture.

## SUSTAINED GRATITUDE IS ETERNAL

To some readers this may seem an unnecessary contradiction of terms. The word "sustained" is used deliberately, for alas, certain types of gratitude resemble flowers which bloom for a short time and then die! It is worthy of attention that on this visit to Bethany, the Lord went to a new home. A man called *Simon, the leper*, invited Him to share a meal, and to that supper Martha, Mary, and Lazarus were invited. There were many Simons in Palestine, and several of them are mentioned in the Bible story. There is reason to believe this Simon might have retained his nickname to differentiate him from others also called Simon. He had doubtless been known as Simon the leper, but after his miraculous cleansing and restoration to society, his friends continued to call him "Simon, the leper." Possibly the cleansing of this man was one of those other miracles mentioned by John (see John 21:25).

Simon was undoubtedly a friend of Martha and Mary; some writers have even suggested he was their father! Knowing that Jesus was approaching, he probably went to Martha to ask a special favor. He explained his indebtedness to the Lord, and expressed a desire to pay back a little of his debt. He would be thrilled if he could entertain Jesus at supper, and would be very appreciative if Martha would take charge of the cooking! Martha and Mary were understanding and very sympathetic. It would be a marvelous change for Jesus. Yes; of course it could be arranged! And that evening, Jesus went to share a meal with one of His outstanding converts. Simon had been saved by the grace of God, and as long as breath remained in his body, he would be grateful to the Lord. This would last for eternity. That same kind of gratitude may be heard in the song of the redeemed mentioned in Revelation 5:9. "...thou wast slain, and hast redeemed us to God by thy blood out of every kindred, and tongue, and people, and nation...." When a man ceases to be grateful to Christ, his soul has died even though his body still lives.

### SACRIFICIAL GIFTS ARE EXPRESSIVE

"There came unto him a woman having an alabaster box of very precious ointment, and poured it on his head, as he sat at meat." Mark describes it as *pistic nard* rendered in our version as "spikenard." Nard is found in Syria and in certain parts of India; from its root a very strong perfume or ointment was manufactured. This had to be imported and was always expensive. Jewish ladies often carried small quantities of perfume in small alabaster boxes or flasks. These were round bottles with a long ornate neck, the orifice of which was sealed. It is not known how Mary came into possession of her treasure. Perhaps her brother and sister gave it as a birthday present; she might have purchased it, or there exists the possibility that some would-be husband had presented it to her. That box of ointment was probably her greatest possession.

Judas complained saying, "Why was not this ointment sold for three hundred pence, and given to the poor" (John 12:5). The word translated "pence" is *denarii*, but to get an understanding of this incident it is necessary to consider the same word used in the feeding of the thousands. When the Lord spoke with His disciples concerning the feeding of the multitude, Philip said, "Two hundred pennyworth of bread is not sufficient for them, that every one of them may take a little" (John 6:7). If Philip's assessment were correct, then the value of Mary's treasure would have been sufficient to feed at least seven thousand, five hundred people, or a half as many again as were fed when Jesus used the lad's loaves and fishes. Mary gave the best thing she had; she might have expressed her devotion with a less valuable gift, and doubtless the Lord would have been pleased. True love never counts the cost of sacrifice. Nothing less than the best can fittingly express the love found in a grateful soul.

## SENSELESS GOSSIP IS EXASPERATING

John suggests the criticism was first made by Judas; Matthew reveals the words were soon repeated by the other disciples. They were insensitive to the feelings of Mary, and thought nothing of the tribute being paid to the Master. They saw only the apparent waste of money. Once again we are reminded of the famous words spoken by Lincoln: "Better to remain silent and be thought a fool, than to speak and remove all doubt." Had the thoughtless disciples looked at Jesus, they would have seen eyes shining with delight, and a face radiant with joyful appreciation. He knew Mary was trying to express the overflowing love of her soul; she was giving to Him the best she had. The Lord looked at her and seemed to see what others missed. His words: "She did it for my burial," suggest the woman realized Jesus was about to die. The disciples had heard His prediction, but she alone understood! If we may use modern terminology, she had no desire to place flowers upon his casket! Her beautiful soul was opening as a flower at sunrise; the disciples resembled flowers closing before a night of criticism and bitterness. Their gossiping tongues were capable of causing pain. Alas, the criticism of disappointed disciples never seems to die.

## SANCTIFIED GIVING IS EXCITING

When a stone is thrown into a pool, it is almost impossible to tell where and when the ripples will end. Even so, when an appreciative person performs an act of kindness, no one can possibly know how far-reaching the action might be. Mary had no idea that thousands of years after her death people would still be talking about what she did in the home of Simon the leper. She would have been very surprised had she been told her gift would inspire millions of others; that her dedication would be a standard of excellence for all Christians. Jesus said, "Wheresoever this gospel shall be preached in the whole world, there shall also this, that this woman hath done, be told for a memorial of her." Her act of kindness made Mary immortally famous. It is impossible to out give God, and it is this realization which makes discipleship the most exciting career in the world.

## SECTION THREE

*Expository Notes on the Treachery of Judas*

**Then one of the twelve, called Judas Iscariot, went unto the chief priests, And said unto them, What will ye give me, and I will deliver him unto you? And they covenanted with him for thirty pieces of silver. And from that time he sought opportunity to betray him (vv. 14-16).**

## THE PREDICAMENT OF THE SANHEDRIN

To the perverted minds of the Jewish rulers, the arrival of Judas must have seemed providential. They had already decided not to arrest Jesus during the Passover feast, and therefore the entire matter was about to be postponed until a more convenient season. Then suddenly Judas arrived, and his offered help solved the problems which had baffled the greatest legal minds in Israel. If one of Christ's closest associates were willing to betray his Master; if discord and division were already disintegrating the Carpenter's followers, then it was feasible that their disunity would mean the destruction of every plan made by the Nazarene. The multitudes throughout the country could hardly be expected to give allegiance to a Man who had failed to unify His twelve closest friends. The suggestions made by Judas removed all difficulties; the traitor was welcomed with open arms.

## THE PRICE OF A SLAVE

Much has been said about Judas, but a few simple headings sum up the tragedy of this poor man. He was *disgusting, desperate, disillusioned, defenseless*, and finally, *dead*. "Modern criticism has endeavored to minimize the crime of Judas, or even to regard him as a hero misunderstood, but the facts are entirely in favor of the traditional view....Being a man of business capacity and skill in the management of money matters, he was appointed treasurer of the little funds at the disposal of Christ and His followers. Half-hearted and self-seeking, his undertaking this office was a snare to which he easily fell a victim. He began by petty peculations, which were not discovered by his comrades (John 12:6), though he must often have felt an uneasy apprehension that his Master saw through him, and that many of His warnings were directed at him (see John 6:64, 70 and 71). He had admitted the demon of covetousness to his breast, and now adhered to Christ for the hope of satisfying greed and wordly ambition" (The Rev. A. Lukyn Williams. *The Pulpit Commentary. Matthew*, Vol. 2, p. 518).

Liberal commentators, assisted by the film industry, have tried to persuade mankind that Judas was a victim of circumstances rather than a diabolical traitor. They assert that the unfortunate man was a diehard Jewish patriot intent on expelling the Roman invaders from his country. He firmly believed that Jesus was a most capable leader who, alas, needed encouragement to strike a blow at the enemy. Therefore, so it has been taught, Judas deliberately created incentives for the Lord, firmly believing that when His life was threatened, Jesus would assert Himself, rally His followers, and strike a death blow at the oppressors of Israel. When his plans misfired, Judas was overwhelmed with remorse and regret, and went out to end his miserable existence. Luke 22:3 states that Satan entered into Judas, and there is reason to believe this would have been an impossibility without cooperation from Judas himself. Even the Lord admitted his former follower was a lost soul, and in the light of that important utterance, the speculation from liberal theologians must be rejected (see John 17:12).

Whatever else might be claimed about this unfortunate betrayer, it remains evident that desperation had deadened his business capabilities. He was content to receive thirty pieces of silver, when a larger amount might have been obtained from the Sanhedrin. The accepted sum of money only equalled the price of a slave. Moses commanded: "If the ox shall push a manservant or a maidservant; he shall give unto their master thirty shekels of silver, and the ox shall be stoned" (Exod. 21:32). Therefore the value of Jesus was reckoned as equal to any servant gored by the horns of an ox. He was of no more worth than a peasant injured on a Judean mountain or an illiterate beggar hurt by a runaway animal in the streets of a Galilean village. There is something awfully sinful, and yet strangely beautiful about this comparison. Jesus was being placed alongside the most valueless human in the country, and that was precisely the reason why He left heaven and came to earth. He wished to be identified with the lowest of mortals, that through His grace, He might eventually take them back to His eternal home.

## THE PURPOSE OF A SINNER

"And from that time [Judas] sought opportunity to betray him." It is almost beyond comprehension that a man who had been close to Christ should drift so far away. Judas, who had been among the twelve sent out to preach the gospel of the kingdom, had become a reprobate. It might be easy to condemn the poor man, but it behooves all critics to examine themselves ere they condemn the traitor who somehow lost his way in the dark. How often have we sacrificed Jesus in order to please ourselves? The Bible says, "Wherefore let him that thinketh he standeth take heed lest he fall" (1 Cor. 10:12).

Judas had become derelict in thought; constantly he sought ways by which to deliver his Master to the enemy. His deed was premeditated and deliberate; he had lost his grip on decency. (See the expository notes on the parallel Scriptures in the author's commentaries on the Gospels of Mark, Luke and John. See also the special homily, "Judas the Gambler," *Luke's Thrilling Gospel*, p. 445.)

### SECTION FOUR

*Expository Notes on the Events Connected With the Last Supper*

**Now the first day of the feast of unleavened bread the disciples came to Jesus, saying unto him, Where wilt thou that we prepare for thee to eat the passover? And he said, Go into the city to such a man, and say unto him, The Master saith, My time is at hand; I will keep the passover at thy house with my disciples. And the disciples did as Jesus had appointed them; and they made ready the passover (vv. 17-19).**

## THE SUGGESTIVE ORDER

"Go into the city to such a man, and say unto him, The Master saith, My time is at hand; I will keep the passover at thy house with my disciples." Other gospel writers supply added information concerning this unique command, but Matthew does not appear to be concerned with mentioning the instructions given to the disciples. It seems obvious that Jesus had previously alerted His unknown friend to the fact that He would need accommodation in order to observe the forthcoming feast. The man was expecting to receive this message, and it is safe to assume that he had made special provision for his honored Guest. A large, furnished upper room was in readiness, and doubtless the two disciples were pleased with what they found. Tradition says the home belonged to the parents of John Mark, and that this home was used at Pentecost and the regular meetings for the members of the early church. It seems important that although the Lord was aware of the terrible sufferings awaiting Him in Jerusalem, He still planned every detail that nothing would be left to chance.

## THE STRICT OBEDIENCE

The required preparations for the Passover feast were numerous. The house had to be carefully cleansed from every particle of leaven; furnishings had to be supplied and sufficient lights added that adequate illumination would be forthcoming. A lamb had to be obtained, and certified by the priests as being clean and acceptable. Bread, wine, and bitter herbs had to be made ready, and many other details had to be meticulously observed. This would take a great deal of time, and therefore it was thought necessary that disciples be commissioned to attend to the legalities connected with the feast. The disciples made their request in the morning, and then worked throughout the day to have everything in readiness for the Master's arrival. They fully expected Him to conform to the usual practice of celebrating Passover, but Jesus had other intentions. As a matter of fact, there was a sense in which He did not celebrate the Passover at all!

## THE STRANGE OMISSION

There is a little uncertainty as to the time and day when the Lord instituted the Last Supper; the usual procedure of slaying the lambs had been extended over several days. Since a quarter of a million lambs had to be slain, and the fact that nearly three million people would be at the feast, certain Mosaic details had been rearranged. Visitors were permitted to live in tents and booths as far away as Bethany. Many teachers believe the death of Jesus took place at the same time lambs were being slain in the temple precincts. If, as we have already considered, the Lord was crucified on the afternoon of Wednesday, then

He may not have kept the Passover at the customary time when millions of other people were celebrating the feast. Another important fact seldom if ever recognized is that Christ's passover was not in alignment with the usual type honored by Jews. The most important element in the Passover observance was the sharing and eating of the slain lamb. This was never mentioned by any of the New Testament writers. As far as we are able to judge, even if Peter and John had prepared a lamb for the occasion, *it was never used by the Lord*. Jesus used the bread and wine, and *substituted Himself for the Passover lamb*. He took the bread and said: "Take, eat; this is my body."

Thus He taught very important truths. (1) The dictates and commands of Moses were reaching the end of their usefulness. The law was to be superseded by grace. (2) Lambs need never again be offered as an atonement for sin. He was to be the Lamb of God to take away the sins of the world forever. (3) As the old era was quickly drawing to conclusion, so the new one was commencing. If the Passover summed up all that had gone before, the communion feast, generally called "the last supper," would foreshadow and express all that lay ahead. Everything had changed, and probably this was one of the reasons why the Christians of the first century abandoned the practice of honoring the Passover and the Sabbath day; they preferred to remember their risen Lord on the first day of the week. Old things had truly passed away and everything had become delightfully new. (See Acts 20:7.)

> Now when the even was come, he sat down with the twelve. And as they did eat, he said, Verily I say unto you, that one of you shall betray me. And they were exceeding sorrowful, and began every one of them to say unto him, Lord, is it I? And he answered and said, He that dippeth his hand with me in the dish, the same shall betray me. The Son of man goeth as it is written of him: but woe unto that man by whom the Son of man is betrayed! it had been good for that man if he had not been born. Then Judas, which betrayed him, answered and said, Master, is it I. He said unto him, Thou hast said (vv. 20-25).

## A LITERAL WONDER

There are several problems connected with the varying accounts of the Last Supper, and these will be considered in the next section of this commentary. Meanwhile our Scriptures introduce us to three important areas of thought. It must ever remain a cause for amazement that, when the Lord ultimately announced the existence of a betrayer, the other members of the party were unaware of the identity of the guilty man.

Their question "Is it I?" reflects the complete surprise with which the utterance was received. The only place of responsibility within the company had been given to Judas, and it appeared inconceivable that he could be the offending brother. All the disciples momentarily questioned their own loyalty, but no one suspected the actual traitor. This means the love of Jesus had completely preserved His secret. His love for John and the rest of the group had been the same as the love shown to Judas. The Lord had known for a long time what would happen at the close of His ministry, but never on any occasion did He permit His secret to escape. How He managed to succeed in doing this will probably remain an inscrutable problem.

## A LAST WARNING

"Then Judas, which betrayed him, answered and said, Master, is it I? Jesus said unto him, Thou hast said." There is no reason to assume that Judas was ever mentally incompetent, and the plainness of the Lord's reply surely revealed that Jesus was aware of what was about to happen. The betrayer had already agreed on the price to be paid for his infamous act. Yet, it was not too late, had he so desired, to renounce his pact, warn Jesus, and try to prevent the tragedy. Alas, Judas had become a human vehicle out of control. The brakes of self-denial had failed; he had allowed Satan to seize the wheel and finally his whole being rushed toward self-destruction. Why did Jesus warn him? The answer can only be that in some amazing way, the Lord loved everybody. Nevertheless, even that kind of compassion remains helpless when a man or woman decides to remain stubborn. There is a limit to everything — even the Grace of God.

## A LINGERING WICKEDNESS

No complete understanding of the events connected with the Lord's Supper is possible, unless all the Scriptures relative to the occasion be taken into consideration. It has often been claimed that the "giving of the sop" was a means by which a host expressed favor toward a special guest. If this be true, then the Lord offered friendship to a man who even at that moment had arranged to become a traitor. For additional expository notes, consult the author's commentaries on Mark, Luke, and John.

And as they were eating, Jesus took bread, and blessed it, and brake it, and gave it to the disciples, and said, Take, eat; this is my body. And he took the cup, and gave thanks, and gave it to them, saying, Drink ye all of it; For this is my blood of the new testament, which is shed for many for the remission of sins. But I say unto you, I will not drink henceforth of this fruit of the vine, until that day when I drink it new with you in my Father's kingdom. And when they had sung an hymn, they went out into the mount of Olives (vv. 26-30).

## THE UNUSUAL TIMING

Throughout the Christian era, endless discussion has taken place in an attempt to reconcile noticeable differences in the gospel records. If, as has already been discussed, the Lord was crucified earlier than the Friday of Holy Week, then the observance of what Jesus called "The Passover" could not have been THE Passover celebrated by all Jews. Many scholars refer to the "Last Supper" as a paschal meal anticipating the true Passover. "...The synoptics are explicit in stating that the Crucifixion took place on the first day of Passover (Nisan 15). There are two possible problems in this connection: the events described in the story of the Passion would have to be compressed within a very short time; the involvement of the Jewish authorities in the sordid business of a crucifixion on the first day of a high festival is difficult to accept. J. Jeremias rejects the difficulties that arise in connection with the crucifixion on Nisan 15...but on the Jewish side, this is held to be a sheer impossibility....Mlle. Annie Jaubert has worked on the premise of two different calendars: an old sacerdotal calendar based on the solar system, and the official lunar calendar in force at the time. According to the solar system, Passover would always fall on a Wednesday; the lunar system would make it a moveable feast. It is therefore suggested that the discrepancy in the Gospels derives from the double system. According to an ancient church tradition, Jesus was arrested on Wednesday, which means that the Last Supper would have taken place on a Tuesday. Mlle. Jaubert's theory has received wide acceptance....But the theory stands and falls with the assumption of two paschal celebrations....At the same time there is wide concensus of opinion that the Last Supper was a paschal meal....One way out of the difficulty would be to assume that the Last Supper was a paschal meal, but in anticipation of the festival, which would mean that the paschal lamb was missing" (J. Jocz. Quoted from *The Zondervan Pictorial Encyclopedia of the Bible*. Vol. 4, pp. 608-609). This conclusion agrees with the suggestion that Jesus was crucified on the Wednesday afternoon, making it possible for His body to remain three days and nights in the grave prior to His resurrection on the first day of the week.

## THE UNIQUE TRUTH

Whatever interpretation might be given to this Scripture, it should be remembered that Jesus said, "With desire I have desired to eat THIS PASSOVER with you before I suffer" (Luke 22:15). Men may refer to this feast as a *paschal meal anticipating the true feast* to be celebrated later in the week, but for Jesus, this was Passover — but with a new meaning. It should be remembered that Peter and John had been sent beforehand to make preparation for the Passover, and there can be no doubt that they did an excellent job. All that was necessary was ready for use when Jesus arrived. "The ceremonial usually practiced was as follows: The head of the family, sitting in the place of honor, took a cup of wine and water mixed (the first cup), pronounced a thanksgiving over it, and having tasted it, passed it round to the guests; the master washed his hands, the others performing their ablutions at a later part of the service; the dishes were placed on the table; after a special benediction had been spoken over the bitter herbs, the master and the rest of the company took a bunch of these, dipped it in the appointed sauce, and ate it; an unleavened cake was broken and elevated with a prescribed formula; the second cup was filled, the history of the festival was proclaimed; Psalms 113-118 were recited, and the cup was drunk. Now began the proper paschal meal with a general washing of hands; the lamb was cut into pieces, and a portion given to each, with a bit of the unleavened bread and bitter herbs dipped in the sauce, called by John (13:26) 'the sop.' At the end of the meal...a third cup, 'The cup of blessing was drunk, and the solemn grace after meat was uttered.'" (Quoted from *The Pulpit Commentary. Matthew*. Vol. 2, p. 520).

It is not difficult to recognize that the celebration of the Last Supper was not the same as that of a regular Passover. If Peter and John, with the cooperation of the unknown householder, had supplied a lamb ready for the feast, we are obliged to ask, "What happened to it?" At the appropriate time, when normally the guests would have each taken a piece of the lamb, Jesus paused to utter an immortal truth. He said in so many words: "I AM THE LAMB; this bread is my flesh; take, eat, and live!" Thus in one glorious moment He signified certain important things. As far as He was concerned, there would never be need again to slay a lamb and observe the Passover festival. The laws of Moses were no longer binding; He was instituting a new festival, not to be observed annually, but "as oft as they did it" it would be a remembrance of Him. His new ordinance was not merely an improvement on the old system; it was something totally new. That possibly was one of the reasons why the observance of the Sabbath was no longer mandatory. The disciples, who had been given a new faith, feast, and hope, decided to celebrate on the first day of the week. Finally, although that decision has been criticized, the fact remains those early Christians were so blessed by God that they "turned the world upside down" with the proclamation of their gospel. It would have been extremely difficult for God to bless preachers whose actions were displeasing in His sight.

## THE ULTIMATE TRIUMPH

Jesus said, "I will not drink henceforth of this fruit of the vine, until that day when I drink it new with you *in my Father's kingdom*." That great utterance resembles a morning star shining in the darkness of a night but heralding the approach of dawn. In spite of unprecedented anguish soon to break the Savior's heart, and the persecution which would threaten the existence of His church, Jesus remained completely convinced the final triumph would belong to His Father. When Christian workers become disheartened and weary in well-doing, they should remember His words. They should consider that He will reign where'er the sun doth his successive journeys run; His kingdom will stretch from shore to shore, till moons shall wax and wane no more.

## SECTION FIVE

*Expository Notes on Christ's Warning to the Disciples and Peter*

**Then saith Jesus unto them, All ye shall be offended because of me this night: for it is written, I will smite the shepherd, and the sheep of the flock shall be scattered abroad. But after I am risen again, I will go before you into Galilee. Peter answered and said unto him, Though all men shall be offended because of thee, yet will I never be offended. Jesus said unto him, Verily I say unto thee, That this night, before the cock crow, thou shalt deny me thrice. Peter said unto him, Though I should die with thee, yet will I not deny thee. Likewise also said all the disciples (vv. 31-35).**

*HIS GREAT COMPREHENSION...''It is written'' (See Zech. 13:7)*

One of the most astounding features about Jesus was the complete composure with which He met and overcame every obstacle in His path. Throughout His sojourn on earth, He quoted the Scriptures, and reminded listeners that God had spoken clearly concerning events to take place. The Lord was aware that nothing had been overlooked in the divine planning, and was content to walk the predetermined pathway. He was one of a kind! No other person ever compared with Him. He searched the Scriptures but if there were any doubt about a course of action, Jesus climbed into the mount of Olives to commune with His Father. Thus did He set an example for all His followers.

*HIS GLORIOUS CONFIDENCE...''...after I am risen again''*

Christ's faith in His Father was indestructible. He knew He would be ''declared to be Son of God with power, according to the spirit of holiness, by the resurrection from the dead'' (Rom. 1:4). When everything seemed to be in jeopardy, Jesus bowed His head, and dismissed His spirit. With the trust of a little child, He was content to place Himself in the arms of God's unfailing kindness, and without anxiety, await the fulfillment of all that was planned before the world began.

*HIS GRACIOUS COMPASSION...''I will go before you into Galilee''*

Although the arrogant, self-confident Peter would deny the Lord; in spite of the fact that the other ten disciples would also forsake Him; Jesus never abandoned them. His statement to Peter, ''But I have prayed for thee'' revealed that even Simon had a place in God's planning (see Luke 22:32). It is encouraging that, although Peter was sometimes irrationally thoughtless, unreliable, and inconsistent, Jesus never abandoned him. This supplies encouragement for every Christian worker, for Jesus also prays that we might succeed. With such a friendly Intercessor, can we really fail? For more detailed notes on the collapse of Simon Peter, consult the author's commentary, *Luke's Thrilling Gospel*, pp. 457-467.

*Expository Notes on the Events in the Garden of Gethsemane*

**Then cometh Jesus with them unto a place called Gethsemane, and saith unto the disciples, Sit ye here, while I go and pray yonder. And he took with him Peter and the two sons of Zebedee, and began to be sorrowful and very heavy. Then saith he unto them, My soul is exceeding sorrowful, even unto death: tarry ye here, and watch with me. And he went a little farther, and fell on his face, and prayed, saying, O my Father, if it be possible, let this cup pass from me: nevertheless not as I will, but as thou wilt. And he cometh unto the disciples, and findeth them asleep, and saith unto Peter, What, could ye not watch with me one hour? Watch and pray, that ye enter not into temptation: the spirit indeed is willing, but the flesh is weak (vv. 36-41).**

*THE TERRIBLE BURDEN...He "began to be sorrowful and very heavy"*

The word translated "very heavy" is *adeemonein* , which according to Thayer means "to be uncomfortable; not at home; to be troubled; distressed." This idea of being away from home suggests "out of one's natural environment." He who had known holiness from eternity was indeed in an alien world!" The pure air of righteousness had been substituted by the smoggy condition of sin. The Lord was fully aware of all the sufferings to be endured, and was cognizant of each and every detail of what lay ahead. The contemplation of the impending events weighed heavily upon His spirit, and it must have been difficult to avoid the depression which would have overwhelmed ordinary men.

*THE TREMENDOUS BATTLE*

During His indescribable anguish, Jesus cried, "O my Father, if it be possible, let this cup pass from me: nevertheless not as I will, but as thou wilt." "Probably there is very much more in this text than at first would appear. What was this cup to which the Lord referred? It was unthinkable that He should be seeking a way to avoid the death of the cross. It was for that specific cause He came into the world, and Hebrews 12:1-2 makes it perfectly clear that when He contemplated going to the Cross, He did so with great joy. He never shirked His responsibilities; He never tried to avoid what He had helped to plan in the earliest of all ages. Therefore the cup could not have meant the cross.

"Hebrews 5:7 makes an important contribution to our consideration. 'Who in the days of his flesh, when he had offered up prayers and supplications with strong crying and tears unto him that was ABLE TO SAVE HIM FROM DEATH, and was heard in that *he feared.*' First, let it be clearly understood that Christ's prayer *was answered.* The cup DID pass from Him. This is something we need to comprehend. The Lord never prayed any prayer but what it was answered; He always prayed in the will of God. This is the first thing to be remembered. The Savior's prayer was answered while a deadly fear gripped His soul. It was not the fear of death — but rather the fear that *He might die too soon.* Reconciliation was to be made through the blood of the Cross; there, the forces of evil would be put to flight. Even Satan knew this, and knowing the time was short, the hosts of evil attacked the Son of God. This was the greatest attempt ever made upon the Lord's life. The onslaught was so severe that blood began to ooze from the Savior's temples. When His life seemed to be in jeopardy, the thought occurred 'Am I to die within sight of my goal?' The cup was the experience of physical weakness, and the Lord's desperate cry for help was answered when the angel came to assist Him (see Luke 22:41-43). The imparted strength enabled Jesus to vanquish the forces besieging His soul, and to proceed calmly toward the realization of His greatest ambition. The Savior's submissiveness was never in doubt. Although He desired to redeem sinners, His yieldedness to His Father was obvious when He said, 'Not my will, but thine be done.' He yearned to save a lost world, but desired even more to please His Father. Only thus could He prove His fitness to become our Redeemer. It *was* the will of God to save Him; and in answer to the Son's prayer, the angel came to do what was necessary." (Reprinted from the author's commentary, *Luke's Thrilling Gospel*, p. 460.)

*THE TRIUMPHANT BENEVOLENCE*

When He found the disciples asleep, He said, "The spirit indeed is willing, but the flesh is weak." He did not angrily criticize His followers; rather, He understood their problem. An unkind word spoken hastily against anyone can become a dagger piercing the soul. It never hurts to be kind to a weary person, and a cup of the refreshing water of kindness can be a means of restoring hope to one about to abandon it. Thus the Lord set a glorious example for all His followers. It behooves us, therefore, to be reluctant to criticize anyone except ourselves.

HOMILY

Study No. 17

## THE WORLD'S GREATEST BATTLE

The life of the Lord Jesus was a time of constant watchfulness against wiles of Satan. One mistake would have been sufficient to wreck the entire plan of God's salvation, and both Christ and His enemy knew it. Through direct methods, when Jesus was promised the kingdoms of the world, and through indirect methods when the spite and bitterness of men endeavored to irritate the Lord, Satan continually tried to overcome the Son of God. "[He] was in all points tempted like as we are, yet without sin" (Heb. 4:15). The nearer Christ went to His Cross and victory, the more desperate became the enemy. It would appear that Satan finally abandoned any attempt to make Christ fall into sin, realizing that in this matter the Lord Jesus was invincible. There remained but one possibility. The Garden of Gethsemane became the scene of the world's greatest conflict, when Satan tried to kill the Savior before the triumph of the cross could be won.

*THE GREAT CONFLICT...How great Christ's subservience to the will of God.*

"And he was withdrawn from them about a stone's cast, and kneeled down, and prayed, saying, Father, if thou be willing, remove this cup from me: nevertheless not my will, but thine, be done" (Luke 22:41). Probably this was the greatest prayer ever offered. The writer to the Hebrews adds a few poignant details: "Who in the days of his flesh, when he had offered up prayers and supplications with strong crying and tears *unto him that was able to save him from death*, and was heard in that he feared" (Heb. 5.7). Obviously, Christ dreaded death, but that could not have been the death of the cross. Calvary and what lay beyond brought great joy to the Lord's heart, for we read in Hebrews 12:2 "... *who for the joy that was set before him* endured the cross, despising the shame, and is set down at the right hand of the throne of God." The death feared by the Savior was the premature death planned by the evil one. If the Lord had died in the Garden of Gethsemane, the triumph of the cross would have been unknown. Therefore Satan directed against the physical resistance of the Lord Jesus every power at his command. In His moments of agonizing strain and weakness, the Lord realized His need, and "the strong crying and tears" brought instant relief.


*THE GREAT CRY...How great Christ's supplication to the heart of God.*

Language is inadequate to describe the spiritual stature of the Lord when, in spite of His intense longing to reach Calvary, He cried, "Not my will, but thine, be done." Yet IT WAS THE WILL OF GOD TO SAVE HIM, for the desires of the Son were in perfect alignment with the will of the Father. Prayer was not a new exercise to the Lord Jesus. Day after day He had communed with God, yet these prayers in Gethsemane were unique. "And being in an agony he prayed more earnestly: and his sweat was as it were great drops of blood falling down to the ground" (Luke 22:44). It would appear that this was a desperate cry for assistance. His lifeblood was being shed too soon. The appeal reached the heart of God, and the prayer was answered. "And there appeared an angel unto him from heaven, strengthening him" (Luke 22:43). This is probably the Bible's greatest portrait of prayer. If only the followers of Christ would emulate the Master's example, revival would begin immediately.


*THE GREAT CONQUEST...How great Christ's succor through the help of God.*

"True prayer is always answered, but if we ask according to the will of God, the answer is always in the affirmative. The coming of the angel provided Jesus with the much-needed strength which enabled Him to overcome the fierce assault of Satan, and ultimately to proceed triumphantly to Calvary. Satan's last great attempt to defeat the purposes of God in Christ failed completely. Exultantly, Paul was able to write: "And having spoiled principalities and powers, he made a show over them openly, triumphing over them in it" (Col. 2:15). The foundations of Calvary's victory were laid in the prayer of Gethsemane. Thus, in a remarkable fashion, God would teach us that life's greatest achievements are only made possible when we seek the place of prayer. A man is never greater than when he kneels before his Maker." (Reprinted from the author's commentary on *Luke's Thrilling Gospel*, pp. 462-463).

He went away again the second time, and prayed, saying, O my Father, if this cup may not pass away from me, except I drink it, thy will be done. And he came and found them asleep again: for their eyes were heavy. And he left them, and went away again, and prayed the third time, saying the same words. Then cometh he to his disciples, and saith unto them, Sleep on now, and take your rest: behold, the hour is at hand, and the Son of man is betrayed into the hands of sinners. Rise, let us be going: behold, he is at hand that doth betray me. And while he yet spake, lo, Judas, one of the twelve, came, and with him a great multitude with swords and staves, from the chief priests and elders of the people (vv. 42-47).

Most of the subject matter contained in these verses has already been examined. However, three simple thoughts remain for our consideration.

## THE PERSISTENT PRAYER...A strenuous conflict!

That Christ prayed three times, using the same words, indicates the emphatic insistence of Jesus in presenting His request. Nothing else would suffice; He knew what was needed, and prayed until He received it. This attitude was seen in the life of Daniel who prayed for three weeks until the answer to his prayer arrived from heaven (see Dan. 10:12-14).

## THE PERSISTENT PROBLEM...A sleeping church!

It must remain a cause for regret that so often the disciples fell asleep when they should have remained awake. They might have seen so many things, and heard so much more from Jesus, had they stayed alert. Alas, this has been a recurring problem throughout the ages. Each time the church has awakened from slumber and gone forth to do the Master's will, times of refreshing arrived from the presence of the Lord. Church history calls this REVIVAL. The text in Luke 9:32 is very thought-provoking. "And *when they were awake* [and not before], *they saw his glory.*"

## THE PERTINENT POSSIBILITY...A stupid Christian!

It would be easy to criticize the early disciples, but ere we begin it might be wise to consider ourselves. The lethargy of slumber is something which attacks each worker for Christ. The body needs rest, but if we lose our enthusiasm for the cause of Jesus and His kingdom, our sleep becomes a disease — sleeping sickness. This is deadly and indicates approaching death. "He that hath an ear, let him hear what the Spirit saith to the churches" (Rev. 2:29).

Throughout the Christian era, all God's servants found inspiration in the Lord's prayer in Gethsemane, and from time to time preached inspired sermons which came from moments of contemplation. I had a friend who was the pastor of the great Wale Street Baptist Church in Cape Town, South Africa. He was the Rev. James Walker, whose influence was felt throughout the country. That dear brother has long since gone to meet his Savior, but his notes on Matthew's Gospel are now on my desk. They were given to me by Dr. Alistair Walker, another of God's choice servants and the son of my old friend. I feel as if I am walking on holy ground when I read James Walker's outline. (1) This was a *Lonely Prayer*. Jesus "went a little farther." (2) This was *Humble Prayer*. Jesus knelt and fell on His face. (3) This was a *Filial Prayer*. Jesus did not pray as later "My God," He said, "O my Father." (4) This was a *Persevering Prayer*. It was uttered three times. (5) This was a *Prayer of Resignation*. Jesus said, "Not my will, but thine be done."

> Now he that betrayed him gave them a sign, saying, Whomsoever I shall kiss, that same is he: hold him fast. And forthwith he came to Jesus, and said, Hail, master; and kissed him. And Jesus said unto him, Friend, wherefore art thou come? Then came they, and laid hands on Jesus, and took him. And, behold, one of them which were with Jesus stretched out his hand, and drew his sword, and struck a servant of the high priest's, and smote off his ear. Then said Jesus unto him, Put up again thy sword into his place: for all they that take the sword shall perish with the sword. Thinkest thou that I cannot now pray to my Father, and he shall presently give me more than twelve legions of angels? But how then shall the scriptures be fulfilled, that thus it must be? In that same hour said Jesus to the multitudes, Are ye come out as against a thief with swords and staves for to take me? I sat daily with you teaching in the temple, and ye laid no hold on me. But all this was done, that the scriptures of the prophets might be fulfilled. Then all the disciples forsook him, and fled (vv. 48-56).

## THE HYPOCRITICAL ACT

The entire world is aware of the treachery of Judas. That he should betray his Master with a kiss is even worse than most people realize.

Throughout the Middle East, it is customary for people to greet each other in this manner. Politicians embrace others, and even when neighbors meet in the streets it is customary for either to embrace the other, and for both — even men — to implant kisses on the other's cheeks. When Judas made his infamous arrangement with the enemies, he used the word *philein* which is the ordinary, everyday word for a kiss. Yet when he actually identified the Savior, another word was used to describe the act. It was *katephileesen*, which is better translated "he ardently kissed him." This was a much stronger word used to indicate a lover's kiss; or a kiss of extreme affection as shown by a mother to her son. Judas enthusiastically embraced the Lord and kissed Him with a passion which appeared to be unmistakable. Thus did he exhibit the depths of infamy into which he had fallen.

## THE HYPOTHETICAL ANSWER

When Jesus said in response to Peter's action, "Thinkest thou that I cannot now pray to my Father, and he shall presently give me more than twelve legions of angels," He uttered truths almost beyond comprehension. A legion was made up of 6,000 soldiers. Therefore, twelve legions would represent 72,000 men. That number would have been more than sufficient to meet the challenge given by the enemies in the Garden of Gethsemane. It is the hypothetical picture behind the statement that is frightening. We are informed in 2 Kings 19:35 "...that the angel of the LORD went out, and smote in the camp of the Assyrians an hundred fourscore and five thousand: and...in the morning, behold, they were all dead corpses." If one angel could slay 185,000 men, we are left to speculate as to the efficiency of twelve legions. By the same computation they could have destroyed 11 billion, 920 million, or nearly three times the population of earth at the time when this commentary is being written. The Lord expressed the truth enshrined in the Negro Spiritual Hymn: "He's got the whole world in His hands" This only emphasized the astounding fact that Jesus was crucified — not because He was sentenced by a judge, but rather because that was the way HE CHOSE TO DIE!

## THE HOLY ASSIGNMENT

"But all this was done, that the scriptures of the prophets might be fulfilled." Once again we are presented with the astounding fact that what was taking place had been planned before time began. The Lord came to earth to walk a predestined pathway, and never for a moment did He deviate from it. His life was lived in alignment with the will of His heavenly Father, and it was because of this fact He became God's lifeline to a perishing world. This should be the standard by which all Christians should pattern their lives. To live for self is to live in vain; to live for Christ is to live again.

## SECTION SEVEN

*Expository Notes on Christ's Appearance Before the High Priest*

**And they that had laid hold on Jesus led him away to Caiaphas the high priest, where the scribes and the elders were assembled....Now the chief priests, and elders, and all the council, sought false witness against Jesus, to put him to death; But found none: yea, though many false witnesses came, yet found they none. At the last came two false witnesses, and said, This fellow said, I am able to destroy the temple of God, and to build it in three days. And the high priest arose, and said unto him, Answerest thou nothing? what is it which these witness against thee? But Jesus held his peace. And the high priest answered and said unto him, I adjure thee by the living God, that thou tell us whether thou be the Christ, the Son of God. Jesus saith unto him, Thou hast said: nevertheless I say unto you, Hereafter shall ye see the Son of man sitting on the right hand of power, and coming in the clouds of heaven (vv. 57 and 59-64).**

## *THE INEXCUSABLE INJUSTICE*

History records that the Sanhedrin was the highest court of the Jews. It was composed of Scribes, Pharisees, Sadducees, and elders of the people. It numbered seventy-one members and was presided over by the high priest. For a trial such as this a quorum was twenty-three. Among its regulations was a requirement that criminal cases be tried and completed during the daytime. Criminal cases could not be transacted during the Passover season at all. Only if a verdict was NOT GUILTY could a case be finished on the day it was begun; otherwise a night must elapse before the pronouncement of the verdict, so that feelings of mercy would have time to arise. Further, no decision of the Sanhedrin was valid unless it met in its own meeting place. All evidence had to be guaranteed by two witnesses separately examined, and having no contact with each other. False witness was punishable by death. In any trial the proceedings began by the laying before the court all the evidence for the INNOCENCE of the accused. The evidence to prove guilt was given later. It is abundantly clear that in their eagerness to get rid of Jesus, the Sanhedrin members broke their own rules.

## THE INSUFFICIENT INFORMATION

When the repeated efforts to find competent accusers failed, the high priest became desperate, and it seemed providential when two volunteers came forward to tell of an incident which had taken place years earlier. Yet, even their speaking about Christ's reference to His resurrection seemed inconclusive, for they could not agree on the details of their story (see Mark 14:58-59). In spite of repeated efforts, the high priest could not find convincing informers, and the case against Jesus should have been dismissed because of inconclusive evidence. The entire proceedings suggested a frame-up — hypocrisy at its worst. Probably the reference to the temple was only made because it suggested a threat against the illicit profits constantly being made by Annas and the priestly family. The Jews had no power to execute prisoners; that was a privilege reserved by the Romans. Therefore, the rulers tried to formulate an accusation which they could bring against Christ when He appeared before Pilate. When bonified testimonials could not be obtained, Caiaphas became desperate, and invoked a law from which there appeared to be no escape.

## THE INSPIRED ILLUMINATION

"And the high priest answered and said unto him, *I adjure thee by the living God*, that thou tell us whether thou be the Christ, the Son of God" (see Lev. 5:1). Under such circumstances a man was expected to answer certain questions, and knowing this, the high priest tried to make Jesus condemn Himself. Americans are aware of the fifth amendment which supplies an escape route for people who appear to be endangering their own defense. Jesus was fully aware of the machinations of His accuser, but with great courage did not turn from His responsibilities. His reply gave clear, convincing proof that He was what He claimed, or the greatest liar ever to testify in a courtroom. When Jesus spoke of His return in power and glory, the priest seemed to have obtained all the evidence necessary to bring a charge of blasphemy against the Prisoner. The rending of the priestly garments was something done in mock horror, but the physical punishment which followed was inexcusable. There was no chance for tempers to cool;

for decisions to be reconsidered; for compassion to emerge. Immediately, they subjected Jesus to physical harm, something banned by their own laws. Yet, the Lord never flinched. He looked beyond to the day of ultimate triumph, when He would return from His place at the right hand of the majesty on high. He knew where He was going, and He was content. Happy are they who follow in His footsteps.

## SECTION EIGHT

*Expository Notes on the Collapse of Simon Peter*

**But Peter followed afar off unto the high priest's palace, and went in, and sat with the servants, to see the end....Now Peter sat without in the palace: and a damsel came unto him, saying, Thou also wast with Jesus of Galilee. But he denied before them all, saying, I know not what thou sayest. And when he was gone out into the porch, another maid saw him, and said unto them that were there, This fellow was also with Jesus of Nazareth. And again he denied with an oath, I do not know the man. And after a while came unto him they that stood by, and said to Peter, Surely thou also art one of them; for thy speech betrayeth thee. Then began he to curse and to swear, saying, I know not the man. And immediately the cock crew. And Peter remembered the word of Jesus, which said unto him, Before the cock crow, thou shalt deny me thrice. And he went out, and wept bitterly (vv. 58, 69-75).**

Readers will possibly be aware that in the author's commentaries on Mark, Luke, and John, much has been said about the collapse of Simon Peter. At great length we have studied many details concerning his sad failure, and the love of Christ, who went in search of the prodigal son! It might be refreshing to discover something new in this strange story. It should be stimulating to remember that however disappointing Peter became, he was not as bad as some of the people who criticized him.

## PETER'S COURAGE

After the attack made upon the servant of the high priest, it would have been prudent for Peter to seek a hiding place, either in the home of a friend, or among the bushes and trees on the Mount of Olives. To go into the palace of the high priest was tantamount to suicide. Had he been recognized by his enemies, he might have been slain even before the maid saw him. In spite of his failure and denial, Peter truly loved the Lord, and it is worthy of attention that when most of the other disciples ran for their lives, Simon Peter went to be near his Lord. That was a very courageous act.

## PETER'S CONCLUSION

Peter went "to see the end." Truly convinced that everything was over; that the hope of seeing the kingdom of heaven established was now only a dream, Peter was determined to witness the final act in the drama. It would appear that his faith had been destroyed, yet, something deep within his soul still yearned for Jesus. The outlook was bleak; the past had been disastrous, but Jesus was still there. Let the other disciples run if they so desired; Peter would see things through, for better or worse, until everything had terminated. It will always seem a tragedy that Peter and his friends forgot the Lord's promise to rise from the dead. So much pain might have been avoided had they paid more attention to the words of Christ.

## PETER CHALLENGED

When the maid recognized Peter to have been in the company of Jesus, she confessed inadvertently that she had either been in one of the Lord's meetings, or she had witnessed the triumphant entry into the city. There is no evidence that she was an enemy of Jesus; she could have been one of His admirers. Had Peter remained silent, he might have made a new friend. Alas, the disciple made his first denial. This was followed by two more failures, and almost before he knew what was taking place, Peter had identified himself with those who were about to crucify his Master. Peter was not equipped to meet such an onslaught from the forces of evil, and yet, *he was there*; the others, who also had professed unfailing allegiance, were hiding in the shadows.

## PETER'S CONSCIENCE

"And when he was gone out into the porch." Had Peter gone a few more yards, he would have been standing beneath the stars with a cold wind blowing upon his flushed face. Why did he leave the fireside, where for a time he had seemed at home? He had denied knowledge of his Lord, and had become a common liar, unworthy of a relationship with Jesus. Peter felt he was a hypocrite, and with shame overwhelming him, went to the door. Why did he stop? Did he feel he was abandoning his

Master? Should he have continued his walk into the night? The most marvelous fact was that even if he were abandoning his Lord, Jesus never abandoned him. Years later Peter remembered, and told his story. He would have appreciated George Matheson's hymn: "O love that wilt not let me go."

## PETER'S CURSING

Did Peter return to the fireside because he was confident his failure would never be repeated? Was he content to play with fire believing he would never be burned? Did he need to remember the words of Scripture: "Let him that thinketh he standeth, take heed lest he fall"? Sometimes, a man is stronger when he feels weak, and weaker when he feels capable of doing anything. Self-confidence can make a man vulnerable. Paul stated that with Christ he could do everything, yet he would have been the first to admit that without Christ he would have been helpless!

## PETER'S CONTRITION

"And he went out, and wept bitterly." The time was probably three o'clock in the morning when the Roman guards were changed. The bugle call heralding the change was known as the *gallicinium*, which in Latin meant "the cockcrow." Most citizens would have been asleep in their beds. It must ever be remembered that Peter had resisted every inclination to sleep. He had stayed throughout the early morning hours, but when the bugle call pierced the silence of the night, Peter remembered the prediction of Jesus and rushed into the darkness to break his heart. His tears softened the hard self-confident clay of his soul. It was from such material that Jesus made the man of Pentecost. (For more detailed expository notes on the collapse of Peter, consult the author's commentary, *Luke's Thrilling Gospel*, pp. 464-467).

# The Twenty-seventh Chapter of Matthew

THEME: *The Trial and Crucifixion of Jesus*

OUTLINE:
  I. The Betrayer of Jesus...*His Turmoil* (Verses 1-10)
  II. The Judge of Jesus...*His Troubles* (Verses 11-26)
  III. The Death of Jesus...*His Triumph* (Verses 27-56)
  IV. The Burial of Jesus...*His Tomb* (Verses 57-66)

## SECTION ONE

*Expository Notes on the Betrayal of Jesus*

**When the morning was come, all the chief priests and elders of the people took counsel against Jesus to put him to death: And when they had bound him, they led him away, and delivered him to Pontius Pilate the governor. Then Judas, which had betrayed him, when he saw that he was condemned, repented himself, and brought again the thirty pieces of silver to the chief priests and elders, Saying, I have sinned in that I have betrayed the innocent blood. And they said, What is that to us? see thou to that. And he cast down the pieces of silver in the temple, and departed, and went and hanged himself (vv. 1-5).**

That was a morning which followed a very short night! If Peter's third denial of his Lord took place at the gallicinium — the bugle call announcing the third watch at three o'clock in the morning — then it was obvious that the priests, Pharisees, and others on the council had taken a few hours rest, and when the morning arrived, assembled again to take their prisoner to the governor. This was necessary, as the Jewish leaders had been deprived of the power to execute criminals. Jesus was bound and led to the residence occupied by Pontius Pilate. This man was the sixth Roman Procurator of Judea, and held this office for ten years under the Prefect of Syria. At the end of a decade he was removed because of cruelty and extortion and banished to Gaul where he committed suicide. The Roman governor usually resided at the fortress in Caesarea, but it was customary, whenever he came to Jerusalem, for him to stay in the magnificent palace of Herod, which was situated on the northwest angle of the upper city. Herod possessed a large house of his own, situated on the east of Jerusalem, and opposite to the castle. Apparently he preferred to stay in his palacious home more than in the governor's mansion. "From the slope of the eastern angle, opposite the Temple-Mount, where the Palace of Caiaphas stood, up the narrow streets of the Upper City, the melancholy procession wound to the portals of the grand Palace of Herod. It is recorded, that they who brought [Jesus] would not themselves enter the portals of the palace, 'that they might not be defiled, but might eat the Passover.'" (Dr. Edersheim. *The Life and Times of Jesus the Messiah.* Vol. 2, p. 566). At this point in the story, we are introduced again to Judas, and three simple but vital details need to be considered.

## HIS SHAMEFUL DISTRESS

"Then Judas...when he saw that he was condemned, repented himself." Judas had probably spent the hours before dawn contemplating the results of his infamous deed. Some teachers claim he hoped Jesus would now assert His authority and deliver Himself from the clutches of the enemies. When the man realized his dreams would not be fulfilled, he became increasingly agitated; his ill-gotten gains seemed to be burning holes in his hands and conscience. He began to know that what he had envisaged was a mirage; something unreachable.

## HIS SADDENING DISGRACE

Probably, although Judas never appreciated the fact, the fellowship with the disciples had been the most joyous experience of his life. He had lived, moved, and had his being with others who shared a common purpose. Doubtless there had been moments of strain and agitation, but his brethren had always been accessible, they had been a glorious preventative of loneliness. Now, suddenly they were gone, and would never again extend welcoming arms. He was terribly alone. What he had accomplished would place an everlasting stigma upon his soul. As long as the human race continued, the name Judas would be an epithet of infamy. His world had become an empty, lonely place.

## HIS SUDDEN DESPAIR

"...he repented himself, and brought again the thirty pieces of silver to the chief priests and elders, Saying, I have sinned in that I have betrayed the innocent blood. And they said, What is that to us? See thou to that." Was Judas trying to make amends? We may never know the answer to that question. When he threw his money into the sanctuary, he proclaimed that nothing could atone for what had been done, nor supply the peace so desperately needed by his tormented soul. He had betrayed his best Friend; he had incurred the wrath of his brethren; he was worse than the filthiest man he had known.

## HIS SICKENING DEATH

"[He] departed, and went and hanged himself." Literally this means "he strangled himself." The Greek word is *apeegzato*, and this suggests Judas climbed to a pinnacle on a hill, and using his girdle, tied one end to a rock, the other to his neck, and then cast himself over the edge of the precipice. Peter (Acts 1:18) supplies a terrible description of that horrifying event. "And falling headlong, he burst asunder in the midst, and all his bowels gushed out." This might have happened because the girdle or belt snapped, being unable to hold the suspended weight of a body. A fragment of an ancient manuscript says that after his fall from the high place, Judas was disembowelled by a passing wagon. Thus *he went to his own place*. This was never said of any other person (see Acts 1:25).

**And the chief priests took the silver pieces, and said, It is not lawful for to put them into the treasury, because it is the price of blood. And they took counsel, and bought with them the potter's field, to bury strangers in. Wherefore that field was called, The field of blood, unto this day. Then was fulfilled that which was spoken by Jeremy the prophet, saying, And they took the thirty pieces of silver, the price of him that was valued, whom they of the children of Israel did value; And gave them for the potter's field, as the Lord appointed me (vv. 6-10).**

## THE PILFRERED EXCHEQUER

The treasury was the common fund used to pay the expenses of the religious services. It was also used for repairs thought necessary in the building itself. The fund was maintained by gifts from worshipers. It is most probable that the thirty pieces of silver used to pay Judas were obtained from this source, as it was extremely unlikely that any member of the Sanhedrin would be willing to sacrifice money to compensate a despicable traitor.

It is interesting to note Deuteronomy 23:18 which appears to relate to impure things being used for the service of God. "Thou shalt not bring the hire of a whore, or the price of a dog, into the house of the LORD thy God for any vow; for both these are abomination unto the LORD thy God." It is thought-provoking that the men who in all probability took the money from the general fund, were unwilling to return it because it had touched the hands of Judas. To say the least, their act was hypocritical.

## A POOR EXCHANGE

"And they took counsel, and bought with them the potter's field, to bury strangers in." There are two explanations of this statement. "The strangers" might have been the Jewish visitors who died while attending a feast. If their bodies were not returned to their place of residence in another land, it would be necessary to inter them in or near Jerusalem. Some teachers believe the term "strangers" referred to Romans and Gentiles who died in the city. The Jews considered their presence in Palestine a source of defilement and a cemetery purchased by "tainted" money would have been a fitting resting place for those unwanted foreigners! It was strange that the life-giving Savior from Galilee was exchanged for a cemetery! Had Jesus been accepted by the nation, there would have been no need for cemeteries. He said, "Whosoever liveth and believeth in me shall never die" (John 11:26)!

## A PROBLEMATIC EXPLANATION

"Then was fulfilled that which was spoken by Jeremy the prophet, saying, And they took the thirty pieces of silver, the price of him that was valued....And gave them for the potter's field, as the Lord appointed me." It is thought that the piece of land in question was situated on the south side of Jerusalem on what was called "The Hill of Evil Counsel." The area had clay suitable for potters and the land had been excavated in all directions. It was unsuitable for agricultural purposes and therefore was inexpensive. Matthew refers to a text which he claimed had been spoken by Jeremiah, but actually the words appear to have been written by Zechariah. "And the LORD said unto me, Cast it unto the potter: a goodly price that I was prised at of them. And I took the thirty pieces of silver, and cast them to the potter in the house of the LORD'' (Zech. 11:13). There is a reference in Jeremiah to the purchase of a field (Jer. 32:7-9) but the price was seventeen shekels of silver. No satisfactory explanation of this apparent discrepancy has ever been offered. A suggestion has been made that the scribe who wrote the copies of the Gospel by hand, remembered that Jeremiah had mentioned the buying of a field, and endeavored to unite both utterances under one name. This may or may not be the case. The possibility exists that Jeremiah might have said something of the kind, for not all that he uttered was written in a book.

## THE PLAUSIBLE EXCUSE

"It is not lawful for to put them [the pieces of silver] into the treasury, because it is the price of blood." The law demanded that any money thought to be unworthy of use for temple services, should be returned to the donor. If this were not possible, or if the man were unwilling to accept the money, it was then to be used for some public project to benefit the community. It was then considered to be a gift from the man, even though he were dead. Hence Peter was able to say of Judas, "Now *this man purchased a field with the reward of iniquity*" (Acts 1:18). The action of the Jewish rulers would have been praised by all the people; they had performed an act which would benefit everybody. It was to be regretted that they never considered they were purchasing a burial plot for the interment of their personal guilt. The statement "as the Lord appointed me" must have connections with a similar utterance found in Zechariah 11:13, "And the LORD said unto me." The tainted money could not be used for any other purpose, therefore it was predetermined, or predestined by God to be used for the purchase of that particular piece of land.

## SECTION TWO

*Expository Notes on Christ's Appearance Before Pilate*

**And Jesus stood before the governor: and the governor asked him, saying, Art thou the King of the Jews? And Jesus said unto him, Thou sayest. And when he was accused of the chief priests and elders, he**

answered nothing. Then Pilate said unto him, Hearest thou not how many things they witness against thee? And he answered him to never a word; insomuch that the governor marvelled greatly. Now at that feast the governor was wont to release unto the people a prisoner, whom they would. And they had then a notable prisoner, called Barabbas. Therefore when they were gathered together, Pilate said unto them, Whom will ye that I release unto you? Barabbas, or Jesus which is called Christ? For he knew that for envy they had delivered him (vv. 11-18).

## A CHALLENGED SAVIOR

To obtain a complete picture of the proceedings at the trial of Jesus, it is necessary to read and compare the accounts supplied by all the gospel writers. Matthew only mentions a few details; the other writers supply additional facts. The examination before Pilate probably took place within the praetorium where Christ was detained by the official guards. The Jews were reluctant to enter the building and their accusations had probably been made outside. The question asked by the governor, "Art thou the King of the Jews?" was most interesting for, as far as we know, Christ had never made such a claim. He had claimed to be the Son of God, and speaking to the woman at Sychar's well, had inferred He was the true Messiah. Yet, although others had referred to Him as "The King of the Jews," He had not specifically said so. Pilate had heard all kinds of reports, but now, face to face with the prisoner, he asked if the rumors were true. Some think there was an element of disdain in his voice — "Can such as you be the Jewish King?" The evidence to support this assertion is inconclusive. Probably he was making an honest inquiry. Jesus replied, "It is as you say!"

## A CONTINUING SILENCE

"And when he was accused of the chief priests and elders, he answered nothing." When Pilate continued his interrogation and received the same treatment — silence — he was amazed; he had never confronted a prisoner such as Jesus. The governor was accustomed to hearing loud protestations of innocence; to watch a man apparently content to die was confusing. The Lord remembered the words of the prophet, and was determined to do as Isaiah predicted. "...he is brought as a lamb to the slaughter, and as a sheep before her shearers is dumb, so he openeth not his mouth'' (Isa. 53:7). Had Jesus retorted angrily, His accusers would have created a noisy brawl, and it would have been tantamount to casting pearls before swine. (See the special homily in the author's commentary, *John's Wonderful Gospel,* p. 95. The Eloquent Silences of Jesus.)


## A CONVENIENT SUBSTITUTE

Little is known of the origin of the custom to release a prisoner at the Feast of the Passover. It is thought it related to the deliverance from Egypt, and thus Pilate referred to it as "Your custom" (see John 18:39). Tradition refers to an earlier incident when a Roman governor, trying to gain favor with the Jews, made this concession. Pilate was desperately trying to find a way by which to deliver Jesus. Remembering the incarceration of a murderous revolutionary named Barabbas, the governor thought a way could be found to indict the criminal and at the same time exonerate Jesus. His conclusions were preconceived and mistaken. Barabbas means "the son of the father," and since the leading rabbis were called "father," it has been claimed the prisoner was the prodigal son of a religious leader. Mark 15:7 says, "And there was one name Barabbas, which lay bound with them that had made insurrection with him, who had committed murder in the insurrection." A worse criminal could not have been found, and there is something suggestive in the fact that Christ took the murderer's place, and his cross, and went to Calvary to die in his stead. Barabbas could have said,"He died for me."


**When he was set down on the judgment seat, his wife sent unto him, saying, Have thou nothing to do with that just man: for I have suffered many things this day in a dream because of him (v. 19).**


According to ancient Christian tradition, the wife of Pilate was named Claudia. She was a convert to Judaism, who later became an ardent Christian. Pilate was seated upon his throne on a raised platform in front of the praetorium, when a servant from his palace pushed through the crowd to deliver a message from his wife. This account is only found in Matthew's Gospel.

HOMILY

Study No. 18

## A GRACIOUS WIFE...Who Believed in Dreams

"The scene was set for the greatest drama in history. At the gates of the governor's palace, an insistent mob clamored for attention. The feast day was at hand, and before it commenced, dirty work had to be done — and done quickly. As the sun arose to send its silvery beams across the darkened sky, the shouts of the people echoed along the cobbled streets. Awakened thus from his sleep, Pilate went forth to the trial of Jesus ignorant of the fact that his own soul would also be tried that day. Losing his balance on the slippery slope of indecision and compromise, the judge began to fall, and every passing hour brought him closer to disaster. How wonderful it is to recall that in those moments God sufficiently loved this sinner to plan a final attempt to save him. In common with all other aspects of redeeming love, this is beyond comprehension.

### HOW GREAT WAS THE GRACE OF GOD

"Pilate's wife lay deep in slumber; she had not yet risen from her bed. Outside, her husband tried to outwit the bigoted people who were beginning to blackmail him, and silently, Christ stood listening. The woman stirred uneasily; she was restless. God had stooped to touch her slumbering eyes, and as she slept, she dreamed of Jesus. Suddenly, awakening with a start, she remembered that Pilate had gone to be the judge of the prophet.

"Trembling with premonitions of disaster, she wrote her urgent message, 'Have thou nothing to do with that just man: for I have suffered many things this day in a dream because of him.' If Pilate had taken her advice, his soul might have been saved. Had he not been so devoid of true understanding, he would have recognized this dream to be a medium of grace. God never ceases His attempt at rescue while there remains a chance to succeed.

### HOW GREAT WAS THE GOODNESS OF A WOMAN

"Possibly the governor dismissed this appeal as an intrusion into his own affairs. His wife should mind her own business! How could she understand the intricacies of this difficult case? These Jews had threatened to tell Caesar, and if a charge of treason should be brought against him, his future would be ruined. He had nothing to lose in crucifying the Prisoner; he had nothing to gain in resisting these arrogant Jews. Let her mind her own affairs! She did not understand. Ah, but she did. If misfortune overtook her husband, she could not escape; irrevocably her life was linked with his. She knew more. She knew that death was not the greatest of all tragedies. It was far better to die in honor than to live in shame. 'Husband,' she would have cried, 'do that which is right. This man is just, therefore stand by him whatever the cost.' Pilate should have been very proud of his noble partner. A good woman is the greatest jewel outside of heaven; a bad woman is the vilest creature outside of hell!

## HOW GREAT WAS THE GUILT OF A MAN

"Rudely brushing aside both the grace of God and the entreaties of his gracious lady, Pilate washed his hands before the multitude, saying, 'I am innocent of the blood of this just person.' Then, in contradiction of his verdict, he sent Jesus to be scourged and crucified. He had washed his hands, but had never touched the soiled places of his soul. To save himself, he sacrificed his Prisoner, and his honor. Yet we are told that within seven years of his deed, a broken, destitute man, removed from high office by the Governor of Syria, alone and unwanted by Caesar, Pilate went out into the darkness of the night to hang himself. His body was found by a workman. Poor guilty man, I feel sorry for him. He met the Savior and refused to love Him. And now it is dark — awfully dark." (Reprinted from the author's book, *Bible Cameos*, pp. 97-98).

**But the chief priests and elders persuaded the multitude that they should ask Barabbas, and destroy Jesus. The governor answered and said unto them, Whether of the twain will ye that I release unto you? They said, Barabbas. Pilate saith unto them, What shall I do then with Jesus which is called Christ? They all say unto him, Let him be crucified. And the governor said, Why, what evil hath he done? But they cried out the more, saying, Let him be crucified. When Pilate saw that he could prevail nothing, but that rather a tumult was made, he took water, and washed his hands before the multitude, saying, I am innocent of the blood of this just person: see ye to it. Then answered all the people, and said, His blood be on us, and on our children. Then released he Barabbas unto them: and when he had scourged Jesus, he delivered him to be crucified (vv. 20-26).**

## THE UNDESERVED SENTENCE

It must always remain an inscrutable mystery that, during the hours of Christ's unprecedented agony, and throughout the ordeal in the palace of His enemy, not one voice was raised in the Lord's defense except that of a woman. Pilate's wife did what she could to influence her husband, but apart from her effort, no other person spoke favorably for Christ. Barabbas was an insurrectionist whose fierce opposition to the Romans was known throughout the land. His villainy was proverbial, and Pilate apparently believed the crowd would choose the miracle-working Jesus instead of the man whose ambition knew no bounds; whose dagger destroyed human life. Pilate underestimated the strategy of his enemies. They circulated among the crowd using persuasive arguments to support their project. After three-and-a-half years of inspired service to the Jewish nation, the only thanks Jesus received was a brutal death. The people cried out, "Crucify him," and of all the sentences pronounced in a court of law, this was the most infamous.

## THE UNWASHED SOUL

"When Pilate saw that he could prevail nothing...he took water, and washed his hands before the multitude, saying, I am innocent of the blood of this just person: see ye to it." The word translated "just" is *dikaiou*, derived from *dikaios*. Dr. Thayer states it means "righteous; observing divine and human laws; one who is such as he ought to be; one who is virtuous keeping the commands of God." These words are a window through which it is possible to look into the soul of the judge. Apparently, Pilate sinned against all he had ever learned. When he washed his hands before the watching crowd, he seemed unaware of the fact that not one spot of the stain on his soul was even touched. He resembled the Pharisees of whom the Prisoner had said, "They were whited sepulchres — clean outside, but filthy within."

## THE UNWISE STATEMENT

"His blood be on us, and on our children." There is reason to believe that a curse settled on the nation that day, and it is problematical whether or not it has ever been removed. Josephus, in writing about the fall of Jerusalem, described how a vast number of Jews died by crucifixion. He said that as far as the eye could see in every direction, there was no sight to be seen except that of crucified Jews. Then he added a footnote to say this judgment fell upon the nation because they had crucified their Messiah! We now know that for two thousand years trouble has followed the Jewish people. The pogroms which became commonplace throughout the Middle Ages, and the concentration camps which made Hitler infamous, reflected what the Jews said long ago, "His blood be on us, and on our children." It is an irrefutable law of God that men reap what they sow.

## THE TERRIBLE SCOURGING

The word used by Matthew was *phragello*, which resembles the Latin word *flagellum*. It referred to the most terrible of all torture weapons, the Roman scourge. "This was no ordinary whip, but commonly a number of leather thongs loaded with lead or armed with sharp bones or spikes, so that every blow cut deeply into the flesh, causing intense pain. The culprit was stripped of his clothes, pinioned, and bound to a stake or pillar, and thus on his bare back suffered this inhuman chastisement" ( *The Pulpit Commentary. Matthew*. Vol. 2, p. 586).

Death by crucifixion was the most painful punishment known to man, and the scourging which preceded it was so horrible that many prisoners died on the rack. Another account from history describes the rack as wider and longer than a man's body. Stripped of all clothing, the prisoner was spread-eagled upon this frame, and by using leather straps attached to the ankles and wrists, the persecutors were able to exert pressure to extend the body to unbearable limits. The whip was then applied to the strained back of the offender, and often the prisoner died before he could be crucified.

### SECTION THREE

### Expository Notes on the Death of Jesus

**Then the soldiers of the governor took Jesus into the common hall, and gathered unto him the whole band of soldiers. And they stripped him, and put on him a scarlet robe. And when they had plaited a crown of thorns, they put it upon his head, and a reed in his right hand: and they bowed the knee before him, and mocked him, saying, Hail, King of the Jews! And they spit upon him, and took the reed, and smote him on the head. And after they had mocked him, they took the robe off from him, and put his own raiment on him, and led him away to crucify him (vv. 27-31).**

*A NIGHT'S ENTERTAINMENT*

"Then the soldiers ... gathered unto him the whole band." The Greek word translated "band" is *speiran*, and it refers to the tenth part of a legion which numbered six thousand men. It is extremely unlikely that six hundred men would be crowded into the common hall of the governor's house. These men had accompanied Pilate to Jerusalem and were responsible for his safety. Unless the entire legion had been temporarily transferred as a precaution against expected trouble at the feast, it is probable that only a small detachment of men was available for what can only be described as a night's entertainment. Perhaps of all the people present throughout the trial and crucifixion of Jesus, these men were the least to be blamed. They were not Jews, and possibly had no knowledge of Jesus or Jewish law. They were conscripts from all parts of the Roman Empire and were possibly very bored with their job. The chance to torment a prisoner was an attractive diversion from the wearisome hours of military duties.

*A NEEDLESS EXHIBITION*

"And when they had plaited a crown of thorns, they put it upon his head, and a reed in his right hand....And they spit upon him, and took the reed, and smote him on the head." The bushes of Palestine are noted for their very sharp, long thorns, and these were twisted into the shape of a crown by the soldiers' gloved hands. The reed was probably a form of eastern bamboo, and each time the soldiers smote Christ on the head, the thorns were driven deeper into His scalp. What those men did to an apparently helpless prisoner was inhuman and without justification. They were barbarians intent on having fun at the expense of a tired, exhausted sufferer. And yet in their blindness they did the only thing which could truly express what God in Christ was about to accomplish. Thorns had always been the emblems of sin; they appeared when the curse came upon the earth. They were meant to remind man that when he reached for fruit, there was always something to hurt; to pierce and cause pain. The soldiers could only take *the emblems* of sin; God took *the actual sins* of the world, and with them crowned the Savior.

*A NOTABLE EXCHANGE*

"And they stripped him, and put on him a scarlet robe....And after that they had mocked him, they took the robe off from him, and put his own raiment on him, and led him away to crucify him.'' It will be remembered that Herod placed ''a gorgeous robe'' on Jesus and sent Him back to Pilate (Luke 23:11). Was Matthew referring to that same robe? Suggestions of another kind may be within the narrative. Jesus, who had been clothed with garments of eternal splendor, had voluntarily lain these aside, and had come to earth ''to be found in fashion as a man.'' This same Jesus was afterward highly exalted, and enthroned at the right hand of the Majesty on high. The soldiers probably thought it would be regrettable if a gorgeous robe were stained by blood and dirt, and therefore removed it, and returned the Lord's garments to His bleeding body. They had no understanding of the glorious truth that Jesus alone was able to replace their filthy rags of self-righteousness with the garments of everlasting salvation. There are times when ordinary things may be significant; a vast area may be seen through a small hole in a fence!

> **And as they came out, they found a man of Cyrene, Simon by name: him they compelled to bear his cross. And when they were come unto a place called Golgotha, that is to say, a place of a skull, They gave him vinegar to drink mingled with gall: and when he had tasted thereof, he would not drink. And they crucified him, and parting his garments, casting lots: that it might be fulfilled which was spoken by the prophet, They parted my garments among them, and upon my vesture did they cast lots. And sitting down they watched him there. And set up over his head his accusation written, THIS IS JESUS THE KING OF THE JEWS (vv. 32-37).**

## A GREAT PRIVILEGE

''And as they came out, they found a man of Cyrene, Simon by name: him they compelled to bear his cross.'' Cyrene was an important city in North Africa; it was for the most part colonized by Jews. They were very wealthy and maintained their private synagogue in Jerusalem. (See Acts 6:9.) It has often been claimed that Simon was a pilgrim from that distant city, and had come to Jerusalem to celebrate the Feast of Passover. However, it has been suggested that he had formerly resided in North Africa, had become a resident in Israel, and had merely made the short journey from his new home in the countryside. It is impossible to be dogmatic about this detail, but there is evidence to support the first suggestion. Possibly he had come from North Africa, had decided to avoid the crowds in the city, and had stayed the night in a hostel along the route.

Mark (15:21) supplies the information that Simon was the father of Alexander and Rufus. It is safe to assume that Mark did this because both sons were known throughout the early church. It would seem that on the memorable day when Simon carried the cross, Jesus captured the Cyrenian's heart. Later that grateful father helped his sons to become Christians. That Simon was *compelled* to carry the cross infers some degree of force was necessary to make him comply with the soldier's command. The word translated ''compelled'' is *heeggareusan*, and this was the term generally used to express the compulsory power exercised by couriers when they requisitioned horses for the transport of royal proclamations. A Roman had only to place the head of his spear on the shoulder of a bystander to conscript the man for immediate service. Obviously, although he may not have appreciated the fact, Simon was apparently in the right place at the right time. It is truly thought-provoking that none of Christ's intimate friends were available for the service required. The greatest privilege ever given to men was afforded to a stranger from a distant country.

HOMILY

Study No. 19

### SIMON THE CYRENIAN...The Most Privileged Man in the World

The entire gospel story may be described as an account of God's giving to man. At Bethlehem He gave His Son to the world; in the ministry of Christ He gave His message to the world; at Calvary He gave His life for the world. Human indebtedness increased daily, yet when the disciples had their greatest opportunity of expressing their gratitude, they miserably failed. There came a day when Jesus urgently needed help; when a cruel cross had crushed Him to the ground. In those moments of supreme opportunity the disciples did not respond, and it was ''a stranger coming out of the country'' who carried the cross after Christ.

### *THE SHOULDERING OF THE CROSS*

Simon the Cyrenian lived in North Africa, but in common with all other people of his race he loved to attend the feasts at Jerusalem. This he was able to do because he had two sons who were capable of managing family affairs while he was away. Greatly excited, Simon completed the long journey and drew near to the city of his fathers. The temple roof glistening in the sunshine; the surging crowds, and the city itself made sacred by the ministry of the prophets, increased the thrill in his soul. He pressed along the street and came to the soldiers who at that moment were seeking the services of a strong man. "And as they came out, they found a man of Cyrene, Simon by name: him they *compelled* to bear his cross (Matt. 27:32). There was no court of appeal against the injustice of the soldiers' request. These men were a law unto themselves, and even the other Jews laughed at the stranger's embarrassment. Simon was probably angry. It seemed inexcusable that they should inflict upon him the indignity of carrying a cross for a malefactor. His arguments were useless — "They compelled him to carry the cross." Perhaps God looked down and smiled. Such service would be amply rewarded. When the cross was lifted, the Savior slowly arose and with quiet dignity looked upon His helper. Sullenly, Simon returned the look, and in seeing the face of Jesus, he looked into the heart of God.

## THE SHAME OF THE CROSS

We can understand the reluctance of the Cyrenian: but another problem arises. Where were the disciples in this hour of crisis? They had promised to be true to their Master; they had vowed to go with Him to prison and to death — where were they now? Probably they were in the crowd watching the unfolding of the sad drama, but when conscience suggested their going to aid the Lord, fear made them cowards. They were ashamed and afraid. To make a public confession of loyalty would invite the scorn of the entire multitude; they therefore left Him to suffer alone. Had any disciple rushed forward to lift the cross, he would have won eternal honors. Alas, they were all ashamed to respond, and the task was left to the man from Africa. He listened to the words addressed to the sorrowful women (Luke 23:28), and then followed to Calvary. He heard the request of the thief, and the response of Jesus; he listened as the Lord prayed: "Father, forgive them, for they know not what they do," and finally marvelled at the confession of the Centurion who said, "Certainly, this was the Son of God." At that time, his anger had died.

## THE SIGHT OF THE CROSS

Was it true? Had he carried a cross for the Son of God? What did it all mean? And perhaps God smiled again. He knows how to reward His workmen, and is never in debt to any man. The work commenced at Calvary was completed in the garden tomb. The news of the resurrection brought new excitement to the city, and more particularly to Simon. Soon he heard another message: "If any man will come after me, let him deny himself, and take up his cross daily, and follow me." When Simon lifted the second cross, he was more than compensated for his task in carrying the first one. Alexander and Rufus are mentioned later in the New Testament, and all Bible teachers agree that these leaders in the church were the sons of the man who carried the cross for Christ. Who led them to the Savior? Why, father, of course. God not only paid His debt, He gave "good measure, pressed down, and running over." He always does. (Reprinted from the author's book, *Bible Cameos,* pp. 123-124.)


## A GRACIOUS PITY

"And when they were come unto a place called Golgotha, that is to say, a place of a skull, They gave him vinegar to drink mingled with gall: and when he had tasted thereof, he would not drink" (v. 34). Historical records mention the fact that a small company of wealthy sympathetic ladies in Jerusalem always prepared an opiate for the criminals about to be crucified. David in Psalm 69:21 had written: "They gave me also gall for my meat; and in my thirst they gave me vinegar to drink." It is generally believed that this event at Calvary was a fulfillment of the ancient Scripture. It is taught that the concoction prepared by the benevolent women was a narcotic of some kind meant to ease the pain of crucifixion, or perhaps to supply strength which would enable the sufferer to endure his approaching ordeal. That Jesus refused to drink it was not an indication of an unsympathetic attitude. He refused because vital Scriptures had to be fulfilled. Had the Lord been drugged or in some kind of a coma, He would have been unable to fulfill what had been predicted. He was determined to drink the cup of anguish to the last drop. However, we should never forget that, even amid the unpleasant events connected with the death of Christ, there existed good and gracious women who desired to help the Man about to be crucified. We would like to know more about that brave little company. They remind us of Elijah who cried in despair, "I only am left." The prophet was mistaken. God always has His delightful servants somewhere, and to meet and know them is a continuing delight.

## A GLORIOUS PREDICTION

"...that it might be fulfilled which was spoken by the prophet, They parted my garments among them, and upon my vesture did they cast lots." This Scripture comes from Psalm 22:18, but its location in that particular psalm introduces the reader to a great area of thought. It would appear that the psalmist was aware of many details connected with the Messiah's death, for in verse after verse he spoke of things unknown among men. David said, "My God, my God, why hast thou forsaken me...They cried unto [me]....He trusted on the LORD that he would deliver him; let him deliver him, seeing he delighted in him....I am poured out like water, and all my bones are out of joint....For dogs have compassed me: the assembly of the wicked have inclosed me; they pierced my hands and my feet." We cannot be sure if primarily these words were spoken by David during the anguish of some spiritual crisis of his own. Yet, a careful examination of the entire psalm encourages the belief that all these things could hardly have happened to David. Surely, the sweet singer of Israel was so close to God, that he became a true prophet.

## A GOVERNOR'S PRONOUNCEMENT

"And sitting down they watched him there; And set up over his head his accusation written, THIS IS JESUS THE KING OF THE JEWS." Often when a criminal was condemned, to be crucified, he was placed in the center of four Roman soldiers. It was then the custom that he should carry the cross beam of his own cross as the upright was already waiting at the scene of crucifixion. The charge on which he was being executed was written on a board which either hung around his own neck or was carried by an officer in front of the procession. Later it was affixed to the cross itself.

It must be recognized that the title written and placed on the cross was hardly an accusation. It was a statement of identification; a claim resented by the Jews. (See John 19:19-22.) It is worthy of attention that it was written in Greek, Latin, and Hebrew. These were the three principal languages of the world; this was a message every nation needed to hear. The royal title might have been rewritten in the language of the poet:

> Go tell it on the mountain,
> Over the hills and everywhere;

Go tell it on the mountain,
That Jesus Christ is KING!

**Then were there two thieves crucified with him, one on the right hand, and another on the left. And they that passed by reviled him, wagging their heads, And saying, Thou that destroyest the temple, and buildest it in three days, save thyself. If thou be the Son of God, come down from the cross. Likewise also the chief priests mocking him, with the scribes and elders, said, He saved others; himself he cannot save. If he be the King of Israel, let him now come down from the cross, and we will believe him. He trusted in God; let him deliver him now, if he will have him: for he said, I am the Son of God. The thieves also, which were crucified with him, cast the same in his teeth (vv. 38-44).**

## THE PRESENCE OF THE MALEFACTORS

"Then were there two thieves crucified with him." Josephus the Jewish historian informs us that brigands were common throughout Palestine. In his book *The Antiquities of the Jews*. Book 16; Chapter 10, paragraph 8, he wrote: "There were robbers that dwelt at Trachonitis; at first their number was no more than forty, but they became more afterward, and they escaped the punishment Herod would have inflicted on them by making Arabia their refuge. Sylleus received them, and supported them with food that they might be mischievous to all mankind, and gave them a country to inhabit and himself received the gains they made by robbery...." The Lord in His parable of the Good Samaritan mentioned that the traveler "fell among thieves, which stripped him of his raiment, and wounded him, leaving him half dead" (Luke 10:30). These bandits were ardently pursued by the Romans, and it now appears the thieves who died with Jesus were caught red-handed during one of their infamous raids. Isaiah had foreseen what would happen at the death of the Messiah for he wrote: "and he was numbered with the transgressors..." (Isa. 53:12).

## THE PERVERSION OF THE MOB

It is interesting to compare the two types of people mentioned in the Scriptures. (1) "And sitting down, they watched him there." (2) "And they that passed by reviled him, wagging their heads." We are told that the Lord was crucified near to the city, and therefore near a highway. There were many people coming and going, and the sight of the crucifixion could easily be seen by the travelers. Some people sat on the hillside watching. Were they meditating? Were they sympathetic? We may never know, but others who were too busy to linger, wagged their heads and scoffed. This also had been predicted, for David wrote: "All they that see me laugh me to scorn: they shoot out the lip, they shake the head, saying, He trusted on the LORD that he would deliver him: let him deliver him, seeing he delighted in him" (Ps. 22:7-8). People who are unable to find time to consider Jesus, advertise their stupidity. Blessed are they who pause along life's highway to look at the Cross and ask, "Why?"

## THE PRELUDE OF A MIRACLE

Matthew said, "The thieves also, who were crucified with him, cast the same in his teeth." It is thought-provoking that he should insist that BOTH thieves cursed the Lord. Maddened by pain, the dying men cursed the day they were born; God for permitting this to happen; the crowd for its tantalizing remarks, and even Jesus, who by His silence put them to shame. The thieves were swearing, Jesus was praying, yet all three were about to die. Blasphemy is a strange language to use when one is approaching eternity! Then, suddenly a thief became attracted to the Man on the adjacent cross. He stared, saw, believed, and made his request. He could not have known that his reactions had been predicted by the prophet who said: "When thou shalt make his soul an offering for sin, *he shall see his seed...*" (Isa. 53:10). The criminal, unlike the prophet, was unable to see the end from the beginning, but he could see Jesus and ask for forgiveness. There may be many things beyond a man's comprehension, but if he can see the Lord, and gently place his hand into the Savior's, he can be safe for all eternity.

**Now from the sixth hour there was darkness over all the land unto the ninth hour. And about the ninth hour Jesus cried with a loud voice, saying, Eli, Eli, lama sabachthani? that is to say, My God, my God, why hast thou forsaken me? Some of them that stood there, when they heard that, said, This man calleth for Elias. And straightway one of them ran, and took a sponge, and filled it with vinegar, and put it on a reed, and gave him to drink. The rest said, Let be, let us see whether Elias will come to save him. Jesus, when he had cried again with a loud voice, yielded up the ghost (vv. 45-50).**

## THE EERIE CONDITIONS

Jesus was probably crucified at nine o'clock in the morning, which was the hour of the morning sacrifice. After He had been on His cross for three hours, darkness descended on the country, for the sun temporarily ceased to shine. Therefore from noon until three o'clock in the afternoon, the Lord endured the impenetrable darkness which had engulfed the land. At three o'clock in the afternoon, the light began to return, and shortly afterward, when the lambs were being slain for the Passover, Jesus dismissed His spirit. Throughout the history of the church, men have tried to explain why the darkness descended upon Israel. Chrysostom thought it to be a token of God's anger against the people who had done such a wicked deed. Others said the withdrawal of the sun's light was evidence that God was about to withdraw His presence from the nation which, hitherto, had been His pride and joy. I like to believe that God was preaching! He who had provided light, life, and healing from the beginning was being temporarily eclipsed. The darkness of a world's sin had hidden the radiance of His lovely face, yet, after three hours of gloom, the sun arose, as it were, from his grave of darkness never more to endure such an experience. God was painting on celestial canvas the greatest scene ever to be witnessed.

## THE EXHUBERANT CRY

"My God, My God, why hast thou forsaken me?" The language used was Aramaic, which in all probability was often used by Jesus. It is of the utmost importance to remember that the word used in the question is *egkatelipoes* — "Why hast thou forsaken me?" This is the aorist tense of the Greek verb denoting "something accomplished — completely finished — in the past!" Literally the text should be: "My God, My God why DIDST thou forsake me? "Whatever happened during the three hours of darkness HAD ALREADY HAPPENED. This cry of the Lord was not one of dejection, grief, nor sorrow. It was an exuberant cry of relief and joy. The light had returned, not only to the land, but to His own soul. He had gone into the darkness that we might stay in the light. Doubtless the question was born of the terrible experience through which He had successfully passed. Habakkuk supplies the answer to the Lord's question. He said, "Thou art of purer eyes than to behold evil, and canst not look on iniquity..." (Hab. 1:13). When the Lamb of God took our sins to the cross, God turned away from the sight, and that was the only time there was a break in the enduring fellowship of the divine family. Jesus temporarily went out of that fellowship, that we, by His grace, might enter it eternally.

## THE EXCITING CLIMAX

"Jesus, when he had cried again with a loud voice, [dismissed his spirit]." Obviously the Lord was in control even to the end. He did not succumb to the tortures of body and soul. However great His sufferings, that did not mean He died because death was unavoidable. When He was ready; when He was certain that all had been fulfilled as the Scriptures predicted, THEN, AND NOT BEFORE, He surrendered His spirit. His life was never taken from Him. Voluntarily, He laid it down as a sacrifice for sin. This is the heart of the Christian gospel and privileged are they who have enough vision to see it, and sufficient courage to preach it.

**And behold, the veil of the temple was rent in twain from the top to the bottom: and the earth did quake, and the rocks rent; And the graves were opened; and many bodies of the saints which slept arose, And came out of the graves after his resurrection, and went into the holy city, and appeared unto many. Now when the centurion, and they that were with him, watching Jesus, saw the earthquake, and those things that were done, they feared greatly, saying, Truly this was the Son of God. And many women were there beholding afar off, which followed Jesus from Galilee, ministering unto him: Among which was Mary Magdalene, and Mary the mother of James and Joses, and the mother of Zebedee's children (vv. 51-56).**

## RENDING THE VEIL

"And behold the veil of the temple was rent in twain from the top to the bottom." This was the ornate veil which separated the Holy of Holies, where God was believed to dwell, from the Holy Place where the priests were permitted to minister. The high priest, on the Day of Atonement, was allowed to proceed beyond the veil. He did so to place the blood of the offering on and before the mercy seat. The rending of the veil indicated that a private footpath had become an open highway! The death of the Savior opened a new and living way to the heart of God. The writer to the Hebrews was therefore able to urge his readers to "draw near, with full assurance of faith, that they find grace to help in every time of need." (See Heb. 4:16 and 10:19.) It is worthy of attention that the veil was rent from the top to the bottom and not from the bottom to the top. The break came from heaven. Had it started on earth, men might have tried to hold the sections together. There is a way that leads to the throne of God. Happy and wise are they who use it!

## RESURRECTING THE VIRTUOUS

"And the graves were opened; and many bodies of the saints which slept arose, And came out of the graves after his resurrection, and went into the city, and appeared unto many." At one special point in His ministry, Jesus described the temporary location of the dead (see Luke 17:19-31). The unrighteous dead went to Sheol or Hades; the righteous dead went to the other half of the same location known as Abraham's Bosom. At that time, sin had not been removed, and tainted by it, even the saints were unable to proceed directly into the presence of God. The atoning death of Jesus accomplished what had never been done, and thus it became possible for Jesus, when He ascended up on high, to lead a multitude of captives to their eternal home (see Eph. 4:8). Today, the saints who die in the Lord do not go to the place which some people call Purgatory; they go immediately into the presence of their heavenly Father. Thus it is written "they are absent from the body and at home with the Lord." (See also 2 Cor. 5:6.) When God opened the graves allowing some of the saints to revisit Jerusalem, He indicated to the world that the power of death had been destroyed.

## RECOGNIZING THE VICTOR

"...the centurion, and they that were with him, watching Jesus, ...feared greatly, saying, Truly this was the Son of God." Many people have asked if this centurion was the same man who earlier sought the help of Jesus on behalf of his sick child. If indeed that were the case, then we see at the cross the climax of a very wonderful story. The captain with his men had witnessed every detail of what had transpired, and their conclusion was obvious. No ordinary man could act as did Jesus. He had called God His Father, and had assumed authority to forgive a penitent thief. He had spoken of a realm called Paradise, to which the dying criminal had been guaranteed an entrance. These were the hallmarks of divinity. As far as is known, the Roman centurion was the first Gentile to be won through the death of Christ. He became the firstfruits of a great harvest.

## REMAINING THE VIGILANT

"And many women were there beholding afar off." It is thrilling to discover that the famous women of the New Testament were not alone. There were many other ladies in the watching group. The men were conspicuous by their absence; the women never left their Lord. Throughout His ministry, in various ways, they had ministered to His needs. They had never become too prominent, and no gossip was ever heard about their traveling with unrelated men. They were careful, considerate, contented and consecrated. They had been near to Him in life; and were determined to stay with Him in death. Although two men gently laid the body to rest, possibly it was the loving hands of devoted ladies which prepared the body for burial. Throughout the Bible story men occupied the prominent places of honor, but it is undeniable that when things became unbearably difficult, the faithfulness of women shone as stars in a very dark sky.

## SECTION FOUR

### Expository Notes on the Burial of Jesus

**When the even was come, there came a rich man of Arimathaea, named Joseph, who also himself was Jesus' disciple: He went to Pilate, and begged the body of Jesus. Then Pilate commanded the body to be delivered. And when Joseph had taken the body, he wrapped it in a clean linen cloth, And laid it in his own new tomb, which he had hewn out in the rock: and he rolled a great stone to the door of the sepulchre, and departed. And there was Mary Magdalene, and the other Mary, sitting over against the sepulchre (vv. 57-61).**

### JOSEPH'S COURAGE

The law given through Moses stated that ''…if a man have committed a sin worthy of death, and he be put to death, and thou hang him on a tree: His body shall not remain all night upon the tree, but thou shalt in any wise bury him that day; (for he that is hanged is accursed of God;) that thy land be not defiled, which the LORD thy God giveth thee for an inheritance'' (Deut. 21:22-23). The laws of the Romans were different. They permitted the bodies of criminals to remain on the cross until they were devoured by ravenous beasts. This was all part of the shame and punishment of criminals. John tells us that Joseph was a disciple of Jesus *but secretly for fear of the Jews* (John 19:38). Matthew affirms that Joseph was a disciple. Other New Testament Scriptures have much to add to the account supplied by Matthew. For example we are told that Joseph did not consent to the foul deeds of the Sanhedrin; the possibility exists that he was not present at the hastily summoned meeting in which Christ was condemned and sentenced to death. We are also informed that Joseph was joined by Nicodemus, another secret disciple, and that together they carried the body of Jesus to the sepulchre. It must ever be remembered that they buried a dead Christ; they did not know Jesus would be resurrected within a few days. Knowing they would be objects of ridicule when they returned to the Sanhedrin, these brave men completed their task.

## JOSEPH'S CARE

Wordsworth made a very suggestive remark when he said, "One Joseph was appointed by God to be guardian of Christ's body in the virgin *womb*, and another Joseph was the guardian of His body in the virgin *tomb*, and each Joseph is called 'a just man' in the Holy Scripture." It is important to remember that those who buried Jesus, according to law, became defiled, and as such were prohibited from participating in the Passover feast. In common with all other Jews, both Nicodemus and Joseph would have prepared for the great event, but when confronted by the problem, which was the more important, Jesus their Master, or observance of ancient ritual? it took only moments for those men to make their decision. Matthew does not supply the details found in the other Gospels. Probably to him they were anticlimactic. His King was dead! That He would rise again, Matthew had no doubt, and the more quickly he could describe the wonder of the resurrection, the happier he would be. He could hardly wait to begin!

There is another inconclusive detail which invites attention. It was customary for relatives of criminals to claim the body of the deceased. The Lord had no relatives close at hand, except *perhaps* Joseph of Arimathaea. An old legend said that Joseph was the uncle of Jesus, and that in requesting the body of the Savior, he was exercising his right as a relative. This may or may not have been true. No one can question the love which inspired the actions of that wonderful man. He had prepared a tomb against the day of his decease; with his money he purchased the clean linen, which in all probability was a fine cloth that had been brought either from India or Egypt. With resolute but trembling hands, he helped carry Jesus to the nearby tomb, and then placed the stone in place so that marauding dogs would not desecrate the burial place. It must always be remembered that Joseph did all that was possible for his dead Master. Doubtless the news of the resurrection made him one of the happiest men in existence.

## JOSEPH'S COMPANIONS

"And there was Mary Magdalene, and the other Mary [see v. 56] sitting over against the sepulchre." It would be nice if we knew what happened to "the many other women" who had been at the crucifixion. For reasons unknown, they had returned to their homes. Yet, two wonderful women stayed as near as was possible to the One they adored. With tearful, wondering eyes they watched the two disciples attending to the funeral, and doubtless decided that as soon as the sabbath restrictions terminated, they would complete what the men had commenced. (See Luke 24:1.) There has been endless discussion about the site of Christ's death and burial, and all visitors to Jerusalem are quickly made aware of the continuing arguments. To this author, at least, the only site in Jerusalem which fits the descriptions supplied by the writers of the Gospels is The Tomb in the Garden — the garden which exists at the foot of the small hill, now a Moslem cemetery. To walk around that place; to enter the tomb cut in the solid rock is truly an unforgettable experience.

**Now the next day, that followed the day of the preparation, the chief priests and Pharisees came together unto Pilate, Saying, Sir, we remember that that deceiver said, while he was yet alive, After three days I will rise again. Command therefore that the sepulchre be made sure until the third day, lest his disciples come by night, and steal him away, and say unto the people, He is risen from the dead: so the last error shall be worse than the first. Pilate said unto them, Ye have a watch: go your way, make it as sure as ye can. So they went, and made the sepulchre sure, sealing the stone, and setting a watch (vv. 62-66).**

## THE UNITED PURPOSE

"The chief priests and Pharisees came together unto Pilate." It seems that they were still scared of Jesus. They had thought death would end His ministry, but now they were haunted by memories. They referred to Jesus as a deceiver; actually they called him "that Vagabond! that useless Person!" It seems strange that they should remember those words of Jesus when so many more had been forgotten. They were afraid that, after all, their cause was threatened. Therefore, in spite of theological differences, they united their forces and made their request to Pilate. They had never feared the disciples during the years of Christ's ministry. The Pharisees had feared Jesus, but the uneducated fishermen from Galilee amounted to nothing! It is surprising to note how they had changed their opinion. Jesus was dead, but those men from Galilee could become a problem. They needed to exercise caution!

## THE UNIQUE PLAN

"...they made the sepulchre sure, sealing the stone, and setting a watch." Sepulchres were blocked by a large stone resembling a cartwheel. This was rolled along a small runway until it reached a niche in the wall. Dogs and other animals were thereby prevented from attacking the body and desecrating the tomb. Acting on the instructions received from Pilate, they sealed the stone with an offical marker, and to make absolutely certain no intruders would spoil their plans, arranged for a military guard to be there throughout the night. Remembering that Jesus had spoken of three days, the priests probably arranged for a succession of guards to be changed at intervals during the specified time. Martha had said that after four days interment, the body of her brother would have become obnoxious. The Pharisees probably thought the same of the body of Jesus. After three days, no one would desire to steal putrefaction!

## THE USELESS PROCEDURE

The men who made those plans were very stupid; there was an excuse for the hired soldiers, but the leaders of Israel should have known better. The disciples had vanished, their faith had been shattered; they were planning to return to the fishing grounds of Galilee. Alas, their King was dead! The greatest of Israel's teachers should have recognized the impossibility of fighting against God. If Christ were what He claimed to be, neither the grave nor the soldiers would prevent His resurrection. If He were a vagabond, an imposter, they had nothing to fear. What they did was useless. The Lord of Life, who inhabited eternity, could never be confined within a stony tomb.

# The Twenty-eighth Chapter
# of Matthew

THEME: *The Resurrection of the Savior*

OUTLINE:
    I. The Radiant Messenger (Verses 1-8)
    II. The Risen Master (Verses 9-10)
    III. The Reporting Men (Verses 11-15)
    IV. The Royal Message (Verses 16-20)

## SECTION ONE

*Expository Notes on the Appearance and Message of the Angel*

**In the end of the sabbath, as it began to dawn toward the first day of the week, came Mary Magdalene and the other Mary to see the sepulchre. And, behold, there was a great earthquake: for the angel of the Lord descended from heaven, and came and rolled back the stone from the door, and sat upon it. His countenance was like lightning, and his raiment white as snow: And for fear of him the keepers did shake, and became as dead men. And the angel answered and said unto the women, Fear not ye: for I know that ye seek Jesus, which was crucified. He is not here: for he is risen, as he said. Come, see the place where the Lord lay. And go quickly, and tell his disciples that he is risen from the dead; and, behold, he goeth before you into Galilee; there shall ye see him: lo, I have told you. And they departed quickly from the sepulchre with fear and great joy; and did run to bring his disciples word (vv. 1-8).**

It is extremely difficult to place in order, chronologically, the arrivals and departures to and from the tomb on that first Easter morning. Many theologians have brought together the complete records as supplied by the four Gospels, and attempts have been made to list events as they occurred on that memorable occasion. Alas, the conclusions have been unconvincing. The story has been read many times, but as we examine it more closely, seven areas of thought await scrutiny. (1) The Suggestive Sequence. (2) The Sudden Shaking. (3) The Scintillating Spectacle. (4) The Stricken Soldiers. (5) The Sublime Statement. (6) The Stirring Sequel. (7) The Special Service. It should be refreshing an beneficial to consider them in order.

## THE SUGGESTIVE SEQUENCE

John indicated that Mary Magdalene came to the tomb, "when it was yet dark" (John 20:1). Matthew said the same woman was accompanied by another lady who was also named Mary. Matthew also indicated they came "as it began to dawn" (Matt. 28:1). Mark said the two women were accompanied by a third whose name was Salome, and that all three arrived at "the rising of the sun" (Mark 16:1-2). The differing viewpoints represent a sequence of extremely interesting events. When the women began their journey to the sepulcher, everything was dark. God had apparently failed them; no one seemed to care; the outlook was bleak and unpromising; but they came in spite of everything. Continuing the account, Matthew implies that as they proceeded on their journey, the darkness began to diminish; dawn was swiftly approaching. Mark completes the account by saying they arrived at sunrise! The texts present a perfect picture of every soul who comes to the Savior. True conversion is often a walk out of the darkness into the glorious light of a new day.

## THE SUDDEN SHAKING

It is not clear if the angel placed a hand on the stone in order to roll it away from the mouth of the tomb, or whether the angelic visitor used the earthquake to do what had to be done. It might easily have been that as the earth began to shake, the huge stone suddenly rolled away, revealing the entrance to the sepulcher. The women had yet to learn that God was capable of dealing with obstacles. Their need was to come in faith; God's responsibility was to use whatever means He had at His disposal to reveal the miracle of the resurrection. Those dedicated ladies would have missed so much had they remained at home. So shall we if doubt be permitted to ruin our vision and shackle our feet!

## THE SCINTILLATING SPECTACLE

Matthew said there was one angel; Mark tells us that the angel was *a young man* (16:5). Luke insists there were two angels (24:4). John mentions the angels as an afterthought, and supplies the information that they were sitting, "one at the head, and the other at the feet, where the body of Jesus had lain." The differing accounts do not imply contradictions; each was telling the story as he saw it. Another writer with keener vision might have said hundreds of angels were present. Not every man sees everything! Luke was quite sure that at the birth of the Savior "a multitude of angels" was present to praise God and say, "Glory to God in the highest, and on earth peace, good will toward men" (Luke 2:13). Throughout the Bible it was commonplace for angels to appear in a form reflecting the glory of God. Only on special occasions was it difficult to recognize such a messenger (see Gen. 18:2). They usually appeared in garments which shone with the splendor of an eternal world. It was this which terrified the soldiers as they kept watch around the tomb of the Lord.

## THE STRICKEN SOLDIERS

It is not inconceivable that some, if not all, of these men had been present when the Lord was apprehended in the Garden of Gethsemane, and that they had not forgotten the awesome display of power when a few words spoken by Jesus paralyzed hundreds of men (see John 18:6). They might also have been present when, at the death of Jesus, the sun ceased to shine, and an earthquake devastated the city. Those soldiers had already been terrified by supernatural events, and the sudden blinding display of celestial brilliance was so frightening, the scared watchers became unconscious. They were victims of circumstance; they obeyed Caesar, but unwittingly fought against God.

## THE SUBLIME STATEMENT

"And the angel answered and said unto the women, Fear not ye: for I know that ye seek Jesus, which was crucified. He is not here: for he is risen, as he said. Come, see the place where the Lord lay." Are we justified in thinking a gentle rebuke was expressed in the words "as he said"? Was the angelic messenger trying to say, "Why are you seeking the living among the dead? Jesus told you what would happen; have you forgotten His prediction so soon? The Lord always honors His word. If you forget His promises, you may spend years seeking satisfaction in wrong places! Why don't you give more attention to the infallible Word of God?" It is difficult to avoid the conclusion that if that angel visited us he would repeat his questions!

## THE STIRRING SEQUEL

"And go quickly, and tell his disciples that he is risen from the dead: and, behold, he goeth before you into Galilee; there shall ye see him: lo, I have told you." It is worthy of note that the first commissioned preachers of the resurrection were women! Men may argue about the place of women within the church, but this fact remains irrefutable; the women were told to do a job because no male disciple was present either to see or hear the angels. The men had failed their Lord. Many times later, the apostles talked themselves hoarse, but the fact remains that when they were urgently needed, the brethren were conspicuously absent. If I were a woman, I think I would be tempted to tell interfering men that they would be wise to get on with their job, and allow us to do ours! Commissioned by a risen Lord, it was impossible to remain silent.

## THE SPECIAL SERVICE

"And they departed quickly from the sepulchre with fear and great joy; and did run to bring his disciples word." The word translated "fear" is *phobou* and basically means "to be terrified." It was the same word used to describe the alarm which gripped the soldiers when they beheld the shining appearance of the angels. Dr. Thayer points out that it is also used to express *reverential obedience* (see Acts 10:2). The women who came to the tomb of Jesus were startled by the magnificent appearance of the angels, but this begat an intense desire to obey God's command and share with others their new happiness. To have remained silent and inactive would have been inexcusable. They RAN to bring the disciples word of the resurrection. The message was thrilling; the need was extremely urgent; to walk on such an errand would have been impossible. Their enthusiasm was contagious, for when the apostles also received a similar command, they never ceased in their endeavor to bring the gospel to a waiting world. Men and movements without a missionary vision are dead even before they die!

### SECTION TWO

*Expository Notes on Christ's Meeting the Women*

**And as they went to tell his disciples, behold, Jesus met them, saying, All hail. And they came and held him by the feet, and worshiped him.**

Then said Jesus unto them, Be not afraid: go tell my brethren that they go into Galilee, and there shall they see me (vv. 9-10).

## THE DELIGHTFUL REASSURANCE

The casual reader might ask why the Lord appeared to the ladies, especially as He did not extend the original commission given by the angel? To suggest that nothing was added would be a misrepresentation of the facts. The women knew exactly what they were told to say, but under questioning would be forced to admit they had not seen the risen Christ. The Lord made His personal appearance to confirm what had been done, and to give to the messengers the thrilling experience of being able to describe facts. They could say as did John, "That which we have seen and heard declare we unto you, that ye also may have fellowship with us: and truly our fellowship is with the Father, AND WITH HIS SON JESUS CHRIST" (1 John 1:3).

## THE DUBIOUS REQUEST

At first glance, Matthew seems to be at variance with John who claimed that Jesus said to Mary, "Touch me not: for I am not yet ascended to my Father..." (John 20:17). Matthew says: "They came and held him by the feet, and worshiped him." Could they not both be correct? Did the women embrace His feet, only to see the Lord stepping back from their encircling arms to deliver the important message mentioned by John? The Lord was in a transitional period between the cross and His becoming our representative before the throne of God. As the high priest of Israel first sprinkled the blood of sacrifice before and on the altar, so Christ "is not entered into the holy places made with hands, which are the figures of the true; but into heaven itself, now to appear in the presence of God for us" (Heb. 9:24). (See the special homily: Mary Magdalene...who was told to keep her distance. *John's Wonderful Gospel*, pp. 423-424.)

## THE DEFINITE REPETITION

The fact that the risen Lord insisted on repeating the commission already given suggests two things — its importance for men and its inspiration from heaven. The disciples who had temporarily lost their faith urgently needed encouragement. They would need to choose between nets used on the Sea of Galilee, and the new ones to be used in catching men and women for Christ. It was necessary for them to understand that the command sent by God through the angel was identical with His own desires. He and the Father were in total agreement; there was no variance within the divine family. The commission was sent from God, delivered by the angel, and endorsed by Jesus. It represented importance of the highest kind.

## SECTION THREE

*Expository Notes on the Infamous Decision of the Sanhedrin*

**Now when they were going, behold, some of the watch came into the city, and showed unto the chief priests all the things that were done. And when they were assembled with the elders, and had taken counsel, they gave large money unto the soldiers, Saying, Say ye, His disciples came by night, and stole him away while we slept. And if this comes to the governor's ears, we will persuade him, and secure you. So they took the money, and did as they were taught: and this saying is commonly reported among the Jews until this day (vv. 11-15).**

## THE SOLDIERS' STORY...Disturbing

It is interesting to note that only some of the soldiers reported to the Sanhedrin members. We can only speculate as to the reason for this. Were the others frightened? Were they content to commission a few of their number to act as representatives for the entire company? Obviously some spokesman had to make the Jewish leaders aware of the events which had taken place during the night. The lives of the guards might be endangered if false accusations were made before Caesar. The soldiers therefore hurried to the city to speak of the earthquake, the appearance of the angels, and the disappearance of the body of Jesus. Doubtless many questions were asked, but the frightened men were unable to supply many additional details. The body had disappeared, and if asked about their inability to prevent this, the harassed men could only tell of the black out which followed the appearance of the shining ones. Maybe heathen superstitions embellished their report, but they remained adamant that, when they awakened from sleep, the body of Jesus had been removed.

It is interesting to consider that the report was never discredited nor denied by the Jewish leaders. They were only concerned with the preservation of their own credibility. They had worked unceasingly to defeat the purposes and teachings of the Nazarene; they could not afford any recurrence of the problems thought to have been destroyed. Actually, they did not worry about the location of the body of Jesus; they were obsessed with the idea of concocting an acceptable explanation of the mysterious events which had taken place in the Garden of Gethsemane.

## THE STARTLED SANHEDRIN...Deciding

They discussed their options. To admit that Jesus the carpenter had risen from the dead was unthinkable. They were sure He could not do this. They could suggest the angel had carried away the body to an unknown destination. No, that would be unwise for it inferred the angel was a supporter of the heretic! If the people believed that explanation, the end results might be worse than the beginning. Jesus was an enemy of God and the State. Yet, how could they explain the disappearance of His body? It had to be somewhere! When one of the members suggested the disciples had stolen it, instantly, the entire council recognized a way of reporting the news. The disciples had stolen the body while the soldiers were sleeping! The Sanhedrin only needed the cooperation of the Romans, and the problem was solved.

## THE SUBTLE SCHEME...Defiling

It might cost money, but how much? If soldiers were found asleep at their post, the penalty was death. To sleep during a period of guard duty endangered the lives of comrades. When the men heard the Jewish suggestion they were surely appalled; to accept the plan was tantamount to signing their death certificate. Their spokesman surely made this perfectly clear. Why should they risk their lives to cooperate with people whose land they occupied? Then the Jews spoke about money — a lot of it. They had bribed Judas with thirty pieces of silver to *put Christ into the tomb*. Now they probably spent much more to explain how Jesus had *left His tomb*. Alas, this Carpenter was becoming a very expensive nuisance! But something had to be done, and the gleam in the eyes of the informers indicated the plan was about to succeed. Should any information reach the governor, the Jews would make themselves responsible for suitable explanations. They would guarantee the safety of the men who had guarded the tomb in the garden. Alas, the corruption of the Sanhedrin increased the unspeakable defilement of all who participated in that abominable plan.

*THE SHAMEFUL SUGGESTIONS...Deluding*

"So they took the money, and did as they were taught: and this saying is commonly reported among the Jews until this day." Matthew did not write his Gospel until decades had passed, and therefore was able to make his observation. It is significant that he said the report was believed AMONG JEWS until this day. Gentiles would have been too wise to accept the lie, knowing that had the soldiers slept, they would have been charged with negligence and executed as a warning to others tempted to make the same mistake. It should be remembered how Jesus said men would love darkness rather than light. He was sure of His facts. Some people prefer to be pleasing before men even at the risk of being obnoxious before God. There are none so blind as those who have no desire to see. The lie was often repeated, and there are people who continue to believe it. Nevertheless, there has never been an explanation how a stolen corpse suddenly began to change the lives of men and women. Then, and now, it might be claimed the greatest evidence for the resurrection of Jesus would not have been in the discovery of His body, but rather in the mystical, but marvelous power that transformed human life.

## SECTION FOUR

*Expository Notes on the Commission to Evangelize the World*

**Then the eleven disciples went away into Galilee, into a mountain where Jesus had appointed them. And when they saw him, they worshiped him: but some doubted. And Jesus came and spake unto them, saying, All power is given unto me in heaven and in earth. Go ye therefore, and teach all nations, baptizing them in the name of the Father, and of the Son, and of the Holy Ghost: Teaching them to observe all things whatsoever I have commanded you: and, lo, I am with you always, even unto the end of the world. Amen (vv. 16-20).**

Matthew was about to complete his manuscript; this was to be his final paragraph. Contemporary writers would describe additional things, for Jesus made other appearances after His resurrection. Matthew remained unconcerned. He had done his job! Originally he began with one absorbing desire — to prove that his Master was the King of Israel. He had done this, and God through the resurrection had endorsed what had been written. Jesus, the Christ, was seated at the right hand of the Majesty on high. Let other evangelists say or write whatever they desired; for Matthew only one thing remained. The kingship of Christ had been established; the King had issued directions regarding future conduct. There remained the task of telling the nations the greatest message ever to be delivered. Matthew seemed to say, "This is what our King desires; listen to His words, and then, get on with the job."

*HIS MOUNTAIN...Sacred*

"Then the disciples went away into Galilee, into a mountain where Jesus had appointed them." Jesus never overlooked details! Some time before the Passover feast, He made arrangements with an unknown friend that the celebration should take place in his house. He had agreed on a sign by which His disciples would be able to recognize the servant who would guide them to the prepared room (see Luke 22:10). We are now told that Jesus personally selected the mountain where He gave final instructions to His friends. Men have since speculated as to the location of that mountain, but probably God decided not to reveal its whereabouts, so that all mountains might become sacred to His children. There is reason to believe that Jesus had been there many times, and the disciples had no problem retracing their steps to the place often sanctified by the presence of their Master.

*HIS MEN...Surveying*

"And when they saw him, they worshiped him: but some doubted." Matthew was quite certain of the accuracy of his report; he was there when it happened! It should be remembered that Jesus made several appearances to His disciples in the city of Jerusalem. Therefore it must seem a little strange that "some doubted." Theologians have tried to explain this by stating many others were present, but Matthew mentions ELEVEN disciples and says, "When THEY saw him, some doubted." Obviously some of the men had unanswered questions in their minds. Yet others looked into His lovely face, and fell adoringly at His feet. Alas, certain people resemble the ancient disciples. They permit doubt to place cataracts on the eyes of the soul, and as a result vision is impaired. Blessed are they who take care of their eyesight. It is never pleasant to walk in the dark!

*HIS MAJESTY...Scintillating*

"And Jesus came and spake unto them, saying, All power is given unto me in heaven and in earth." He did not say "Power is given unto me." He said, "ALL POWER is given unto me." Jesus claimed to be the supreme executive of the divine family. Every inch of territory, not only on the planet earth, but throughout the innumerable far-flung planets in outer space, had become part of His domain. The carpenter of Nazareth, who spent years making and repairing farm vehicles, was now to be seated far above principalities and powers in heavenly places. Matthew must have been thrilled as he contemplated this glorious fact. He had written about the Messiah, and his messages had been endorsed by God. There was no cause for amazement in the fact that fishermen fell at Christ's feet to worship Him. Angels had done this from the beginning of time, and ten thousand times ten thousand, and thousands of thousands will do it throughout eternal ages. Matthew could have been excused had he thrown his pen into the air as he cried, "Glory be to God: He's marvelous!"

## HIS MISSION...*Stimulating*

"Go ye therefore, and teach all nations, baptizing them in the name of the Father, and of the Son, and of the Holy Ghost." Jesus, having died to save a lost world, now wished that all men everywhere should be made aware of what had been done. This was not a time for celebrating the resurrection, nor mourning His departure to another world. A great amount of work had to be done, and nothing should be permitted to prevent the observance of His commandments. The word translated "teach" is the Greek word *matheeteusate* which would be better translated "disciple of all nations." That would mean "make them as you are. You are My disciples. Go therefore and do for others what I did for you." That glorious commission has much to teach all followers of Christ. Jesus seemed to be drawing attention to certain important facts. He had found them; instructed them; loved them; exercised patience dealing with their inconsistencies, and had been willing to give all He possessed to help them. This was the standard of excellence by which the disciples were to measure the value of their ministry. As He had done for them, they should do for others. This would be the only way to make genuine disciples.

## HIS MESSAGE...*Strengthening*

"...lo, I am with you always, even unto the end of the world. Amen." Perhaps this was the most potent of all the Lord's promises. Uneducated fishermen and others of their type were being sent to challenge the might of Caesar's empire; the problems awaiting them beggared description. Often they would be confronted by the greatest heathen scholars; unfriendly tribunals would sentenence many of them to death. They would be fed to hungry lions in the arena, tortured, and burned to amuse the emperor's guests. The problems of world evangelism would appear to be insurmountable, but at all times the preachers should remember that even the darkest night would have one brilliant star of promise. Jesus said, "I will be with you always, even unto the ends of the age." It would be easy to recognize His presence in the sunshine when success recompensed their labor, but they were to look more closely when darkness and doubt overshadowed their efforts. Always, somewhere in the shadows, they would find Jesus. They would never be alone. Matthew must have been very thrilled when he wrote his final message. It is easy to see him leaning back on his bench, perusing his words, and then completing his manuscript by saying a very loud "AMEN!"

# BIBLIOGRAPHY

*Amplified New Testament.* Grand Rapids: Zondervan Publishing House, 1958.

Edersheim, Alfred *Life & Times of Jesus the Messiah.* Grand Rapids: Wm. B. Eerdmans Publishing Co., 1972.
*Eusebius Ecclesiastical History.* Grand Rapids: Baker Book House, n.d.

Gaebelein, Arno C. *Gospel of Matthew.* Neptune, New Jersey: Loizeaux, 1961.
Geikie, Cunningham *The Life and Words of Christ.* New York: D. Appleton & Co. 1880.
Godet, Frederic L. *Commentary on Luke.* Grand Rapids: Kregel Publications, 1981.

Josephus, Flavius *The Complete Works of Flavius Josephus.* Grand Rapids: Kregel Publications, 1960.

Keller, Werner *The Bible As History.* New York: William Morrow & Company, 1956.

Liddell, Henry G. & Scott, Robert; editors. *Greek English Lexicon* 9th ed. New York: Oxford University Press, 1940.
*Living Bible Paraphrased.* Wheaton: Tyndale House, 1971.

Marshall, Alfred *The Interlinear Greek-English New Testament.* Grand Rapids: Zondervan Publishing House, 1958.
Morgan, G. Campbell *The Gospel According to Matthew.* Old Tappen, New Jersey: Fleming H. Revell, 1939.

*New English Bible.* New York: Oxford University Press and Cambridge University Press, 1961.

Phillips J.B. *New Testament in Modern English.* New York: Macmillan, n.d.
Powell, Ivor *Bible Cameos.* Grand Rapids: Kregel Publications, 1985.
_____ *Bible Highways.* Grand Rapids: Kregel Publications, 1985.
_____ *Bible Pinnacles.* Grand Rapids: Kregel Publications, 1985.
_____ *Bible Treasures.* Grand Rapids: Kregel Publications, 1985.
_____ *Bible Windows.* Grand Rapids: Kregel Publications, 1985.
_____ *John's Wonderful Gospel.* Grand Rapids: Kregel Publications, 1983.
_____ *Luke's Thrilling Gospel.* Grand Rapids: Kregel Publications, 1984.

_____ *Mark's Superb Gospel.* Grand Rapids: Kregel Publications, 1985.

_____ *What in the World Will Happen Next?* Grand Rapids: Kregel Publications, 1985.

*Pulpit Helps.* Chattanooga, Tenn.

Reader's Digest *Great Encyclopedic Dictionary,* n.d.

Ryle, J.C. *Expository Thoughts on the Gospels.* Grand Rapids: Zondervan Publishing House, n.d.

Spence, H.D. and Exell, Joseph S., eds. *The Pulpit Commentary, Matthew.* Grand Rapids: Wm. B. Eerdmans Publishing Co., 1950.

Strong, James *Exhaustive Concordance of the Bible.* Nashville: Abingdon Press, 1890.

Tenney, Merrill C., ed. *The Zondervan Pictorial Encyclopedia of the Bible,* 5 Volumes. Grand Rapids: Zondervan Publishing House, 1975.

Thayer, Joseph H. *The Greek-English Lexicon of the New Testament.* Grand Rapids: Zondervan Publishing House, 1983.

Thomson, J.A. *The Land and the Book.* New York, Harper and Brothers, 1869.

Unger, Merrill F. *Unger's Bible Dictionary.* Chicago: Moody Press, 1957.

# BOOKS BY IVOR POWELL

## BIBLE CAMEOS
These eighty graphic "thumb-nail" sketches are brief biographies of Bible people. Pungent and thought-provoking studies.

## BIBLE GEMS
You will be captivated by the warm and practical style of these mini-messages with an ample supply of sermon starters, illustrations and deep truths from God's Word.

## BIBLE HIGHWAYS
In this series of Bible studies, Scripture texts are linked together, suggesting highways through the Bible from Genesis to Revelation.

## BIBLE PINNACLES
A spiritual adventure into the lives and miracles of Bible characters and the meaningful parables of our Lord.

## BIBLE TREASURES
In refreshingly different style and presentation, these eighty Bible miracles and parables are vividly portrayed.

## BIBLE WINDOWS
Anecodotes and stories are, in fact, windows through which the Gospel light shines, to illumine lessons for teachers and preachers.

## MATTHEW'S MAJESTIC GOSPEL
You will find almost everything you need in developing sermons: theme, outline, expository notes, preaching homilies. A treasure-book of hands-on help in communicating God's truth to today's Christians.

## MARK'S SUPERB GOSPEL
This most systematic study offers expositional, devotional and homiletical thoughts. The enrichment gained from the alliteration outlines will create a desire for more truth.

## LUKE'S THRILLING GOSPEL
In this practical and perceptive commentary, there is a gold-mine of expository notes and homilies.

## JOHN'S WONDERFUL GOSPEL
Another verse-by-verse distinctively different commentary with sermonic notes and outlines.

## THE AMAZING ACTS
The Acts of the Apostles become relevant for today in this most helpful exposition.

## WHAT IN THE WORLD WILL HAPPEN NEXT?
An unusual work on prophecy dealing especially with the return of Christ to earth and the nation of Israel's future.